The Governors–General

The Institute of Early American History and Culture
is sponsored jointly by
The College of William and Mary
and The Colonial Williamsburg Foundation.

Publication of this book has been assisted by a grant
from the Prescott Jennings Charitable Trust.

The Governors-General

The English Army and the Definition of the Empire, 1569–1681

by Stephen Saunders Webb

Published for the Institute of Early American History and Culture
Williamsburg, Virginia
by The University of North Carolina Press
Chapel Hill

Both the initial research and the publication of this work were made possible in part through grants from the National Endowment for the Humanities, a federal agency whose mission is to award grants to support education, scholarship, media programming, libraries, and museums, in order to bring the results of cultural activities to a broad, general public.

Library of Congress Cataloging in Publication Data

Webb, Stephen Saunders, 1937–
    The Governors-General.

    Includes index.
    1. Great Britain—Colonies—Administration.
    2. Military government of dependencies.   I.   Title.
    JV1061.W4   325'.31'0941   78-8746
    ISBN 0-8078-1331-1

To my parents

Contents

A Note on Style

In the documentation for the work that follows, the year is taken as beginning on January 1, but the Old Style month and day are retained. Double dates are given either when the original correspondence is dated in both the Old and the New Styles or when there is some ambiguity about the year of the document in question (as is often the case with calendared items). The words of quotations are modernized and regularized in spelling, modern ornothography is imposed on personal names, random capital letters are reduced to lowercase, and abbreviations are expanded, save in those cases where any of these aspects of the original document reflect the character of the author or significantly affect the interpretation of the document.

Illustrations

English Garrison Government in Britain and America, 1569–1763

Since 1924 Charles M. Andrews's conceptions, most concisely contained in his essay entitled "Conditions Leading to the Revolt of the Colonies," have controlled historians' understanding of the nature of the English empire before the American Revolution. Andrews declared:

The year 1763 has always and rightly been considered a great turning point in the history of America's relations with the mother country. . . . By her victory over France, Great Britain obtained peace and a securely established imperial status. . . . In the past men had spoken of "empire," meaning the self-sufficient empire of the mercantilists rather than a thing of territory, centralization, maintenance, and authority. After 1763, however, territorial empire came into real and visible existence, and writers, both British and colonial, became aware that "imperialism" meant something more than commerce and colonies and that the colonial problem, with which they were familiar only in its mercantile aspects, had taken on a distinctly territorial and political form.

The "new and untried policy of imperialism," Andrews pointed out, had "autocratic" and "paternal" elements. Its promoters "advocated the use of force or the employment of a policy of coercion." After 1763, therefore, "British statesmen affronted in one way or another the colonies in America, because they were thinking in terms, not of the accepted mercantilism but in those of the new imperialism."[1]

Andrews both summarized and reinforced the individualist, capitalist views about the colonies held by his pioneering historical generation. So he persuaded virtually all subsequent historians of early America that imperialism was inaugurated only after 1763 and that imperialism was not in accord with "the principles or methods of the old British colonial policy." Indeed, in his final statement on the subject, published in 1938, Andrews asserted

---

1. Charles M. Andrews, *The Colonial Background of the American Revolution*, rev. ed. (New Haven, Conn., 1931), 122, 123, 126–127, 128.

that, in the classic sense of rule and control by a state over dependencies, "imperial and imperialism have no place in the vocabulary of our early history."[2]

Historians have since questioned the significance of the year 1763 as a turning point in British policy toward America, and they have debated the degree of change from mercantilism to imperialism that occurred during and after "the great war for the empire," but they have nonetheless continued to acquiesce in Andrews's fundamental dictum: before that war, England's had been a "commercial and colonial policy"; during or after that war, it was suddenly altered into a military and metropolitan policy, with revolutionary results. Thus historians have continued to assess the Anglo-American empire in a commercial framework, burdened with whig political assumptions and late nineteenth-century economic concepts. Historical presentism, political partisanship, and goldbug economics have obscured the social, political, and economic realities of Anglo-America before 1763 and have even restricted our understanding of the roots of the Revolution, for whig-capitalist orthodoxy celebrates the rise of the patriots without explaining the existence of the loyalists.[3]

It is the intent of this book to establish that, from the beginning, English colonization was at least as much military as it was commercial. The forces fostering imperial attitudes and institutions are most clearly visible in the political role of the English army and in the administrative careers of its officers commanding colonies—the governors-general. Their imperial influence was coeval with colonization itself. The empire that they organized originated almost two centuries before 1763. After a century of development, this English empire achieved a constitutional definition in 1681 that prevailed until 1783. In Anglo-America from

2. *Ibid.*, 129; Charles M. Andrews, *The Colonial Period of American History* (New Haven, Conn., 1934–1937), IV, 7, 1. Here (pp. 5, 7) we also find the decisive statements: "England's interest in these colonies was not political but commercial," and " 'colonies' were not looked upon as the stuff: out of which an empire was to be made, but rather as the source of raw materials. . . . No one at this time took any other view." The view that Andrews summarized was earlier expressed by George Louis Beer; see *The Old Colonial System, 1660–1754*, Pt. I: *The Establishment of the System, 1660–1688* (New York, 1912), vii. Beer defined "colonial system" as "that complex system of regulations whose fundamental aim was to create a self-sufficient empire of mutually complementary economic parts."

3. For the continued dominance of the "commercial and colonial" interpretation of Anglo-American history, see the following recent, representative, and well-regarded works: Michael Kammen, *Empire and Interest: The American Colonies and the Politics of Mercantilism* (Philadelphia, 1970), esp. chapter 1; Alison Gilbert Olson and Richard Maxwell Brown, eds., *Anglo-American Political Relations, 1675–1775* (New Brunswick, N.J., 1970), esp. fig. 2; and Thomas C. Barrow, *Trade and Empire: The British Customs Service in Colonial America, 1660–1775* (Cambridge, Mass., 1967), esp. 1–3.

1569 until 1783, commercial considerations, while always present, were dominant only occasionally. More often the imperial ethos—social order, political loyalty, economic discipline, military preparedness—prevailed in English thinking about the provinces.

Of course, the empire had commercial as well as bureaucratic and military bases, but it should not be forgotten that the provincial executives of the crown were able to make political and social capital of the mercantile acts of trade and navigation. Moreover, these acts promoted prerogative politics by binding the richest and most influential colonial traders to the merchant-capitalists of the metropolis, many of whom were courtiers to the core: bankers to the crown, agents of the governors-general, advocates of comprehensive and aggressive imperial policies. It was their commercial enemies—outsiders and outport merchants, interlopers and illegal traders, mercantile misfits both in England and in the colonies—who objected alike to London-dominated trade and imperially dictated politics and who supported both a freer trade and more autonomy for the colonies. Thus even the commercial elements of the Anglo-American society—so homogeneous in the whig-capitalist assessment by Andrews—were deeply divided along imperial and mercantile lines.

The coexistence of these policy extremes, imperial and mercantile, and their continual competition for political influence, demand a revision in the terms of Anglo-American analysis. It is time to end the commercial and colonial monopoly of interpretation. Therefore the present volume reassesses Anglo-America in terms of the fact of empire, a fact embodied in the governors-general and applied in the British Isles as in America by garrison government.[4]

The essential element in the definition of empire is the imposition of state control on dependent peoples by force. The instrument of that imposition is the army. There are no empires without armies. Three militant phases thus constituted the formative period of the "old empire." First, the military foundations of English empire were built by the Tudor monarchs, on the continent, at home, and in Ireland. Then "garrison government"—militarized

4. Of course, English attitudes toward the colonists (and vice versa) were also shaped by the ties of family and of place: the Modyford cousinage spanned the empire; Bishops Waltham meant as much as Green Spring to Francis Morrison. And ideologies, classical and Christian, were ever present. The growing English state, however, incorporated into itself the energies of family "interests" and religio-social ideas. Families joined the new bureaucracies, and ideologies were written into imperial orders. All of these influences, therefore, tended to promote Anglo-American empire at least as much as they enhanced transatlantic commerce or as they independently affected events.

and centralized provincial administration—was developed in England, particularly during the civil wars and the Interregnum. And, last, throughout the Protectorate and during most of the Restoration, paramilitary power relationships were applied over ever-widening territorial areas, first in the British Isles and then in England's overseas provinces. The result was that, by 1681, Anglo-American relations were dominated by an imperial system whose principal agents were the governors-general. These officers of the English army constituted nine-tenths of the royal provincial governors during the adolescence of the old empire, that is, between the Restoration of the monarchy in 1660 and the death of King George I in 1727.

The maturation of that empire, in the period 1681 to 1722, and its key event, the imperial achievement of Marlborough's governors-general, is the subject of this volume's immediate sequel. Here we may only note that, by 1727, garrison government and its development by Marlborough's subordinates, was being overlaid, if not undone, by the commercial and colonial policies long advocated by "country" politicians and whiggish merchants. These policies were at long last effected by the Walpole regime. The renewal of imperial war after 1739, however, ended this era of unsalutary jobbery. Once again, armed authority and imperial control were set against commercial motivation and colonial autonomy. "The great war for the empire," between 1754 and 1763, at last achieved the imperial ambitions of two centuries, but at the price of provoking the resistance of the colonial elites and the revenge of imperial rivals that combined as the American Revolution.

Such is the conceptual structure within which appears this study of the role of the governors-general in the creation of the first English empire. In the course of fourteen years largely devoted to this work, I have incurred innumerable debts to family and friends, to readers and editors, and to institutions of learning. The line between life and work long ago evaporated. Those who have contributed to the one, assisted the other. If only the conventional acknowledgments are made here, others to whom I am profoundly indebted will please accept this statement of my heartfelt thanks.

The concepts of Anglo-American association that pervade this work date from an honors thesis written in 1958–1959 at Williams College under the guidance of John G. Sproat and Frederick Rudolph. In 1962 the encouragement of David S. Lovejoy and Charles Mullett led me to develop the institutional and the eighteenth-century aspects of this subject. The larger outlines of the work, and the first full-time research for it, were supervised by Merrill Jensen and refined by his criticism and that of my colleagues in his seminar at the University of Wisconsin. Mr. Jensen's respect for the integrity of the sources, and his social idealism, are traits that I hope are reflected in this work. There ensued a doctoral dissertation which treated some early eighteenth-century aspects of garrison government. It was supported by a University of Wisconsin Fellowship and was assisted by the librarians of the Wisconsin State Historical Society and the Manuscript Division of the Library of Congress.

The present volume reaches back four generations from the period of the dissertation. The research for it was largely conducted between 1965 and 1968, while I was a Fellow of the Institute of Early American History and Culture. A grant from the Penrose Fund of the American Philosophical Society also helped support my research in English archives. The staffs of the then British Museum, the Public Record Office, the Institute for Historical Research, and the Bodleian, National Maritime, and Pepysian libraries all are due many acknowledgments for their helpful courtesies and scholarly assistance. Special thanks are rendered to the household officers and staff of his late grace, the Duke of Marlborough, for generous assistance at Blenheim Palace, details of which await a more appropriate place, and to the Resident of Dyrham Park, Gloucestershire. For patient and learned assistance in ordering the results of this research, I must give grateful notice to the work of the staff of the Institute during my tenure there, in particular to Lester J. Cappon, Stephen G. Kurtz, Thad W. Tate, W. W. Abbot, James Morton Smith, and my colleagues in the Institute Fellowship. In more recent years, the extraordinary sensitivity and perception of Norman S. Fiering have done much to shape this work. Portions of it appeared in the *William and Mary Quarterly*, having benefited from the astute advice of Michael McGiffert. The copy editing of Joy Dickinson Barnes and Gretchen Oberfranc is acknowledged with thanks. Also under Institute auspices, Richard S. Dunn gave the manuscript his profound and searching attention. Malcolm L. Call, of the University of North Carolina Press, has been supportive and discerning in his relation to this work.

The reduction and revision of the manuscript largely occurred during two leaves of absence from Syracuse University in 1971–1972 and 1974–1975. Authorizations, arrangements, and financial aid for these leaves came from the successive Deans of the Max-well School, Alan K. Campbell and Guthrie S. Birkhead; from David Bennett, Chairman of the Department of History; and from Donald E. Kibbey, Vice President of the University.

These years were spent as a Fellow in the Charles Warren Center for Studies in American History, Harvard University. A generous grant from the National Endowment for the Humani-ties, during my term as a Junior Humanist Fellow, made it possible for me to take up the first Warren Center award. The collections and the superb staff of the Harvard College Library were of great help to me in completing this work. Inestimable assistance was given by my colleagues and advisors at the Charles Warren Center. First among them has been Bernard Bailyn. Since his term as chairman of the Council of the Institute of Early American His-tory and Culture in 1966, Mr. Bailyn has simultaneously chal-lenged this work and encouraged its author. The articulation of concepts herein is in large measure a response to Mr. Bailyn's profound and persistent questioning. To Donald Fleming, Wallace MacCaffrey, and Oscar Handlin I make acknowledgments for criticisms both helpful and stimulating. In two visits to the Charles Warren Center, J. H. Plumb conveyed his exciting ideas and gave memorable advice. Quondam Fellows of the Warren Center have continued to offer me both important suggestions and intellectual communion. To single out individuals from so distinguished a group is invidious, but I owe special thanks to Pauline Maier and Henry D. Shapiro. Finally, in the Cambridge community, I am grateful for the generous hospitality of Leverett House and Adams House, their Masters and their House Secretaries.

For nine years the officers, members, and guests of the Co-lumbia University Seminar in Early American History and Culture have offered me intellectual stimulation and social companionship. They have listened, with varying degrees of patience, to portions of the present work, and shared their own ideas and enthusiasms with me. To them, a former chairman's thanks.

Formal recognition is due the British Library, the Public Rec-ord Office, and the Library of Congress for the use of materials to which they hold crown or common law copyright. I acknowledge with thanks the permission of the owners of the Papers of Francis, Baron Howard of Effingham (deposited in the Library of Con-gress), the Marquis of Bath (Secretary Coventry's Manuscripts at Longleat), the Henry E. Huntington Library (Blathwayt Manu-scripts), and the Institute of Jamaica (Phillips Manuscript 11009), to cite and to quote from papers in their possession. Parts of this work appeared in the *William and Mary Quarterly*, 3d Series, XXIX (1977), 1–31, as "Army and Empire: English Garrison Government in Britain and America, 1569 to 1763."

Through every stage of this work, from its inception to the present, Linda Ward Mellichamp Webb has been my dear companion and severe critic. Mere words cannot describe my reliance upon her unvarying support. Our sons, Peter S. M. Webb and Thomas S. M. Webb, have grown up with this work, from quiet resentment, through resigned tolerance, to critical understanding. Their patience was appreciated; their growth is a joy.

That fundamental contributions to this work have been made by my parents is obvious enough, but they have done more than shape the author's being and mind. They have read and, gently but unrelentingly, criticized every major revision of the much larger manuscript of which a part is here presented. To them, this volume is dedicated.

PART I Military Administration
in the British Isles, 1569–1676

CHAPTER 1

Garrison Government

Charles II was the most absolute king in the history of England.[1] His brother James II was a tyrant. Yet historians have told us little of the mechanics or meaning of their sovereignty. The usual explanation of the restored monarchy's tightening grip on England, and on its empire, is that the havoc of the civil wars created such fear of anarchy in Englishmen that they accepted every absolutist act short of Roman Catholic counterrevolution as the price of civil peace and social stability. This view is demonstrably untrue. Riots, risings, and rebellions against the restored monarchy repeatedly manifested Englishmen's unassuaged thirst for liberty and continually reinforced the government's fear of revolution. That fear inspired absolutism. The coup that toppled the arbitrary regime in 1688 proved that the Stuarts could hold on to sovereignty only as long as they could hold down the many who did not accept their absolute authority.

This absolutistic executive was the imperial government. The regimes of Oliver Cromwell and Charles II fully established the prerogative for the first time in the scattered settlements across the Atlantic. In America and the West Indies, as in the British Isles, Cromwell and the later Stuarts sought to end a century of rebellion by reducing local self-government. Their tool was an armed prerogative, an authoritarian politics developed during the civil wars, the royal exile, and the Interregnum. Entrenched corporate privilege, the self-rule of the local elites who were ensconced in judicial and legislative bastions, limited the executive's gains. Nonetheless, the successes of Cromwellian and Stuart sovereignty underlay the subsequent dominion of the central government over the provincial oligarchies and of the executive over the central government. Even more powerful in its American (and British) provinces than in England itself, the English executive confirmed the centralized, militarized, imperial tradition in Anglo-American politics. Imperial, not commercial, values finally dominated the war-wracked, socially rent American polities of the late seventeenth and early

1. David Ogg, *England in the Reign of Charles II*, 2d ed., 2 vols. (Oxford, 1955–1956), II, 455, 459.

eighteenth centuries. "Salutary neglect" neglected imperial order, but after 1739, revitalized order incited the American Revolution.

The American Revolution was thought out and fought out in terms of the seventeenth-century struggle against Stuart absolutism. Thence came, for example, that fear of executive conspiracy against the liberties of the people, recently reidentified as a central source of American alienation from the empire.[2] This fear reflected reality. The officers and governors who ruled British towns and American colonies were the instruments of an overweening prerogative power, the agents of an actual executive conspiracy. The fears of our fathers rested on the firmest foundations: their revolution was a reaction to a century and a quarter's experience of a militarized executive.

Fear's foundations were the English "Guards and Garrisons," the standing regiments and town garrisons that bred the soldier-executives of British cities and American colonies. Through the military government of garrison towns, the English executive bypassed the corporate structures of traditional local government and weakened the autonomy of its gentry-and-merchant ruling class. Acting as governors, royal army officers imposed the crown's military and political will directly on the cities, the centers of subject populations. Garrison government expressed the growing force of the national executive in strategic seaports, border fortresses, and political capitals in the British Isles. From Britain and from Ireland, garrison government was transplanted to America. Army officers, all of them garrison veterans and many of them town governors, constituted almost nine-tenths (87.5 percent) of the 206 colonial viceroys commissioned between 1660 and 1727.[3]

The formative experiences of the governors-general in the garrisons were supplemented by the influence of their "regimental connections." These military associations of aristocratic patronage, territorial loyalty, shared services, and personal companionship were especially characteristic of the English army before 1660 and after 1685. Between these dates, the Guards units constituted the leading regimental connections. Their patrons were the commander-in-chief and his captain general. Their territory was the capital. Their services were political. Their officers were most likely to be commissioned governors and generals of the provinces of empire.

2. Bernard Bailyn, *The Ideological Origins of the American Revolution* (Cambridge, Mass., 1967), 90–91, 95, 112–117, 119, 150, 158–159, and Bailyn, "The Origins of American Politics," *Perspectives in American History*, I (1967), 84, 104–107.
  3. See the Appendix.

Besides garrisons and regiments, the bodyguards and household staffs of Cromwell and of his general, George Monck, of Charles II and his brother James, provided martial men to govern the empire. These soldiers were politically active and prerogative-minded. Their careers usually encompassed diplomatic as well as military and political services. Their personal loyalty to the head of state, their political reliability, and their physical proximity to the nation's military leaders made officers of these rulers' households favored candidates for the garrison governorships that extended central sovereignty to the provinces. During most of the seventeenth century, garrison government was the innovative institutional model for the expansion of English executive authority. England's garrison governors became America's governors-general.[4]

The Interregnum and Restoration sovereignties inherited the institution of "governor" after it had been defined by the Tudors' monarchical assertiveness and strengthened by the war with Spain. The Elizabethan executive knew that the frontiers of the British Isles lay in northern France, in the Low Countries, and in Normandy and Brittany. In the dozen years after 1585, fifty thousand English troops were sent overseas to advance English interests in northern Europe and to support the enemies of Spain. The captains of these English military companies became the professional officers of a royal army. Their services centered on garrisoned cities and on these cities' citadels, both commanded by "governors." Often the crown recalled its officers from the military government of these towns to build and to command the new English coastal fortifications against the repeated invasion efforts of Spain.[5]

These officers became the local agents of royal authority and

4. See my introduction to the Appendix.
5. On the English understanding of the political and strategic importance of the fortified cities, see Sir George Carey to Sir Robert Cecil, Aug. 2, 1593, Nov. 4, 1597, Historical Manuscripts Commission, *Calendar of the Manuscripts of the Most Hon. the Marquis of Salisbury . . . Preserved at Hatfield House, Hertfordshire*, 22 vols. (London, 1883–1970), IV, 346, VII, 469–470 (hereafter cited as HMC, *Salisbury*). On the transfer of the garrison strategy to England, as recommended by a committee of Low Country veterans, see *ibid.*, II, 42. For the English military government of Flushing, Sluys, and Brill, see the case of Sir Ferdinando Gorges below and HMC, *Salisbury*, IV, 293, 503, 512, 581, V, 450, VI, 538–539, VII, 13, 57. Sir John Oglander, *A Royalist's Notebook: The Commonplace Book of Sir John Oglander, k.t., of Nunwell*, transcribed and ed. Francis Bamford (London, 1936) (hereafter cited as Oglander, *Royalist's Notebook*), contains the example of Lord Conway, common soldier in the Low Countries, captain and lieutenant governor of Brill, secretary of state, and captain of the Isle of Wight. See C. G. Cruickshank, *Elizabeth's Army*, 2d ed. (Oxford, 1966), for the soldier's oath of obedience (appendix, p. 6) and on the strategic situation (esp. pp. 14–15). For the numbers of troops, see *ibid.*, 290–291, and R. B. Wernham, "Elizabethan War Aims and Strategy," in S. T. Bindoff *et al.*, eds., *Elizabethan Government and Society: Essays Presented to*

military discipline. They imposed social as well as soldierly order. Wherever royal officers added new political prerogatives to traditional military responsibilities, the customary titles of "captain" of troops, "keeper" of forts, "constable" of castles, and "lieutenant" of royal citadels were subsumed under the broader label, "governor."[6] The governors' monarchical loyalties and growing responsibilities pitted these new, military, statist executives against the traditional, civilian, local governing castes that operated through town corporations, county courts, and militia lieutenancies. Garrison government challenged local elites everywhere in the empire for the next two centuries.

The Tudor Prerogative Asserted: The Case of Sir George Carey

The rise of this new type of civil-military leader in England was exemplified by the career of Sir George Carey. Carey added military professionalism to the court influence he inherited from his father; in just six years, he transformed the ancient military captaincy of the Isle of Wight into a politically comprehensive government. Appointed captain general of the island, he became governor-in-chief as well. In the process, Carey defined the characteristics of the crown's provincial executive.

In attitude and action George Carey was his father's son. Like Henry Carey, the first Baron Hunsdon, George was apprenticed to war and rose in the royal service through military distinction. At twenty-two he served under his father's command in the cold campaign of 1569–1570 against the rebellion of the northern earls. These archaic nobles were the victims of a modernizing monarchy. The crown sought stability and security for its obedient subjects, but royal troops looted the lands and hung the followers of aristocratic rebels against centralized authority. Ruined feudal castles

---

Sir John Neale (London, 1961), 348. The figure given is conservative. It does not include either the 40,000 troops sent to Ireland in the years 1590 to 1601 or the 3,300 troops sent to the Netherlands in 1602. On the command of these troops, see Sir John Neale, "Elizabeth and the Netherlands, 1586–7," in his *Essays in Elizabethan History* (London, 1958), 170–201, and the career of Gorges, discussed below.

6. HMC, *Salisbury*, II, 200, IV, 49, VIII, 343; HMC, *Calendar of the Manuscripts of the Marquess of Ormonde, K. P., Preserved at Kilkenny Castle*, 2 vols., N.S., 8 vols. (London, 1895–1899, 1902–1920), N.S., I, esp. 402–403 (hereafter cited as HMC, *Ormonde*). The "lieutenancy" of Portsmouth became a "government" on the appointment of Capt. Sir Charles Blount; HMC, *Salisbury*, VI, 240, VII, 463–464.

and strengthened royal citadels manifested the transfer of sovereignty from noblemen to the state. The strongholds of the old aristocracy, which had dotted the margin of the Border hills, literally collapsed after the northern rebellion. From pele tower and castellated house, the queen's men tore off the lead roofs and carried down the glass windows to embellish their own lowland mansions.

These modern, unfortified Elizabethan country houses were not set on steep hills or in narrow passes but in broad plains and fertile vales. They were not isolated and independent. Rather, they were dominated by the fortified cities—Carlisle, York, Newcastle, Chester—that bestrode the major trade routes. The command of these cities had passed to a new class of administrators: royal military governors. Under the royal governors, garrisons of professional soldiers held these cities in 1569, even against the will of their inhabitants. These garrisons and their governors were supplied with soldiers, munitions, and the orders of the crown, from the royal fortress of Berwick-upon-Tweed.[7]

Berwick became the major base of the crown's domestic, political police actions in the northern counties while it still sustained its ancient role as the anchor of the Scots Border defenses. By 1568, when Queen Elizabeth commissioned her cousin Lord Hunsdon as Berwick's first governor, the city was England's "greatest military post." Its "governor was at once military commander, civil governor, and diplomat, with some hundreds of men under his command," even while "the other English garrisons, usually numbering no more than a dozen men, were scattered in the coastal fortresses each under its own captain."[8]

7. R. R. Reid, "The Rebellion of the Earls, 1569," Royal Historical Society, *Transactions*, N.S., XX (1906), 175; Wallace MacCaffrey, *The Shaping of the Elizabethan Regime* (Princeton, N.J., 1968), 343; [Sir Cuthbert Sharp, ed.], *Memorials of the Rebellion of 1569* (London, 1840), 76, 117n, 160–161n, 219, 413. The crucial evaluation is by Sir Francis Knollys to Cecil, Sept. 17, 1568, noting that "the landlords have retired themselves within the land," left their castles to decay, and, by raising rents, destroyed the military will and armigerous quality of their tenants. "Were it not for the garrison of Berwick the Scots might spoil the Border of England at their pleasure"; see Joseph Stevenson *et al.*, eds., *Calendar of State Papers, Foreign Series, of the Reign of Elizabeth*, 16 vols. (1863–1909; repr. Nendeln, Liechtenstein, 1966), *1566–1568*, no. 2534 (hereafter cited as *Cal. S.P. For.*).

8. *Cal. S.P. For., 1566–1568*, nos. 2335, 2453, 2454, 2496, 2571; Sharp, ed., *Memorials*, 331; Reid, "Rebellion of the Earls," RHS, *Trans.*, N.S., XX (1906), 176, 179, 180; John Scott, *Berwick-upon-Tweed: The History of the Town and Guild* (London, 1888), 131, 133, 136–137 (note especially the recommendations of the captain in 1552 that he, the council, and the garrison "choose a burgess to Parliament as done in Calais, since the burgesses chosen by the Freemen little regard the profit of the soldiers"), 140, 141–144, 147–160 (by 1559 the greatest part of the garrison was 1,198 harquebusiers), 162–163, 167–168. The precision of the contemporary distinction between "governor" and "captain" is reflected in the quoted passage from Wallace T. MacCaffrey's lucid essay, "Place and Patronage in

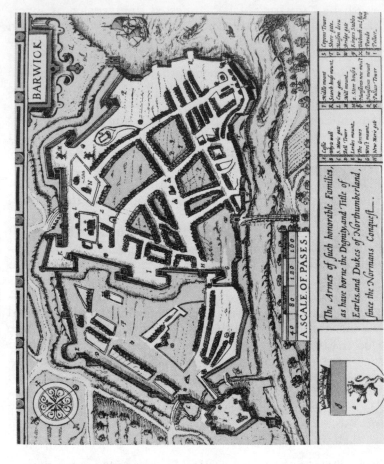

City Plan of "Barwick." From "Northumberland" in 1610, fol. 89v–90r of
John Speed's atlas, *The Theatre Of The Empire Of Great Britaine: Presenting
An Exact Geography of the Kingdomes of England, Scotland, Ireland and the Isles
ajioyning* . . . (London, 1611).

It was chiefly the royal soldiery, citadel, and governor of Berwick that enabled Elizabeth's government to survive its "time of testing," the rising of the northern earls, which broke out early in November 1569. Berwick's harquebuses and horses provided the royal army with its margin of superiority over the rebel bows and bills (the earls had appealed in vain for Spanish harquebusiers from Flanders). The feudalists' lack of ordnance made the royal cities and citadels safe from the "rank riders" of the Border lords. Thus it was royal firepower that forced and determined the decisive battle in which the Careys distinguished themselves: Naworth.[9]

To Naworth Castle, the stronghold of the Dacres and the seat of the rebellion, marched Governor Hunsdon of Berwick, his deputy, his son George Carey, and the captain of Newcastle. Followed by fifteen hundred men, they filed through snow-filled passes by night to obey the queen's order to arrest Leonard Dacre, the champion of Mary Stuart, the old religion, and the northern feudal tradition. But the beacons of Dacre's dependents flared from every hilltop, "so as by day light," Hunsdon wrote, "I came byfor Naworth." From his castle's wall, Dacre defied the governor. Then, all around him, Hunsdon saw "every hyll full on men, bothe horsemen and footmen, krynge and showtyng, as they had been mad." Outnumbered two to one, Hunsdon's little army tried to retreat to the safety of Carlisle before the arrival of the Scots reinforcements promised to Dacre, but Dacre and his hordes followed and surrounded the royalists. At the first ford, the borderers attacked Hunsdon's harquebusiers and were shot down. Then the governor charged the broken ranks at the head of his cavalry, slaying and capturing hundreds. Hunsdon's horsemen pursued Leonard Dacre from the battlefield into an exile from which he never returned.[10]

Elizabethan Politics," in Bindoff *et al.*, eds., *Elizabethan Government*, 107. The first reference to a "governor" of Berwick relates to Carey and is dated Mar. 25, 1569; see Robert Lemon *et al.*, eds., *Calendar of State Papers, Domestic Series, of the Reigns of Edward VI, Mary, Elizabeth and James I, 1547–[1625]*, 12 vols. (1856–1872; repr. Nendeln, Liechtenstein, 1967), *1547–1580*, 331 (hereafter cited as *Cal. S.P. Dom.*). See also MacCaffrey, *Elizabethan Regime*, 343.

9. MacCaffrey, *Elizabethan Regime*, 352; J. B. Black, *The Reign of Elizabeth, 1558–1603*, 2d ed. (Oxford, 1959), 144. Hunsdon, asking for the continuation of the garrison at wartime strength, told the queen that such manpower would have prevented the rebellion that had cost so much to suppress (Sharp, ed., *Memorials*, 126). The *Memorials* detail the role of the Berwick garrison (pp. 17, 67, 74n, 84, 92, 103), with particular references to the cities (pp. 77, 82, 90). In fine, the rebels, attacked by "superior forces on the south, and by the garrison of Berwick on the north," abandoned their ragtag "infantry" and rode hard for Scotland (p. 382). See the role of the Gowers at Newcastle (p. 23n) in the forcible administration of the North for the crown, the relation of which continues below in chapter 2.

10. Hunsdon's own report to Cecil is dated from Carlisle on the night of the battle and is supported by other accounts (Sharp, ed., *Memorials*, 219–222). The rebels were con-

Naworth Castle surrendered two days later to mere messengers sent from Carlisle by Hunsdon. Inherited by the Howard family, descendants of Dacre daughters, Naworth became a noted country house for Charles Howard, the first earl of Carlisle. The age of feudal castle and dependency was past, and the Howard holders of Naworth found authority instead in their exercise of royal commissions as governors of Carlisle and as commanders of its royal garrison. Emblems of shifting sovereignty in the North antedated Charles Howard's career, however. Governor Hunsdon himself had captured the guidon of the Dacres, the red bull, "which I trust the law of armes will allow me too beare." So his son George did after him.[11]

Late in the starving spring that followed this bitter winter, the lord general of the queen's northern forces knighted George Carey for his service against the Scots. In 1575 Sir George was commissioned constable of Bamborough Castle. In 1580 he acted as the queen's political interrogator in the Tower. From 1582 Carey also personified royal order as marshal of the court, and in that year he became captain general of the Isle of Wight and constable of its mouldering citadel, Carisbrooke Castle.[12]

The new captain general quickly exhibited his political intent. In 1584 Sir George secured for Newport, the island's commercial center, a corporate government and borough representation in parliament. The burgesses reciprocated by granting Carey control of a seat. Except during the period of prerogative decay in the early Stuart era, commanders of the island retained the borough nomination. In years to come, either their favor or royal command placed in parliament as member for Newport such military servants of the crown as John Churchill, afterward duke of Marlborough, William Blathwayt, secretary of war and plantations, and Blathwayt's client Colonel Joseph Dudley, deputy governor of the island and subsequently captain general and governor-in-chief of Massachusetts during the period of Marlborough's ascendancy. Captain General Carey himself sat for Newport, serving with other old

---

demned by a specially empowered royal commission (which included the lieutenant general [Gov. Hunsdon] and the queen's attorney general) and were hung in their native villages (pp. 225–232), a process that exactly anticipated the repression of 1663; see chapter 2 below.

11. See chapter 2 below for Carlisle's career. On the inheritance, see Sharp, ed., *Memorials*, 224.

12. On winter's woe, see Gov. Hunsdon's report from Berwick that he had left the rebel nobles neither "Castell standing for themselfs, or house for any of ther people" (Sharp, ed., *Memorials*, 237). See also *ibid.*, 116n, 233–240; *Dictionary of National Biography*, s.v. "Carey, Sir George"; MacCaffrey, *Elizabethan Regime*, 343, 345, 348–349, 350–351, 477.

soldiers on parliamentary committees for veterans' benefits.[13]

Carey not only strengthened the political bonds between his province and the nation, but also inaugurated gubernatorial control of passports, gathering of intelligence, seizure of hostile pirates, and official financing of friendly ones. He incorporated into his command such disparate props for social stability as the control of grain trading and the regulation of local churches. As captain general, Carey called for royal reinforcements for the Protestant cause in the Low Countries. It was the first line of Wight's defense. He arranged for the troops' transportation, via Cowes, and he fortified the island's coasts. Carey attempted to remodel adjacent mainland militias as well as his island forces. His influence over crown appointments of officers to the south coast militias intensely annoyed the local magnates. Sir George combined all his executive activities in his defense of Wight against the Spanish Armada.[14]

The symbol of this defense, and of Carey's paramilitary politics, was his citadel, Carisbrooke Castle. If the castle could be modernized, Sir George asserted, the Isle of Wight would "be the strongest island of Christendom, and thereby stand ever assured to the crown of England." His artillery bastions do still stand at Carisbrooke, flanking Roman wall and medieval tower. Carey's contributions to Carisbrooke Castle are the finest English example of the military revolution of the Renaissance: the combination of war, mathematics, and architecture. Sir George expressed in stone a new age of war, a new logic of power politics. The huge new kitchen of Carisbrooke, the enlarged medieval hall, the two-story block of "Officer's Quarters," all manifested hospitality, pomp, bureaucracy—the expressions of resident, royal, military leadership.[15]

13. *DNB*, s.v. "Carey"; Richard Worsley, *The History of the Isle of Wight* (London, 1781), 114; Gertrude Ann Jacobsen, *William Blathwayt: A Late Seventeenth Century English Administrator*, Yale Historical Publications, Miscellany, XXI (New Haven, Conn., 1932), 219ff; Everett Kimball, *The Public Life of Joseph Dudley: A Study of the Colonial Policy of the Stuarts in New England, 1660–1715* (New York, 1911), 69; Richard Ollard, *Man of War: Sir Robert Holmes and the Restoration Navy* (London, 1969), 193; Committee for Relief of Maimed Soldiers and Mariners, Mar. 8–24, 1593, HMC, *Salisbury*, IV, 295.

14. *DNB*, s.v. "Carey"; Lt. John Dyngley to Carey, Apr. 13, 1585, Carey to Sir Francis Walsingham, June 25, July 15, Dec. 2, 1585, to council of state, Mar. 18, 28, Apr. 23, 1587, requisition by Carey, Mar. [?], 1587, reasons Spaniards would prefer to land at Isle of Wight, [May] 1588, Lord Henry Seymour to Walsingham, June 17, July 20, 1588, Sir William Wynter to Walsingham, July 27, 1588, *Cal. S.P. Dom., 1581–1590*, 237, 247, 252, 290, 387, 394, 398, 406, 400, 486, 490, 506, 514; opinion of Lord Grey *et al.* in reference to a Spanish invasion, Mar. [?], 1588, *Cal. S.P. Dom., 1580–1625*, 248.

15. Carey to Cecil, Oct. 29, 1597, HMC, *Salisbury*, VII, 451; Dyngley and Anthony Dillington to council of state (with inventory, survey, and plan of Carisbrooke Castle), Apr. 27, 1583, Carey to Walsingham, Jan. 30, 1584, Mar. 2, 1586, *Cal. S.P. Dom., 1581–1590*, 107,

"I will lose my life before my government," declared Sir George, and, on the eve of the Armada's appearance, the queen commissioned him governor of the Isle of Wight. This declaration of royal authority in their island infuriated the local oligarchy. The captain general and governor, or governor-general, labeled their protest "mutinous," and the privy council thereupon imprisoned the most prominent protestors. In the governor-general's presence the remaining gentry were compelled to tear up their petition against his authority. Repressed but not reconciled, local leaders insisted that the governor-general's command was "arbitrary," that is, not approved by themselves. "Mutinous" and "arbitrary" became the ritual watchwords of future feuds between royal military executives and the local elites they challenged. But there was no ignoring the reality of social and civil power that Governor Sir George Carey had added to the traditional military role of captain general. [16]

The Armada threat, Carey's own high social rank, "and his consciousness of support from the Government" led Sir George to assert royal political control of the island in military terms—"to subject them to the military power," as the islanders put it. The resulting protest of the gentry, especially those concerned in trade and commerce, typified the continuing conflict between the prerogative and the law, between the ruler's rights and the subject's liberties, between public necessity and private property. Such were the constitutional expressions of the power struggle between royal governors and local elites that was sustained for two centuries in England and its emerging empire. [17]

In the significantly titled "Demands by the Gentlemen of the Isle of Wight for Reformation of a Certain absolute Government lately assumed by the Captain there, tending to the Subversion of the Law, and to the taking away of the natural freedom of the Inhabitants there," members of the gentry denied that the "cap-

---

156, 309; W. H. Long, ed., *The Oglander Memoirs: Extracts from the Mss. of Sir J[ohn] Oglander* (London, 1888, 5, 23. See the wonderful story of Carey's four oaks party and Oglander's praise of Sir George's hospitality, in Oglander, *Royalist's Notebook*, 88–91. Also see Sir Charles Peers, *Carisbrooke Castle, Isle of Wight*, 2d ed. (London, 1948), 15 and map.

16. Carey to Cecil, Oct. 29, 1597, HMC, *Salisbury*, VII, 451; Carey to Walsingham, June 14, 1588, *Cal. S.P. Dom., 1581–1590*, 488. By 1595 the governor and captain of the Isle of Wight was also governor of all the castles and fortresses on the island, constable and doorkeeper of Carisbrooke, steward, surveyor, recorder, and bailiff of all the royal manors and lordships, and holder of all other offices of profit on the island that were or should have been in royal hands; see governor's commission, State Papers, class 44, piece 29, 141, 142, Public Record Office (hereafter cited as S.P. 44/29).

17. Oglander, *Royalist's Notebook*, 91, 91n; Worsley, *Isle of Wight*, 97; Long, ed., *Oglander Memoirs*, 5.

tain" possessed any judicial, magisterial, or civil role. With the law, they insisted, the captain had nothing to do. But even as captain general, Carey had served writs, held hearings in which he selected and applied the law, and passed judicial sentences. While continuing to exercise judicial powers himself, Carey, when he became the governor-general, made manifest his contempt for the common law and for lawyers by his brutal treatment of the Isle of Wight's first attorney. That unfortunate man was, by Sir George Carey's command, "with a pound of candles hanging at his breech lighted, with bells about his legs, hunted out of the island."[18]

The governor-general's violent disregard for the law of property was matched by the island oligarchy's vehement insistence that anything to do with private property was beyond the captain's purview. Acting as captain and governor, however, Carey made good his claim that the general welfare of the island required not only that he protect his command militarily but also that he unite it socially and regulate it economically. Carey thus used his military authority to commission privateers (acts that merchants considered inimical to peaceful trade). He impressed both transport and labor for fortifications. As governor-general, Carey also controlled the port by imposing embargoes on ships and food cargoes and by licensing, for a fee, both ships and passengers. Most intrusive on the island's political economy was the "governor's" application of royal rules of survey and escheat to landed estates in his government.[19]

To move from mere military defense of the island's fortifications to the dominance of its land, sea, and law was to move from protecting the island to governing it. Controlling persons and property, the governor-general not only could command the resources necessary to protect his province but also could compel the obedience of even its wealthiest inhabitants. Faced with this threat to elites' liberty, the leader of the defiant gentry told his neighbors "that he neither could nor would brook Sir George Carey's Government, and that, if the abuses complained of were not redressed, he would seek a remedy with his poniard, at the same time shouting out in a seditious manner, liberty! liberty!" To Sir George himself the provincial magnate said "that we wanted

18. "Demands," in Worsley, *Isle of Wight*, 97–100; Long, ed., *Oglander Memoirs*, 21.
19. Worsley, *Isle of Wight*, 98–100. In contrast with the merchants, who considered privateering to be inimical to peaceful trade, some landed gentlemen welcomed the privateers because they brought cheap goods to the island and provided a market for island produce at high, cash prices. For colonial parallels see chapter 4, n. 25, below. Escheat and survey also became powerful political tools for overseas governors; see Part III for cases in Virginia.

no governor, neither would we permit any but our sovereign, but, if he would needs be a governor, then he should go into the West Indies amongst the base people." Carey's opponent recognized that the political result of governorship was the local exercise of royal sovereignty but, significantly, insisted that the office was appropriate to the crown's unlimited authority over England's castoffs, its colonists.[20]

The queen's privy council jailed Carey's critic for speaking treason: he had exposed the threat of royal rule to private property. Carey replied to this critic, as governors-general afterward habitually would, by labeling him a religious or a political subversive, "either a papist or a misliker of the present state," a weak-minded member of a factious minority misled by the "lewd persuasions of some few" malcontents. He himself, however, the governor-general claimed, was legally justified in his acts against property by his instructions and commission from the crown, and, Carey added, he was morally supported by public necessity. "My government in that place," Carey affirmed, is "what hath been given me in charge by her Majesty, what is warranted by my patent, and what I shall find to be good for the benefit or strength of the country."[21]

After all, Carey represented the sovereignty of the state in the locality. Governors-general continued to resist the hegemony of the local elites, both gentry and merchant, with whom the central government competed for provincial power. Yet Richard Worsley, the native historian of the Isle of Wight (who by his notable local lineage and his combination of perspicuity, political passion, and provincialism remarkably resembled Virginia's Robert Beverley and Jamaica's Edward Long), contended that, despite the crown's support of Carey against the provincial gentry, political powers "were never afterwards claimed, either by Sir George Carey or his successors." This statement is inaccurate with regard to Carey, as the governor's activity in the 1590s demonstrated. Neither does it do justice to the authority of Carey's successor, the earl of Southampton, who was titled "governor" even by the most dissident islanders.[22]

20. See n. 21 below.
21. Worsley, Isle of Wight, 100–106; Oglander, Royalist's Notebook, 91; n. 15 above.
22. On Carey (Hunsdon) as "Our most worthy Captain and Governour," see Long, ed., Oglander Memoirs, 6, also 65–71 and notes.

It was not until the end of the reign of James I that the spreading paralysis of royal power restricted the regality of crown commanders in the island. Then army officers, who had become absentee governors, gave way to nobles, who were drunken ones. Drams replaced drums as the emblems of island administrations. The result, or so an island gentleman boasted, was that during Lord Conway's term from 1625 to 1631, "that word *Governour* we have now caused to be clean abolished, if after ages will so keep it, for there is no readier way to enthrall the island than by making the Captain too great, above all things keep Westminster and Winchester Hall open for us, and let him assume nothing to himself but martial discipline."[23]

"After ages," however, could not exclude the national executive, keep legislature and law supreme, or confine the governor to the castle and the drill field. In 1647 Colonel Robert Hammond, formerly Sir Edward Massey's subordinate in the garrison government of Gloucester, became captain and governor of the island. His experience in military government, together with the crisis created by King Charles's incarceration in Carisbrooke Castle, revived much of the power exercised by Tudor governors. A full reconstitution of royal authority, one that extended to land survey and to the recovery of some of the royal estates alienated by the earlier Stuarts, awaited the restoration of the monarchy by General Monck and the administration of the island by Thomas, Lord Culpeper (before his term as captain general and governor-in-chief of Virginia). Then the commissions and instructions of the later Stuarts to their officers and governors expanded to imperial dimensions the civil jurisdiction that Sir George Carey had first added to the military captaincy of the Isle of Wight.[24]

As governor and general, Sir George Carey had been typical of the Tudor "governors of the public weal" who combined the ancient military powers and titles of "captain" and "general" with the nationalist political authority of "governor-in-chief." These governors-general asserted locally the will of the more powerful state that was to centralize old England's government and to colonize a new England overseas.[25]

---

23. Worsley, *Isle of Wight*, 106; n. 13 above.
24. Worsley, *Isle of Wight*, 135, 136*ff*; Robert Latham and William Matthews, eds., *The Diary of Samuel Pepys* (Berkeley and Los Angeles, 1970–   ), VI, 317 n. 1; chapter 5 below.
25. Sir Thomas Elyot, *The Governour* (London, 1937 [orig. publ. London, 1531]), xxxi.

The Stuart Prerogative Assailed:
The Case of Sir Ferdinando Gorges

"The grand old man" of American colonization, Sir Ferdinando Gorges, succeeded Sir George Carey as the commander of England's Channel defenses. Gorges's career, after its first few Elizabethan years, was marked by failures that symbolized the decay of garrison government under the early Stuarts, just as Carey's successes had epitomized its Tudor growth.

Carey's succession to the barony of Hunsdon in 1596, his subsequent commission as captain of the royal bodyguard, and his appointment as lord chamberlain kept him from all but emergency residence at Carisbrooke Castle. As the new Lord Hunsdon left for London, he was succeeded in the coastal defense command by that thoroughly professional officer Sir Ferdinando Gorges.[26]

The queen recalled this honored veteran of eight years' service in France and the Netherlands from the deputy governorship of Brill to "take charge" of her new fort and its garrison at Plymouth. The queen made the appointment despite the repeated protests of that locality's leaders, who wanted no commanders at Plymouth save themselves. But the threat from Spain placed a premium on experience in war, and Gorges had a high reputation among his contemporaries for military skill. Gorges also displayed the soldier's urge toward empire that stems from military lust for strategic territory, for increased national wealth to support larger military expenses, and for military commands in conquered countries. Imperial commands carried with them salaries and perquisites provided from the revenue that the conquest brought to the conquering state. Such imperialism already had infused Sir Walter Ralegh's plans for overseas English expansion and permeated the American projects of such veterans of England's intervention in the Low Countries and Ireland as Sir Humphrey Gilbert, Sir Thomas Dale, and Sir John West, as well as the American plans of Gorges himself.[27]

26. Andrews, *Colonial Period of American History*, I, 90; Hunsdon to Cecil, Oct. 28, 1600, HMC, *Salisbury*, X, 367; *DNB*, s.v. "Carey."

27. Gov. Thomas, Lord Burgh, to the earl of Essex, Aug. 12, 22, 27, Oct. 8, 1595, William Stallenge to Cecil, Sept. 23, Oct. 17, 1595, HMC, *Salisbury*, V, 314–315, 337–338, 349–352, 406–407, 386–387, 418; Sir Francis Coke to Sir John Coke, July 27, 1626, Mar. 5, 1628, Historical Manuscripts Commission, *The Manuscripts of the Earl of Cowper, K. G., Preserved at Melbourne Hall, Derbyshire*, 3 vols. in 2 (London, 1888–1889), I, 276, 340 (hereafter cited as HMC, *Cowper*); Richard Arthur Preston, *Gorges of Plymouth Fort: A Life of Sir Ferdinando Gorges, Captain of Plymouth Fort, Governor of New England, and Lord of the Province of Maine* (Toronto, 1953), 22–23, 25–28, 31–50.

Whether in old or new England, however, Gorges's administrative career was a failure. Sir Ferdinando was a brilliant tactician but a poor politician: "captain" of Plymouth Fort, he never became "governor" of Plymouth. Gorges's failure was the image of Carey's success, reversing the results of that fundamental conflict of interest between crown and corporation, executive and oligarchy, prerogative power and provincial liberty, that had underlain Carey's confrontation with the gentry of Wight and that incited the continued contention of royal representatives with local elites.

Gorges's political failures instanced the inability of the early Stuarts to maintain the provincial authority won by the Tudor monarchy. As the fears of foreign invasion that had inspired and justified the extension of Tudor authority faded, Gorges's authority as a royal representative diminished. The central government's pacificism permitted the reassertion of legalism and localism, of law and liberty. "Peace and law have beggared us all," said one soldierly royal administrator.[28]

The court's collapse was most pronounced in military administration. For European monarchies, effectiveness in national defense had become the supreme political test, just as it was their greatest source of power. King James I, however, "never made use of soldiers, as never loving them or their profession, which was the cause that the gentry followed the course of the time—*regis ad exemplar totus componitur orbis.*" Thus when this cowardly king, or so his subjects thought him, was succeeded by his unmilitary son, Charles I, the new king "much wanted for Commanders" against Spain. The few veterans—sacrificed on the Isle of Ré to the incompetence of Buckingham and to the army of France—were succeeded by field officers who "were men of neither worth nor fortunes, and Captains such young men as never saw a sword drawn—fiter for a May-game than to command an army" or to govern a province.[29]

Sir Ferdinando Gorges was no raw recruit, however, and in the first, Elizabethan, wartime years of his service as captain of Plymouth Fort, he had acquired many of the insignia of executive influence. He built a modern fort containing a house for himself and barracks for his men. Gorges's citadel was financed from local customs duties—in keeping with the crown's fiscal ideal of directly

28. The court scoffed at the danger of invasion, despite the fears of such exposed subjects as those on the Isle of Wight (Oglander, *Royalist's Notebook*, 51–54). See also *ibid.*, 47–48, and Long, ed., *Oglander Memoirs*, 20–21, 193.

29. To the quotations from Long, ed., *Oglander Memoirs*, add the account of the Ré expedition in Godfrey Davies, *The Early Stuarts, 1603–1660*, 2d ed. (Oxford, 1959), 38, 65–66.

converting provincial resources into national strength, an ideal the crown held up to all its dependencies, at home or overseas.[30]

Sir Ferdinando's fort faced the sea. Like all English imperialists, he knew that:

Needs must we all their Tributaries be,
Whose Navies hold the Sluces of the Sea.
The Ocean is the Fountain of Command,
But that once took, we Captives are on Land.

And like every provincial commander, Gorges wanted ships of the royal navy assigned to extend his authority. Lacking them, he impressed sailors from Plymouth and its satellite towns (over the protests of merchants and shipowners) to man the privateers and transports that he financed and that he sheltered beneath his fort. Sir Ferdinando pointed out—as governors of Jamaica, Tangier, and New York did afterward—that when England could not afford naval support for its outposts, those outposts must rely on private men-of-war. Like his proconsular descendants, Gorges argued that privateers could best be financed by raids on Spanish commerce in those American seas that never knew peace.[31]

Despite the public service Gorges's privateers performed, the crown denied its captain of Plymouth Fort the vice admiral's commission characteristically given to governors and held, for example, by Carey. Instead, Sir Ferdinando acted in prize matters, intelligence collection, and coastal defense in joint commission with the mayor and a leading merchant of Plymouth. Gorges was not encouraged to exercise the wartime initiative that increased executive influence. Indeed, he was not permitted to do what he thought was "fit to be done for my countries good." Nor were he and his fellow commissioners regularly reimbursed for their expenses in the state's service. The frustrated captain concluded, "My being here is to no purpose if I may neither have ample au-

30. On the fort and its financing, see Gorges to Cecil, Mar. 28, 1596, Stallenge to Cecil, Aug. 15, 1596, Gorges to Lord Burghley, Sept. 27, to Cecil, Oct. 20, 23, 1597, HMC, Salisbury, VI, 119, 336–337, VII, 403, 438, 441–442; Preston, Gorges of Plymouth Fort, 55, 58–59, 124–126.

31. Andrew Marvell, "The First Anniversary of the Government under O.C.," ll. 367–370. On naval activities, see Preston, Gorges of Plymouth Fort, 128, 131, 133; Stallenge to Cecil, July 20, 1596, HMC, Salisbury, VI, 271; also Gorges to Cecil, Aug. 7, 8, Nov. 2, 1596, Gorges and Stallenge to the lords of the council, Aug. 9, 1596, [Gorges] to the lord treasurer, Sept. 8, 1596, ibid., 321–322, 325, 466–467, 326–327, 374. On English pirate-privateers and their support in the West Indies, see Gorges to Salisbury, May 18, 1605, Mar. 1607, James Phinney Baxter, ed., Sir Ferdinando Gorges and his Province of Maine, 3 vols., Publications of the Prince Society, XVIII–XX (Boston, 1890), III, 116, 164.

thority nor sufficient means to discharge that for which I came."[32]

The fort was the bastion of Gorges's military authority as well as of his naval pretensions. From his headquarters at Plymouth Fort he commanded the town militia and acted as the first professional military advisor to the lord lieutenant of Devonshire (a post later held by another soldier-administrator of New England, Sir Edmund Andros). Gorges, however, could not make his authority over the townsmen independent of the county militia lieutenancy (unlike officers afterward commissioned "governor" of Plymouth). Even when the country magnates did not check Gorges, the townsmen often refused to obey his orders. He asked in vain for a royal commission broad enough to eliminate "all cavil or contradiction of so ignorant and stubborn a people." Merchants and country gentlemen alike were awful officers. According to Gorges, they were "divided amongst themselves" by political faction and social jealousy. Their lack of military experience made them "ignorant of what they ought to do." The local elite valued their popularity more than the public good and therefore did not demand hard service of their men. "The people themselves, (I mean the men appointed to arms)," Gorges complained, were "a raw multitude, without either use of their arms or knowledge of any order." Naturally, Gorges sought to substitute professional officers like himself for the local amateurs. He tried to exempt his veteran garrison company from any control by the local magistracy, denying the magistrates' right to arrest his troops for debt or even for felony. He rejected local control, but Gorges nonetheless tried to compel the locality to feed, warm, and quarter his men. He conscripted recruits for his ranks from the townspeople and took town munitions and construction material for the fort. In this hated citadel, guarded by his garrison, Captain Gorges insisted that both county and town militia store their weapons.[33]

32. On the vice admiral's commission, see Preston, *Gorges of Plymouth Fort*, 68; the commission to Christopher Harris, n.d., and Gorges to Cecil, Oct. 5, 1586, Mar. 28, 1597, Baxter, ed., *Gorges*, III, 3 n. 518, 26–27; Stallenge to Cecil, Aug. 2, 1596, Gorges to Cecil, Sept. 10, 1596, Capt. Christopher Croft to Cecil, Nov. 6, 1596, HMC, *Salisbury*, VI, 315, 377, 473, also VII, 7.

33. On militia command in the town, see Gorges to Cecil, June 5, July 10, 1596, Aug. 25, 1599, HMC, *Salisbury*, VI, 209–210, 255, IX, 323. On professionals and privilege, see "The Matter in Difference between the Town of Plymouth and Sir F. Gorges," in Baxter, ed., *Gorges*, III, 14–16; the mayor and inhabitants of Plymouth to the privy council, 1596, Essex to the privy council, Aug. 14, 1597, Lord Mountjoy to Cecil, Oct. 25, 1597, Gorges to Essex, Nov. 6, 1597, to Cecil, Aug. 25, 1599, HMC, *Salisbury*, VI, 561, VII, 352, 443–444, 472–473, IX, 323; Gorges to the privy council, Dec. 5, 1597, Baxter, ed., *Gorges*, III, 45; Preston, *Gorges of Plymouth Fort, passim*, esp. 84, 85, 88. See also n. 37 below.

The legality of garrison government such as Gorges's is left obscure by such scholarship as exists on martial law. Civilian legal commentators even assert that no such law existed in Gorges's time. Yet at all periods the prerogative of the sovereign included command of the troops enforced by military tribunals. In time of war the crown could assert its military authority over civilians as well as soldiers. The Tudors had extended monarchy's martial jurisdiction to times when invasion was merely feared or insurrection only apprehended: "They made use of the obscurity of the law to assume the powers which they considered to be necessary for the maintenance of peace."[34]

Garrison commanders, ofttimes governors, exercised these powers as the crown's agents. The most politically effective part of this martial authority was a governor's exclusive jurisdiction over crimes committed by his soldiers—an authority that could be an instrument of political terror as well as of martial discipline. In 1625 Plymouth was particularly named by Charles I as being subject to his new code of martial law. Thus Gorges's government was especially reflected on in 1628 by parliament's Petition of Right, which insisted that "no man ought to be adjudged to death but by the laws established in this realm" by parliament.[35] The royal rebuttal, issued on the eve of civil war, took the form of new articles of war. They reiterated the prerogative's political reliance on force. "The soldier may bring the country to reason," royal army officers felt sure, but, they asked, "who shall compell the soldier" if the parliament could declare the king's martial law illegal? The governor-general of the Isle of Wight, Lord Conway, solicited royal orders to hang a few lawyers by way of example to those who upheld parliamentary law and opposed the crown's martial prerogative. Impending civil war made it clear that the king's military authority was the foundation of royal power.[36]

Thus the constitutional lines were drawn between the rival forms of law: parliamentary statutes applied by a civilian magistracy; royal decrees enforced by military governors. Within these lines, the struggle of the king's governors-general with gentlemen justices or corporation officers would continue beyond the civil wars and throughout the empire. The royal refusal to support Gorges against Plymouth's elite anticipated the failure of royal

34. W. S. Holdsworth, *A History of English Law*, I (London, 1903), 337–340.

35. Charles M. Clode, *The Administration of Justice under Military and Martial Law* (London, 1872), 57, 20–25.

36. Alexander Fraser Tytler, *An Essay on Military Law and the practice of Courts Martial* (Edinburgh, 1800), 15–16, 61–70.

authority in the civil wars. In parallel fashion, Gorges's own failure to apply his royal commission as governor-general of New England contributed to the delay in imposing imperial executives in America. Sir Ferdinando's defeats, in Plymouth and in New England, were less his own than they were symptoms of the political, financial, diplomatic, and moral bankruptcy of the Stuart court. The institutional corruption of the royal government had rotted the nation's political fabric.

In the civil war that tore that fabric to pieces, Plymouth, menaced by no effective threat from the citadel or its current captain, declared for parliament and so for local self-government. The former captain of Plymouth Fort, Sir Ferdinando Gorges, came out of retirement to raise a troop of cavalry for the king. He won one last military distinction, planning the capture of Bristol for Prince Rupert's army. But Gorges's recognition that parliament's cause, if it were not more correct, was certainly more powerful than Charles I's, reinforced the lesson of a military lifetime: "The negligent and unarmed are always a prey to the vigilant and powerful." The king's cause was the former. His aged captain, Sir Ferdinando Gorges, went home to poverty and death. Other officers—both royalist and parliamentarian—younger, better armed, and more aggressive than Gorges, took command of the garrison governments that sprang up like mushrooms in the darkness of civil war.[37]

Civil War and the Growth of Garrison Government: Three English Cases

Seventeenth-century war centered on cities, the regional centers of trade, finance, and politics. They stood strategically at road junctions, river crossings, or harbors. In England they retained enough of their medieval walls and militia traditions to require full-scale sieges to capture them, but cannon for sieges were often wanting. Economy, topography, and weaponry thus made control of the cities the key to civil war supremacy. Their crumbling citadels on commanding sites suddenly ceased to be stone quarries. During the wars of the 1640s, the citadels reverted to their original

37. Instructions to Gorges, 1599, Sir John Gilbert to the privy council, Nov. 6, 1601, HMC, *Salisbury*, IX, 431–432, XI, 481–483, Preston, *Gorges of Plymouth Fort*, 70–72, 77–78, 83, 86, 88, 89, 92, 95; navy paper, July 16, 1602, HMC, *Cowper*, I, 42; Baxter, ed., *Gorges*, III, 60, 64–66. Gorges's civil war career is described in Preston, 341–342, 343–344.

function of ensuring the obedience of the local population to the orders of the castellan. Now, if not previously, he became a "governor." The outcome of the civil wars depended upon which central government, or whose governors, could control these centers. Desperately competing executive and legislative sovereignties reduced previous restraints on their military champions. The government sensitivity to local self-interest that had crippled Gorges now atrophied: "These were the days of sword-law."[38]

Out of this period of garrison government came Cromwell's and Charles II's generation of Anglo-American governors-general. They represented all of the major religious, national, and political divisions of the empire's internecine strife. Some were Presbyterians (Sir Edward Massey of Gloucester and, nominally, of Jamaica); some were Independents (Colonel John Hutchinson of Nottingham); and some were *politiques* (Major General Charles Howard of Carlisle and Jamaica). Some served in Scotland with Colonel George Fenwick of Connecticut and Edinburgh or with Lieutenant Colonel William Brayne of Inverlochy and Jamaica. Some marched through Ireland with Colonel George Cooke of Massachusetts and Wexford or with General Robert Venables of Ulster and Jamaica. Some governors-general were royalists, others parliamentarians or Cromwellians. From European careers as soldiers of fortune, from the ranks of crown retainers, or, at a later date, from the regiments of the New Model, these officers came to government, ousting local magnates from town governorships and castle captaincies. Veteran professional military men, often new to the regions they ruled, these governors acquired broader commissions over larger territories backed by more effective forces than had their titular predecessors. What gave life to their commissions was that all of these civil war officers had experienced the "neces-

---

38. Rev. John Webb and Rev. T. W. Webb, eds., *Military Memoir of Colonel John Birch, Sometime Governor of Hereford in the Civil War . . . Written by Roe, His Secretary*, Publications of the Camden Society, N.S., VII (Westminster, 1873), 110. For this metropolitan strategy and its prevalence through the Restoration, see Samuel Rawson Gardiner, *History of the Commonwealth and Protectorate, 1649–1660*, 3 vols. (London and New York, 1894–1901), III, map opp. 340; S.P. 44/20, 55–60; S.P. 44/58, 9–11; S.P. 44/60, 18–20; S.P. 44/68, 28–30; Charles Dalton, ed., *English Army Lists and Commission Registers, 1660–1714*, 6 vols. in 3 (1891–1904; repr. London, 1960), I, 10–16, II, 66. On the citadel and the governance of cities, see B. H. St. J. O'Neil, *Castles: An Introduction to the Castles of England and Wales* (London, 1954), 2–3, 6, 23–24. In the case of Plymouth, the inability of "the fort by Plymouth" to enfilade the streets of the town was complained of in reports by Frederick Genebelli, the queen's engineer in Gorges's time; the engineer called for a citadel "against" the town on the model of those that European princes "have builded for their security" (HMC, *Salisbury*, XII, 555–556). The Plymouth citadel's lack of command was corrected by Charles II (S.P. 44/17, 168–169).

sity" of the "arbitrary and extensive power" that provoked the jealousy of local elites.[39]

Of course, every dispute between one of these paramilitary proponents of state authority and the traditional provincial elite also reflected personal resentments between the governor and his rivals for power. Civil war licensed human malice generally. More particularly, governors often personified family feuds or took a side in the ancient struggles of urban oligarchies with the gentry of adjacent counties. But the disruptions of long wars and of profound social upheaval were transformed by pressure for political reform into institutional change and growth. Together, war and reform infused some of the petty personal contests between the military governors and the local elites with the pervasive conflict of metropolitan with provincial values.[40]

All of the officer-governors faced demoralized, ofttimes dissident populations as well as disgruntled oligarchs. From their citadels they threatened their opponents with their garrisons. But the executives also used more politic methods of persuasion to enlist the energies of townsmen and the resources of the metropolitan region in the service of whichever central government the governor represented.[41] The townsmen, however, who "had lived free, and plentifully of themselves, could not subject themselves to government." When the king's representative took the town magazine —the activities of Lord Dunmore's marines at Williamsburg and General Gage's redcoats at Lexington and Concord suggest the longevity of this tactic in the struggle between prerogative and province—or a parliamentary partisan quartered troops in townsmen's homes, the localities raised forces for self-defense. "Having taken up the sword," they then "saw it was not safe to lay it down again, and hold a naked throat to their enemies whetted knives."[42]

39. Appendix, nos. 45, 51; chapter 4 below; Birch, Military Memoirs, 109.

40. On the country gentry-merchant oligarchy interconnections and rivalries, see Wallace T. MacCaffrey, Exeter, 1540–1640: The Growth of an English County Town (Cambridge, Mass., 1958), esp. 244–245, 246–247, 249, 274–275, 278, 281. For the elevation of the provincialism of the local elites into the ideology of the "country party," see Perez Zagorin, The Court and the Country: The Beginning of the English Revolution (New York, 1970), esp. 83–84, 331–333.

41. On the problems of royalist and parliamentary governors in Hereford, see Webb and Webb, eds., Military Memoirs of Birch, esp. 31, 109, 110. On military confiscation or "contributions" as a financial basis for government, see n. 61 below and chapter 2.

42. Lucy Hutchinson, Memoirs of the Life of Colonel Hutchinson, Governor of Nottingham Castle and Town . . . , ed. Rev. Julius Hutchinson, rev. C. H. Firth, new ed. rev., 2 vols. (London, 1906 [orig. publ. London, 1806]), 156, 81–83, 86–87, 91, 100, 105–106, 106n, 111, 124 (hereafter cited as Hutchinson, Memoirs); Special Passages (London), no. 3, Aug. 22–29, 1642, printed in Hutchinson, Memoirs, 394.

No locality could long keep up its forces without government aid, however, and all wanted some semblance of legal authority for their military activity. To secure aid and authority, each community became a nominal supporter of the parliament or the king. The sovereign they chose then appointed a council or committee for civil administration from among the local notables and (either directly or through its regional general officer) commissioned a military commander, or "governor," for the metropolitan area. Unwillingly yoked, the governor and council each sought support both from the central sovereignty and from the local assembly— the town meeting, or "hall." In the Aristotelian terms of the time, both "monarchy" and "democracy" played larger parts in provincial politics, because of the institution of garrison government, whereas "aristocracy" (and "oligarchy") were given smaller ones. Such was the legacy of civil strife, first in war-wracked England itself, and then elsewhere in an empire everywhere and always stressed by growth and conflict.[43]

Hutchinson in Nottingham: Arming the Civil War Executive

In Nottingham the local parliamentary committee chose Colonel John Hutchinson as governor. He moved to modernize the castle on its crag above the town, adding outworks and bastions whose cannon, taken from the town magazine, commanded the streets within the city walls as well as the meadows outside them. The governor had barracks and a residence built. His followers filled storage caves in the castle rock. Four hundred men of the poorer and middling sorts—many of them religious radicals— sent their families to outlying villages and came in with their movable goods to join the governor's garrison. The governor had created a citadel from which he and his garrison could command the city.[44]

Appalled by the establishment in their midst of that very military power that they had armed themselves to avoid, the town notables "mutinied." The aldermen called the hall into session. In this local assembly, the oligarchy threatened to storm the castle,

43. Of course, the classic definitions are those of Aristotle himself, especially in Book IV, chapter 7 of the *Politics*, although it is my impression that "oligarchy" was a less favored term of 17th-century political analysis than were the triumvirate, "the one, or the few, or the many" (Bk. III, chap. 7), and these in their favorable forms: kingship, aristocracy, and polity (commonwealth).

44. See George Charles Deering, *Nottinghamia Vetus et Nova; or, an Historical account of the ancient and present state of the town of Nottingham* (Nottingham, 1751), for plans and views of the town and castle. See also Hutchinson, *Memoirs*, 124–126, 131–132.

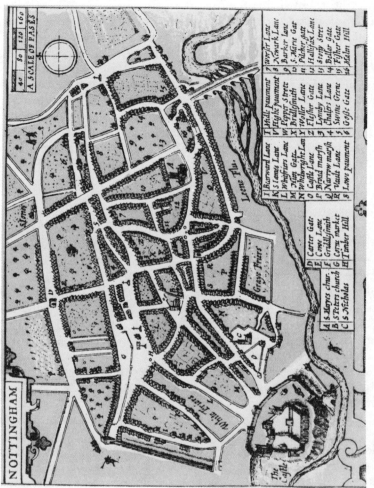

City Plan of "Nottingham." From "The Countie of Nottingham," in 1610, fol. 65v–66r of John Speed's atlas, *The Theatre Of The Empire Of Great Britaine: Presenting An Exact Geography of the Kingdomes of England, Scotland, Ireland and the Isles ajoyning . . . .* (London, 1611).

recapture the town ordnance, use it to defend the town of Nottingham (not just its citadel), and thus put an end to garrison government. At this moment, the governor entered the town hall at the head of his soldiers, seized fourteen of the leading dissidents, and sent them off to prison. On a dark night soon after, the imprisoned aldermen's colleagues opened the town gates to waiting royalist troops. The king's cavaliers plundered their way up the streets; the parliament's governor fired the castle cannon down them. Finally, a relieving force drove off the invaders. The outraged governor then jailed the remaining "malignant" aldermen in the castle. His troops looted their houses. No one now interfered when the garrison tore down the hedges, the houses, and the church that had cluttered the citadel's field of fire.[45]

Various authorities offered to the seemingly victorious governor commissions for the government of the county, the city, and the castle of Nottingham, together or in combinations. Colonel Hutchinson delayed his acceptance, however, for he still feared the personal jealousy of the town leadership, and he recognized the force of the townsmen's hopes for continued local autonomy. For political and military support, Hutchinson had only the undisciplined, often impoverished religious radicals who made up most of his garrison. At last the governor accepted commissions from the parliament and from its general, Lord Fairfax. These authorizations gave him "power and command" over the civil government of the town, and they reiterated his military authority.[46]

The expansion of the governor's jurisdiction abridged that of the committee of notables. They protested their demotion, but to no avail, for Colonel Hutchinson refused to accept a divided or degraded command. The governor then summoned a council of war (the committee plus the governor's military staff and other officers resident in the town) to prepare an agenda for the town meeting. To both council and commonalty Hutchinson made the military executive's traditional pledge: he would protect the town if the townspeople would pay taxes and obey his orders. The council authorized the taxes that the governor requested, and his troops collected these assessments.[47]

Defense was more difficult. At the first opportunity, dissident townsmen again opened their gates to the enemy. When the garri-

45. Hutchinson, *Memoirs*, 126, 141–144, 147, and Hutchinson's letter of Jan. 16, 1644, pp. 418–420. Col. Hutchinson's forcible dispersion of the town assembly can be noted as a miniature of Gen. Cromwell's dismissal of parliament.

46. *Ibid.*, 154, 156–157.

47. *Ibid.*, 157–158, 163, 128.

son counterattacked from the castle, the retreating cavaliers tried to set the town afire. The near loss of the town forced parliament to recognize that "Nottingham is a place of that importance, both in regard of that pass, being seated on the river of Trent, and in regard of the situation in relation to the neighboring counties," that its defense should be promoted by expanding both the governor's territorial jurisdiction and his authority over the civil life of the town.[48]

The Nottingham committee immediately challenged Governor Hutchinson's exercise of executive power in taxation, trade, and politics. He replied that "since he saw his condescensions did but encourage them to wrest off all things from him, and to question all his dues, he would now expect that full observance from them all, that was due from the officers of a garrison to the governor." At the same time, Colonel Hutchinson asked General Fairfax to make all troops resident in Nottingham part of his garrison, in order to ensure the monopoly of force by which he governed. Fairfax agreed. Then, when the local elite refused to implement his orders, the governor made his soldiers his civil agents. This militarized staff was both more obedient and more obeyed than the old officials because, to reinforce military discipline and thereby to promote effective government, General Fairfax had granted Governor Hutchinson court-martial jurisdiction over Nottingham. The governor used this power to try without jury and to execute without appeal even civilians whom he considered deserters and saboteurs. When the disaffected Nottingham magistrates tried to use civil process as a weapon against his men, Governor Hutchinson forcibly freed them from the local courts and jails.[49]

Just as the officer-governor had appealed to his military superior for court-martial authority, so the Nottingham committee (like anti-executive Americans afterward) petitioned the national legislature to vindicate their civilian authority. They asked parliament to grant local leaders exclusive control of matters political, social, and religious. They demanded that the legislature reduce the power of that upstart military executive, "the Governor," who "began these differences by his high demands." While this petition was pending in the distant capital, the anti-executive elite, led by the town's mayor, treasurer, physician, and member of parliament, tried to build their own armed force by subverting troops from their obedience to the governor. The threat of mutiny compelled

48. House of commons to Lord Fairfax, Apr. 29, 1643, house of commons order of Jan. 15, 1644, *ibid.*, 402–403, 417, also pp. 165–168, 168–169.
    49. *Ibid.*, 170, 171, 173–174, 177, 182, 182n, 432, 434.

Hutchinson also to appeal to the national authority in London. The governor sought "a resolution . . . whereby his power and their duty might be defined, that he might know wherein he was to command them in his garrison, and they to obey him." The local leaders, a committee majority, replied that "such a power given to a governor, would not consist with that which belonged to a committee." They insisted that the local citizens and militia look to their traditional and natural superiors, the committeemen, for leadership. Both the elite and the commonalty, the committee claimed, "have been so discouraged and provoked by the impious commands and passionate and violent Carriage of the Governor, that they will rather lay down their arms and quit the Garrison then endure such slavery." Therefore, the committee majority asked "that the government of the garrison may be fully and speedily settled in this Committee." They tried to prejudice the executive in Westminster's eyes by provoking him to some outrageous political act. Simultaneously, by continuous obstruction, they hoped to exhaust his will to rule and to force his resignation.[50] Such were the tactics used by local magnates against metropolitan officer-governors for the next five generations. Repeated and exact parallels pervaded the administrative histories of localities throughout the British Isles and the provinces overseas. These contests of executives with elites acquired ever larger ideological meaning, social impact, and political importance, until they culminated in an anti-imperial revolution.

Despite provincial opposition, Governor Hutchinson, like so many later military administrators, clung to his executive post out of political pride and desire for personal profit. Also like his successors, the governor felt obliged to use his official powers to protect his loyal officers and his political allies. Admittedly, he also enjoyed keeping down his opponents. But above all Hutchinson believed that his exercise of executive authority offered "protection, liberty, and real advantage" to the people of his province. He would resist both the physical menace of martial enemies without and the social and political pretensions of "Sir Politic Would-Be" oligarchs within.[51]

50. *Ibid.*, 200; petition to the committee of both kingdoms, [Nov. 14, 1644], W. T. Baker, ed., *Records of the Borough of Nottingham . . .* , V, *1625–1702* (London, 1900), 227–228. In the town meeting of Dec. 18, 1643, the committees tried to distinguish between "martial" affairs of the town, admittedly the governor's province, and their own reserved powers (Baker, ed., *Nottingham Records*, 221–222). The vast extent of the corporation's self-government, vis-à-vis both county and king, is outlined in their charters (Deering, *Nottinghamia*, 103–115), but the published edition omits the period from James I to Charles II. See also Hutchinson, *Memoirs*, 190, 192, 194, 196, 197, and Baker, ed., *Nottingham Records*, 230–231.

51. Hutchinson, *Memoirs*, 195, 197, 198, 198n, 200.

Yet Colonel Hutchinson's self-assurance did not blunt the hostility of Nottingham's local elite, any more than that of later proconsuls prevented provincial leaders from attacking them. The townsmen's biased financial audits, their prompting of the Presbyterian pulpits to "invectives against governors and arbitrary power," their resistance to the military quartering, requisition, and impressment that menaced their property and their prestige, all pioneered provincial tactics of opposition to executive prerogative. When the governor held stubbornly on his way, the local leadership tried to escalate the anti-executive political campaign in a manner often used afterward by provincial elites: they broadcast complaints to their economic, religious, and parliamentary allies in London, denouncing the governor as "violent and passionate" (as indeed any military absolutist was in the estimation of provincial politicians). As usual, the national authority replied that soldiers are habitually violent and added that the committee's obstructionism would make any executive passionate. Then the men of local consequence made the ultimate accusation against an officer and governor: Colonel Hutchinson (and other "Castillians") "had betrayed the town and castle, and were ready to surrender them to the enemy." This charge, used often in later years, was designed to justify revolution against the alleged traitor. With such serious charges abroad, the government perforce called both the executive and his accusers to London. They appeared before Sir Henry Vane's subcommittee of the committee of both kingdoms. Nottingham's mayor, its member of parliament, and the city committeemen put their case honestly: they asked to rule the town themselves; they demanded the recall of the governor.[52]

Instead of acceding to the local leaders' demands, the Vane committee vindicated Colonel Hutchinson. In November 1644 they imposed a formula for the distribution of power in the locality, a formula that survived the Restoration to appear ultimately in royal governors' commissions as the definition of the role assigned to provincial councils overseas. The governor, the Vane committee specified, must have planning initiative. He had then to secure the advice and consent of the committee (or council) to his proposals. Consent was to be facilitated by a new set of committee appointments that increased the number of ex officio and military committeemen and so expanded executive influence in the advisory body. Once the (reformed) committee consented to a plan, the governor was given absolute control of its execution by the garrison. And he could, as could later proconsuls, extend his influ-

52. *Ibid.*, 203–204, 207–208.

ence by marching his men beyond the bounds of his government. Defeated, most of the old committee fled from Nottingham before the governor returned.[53]

Colonel Hutchinson backed his formal authority to command with personal qualifications. He had a "noble spirit of government," a "native majesty" that carried "an awe in his presence that his enemies could not withstand . . . an awe that made him to be equally feared and loved." This poise was in part military. Trained in arms from his school days, Hutchinson was adept at "the military art." He "naturally loved the employment," which "suited his native active temper." He evinced "a mutual delight in leading those men that loved his conduct." The men accepted his discipline as impersonal and designed for the general good. Because he "exercised his authority in no way but in keeping them to their just duty, they joy'd as much in his commands as he in their obedience." Social sanctions and conventions, as much as military ones, supported Governor Hutchinson's command. He was dignified and decorous, but also affable and accessible to both soldiers and subjects. Self-assured without being arrogant, Hutchinson kept the state appropriate to his station in an age of display, but he did not let his hospitality degenerate into debauchery. Neither did he permit his politic quest for popularity to descend into demagogy. Although in dealing with his subjects he was supported by soldiery and was dignified by status, the governor nonetheless relied on discussion rather than force or commands whenever possible. He sought "rather to convince them by reason than compel them to obedience." That Hutchinson was always proud and passionate, and often violent, unscrupulous, and unfeeling, lent to his government the elements of fear and inhumanity required to exact obedience from the opposed, the slothful, and the uncaring. Qualities such as Hutchinson's, albeit less abstract, less idealized, and more diffuse, constituted the character of every successful officer and governor. These command characteristics persuaded men of the beneficence of their governors and of the necessity of obedience to executive authority, at least in those times of crisis "when any public necessity superseded the mutiny of those private lusts, whereby all men naturally, but especially vulgar spirits, would cast off their bridle, and be their own only rulers."[54]

Hutchinson's political problems typified those of garrison government in England during the Interregnum and later through-

53. *Ibid.*, 214–215, 220, 222; report of the committee of both kingdoms (Vane subcommittee), Nov. 11, 1644, *ibid.*, 427.
54. *Ibid.*, 24, 27, 28, 29–30, 41–42, 224–225, 297.

out the empire: "Almost all the parliament-garrisons were infected and disturbed with like factious little-people, insomuch that many worthy gentlemen were wearied out of their commands." Admittedly, some officer-governors "as violently curbed their committees as the committees factiously molested them."[55] The disease of political faction was bred by legitimate differences of national and local viewpoints. If faction was further fed by religious rivalries in places under parliamentary control, it also throve in religiously conformist and royalist garrison governments such as that of Barnstaple.

Apsley in Barnstaple: Royalist Executive

While royal governor of the town and garrison of Barnstaple, Sir Allen Apsley (afterward prominent in imperial administration under the earl of Clarendon and the duke of York) struggled with his local council on the king's behalf. Apsley was one of six brothers who, encouraged by the example of their father, the lieutenant of the Tower of London, all became professional soldiers. Born in the Tower in 1616, Apsley completed his Netherlands apprenticeship in arms just in time to help raise the royal standard at Nottingham in August 1642. Notorious for his storm and sack of Tiverton, famous for his relief of besieged Appledore Fort, Sir Allen became Sir John Berkeley's lieutenant governor in Exeter after that city fell to the royalists.[56]

When the nearby Devon town of Barnstaple refused the "contributions" demanded of it by the conquering king's army, Apsley was sent to discipline "the refractory town" as its governor. He quickly refurbished the signposts of military rule: he reorganized the town militia, dictated the corporation's election of a royalist as militia captain, refortified the castle at one end of the town, and built the "Great Fort" at the other. These fortifications were esteemed by some royalists as the most formidable in England. They wholly dominated the town, made it untenable by any enemy, and placed its resources in men and material at the governor's disposal. The town corporation protested every aspect of the governor's "arbitrary and oppressive authority," which included impressment and martial law as well as forced militia reform and menacing fortifications. Governor Apsley thereupon imprisoned

55. *Ibid.*, 227.

56. *Ibid.*, 10–11, 227–228, 227n, 243–244, 334n; Deering, *Nottinghamia*, 246; *DNB*, s. v. "Apsley, Sir Allen, (1616–1683)"; Richard W. Cotton, *Barnstaple and the Northern Part of Devonshire during the Great Civil War, 1642–1646* (London, 1889), 299, 348–349.

eight of the burgesses and drove their clerical allies from Barn-staple's pulpits. Sir Allen's well-fortified authority so impressed Sir Edward Hyde (subsequently the earl of Clarendon) that he brought the prince of Wales (afterward Charles II) to the shelter of Barnstaple. Only the approach of Fairfax's and Massey's over-whelming forces compelled the prince and his council to flee.[57]

This emergency led Barnstaple's governor to complete his work of command. He tore down the houses that enfiladed his defenses and leveled a church steeple that overlooked his fortifica-tions. He ordered the church bells melted down and cast into can-non. He secured royal orders to appropriate local customs revenue to his own use. He called on the countryside for further "contribu-tions" of cash and grain "for the use and supply of his Highness his army." Those who failed in "the payment and full performance thereof by the time appointed [three days], they must expect to have a party of my Lord Gorings Horse sent to them for the bringing of the same." The threat of a visit from a unit of what even its leaders admitted was "a dissolute, undisciplined, wicked, beaten army" got the governor the provisions that helped him defend his command, including the strategic Taw bridges, against a blockade and siege of forty-nine days.[58]

Barnstaple was the last major town in the West to hold out for the king. The terms of its surrender, in April 1646, after all hope of relief was gone, protected Governor Apsley in his profits and person and exempted him from prosecution in the courts for his executive and military acts as governor. He retired with honor to the custody of his brother-in-law, John Hutchinson, the parlia-ment's governor of Nottingham. Colonel Hutchinson made sure that his party kept their treaty with his brother and fellow gover-nor, despite the protests of Barnstaple's angry oligarchs. Apsley would return the favor when the wheel of political fortune turned in 1660.[59]

In short, whether the governors were royalists or parliamen-

57. Local magnates served as royal county commissioners. "Instead of forming and pursuing any design for raising of men or money, [they] were only busy in making objec-tions, and preparing complaints, and pursuing their private quarrels and animosities against others. So they brought, every day, complaints against this and that governor of garrisons." For this generalization, and for Barnstaple's particular obstreperousness, see Edward Hyde, earl of Clarendon, *The History of the Rebellion and Civil Wars in England . . .* , new ed., 3 vols. (Oxford, 1819 [orig. publ. Oxford, 1704]), II, pt. ii, 832, 875–877, 886–889; Cotton, *Barnstaple*, 347, 350–351, 352, 353, 367, 375–379, 506.

58. Cotton, *Barnstaple*, 431, 433, 439, 446, 448–449, 450, 456–458. Cotton also reprints the order of Feb. 8, 1646 (p. 470).

59. Treaty of Apr. 12, 1646, *ibid.*, 512–515; Hutchinson, *Memoirs*, 236, 243–244, 247, 286, 286 n. 2; *DNB*, s.v. "Apsley."

tarians, the personal and professional interests of these men as officer-executives and as a central government's local representatives invariably conflicted with the economic interests and status aspirations of the locally dominant gentry and merchants. The struggle between officers and oligarchs, executives and elites, was not just an English issue, nor was it limited to the civil war period. It shaped much of England's imperial politics in the era of enhanced executive authority after 1654.

Massey in Gloucester: "The perfect work of a souldier"

The desirability of a powerful national sovereign, that is, the appeal of political unity, was inversely proportional to existing social order and stability. To combat civil war and to redress social chaos required unity of command. This was locally achieved by the concentration of power in the hands of military governors. Edward Massey was a noteworthy example of these powerful officer-executives. He had returned from war in the Low Countries to serve as a royalist engineer and a lieutenant colonel of parliamentary infantry before becoming governor of Gloucester. Isolated from the national capital by distance and by enemy forces, military governments like Massey's grew local roots. And their links to London also were remarkably similar to those of colonial commands. The Gloucester of Massey's regime was "a branch almost divided from the main stock, and hath been put to live and act of itself; nevertheless a branch still, and enlivened by the Authority of the Kingdome's sovereign power, from which it receives an influence both of support and guidance; but its distance from the fountaine of power had derived upon the Trustee a more free command, and made way for the perfect work of a souldier both in counsel and action, which is the way to make such commands both active and prosperous."[60]

"The perfect work of a souldier" depended on Massey's physical and political control of his urban base. Originally bereft of the apparatus of authority—judges, tax collectors, statutes, and the like—the governor appointed soldiers to do the work of civil offi-

---

60. *DNB*, s.v. "Massey, Sir Edward"; John Corbet, *An Historicall Relation of the Military Government of Gloucester: from the beginning of the Civill Warre betweene King and Parliament to the removall of Colonell Massie from that government to the command of the westerne forces* (London, 1645), 5 (citations are from the British Library copy). A reprint of Corbet is in John Washbourn, ed., *Bibliotheca Gloucestrensis: A collection of scarce and curious tracts relating to the County and City of Gloucester . . . published during the civil war*, with a historical introduction by Rev. John Webb, 2 vols. (London and Gloucester, 1823–1825).

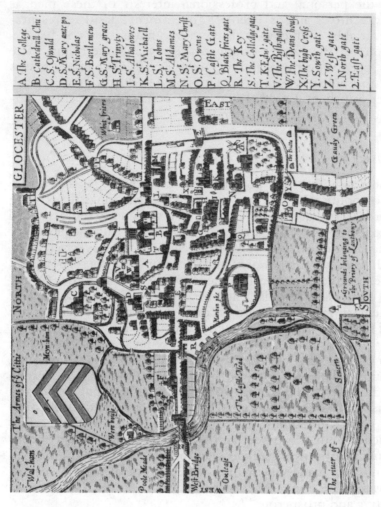

City Plan of "Glocester." From "Glocestershire." in 1610, fol. 47v–48r of John Speed's atlas, *The Theatre Of The Empire Of Great Britaine: Presenting An Exact Geography of the Kingdomes of England, Scotland, Ireland and the Isles ajioyning . . .* (London, 1611).

cials and substituted necessity for law. He imposed the taxes his troops collected. Together with his committee, he elicited loyalty oaths, jailed political opponents, answered petitions from the local population, and, occasionally, paid his troops. He was quick to quell his committeemen when they tried to limit his power. He considered them to be a council of war whose function was to advise him as commander-in-chief, to execute his orders, and to extend his authority, not to check it. This view of governmental committees (or councils) remained common among commanders-in-chief, whether kings or governors. It was always objected to by the councillors, whether urban, provincial, or national.[61]

War reduced the prestige and power of the members of the "councilliar" class, devaluing their estates and discrediting their peacetime political experience. The political disruption of civil war in the British Isles (like the social disorder of newly established communities in America) offered military executives the opportunity to build popular political constituencies. Thus officer-governors found local support for their authority and local allies against both the merchant magistrates in the councils and committees and the county gentry in the militia lieutenancies. Just as popular governors subordinated oligarchical councillors in law and finance, so military governors made it clear that gentry lieutenancy was "a kind of command suitable only to the infancy of Military affairs, and the whole business [of military command, militia included] was devolved on the soldier."[62]

"The true Commons of the Realm," as the governor's partisans labeled the middling sort of people, took the part of the executive. They opposed the "powerful Gentry, who for the most part care not to render themselves the slaves of princes," or of the prince's viceroys. The gentry preferred to continue to "rule over their Neighbours as Vassals." The middling sort also feared "the dregs of the people," who often resented government and always envied those next above them in the social scale. Against both the disorder of the mob and the selfish rule of the powerful gentry, the middling sort turned to the (hopefully) non-partisan and (usually) non-native governor. A soldier such as Massey typified their ideal:

61. For the struggle between the governor, who sought to discipline and pay his troops, and the committee, who defended the rule of law and the integrity of their pocketbooks, see Rev. Webb's introduction and note to Washbourn, ed., *Bibliotheca Gloucestrensis*, xlvi, 115n, also xciii, xciv, xcv, xcviii–xcix. On military confiscation as the fiscal basis of garrison government, see *ibid.*, lxxxvi; Baker, ed., *Nottingham Records*, V, 225, 234, and esp. 212–219, where the amounts assessed (by ward and person) and their use (for wall repair, light and fire for guards) are given. See also n. 66 below and the case of Jeffreys in chapter 2.

62. Corbet, *Military Government of Gloucester*, 25, 26, 36, 39.

he was the representative of a sovereign comfortably distant, the competitor of class rivals uncomfortably close, and the spokesman of public interest and national security. Andrew Marvell voiced their feelings on executive government:

> 'Tis not a Freedome, that where All command;
> Nor Tyranny, where One does them withstand:
> But who of both the Bounders knows to lay
> Him as their Father must the State obey. [63]

Massey was an absolute military executive, but his political effectiveness stemmed from his recognition that force had to be reserved for the crises of war and politics. Like most governors, Massey had so few troops from his divided command, so little money from his devastated province, and such sporadic support from Westminster, that persuasion had to prevail. Massey had no choice but to employ much reasoning, backed by a bit of force—a policy that in him, as in many of his successors, was called "moderation": "The people never groaned under the Governor's power; their voluntary submission was a witness to his moderation. And this authority had more of entreaty than constraint, only the Sword had some influence of fear upon the injurious."[64]

Massey's moral and physical authority in Gloucester enabled him to extend his jurisdiction, and that of parliament, over a growing area. Early in 1643 the governor and his troops captured three of the neighboring royalist garrisons that had hemmed them in. Massey then led his garrison and the city militia out to join Sir William Waller's forces in a pitched battle against a new menace to his frontier garrison—Welsh invaders. After that battle Massey marched fifteen hundred prisoners into Gloucester, and parliament commissioned him as governor in his own right (rather than as deputy to the colonel of his regiment, the earl of Stamford).[65] A base for a royalist counterattack against Massey's fortress was created when Prince Rupert took Sir Ferdinando Gorges's advice and thereby captured Bristol. Massey's subsequent defense of Gloucester against the royalists was probably the most important of the war: only the month lost to the governor's stubborn resistance prevented King Charles from marching on London. From the capital it had preserved, Gloucester was relieved at the last possi-

63. *Ibid.*, 9, 14; Marvell, "The First Anniversary of the Government under O.C.," lines 279–282.

64. Corbet, *Military Government of Gloucester*, 58; Sir Charles Firth and Godfrey Davies, *The Regimental History of Cromwell's Army* (Oxford, 1940), xix–xx.

65. Webb, in Washbourn, ed., *Bibliotheca Gloucestrensis*, xxxvi–xxxvii, xl.

ble moment. As its governor, Massey deserved and received the thanks of parliament, £1,000 for himself, pay for his garrison, and arms and reinforcements for his exhausted command.[66]

Then Massey returned to the offensive. In the spring of 1644 he stormed five royalist garrisons in eighteen days before running out of men and money. By the autumn, the governor could no longer man the conquests he was making, and so he periodically remade them, in hand-to-hand combat. "Active" Massey, he was labeled. To take advantage of his obvious abilities and to give the governor a long-promised promotion, parliament appointed him major general of the five-county Western Association in May 1645. Major General Massey left Gloucester to assist Fairfax in the conquest of the West (his brigade compelled Apsley's surrender of Barnstaple). He did not return to the city as governor for more than a decade.[67]

From July 1646, General Massey sat for Gloucester in parliament. When the first civil war ended in the autumn of that year, Massey lost his field command and became a leading opponent of the religious and political radicalism supported by the New Model army. The Presbyterians in parliament appointed Major General Massey to command the London militia against the army. The army's twenty thousand troops were irresistible, however, and it seized London and parliament on August 4, 1647. Massey fled to Holland, the first of his four dramatic escapes from Cromwell's army in the next decade. He was one of the few Englishmen given a command in Charles II's and the Scots Presbyterians' abortive invasion of England in 1651. He served as lieutenant colonel of cavalry, lieutenant general, and governor of Kirkcaldy. Wounded and captured before Worcester, Massey escaped again, this time from the Tower of London. He joined the diplomatic service of Charles II, but the coils of diplomacy and the pointless bitterness of exile politics literally sickened him. The general wanted to act "with my sword in my hand against His Majesty's enemies." So

66. Preston, *Gorges of Plymouth Fort*, 341–342, 343–344. On the siege of Gloucester, see *DNB*, s.v. "Massey"; Firth's introduction to Hutchinson, *Memoirs*, 118–183; Webb, in Washbourn, ed., *Bibliotheca Gloucestrensis*, xlvii–l, lxxii, and documents appended. Clarendon stressed the garrison strategy in his explanation of the decision to attack Gloucester as the key to control of the Severn trade route and to the area as a source of "contributions" (*History of the Rebellion*, II, 312*ff*).

67. On the capture of royalist garrisons, see Webb's narration of 16 skirmishes, Nov. 1643–May 1644, in Washbourn, ed., *Bibliotheca Gloucestrensis*, lxxxi, also lxxxvi–lxxxviii. Webb also discusses the deficiencies of men and money (pp. lxxvi, lxxix–lxxx, lxxii, lxxxiv); note the governor's own support of a company of infantry and a troop of cavalry (p. lxxxiii). Massey's services as a general of the Western Association are sketched by Webb, *ibid.*, cix, and Firth and Davies, *Regimental History*, xix–xx.

he returned to a life of plot, skirmish, betrayal, and escape as a leading organizer of English Presbyterian resistance to the Protectorate.[68]

King Charles was obsessed with the need to command county seats and seaports, and Gloucester in particular, so he commissioned Massey as governor of that city in January 1660. Massey's new term began when he seized the city in March. As Clarendon had said, "When the time is ripe for action, there will be very few things more hopeful, and fill the hearts of the people better, . . . than to hear that Gloucester is defended for the king by Massey." General Massey's return was "one of those revolutions which providence brings about"—dramatic testimony to the role of soldier-executives in restoring the monarchy that they would maintain henceforward, both at home and overseas.[69]

For his part in restoring the monarchy, parliament voted Massey £4,000. The king knighted him and added the governorship of Jamaica to his command of Gloucester. Although Massey did not go out to Jamaica, his influence was already indirectly manifest in the colony through the powerful clique of his officer protégés in the island government. Their martial tutor continued to serve Stuart imperialism at home. He was the royal governor of Gloucester, a member of parliament from that city, and the last colonel of the famous "Tower Regiment," which he disbanded at Gloucester. He served England's overseas interests as well, as commissioner of prizes, as colonel of a regiment of foot in the second Dutch war, and as commander of a company of foot in England's Irish colony.[70]

68. Washbourn, ed., *Bibliotheca Gloucestrensis*, appendix XXII (A); Hutchinson, *Memoirs*, 246. See also Samuel Rawson Gardiner, ed., *Letters and Papers Illustrating the Relations between Charles the Second and Scotland in 1650*, Publications of the Scottish Historical Society, XVII (Edinburgh, 1894), 114; John Lilburne to Cromwell, Mar. 23, 1654, C. H. Firth, ed., *Scotland and the Protectorate: Letters and Papers Relating to the Military Government of Scotland from January 1654 to June 1659*, Publications of the Scot. Hist. Soc., XXI (Edinburgh, 1899), 59; David Underdown, *Royalist Conspiracy in England, 1649–1660* (New Haven, Conn., 1960), 14, 231, 236, 242, 248–249.

69. Hutchinson, *Memoirs*, 267; Matthew Rowe to William Cadogan, Jan. 23, 1649, anon., Mar. 21, 1651, Massey to the king, Feb. 21, to Ormond, Mar. 13, Apr. 3, 24, 1653, HMC, *Ormonde*, II, 87, N.S., I, 166, 268–269, 272–273, 278–282, 285–288. See the Gloucester town register for Dec. 2, 1657, in Washbourn, ed., *Bibliotheca Gloucestrensis*, cxxix, also appendix XXII (B–G). Webb discusses Massey's activities, *ibid.*, cxxix–cxxxi (he also cites Clarendon to Mordaunt, May 9, 1659; see Clarendon, *History of the Rebellion*, III, 464); similarly, Underdown, *Royalist Conspiracy*, 258, 261–263, 302, 308, 309. See also the king to Maj. Gen. Massey, Jan. 14, 1660, Clarendon, *History of the Rebellion*, III, 646–647; the king to Massey, Mar. 3, and to "my friends," Mar. 11, 1659, Sir H. Moore to Clarendon, May 27, 1659, Capt. John Nicholas to Maj. Gen. Charles Fleetwood, July 13, 1659, Massey to Clarendon, Nov. 14, 1659, Feb. 10, 17, 1660, F. J. Routledge, ed., *Calendar of the Clarendon State Papers*, Vol. IV, *1657–1660* (Oxford, 1932), 152, 156, 216, 273, 433, 555–556, 564.

70. C. H. Firth, ed., *The Narrative of General Venables, with an Appendix of Papers Relat-*

The Irish Experience of Garrison Government

In addition to Sir Edward Massey, officers on the Irish establishment included such imperial figures as General Monck (now the king's captain general and the duke of Albemarle), Sir Charles Wheeler (afterward governor-general of the Leeward Islands), both William Penns, and Lieutenant Colonel James Mutlow (whose Guardsman brother would command in Virginia). These were for the most part sinecure appointments. King Charles used them to keep in pay supernumerary English officers (and a reserve of troops), as military insurance against renewed civil war in England and Scotland. Ireland sustained royal forces that the king's English revenue could not afford and that his English parliament would not permit. Soldiers from Irish garrisons periodically reinforced the king's forces in England, Scotland, France, and the overseas dominions. The English army in Ireland also served to hold down the "natives," as the English called the Irish, by garrisoning the most strategic seaports and the provincial capitals. In Ireland, as in American colonies, the English army of occupation labored on its commanders' "plantations." And in Ireland, as in other garrison governments, company commanders contracted for their soldiers' uniforms and food and issued their pay. Fraud in each area put uncounted pounds in captains' pockets.[71]

Corrupt as it was, English garrison government in Ireland systematically suppressed the native population. Many an imperial officer learned sharp lessons there in forceful colonization and martial government. Massey's generation was preceded in Ireland (and in America) by such veterans of the civil wars as Colonel Thomas Dongan of Dublin, Tangier, and New York, and Colonel William Moore and General Robert Venables of Ulster and Jamaica. It was succeeded by such junior officers as Richard Ingoldsby and Benjamin Fletcher (both of whom commanded in Athlone and New York), Lionel Copley (of Dublin and Maryland), Edmund Andros (of the Irish Guards and a half-dozen colonial commands), and William O'Brien, Lord O'Brien and second earl of Inchiquin

---

ing to the *Expedition to the West Indies and the Conquest of Jamaica, 1654–1655*, Publications of the Camden Society, N.S., LX (London, 1900), xii, xvii; chapter 4 below; Firth and Davies, *Regimental History*, 307; Dalton, ed., *English Army Lists*, I, 66.

71. HMC, *Ormonde*, I, 241–242, 244–245, II, 192, 194. Some of Massey's land claims may have dated from his services in Ireland under Ormond in 1640 (*ibid.*, I, 122, also 263, 269, 305, 310, II, 196, 200, 303, 309); see also Thomas Carte, *The Life of James Duke of Ormond . . .* , new ed., 6 vols. (Oxford, 1851 [orig. publ. Oxford, 1735–1736]), V, 60. On the use of Irish forces in Great Britain, see, for example, HMC, *Ormonde*, for the expedition from York and Ulster against the Scots (I, 268) and for recruits for the king's forces in England (I, 400).

(of Boyle, Tangier, Bandon, and Jamaica). If the faintest credence can be given to the statistics of the partisan observers of this tortured time, when these veteran commanders of Ireland went to command overseas, they found thousands of enslaved, imprisoned, indentured, and exiled Irish in the colonies. The Irish bondsmen were a turbulent, embittered population. Their memories of forceful solutions to social and political problems were just as keen, if not so articulate, as those of their oppressors, England's officers and governors.[72]

For both victors and victims of the Anglo-Irish struggle, unforgettable lessons—"the shame and plague of both the land and age"—rose out of the coincident terrors of the Irish rebellion and the English civil wars. In the winter of 1641 and 1642, every Irish town within a dozen miles of Dublin was pillaged and burned by the capital's garrison, "which as it comforted the soldiers, so it laid a mark of his Majesty's indignation, with terror to others, on those inhabitants for their defection." As always, the command of the garrison was disputed between a council of provincial magnates and the royal military governor.[73]

The governor and council disputed which of them should exercise executive and martial authority, but they agreed on what that authority must include: not only the ultimate power to hang prisoners without trial (thus saving food and making room for more prisoners), but also more mundane military authority, that is, power to police the movements of passengers and of letters through the seaports and to seize estates from which to arm, feed, clothe, and shoe the troops who were the instruments of English authority. Divided authority left the troops "in such nakedness that it is even a shame and dishonor to the State." If the soldiers had shoes, however, they could march to man garrisons on the frontiers of English settlement. From frontier forts, the garrison patrols could seek the native rebels in their "fastnesses, bogs, and woods," as, in the 1640s, Sir John Berkeley's men did in Connaught and his brother Sir William's soldiers did in Virginia.[74]

In time, the party allegiance of the English conquerors of Ireland largely shifted from king to parliament, but their tactics against the native Irish did not alter. Colonel George Cooke had learned bush fighting and scalp collecting—an efficient New World

72. Richard Bagwell, *Ireland under the Stuarts and during the Interregnum*, 3 vols. (London, 1909–1916), II, 210, 213, 345–346, 346n.
73. Lords justices and council to the lord lieutenant (Ormond), Feb. 12, 1642, HMC, *Ormonde*, I, 71, also 57–58, 72–73, 73–74.
74. *Ibid.*, 74, 101–102.

improvement on Ireland's cumbersome headhunting—in war against the natives of New England before he applied these lessons to those of Ireland. This former speaker of the Massachusetts house of deputies and captain of the Bay colony's artillery company raised a regiment in England for the Irish wars and became governor of Wexford, with his regiment as his garrison. Their record is terribly typical of the racial, religious, and colonial war of conquest in which they fought. After the English garrison of Enniscorthy was surprised and slaughtered by the Irish, Governor Cooke stormed the place and executed its Irish defenders. More of the governor's time was taken up with a regular army's perennial pursuit of guerrillas. Failing their capture, the army destroyed the natives' food supply and shelter, the resources that supported guerrillas. Colonel Cooke described a search-and-destroy operation in a letter of March 1652:

In searching the woods and bogs, we found great store of corn, which we burnt, also all the houses and cabins we could find: in all which we found great plenty of corn. We continued burning and destroying for four days: in which time we wanted no provision for horse or man, finding housing enough to lie in; though we burnt our quarters every morning, and continued burning all day after. He was an idle soldier that had not either a fat lamb, veal, pig, poultry, or all of them every night for his supper.

A month after this, the Irish ambushed Cooke and killed him. The parliamentary committee forgot their political jealousy of the military governor and reported to Westminster that "the merit of the gentleman was very great in his zeal to God, and your service, and in his activity and valour against the common enemy, in which he hath been sundry times successful."[75]

Even more "successful" in this war of atrocities was Colonel Cooke's superior, General Robert Venables, the commander of Ulster. Venables began his military service in England during the first civil war, becoming a colonel and the governor of Liverpool in 1648. The Irish rebellion of 1649 led Venables to recruit an English regiment to help suppress the outbreak. After raising the siege of Dublin, Venables and his regiment were even more bloodily distinguished at the storm of Drogheda. Brigaded under Venables's command with three additional regiments, his troops joined the

75. Firth and Davies, *Regimental History*, 579–581. On guerrilla warfare in Ireland, see Bagwell, *Ireland under the Stuarts*, II, 280–281, 295–297, 300. Bagwell also discusses the storm of Enniscorthy, the hoped-for migration of New Englanders to the Cromwellian plantations in Ireland, and the active influence, via Col. George Cooke and other returned colonists, of the New England experience on the plantation system in Ireland (*ibid.*, II, 215, 316, 340). Note the reversal of the long-recognized Irish influence on American plantation.

forces of Sir Charles Coote (the uncle of Richard Coote, earl of Bellomont and governor of New York, New Jersey, and Massachusetts) in a three-year campaign to reduce royalist and Irish garrisons in Ulster. Venables's veterans fought in five regular sieges and two pitched battles before settling down to colonize the Ulster lands they received in lieu of pay and, being Independents, to quarrel with the Ulster Presbyterian ministers. Threatened with transportation to America, some Presbyterians took loyalty oaths:

> Then let's subscribe, and go thorough stitch,
> As long as we are governed by a soldier's switch.

The soldier's switch was needed. As long as he remained in Ireland, Venables had to march his men out from their plantations against the elusive native guerrillas. Finally, in December 1654, as C. H. Firth put it, "Venables had the ill luck to be appointed general of the forces sent to attack the Spaniards." Like so many of the Irish he had overcome, Venables was himself transported to the West Indies. There he captured Jamaica as England's imperial outpost in the Caribbean and once again settled English soldiers on plantations cut from conquered territory.[76]

Conquest, expropriation, and forced transportation of displaced populations remained meaningful terms in the harsh language of Irish politics during the Protectorate. So Thomas Dongan and his family found to their cost. Charles II acknowledged in 1653 that his fellow exile Colonel Dongan had "served during the recent war in Ireland, with great intrepidity, skill, and loyalty, as Colonel and quartermaster-general of the royal army." But after that army was defeated and dispersed, soldiers of the English Protestant commonwealth drove the Irish, Roman Catholic, royalist Dongans from their ancestral lands near Dublin into a Connaught Catholic reservation. Expropriated, Dongan became expatriated also. Turning to the traditional refuge of landless gentlemen, he parlayed his military experience and the recommendation of his royal commander-in-chief into a lifetime military career, which included French and Irish regimental commands and garrison governorships in Tangier and New York.[77] The loyalty of necessity,

---

76. Bagwell, *Ireland under the Stuarts*, II, 197, 209, 236, 270, 287, 288, 305–306, 341–342; verses by Charles Staynings, in Mary Anne Everett Green, ed., *Calendar of State Papers, Domestic Series, 1649–[1660]*, 13 vols. (1875–1886; repr. Vaduz, Liechtenstein, 1965), *1654*, 282 (hereafter cited as *Cal. S.P. Dom.*); Firth and Davies, *Regimental History*, 666–667; Firth, ed., *Narrative of Venables*, viii–ix, 2–3.

77. Charles II, passport, July 25, 1653, HMC, *Ormonde*, I, 11. See also *ibid.*, 152, II, 133, 249–253. Fleetwood to Thurloe, Aug. 2, 1654, also proposed a "free-fire zone" for Scotland, since he had used one successfully in Ireland; see Thomas Birch, ed., *A Collection of the*

the French connection, and the mercenary experience that made Irish Catholic soldiers so valuable to the Stuart kings also made officers and governors such as Dongan profoundly suspect to the libertarian, Francophobe, Protestant parliamentarians and provincials of England and its empire.

The restoration of the Stuart monarchy increased religious tolerance, decreased political violence, and so reduced Irish traumas. But two Irish native revolts and two English civil wars had riveted garrison government on to Ireland. Governors and garrisons were the symbols and safeguards of England's conquest. The conquerors' commander was the king's lieutenant and governor-general. He "held the sword" in Dublin Castle, the key to the kingdom and twice in twenty years the last refuge of English authority in Ireland. Ireland's viceroy, its governors and occupation forces, not only set administrative examples for the rest of England's empire but also provided it with officer-administrators.

In 1677, at the beginning of his third term as governor-general of Ireland, James, duke of Ormond, was asked for passports, long a gubernatorial responsibility. He refused to issue them "till I should have received the sword" of state. With "this sword, the instrument of conferring military honour and the emblem of inflicting punishment," again in hand, the viceroy set out to reform the military government of Ireland. Ormond voiced the complaint echoed by almost every later governor-general: "Our army is too little, our forts ruined, and our magazines almost empty." As governors-general also always did, Ormond blamed his predecessor for this unpreparedness, exclaiming "how empty he left the stores, how ruinous the store houses and forts, and how utterly unprovided the whole kingdom of all things that belonged to war, but the bare bodies of men; and very many of those antiquated and unserviceable."[78]

Ormond's complaints, like his life experience, testified to his sense of the army's centrality in imperial government. His profes-

State Papers of John Thurloe, Esq; Secretary, First, to the Council of State, And afterwards to The Two Protectors, Oliver and Richard Cromwell, 7 vols. (London, 1742), II, 516 (hereafter cited as Birch, ed., Thurloe S.P.). On transportation and its execution by martial law, see Bagwell, Ireland, II, chapter 37, esp. 318, 323, 325, 333.

78. Orrery to Ormond, Dec. 3, 1678, and "A Diary of Events in Ireland from 1685 to 1690," entry of Jan. 9, 1686, HMC, Ormonde, N.S., IV, 260, VIII, 345; Hutchinson, Memoirs, 76. See also Bagwell, Ireland under the Stuarts, III, 101–102; Ormond's speech to parliament, Sept. 27, 1662, Carte, Ormond, V, 34; Ormond to Sir Robert Southwell, Nov. 11, 1678, Aug. 24, 1679, HMC, Ormonde, II, 279, 291.

sional attitude toward that army was equally evident in his lament that,

For some time past, commands have either been given or perhaps sold to those who have been strangers to the army or they have been trucked for betwixt the officers so at last some body came in for money, whereby good officers who wanted dexterity, money or favour were never advanced nor could volunteers, who carry pikes in the regiment, ever come to be ensigns, to the great discouragement of all those who have a mind to learn the trade; this I have begun to reform and hope to effect it if I am not imposed upon from the other side [England], as I hope I shall not [be]; considering how much it imports the discipline of an army to have a due succession observed.[79]

As military discipline and loyalty depended upon the general's control of promotion, so the control of provincial patronage, the ability to resist interference from Whitehall, was the essence of any governor's power. Ormond's enormous prestige consolidated his appointive power and, together with his obvious desire to "find out a man of experience and acquainted in arms" to fill each of his executive positions, reinforced the martial character of Ireland's executives. The governor-general, for example, successfully resisted the grant of a town government "to one who I have heard to be a better Parliament man than a soldier whilst we have so many old officers who have come to the stations they are in by degrees and the expence of time and blood."[80]

With the help of his veteran soldier subordinates, Ormond not only fulfilled his duty to hold down the Irish but also supplied King Charles with the means for military repression elsewhere in the British Isles. Yet he did so against Anglo-Irish opinion. When the Scots rose in 1679 and the governor-general was called on to list the troops he could send against the rebels, he acknowledged that "it is not unusual to require from Governors of garrisons and provinces an account of what men they can spare towards a campaign," but he noted that the provinces of Ireland, like those else-

79. Ormond to Southwell, Nov. 6, 1677, HMC, *Ormonde*, II, 265.
80. Ormond to Sir William Temple, Sept. 28, 1680, Carte, *Ormond*, V, 146; Ormond to Southwell, Feb. 24, 1678, HMC, *Ormonde*, II, 268. The centrality of the army to government in Ireland was affirmed at the end of Ormond's term, as it had been at the outset. To catholicize that army, Ormond was removed; see the king, the duke of York, and the earl of Rochester to Ormond, Oct. 19, 21, 23, 1684, Carte, *Ormond*, V, 166–168. Ormond's letter to the king, Oct. 26 (*ibid.*, 170), pointed out that the government was now "supported by such a force, that an attempt to disturb it may not seem easy" for the first time in 40 years. This was an eloquent statement of the authoritarian accomplishment of the Stuart regime. See also Carte, *Ormond*, V, 176, and Bishop Gilbert Burnet, *Burnet's History of My Own Time*, ed. Osmund Airy, 2 vols. (Oxford, 1897–1900), II, 449–450 (hereafter cited as Burnet, *History*).

where in the empire, disliked the dispatch abroad of their garrisons. Provincials correctly complained that "these men they have fed in times of peace and safety are taken from their defence in times of danger." Ormond believed, however, that most of this opposition sprang from political malice toward the monarchy and from provincial ignorance of imperial needs. Both the provincial complaints and the gubernatorial deprecation of them were to be repeated many times in colonies across the Atlantic.[81]

Ireland's viceroy requested what every governor required, the support of royal commands for the government of his province, "which I think needs only authority and directions to provide for its own security." Provincial ability to obey those orders, however, whether for self-defense or domestic pacification, was reduced in Ireland, as in other colonies, by the English exchequer's control of the provincial treasury. Payoffs to parasites at Whitehall drained away the money that the governor-general and his advisers designed for Ireland's weapons, stores of war, and army. Similar sapsucking followed the extension of English exchequer authority to colonies across the Atlantic. Strong commanders would be militarily, and so politically, crippled by English requisitions for purposes unconnected with provincial defense, requisitions inimical to the basic political equation of imperial government: the exchange of obedience for protection. The incompatibility of the unjustified profits of English politicians with the effective assertion of England's prerogative overseas was a permanent problem of empire.[82]

Ormond, like other and lesser provincial governors-general, was also afflicted by another imperial dilemma: the opposed requirements of the rules of law and of force. Ireland's ruler recognized, for example, that it was illegal to quarter his troops on his subjects, to seize their private property, and to exercise martial law over the army in peacetime and over civilians during emergencies, without any commission to do either. The custom of governors-general, the law of necessity, the benefits of social stability, and the

81. For the pursuit of tories by Ormond's troops, see Bagwell, *Ireland under the Stuarts*, III, 91–92, 142–144, 147, 177–178. See also Ormond to Southwell, June 17, 1679, HMC, *Ormonde*, II, 288; instructions for James, duke of Ormond, lieutenant general and governor-general of Ireland, S.P. 44/4, 52, 60–61. Note that James II used the Irish army in England in 1685 and 1688, as did William III in 1697.

82. Ormond to Southwell, June 23, 1679, Southwell to Ormond, Mar. 16, 1678, June 17, 21, 1679, HMC, *Ormonde*, II, 288–289, N.S., IV, 415, 524–527; Ormond to the duke of York, May 27, 1681, Carte, *Ormond*, V, 162–163. Stephen Saunders Webb, "William Blathwayt, Imperial Fixer: Muddling Through to Empire, 1689–1717," *William and Mary Quarterly*, 3d Ser., XXVI (1969), 414–415, gives a later example of this conflict.

blessing of provincial peace, Ormond argued, all drove him to such illegal—but inevitable—acts. Therefore the viceroy not only defended his own militant administration but also quickly quashed town corporations' complaints against the allegedly illegal acts of his subordinates, their military governors. While in commission, governors-general and their military subordinates were spared suits at law by their status as soldiers of the king. Retiring executives, Ormond included, often sought a royal pardon for their actions in office before they laid down the sword of command and again became liable to the rule of that civil law they had so often ignored.[83]

An Irish viceroy's often extralegal commands were executed by a variety of subordinate military administrators. Each of them exercised part of the governor-general's prerogative. When these officers eventually assumed provincial commands overseas, their sense of the executive role reflected their Irish experiences. Those army officers who had been commissioned as governors of Irish coastal cities had supervised the movement of private persons, taken custody of prisoners of war or state, distributed prize goods, and commanded troops and transports. Often they had acted as vice admirals, and sought boat allowances, station ships, and crews from the royal navy in order to police and protect their harbors. To control port cities and populations, to maintain citadels and batteries, these governors had asked for additional troops and larger ordnance, more matériel, and money. They had requested, usually in vain, their arrears of pay and those of their men. When soldiers mutinied because of bad treatment, the governors had shipped them off to fill up the king's regiments in England or in France. Occasionally, when menaced by the approach of the muster master, these local governors recruited replacements for their garrison companies.[84]

Always the governors tried to reduce their military dependence on the local militia and to increase their legal independence of the local magistrates. The officer-executives quartered troops

83. Ormond to Southwell, Nov. 8, 1679, HMC, *Ormonde*, II, 294–296; see the identical rationale—that necessity justifies martial law and military police—presented by Lord Lieutenant Essex, in Bagwell, *Ireland under the Stuarts*, III, 117. On (illegal) quartering as a guarantee of political security, see Ormond to the earl of Orrery, Sept. 20, 1677, Carte, *Ormond*, V, 52, also 64, 67–68, 69, 75–76; the earl of Ossory to Ormond, Sept. 20, 1679, HMC, *Ormonde*, N.S., V, 211. On martial law, see Carte, *Ormond*, V, 90, and on governors' relations with corporations, see Ormond to Ossory, Dec. 10, 1679, HMC, *Ormonde*, N.S., V, 252.

84. On the requirements of coastal governments, see especially Maj. Nicholas Bayly (Baily) to Ormond, Feb. [?], 1664, and Ormond's following letters and orders, HMC, *Ormonde*, I, 295–299. See also Bayly to [?], Sept. 12, 1668, *ibid.*, N.S., III, 286, and the case of Col. John Spencer, in n. 85 below.

on private citizens or taxed them to pay for heat, light, and beer for troops in barracks. Their soldiers often robbed and occasionally murdered townspeople. Soldiers' cheap labor always competed with that of the townsmen. All these military provocations set local magistrates against garrison commanders on the judicial benches they shared. Not only did the magistrates reflect the townsmen's dislike of troops, but they also resented their own military subordination to the governor. Governors marched the town militias (including their magistrate-officers) to the provincial musters and there drilled them in the use of arms drawn for the occasion from the governors' magazines. Decades of native rebellion and years of civil war had driven military governors thus to convert each garrisoned town into a "place of strength," for the "better security of the King's friends upon any occasion," despite the apathy of the population and the enmity of the oligarchy.[85]

Enmity and apathy made military coercion essential. James II's military engineer and surveyor, Colonel Thomas Phillips, observed of Ireland's cities that the subversive influence of multitudes of "ill-minded people" was compounded by an utter absence of public spirit: "The business of most people here is nothing but getting of money without the least regard to their Prince's service." This centurion's disapproving comments on burgesses' mercenary loyalties underlay his recommendations—repeated so often in imperial reports from America—that the king reinforce or construct citadels to command the provincial capitals, build additional batteries to protect and to control shipping in the harbors (and so to secure royal customs revenue), and, finally, to demand a better account of the uses made of that royal revenue. For the surveyor noted, as imperial auditors always did, that money allocated to provincial governments for public works invariably found its way into private pockets.[86]

85. Thomas Phillips to the earl of Dartmouth, Feb. 26, 1685, Historical Manuscripts Commission, *The Manuscripts of the Earl of Dartmouth*, 3 vols. (London, 1887–1899), I, 122 (hereafter cited as HMC, *Dartmouth*). Of the many Irish governors' administrations, two typical ones are documented here. The first, that of Col. Thomas Trafford, governor of Trim, covers the civil war period. Note that his actions precisely parallel those of Massey at Gloucester; see HMC, *Ormonde*, II, 28–31, 32–33, 38, 41–42, 44–45, 46, 47, 48, 49, 56, 58, 110–112, N.S., I, 263–264. Gov. John Spencer, of Galway, and some of his colleagues exemplified the Restoration governments, recalled Gorges's efforts at Plymouth, and fully anticipated those of Andros in New York; see HMC, *Ormonde*, I, 267, 268, 275, 277, 302, 333, II, 188, 198, N.S., III, 229–230, 235–237, also I, 255, 257. See also Carte, *Ormond*, V, 64–65.

86. Phillips to Dartmouth, Feb. 26, 1685, HMC, *Dartmouth*, I, 122, also 124*ff*; Dalton, ed., *English Army Lists*, I, 226, II, 113, III, 304, 305n. Note the similar status and motivation of Roman imperial auditors in Britain and such English auditors as John Lewin in the province of New York.

Ireland's garrison government displayed administrative as well as fiscal failings. At the levels of both garrison and province, military administrators were often absent, sometimes without leave. Subalterns commanded in their stead. Lord John Berkeley, the lax president of Connaught, left his own troop of cavalry to the care of Cornet Benjamin Fletcher. The only merit of the practice was that such subordinates learned to meet foreign and domestic dangers with the ill-paid men of the "independent" (unregimented) companies that formed most garrisons. These nuclei of English troops sustained the settlers' morale and provided them with a rallying point in emergencies. As Governor-General Ormond said, "I have to spread the army very thin to keep the Tories [Irish guerrillas] in awe and the English in heart." This use of unregimented companies in support of English colonization, and these independent companies' peculiarities of discipline, recruitment, and quartering, characterized the garrisons of other overseas provinces throughout the empire.[87]

Benjamin Fletcher, for example, acquired appropriate imperial experience in the ten years he took to become captain of an independent company. He lost that command in James II's expulsion of Protestant officers from Ireland in 1685, joined the military coup of 1688 against the Catholic king, and returned to Ireland in the army of that Protestant soldier, William III. The king so approved of Fletcher's field command that he commissioned him governor-general of New York: "His Majesty Having of his own choice in considering of his Services during the whole war of Ireland taken him out of Colonel Beaumont's Regiment where he was Major and sent him to New York as a person very fit to manage the War in those parts."[88]

---

87. Carte, *Ormond*, V, 91. Note the mutiny of the unpaid Carrickfergus garrison and Ormond's efficient suppression of it (Bagwell, *Ireland under the Stuarts*, III, 68–69). Lord Robartes, as Ireland's governor-general, required even commanding officers to reside at their posts all but three months a year, much to the discomfort of Lord O'Brien, who had to take up his duty in "the devilishest Tory country in Ireland" in 1669, prior to his governments of Tangier and Jamaica (*ibid.*, 326; O'Brien to Temple, Sept. 28, 1680, Carte, *Ormond*, V, 146).

88. "A list of the persons received into his majestie's army in Ireland since 1662," "A list of the quarters of the army April 20th, 1668," "A list of the officers in the year 1672, showing which of them are now in the army," Aug. 29, 1677, HMC, *Ormonde*, I, 355, II, 195, 204; Fletcher's English commission, Sept. 12, 1688, Dalton, ed., *English Army Lists*, II, 162; William Blathwayt to the lords justices, Aug. 8, 1695, Additional Manuscripts 9722, 89–90, British Library (hereafter cited as Add. MSS). See also S. S. Webb, "Blathwayt, 1689–1717," *WMQ*, 3d Ser., XXVI (1969), 395–396. The favorable report on Fletcher's regimental performance is reprinted in Dalton, ed., *English Army Lists*, III, 106–107, 107 n. 2. From the first civil war onward, the commanders of important garrison governments ranked as colonels of the regular army; note Fletcher's brevet as colonel on his appointment to New

King William's promotion of Fletcher from military service in Ireland to be colonel and governor of New York continued a well-established tradition of imperial government: Fletcher's predecessors in command of the province, Colonel Thomas Dongan and Major Edmund Andros, had also held Irish commands prior to their New York governments. Likewise, officers of the Irish army went out to bring order to England's imperial conquests in Africa and the West Indies. So did veterans of the English occupation of Scotland, such as George Fenwick.

Scotland under Military Government, 1650–1654

A lawyer, George Fenwick had gone to Connecticut in 1636 as the agent of the Warwick patentees. He was titled "governor" of the fort, town, and houses at Saybrook. The fort and blockhouse had been built to inaugurate the settlement in 1635, but "Saybrook lost much of its military character by 1641." By that time, also, it was evident that the Puritan patentees, now powers in the Long Parliament, no longer stood "tiptoe in our land ready to pass to the American strand." They would lead no new mass migration to New England. Governor Fenwick therefore arranged for the nascent Connecticut colony to maintain the fort. After he had served briefly as a Connecticut magistrate and had been one of that colony's commissioners to the United Colonies, he made over the whole settlement to Connecticut. Fenwick returned to England, where he became a member of parliament, served on its committee on plantations, and buckled on the armor of righteousness.[89]

Fenwick's militia regiment won fame for itself and its colonel at the outbreak of the second civil war, fighting in battle and siege under Major General John Lambert's command. Given this military experience, Fenwick served a further apprenticeship in garrison government as deputy governor of Berwick, that prototype Tudor citadel, the administration of which trained such future

---

York. See Hutchinson, *Memoirs*, 275; Ollard, *Sir Robert Holmes*, 194; S. S. Webb, "The Strange Career of Francis Nicholson," *WMQ*, 3d Ser., XXIII (1966), 514 n. 2; Col. Daniel MacKinnon, *Origin and Services of the Coldstream Guards*, 2 vols. (London, 1833), I, 121, 150.

89. Charles M. Andrews, *The Beginnings of Connecticut, 1632–1662*, Connecticut Tercentenary Pamphlet Series, XXXII (New Haven, Conn., 1934), 60–61, gives this characteristically backhanded acknowledgment of Saybrook's "military character." See also *Dictionary of American Biography*, s.v. "Fenwick, George"; Firth and Davies, *Regimental History*, 387–388.

governors-general as Edward Nott of Virginia. Besides his extensive refortification of Berwick, Colonel Fenwick's economic policy was "the observed of all observers." The deputy governor tried to keep tariffs low. He pointed out that the high customs ordered by parliament would put Berwick at a competitive disadvantage with the neighboring Scots: "The trade will wholly be lost, the town left desolate, and the Scots enriched by our ruin," Fenwick wrote. He argued that Berwick's strategic importance and its role in England's national economic rivalry with Scotland justified favorable customs treatment for his government.[90] Fenwick's brief was copied by many English officers commanding governments after 1660, when England's dependencies generally suffered from the same London-inspired, mercantilistic regulations here opposed by Berwick's governor.

Colonel Fenwick also displayed gubernatorial characteristics when he used his extensive local influence to raise troops for the war in Ireland. For this recruitment, and for his work collecting intelligence, Fenwick received the formal thanks of the council of state. Thus Cromwell chose a well-known military executive when he took Fenwick with him into Scotland. In December 1650, Cromwell commissioned Fenwick governor of Edinburgh. From the Scots capital and its seaport, Leith, Governor Fenwick undertook aggressive patrols, and his successful attacks on enemy garrisons fully met the ferocious standards of the time. Indeed, Fenwick's orders to civilians against harboring guerrillas have an uncomfortably modern sound. The Scots irregulars ("moss-troopers"), Fenwick declared, relied on "Protection, Countenance, and Assistance from the Inhabitants of the Country." He ordered collaborators punished "by burning of their Houses." If natives were taken in arms, they were to be executed. Death, as Fenwick's commander put it, would render hostile inhabitants less likely to repeat their error.[91]

90. Fenwick to the commissioners of customs, June 6, 1650, Cal. S.P. Dom., 1650, 192–193. Fenwick also established a public granary, a commonplace executive effort to keep the populace quiet by keeping the price of bread down in times of scarcity (council of state proceedings, May 27, 1650 [no. 2], ibid., 175). See also council of state to Mr. Walley, Oct. 27, 1649, council of state proceedings, Dec. 3 (no. 10), 8 (no. 17), 1649, ibid., 1649–1650, 366, 421, 430–431, regarding money and matériel sent to Fenwick for fortification, and Firth and Davies, Regimental History, 388. On Berwick's garrison government as a school for imperial administrators, see the Appendix, introduction and no. 204.

91. Council of state proceedings, Aug. 24, 1650 (no. 8), Cal. S.P. Dom., 1650, 303. On recruiting, see council of state proceedings, Nov. 24, 1649 (no. 13), ibid., 1649–1650, 405. Venables's forces in Ulster were recruited by Fenwick (Firth and Davies, Regimental History, 388–389). See the proclamation against moss-troopers, Aug. 27, 1651, in C. H. Firth, ed., Scotland and the Commonwealth: Letters and Papers Relating to the Military Government of Scot-

As a base for his punitive expeditions, Fenwick built at Leith one of the greatest citadels of the age. While it protected the strategic port, this fortress also constituted a continuing military and economic challenge to its neighbor, dissident Edinburgh. The fortified complex included the governor's house, storehouses, barracks, and a chapel. Protected by modern walls, entrenchments, and batteries, the citadel embodied physical and political power in a form that many governors-general overseas subsequently tried to emulate.[92]

Other aspects of Governor Fenwick's administration did more than fortification and pacification to expand the dimensions of governorship from the mere command of garrison troops to the government of metropolitan, of provincial, and, finally, of imperial societies. Making civil use of military tools, the governor used courts-martial not only to punish civilians trading with the enemy but also to break economic monopolies and to oppose Edinburgh's municipal exclusiveness in trade. He ordered his courts-martial to protect consumers by regulating the prices, labeling, and vending of food and fodder. Also enforced through the military courts was Governor Fenwick's famous "Proclamation concerning Lighting and Cleaning the Streets," which, among other things, prohibited Edinburgh's odoriferous rain of sewage from the upper stories of houses. "Proclaimed by beat of Drum" to garrison and citizens alike, Fenwick's orders, even that forbidding the marriage of his soldiers to native women and banishing barmaids, all had obvious military utility.[93] These orders also exemplified the expansion of the officer-governor's jurisdiction into economic and social spheres under the spur of his garrison's needs, his nation's interest, and his own broadening social concerns.

The developing social philosophy of the English military governors in Scotland would be carried overseas. It sought to "free the poor commoners, and make as little use as can be either of the great men or clergy." The soldier-executives successfully courted a relatively broad constituency to reduce the influence of their rivals for power, the traditional ruling classes. One native son, who deplored the petty tyrannies of the Scots nobility and "the peevishness, the ill nature, and the ambition of many hot clergy-

---

land from August 1651 to December 1653, Publications of the Scot. Hist. Soc., XVIII (Edinburgh, 1895), 318–319. See also Firth, ed., Scotland and the Protectorate, 113.

92. Firth and Davies, Regimental History, 390–391.

93. See Firth, ed., Scotland and the Commonwealth, xxxiv, 322–323, 344–345, 346–348, 358, for proclamations: against trading with the enemy; regarding the price of hay, and the marking, marketing, and price of bread; and concerning butchers, ferry fees, the streets, marriage, and barmaids.

men," praised English military rule: the pay of garrisons fueled the economy, "there was good justice done, and vice was suppressed and punished, so that we always reckon those eight years of usurption a time of great peace and prosperity." These were the results of Governor Fenwick's expanding use of the military courts as social and economic monitors, his supervision of education, and his regulation of religion. These were political instruments as well as the tools of public peace, economic prosperity, and military security. Nationally, military commissions for regulating Scotland's universities, clergy, and administration all manifested the public, institutional concerns of the military executive.[94]

Fenwick's activity reflected the social formula especially characteristic of the more professional and less aristocratic sort of officer-governors. They first became prominent in the Cromwellian provinces and were predominant under Marlborough. They embodied the state's assertion of military discipline in place of upper-class rule, an assertion designed to win the political support of the middle social ranks for garrison government. The ark of this vision—public interest imperially determined—ran onto the rocks of national, racial, and religious hatreds in Scotland and sank, weighted down by the costs of the garrison government required to administer social discipline and maintain physical security.[95] Nonetheless, the combination of military government, social discipline, and popular appeal—"prerogative politics"—underlay executive assertiveness in England's empire until at least the end of the second decade of the eighteenth century. Prerogative politics enjoyed an even larger measure of success in conquered Jamaica, Virginia, and New York than it did in conquered Scotland or Ireland, for the young royal provinces in the New World had at once a greater need for the social cement that garrison government provided and less of the developed political consciousness that it offended than did the British kingdoms.

The interconnection of England's British and American conquests and colonizations, and the identity of the administrative

94. *Ibid.*, xxxiii–xxxv, xxxiii–xxxiv, xxxvi*ff*, 44–45, 214n; council of state proceedings, June 14, 1654 (no. 23), *Cal. S.P. Dom., 1654*, 211; Burnet, *History*, I, xxxiv, 108–109, 186, 195. This social rationalization by the English conquerors of Scotland closely resembled the one they had used for 75 years in Ireland (Nicholas P. Canny, "The Ideology of English Colonization: From Ireland to America," *WMQ*, 3d Ser., XXX [1973], 597).

95. The Presbyterian church remained the particular bulwark of the challenged traditional establishment. See the telling analysis by Firth, ed., *Scotland and the Commonwealth*, xxxiv–xxxvii, and an example in S. S. Webb, "Francis Nicholson," *WMQ*, 3d Ser., XXIII (1966), 522–523, 529–531, 536, 537–541.

attitudes of the conquerors and colonizers in both cases, were again evident in Cromwell's and Monck's choice of a veteran of Scots garrison government to lead an English army of occupation in the settlement and socialization of Jamaica. That veteran governor was Lieutenant Colonel William Brayne. His regiment had been the spearhead of Cromwell's advance into Scotland. It helped crush the Scots in July 1651, garrisoned Perth, and built a citadel there. Its patrols decimated Highland clans and eliminated enemy garrisons. Brayne's loyalty to his superiors and his skill in administering his regiment led to his increased responsibilities in garrison government. He gathered a thousand soldiers from English garrisons in Ireland and shipped them to Scotland to resist the Scots rebellion of 1654.[96]

Eighteen ships brought these troops to Inverlochy, the heart of the enemy's country and the bleak and hostile site of Colonel Brayne's new government. His troops lived aboard ship while they built a fortress and barracks. From this citadel, Brayne's garrison pacified the Highlands with fire and sword. Houses were burnt, crops destroyed, their defenders killed, "so that the whole Highlands, in all probability, will be laid waste." By winter, the governor of Inverlochy reported that "this place, which was their safe place of retreat and recruit, is now very peaceable, and in a posture of defence, and with the force of the garrison, will be able to oppose any [force] they can bring."[97]

Perhaps Brayne confused desolation with peace, but Inverlochy was the key to both. Its construction and maintenance depended upon the remarkable cooperation between Governor Brayne and the naval captains who cheerfully and competently transported enormous quantities of food, munitions, and stores to Inverlochy from distant depots in the garrison towns of Chester and Carrickfergus. They carried Brayne's troops on coastal raids, cleared enemies—"pirates," they called them—from the shipping lanes, built a supply ship at Inverlochy for the garrison's service, and faithfully supported Brayne's government through the worst of the North Atlantic winter.[98] Difficult duty in response to an

96. Firth and Davies, *Regimental History*, 489–491; Birch, ed., *Thurloe S.P.*, II, 111, 113–114, 285, 295; *Cal. S.P. Dom., 1654*, 150.

97. Firth, ed., *Scotland and the Protectorate*, xx; Brayne to the admiralty committee, Dec. 11, 1654, *Cal. S.P. Dom., 1654*, 408–409.

98. Firth, ed., *Scotland and the Protectorate*, reproduces a manuscript plan of the fort (p. xxxviii) and discusses the strategic importance and logistical challenge of the garrison (pp. xxxviiiff). See also Monck to Cromwell, Aug. 5, 1654, Lord Broghill to Thurloe, Feb. 4, 1655, Birch, ed., *Thurloe S.P.*, II, 527, IV, 500. On the establishment of the garrison, see *Cal. S.P. Dom., 1654*, 260–262 (nos. 46–52iv), 270, 317–318, 367, 382, 408–409, 558. There were

isolated governor's orders was the highest testimony to the Protectorate's martial discipline and esprit de corps. Later governors and governments overseas were almost equally dependent upon English naval support, but they were often denied it by the social and service rivalries ascendant throughout the Restoration. Part of the credit for this unique naval-military cooperation must go to Colonel Brayne. The governor effectively combined conciliation and command (as his career in Jamaica would again demonstrate). He was, as even a subject Scot admitted, "an excellent wise man."[99]

The administrative tools of this capable executive were by now typical of garrison government. First, he established a monopoly of force. He held the weapons of the local populace in his magazine, secured bonds from their leaders to keep the peace, required passes and passports to control movement in his district, and levied local taxes in money and firewood to sustain his garrison. He thus made his garrison the only disciplined, well-armed, mobile force in the region he governed. The governor administered justice to both the garrison and the local population through his court-martial, which made civil and criminal as well as military judgments. Colonel Brayne's instructions asserted that only force had ever compelled obedience to law in the turbulent Highlands. "For the remedying of which disorders and civilizing of the said people," Brayne was ordered to use all "good and convenient ways to bring the inhabitants . . . to a more civil life and conversation." The governor did exercise his "utmost endeavors for keeping the public peace." In return for his Scottish subjects' peaceable behavior, he tried to protect their lives and property both from their neighbors and from the garrison. The result, as one Scot observed, was that "where there was nothing but barbarities . . . there is not one robbery all this year; although formerly it was their trade they lived by to rob and steal."[100]

General Monck insisted that the Protector promote this judicious and successful officer-governor. Colonel Brayne hoped that

---

hitches serious enough to threaten the garrison with starvation; see Birch, ed., *Thurloe S.P.*, II, 405–406, 516.

99. J. Drummond to Thurloe, Jan. 8, 1656, Birch, ed., *Thurloe S.P.*, IV, 401 (also cited by Firth, ed., *Scotland and the Protectorate*, 491).

100. Monck's instructions to Brayne as governor, June 6, 1655, Birch, ed., *Thurloe S.P.*, III, 520–521; treaty with Evan Cameron of Lechiel, May 1655, Firth, ed., *Scotland and the Protectorate*, 276–280, esp. 277–279. See also Monck to Lambert, Apr. 5, 1655, *ibid.*, 262, also xxxiii, xxxvi, xxxix, 293, 304; Birch, ed., *Thurloe S.P.*, IV, 401; and Firth and Davies, *Regimental History*, 491. Bishop Burnet recalled that "the country was kept in great order: some castles in the Highlands had garrisons put in them, that were careful in their discipline, and so exact in their rules, that in no time the Highlands were kept in better order than during the usurption" (*History*, 108).

he might get paid. He went to London and found that the prestige he had won in the most remote garrison government of Great Britain had earned for him a yet more distant (and still unpaid) command. Cromwell ordered Brayne to pick a regiment of veterans from the army in Scotland and with them to secure and civilize Jamaica, England's newly conquered province and the key to Cromwellian imperialism.[101]

Garrison Government in the British Isles

As Brayne's career demonstrated, the office of governor-general and the forms of garrison government had acquired institutional definition and political power in the three generations prior to the Restoration. Their essential characteristics were military. In strategically important governments, a citadel housed a military executive and his staff of officer-administrators. Together with their garrison, they militarized and nationalized provincial politics by creating a local political and police presence for the national executive. As provincial proconsuls, the governors-general steadily increased their power relative to that of the traditionally dominant local elites. Thus they enhanced the regional authority of the national government that commissioned and instructed the governors-general and provided their garrisons. Although the civil wars destroyed such instruments of the crown's provincial control as the prerogative courts and the council of the North, the wars at the same time amplified the political and military importance of the authoritarian institution of the governors-general and their garrison governments. From being the captain-caretakers of crumbling medieval castles, royal military executives became regional military and naval administrators, financial agents, election managers, economic regulators, and magistrates, both civil and military. Officers became, in a word, governors.

The governors-general represented a national government of mutable political purpose and variable physical power. The martial, material, and political support that the central authority supplied its officer-executives in the localities was always less than they thought they needed to enforce its orders effectively. But the nationalist, ultimately imperialist, aspiration that governors-general

101. See n. 94 above and chapter 4 below. Broghill praised Brayne as an officer "of parts, honesty and affection to the government" in a letter to Thurloe asking him to secure £1,000 in arrears owed to Brayne, Feb. 4, 1656, Birch, ed., *Thurloe S.P.*, IV, 500.

forcefully expressed vastly amplified the local influence of the English executive.

Political dynamics as well as institutional structures developed in the formative period of English imperialism. Between 1569 and 1681, the period in which the executive institution of the governor-generalcy was established, there also matured oligarchy's institutional counterweight, the magnate council. These two institutions, and the political dynamic between them, were identical in function, and in some cases in personnel, to the governor and council system as it was imposed on English imperial governments in America.

The imposition of political structure, military discipline, and national usefulness on such ancient agencies of local authority as military captaincies and elite councils were some of the institutional products of the rise of garrison government. Increased provincial involvement in national politics was another result. The governor-general's self-interest lay in building a local power base and representing it to the central government. To preserve its accustomed hegemony, the local elite found that it had to compete with the governor in securing the capital's recognition of local needs. The traditional rulers also found that the most effective way to attack a governor-general was to appeal against him to the source of his authority, that is, to exploit political enmities in the capital. The presence of the executive in the provinces thus inspired two sets of new links to the metropolis: one via the governors-general and their superiors, the other through these executives' elitist opponents and their representatives: legislative, councilliar, and economic. The importance of these ties between British localities and London—inspired by garrison government, nationalizing domestic society and politics—was more than matched in the overseas provinces. In America and the West Indies, such links became the first effective governmental bonds of empire.

CHAPTER 2

Officers and Governors

The Roots of Stuart Absolutism

In October 1659 an army faction turned out what remained of the parliament of England. "We had now no Government in the Nation," John Evelyn lamented, "all in Confusion, no Magistrate either owned or pretended but the soldiers and they not agreed." Led by General Monck, those soldiers who believed in civil authority as the prerequisite of social stability restored the monarchy. The king-in-parliament, they hoped, would veil the politics of armed force with a semblance of traditional authority and of customary social sanction. But the clothes of constitution and of law could not conceal the reshaped body politic, force-fed during twenty years of civil war and revolution. The political predominance of military might, "the sword that will give the law to law," could not be wished away.[1]

Charles II, however, tried to end military rule. Initially, he associated his own restoration with that of the unarmed state of 1637. He hastily disbanded the army of his enemies, conciliating the soldiers with their arrears of pay and a cash gratuity. He opened the skilled trades to them by suspending all apprenticeship rules. To a degree, this policy was successful: "Wherever was to be found a carter more steady, a blacksmith more industrious, a workman more sober, he was a soldier of the old army." But the steady carter was a good courier for anti-monarchical conspirators. The industrious blacksmith forged new weapons for republicanism or religious dissent, because King Charles could not keep the promises of political forgiveness and religious toleration that underlay his restoration. Even before his coronation, "fanatic" cavalry raided the arsenal at Newcastle. Coal from Newcastle heated London. Control of the coal port had stoked the fires of English

---

1. E. S. de Beer, ed., *The Diary of John Evelyn* (London, 1959), entry of Oct. 11 [/13], 1659; C. H. Firth, *Cromwell's Army: A History of the English Soldier during the Civil Wars, the Commonwealth and the Protectorate* (London, 1902), 371–381.

politics in 1639. When Newcastle was again attacked in 1660, even royalists feared that "the government will not last a year."[2]

Almost as threatening as the strength and fanaticism of his armed enemies were the weakness and disunity of the king's military allies. The royalists who had shared the Stuart exile and the Presbyterians and *politiques* who engineered the Restoration still stood in armed ranks, distrustful of each other, but asking similar satisfaction from the king. The soldiers of both the restored king and the restoring general demanded that their units be retained to support the monarchy (and to feed themselves). Overseas, the military agents of the English executive, now royal authorities, also demanded continuance of their status and pay.[3] Dunkirk, for example, Cromwell's imperial legacy across the Channel, was rotten with royalists who resented their king's neglect and with republican troops who had been exiled by the Protector because he knew that they hated government "by a single person," whether dictator or monarch. Garrisons like this festered at a distance, some as far off as Jamaica, but even the security of London, the seat of sovereignty, was threatened by the dual military legacy of the Protectorate's dictatorship: the presence of ex-Cromwellian soldiers and the absence of a garrison of loyal troops. Whenever the as yet uncrowned king left London with his court of royalist soldiers, members of the capital's Presbyterian, Anabaptist, or Fifth

2. Allen B. Hinds, ed., *Calendar of State Papers and Manuscripts Relating to English Affairs, Existing in the Archives of Venice, and . . . Northern Italy*, Vol. XIII, *1659–1661* (London, 1931), 199, 200, 202 (hereafter cited as *Cal. S.P. Ven.*). The saying is that of Pepys's friend Blackburne, as paraphrased in Wilbur C. Abbott's ferocious analysis of "English Conspiracy and Dissent, 1660–1674, I," *American Historical Review*, XIV (1908–1909), 503. See also Leopold von Ranke, *A History of England Principally in the Seventeenth Century*, III (Oxford, 1875), 372. For the old army's pledges, see Firth's magisterial chapters on "Religion" and "Politics" in *Cromwell's Army*, and Burnet, *History*, I, 158–162, 279–281, 289. Burnet also discusses the search for the status quo ante bellum (pp. 276–277). On Newcastle as a developing seat of garrison government, see chapter 1 above. The potential for an old army rising haunted the first six months of the Restoration. See *Cal. S.P. Ven., 1659–1661*, 204, 207; *ibid., 1661–1664*, 161, 190–191, 267; K.H.D. Haley, *The First Earl of Shaftesbury* (Oxford, 1968), 143; Ogg, *Charles II*, I, 156; [William Dicconson], *The Life of James the Second . . . Collected Out of Memoirs Writ of his Own Hand . . .* , ed. Rev. J. S. Clarke, 2 vols. (London, 1816), I, 435; Hutchinson, *Memoirs*, 321; and Burnet, *History*, I, 326, 355. The attack on Newcastle and one on Berwick are further detailed by William Delavalle to Edward Grey, Jan. 10, 1661, deputy governor and captains of Berwick to Gov. Lord Widdrington, Apr. 24, 1661, Mary Anne Everett Green and F. H. Blackburne Daniell, *Calendar of State Papers, Domestic Series, of the Reign of Charles II [1660–1685]*, 21 vols. (1860–1938; repr. Nendeln, Lichtenstein, 1968), *1660–1661*, 470, 572 (hereafter cited as *Cal. S.P. Dom.*); Ranke, *England*, III, 355; Abbott, "English Conspiracy and Dissent, I," *AHR*, XIV (1908–1909), 504.

3. C. H. Firth, "Royalist and Cromwellian Armies in Flanders, 1657–1662," RHS, *Trans.*, N.S., XVII (1903), 67–119; Sir Frederick W. Hamilton, *The Origin and History of the First or Grenadier Guards . . .* , 3 vols. (London, 1874), I, 9, 40, 43; Lord Rutherford to Nicholas, July 8, 1662, *Cal. S.P. Dom., 1661–1662*, 432.

Monarchy congregations met with cashiered Cromwellian officers to organize militant resistance to the restoration of church and king.[4]

These disbanded, dissenting veterans were only somewhat less menacing to the monarchy than their comrades still in arms. King Charles paid off regiments and reduced town garrisons as soon as he collected the taxes authorized for this purpose by the Convention Parliament. But fewer foes and more money would not suffice to save a prince who was denied military power. The king dissolved the parliament in January 1661 because it would not acknowledge his absolute control of the armed forces. That is, parliament still refused to settle the "decisive issue" of the civil war in the crown's favor. Moreover, the parliament had not enacted any of the king's promises of religious toleration or political pardon, the conditions of his restoration. The fault was the legislature's, but the hatred accrued to the king. To protect his restoration, therefore, Charles II had also to restore the most important and enduring political invention of the civil wars and Interregnum: the standing army. He reluctantly agreed with his generals "that in the last resort it is with an army, not with the lawyers, that the sovereign controls multitudes."[5]

On Sunday, January 6, 1661, King Charles was in Portsmouth, seeing his mother off to France. In London, Thomas Venner, a cooper recently returned from New England, tapped the Sabbatarian wrath of the Fifth Monarchy men. They seized St. Paul's to announce the reign of their king, Christ. Passersby were challenged to declare which king they were for. "King Charles," said one Londoner. He was shot through the heart. But the City did not respond to this forceful eloquence. Venner's men went into hiding until Wednesday. They emerged to attack Sir Philip Howard (afterward named governor-general of Jamaica), who had rallied his troop of General Monck's bodyguard to protect the king's peace. At first, Howard's cavalry were badly beaten by the "mad courage" of the men fighting for King Christ. Finally, the Guards drove the fanatics into a tavern. Afraid to use firearms lest the people hear them and rally to Venner, the besiegers chopped a hole through the roof and dropped through it to cut down Venner's men. None surrendered. Twenty-six were slain. Nine badly

4. See n. 3 above; informers' reports, Jan. 8, 1661, William Williamson to Sir John Mennes, Apr. 1, 1661, the king to the officers of the militia of London [draft], [Apr. 3], 1661, *Cal. S.P. Dom., 1660–1661*, 471, 561, 563.
5. See n. 2 above; Ranke, *England*, III, 333; Ogg, *Charles II*, I, 144.

wounded survivors were overpowered, tried for treason, and executed. Their heads, and the butchered quarters of their bodies, were nailed up around London as bloody scarecrows to rebellion.[6]

At last alarmed "for the safety of his person and the security of the government," and pressed by his bellicose brother James, King Charles stopped disbanding the army. He kept General Monck's own units of cavalry and infantry in arms. He commissioned their commander as captain general and created him duke of Albemarle. To multiply his police power and to insure that Albemarle's army remained loyal, the king raised twice as many royalist veterans. In both the duke's Guards and the king's, there was an unmilitary predominance of cavalry over infantry. Moreover, there was no foreign war to excuse army expansion. Clearly, these troops were designed to be an elite mounted police, not a field force. The troops and regiments of the Guards in London, and the reinflated companies of the garrisons in provincial ports and county towns, were simply "an armed police for the carrying out of the oppressive laws against dissenters," both religious and political. The king now commanded twenty-eight hundred professional soldiers in London alone. This was "not an excessive number," the Venetian ambassador observed, "but noteworthy by comparison with the way in which kings used to live, who had no troops of any kind except a few *arcieri* for show." Charles II was suddenly the most potent peacetime prince in English history.[7]

To protect his coronation, the king ordered the old soldiers

6. "Vennerian" became a byword for "anti-monarchist." As late as 1708 it was used by Gov.-Gen. Thomas Handasyde of Jamaica to describe his opposition; see Handasyde to the council of trade and plantations, Mar. 31, 1708, W. Noel Sainsbury *et al.*, eds., *Calendar of State Papers, Colonial Series* (London, 1860–), *America and West Indies, 1706–1708*, 714 (hereafter cited as *Cal. S.P. Col.*). On this episode of rebellion, see [Dicconson], *James the Second*, ed. Clarke, I, 388–390; Nicholas's notes concerning Mr. Ratcliff, June [Jan.?] 12, 1661, [Nicholas] to Sir Henry Bennet, Jan. 10, 17, 1661, and to Sir Henry De Vic, Jan. 18, 1661, "Proclamation for restraining all seditious meetings . . . ," Jan. 10, 1661, Sir John Finch to Lord Conway, Jan. 11, 1661, information against Capt. Edw. Short, Jan. 15, 1661, lists of 16 prisoners, Jan. 16, 17, 1661, list of 22 traitors, Jan. 17, 1661, *Cal. S.P. Dom., 1660–1661*, 470, 476, 470–471, 474, 475, 476; Ranke, *England*, III, 357–359; *Cal. S.P. Ven., 1659–1661*, 239–240; Burnet, *History*, I, 279. To Christopher Hatton (afterward governor of Guernsey), Sir Charles Littleton described the rising and his association with its repression on the eve of his departure to be deputy governor of Jamaica, Aug. 31, 1661; see Edward Maunde Thompson, ed., *Correspondence of the Family of Hatton . . .*, 2 vols., Publications of the Camden Society, N.S., XXII–XXIII (Westminster, 1878), I, 22–23.

7. [Dicconson], *James the Second*, ed. Clarke, I, 390, 427; Sir John Finch to Lord Conway, Jan. 11, 1661, "Establishment of forces to be raised for the safety of His Majesty's person and government," Jan. [26], 1661, *Cal. S.P. Dom., 1660–1661*, 471, 489; Ranke, *England*, III, 359–360; Hamilton, *Grenadier Guards*, I, 43; *Cal. S.P. Ven., 1659–1661*, 255; *ibid., 1661–1664*, 84; Max Beloff, *Public Order and Popular Disturbances, 1660–1714* (London, 1963), 144; Charles M. Clode, *The Military Forces of the Crown; Their Administration and Government*, 2 vols. (London, 1869), I, 54.

out of London, checked access to the capital's citadel, the Tower, and stationed his Life Guard of cavalry along the processional route. So circumscribed, Coronation Day, April 23, 1661, passed peacefully in the capital. In other English cities, however, celebration of the monarchy's restoration incited violent protests. In the kingdom's northern citadel, Berwick, the Anabaptists had forecast "a joyful day before the coronation." On the dark night of April 22, they attacked the magazine. A strong sentry fought free of the attackers and fired his musket. The garrison companies rallied to their colors, beat off the attackers, closed the town gates, manned Berwick's walls, and conducted a house-by-house search, arresting eighteen men.[8]

Berwick was safe for the moment, but the attack, like that on Newcastle, reminded a generation of civil war veterans of the critical political importance of arms depots and citadels. The king's lieutenants reported that if rebels could seize some stronghold, they could quickly rally to it some of the tens of thousands of men trained in civil war. Then ambitious leaders of more than local influence would emerge to direct the entrenched rebels in the use of the growing popular discontent with the restored monarchy. For the combination of royal debauchery with royal taxation, the incompetence of the king's government at home and its impotence abroad, had disgraced the king and deflated national pride. Even the best friends of monarchy were disappointed by the tawdry reality that mocked the royalist refrain: "All will be well when the king enjoys his own again."[9]

When loyalty ceased to be freely offered, it might be forcibly imposed. But military officers were needed to impose royal rule. The officer corps was the major source of trained administrators available to the government. It was divided into at least five factions, however, two "old army" and three monarchist. From the Interregnum there survived unreconstructed republicans and devoted Cromwellians, mostly in garrisons overseas and in Albemarle's partly Presbyterian, thoroughly professional legions, largely in

---

8. The expulsion of old soldiers was simple retaliation for the like measure against cavaliers under Cromwell; see Gardiner, *Commonwealth and Protectorate*, III, 194.

9. On the relationship of places of strength to successful rebellion, see the earl of Annandale to the deputy lieutenants of Westmoreland and Cumberland, Nov. 25, 1666, Sir Edward Musgrave to Sir Philip Musgrave (gov. of Carlisle), Nov. 26, 1666, *Cal. S.P. Dom., 1666–1667*, 288, 290; Abbott, "Conspiracy and Dissent, I," *AHR*, XIV (1908–1909), 527; *Cal. S.P. Ven., 1659–1661*, 247; *ibid., 1661–1664*, 180, 212. On cavalier disappointment, see Burnet, *History*, I, 176, 287–289; but see also Latham and Matthews, eds., *Diary of Pepys*, VI, 330 n. 1. See Burnet, *History*, on the loss of reputation abroad (pp. 302, 305) and on military dispositions (pp. 280–281, 326).

garrisons at home. Their new commander-in-chief, Charles II, would have had to become respectable to satisfy the former and combative to win the latter's confidence, but he was neither. Even among the royalist officers, the king's men quarreled with his brother James's backers, and wartime exiles resented the stay-at-homes. All of these military factions were socially split. Wealthy army grandees, now ennobled, and well-born royalist aristocrats, now politicized, shared class-bound and traditional views of how and whom the government ought to serve. By contrast with these traditionalists, the professional men who had by force of civil war become career soldiers and administrators, whether for king or commonwealth, were more flexible politically and more tolerant of social variety and aspiration in those they ruled. These professionals were the most intelligent and, when not crippled by their lack of social status, the most effective members of the royal military and imperial officer corps that developed during the reign of Charles II.[10]

All of these royal officers and governors were, at least nominally, the ideological enemies of the thousands of Cromwellian and republican soldiers who peopled their English and American governments. Yet the political behavior of all these English military men—aristocrats, grandees, or professionals; the general's men, the king's men, or the duke's men; royalists, *politiques*, or republicans—was startlingly similar: "They all handled the Sword and are expert in War." By 1660 English troops were imbued with the professional military principles that dictated the development of an empire in depth during the latter half of the seventeenth century.[11]

The Principles of Military Administration

A characteristic expression of these shared professional principles was written by the governor of Hull, Richard Elton. His work, *The Compleat body of the Art Military*, appeared in a second edition in 1659, just before its author tried to capture the city of Carlisle on behalf of the army. Elton was balked by Carlisle's

10. Burnet, *History*, 352; *Cal. S.P. Ven., 1659–1661*, 187–188.
11. Song of Solomon, 3:8, was a text appropriately used by an officer-governor, for which see the title page of Lt. Maj. Richard Elton's *The Compleat body of the Art Military; exactly compiled, and gradually composed for the foot* . . . (London, 1650), 2d ed. (London, 1659). Citations are to the Houghton Library's copy of the second edition, which contains hostile emendations and annotations by a royalist reader.

governor, Major General Charles Howard (who had just joined General Monck in declaring for a parliamentary government and who, in addition, was conspiring to restore King Charles by force). Elton's attack on the regional capital and Howard's defense of it alike attested to the political importance of the military. Elton defined that importance institutionally, and he dedicated his work of military definitions to Lieutenant Colonel Edward D'Oyley and Thomas Noell, officers who, like Howard, afterward applied Elton's military prescriptions to the government of provinces overseas.[12]

Elton's *Art Military* reflected ruling-class ideas of estimable popular behavior. The army's common people were its privates. The *Art Military* condemned their quarrels, disobedience, curses, lies, and drunkenness. These prohibitions forbade the turbulence, defiance, and turpitude feared by all of the "better sort," whether military "commissioners" or civilian rulers. In the interest of social order, Major Elton urged privates to be frugal, content with their wages, religious, and obedient.[13]

While it reiterated traditional social restraints, the *Art Military* also indicated ways in which the army modified traditional values and so opened imperial careers to men of administrative talent. The military elite was at once more responsible to superiors and more open to new blood than was the traditional ruling class. The first duty of every officer was loyalty to his class and to his superior, yet the officers were to be recruited from upwardly mobile apprentices in arms. Each of these gentlemen volunteers, therefore, "ought truly to love, respect, and obey his Captain, and stick close to him, vindicating him upon all just occasions, when he shall be wronged, and injured by any mutinies of the common soldiers or others." The volunteer's reward was not just his full pay, without the deductions for clothing and quarters that were made from privates' wages, but the more enticing prospect of promotion. Many a future governor-general received his first military training as "the gentleman of a company" and thereby won an entry into public life unsupported by particularly elevated birth or by very much wealth.[14]

Promotion to commissioned rank, however, did not lessen the military gentleman's obligations to obey and support his supe-

12. Firth and Davies, *Regimental History*, 152, 522–525, 557; *DNB*, s.v. "Howard, Charles."

13. Elton, *Art Military*, 176.

14. *Ibid.*, 177, Preston, *Gorges of Plymouth Fort*, 25; Oglander, *Royalist's Notebook*. See also Ormond's comments in chapter 1 above.

riors. Rather, it required the officer to learn and observe the limits of his new power. Lieutenants, for example, were told by Elton not to assume authority in the presence of their captain. Instead, they were to learn the captain's purpose during peacetime so that they could better execute it in battle. Even colonels were to be subservient to their superiors, governors and general officers, paying them the "like respect and observance as he himself expecteth, (and that justly), from all inferiors to him." The army exalted the hierarchical principle of the age into inviolable law.[15]

Hierarchy and paternalism were linked in the mind of the age. Naturally, the author of the *Art Military* drew on the paternal image of authority to explain and to vindicate military officers' authority. Military responsibility mandated social paternalism, whether in command of a company or a colony. The captain was "to have a fatherly care of his Souldiers," looking after his sick and wounded men, providing the able-bodied with food, weapons, and pay, and acting as umpire and judge. "His care must be to execute justice, appease quarrels, punish offenders; by doing whereof," Major Elton asserted, "he will maintain the *honour* and *dignity* of his place." The ideal father-commander was evenhanded, courteous, even kind to his subordinates. But he was never familiar. He exemplified the values of military society by being religious, temperate, wise, loyal to his trust, and courageous in battle.[16]

Embodying *virtu*, the officer also rewarded it. Captains controlled the recruiting of their company's soldiers and the appointment of its subalterns, just as colonels controlled company grade appointments. Both captains and colonels recognized, as Elton affirmed, that "every Officer and Souldier in a *Regiment* is worthy of Honour, Pay, and Encouragement according to his Merit and Seniority." The military emphasis on merit, on professional ability as a criterion of promotion and rank, was at odds with a nominally static social system rooted in inheritance and wealth. The social and political ascent of officers by dint of personal merit was one result of the social responsiveness inherent in military command.[17] Another was attention to the needs and opinions of inferiors. Officers dealt daily with armed commoners (as governors would rule armed colonists). Privates revenged themselves on unduly harsh

15. Elton, *Art Military*, 181–182; Maurice Ashley, *Cromwell's Generals* (London, 1954), 199.

16. The standard expression of authoritarian paternalism is Sir Robert Filmer, *Patriarcha* (London, 1680), especially the sections quoted in David C. Douglass, ed., *English Historical Documents*, Vol. VIII, Andrew Browning, ed., *1660–1714* (New York, 1953), 70–72. See also Elton, *Art Military*, 184–187.

17. Elton, *Art Military*, 184, 187.

or rigid superiors by shooting them in the back on the day of battle. An army officer's need to retain the respect and even affection of his men forced him to seek ways in which to make the arbitrary, often unpopular orders of his commander-in-chief, the sovereign, acceptable to subordinates. Officers' mediation between sovereign and subject trained commanders for government, but it also imposed a dilemma on governors-general like Charles Howard, who "loved to be popular, and yet to keep up an interest at court; and so was apt to go backward and forward in public affairs." Such political officers were, as Major Elton also defined himself, "*Militares Magistre*." Their particular political contribution was to implement the army's social idealism.[18]

The public morality of the military—expressed in regulation of prices, wages, and behavior—was designed to secure popular support for military government, in Scotland for example, or in Virginia. This regulation was the special responsibility of the marshals. The provost marshal, or marshal general, Elton observed, not only disciplined soldiers, but also enforced the governor's, colonel's, or general's regulations regarding such hangers-on as camp followers and sutlers. In addition, the articles of war authorized the marshal to set food prices and drinking hours in civilian places that served soldiers, to preserve order in the camp, and to impose orthodox religious observances. All of these regulatory functions made the marshal, whether in camp or garrison, capital or colony, London or the Leeward Islands, the starkest symbol of the army's social influence. Consequently, the provost marshal was the military officer most hated by the growing class of individualistic, profit-minded, irreligious merchant-capitalists. To end the executive's use of the martial law that the marshal enforced became the goal of capitalist representatives in the legislatures of the empire.[19]

18. Burnet, *History*, II, 277; inscription on John Droeshout's engraving of a portrait of Elton by "W.S.," Elton, *Art Military*, frontispiece.

19. The marshal's office, as described by Elton, *Art Military*, 179, existed in garrisoned places across the empire. For London, see the commission to Gilbert Thomas, Feb. [?], 1665, *Cal. S.P. Dom., 1664–1665*, 229–230, and the petition of Thomas (provost marshal), Feb. [23?], 1667, *ibid., 1666–1667*, 528. For Guernsey, see Sir Jonathan Atkins to Williamson, Apr. 23, 1670, *ibid., 1670*, 179–180. For Jamaica, see Sir Thomas Modyford to commissioners, [Dec.] 1671, minutes of the council of Jamaica, Jan. 15, 1674, *Cal. S.P. Col., 1669–1674*, nos. 704, 1206, and chapters 4 and 5 below. For Barbados, see petition of Edwin Steed [Nov. 19], 1673, report of the council for trade and plantations, Mar. 8, 1674, *ibid.*, nos. 1167, 1238, and Charles M. Andrews, *British Committees, Commissions, and Councils of Trade and Plantations, 1622–1675*, Johns Hopkins University Studies in Historical and Political Science, Ser. XXVI, nos. 1–3 (Baltimore, 1908), 52, 149. And for the Leeward Islands, see Gov. Sir Charles Wheeler to the council for foreign plantations, Dec. 9, 1671, *Cal. S.P. Col., 1669–1674*, no. 680 (as Wheeler explained the political expansion of the military office in the Lee-

Whereas the marshal enforced a code of military and moral conduct derived primarily from the corporatism and paternalism of the past, the quartermaster, as Elton depicted him, exemplified the martial strengths of the absolutist and bureaucratic future. Professional planning and systematic administration were the hallmarks of his office. The quartermaster selected campsites and scouted battlefields, designed field fortifications and assigned quarters to troops in garrison. To supply the forage that fueled a horsepowered army, he scoured the countryside in wartime or, in peacetime, negotiated contracts. In short, the quartermaster managed the material and mathematical aspects of army administration. His organizational duties and intellectual skills marked this staff officer as the advanced guard of modernized army and imperial administration. The quartermaster forecast government by military technicians— staff officers such as William Selwyn and Alexander Spotswood —who would ultimately displace well-born courtier-commanders —the Lords Windsor, Culpeper, and Howard of Effingham—as the dominant type of governor-general in England's empire.[20]

If the administrative future belonged to the quartermasters, the military administration of the Interregnum and Restoration belonged to the majors, labeled by Major Elton "the eyes, hands and feet" of every regimental and garrison staff. The successful major developed a capacity for organizing numbers of men and for grasping data about them. Pressed for time, working in difficult terrain and in the midst of battle, he wrote orders about men and matériel. He had to cultivate many of the skills of his subordinates, the quartermasters, in transportation, provisioning, housing, and fortification. In addition, the major assigned daily work to the troops, mapped march routes for his regiment, and set its companies in the appropriate order for quarters, camp, or battle. His was the chief administrative rank in the seventeenth-century army, "the greatest Affairs of the Regiment being carried forth by the Major." It was as regiment, town, or brigade majors that officers such as Henry Norwood, Edmund Andros, Benjamin Fletcher, Robert Hunter, and Edward Nott achieved the administrative reputations that underlay their promotions to command colonies as colonels.[21]

---

wards: "The office of High Sheriff in England bears the name of the Provost Marshal"). See also the petition of Sir Francis Clinton, *ibid.*, no. 917; Firth, *Cromwell's Army*, 282–285; J. R. Western, *The English Militia in the Eighteenth Century: The Story of a Political Issue, 1660– 1802* (London and Toronto, 1965), 48. On Scotland, see Western and chapter 1 above; on Virginia, see S. S. Webb, "Francis Nicholson," *WMQ*, 3d Ser., XXIII (1966), 530–531.

20. Elton, *Art Military*, 179–180.
21. *Ibid.*, 183, 184.

The colonel's function was executive, Elton wrote, as distinguished from the administrative role of the major. The colonel, or, in his absence, the lieutenant colonel, helped formulate military plans as one of the general's council of war. It then became the colonel's duty to execute that plan, whether or not he agreed with it, in order "to express his obedience to his *General*, although it be a service that corresponded not with his own opinion at the first. . . . " In the general's court-martial or in his own, the colonel examined and judged those who were indicted by the marshal or by the company captains for offenses against the articles of war. Perhaps the colonel's most important task was to discipline both his own men and, as much as possible, the neighboring civilians. "At all times," Elton wrote, the colonel was "to be diligent in suppressing of *Mutinies*, even in their first growth by a discreet punishment of the principal offenders, for prevention of further mischief." "Mutiny" could be civilian, but it was still the officer's responsibility to quell it, as Sir Philip Howard's resistance to Venner's rebellion or Herbert Jeffreys's suppression of the Derwentdale Plot demonstrates.[22]

Officers commonly applied military discipline to urban civilian populations. Metropolitan discipline, Elton observed, was the duty of the military officer who ranked as colonel and who was entitled "governor." In the largest English garrisons, or in the most important overseas colonies, governors-in-chief were also commissioned as general officers. Just as governors were automatically highly ranked as regular military officers, so senior military officers filled almost all governorships, whether in the British Isles or overseas.[23] Thus an office that is now considered essentially civilian was fundamentally military in Cromwell's England, in that of the later Stuarts, and so also in England's empire.

The superior rank of the officers who commanded as governors reflected their substantial responsibilities under the Protectorate and throughout the Restoration. Town (and colonial) garrisons commanded by officer-governors were an alternative to

22. *Ibid.*, 185. Note Bishop Burnet's very similar language in his eulogy of Gen. Hugh MacKay, quoted in Browning, ed., *English Historical Documents, 1660–1714*, 930.

23. Elton, *Art Military*, 187–189; "Lord Gerard's instructions," June 15, 1667, *Cal. S.P. Dom., 1667*, 190; rules and directions as to the precedency of the several regiments and their officers, May 28, 1673, *ibid., 1673*, 305; the king to Prince Rupert, Aug. 15, 1674, *ibid., 1673–1675*, 334–335; Sir J. Williamson to Sir Bernard de Gomme, Feb. 16, 1678, *ibid., 1677–1678*, 651; S.P. 44/31, 138b–139. For the officers who served as colonial governors and for their English commands, see the Appendix. For the garrison governments in England, see chapter 1 above; Dalton, ed., *English Army Lists*, I, 10–16, and the commission registers, *passim*; and MacKinnon, *Coldstream Guards*, I, 121.

regiments as a form of multi-company military organization. If a garrison numbered two companies or more, the colonel-governor (or governor-general) usually sought the king's appointment of one of his captains as a town-major (or major general). This officer was to a government what a major in the field was to a regiment: a regulator and an administrator. The town-major mustered the garrison companies. He organized the nightly patrols by the garrison's musketeers, who quelled all turbulence in the town after the "tap too" was beaten, arrested anyone who seemed dangerous to town peace or garrison security, and confined these prisoners to the guardhouse until the governor disposed of them. The guardhouse was the rallying point of the guards manning the main gate, and it was the post of the officer of the watch. The main guard and its officer were posted by the major, according to the governor's orders, as were lesser gate guards and wall patrols. Majors thus were the chief instruments by which governors carried out their primary responsibility: to preserve the town's peace from all enemies, civil or military, domestic or foreign. Even natural hazards were fought by the garrison, for the town guard served as firefighters as well as police and security forces. At dusk, after setting the guard, the major formally locked the gates of the town and ceremoniously conveyed to the governor the keys of the city.[24] The keys were the emblem of a governor's authority over the town, the symbol of the military's role in metropolitan control. Carried from the gate to the governor, the keys to the city marked the powerful place of the army officer in later seventeenth-century politics and administration.[25]

Governor, town-major, provost marshal, sentinel, guard, and patrol, such were the garrison roles as Governor Elton described them at the end of the second civil war. They had not changed when the second edition of Elton's work came out in the last year of the Protectorate. Two years later King Charles replied to the rash of risings in his three kingdoms by starting the restoration of

24. Elton, *Art Military,* 187, 188, 190. See the examples of town-majors in S.P. 44/69, 170, 183. On colonial major generals see: for Jamaica, S.P. 44/20, 7, the council of St. Christopher to the privy council plantations committee, July 12, 1680, *Cal. S.P. Col., 1677–1680,* no. 1441, and chapters 4–6 below; for Virginia, account of the establishment for Virginia, Feb. 15, 1678, *ibid.,* no. 602, and Treasury Group, class 64, piece 88, 75–76, P.R.O. (hereafter cited as T. 64/88). See also chapters 7 and 8 below. Note the commission of Thomas Dongan as major general on his appointment to the Tangier command, May 1, 1678, prior to his New York command (S.P. 44/44, 99, 105).

25. On the keys to the city, see the commissions to Capt. Herbert Jeffreys and Lord Frescheville, June 18, 1667, *Cal. S.P. Dom., 1667,* 209, and the case of Jeffreys (afterward lieutenant governor of Virginia) in chapter 3 below.

Cromwell's system of garrisoned provincial strongholds and strategic seaports that over the next five years became the fortress of the restored monarchy. Thus the position of the governor and of lesser officers, and their ideology, all as described in Elton's *Art Military*, were replanted as roots of Stuart absolutism. The royal revival of garrison government reconfirmed the political commands of officer-administrators. Their forceful rule produced exile populations whom they would rule once more across the Atlantic. As governor and exiler, under both Oliver Cromwell and Charles Stuart, in England, in Scotland, and in Jamaica, Charles Howard, earl of Carlisle, was a commanding figure.

The Case of the Earl of Carlisle, Military Administrator

The Cromwellian Period

Charles Howard's royal commissions were premised not only on the traditional qualifications of gentle birth, great wealth, and long residence in the north country, but also on a career somewhat surprising in a royal officer: a decade of military service under Oliver Cromwell. Howard had been captain of the Protector's own Life Guard, and he had commanded one of the military districts that epitomized Cromwell's dictatorship. The portrait of this trusted Cromwellian-turned-royalist commander shows a face sensitively handsome and somewhat sad—a startling combination of youth and experience—framed by the finest armor and richest brocade.[26]

Wealth and war were Howard's hallmarks. When he was seventeen, in July 1645, his guardians sent him away from his war-threatened home, Naworth Castle in Cumberland, the scene of Governor Hunsdon's victory over the rebel earls. His ship was wrecked only a few hours out of port, however, and the royalist cavalry who rescued him were attacked the same night by parliamentary troopers. Howard was sent prisoner to London, where he was forced to compound for his estates by paying parliament £4,000, was converted to Protestantism, and then was married to the daughter of Edward, Lord Howard of Escrick, a Protestant par-

26. The portrait appears as the frontispiece of [Guy Miege], *A Relation of Three Embassies . . .* (London, 1669).

liamentarian peer. Not until September 1646 was Charles Howard finally permitted to pass the ports on his grand tour.[27]

On his return, "having taught his necessity to reason thus," Howard became an ardent parliamentarian—and he made sure that his religion, whatever it might be, never again came to public notice. He defended Naworth Castle against royalist attack in October 1648. A month later he was able to ally himself to the personification of the new order by entertaining Cromwell. Howard's gift to Cromwell's new governor of the city of Carlisle, a pair of pistols, betokened the governor of Carlisle's and Howard of Naworth's joint efforts to police the Borders. Pistols and patrols made manifest Howard's recognition that the governments of England, in his lifetime at least, were essentially "the armed forces providing ultimate sanction for the enforcement of law and order." His own police service, his local influence, the patronage of his influential father-in-law, and the favor of General Cromwell led to Howard's appointment as high sheriff of Cumberland in 1650. Within the year, Cromwell made him governor of Carlisle.[28]

In April 1651, Governor Howard left his residence in the Carlisle citadel to take command of Cromwell's newly organized Life Guard. At Worcester, Captain Howard "received divers sore wounds" when he led the charge of the Guards into "a place of much danger." As "Captain Howard of Naworth, captain to the life guards of his excellency," he became a familiar public figure, commanding the Life Guard at the Protector's installation, proving on the parade ground and on the battlefield, in garrison and on patrol that "ceremony and order, with force, governs all."[29]

Howard demonstrated that forceful abilities led to political power when he represented Westmoreland in parliament and served in the council of state in 1653. He was returned for Cumberland in 1654 and 1656. In the latter session he joined the committee for trade and presumably participated in its discussions of recently conquered Jamaica. Howard had joined in like deliberations the previous year as a member of the military council for Scots government. The peak of his political influence during the Protector-

27. The best account of Howard's early life is C. Roy Huddleston's introduction to *Naworth Estate and Household Accounts, 1648–1660*, Publications of the Surtees Society, CLXVIII (Durham, 1958), esp. x.

28. Howard's religious elusiveness is recorded in John Gough Nichols, ed., *The Autobiography of Anne Lady Halkett*, Publications of the Camden Society, N.S., XIII (London, 1875), 36ff; Huddleston, ed., *Naworth Accounts*, xi, 94; Firth and Davies, *Regimental History*, 510; Ogg, *Charles II*, II, 486.

29. *DNB*, s.v. "Howard, Charles"; Huddleston, ed., *Naworth Accounts*, xii. The duke of Newcastle's statement ("ceremony and order . . . ") is quoted by Ogg, *Charles II*, I, 145.

The Right Hon:^ble Charles, Earle of Carlisle, Vicount Howard of Morpeth, Baron Dacre of Gilsland. Lord Lieutenant in the Counties of Cumberland, and Westmoreland, and one of the Lords of his Majesties most Honourable Privy Councell, etc.

"The Right Honble. Charles, Earle of Carlisle. . . ." Engraved frontispiece of Guy Miege, *A Relation of Three Embassies* . . . (London, 1669), reproduced by permission of the Houghton Library, Harvard University, Cambridge, Mass.

ate came when he was summoned to Cromwell's house of lords in December 1657.[30]

Howard's military activity in support of the central government had steadily increased during this whole period of his rising political power. Political offices rewarded his armed efforts. After guarding Cromwell's installation, Captain Howard went home to Naworth in the spring of 1654 to see to his estates. He was welcomed by a Scots raid over the Border. His retaliation against the moss-troopers was the subject of a report by the commander-in-chief for Scotland, General Monck, to Cromwell. Howard's patrols were so effective, Monck wrote, that "I shall nott feare any insurreccion behinde mee." Monck ordered the captain to extend his patrols across the Border into Galloway, and he added two troops of cavalry to Howard's command. At month's end, Howard led four troops north to cover Monck's communications with Glasgow, relieving Lieutenant Colonel Brayne to move into the Highlands (where he achieved the distinction that led him to Jamaica and death). To patrol the Border, Howard mounted as dragoons companies of infantry from the garrisons of Carlisle and Berwick. He used these troops to arrest political opponents of the Protectorate, to hunt down those who escaped from jail, and to prevent public assemblies. In August, Howard, Governor Fenwick (of Connecticut and Berwick fame), and General Monck were named commissioners to govern the Border.[31]

Howard commanded in Scotland as colonel of cavalry during the winter of 1654–1655. In March he moved south again, adding another two troops to his mounted police and stationing them in the family village of Morpeth. Howard used the augmented force to curb local risings, so that he was able to report to the Protector in June 1655: "We have imprisoned the most dangerous, and taken bond of the rest of the disaffected in these northern parts. There

30. That the major generals and their deputies were all members of parliament in 1656 attests to the political effectiveness of their military control. See David Watson Rannie, "Cromwell's Major-Generals," *English Historical Review*, X (1895), 500; B.L.K. Henderson, "The Commonwealth Charters," RHS, *Trans.*, 3d Ser., VI (1912), esp. 139–142. See also Birch, ed., *Thurloe S.P.*, IV, 383, index entry. For Howard and the English committees, see Andrews, *British Committees*, 40; *The Journals of the House of Commons*, 32 vols. (London, 1547–1770), VII, 442, 452, 460. Howard's brother-in-law, the scoutmaster, major general, and former New Englander, George Downing, also served on the trade and navigation committee. For the committee of the military government of Scotland, see Birch, ed., *Thurloe S.P.*, IV, 41.

31. Monck to Cromwell, May 9, 21, 30, 1654, Firth, ed., *Scotland and the Protectorate*, 103, 108, 113; council of state to Robert Shafton, Apr. 14, 1654, council of state proceedings, July 6 (nos. 3, 12), Aug. 8 (no. 7), 1654, council of state to Howard, July 6, 1654, *Cal. S.P. Dom.*, *1654*, 100, 244–245, 290, 245–246.

are several who I wish might be sent to the Barbadoes, both men of fortune and others, being, such, whose principles and temper fitt them for disturbance upon any opportunity."[32] Besides noting the coercive potential of colonies, Howard bolstered his own political position by repressing the men who were his rivals for power and the enemies of the Cromwellian state.

Even before he became deputy major general for the region, Howard used his regional preeminence in the government's police to justify his monopoly of nominations to office, both militia and civilian, in Cumberland and Northumberland. Next, Howard sought to secure "senatorial courtesy," that is, the assurance of the central government that it would make no appointments whatever in his bailiwick without first consulting him. Howard's assertion that "none ought to put themselves upon us but by our general consent" was a slogan universally adopted by provincial governors-general and their courtiers at home and overseas. The efficacy of their rule depended in large part on their control of the central government's local patronage.[33]

Once Howard's local position was assured by the appointment of his partisans, this "faithful and obedient servant" of the Protectorate asked orders "for this disposing of myself to such service and employment as his highness shall require." In August 1655 he was named as the third of the nine commissioners for the civil government of Scotland. This appointment provided Howard with a well-paid apprenticeship to General Monck, that master of forceful government, and to Roger Boyle, Lord Broghill, a brilliant administrator. Service with these two senior members of the Scots council exposed Howard to problems of finance, patronage, religious and naval organization, collection and evaluation of intelligence, repression of civil disturbance, and the military foundations of colonization.[34]

The commissioners' first act was to remodel the corporations that governed Scotland's cities, the most potent political parts of the nation. Here Howard was set an example for his own reconstruction of the city corporation of Carlisle in July 1656, as well as

32. Col. Charles Howard to the Protector, Newark, June 20, 1655, Birch, ed., *Thurloe S.P.*, III, 568.

33. *Cal. S.P. Dom.*, *1654*, 318; Birch, ed., *Thurloe S.P.*, IV, 71–72; Burnet, *History*, I, 144.

34. Birch, ed., *Thurloe S.P.*, IV, 72, 526, and Broghill's letters, *passim*; Monck to Cromwell, Sept. 13, 1655, Firth, ed., *Scotland and the Protectorate*, 306, also 306 n. 3. Broghill (afterward, first earl of Orrery) and Howard were Burnet's Restoration informants about Cromwellian affairs, and particularly about the military government of Scotland (*History*, I, 115).

for his role in the remodeling of the constitution of Jamaica twenty years after. Recasting or reducing the power of these centers of local self-government in the interest of centralized, militarized administration made it all the more essential that the officer-governors of Scotland recruit influential local personages as justices of the peace through whom to govern. Howard personally attended to this task of political recruiting in the three counties where he was named a justice of the quorum. There he also helped to redefine political boundaries. The institution and exercise of central power in the provinces remained Colonel Howard's lifelong concern and career. To reduce formal resistance to that power, the commissioners for Scotland refused tenure to judges. This attack on judicial independence both reflected Howard's attitude toward judges as biddable executive tools and anticipated his dismissal of the entire Jamaica judiciary for political disobedience during his subsequent governor-generalship.[35]

The colonizing of Jamaica directly concerned Howard as one of the council for Scotland. Cromwell instructed the councillors to scour every Scots shire for the poor, the criminal, and the rebellious and to transport them to Jamaica. The expanding English state would profit by the labor in the West Indies of this manpower now wasted in Scotland, Cromwell wrote. Equally important, he asserted, the cause of the gospel would benefit by the strength these forced recruits would add to England's campaign in the American theater against the inquisition of Spain. To pay for the cost of transporting the impressed Scots, the commissioners were to levy an additional tax on their subjects, and they were to turn over the money to the governor of Inverlochy, Colonel William Brayne, who would administer it for this good and imperial cause.[36]

The commissioners delayed acting on these instructions while Lord Broghill reported the problems that, in the view of the commissioners, hampered Cromwell's colonization proposals. If Scots were impressed to settle the West Indian conquest, Broghill warned, "it will put the country in a flame." Instead of indiscriminate impressment of ne'er-do-wells, Broghill suggested that three classes of colonists be sought: soldiers, planters, and women. After con-

35. Birch, ed., *Thurloe S.P.*, IV, 741; "Lists of Justices of the Peace . . . ," in Firth, ed., *Scotland and the Protectorate*, 310 (Berwickshire), 311 (Dumfriesshire), 315 (Roxburghshire). On the Carlisle remodeling, see Gardiner, *Commonwealth and Protectorate*, III, 291, and Henderson, "Commonwealth Charters," RHS, *Trans.*, 3d Ser., VI (1912), 134. For denial of judicial tenure, see Birch, ed., *Thurloe S.P.*, IV, 268.

36. Instructions for the council of Scotland, [1655], Birch, ed., *Thurloe S.P.*, III, 496–498. See also *ibid.*, IV, 500.

sulting with his colleagues, Broghill advised that General Monck be permitted to nominate "some eminent person" to be commissioned by the Protector to raise a new regiment for service in Jamaica. The "eminent person" was Colonel Brayne, whose career as the colony's general followed. His settlement pattern, the population derived from his troops, and the ruling class that had developed from his officer corps, all were still present, even prevalent, in Jamaica when Brayne's colleague Charles Howard finally succeeded him as the colony's governor-general.[37]

The procurement of planters was Broghill's next concern. He suggested the tactic that Cromwell adopted in his famous proclamation "relating to Jamaica" and that Brayne implemented to expand the conquered colony's civilian population. On behalf of the Scots council Broghill advised that "for such as you desire to have as planters, nothing will be likelier to engage such, then to let them have as good conditions, as any have had, which are already planted in any of the West-India plantations . . . and on assurance that the soldiery there shall protect and guard them; to which if you add free transportation thither . . . many believe you may get some considerable numbers from hence; tho' before I believe it, I must see it." As it happened, the "considerable numbers" were lured from other West Indian colonies, not from Scotland, by promise of free land, naval transport, political privilege, and military protection. But the discussions by Cromwell's military commissioners for the civil government of Scotland had produced the policy that stimulated civilian as well as military settlement in Jamaica. As for women, they and vagabonds were to be sought in Ireland as well as in Scotland and were to be sent out with Colonel Brayne. Some did actually go with the fleet when crop failure left them with the choice between Jamaica and starvation.[38]

Not only in Jamaica and in Scotland, but in England also, Howard acted as a military administrator for the Protector. He had left the command of Cromwell's Life Guard in 1654 to become a colonel of cavalry in Scotland. After returning to the Guard from September 1655 until February 1656, he again resigned his command in order to represent the Protectorate in the north of England as governor of Carlisle, commander of the Border cavalry, and colonel of a regiment of foot. This last unit was especially

37. Broghill to Thurloe, 7ber (Sept.) 18, 1655, *ibid.*, IV, 41. See also the tenth instruction for the council, *ibid.*, III, 498; *ibid.*, IV, 500; and Part II below.
38. Broghill to Thurloe, 7ber (Sept.) 18, 1655, *ibid.*, IV, 41. See also *ibid.*, III, 753, and Part II below. Some of Fenwick's men were also proposed for the Jamaica service (*ibid.*, IV, 73).

useful in executing the orders Howard issued as an officer in the system that marked the apogee of Cromwellian military dictatorship: the "government by Bashaws" of the major generals.[39]

Commissioned in November 1655 as deputy major general to the absent Major General John Lambert, Howard was responsible for the political and military security of Cumberland, Westmoreland, and Northumberland (the very counties he would command as Charles II's lieutenant general). The seat of his command was Carlisle, where he was governor and where his regiment's major served as deputy governor and town-major. Three companies of Howard's regiment composed the Carlisle garrison. His lieutenant colonel was governor of the great citadel of Berwick and commanded five companies of Howard's regiment as his garrison. The district between the garrisons was policed by the remaining companies of the regiment (stationed in two town garrisons) and by the major general's locally raised and paid mounted police.[40]

What majors were to towns or regiments, major generals were to provinces or to colonies. Indeed, one-half of the instructions given the Cromwellian major generals were simply provincial versions of the duties prescribed for town-majors in Elton's *Art Military*. The major generals were to maintain public order in their districts, "suppressing all Tumults, Insurrections, Rebellion, or other unlawful Assemblies." They were responsible for external as well as internal security—for protecting their provinces from "all Invasions from abroad." They were to disarm the disaffected, whether Catholic or royalist, and deposit their weapons "in some adjacent Garrisons." They were to patrol city streets and county ways against "Thieves, Robbers, Highwaymen and other dangerous persons."[41]

39. *Ibid.*, IV, 117, 177; Rannie, "Cromwell's Major-Generals," *EHR*, X (1895), 471–506, esp. 478. Note that the accounting system imposed on the major generals was effective administrative training (*ibid.*, 488–489).

40. Note that by 1666 all the garrison towns of the Cromwellian major generals were regarrisoned by royal troops. See Firth and Davies, *Regimental History*, 522; Gardiner, *Commonwealth and Protectorate*, III, map opp. 340; Charles II's instructions to the earl of Carlisle, Nov. 23, 1666, note of powers granted to the earl, Nov. [?], 1666, *Cal. S.P. Dom., 1666–1667*, 282–283, 283; Dalton, ed., *English Army Lists*, I, 10–16, and nonregimental commissions and commission registers, *passim*. On the major generals' police, see Western, *English Militia*, 8.

41. The instructions to the major generals appeared in the *Mercurius Politicus* and the *Public Intelligencer* from Dec. 20, 1655, through Jan. 3, 1656. They have been collected and reprinted as appendix A of Sir James Berry's and Stephen G. Lee's *A Cromwellian Major General: The Career of Colonel James Berry* (Oxford, 1938), 275–279. The expansion of these instructions, especially with regard to taxation and political discipline, is narrated by Gardiner, *Commonwealth and Protectorate*, III, 175–177, 180. Compare Elton, *Art Military*, 184, 187, 188, 190.

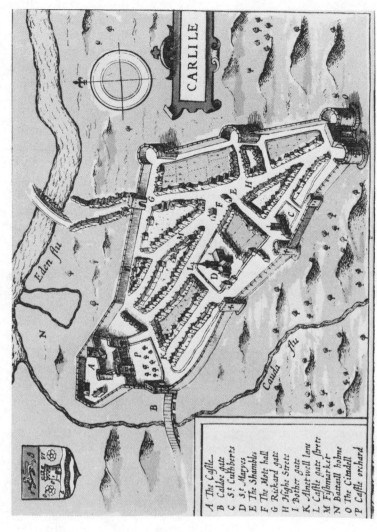

City Plan of "Carlile." From "Cumberland And The Ancient City of Carlisle Described" in 1610, fol. 87v–88r of John Speed's atlas, *The Theatre Of The Empire Of Great Britaine: Presenting An Exact Geography of the Kingdomes of England, Scotland, Ireland and the Isles ajioyning . . .* (London, 1611).

It was the political and moral duty of a major general such as Charles Howard that distinguished his role from the security services of a town-major like Edward Nott. Politically, "the new police system of which the major-generals were to be the heads" was charged with keeping "a strict eye upon the Conversation and Carriage of all Disaffected persons." These dissidents the major generals were to tax, to fine, and, if necessary, to exile to a colony. Moreover, the major generals were to discover "all the idle and loose people" in their provinces, so that they could be "apprehended and transported to foreign parts, where they may earn their living by their labor." Colonel Howard managed this political and social purge with some ease, sending royalists to Barbados, and vagabonds, thieves, and the like to Jamaica. The influence of the major generals did not end with their brief reign. Almost every aspect of their duties, from civil police to all-seeing moral monitor, found its way into the instructions given colonial governors-general after 1660. Howard might have been surprised by the similarity of his orders for the major generalcy of the North in 1655 and for the captain generalcy of Jamaica in 1678, had he not applied his northern experiences as a member of the privy council's plantations committee, which wrote his Jamaica instructions.[42]

The major generals exemplified the ongoing military effort to discipline society as if it were an army unit, but most of them lacked traditional ruling-class qualifications. Even the common people were irritated at being ruled and commanded by those of their own sort, and people of good birth despised the base-born major generals. As a well-born and wealthy gentleman with deep and ancient roots in the North, Colonel Howard understood the opprobrium of his peers and was uncomfortable under it. He agreed with his commander, General Monck, that civilian authority over the army, exercised by members of the traditional elite, was preferable to "the arbitrary power of such proud rebels as Lambert," Howard's arriviste superior. Certainly Charles Howard grew to recognize that traditional social authority could be mobilized to stabilize the nation only through the customary forms of king, lords, and commons. He failed, however, to persuade Oliver Cromwell to take the crown, and he found Richard Cromwell unable to assert civilian authority against army rule—although Howard himself offered to arrest General Lambert. Howard's support of the house of Cromwell made him the object of both republican and

42. Berry and Lee, *James Berry*, appendix A; Gardiner, *Commonwealth and Protectorate*, III, 181; Colonial Office, class 138, piece 3, 198–214, 216–251, P.R.O. (hereafter cited as C.O. 138/3).

army enmity. On the fall of Richard Cromwell, Howard lost all of his commands and was arrested for treason.[43]

The Earl of Carlisle under King Charles II

When the Cromwellian executive failed, its officers allied themselves with the royalist exiles to work for the restoration of the monarchy. On his release from prison in August 1659, Howard helped organize the royalist rising planned for that month. General Monck thus signaled his own monarchist intentions on February 25, 1660, when he commissioned Howard as governor of Carlisle and colonel of an infantry regiment. Naturally, the governor of Carlisle represented that city in the Convention Parliament. Monck also saw to it that the restored king immediately named Colonel Howard to his privy council and that King Charles placed the security of the Borders once more in Howard's hands by commissioning him lieutenant general of Cumberland and Westmoreland.[44]

Garrison Government in the North

On the very day of his appointment, Howard was at work "settling" the trained bands, in obedience to the royal policy that emphasized the political role of militia and decreased that of the professional troops who had been the terror of the land. The king ordered Howard to lessen the number of regular soldiers in his garrison at Carlisle, and here, as in other garrison governments, the king also tried to rescind the political power of the army by reducing the governor of the town to the rank of captain of a garrison company. As it was beneath his dignity to hold the lesser post himself, Howard secured it for one of his own veteran subordinates.[45]

43. Gardiner, *Commonwealth and Protectorate*, III, 189; Rannie, "Cromwell's Major-Generals," *EHR*, X (1895), 498–499, 500; Maj. Gen. Lilburne to Thurloe, from York, Aug. 9, 1656, Birch, ed., *Thurloe S.P.*, V, 296; Hutchinson, *Memoirs*, 317; Firth and Davies, *Regimental History*, 54.

44. [Dicconson], *James the Second*, ed. Clarke, 281. Note Evelyn's parallel analysis of Monck's motives (Beer, ed., *Diary of Evelyn*, entry of Feb. 11, 1660). See also *DNB*, s.v. "Howard, Charles"; Ogg, *Charles II*, I, 26; Firth and Davies, *Regimental History*, 57, 209. "The neck of the fanatic party was broken" by the adherence of the critical governors and garrisons to Monck. Among those prominently mentioned were Gov. Howard and his Carlisle garrison; Sir John Barewick to Sir Edward Hyde, Mar. 19, 1659, Howard to Cromwell, Birch, ed., *Thurloe S.P.*, IV, 861, 340, and see esp. III, 568.

45. Petition of Sir William Dalston, Sept. [?], 1660, Howard to Nicholas, Sept. 6, 1660, George Williamson to Joseph Williamson, Oct. 16, 1660, *Cal. S.P. Dom., 1660–1661*, 259,

Charles II soon recognized, however, that to survive as sovereign he would have to make use of the tools of paramilitary government. He restored the governorship of Carlisle, but he did not recommission Howard as governor. The royalist gentry of the North had suffered under General Howard's government and vigorously opposed his reappointment. Thus, the government of the city and garrison of Carlisle passed to the Musgraves, feudal enemies of the Howards and prominent victims of Charles Howard's earlier military government.[46]

When he lost the garrison government, Howard also lost control of one of the borough's seats in parliament. In the new parliament, Sir Philip Howard, Charles's brother (and designated successor in Jamaica) and captain of Albemarle's (Monck's) Life Guard, retained one seat for the Howard family, but Charles Howard's town-major was displaced from the second seat by Sir Christopher Musgrave, the son of the new governor, captain of one of the garrison companies, and afterward a captain in the king's First Guards. Enemies though they were, Howard and Musgrave alike bespoke army influence in parliament. They typified royal government's reliance on both Anglican royalist officers and Presbyterian followers of the captain general, Albemarle. The Carlisle delegation exemplified the union of these two conservative, largely militarist factions against the "fanatics"—religious zealots, republican partisans, and unreconstructed army men.[47]

313; Howard to Sir George Fletcher, May 9, 1662, Historical Manuscripts Commission, *The Manuscripts of S. H. Le Fleming, Esq., of Rydall Hall* (London, 1890), 28 (hereafter cited as HMC, *Le Fleming*).

46. That the crown was deliberately readopting the methods of the major generals' era is suggested by Western, *English Militia*, 11, 12–13. The garrisons restored in the North were those of Lilburne's district—Berwick, Carlisle, and Tynemouth. On Carlisle, see Thomas Smith to J. Williamson, Oct. 1, 1660, *Cal. S.P. Dom., 1660–1661*, 303–304; Sir Edward Musgrave to Williamson, Apr. 9, 1672, *ibid., 1671–1672*, 294–295. Note the parallel case of Chester, where a military man was removed to satisfy the local gentry and a local royalist worthy substituted (deputy lieutenants and others of Cheshire to Albemarle [Monck], July 16, 1663, Bennet to Sir Evan Lloyd, Oct. 15, 1663, *ibid., 1663–1664*, 205, 303). As a technique of reintroducing royal authority following a political crisis, this method was to become commonplace in colonial governments.

47. Ogg, *Charles II*, I, 189, ranks Howard with Albemarle (Gen. Monck) and the earl of Sandwich (Adm. Montague) as "old servants of the Commonwealth." A new label seems required, however, for the martial factions of Albemarle's (Cromwellian) men vis-à-vis the duke of York's (royalist) men and the parallel religious parties of comprehension and exclusion. Howard, in both the former camps, was increasingly and particularly associated with Lord Holles and the "Presbyterians." See John Dodington to Williamson, [Dec. 9], 1668, *Cal. S.P. Dom., 1668–1669*, 94, and Haley, *Shaftesbury*, 12, 17, 18. On the political situation in the Carlisle corporation, see M. Creighton, *Carlisle* (London, 1889), 162, and R. S. Ferguson, ed., *The Royal Charters of the City of Carlisle* (Carlisle, 1894), xxxvi. See also n. 69 below.

The Howards' loss of influence at Carlisle was offset when, at the coronation of Charles II, Charles Howard was created earl of Carlisle and Baron Morpeth, thereby adding to the power of the "Presbyterian Party" in the house of lords and confirming Carlisle's grip on two seats at Morpeth, part of his extensive parliamentary interest in the region of his lieutenant generalcy. When the king created Charles Howard an earl, he confirmed the barony granted to Howard by Cromwell in 1657. Thus in 1661 Howard's escutcheon blazoned both Charles Stuart's militant determination to support his monarchy and his adoption of Oliver Cromwell's military methods and men.[48]

The authoritarian utility of this executive-military combination became more apparent as the king played upon the legislators' fears in order to increase his military resources. Aroused by royal reports of the attempted rebellion of dispossessed officer-landlords in Ireland, the resistance of Covenanters to episcopacy in Scotland, and the plotting of English sectarians against the repressive Anglican government, the Cavalier Parliament authorized militia taxes and granted the crown full military authority. The new earl of Carlisle used that authority to remodel the command structure of the northern counties, and he spent the additional taxes to pay his select militia for their service against the "fanatics." He took special care to clear the political reputation of his seasoned officers. One such was John Tongue, whom Carlisle commissioned muster and drill master for his militias. Soon afterward, Carlisle secured Tongue a captaincy in Lord General Albemarle's Guards (which led to Tongue's command in the expeditionary force sent to Virginia in 1676). The earl also obtained leave for a number of his officers, among them Francis Watson, quartermaster of Sir Philip Howard's (Albemarle's own) troop in the royal Horse Guards, later major general under Captain General Carlisle in Jamaica, and subsequently commander-in-chief of that colony. Watson's leave, and that of other royal officers of Carlisle's staff, enabled them to join the household that accompanied the earl of Carlisle on his embassy to Russia in June 1663.[49]

48. See the estimate of the parliamentary influence of private individuals and Sir Richard Wiseman's later "Account of the House of Commons," 1676, printed in Andrew Browning, *Thomas Osborne, Earl of Danby and Duke of Leeds, 1632–1712*, 3 vols. (Glasgow, 1951), III, 83, 102.

49. *Cal. S. P. Ven., 1661–1664*, 252; deposition of David Evans, May 7, 1661, *Cal. S. P. Dom., 1660–1661*, 582; warrant to the commissary general of musters, June 12, 1663, *ibid., 1663–1664*, 168.

Plot and Repression, 1663

The "advantage to the other party of the Earl of Carlisle's going away" on an embassy to Russia was the opportunity that the lieutenant general's absence gave for the organization of widespread resistance in the North to royal authority. Particularly provoking were the religious regulations of the "Clarendon code." On August 3, 1663, the earl of Carlisle's brother-in-law, Sir Thomas Gower, the high sheriff of Yorkshire, reported to the captain general, Albemarle, the results of his own "unwearied watchfulness" and the discoveries of his "excellent system of espionage." For six months Gower had been collecting ever more alarming intelligence. At first Gower refused to believe it, but now he had been told the names of the plotters, the date of their projected rebellion, and their objectives. Officers of the old army aimed to capture York during the assizes in August. The captured northern capital would then serve as headquarters for a chain of insurrections in the North and in Scotland. When the king's Guards marched north to fight the rebels, London would rise behind them.[50]

Gower's report of this plot led King Charles, as he prorogued parliament, to question "if he would live to meet them again." Since the king's animal spirits were notoriously robust, his reference to the threat of rebellion was understood. The military

50. Sir William Blakeston to Gower, Aug. 8, 1663, *Cal. S.P. Dom.*, *1663–1664*, 234. Gower, together with Carlisle's other brothers-in-law—Sir Jonathan Atkins (of the Guards and the governments of Guernsey, Rochester, and Barbados), Sir George Downing (scoutmaster general, diplomat, and author of the Navigation Act of 1660), Adm. Sir John Lawson, and the earl of Leven—constituted a Carlisle connection of obvious force in imperial politics and war (Huddleston, ed., *Naworth Accounts*, xiii). On Downing and his protection by Carlisle at the Restoration, see Burnet, *History*, I, 356. Abbott, "Conspiracy and Dissent, I," *AHR*, XIV (1908–1909), 521, labels Gower "governor" of York, but I have not found his commission. Henry Gee, "The Derwentdale Plot, 1663," RHS, *Trans.*, 3d Ser., XI (1917), 135, documents the titles used here. Unfortunately, Gee had not seen Abbott's work on the same subject. See Gee, *ibid.*, 127, on the motives for the rising, and pp. 130 n. 1 and 134 for reference to Gower's diary of the plot (deposited in S.P. 81/77). Gower was a civil warrior of vast experience, having joined Charles I before the walls of Hull (Anchitell Grey, ed., *Debates of the House of Commons from the year 1667 to the year 1694* . . . , 10 vols. [London, 1763], I, 4n). For the conspirators' strategy, see Abbott, 521. For Gower's evidence, see Gee, 134, and citations. The conspirators' committees of correspondence both in London and the North were predominantly military, according to Gee, 122–123, 135, and Sir Philip Musgrave to Gower, Oct. [?], 1663, *Cal. S.P. Dom.*, *1663–1664*, 322. The authorities thought the plotters "only formidable from the disbanded officers and soldiers among them." On the combination of repressive law and taxation, and on the use of these tax moneys to support militia enforcement of the coercive legislation, under the chain of command from the king to Carlisle and Gower, see: Abbott, 521; order by the king, June 1661, the king to [the lord lieutenants of counties], Dec. 27, 1662, *ibid.*, *1661–1662*, 27, 603; Carlisle to the deputy lieutenants of Cumberland and Westmoreland, n.d., the king to Carlisle, Dec. 19, 1662, Jan. 29, 1664, lords of the council to Carlisle, Feb. 12, 1663, HMC, *Le Fleming*, 6, 29, 32, 30; Browning, ed., *English Historical Documents, 1660–1714*, 775–796.

committee of the cabinet met, under Albemarle's presidency, and dispatched Lord Frescheville and Captain Herbert Jeffreys to York at the head of detachments from the Guards. The earl of Carlisle, the king's lieutenant in the North and Albemarle's trusted subordinate, had just sailed for Russia. The captain general did manage to get some help from the eighty-man ambassadorial party, however, when one vessel of Carlisle's convoy was driven back into Burlington for repairs. Sheriff Gower rode to Burlington and warned his fellow Carlislean, Quartermaster Watson, of this "new meeting of fanatics." When the duke of Albemarle learned of his quartermaster's return, he ordered Watson to hurry back to London to recruit their troop and so relieve royalist units of the Guards for duty in York. The Guards marched into York on the very day scheduled for the coup. Directed by Sir Thomas Gower and assisted by the select militia he had brought into town, Frescheville's and Jeffreys's units of the royal Guards made more than one hundred arrests, and so prevented both the imminent rising and an alternative arranged for September.[51]

Some of those arrested were "persuaded" to disclose the final stage of the insurrection, set for October 12. The conspirators planned to surprise the strategic towns of Nottingham and Gloucester, thereby securing the crossings of the Trent and Severn. To open communications with their co-conspirators in Scotland, they would capture Newcastle. The plotters presumed that the Guards still in London would be sent out to recapture these strategic towns, thus exposing the city, Whitehall, the king, and his ministers to the rebels' London associates.[52]

Gower's latest information roused Charles II's government to desperate efforts. While the king's and Albemarle's battalions of the Guards were put on the alert in London, a dozen additional Guards companies—formed during the royalist exile and recently

51. For the march of troops to York, see, in addition to the citations here, chapter 3 below. Carlisle's situation is described by Miege, *Three Embassies*, 5, 12, 17–18. See also the order for continuance of the establishment of forces, [May 19], 1663, the information of Capt. Robert Atkinson, Nov. 26, 1663, *Cal. S.P. Dom., 1663–1664*, 143, 352; Abbott, "Conspiracy and Dissent, I," *AHR*, XIV (1908–1909), 522; Gee, "Derwentdale Plot," RHS, *Trans.*, 3d Ser., XI (1917), 137. Gee also details the situation at York and the timely arrival of the regulars from London (p. 136).

52. The chief plotter was a former parliamentary colonel and deputy governor of Newcastle (Gee, "Derwentdale Plot," RHS, *Trans.*, 3d Ser., XI [1917], 129). For the strategic importance of these towns in a civil war, see Firth and Davies, *Regimental History*, esp. 89, 138, 169, 289, 275, 432, 440, 461 (on Newcastle). Also on Newcastle, see Burnet, *History*, I, 45; Latham and Matthews, eds., *Diary of Pepys*, VIII, 285 (entry of June 29, 1667), 285 n. 5. On Gloucester, see chapter 1 above; Gee, 136–137; Abbott, "Conspiracy and Dissent, I," *AHR*, XIV (1908–1909), 522.

brought over from Dunkirk with just such a contingency in mind —were ordered to the other garrison towns (as Jeffreys had been sent to York). The Guards thus provided the military means of re-establishing the garrison governments of the Interregnum. To disarm the local allegiances that might limit military repression, and to exploit urban-rural jealousies, select city-trained bands were marched out from the garrisoned towns into the most disaffected areas of the countryside. The trained bands were replaced in these towns by units of veteran royalist volunteers hastily raised by the county militia lieutenants.[53]

Despite the government's thorough precautions, no fewer than three northern risings occurred on October 12. Each was led by a captain of the old army in command of as many as three hundred men. Shut out from the regarrisoned towns, the rebels built entrenchments and hoped to attract to them a multitude of the discontented. They did not come. Instead, the forces of the crown arrested an uncounted number of the rebels. Eighteen of them were executed in a batch at York, under the watchful eye of Captain Jeffreys. A scattering of exemplary executions of three or four men each took place in the northern cities that had been the objects of the conspiracy. The death toll reached at least thirty, and the scope of the example was extended by dismembering the victims. The Great North Road was signposted with heads, warnings to potential rebels.[54]

Somewhat more fortunate were the twenty prisoners seized as likely leaders of the rising and shipped off from the Tower "to any plantation except New England and Virginia." The crown saw no need to reinforce New England dissidence with skilled soldiers and practiced plotters against royal authority. As for Virginia, Quaker riots in the west of England against Sir William Berkeley's repression of their co-religionists in the Old Dominion had alerted the crown to the difficulty Berkeley's regime was having in holding down the multitudes of religious enthusiasts sent there since 1657 by Charles Howard and other English provincial governors. Moreover, in 1663 Virginia's government was menaced by a rebellion of the former Cromwellian soldiers now bound to servitude in the colony. The massive transportation of the previous

53. S.P. 44/2, 31, 36; Hamilton, *Grenadier Guards*, I, 90–93; [Dicconson], *James the Second*, ed. Clarke, 391; *Cal. S.P. Ven., 1661–1664*, 202–203, 212, 214, 219, 245, 267, 269–270; Sir Philip Musgrave to Williamson, Nov. 9, to Bennet, Nov. 9, 1663, *Cal. S.P. Dom., 1663–1664*, 332; Gee, "Derwentdale Plot," RHS, *Trans.*, 3d Ser., XI (1917), 139.

54. Gee, "Derwentdale Plot," RHS, *Trans.*, 3d Ser., XI (1917), 139–140; Abbott, "Conspiracy and Dissent, I," *AHR*, XIV (1908–1909), 523, 524.

two years had to be stopped in the interest of continental American security. The prohibition on the shipment of religious dissidents to Virginia and New England was written into the Conventicle Act of 1664.[55]

Dangerous as religious and political prisoners were to colonial stability, the Atlantic prevented their direct attack on royal authority. Therefore transportation, primarily to the West Indies, was retained as a tool of political police. For example, when the earl of Carlisle returned from his embassy in Russia and was appointed to head the royal commission for policing the Borders, he agreed with his deputy that imprisonment of the Quakers would not repress them unless the authorities also resorted to "the executive part, transportation." Carlisle wanted, and ultimately received, royal orders not only to transport religious dissidents and convicted felons to the plantations, but also to ship off to America anyone of "notorious ill-fame." Under such a broad rubric, any person who displeased the authorities was liable to what was, in the eyes of most Englishmen, a fate worse than death. As Carlisle pointed out, during his police work for the Protectorate he had condemned to death one hundred criminals in less than three years, only to find that sending thirty convicts to the plantations was a much greater deterrent to crime. The notoriety of the colonies is patent here, as is Carlisle's knowledge of the colonial demand for labor. In 1662 he had used ships of the royal navy and the agency of the colony's first royal governor to send out to his Jamaica plantation thirty bondsmen, servants he himself would follow as governor-general.[56]

55. The king to Sir Thomas Bludworth and Sir William Turner, Dec. 19, 1662, *Cal. S.P. Dom., 1661–1662*, 596. The limitations on transportation were afterward generalized in the penalty clause of the Conventicle Act, 16 Car. II, cap iv. Political prisoners were a small fraction of the number transported "to the plantations in America" in these years, the bulk being more offensive to authority for religious dissent than for political opposition (*Cal. S.P. Ven., 1661–1664*, 209). In addition to previous examples, see Andrews, *British Committees*, esp. 70–71, and Abbott Emerson Smith, *Colonists in Bondage: White Servitude and Convict Labor in America, 1607–1776* (Chapel Hill, N.C., 1947; repr. Gloucester, Mass., 1965), chapters 8, 9, and p. 309. The rebellion of the old soldiers bound to servitude in Virginia is discussed by Richard B. Morris, *Government and Labor in Early America* (New York, 1946; repr. New York, 1965), 173–174.

56. Lowther to Williamson, Aug. 10, 1665, *Cal. S.P. Dom., 1664–1665*, 513; Carlisle to Arlington, Jan. 1, 1666, *ibid., 1665–1666*, 186. Carlisle's actions were those enjoined on the major generals; see Berry and Lee, *James Berry*, 276, and Gardiner, *Commonwealth and Protectorate*, III, 176. According to Ludlow, the major generals threatened "such as would not yield a ready submission to their orders with transportation to Jamaica or some other plantations" (Ludlow's *Memoirs*, quoted in Rannie, "Cromwell's Major-Generals," *EHR*, X [1895], 500); see also the instructions to Monck, Apr. 6, 1654, for the transportation "to foreign English plantations," of all "enemies now in arms in the Highlands" (*Cal. S.P. Dom., 1654*, 85).

Carlisle's advocacy of transportation accurately reflected this martial earl's attitude toward what was euphemistically called the "liberty of the subject." He had fought at Worcester, whence hundreds of defeated royalists had been summarily shipped off to the plantations, penned with livestock during the voyage, and doomed to five years' slave labor on a diet of potatoes and water. Howard had known then, as he wrote in 1667, that there were objections to sending prisoners overseas without charge, trial, conviction, or sentence, but "the integrity of the work must justify it." The earl repeatedly pled "the public good in an extraordinary case" to justify what was a commonplace abuse of the English executive's political authority and physical power. Such practices convicted King Charles, his heir, and his chancellor, as well as Cromwell and Carlisle, of transferring arbitrary government from England to the empire. These imperial executives bolstered absolutism in both the realm and the dominions by transporting accused men "beyond the seas," that is, to lands out of the reach (as parliament protested and as the executive asserted) of English law. Many commentators not only feared the debasement of Englishmen's personal legal protections by transportation, but also apprehended the negative effects of a prisoner population on colonial society. In the practice of disciplinarians such as General Carlisle, however, England's political and social purge took precedence over both English legal rights and colonial social stability.[57]

The Dutch Wars and Domestic Discipline, 1665–1678

No sooner had the government made itself authoritative at home than, in the spring of 1664, domestic peace was threatened by foreign war. The war with the Dutch provided the enemies of the English crown with "a source of money, arms and supplies, a base of operations, and a possible ally." In the resulting security crisis, the earl of Carlisle played his usual active role on behalf of national authority. He had returned from Russia, Sweden, and Denmark to Naworth in the summer of 1665. There he took up the duties of his multi-county militia lieutenancy, his vice admiralty, and his commissionerships of prizes and Border security. This set of military-executive offices gave institutional focus to the earl's three

57. Carlisle to Arlington, Jan. 1, 1666, *Cal. S.P. Dom., 1665–1666,* 186; Gardiner, *Commonwealth and Protectorate,* III, 196. For the legalization of this long-standing practice, see Ogg, *Charles II,* II, 488–489; Matthew Mackaile to Sir John Frederick, [Aug. 2?], 1678, *Cal. S.P. Dom., 1678,* 340; and instructions to the council for foreign plantations, paragraph 10, July 30, 1670, Andrews, *British Committees,* 120–121. Note such instances as the transportation of 52 Scots to Virginia following the rising of 1678 (the king to Culpeper, Jeffreys, and the council of Virginia, Dec. 17, 1678, *Cal. S.P. Col., 1677–1680,* no. 850).

public preoccupations during the next dozen years: the commercial prosperity of his earldom, the Border region, and the English nation; issues of political and military police; and the Howards' feud with the Musgraves.[58]

The demands and dangers of the war with the Dutch emphasized the military character of all of the earl's offices. His vice admiral's commission made Carlisle responsible for the protection of shipping, especially that of the Newcastle coal convoys. His pleas for royal naval vessels to fight the convoys through to London were punctuated by reports of gunfire at sea. Each convoy cleared the coal ports only to encounter the Dutch blockade squadron. Like his call for naval escorts, the vice admiral's request that royal ships be stationed under his command to protect local commerce anticipated the demands of his colonial counterparts, those of the royal governors-general who served as vice admirals. In England, as elsewhere in the empire, vice admirals tried to preserve the naval traffic that they taxed to support their provincial governments. They all also shared in the prizes condemned by their admiralty courts. In Carlisle's case, prize ships cheaply purchased after condemnation carried the coal and timber from his extensive estates to London, thus adding personal incentives to the earl's official interest in naval security.[59]

Throughout the empire, vice admirals like Carlisle had to impress seamen to man the convoys. Port officers in the northern admiralty district begged for the personal visits of the earl—"who is much honoured and loved amongst all people in those parts"— in order to bring seamen out of hiding. Carlisle benefited even from fugitive seamen, for they worked in his mines or volunteered to march as soldiers under the banner of this famous commander. He proposed that he reconcile his admiralty and army responsibilities by enlisting these men in regiments and then leading them to service at sea.[60]

58. Abbott, "Conspiracy and Dissent, II," *AHR*, XIV (1908–1909), 696; Gee, "Derwentdale Plot," RHS, *Trans.*, 3d Ser., XI (1917), 142; [L. B.] to Bennet, Aug. 20, 1664, *Cal. S.P. Dom., 1663–1664*, 671; statement of prize sums, [1664?], *ibid., 1664–1665*, 147; Carlisle's commission of June 20, 1667, Dalton, ed., *English Army Lists*, I, 88. See also the newsletter of June 18, 1667, in HMC, *Le Fleming*, 50.

59. Petition of Carlisle to the king, Mar. 14, 1663, *Cal. S.P. Dom., 1663–1664*, 76; Lowther to Williamson, Aug. 10, 1665, Sir William Coventry to Arlington, Aug. 12, 1665, *ibid., 1664–1665*, 513, 514; two warrants to the commissioners of prizes, Apr. 26, 1667, Coventry to the navy commissioners, May 18, 1667, Carlisle to Williamson, July 13, 24, 1667, petition of Carlisle and Widdrington, July [?], 1667, warrant to Carlisle, July 31, 1667, Richard Forster to Williamson, Aug. 2, 1667, Richard Bower to Williamson, Aug. 7, Oct. 16, 21, 1667, *ibid., 1667*, 55, 105, 289, 321, 345, 355, 365, 530, 537; recommendations to the lords commissioners of the treasury, Nov. 26, 1671, *ibid., 1671*, 586; Huddleston, ed., *Naworth Accounts*, 10, 67, 115, 139.

60. Forster to Williamson, July 10, 13, 17, 1666, Carlisle to Williamson, July 21, 1666,

As military service by land and sea were linked, so both affected political security. During each summer of the war, the level of domestic unrest depended on a great naval battle. If the Dutch could decisively defeat the English fleet, they would be able to supply material support for an English insurrection. Thus the duke of York's victory off Lowestoft in June 1665 had a double domestic effect: it cut off the "Rathbone" plotters from Dutch support, and it freed the duke himself to march north against the rebels. He was met at York by the earl of Carlisle, who had raised and paid select militia companies "to support his majesty's authority." The duke and the earl, veteran commanders both, then organized military forces to control the adjacent parts of Scotland. Carlisle also acted on the king's orders to take peace bonds from "all persons of a seditious temper," or else arrest them.[61]

The indecisive meeting of the battle fleets in 1666 meant that invasion was still possible, insurrection still prepared. Carlisle not only received the usual orders to keep an eye on the seditious sorts in his lieutenancy but also accepted a commission to raise a troop of regular cavalry to assist him. (He was one of three sometime American officer-governors who enlisted a troop at this time.) Recruits flocked to the standard of this popular commander. The earl reported that he had raised and mounted his troop in two days. He had had to turn away a hundred additional mounted volunteers. In a few days, Carlisle said, he could organize a regiment of cavalry as well as one of infantry. It was this ability of martial magnates to draw out local manpower for the crown that kept noble colonels prominent for so long in the royal army. The earl of Carlisle used his eager troops to protect both the seacoast from Dutch raiders and the royal authority from English fanatics: such was the dual responsibility, for external protection and internal peace, of every provincial executive in England's empire.[62]

Daniel Fleming to Williamson, July 27, 1666, Cal. S.P. Dom., 1665–1666, 518, 530, 546, 561, 582; lords of the council to Carlisle, Oct. 14, 1664, Feb. 17, 1665, Mar. 26, 1672, Apr. 9, 16, 1678, Carlisle to the deputy lieutenants of Westmoreland, Feb. 2, to Fleming, Feb. 21, 1665, to the deputy lieutenants of Cumberland and Westmoreland, Apr. 2, 1672, to Fleming and the deputy lieutenants and justices of Westmoreland, Apr. 26, 1678, Fleming to Carlisle, [Feb. 1672], HMC, Le Fleming, 33, 34, 90, 144, 89.

61. Abbott, "Conspiracy and Dissent, II," AHR, XIV (1908–1909), 696; [Dicconson], James the Second, ed. Clarke, 421–422; Charles II to Carlisle, May 4, 1665, June 25, July 13, 1666, Fleming to Williamson, Aug. 21, 1665, HMC, Le Fleming, 36, 40, 38; Coventry to Arlington, Aug. 12, to Williamson, Aug. 14, 1665, Lowther to Williamson, Aug. 17, 1665, Cal. S.P. Dom., 1664–1665, 514, 517, 521.

62. For these troops, see Dalton, ed., English Army Lists, I, 59–62 (1666), 76–77 (1667). Their captains included Sir John Reresby, the governor of York; Carlisle; Col. Charles Wheeler (afterward of the Leeward Islands); Sir Tobias Bridge (about to sail for the West In-

As Carlisle grew older, however, and as he saw feebler risings foiled with growing ease, he became convinced of the essential stability of English society. He grew increasingly reluctant, therefore, to unsettle his province by excessive ferocity toward the political and religious opponents of the government. To be sure, as the king's lord lieutenant, he continued to play on fear of the fanatics as a means to military and political ends, such as the recovery of that jurisdiction over Berwick that he had previously possessed as the Protector's major general. He also obeyed royal orders to use his forces "to watch suspected persons and to secure the more dangerous, especially such as keep horses or arms above their rank." While he obeyed royal orders to seize these people, Carlisle did so only when he recognized a local emergency. He promised to "secure the peace," but "with the least oppression."[63]

After nearly twenty years in the service of the state, Carlisle had struck a balance between the imposition of stabilizing central authority on the province and the admission of enough provincial freedom to enliven the local economy and to make local government functional. One last episode of unrelieved repression intervened, however, before Carlisle's desire to balance the needs of the prerogative with those of the province—and so to be powerful both in court and country—produced a shift toward "popularity" in the earl's parliamentary and imperial politics.

A single officer escaped to alarm the nearest royal garrison, the one at Carlisle, when at daybreak on Thursday, November 15, 1666, some four hundred Scots Presbyterians stormed into Dumfries, Galloway, and captured their persecutor, the noted military theorist Sir James Turner—and most of his troops—in bed. When messengers sent by John Tongue from the Carlisle garrison arrived in London on Tuesday evening, the court was dancing. King Charles turned to the earl of Carlisle, commissioned him lieuten-

---

dies in command of the Barbados Regiment); and Lord Windsor (recently returned from the government of Jamaica). The king suggested as well that Carlisle have "a regiment in view," which he finally raised in 1673. See Carlisle to Williamson, July 21, 28, 1666, Fleming to Williamson, July 27, 1666, *Cal. S.P. Dom., 1665–1666*, 561, 587–588, 582; Forster to Williamson, July 12, 1667, *ibid., 1667*, 289; Western, *English Militia*, 44–45.

63. The king to Carlisle, July 13, 1666, HMC, *Le Fleming*, 40; Carlisle to Williamson, July 28, 1666, *Cal. S.P. Dom., 1665–1666*, 587–588. In his letter to Williamson, Carlisle did not mention the Battle of Sheerness on July 25, where the victory of the English fleet removed all threat of invasion. He did go on arresting political suspects in emergencies, although he held them only briefly and released rather than transported them (Fleming to Williamson, Sept. 15, 1666, *ibid., 1666–1667*, 127–128). That Carlisle was typical of his officer class both in his coercive activities up to this time and in his repugnance toward repression during the decade from 1669 to 1679 is apparent from Western's discussion of attitudes toward use of the militia as political police (*English Militia*, 48–49, 50–51).

ant general of the royal army and commander-in-chief of all the Border militias, ordered him to lead five hundred of the royal cavalry north, and gave him authority to command royal garrisons both north and south of rebel territory. Governor Fenwick's citadel at Leith was rearmed to counter both the rebels and the Dutch fleet reportedly lying offshore to support the rising. The governors of Carlisle, Berwick, and Tynemouth, whose arsenals had recently been resupplied for just such an emergency, furnished ammunition to the converging royal forces.[64]

Meanwhile the rebels demonstrated the political use of places of strength and the perennial appeal of the slogans of civil war. At the captured garrison town of Dumfries they rallied several thousand men. From Dumfries the rebels issued a call for liberty of conscience and for freedom from taxation, slogans that the authorities correctly feared would be popular far beyond the Borders. The rebels then advanced to within two miles of Edinburgh before the royal forces concentrating there forced them to fall back to the Pentland Hills on Wednesday, November 21. On that day the earl of Carlisle passed through York at the head of the royal cavalry. His troops cut off rebel movements to the south, while the assembled militias of the Scots gentry blocked their northern retreat. The rebels turned to face the royal troops marching out from Edinburgh. Five hundred rebels were killed on the Pentland Hills. The royalists lost hardly a man, and they captured some three hundred of the government's enemies. One in ten of the prisoners was executed. They were fortunate compared with those who were tortured or sold into the long death of colonial servitude. By Friday night, November 23, less than two weeks from the day the rebels stormed Dumfries, the earl of Carlisle was relaxing in Naworth Castle. As Carlisle's Scots agent observed, "A poor mercenary, red-coated soldier, as [the fanatics] call them, will for 8d. a day venture to the cannon's mouth to the risk of his life, which is much more than the loss of a little silver." Short of silver the Restoration governments often were, but they were never again short of the soldiers required to repress domestic discontent.[65]

64. Abbott, "Conspiracy and Dissent, II," *AHR*, XIV (1908–1909), 705; Fleming to Williamson, Sept. 15, 1666, William Fielding to Sir Philip Musgrave, Nov. 15, 1666, instruction and note of powers to Carlisle, Nov. 23, 1666, J. A. to Robert Washington, Nov. 23, 1666, R[obert] M[ien] to Williamson, Nov. 24, 1666, Annandale to the deputy lieutenants of Westmoreland and Cumberland, Nov. 25, 1666, H. M[uddiman] to George Powell, Nov. 29, 1666, *Cal. S.P. Dom., 1666–1667*, 127–128, 262, 282–283, 283, 284, 288, 299. On Turner, who "was a learned man; but had been always in armies, and knew no other rule but to obey orders," and on the revolt, see Burnet, *History*, I, 377–383, 417–426, 440.

65. Annandale to Sir Edward Musgrave, Nov. 20, 1666, Mien to Williamson, Nov. 20,

Six months after the Dumfries rising, the government's new prestige was badly shaken by the brilliant, though momentary, success of the Dutch raid on the royal fleet laid up in the Thames. The captain general, Albemarle, delegated to the earl of Carlisle the belatedly organized but finally effective defense of the river and dockyard. Thus Albemarle associated his veteran subordinate with his own renewed reputation as England's bulwark. Then the earl of Carlisle raced north once more to meet the double danger of Dutch invasion and domestic rebellion. He was anxiously awaited, even by his hereditary enemy, Sir Philip Musgrave, the governor of Carlisle, who received the lieutenant general at the city gates with full military compliments. Carlisle's feverish efforts to raise troops and to ready the defenses of the northeastern coasts against invasion ceased in July 1667, when the Peace of Breda brought to England a degree of domestic tranquility unknown for a generation.[66]

Peace relaxed the economic, military, and police pressures on the earl of Carlisle and left him free to concern himself with poli-

---

27, 28, 30, 1666, [H. Muddiman] to John Witty, Nov. 24, 1666, Fleming to Williamson, Nov. 26, 1666, Sir Edward to Sir Philip Musgrave, Nov. 26, 1666, [T. Corie] to Williamson, Nov. 28, 1666, Joseph Mascall to Williamson, Nov. 28, 1666, Forster to Williamson, Nov. 30, 1666, *Cal. S.P. Dom., 1666–1667*, 275, 295, 301, 285–286, 289–290, 295, 296, 302; Tongue to Sir William Carleton, Nov. 15, 1666, HMC, *Le Fleming*, 42–43; Joseph Binckes to Arlington, May 5, 1670, *Cal. S.P. Dom., 1670*, 199. The most eloquent evocation of the dark penumbra of fanaticism and inquisition, riot and repression, is Burnet's *History*, I, 417. Anxious not to give the Scots regime credit even for effective suppression, Burnet reported that only 130 rebels were captured and 40 killed in battle. But his execution figure (45) is higher than any other source's.

66. Abbott, "Conspiracy and Dissent, II," *AHR*, XIV (1908–1909), 709, 710 n. 86; *Cal. S.P. Dom., 1666–1667*, 73, 130, 189, 200–201; *ibid., 1667*, 216, 217, 219, 233–234, 249(2), 258–259, 263, 266, 267, 286; Historical Manuscripts Commission, *The Manuscripts of J. Eliot Hodgkin, Esq., F.S.A. of Richmond, Surrey* (London, 1897), 301; HMC, *Seventeenth Report*, Pt. V, 7, 9, 12, 14; HMC, *Manuscripts in Various Collections*, Vol. II, *The Manuscripts of Sir George Wombwell, the Duke of Norfolk, Lord Edmund Talbot, Miss Buxton, Mrs. Harford and Mrs. Wentworth of Woolley* (London, 1903), 6, 12, 26, 124–125, 381; HMC, *The Manuscripts of Lincoln, Bury St. Edmund's, and Great Grimsby Corporations; and of the Deans and Chapters of Worcester and Lichfield, &c.* (London, 1895), 368; Latham and Matthews, eds., *Diary of Pepys*, VII, 254–272, 275, 278 (entries of June 8, 10–14, 17, 19, 1667); Western, *English Militia*, 42ff. For Carlisle's activities, see Grey, ed., *Debates of the House of Commons*, I, 27n; commissions to Carlisle, June 18, 20, 1667, Charles II to the mayor, etc., of Newcastle, June [20], 1667, Arlington to Sir John Duncombe, June 20 [?], 1667, Forster to Williamson, June 28, 29, July 2, 4, 1667, Humphrey Pibus to the navy commissioners, June 29, 1667, Carlisle to Williamson, July 4, 1667, Sir Philip Musgrave to Williamson, Aug. 22, 1667, *Cal. S.P. Dom., 1667*, 208, 214, 242, 243, 259, 266, 247, 265, 409–410. This disaster of unpreparedness increased the influence of the militarists, especially York, Rupert, and Albemarle; see [?] to Viscount Conway, June 15, 1667, *ibid.*, 189. Carlisle's dominance of the northern command was reported by the officer-governor of Newcastle (Col. Edward Villiers to Williamson, July 1, 1667, *ibid.*, 255). See also the lords of the council to Carlisle, June 11, 1667, newsletter of June 18, 1667, Carlisle to Sir George Fletcher, June 24, 1667, HMC, *Le Fleming*, 49–50, 50; S.P. 44/17, 244–245; S.P. 44/20, 150, 164.

tics. As provincial executives did everywhere in the empire, the earl used his military patronage to strengthen his political partisans. Likewise, Carlisle used his position as the presiding justice in each county of his lieutenancy to favor his supporters in lawsuits and to assist them in the tax collectorships he helped them obtain. Finally, he employed nearly every political device of an unusually unscrupulous age to win his lifelong feud with Sir Philip Musgrave and so to regain the governorship of Carlisle for the Howards.[67]

The earl of Carlisle's regional success thus was not based solely on his wealth in northern land, mines, mills, and herds, and the associated "interest" of his family; it also grew from his role as the central government's "man of business" in the North. Carlisle's continuing efforts in convoy organization, in fortification, and in militia reform led the government to make an unusual military and political concession to the Howards. In December 1668 the king named Carlisle's heir, Lord Morpeth, as joint lord lieutenant, with his father, of Cumberland and Westmoreland. Each lieutenant received authority to act alone when the other was "beyond seas." Not only did the appointment preserve the Howard influence in the North when the earl was serving abroad, it enabled Lord Morpeth to take local action against the Musgraves at times when it was impolitic for the earl of Carlisle to do so.[68]

By March of 1676 the Howard-Musgrave feud had refocused on the city of Carlisle's garrison government, and on its political function in what Governor Sir Philip Musgrave called "the matter betwixt Lord Carlisle and us." He boldly reminded Carlisle of earlier Musgrave triumphs over the Howard interest: "I have struggled with greater difficulties in the like kind than yet I meet with, and my integrity brought me safe off from the snares laid for me." But age was laying a snare the old governor could not escape, and the earl of Carlisle relentlessly pursued his program of power, "the method I have many years proposed to myself of reconciling my neighbors and impartially settling matters to right between them." That was one way of summarizing Carlisle's whole career in the North since 1649. Even though John Tongue—who as muster

67. Carlisle to Williamson, Mar. 10, 1666, John Waring to Thomas Bromhall, July 13, 1666, *Cal. S.P. Dom., 1665–1666*, 293, 531; *ibid., 1666–1667*, 144; nn. 69–73 below.

68. Warrant for a commission to Carlisle, Jan. 4, 1668, order by the English commissioners for trade with Scotland, Feb. 12, 1668, Maj. Jer. Tolhurst to Carlisle, July 10, 1668, *Cal. S.P. Dom., 1667–1668*, 156, 226, 511; commission for Carlisle and Morpeth, Dec. 3, 1668, *ibid., 1668–1669*, 88; *ibid.*, 150, 163, 164–165, 196, 198, 308; Lowther to Fleming, July 6, 1680, Fletcher to Fleming, Nov. 24, 1680, Fletcher to Carlisle, Apr. 21, 1683, Carlisle to Fletcher, Apr. 23, 1683, HMC, *Le Fleming*, 169, 174, 191.

master had been Carlisle's chief aide in disciplining the earl's potent political allies, the select militia—was gone to a command in the Virginia expedition, Carlisle's power was greater than ever. Governor Musgrave angrily argued that "it is now manifest enough that L[ord] C[arlisle] designs to continue matters in these counties in the same way he pretends to dislike. Arbitrary actings are not discouraged, if they may serve a turn, popularity industriously sought."[69]

That elite opponents could malign Carlisle as at once "arbitrary" and "popular" suggests something of the class and personal bases of their opposition to him. The earl exhibited the usual officer-executive combination. He was "arbitrary" in that he used the military and judicial prerogative delegated to him by the crown to monopolize provincial administration. His administration was "popular" in that it was widely approved of by the governed both as anti-elitist and as demonstrably concerned with "the public good." Elites all over the empire called such officer behavior "arbitrary" and deplored its "popularity" among the classes they exploited, classes whom governors-general claimed to cultivate as the true strength of the state.

The issue between the officer-administrators and their rivals was seldom settled in the provinces. In the case of the Carlisle governorship, the Musgraves proclaimed in vain their determination to resist the earl of Carlisle's "zeal to secure the government." The crown had already chosen him as its agent to assert the prerogative in Jamaica and, in February 1678, insured the earl's cooperation in garrison government overseas by commissioning him "commander and governor of the town and castle of Carlisle," by making him captain of a company in the garrison, and by appointing his son as a garrison captain and deputy governor of Carlisle. After nearly twenty years, Charles, earl of Carlisle, had recombined, under the aegis of the crown, all the offices of power in the North that he had held under Cromwell.[70]

---

69. Musgrave to [Williamson], Mar. 2, Aug. 17, Oct. 9, 1676, to Carlisle, July 17, 1676, to [?], [1676?], *Cal. S.P. Dom., 1676–1677*, 2, 284, 358, 229–230, 483. On Tongue, see the certificate by Carlisle in favor of Tongue, May 17, 1663, *ibid., 1663–1664*, 142; William Fielding to Musgrave, Nov. 15, 1666, *ibid., 1666–1667*, 262; the king to Carlisle and Morpeth, Nov. 7, 1676, *ibid., 1676–1677*, 407; and nos. 884, 885, 885A, 1301, 1307, 1310, 1344, 1485, 1486, 1519, HMC, *Le Fleming*, 60, 89, 90, 96, 106, 111. Both Carlisle's brother Philip and Musgrave's son Christopher are listed in "A Seasonable Argument . . . Or a List of the Principal Labourers in the Great Design of Popery and Arbitrary Power . . ." (1677), in Browning, ed., *English Historical Documents, 1660–1774*, 239.

70. Sir Christopher Musgrave to Williamson, Dec. 16, 1677, warrant for a grant to Carlisle, Feb. 15, 1678, commissions to Carlisle and Morpeth, Feb. 25, 1678, *Cal. S.P. Dom., 1677–1678*, 512, 649, 677; Dalton, ed., *English Army Lists*, I, 228. The companies raised for

Three months after he won back the governorship of his name city, the earl of Carlisle went out to govern the king's dominion of Jamaica. His military titles and duties there, and those of his staff, were those they had held in garrison government at home, writ large.

Paramilitary politics took physical form in the governor-general's independent company of infantry for the island garrison. That troops were the usual instruments of executive authority was reiterated by conferring the command of a second company of regulars on Carlisle's English regimental major—now the lieutenant governor and lieutenant general of Jamaica—Sir Henry Morgan.

The precepts of soldierly sovereignty were underlined again by a commission to the earl's old servant, Major Francis Watson, his brother Sir Philip's quartermaster in the duke of Albemarle's Life Guard. Commissioned major general of Jamaica, Watson carried out the military and civil duties of the majority as described by Major and Governor Richard Elton and amplified by such officers and governors as that (deputy) major general, Charles Howard. After he reshaped Jamaica's militia as a member of Carlisle's staff, Major General Watson acted as governor-general at the time of the so-called Glorious Revolution and tried to recast Jamaica's government into a supremely military mold.[71]

The members of this general staff for the command of Jamaica were paid as officers of the English army. The regular soldiers of the island garrison and an ordnance officer (in charge of a government arsenal for Jamaica) were also on the English army establishment. Early in May 1678 the Jamaica general staff joined their troops on board ships of the royal navy bound for their garrison government. On the down-Channel voyage, Captain General Carlisle put into Plymouth to inspect the "Royal Citadel" that King Charles II had just built, "which fortifications he very much commended."[72] Since the days of King Charles I and Sir Ferdinando

---

garrison duty in 1678 were the largest since 1660 and reflected the establishment intended to meet a civil war; see the warrant to Sir Thomas Chicheley, Jan. 14, 1678, *Cal. S.P. Dom., 1677–1678*, 573–574.

71. For the formulation of a military establishment for the West Indies, see the warrant to Carlisle and the commissions to Carlisle, to Morgan, Ralph Fetherstonhough, and Usher Tyrell, to Elias Markham and John Tolderoy, and to Watson, Jan. 13, 1678, notes by Williamson, Jan. 22, 1678, *ibid.*, 571, 590. On Watson, see also the warrant to the commissary general of musters, June 12, 1663, *ibid., 1663–1664*, 168; the commissions to Watson, May 11, June 25, 1673, *ibid., 1673*, 235, 393; and chapter 6 below.

72. Warrant to Lemuel Kingdon (paymaster to the forces), [Dec.] 1677, estimate of transportation charges to Jamaica, Mar. 1678, *Cal. S.P. Col., 1677–1680*, nos. 544, 643;

Gorges, his captain of Plymouth Fort, how far English government had come toward absolutism.

Imperialists Opposed: Carlisle versus York

Governor-General Carlisle sailed for Jamaica on the crest of a wave of imperialism that had been building for eleven years. The restoration of garrison government by 1667 had made the crown tyrannically triumphant over domestic dissent, but the government of Charles II was so feeble overseas, in war, in trade, in empire, as to threaten even its domestic credibility. King Charles had set out to remedy this imbalance by a foreign and imperial policy that would reinforce his authority at home. Paradoxically, the earl of Carlisle was both an agent of that policy and an opponent of its greatest champion, the king's brother and heir, James, duke of York.[73]

When parliament assembled in January 1674, the earl of Carlisle's credit in court and country made him prominent among the opponents of the duke of York's succession. Carlisle was a leader of the party of Protestant peers who had been parliamentarians or Cromwellians before 1660. James identified them as "the Presbyterian and Commonwealth gang" and as his most determined and powerful enemies. As early as 1667, Carlisle had allegedly proposed displacing James in the succession by legitimizing the king's bastard son, the duke of Monmouth. The earl did help pass the Roos divorce bill. This set a precedent for a possible royal divorce, and so for King Charles's remarriage, which, it was hoped, would produce an heir to lower James in the succession. In 1674 Carlisle openly attempted to have Charles II legitimize Monmouth. As the duke of York complained, "The Earls of Carlisle and Shaftesbury were two of the chiefest managers in this business, and they had the confidence, not to say impudence, to tell the King, that if he would consent to have the thing done, they would undertake to find witnesses to prove the Duke of Monmouth's legitimacy."[74]

Charles II to Chicheley, Feb. 22, 1678, *Cal. S.P. Dom., 1677–1678*, 667; Richard Watts to Williamson, Apr. 24, 26, May 8, 1678, Philip Lanyon to Williamson, May 17, 1678, *ibid., 1678*, 132, 134, 163, 177. William to Daniel Fleming, Feb. 19, 1678, HMC, *Le Fleming*, 143, is an example of Carlisle's recruitment of aides from his lieutenancy.

73. Note the decadent symbol of Dunkirk and the discussion in *Cal. S.P. Ven., 1661–1664*, 202–203, 204–205. See also chapter 3 below and "J'ai vendu Dunkerque" (1664), in George deF. Lord *et al.*, eds., *Poems on Affairs of State: Augustan Satirical Verse, 1660–1714*, I (New Haven, Conn., and London, 1963), 419.

74. [Dicconson], *James the Second*, ed. Clarke, 441–442; Abbott, "Conspiracy and Dissent, II," *AHR*, XIV (1908–1909), 711–712; Haley, *Shaftesbury*, 277–280.

The king refused his consent, not from any motives of delicacy, but out of a powerful conviction that a truly legitimate hereditary succession was necessary to authenticate the royal prerogative. James's enemies, Carlisle prominent among them, had to take other measures to provide a Protestant succession.[75]

When a bill was proposed to require the education of James's children as Protestants, Carlisle seconded it. To ensure the ultimate succession of these Protestant princesses, afterward the queens Mary and Anne, Carlisle added a clause that forbade any royal (that is, James's) marriage to a Roman Catholic without the prior consent of parliament. Small wonder that to seek a wife in Sweden the widowed James chose his own servant, Major Edmund Andros, instead of using the crown's usual envoy to that kingdom, the earl of Carlisle. The earl of Halifax moved to add to the succession bill a clause to disarm James's presumed partisans, all English Roman Catholics and even those merely suspected of being papists. Carlisle had already ordered this done in the four counties of his lieutenancy. Finally, the earl of Carlisle moved that any English prince who married a Roman Catholic be prohibited from succeeding to the throne. The penalty clause was lost, but Carlisle had forecast the Exclusion Crisis.[76]

At this point, the earl's attacks on the Catholic heir again became matters of rumor rather than of record. It was said that Carlisle and Shaftesbury proposed a special act of parliament to disband the duke of York's regiment (a fact that, if true, explains the enmity against Carlisle exhibited by that regiment's colonel, Sir Charles Littleton, and by Littleton's party in his former government, Jamaica). It was further alleged that in 1674 the earls of Carlisle and Shaftesbury were prepared to impeach the duke of York on a charge of high treason. The king, however, killed all pending bills by proroguing parliament. More than that, Charles II made it clear that rather than lose the royal prerogative, in

75. See n. 47 above; Haley, *Shaftesbury*, 277–280, 357; Burnet, *History*, I, 469, 471–472; and [Dicconson], *James the Second*, ed. Clarke, 426, 490. In 1668 the duke's army and admiralty commands were attacked as politically dangerous (*ibid.*, 434). Following the death of Capt. Gen. Albemarle, an attempt was made to shift control of the army, and so of the state, to Carlisle's candidate for the throne, the duke of Monmouth, by commissioning Monmouth as captain general (*ibid.*, 495–496). For Pepys's comments, see Latham and Matthews, eds., *Diary of Pepys*, VI, 321, VII, 324, 332, 434 (entries of Dec. 6, 1665, July 7, 12, Sept. 11, 1667), and notes.

76. *Journals of the House of Lords*, XII, 618; Haley, *Shaftesbury*, 359, 360–361; proclamation against papists, Nov. 10, 1678, *Cal. S.P. Dom., 1671*, 514, 528; Charles II to Carlisle, Nov. 24, 1666, lords of the council to Carlisle, Sept. 30, 1678, HMC, *Le Fleming*, 43, 148. For Andros's mission to Sweden, see Add. MSS 29553, 331, 336.

particular the hereditary succession, he would fight a civil war. Pointing to the crown's monopoly of military force, the king indicated that he expected to win that war.[77]

Political realist and military professional that he was, Charles Howard had bowed to the possessors of physical power throughout his public life. His colleague Shaftesbury demanded the return of "that liberty we and our forefathers have enjoyed until these last forty years, of being free from guards and mercenary soldiers, it being the inseparable right of a free nation that they themselves, and no separate number of paid or hired men, should have the guard of their own prince, government and laws." He pointed out to the earl of Carlisle, and to the rest of their peers, that if the king had a standing army, he would not require the aristocracy in order to govern. The executive tool of the governor-generalcy was a major illustration of what Shaftesbury feared. Military administrators at the head of disciplined legions could displace from public authority the hereditary nobility and their customary clients, as they had under Cromwell. Despite Shaftesbury's argument, Carlisle knew from personal experience that unarmed governments could never return. Like officer-governors in many parts of the empire, the earl had himself used the politics of professional force to bypass or to coerce local elites in the interest of a national sovereignty. So he had made that interest his own. When the king's ministers wondered out loud to their master if another insurrection might not be useful in order to place the king in "such a condition of armes both by sea and land as might incourage you to speake boldly if [parliament] should deny you," Carlisle decided that it was prudent to rejoin the political side with the big battalions. The Howard family's speculative investment in opposition politics was left to Lord Morpeth's management.[78]

---

77. Disbanding the duke of York's own regiment was a logical counter to the Stuart plan for a pro-Catholic coup in pursuance of the Treaty of Dover (whereby officers high in the duke's favor were to control Yarmouth, Plymouth, Hull, and Berwick, while the duke himself would command the Portsmouth garrison); see [Dicconson], *James the Second*, ed. Clarke, 443, and Haley, *Shaftesbury*, 361–362.

78. Shaftesbury's instructions to his supporters in parliament, 1681, and "A Seasonable Argument," in Browning, ed., *English Historical Documents, 1660–1714*, 256, 237–249. See also Haley, *Shaftesbury*, 391, 395, 444–445, 449, 451. Danby's memorandums to the king, Apr. 4, 1677, about the duke of York, [Sept. 1679], Browning, *Danby*, II, 68–69, 89–91. For Morpeth's opposition career, see Lowther to Fleming, Jan. 22, 1680, HMC, *Le Fleming*, 178; Ferguson, ed., *Charters of Carlisle*, xxvi; Creighton, *Carlisle*, 163; Fletcher to Col. Legge, July 10, 1682, Philip Musgrave to Dartmouth, Dec. 30, 1688, HMC, *Dartmouth*, I, 75–76, 245.

The Jamaica Debate

Carlisle's appointment as governor-general of Jamaica marked his conversion from the opposition. In January 1674 the king announced his intention to make the earl the "person of honour" and of absolute authority who had been so often called for to assert the prerogative in the Caribbean province. Ever since Venables's conquest of the island in 1655, Carlisle had been concerned with reinforcing Jamaica's garrison and with developing its plantation. He had been nominated as governor-general in 1671. Three years later the king ordered the Shaftesbury council for foreign plantations, in its dying days, to consider the earl's commission and instructions as governor-general and those of his regimental major, Henry Morgan, as deputy governor.[79]

The debate over these instructions spanned the next four years. The issue was the shape that English partisan politics would give to the colonial constitutions. Just as Shaftesbury and his aide John Locke (the secretary of Shaftesbury's plantations council) attacked the royal prerogative and tried to bolster the governmental power of the parliamentary classes in England, so they sought to reduce the administrative and military powers of the king's viceroys overseas and to exalt the influence of the colonial councillors. Prerogative-minded ministers questioned this design in 1674. By 1678 they had wholly reversed it. The two political extremes were outlined by the two sets of commissions and instructions for the government of Jamaica that were prepared for the earl of Carlisle. The first was written in 1674, the second in 1678. The issues they defined were still the objects of imperial controversy a century later.[80]

79. Commissions and instructions for Carlisle and Morgan, Jan. 23, Mar. 23, 1674, *Cal. S.P. Col., 1669–1674*, nos. 1212, 1251–1255, also Lt. Gov. Thomas Lynch to Dr. Worsley, July 8, 1673, *ibid.*, no. 1115. See also Add. MSS 11410, 258; A. P. Thornton, *West-India Policy under the Restoration* (Oxford, 1956), 148; proceedings of the council for foreign plantations, Feb. 10, 1674 (from *Shaftesbury Papers*, Div. X, 8[8]), in Andrews, *British Committees*, 148–149; Haley, *Shaftesbury*, 364.

80. The council for foreign plantations's statement of reforms appears in Sir Jonathan Atkins's commissions of Dec. 19, 1673, and in Carlisle's (i.e., Vaughan's) commissions of Mar. 23, 1674, *Cal. S.P. Col., 1669–1674*, nos. 1185, 1186, 1251, 1252; in C.O. 138/1, 171–177, 177–185; and in Locke's explanation of the reforms to Arlington, Jan. 6, 1674, *Cal. S.P. Col., 1669–1674*, no. 1197. See the fuller discussion and citations in chapter 5, nn. 80 and 81, below. Burnet's sketch of Shaftesbury (*History*, I, 172–174) includes a symbol of the whig leader's attitude toward the liberty of the subject and toward the colonies: Shaftesbury successfully opposed a bill that would have required mandatory transportation to the colonies as the penalty for petty larceny. The contrast with Carlisle's attitudes toward convicts and colonies, and with those of the whole military executive, is notable.

In 1674 the Shaftesbury council tried to establish in Jamaica a proto-whig program of colonial government. The instructions they wrote for Carlisle made the colonial councillors independent of the governor and dependent on Shaftesbury's council for their appointment. The councillors themselves could veto the governor's suspension of any of them from office. Extension and definition of judicial tenure was intended to protect the rule of civil law in a colony notoriously subject to martial law. The Shaftesbury council took from the governor-general his unilateral power to declare martial law in effect. That the governor-general would also have to share all of his instructions with the colonial council indicated the role the Shaftesbury council expected its provincial counterpart to play in checking the power of "monarchy" and in expanding that of "aristocracy." It was precisely this program of 1674 that John Locke tried to renew when he returned to the administration of the colonies in 1696.[81]

The intervening years witnessed the triumph of the royal prerogative in the government of the empire (a triumph in which the events of 1688–1689 were merely a temporary setback). Carlisle himself turned from accepting in principle Shaftesbury's instructions of 1674 to enforcing in actuality those prepared by the plantations committee of the privy council, which replaced the Shaftesbury council in 1675.

The reconversion of Carlisle and of English policy from mercantilist to imperialist began between March and November of the Shaftesbury council's last turbulent year, when Lord Vaughan was substituted for Carlisle as governor of Jamaica. Vaughan took out to the colony the restricted executive powers of the 1674 commission. He even improved upon its anti-monarchical intent by permitting the assembly to challenge the crown's fiscal prerogative. No sooner had Vaughan arrived in Jamaica, however, than the authors of the policy he embodied fell from power at home. The Shaftesbury council was replaced by the privy council committee for plantations, inspired by a minister of absolutist intent, the earl of Danby, and increasingly influenced by that most royalist of princes, James, duke of York. By April 1675 it was public knowledge that Carlisle would replace Vaughan and that he would be ordered to impose on the provincial government an executive he-

81. Carlisle's commissions, Mar. 23, 1674, *Cal. S.P. Col., 1669–1674*, nos. 1251, 1252; C.O. 138/1, 171–177, 177–185; S. S. Webb, "Francis Nicholson," *WMQ*, 3d Ser., XXIII (1966), 535–536.

gemony that would break the Shaftesburean shackles on Jamaica's viceroyalty.[82]

In the new Jamaica constitution the status of the colonial council was dramatically diminished. Councillors' names were omitted from the public commission to the governor-general and their authority thereby reduced from equality of origin with his. Instead, the councillors were listed in the governor-general's instructions, and these were not necessarily to be read to the council. The governor no longer had to secure councillors' consent to his suspension of one of their number from office, nor did he have to offer any reason for his action. The political power of the prerogative was amplified, and the influence in government of both common law and statute was drastically reduced, by conferring on the governor-general full power to rule by martial law. Finally, the imposition of a legislative model based on Poynings's Law would eliminate the authority Jamaica's legislature had acquired during the country regimes of the previous decade. The commission of 1678 shifted the primary roles in lawmaking from the parliamentary classes—represented in the colonial lower house and by the country members of the council—to the king, his governor-general, and their courtiers in the council.[83] These new orders again demonstrated how vulnerable the plastic colonial constitutions and imitative colonial societies were to English political conflicts and social contests.

---

82. Andrews, *British Committees*, 111–113, 151; notes by Williamson, Oct. 30, 1677, *Cal. S.P. Dom., 1677–1678*, 433; Haley, *Shaftesbury*, 263–264, 376; E. E. Rich, "The First Earl of Shaftesbury's Colonial Policy," RHS, *Trans.*, 5th Ser., VII (1957), 47–70; Beer, ed., *Diary of Evelyn*, June 23, 1673.

83. C.O. 1/43, no. 185ff, 370–371; Carlisle's commission, Mar. 1, and instructions, Mar. 30, 1678, C.O. 138/3, 198–214, 216, 251.

CHAPTER 3

The Grandee, the Courtier, and the Professional

The Case of Lord Culpeper, Courtier

Carlisle and Culpeper Contrasted

Ambitious, avaricious, and *politique* grandee though he was, the earl of Carlisle worked diligently and responsibly in the paramilitary administrations of both Oliver Cromwell and Charles Stuart. These admirable traits, and Carlisle's ability to combine his own best interests with those of the English state and empire, contrast favorably with the character of his royalist counterpart, the courtier Thomas, Lord Culpeper. Culpeper's erratic, irresponsible, and greedy administrations of garrison governments on both sides of the Atlantic were forgiven by King Charles II and Lord Chancellor Clarendon in deference to the memory of Culpeper's father, their comrade and counselor in exile, John, Lord Culpeper, master of the rolls. The master lived to see his king restored, but enjoyed only briefly his own high place in monarchical government. Culpeper's death conferred on his son Thomas the barony of Thoresway, a broken fortune, and the crown's indebtedness to those who bore the Culpeper name. Thomas was lavishly supported by Charles II until, in the king's declining years, regal authority passed to James, duke of York, who had long been displeased with Culpeper's disservices to royal authority. James Stuart's chief imperial bureaucrat, William Blathwayt, the auditor general of the imperial revenues and the secretary of war and plantations, was equally offended by Culpeper's cavalier attitudes toward work and money. The duke and the secretary therefore saw to it that Culpeper's theft of £9,300 from the Virginia treasury was his last act as a royal official.

Lord Culpeper's calamitous career overlapped the earl of Carlisle's Restoration commissions. The differences between these two aristocratic administrators lay not only in their personal abilities but also in their opposed political principles. The public-minded and popular earl fostered a concept of a secular state and its institutional executive that was the antithesis of the selfish and hated baron's fervently personal devotion to a divine-right monarch. Lord Culpeper, though always an intelligent man and occasionally a charming one, was a courtier of the narrowest sort, at least as long as King Charles favored him. When he was out of favor, Culpeper proclaimed country principles. Despite his political cunning and oratorical power, however, Culpeper was apparently devoid of concern for the welfare of kingdom or empire. Yet he was like Carlisle in that both men were officers of the royal army who built administrative careers in garrison government in England and then played active roles in the extension of its arbitrary political implications to the American colonies. As vice-president of the Shaftesbury council for trade and plantations, Culpeper helped compose Carlisle's "countrified" 1674 instructions. In 1678 his own orders for Virginia were revised in conformity with Carlisle's absolutist orders for Jamaica. And both of these governors-general were central figures in the construction of the ensuing compromise between armed English authority and adamant colonial autonomy.

Culpeper at Carisbrooke

Six years Carlisle's junior, Thomas Culpeper was too young to fight or to govern during the civil wars or the Interregnum, but he was not too young to suffer from them. He grew up in penny-pinching exile, much of it at the court of Charles Stuart, itself fiscally impoverished but rich in vice. In 1659, an exile, Culpeper married a Dutch girl who brought him neither wealth nor lineage. When Thomas came back to England in 1660, he left his bride at Leeds Castle, the decrepit seat of the ruined Culpeper estate in Kent, while he went to live at court with his mistress, the much maligned Susanna Willis. In that year of royal restoration, for which he had worked and waited through eleven years of exile, John, Lord Culpeper, died. He left his son a title of honor, a purse emptied in support of the king, and a landed estate of notoriously small size. A post in government had to be found for the new Lord Culpeper, if only, as King Charles said, "as a reward for the Services done Our Royall Father . . . and Our Self by his deceased Father of whome Wee retane a gratious and favourable sence."[1]

1. For the sad state of Leeds Castle, see John Evelyn to Samuel Pepys, Oct. 3, 1665, *Cal. S.P. Dom., 1665–1666*, 3, and for the paltry estate, see Sir John Mounson to Williamson, June 25, 1667, *ibid., 1667*, 229. Culpeper did not get his father's mastership of the rolls; he held only the reversion to it, which he sold in 1677 to Danby (Browning, *Danby*, I, 358,

In October 1661 the king commissioned Culpeper "Captain of the Isle of Wight and Carisbrooke Castle . . . and all other Castles and forces in the same Island." Charles permitted his captain to appoint a deputy and to recruit a garrison for Carisbrooke and also conferred on him the custody of all royal manor and park land on the island. The profits of the captaincy were substantial, at least if the collector's hands were grasping enough: Culpeper enclosed the park and garnered his share of the royal dues with unprecedented rigor. The duties of the captaincy, for which Culpeper was so well paid, were military and constabulary. His lordship, however, was too busy in London primping for the coronation ceremony to bother to come down to the island and examine the Cromwellians seized there by his deputy—prisoners who were prepared to warn the royal authorities of the old army attack that was launched soon afterward against the lord lieutenant of Ireland. Culpeper also left the arrest and interrogation of religious dissidents to his subordinates. When the Dutch war came, the captain had to secure a letter of confirmation from the king before the islanders would believe that he had actually represented their military needs to the government. In the same letter, the king ordered the islanders to obey his captain's commands for recruitment and fortification.[2]

War compelled the captain's presence in his province and increased his responsibilities there. The repair of castles and the erection of earthworks competed for his attention with "the internal regulation of the island." The association of foreign war with domestic dissent was as apparent on the Isle of Wight as it was in other exposed regions of England. Quakers and Commonwealthmen plagued the island's royal authorities. While he left prosecution of local dissidents to the island justices, Culpeper himself

---

362). He did receive nominations to some of the Six Clerks places in the Rolls Office, places with a market value of at least £1,500 each. See S.P. 44/10, 34–35, P.R.O. (quoted); the king to [the master of the rolls?], June 21, 1665, *Cal. S.P. Dom., 1664–1665*, 438; *ibid., 1675–1676*, 502; the king to Sir Harbottle Grimston (master of the rolls), June 28, July 28, 1676, *ibid., 1676–1677*, 193, 248; warrant to the master of the rolls, Sept. 1678, *ibid., 1678*, 437; and Danby to the lord treasurer, Feb. 28, 1685, Browning, *Danby*, II, 113. See also S.P. 44/68, 38; Add. MSS 29559, 138, 147.

2. Warrants to Culpeper, July 27, Aug. 28, 1661, *Cal. S.P. Dom., 1661–1662*, 46, 73; commission to Culpeper, MS All Souls, 233, Bodleian Library, Oxford; the king to [the gentlemen of the Isle of Wight], June 15[?], 1664, *Cal. S.P. Dom., 1663–1664*, 616. On the Irish plot, see Abbott, "Conspiracy and Dissent, I," *AHR*, XIV (1908–1909), 518–520; Bagwell, *Ireland under the Stuarts*, III, 34–39; Ormond to the earl of Anglesey, Nov. 29, 1678, HMC, *Ormonde*, N.S., IV, 251–253. Culpeper's indifference to the plot and to other administrative tasks is documented in the information by Col. Walter Slingsby (deputy governor of the Isle of Wight), July [?], 1663, [Slingsby to Muddiman], Nov. 8, 1663, Slingsby to Williamson, Dec. 16, 1663, *Cal. S.P. Dom., 1663–1664*, 202, 332, 377.

dealt in summary fashion with outside agitators by impressing them "for Guinea or the sea service." Impressment orders were addressed to Culpeper as vice admiral. As a deputy of the lord high admiral, the duke of York, Culpeper also licensed privateers and shared in their prizes. He even helped to inaugurate hostilities with the Dutch when he obeyed the duke's orders to seize Dutch ships in island ports, in retaliation for the impounding of a royal mast ship in the Netherlands.[3]

The strategic importance of Culpeper's command as an invasion site had been recognized in Roman times and had since been reemphasized in every period of foreign war by such commanders of the island as captain and governor Sir George Carey. Wight's inviting position was especially apparent when England faced so formidable a sea power as the United Provinces. Moreover, as invasion threatened, the Quaker agitation increased, for Captain Culpeper had put even women in the castle prison and had shipped those who would not pay his half-crown fine off to Bridewell to die.[4]

King Charles decided to reinforce his captain against both the Dutch and the dissidents with a company of the Guards. Under the command of Ensign Edmund Andros, one hundred Guardsmen sailed to the Isle of Wight to obey Culpeper's commands, whether to defend the island or to repress its people. No sooner had these future colonial commanders joined forces than a false alarm of a Dutch landing sparked an explosion of the islanders' hatred for their captain. A mob of militiamen seized the bridle of Culpeper's horse as he rode up to command them. They berated him about the island's military unpreparedness and raged at his enclosure of the royal park, their traditional pasture and woodlot. Captain Culpeper broke free of the mob, his troops restored order, and he imprisoned the local mayor for resisting his authority.[5]

But the scope of Lord Culpeper's authority was not clear. He was the "captain" of the island, not its "governor." He was nonetheless ordered to act in the civil as well as in the military affairs of

3. Instructions to Culpeper, June 15, 1664, Cal. S.P. Dom., 1663–1664, 616; earl of Sandwich to [Bennet], Sept. 22, 1664, Slingsby to [Williamson], Oct. 29, Dec. 10, 1664, Coventry to Bennet, Nov. 19, 1664, Thomas Middleton to [Pepys], Mar. 27, 1665, ibid., 1664–1665, 15, 47, 108–109, 79, 276; S.P. 44/17, 182. Capt. Alexander Culpeper, afterward his brother's surveyor general in Virginia, was his deputy vice admiral on the Isle of Wight. He represented Lord Culpeper in the investigation of maritime murders and the like (John Lysle to Williamson, Aug. 27, 1666, Cal. S.P. Dom., 1666–1667, 70).
    4. Slingsby to [Williamson], Dec. 10, 1664, Cal. S.P. Dom., 1664–1665, 108–109.
    5. Two warrants to Sir John Talbot, Sept. 11, 1665, ibid., 1664–1665, 560; Slingsby to Williamson, Nov. 8, 1665, ibid., 1665–1666, 46.

his captaincy. Indeed, these two administrative spheres were inseparable, as the crisis of the Dutch war and the island insurrection
made clear even to the crown's most determined champions of
civil government, the lords chancellor and treasurer. These leading
officers of state, the earls of Clarendon and Southampton, had
been King Charles's chief supporters in his effort to turn the constitutional clock back to the halcyon days before the civil war.
Whenever they could, these ministers did away with the office of
governor and reduced the garrison companies. Thus the chancellor
and the treasurer tried to erase the provincial symbols and to eliminate the physical implements of the usurpers' garrison government. The particular targets of these civilians' enmity were General
Monck's martial followers whom he had had ensconced in the
governorships. Their dismissal pleased Chancellor Clarendon politically, while Treasurer Southampton rejoiced at saving their pay
and allowances for the sovereign's shaky exchequer.[6]

The abolition of governorships reduced royal expenses, but it
also diminished royal authority. Lord Culpeper now tried to resume that authority in the Isle of Wight by reclaiming the title of
"governor." As the islanders protested:

The said Lord Culpeper, your Majestys Captain of the said Isle, assuming
to himself . . . the additional title of Governor of the said Isle . . . doth
exercise an arbitrary power in the said island, frequently intermeddling in
the civil government thereof, by giving a disturbance to the proceeding
and due execution of your Majesty's laws, . . . and hath sometimes proceeded so far, as by his sole, arbitrary power, to imprison the persons of
some of your Majestys good subjects in a noisome dungeon in Carisbrooke castle, to their great grief and discouragement, and contrary to
your Majestys good laws.[7]

The islanders' protest, Chancellor Clarendon lamented, had
"awakened a sleeping lion, by acquainting the king with his right."
King Charles ordered his secretary of state to reject the protest

6. [Dicconson], *James the Second*, ed. Clarke, 391. The Southampton-Clarendon opposition to military government is detailed in Burnet, *History*, I, 279–281.

7. The protest is printed in Worsley, *Isle of Wight*, 136–137, and calendared in *Cal. S.P.
Dom., 1665–1666*, 350. In reply to the charge of unlawful behavior, Secretary of State Arlington assured the islanders that illegality would not be protected by the king, but he also
noted that the king did not believe that Culpeper had "misbehaved himself" (Arlington to
Sir Robert Dillington and Sir Robert Worsley, Apr. 12, 1666, *ibid.*, 350). Even the otherwise
sympathetic Lord Chancellor Clarendon wrote that "as to the imprisonment, there is nothing of weight in it." He admitted only that, at most, "my Lord may probably have been a
little rash" (Worsley, *Isle of Wight*, 139). In view of the chancellor's own policy of political
imprisonment, and Culpeper's custody of some of these political prisoners in Carisbrooke,
Clarendon's answer is not very surprising. See also the king to Culpeper, Aug. 21, 1666,
Cal. S.P. Dom., 1666–1667, 55, and *ibid., 1667–1668*, 48.

both as imprudent—being apt to arouse public feeling in what was already a time of popular unrest—and as disrespectful to the royal commission held by his officer Lord Culpeper. Then, in July 1666, the king-in-council commissioned Culpeper governor and captain of the Isle of Wight. To make that government effective (and even more profitable), King Charles also commissioned Lord Culpeper captain of a company of royal infantry. By these actions regarding the Isle of Wight, and by parallel decisions that followed for other jurisdictions, the king demonstrated his recognition that his monarchy, restored by force, could not rely on cliques of provincial gentry to rule a restive people. He therefore adopted the paramilitary instruments of state sovereignty developed in the Interregnum and epitomized by the office of governor.[8]

That this realization should make Culpeper a governor was doubly ironic. For one thing, the anti-militarist ministers, Clarendon, Southampton, and Ashley (afterward the earl of Shaftesbury), disapproved of the reinstitution of the office. For another, the new governor was admittedly incapable. If he had not been promoted, he would have been replaced. On a visit to the island, the king himself had observed that Culpeper "was not respected by the gentry as became his government." King Charles was "unwilling to put persons to employments not suitable to their capacities. . . . And finding this a place not so proper for his command, he intended to remove him to some employment fitter for him." Now, however, in order to vindicate the royal authority and demonstrate its power to uphold its commissioned officers, the king sent Culpeper from London back to the island as its governor.[9]

He was followed to his command by his new infantry unit, a hundred men led by tough Cromwellian sergeants. They were supported by an engineering staff and by ordnance personnel who upgraded island fortifications and restored the island's lesser castles. Three mainland militia companies and a cavalry troop also joined Culpeper's garrison. The governor was ordered to use these forces to discipline the obviously disordered island militia and "to hinder all mutinous and seditious petitions." The king took care to support his governor's political and military authority verbally as well as militarily. He assured the islanders that he was satisfied with Lord Culpeper's vigilance both as captain and as governor. The king lavished praise on the governor's dragoons, that is, his

8. Worsley, *Isle of Wight*, 138; Arlington to Dillington and Worsley, Apr. 12, 1666, order-in-council, July 6, 1666, commission for Culpeper, July 10, 1666, *Cal. S.P. Dom., 1665–1666*, 350, 504, 522; Dalton, ed., *English Army Lists*, I, 70.
9. Worsley, *Isle of Wight*, 138–139.

mounted police. Their patrols of the island fulfilled the royal responsibility for military security and enforced the crown's corresponding political authority. King Charles asked that the islanders repay his dispatch of a garrison, and also "contribute to their own safety," by building fortifications. This royal demand afterward became all too familiar in threatened provinces of the empire overseas.[10]

Despite the damage it did to the cause of local self-government, the islanders' petition had elicited the military protection they demanded. The king even ordered more able professional soldiers to be ready to supersede Culpeper in command in case of an invasion. This responsive pattern was often repeated. The crown disapproved of protests by local elites against the exercise of the royal authority in their province. Nonetheless, the central government acceded to local demands for protection and justice. Imperial authority was reinforced both by practical response and by political reaction.

As for Governor Culpeper, the ministry thought him "not to blame to be willing to leave the command of a place where he is not respected." As soon as the war ended, Culpeper was permitted to begin negotiations to sell his enhanced jurisdiction to an officer more able to administer it. After protracted bargaining, that famous "man o' war" Sir Robert Holmes succeeded to the government in December 1668. Lord Culpeper, his successor said, had let the fortifications crumble, had allowed the garrison to run away, and had pocketed both the construction allowance and the soldiers' pay. But the salary, the prizes, the profits of "justice," and the use of royal lands—as well as the embezzlement of military funds and the sale price of the governorship itself—had made Lord Culpeper rich enough to erase crown officers' complaints against him by the first of several substantial personal loans to King Charles. The former governor, wealthier, perhaps wiser, but certainly no more scrupulous, now looked to the empire overseas for his future official advancement and personal profit.[11]

10. *Cal. S.P. Dom., 1670*, 588; S.P. 44/17, 200, 214; Dillington to Williamson, July 14, 1666, *Cal. S.P. Dom., 1665–1666*, 533–534; Sir Thomas Clarges to Williamson, Aug. 2, 1666, warrant to Clarges, Aug. 3, 1666, the king to Culpeper, Aug. 21, Dec. 18, 1666, to [the governor of the Isle of Wight], 1666[?], warrant for additions to the garrison of Sandown Castle (Wight), Jan. 19, 1667, warrant to Lord Robartes, Feb. 14, 1667, *ibid., 1666–1667*, 6, 7, 55, 315, 413, 461, 515; the king to Culpeper, June [?], 1666, *ibid., 1670*, 708–709.

11. Clarendon's remark on Culpeper's departure is in Worsley, *Isle of Wight*, 139. For the sale discussions and for the duke of York's possible influence in replacing Culpeper with Holmes, see newsletters of Sept. 15 and Dec. 15, 1668, in HMC, *Le Fleming*, 59, 61, and the note of Holmes's appointment, Dec. [?], 1668, *Cal. S.P. Dom., 1668–1669*, 118. The mili-

Culpeper and the Council for Foreign Plantations

The continuing campaign to make England's scattered colonies into an empire—to insist that they "understand that they are to be look'd upon as united, and embodied, and that their head and Centre is here"—was crippled for some time by the fall of Clarendon. For England itself, the lord chancellor had abhorred garrison government, and some saw his fall as King Charles's apology to the prerogative party for failing to capitalize more completely on the Cromwellian legacy of an armed executive. Clarendon, however, had limited his legalism and traditionalism to England. Much different was his attitude toward England's colonies. They, he asserted, "ought not and cannot subsist but by a submission to and protection from his Majestie's crown and government." Clarendon's subordination of colonial welfare to English politics led him to use the plantations as political prisons and to assign their governments as political prizes. Such shortsighted actions exemplified the personal politics that made the chancellor's tenure as resented as it was long—for when the Restoration government first failed to meet the expectations of its supporters and then suffered humiliating defeats at the hands of its enemies, the doctrine that "the king can do no wrong" meant that all the blame would be piled on the doorstep of Clarendon's "Dunkirk House." The embarrassment of the Dutch raid on the Thames was converted into the chancellor's disgrace, impeachment, and exile:

> Pride, lust, ambition, and the people's hate,
> The kingdom's broker, ruin of the state,
> Dunkirk's sad loss, divider of the fleet,
> Tangier's compounder for a barren sheet,
> This shrub of gentry, marri'd to the Crown
> (His daughter to the heir), is tumbl'd down.

---

tary decay of the island is detailed in Holmes's petition of Mar. 23, *ibid.*, 244. Culpeper claimed, 11 years after the fact, that he had spent £1,613 12s. 5½d. more than the king had paid him (reference to the lords of the treasury of Culpeper's petition, Sept. 9, 1679, *ibid., 1679–1680*, 239). For one of Culpeper's loans to the king (here £1,090), see the warrant to repay Culpeper, [May 4], 1668, *ibid., 1667–1668*, 374. On Holmes, see Ollard, *Sir Robert Holmes*, and, more pithily, Andrew Marvell's *A Seasonable Argument* (1677), which describes Sir Robert as "first an Irish livery boy, then a highwayman (a pirate would be nearer the mark), now Bashaw of the Isle of Wight, the cursed beginner of the two Dutch wars" (quoted in Lord *et al.*, eds., *Poems on Affairs of State*, I, 247 n. 83). Culpeper's imperial ventures included the Virginia grant of 1669 (*Cal. S.P. Col., 1669–1674*, 152) and the Northern Neck proprietary (*Virginia Magazine of History and Biography*, XXXIII [1925], 354).

Clarendon's enemies, Shaftesbury chief among them, were left to replace his monarchical and imperial attitudes toward the plantations with their own oligarchical and mercantile ideas.[12]

On Shaftesbury's initiative, King Charles commissioned a select, salaried council for foreign plantations in July 1670. The council was to advise the king and the privy council on colonial matters. In March 1671 an infusion of unsalaried grandees increased the council's stature. At the same time, the secretary of state (Henry Bennett, the earl of Arlington) paid off a political debt by adding Lord Culpeper to the council as a salaried member. "This Noble Lord," it was said of Culpeper, "was skillful in all the Ways of getting Money, and never let slip any Opportunity of doing it," as he demonstrated by having his salary backdated to July 1670. This was the date of the council's commission, but it was a month before its actual organization—and it was eleven months before Culpeper attended a meeting.[13]

He missed little business. In its first year, the council read petitions from the colonies, collected information about their economic production and governmental structures, and reported summaries of its findings to the privy council. But the council for foreign plantations exercised little discernible influence on policy until the functions of the moribund council for trade were added

12. "Overtures touching the Council to be erected for Foreign Plantations," Egerton MS 2395, 272–275, also 270–271; Add. MSS 11411, 3–3b; *Cal. S.P. Col., 1661–1668,* 24, 25, 30–32; report of the council for plantations to the king, Apr. [?], 1661, quoted in Percy Lewis Kaye, *English Colonial Administration under Lord Clarendon, 1660–1667,* Johns Hopkins University Studies in Historical and Political Science, Ser. XXIII, nos. 5–6 (Baltimore, 1905), 32. Contrast Shaftesbury's (and Locke's) instructions to the council, Sept. 27, 1672 (Andrews, *British Committees,* 108–109, 127–132; Latham and Matthews, eds., *Diary of Pepys,* entry of Sept. 1, 1672), with the duke of York's program, as expressed in the additional instructions for the council, Aug. 1, 1670 (Andrews, *British Committees,* 124–126) and as applied to corporations and local autonomy (J. H. Sacret, "The Restoration Government and Municipal Corporations," *EHR,* XLV [1930], 249–250, 257). See also Burnet, *History,* I, 444–463. The quoted lines of poetry are from "The Downfall of the Chancellor," in Lord *et al.,* eds., *Poems on Affairs of State,* I, 158.
13. Andrews, *British Committees,* 96–97; Ralph Paul Bieber, "The British Plantation Councils of 1670–4," *EHR,* XL (1925), 93, 95, 98 n. 1; Rich, "Shaftesbury's Colonial Policy," RHS, *Trans.,* 5th Ser., VII (1957), 51; Haley, *Shaftesbury,* 258. On Arlington's appointments see Beer, ed., *Diary of Evelyn,* entries of Feb. 29, 1671, and June 23, 1673. Note Arlington's association with Culpeper as his liaison with the council for foreign plantations (*Cal. S.P. Col., 1669–1674,* 334, 448). The appreciation of Culpeper's fiscal finesse is by Robert Beverley, *The History and Present State of Virginia,* ed. Louis B. Wright (Chapel Hill, N.C., 1947), 89. On the subject of salaries, see also the warrant to the attorney general for Culpeper's salary, Mar. 4, 1672, *Cal. S.P. Dom., 1671–1672,* 176; MS All Souls, 233 (which also gives a warrant, dated Oct. 1673, for Locke's salary, although Bieber says that he was not paid); and Beer, ed., *Diary of Evelyn,* entry of May 26, 1671. Culpeper managed to collect his salary of £500 per annum from Dec. 1670 at least. Many more faithful members seem never to have been paid. Culpeper himself did not actually attend the council until May 26, 1671.

to its responsibilities in September 1672. Shaftesbury became president of the combined body, just as his break with the monarchy was becoming public, and Culpeper was named vice-president, at an increased salary of £700 per annum. The expanded and revitalized council began to develop definite views of its own on the proper shape of plantation affairs and to write these views into the commissions and instructions of the royal governors.[14]

Under pressure of the Dutch war, the council for trade and plantations even made military plans. As the most senior army officer sitting at the council board, Culpeper planned the recapture of New York. The council adopted in its entirety Culpeper's detailed recommendations for an expeditionary force of warships and regular troops, supported by merchant auxiliaries taken from the Chesapeake convoy and by a militia made up of the convoy's seamen and passengers. The restoration of New York under the treaty of March 1674 aborted this operation, but the planning for it offers a suggestive glimpse of Culpeper's martial vision of himself and of the potential use of Virginia's resources to strengthen England's empire elsewhere on the American continent. He also helped the council to recognize the enormous commercial and strategic potential of New York harbor. Other councillors had pointed out to him the colony's political role as a counterweight to New England and its commercial importance as a source of grain, timber, and livestock for the West Indies.[15]

Culpeper shared the council's expanding breadth and sophistication in political and economic analysis—qualities that would be reflected in his own colonial career in Virginia (the soil of which had been granted to Culpeper and Arlington in February 1672). As a councillor, Culpeper was neither politically nor strategically incapable (however venal, devious, and self-serving his administrations turned out to be). He merely required the potential of personal profit to move him from fine words to concrete acts. As the sponsor of a prospective (and presumably grateful) provost marshal for Barbados, Culpeper entered with heightened interest into the council's discussion of that colony's executive structure. He was rather

14. "Heads of Business of Councils, 1670–1674: Council for Foreign Plantations, 1670–1672," in Andrews, *British Committees*, 133–134. On the work and interests of the councils and on the establishment of the council for trade and plantations, see *Cal. S.P. Col., 1669–1674*, nos. 470, 512, 822, 903, 923, 943, 992. The new council's secretary admitted the laxness of the old council in his letter to Sir Thomas Lynch, Oct. 8, 1672, *ibid.*, no. 943. See also Beer, ed., *Diary of Evelyn*, entries of Sept. 1, Oct. 13, 24, 1672.

15. "Opinion and humble advice" of the council for the retaking of New York, Nov. 15, 1673, *Cal. S.P. Col., 1669–1674*, no. 1165; Beer, ed., *Diary of Evelyn*, entries of May 26, June 4, 20, July 4, 1671, Sept. 15, 1673.

rudely rebuffed by his colleagues, who demanded something more reliable than Culpeper's recommendation before nominating any-one to an office of profit in the wealthiest of England's colonies. Perhaps it was personal pique, then, and not prerogative principle, that kept Culpeper from signing the council's draft commission that reduced the governor-general's martial and judicial powers and elevated the authority of the Barbadian, or, as contemporaries said, "Barbarous," councillors.[16]

Colonial councils were seen by Shaftesbury and Locke as important governmental instruments of their attack on the pre-rogative, as well as sources of patronage places for affluent backers of Shaftesbury's bid to control the City. Shaftesbury's political allies from the London merchant community, or their colonial clients, comprised a significant portion of these councils. But this political marriage of Villiers House with the Exchange—the union of the council for trade and plantations with the merchants and with the City corporation—backfired, for it both lessened the council's administrative usefulness to the crown and bound the council to Shaftesbury's failing political fortunes. Ostensibly, the Shaftesbury council was the victim of an economy drive. It was easy for Lord Treasurer Danby to economize at the expense of his greatest political enemy.[17]

Before the council closed shop in December 1674, it charted a reform of Jamaica's government on the same principles that it had imposed on Barbados. On instructions from the king, Culpeper introduced into the Jamaica debate the king's demand that the crown control colonial legislation. Culpeper also secured a hearing for the earl of Carlisle, who offered suggestions regarding his forthcoming commission. Both Carlisle and Culpeper withdrew from the council's discussions, however, when King Charles dis-missed the council's president, Shaftesbury, from his higher of-fices. Carlisle, although he retained his long-standing reversion to the Jamaica governorship, let the current commission pass to John,

16. *Cal. S.P. Dom.*, *1671–1672*, 206; *Cal. S.P. Col.*, *1669–1674*, nos. 769, 770; proceed-ings of the council, Feb. 17, 1674 (from *Shaftesbury Papers*, X, 8[9]), in Andrews, *British Committees*, 149; draft commission for Sir Jonathan Atkins (as governor of Barbados), Dec. 19, 1673, *Cal. S.P. Col.*, *1669–1674*, no. 1185. Alexander Culpeper was named surveyor general of Virginia, Oct. 25, 1671 (*Cal. S.P. Dom.*, *1671*, 538).

17. The Shaftesbury-Locke theory of provincial councils was expressed by Locke in a letter to [Arlington], Jan. 6, 1674, *Cal. S.P. Col.*, *1669–1674*, no. 1197. Compare the names in Haley, *Shaftesbury*, 238, 240, with the councillors and their London merchant patrons listed in the index to Vincent T. Harlow, *A History of Barbados, 1625–1685* (Oxford, 1926). See also Lt. Gov. Lynch (of Jamaica) to Dr. Worsley, Aug. 12, 1673, and the commission re-voking Shaftesbury's appointment, Dec. 21, 1674, *Cal. S.P. Col.*, *1669–1674*, nos. 1130, 1412.

Lord Vaughan. This infamous anti-Clarendonian and future whig was welcome to attempt to apply Shaftesbury's plans at a time when the court was increasingly aware of and hostile to their political purpose: weakening the imperial prerogative. As for Culpeper, in June 1675 he secured the reversion to Sir William Berkeley's governorship of Virginia.[18]

The Prerogative and the Proprietor

Although he had been vice-president of the council that had grafted Shaftesbury's oligarchical ideas of governance onto colonial constitutions, Lord Culpeper nonetheless emerged from the wreck of the earl's council to become a reluctant agent, and ultimately a victim, of the royalist reaction in imperial affairs that was both led and personified by his royal highness, the duke of York.

The duke disapproved of colonial grants to private proprietors, for they diminished royal authority. He pressed Culpeper to resign his territorial claims in Virginia. In 1674 this negotiation produced a court, imperialist counterstatement to the country, mercantile policies that Shaftesbury and Locke had put forward in the reports of the council for foreign plantations. The imperialist reply insisted that the crown ought not to parcel out the plantations into small, weak, uncoordinated, and uncontrollable proprieties, or abandon them to merchant politicians. The non-government of absentee proprietors and the self-serving factionalism of merchant functionaries should be everywhere replaced by the responsible rule of resident royal officials. A governor-general would concentrate each colony's allegiance on the crown. The imposition of a viceroy would thus eliminate the confused and conflicting loyalties inherent in the mercantilists' "double jurisdiction"—parliament as well as the crown. The colonists were not represented in parliament, the imperialists observed, but in any case the governor-general was the best representative of his province to the sovereign. And the king, not the parliament, was head of the empire.[19]

18. Commission revoking Shaftesbury's appointment, Dec. 21, 1674, draft commission and instructions for Carlisle (i.e., Vaughan), Mar. 23, 1674, commission to Vaughan, Apr. 3, 1674, answer of the president and council of Barbados to the assembly of Barbados, July 23, 1674, revocation of Lynch's commission to Jamaica, Nov. 3, 1674, Coventry to Culpeper, Nov. 20, 1674, council for trade and plantations to King Charles, Nov. 24, 1674, instructions for Vaughan, Dec. 3, 1674, *Cal. S.P. Col., 1669–1674*, nos. 1412, 1251–1252, 1259, 1329, 1374, 1386, 1392, 1398; proceedings of the council, Feb. 10, 1674 (from *Shaftesbury Papers*, X, 8[8]), in Andrews, *British Committees*, 148–149; Grey, ed., *Debates of the House of Commons*, I, 33–36, 35n; Burnet, *History*, II, 6, 17, 36, 37, 42–43, 82–83.

19. For the 1669 Virginia grant to Culpeper and Arlington and for its partial settlement

The imperialists' authoritarian model of provincial government was that pioneered in Ireland. Now being transferred to Jamaica, the "Irish model" would shape a new Virginia constitution as well. The Old Dominion must be made an imperial *cordon sanitaire*, "for the New England disease is very catching." Therefore, the duke of York agreed to help the Virginians rid themselves of proprietors, Arlington and Culpeper in particular, and to encourage Virginia's increased dependence upon the crown.[20]

Yet Lord Culpeper, proprietor and enemy of centralization, was already designated as Virginia's next governor. As long as he could, Culpeper delayed facing the contradiction between his plans for proprietary profit and the duke of York's insistence that Virginians "have no other dependence but on the crown." Sworn in as governor of Virginia for life on July 20, 1677, Culpeper promised to sail by the end of September. September passed. The secretary of state promised that Culpeper's arrival in Virginia, "according to His Majesty's especial injunction and the assurance his Lordship hath given, shall be by Christmas next without fail." Two years after this arrival date, Culpeper had still not embarked for the Old Dominion.[21]

During Culpeper's long delay, the royalist program of imperial centralization crystallized in the earl of Carlisle's instructions, most particularly in the clause that ordered him to impose on Jamaica the Irish legislative model of Poynings's Law, and Culpeper himself became an agent of the imperial prerogative to try to protect his private proprietary. Culpeper was involved in writing Carlisle's instructions. The "Jamaica Minutes Given by Lord Culpeper" record the orders given by the king-in-council to Secretary

in Feb. 1672, see *Cal. S.P. Col., 1669–1674*, nos. 769, 770. On the duke of York's involvement, see Col. Francis Moryson to Culpeper, Apr. 14, 1677, commissioners for Virginia to Mr. Watkins, Apr. 14, 1677, *ibid., 1677–1680*, nos. 184, 185. See also *ibid., 1675–1676*, nos. 403, 602–603, 604, 696–697, 701, 708, 834, 835; chapter 8 below; and Stephen Saunders Webb, " 'Brave Men and Servants to His Royal Highness': The Household of James Stuart in the Evolution of English Imperialism," *Perspectives in American History*, VIII (1974), 70.

20. "Memoirs of his Royal Highness," Coventry Manuscripts, LXXVII, n.p., Longleat House, quoted from the microfilm copy at the Library of Congress, Washington, D.C., by the kind permission of Lord Bath; *Cal. S.P. Col., 1677–1680*, nos. 308, 360, 384, 388.

21. Journal of the privy council plantations committee, Aug. 2, Sept. 11–12, Oct. 9, 25, 1677, Dec. 21, 1678, order of the king-in-council, Nov. 16, 1677, *Cal. S.P. Col., 1677–1680*, nos. 377, 412, 425, 457, 855, 480. See also n. 32 below and Add. MSS 25120, 136, 145. Most important, see Culpeper's and Coventry's memo for "adding the general heads and powers agreed on in my Ld Carlisle's commissions and instructions as a pattern . . . ," Coventry MSS, LXXVII, 258–259. In at least one instance, the flow of constitutional influence was reversed: the commission of oyer and terminer for Virginia provided precedent for the one issued for Jamaica under Carlisle (Journal of the privy council plantations committee, Nov. 20–29, 1677, *Cal. S.P. Col., 1677–1680*, no. 485).

Coventry to prepare the earl of Carlisle's 1678 commission as captain general and governor-in-chief of Jamaica. One politically potent phrase declared "that the powers may be as full as L[or]d Windsor's and Sir Thomas Mudiford's and Sir Thomas Lynch's." The plenary power, both military and civil, of the first royal governors of Jamaica was to be restored. The Shaftesbury-Vaughan constitution for Jamaica was to be erased. What was done to Jamaica government dictated the orders to the governor-general of Virginia. Culpeper, as the memorandum demonstrates, had become the prerogative's agent, writing orders to restore executive authority in England's major colonies.[22]

Now Culpeper sought the physical means by which he could enforce royal rule and so control his profitable province. He asked that, as the king's governor-general of Virginia, he be given command of military weapons to ensure constitutional reform, in amounts equal to those allocated to Jamaica's viceroy. Virginia was, Culpeper wrote, "a Colony of greater extent [than Jamaica] and [of] more advantage in point of the customs and yearly revenue to the Crown." This broad royal dominion and large crown revenue, Culpeper argued, deserved the military protection that would also help to secure political subservience. In these overseas provinces, just as in Culpeper's Isle of Wight governorship or in Carlisle's command of his title town, the reformed executive ought to command an infantry company. In the colonial (as in the English) governments, such a company would provide perquisites for its captain, the governor-general, as well as enforce his commands. Personal profit and political power alike required this extension of what was a normal part of garrison government in the British Isles to royal colonies overseas. Garrison companies introduced royal troops to Jamaica, but that colony had already been militarized by the Cromwellian army units that were the bases of English settlement in the island and by Jamaica's uniquely powerful militia. In Virginia the punitive expedition of 1676 had recently revived the paramilitary politics of the colony's origins, and veterans of that expedition were enlisted as Lord Culpeper's garrison staff and companies.[23]

Not only were the captain generals of Virginia and Jamaica to

22. "Jamaica Minutes Given by Lord Culpeper," Coventry MSS, LXXVII, 312; *Cal. S.P. Col., 1677–1680*, no. 855. See also n. 21, above.

23. Commission to Culpeper to be a captain of a company raised in Virginia, [presumably from Jeffreys's men], Aug. 26, 1678, *Cal. S.P. Dom., 1678*, 379; journal of the privy council plantations committee, Dec. 20, 1678, *Cal. S.P. Col., 1677–1680*, no. 852. That Culpeper saw his company as income enhancement appears in his memorandum of Dec. 9,

command companies; so were their lieutenant generals and lieutenant governors, the veteran soldiers Sir Henry Chicheley of Virginia and Sir Henry Morgan of Jamaica. The "generals," as the
governors-in-chief were popularly termed, also commanded major
generals who were to drill and discipline the colonial militias. In
addition to three general officers each, the Jamaica and Virginia
military staffs included surgeons and chaplains. The governors-
general also obtained military supplies for their governments. Carlisle received artillery and an ordnance officer to service it. Culpeper
was especially anxious to get two hundred sets of dragoon equipment with which to convert his infantry companies into troops of
mounted police, modeled on his Isle of Wight dragoons and, like
them, more suitable than foot soldiers for impressing the majesty
of royal government upon Virginia's scattered plantations and de-
batable frontiers.[24]

Apart from the military support he brought from England,
Lord Culpeper could expect the political backing of part of Virginia's provincial oligarchy, the "Green Spring faction," so named
for its headquarters, the Berkeley plantation. Culpeper's kins-
woman Frances Culpeper first married Governor Sir William
Berkeley, then, after his death, allied herself with the most vocif-
erous of the "Green Spring Cabal," Philip Ludwell. Alexander
Culpeper, surveyor for his cousin's proprietary lands, also served
as Governor Berkeley's English agent, the "great Sollicitor" of
the "Green Spring Interests," and as the chief aide of John, Lord
Berkeley, in the effort to rebut the royal commissioners' testimony
that Sir William and his party were contemptuous of royal authority. The question for Lord Culpeper was whether, as the king's
governor-general, he dared profit by the support of "that faction"
whose power existed both at the cost of the king's authority in
Virginia and to the detriment of the public good of the colony.[25]

"That faction drive on those violent courses" that under Sir
William Berkeley's regime had "proved so fatal to this poore Coun-

---

1677, Coventry MSS, LXXVIII, 144. The crown's acquiescence in this view is expressed in
the orders of the king-in-council, Nov. 24, 1677, Dec. 20, 1678, Cal. S.P. Col., 1677–1680,
nos. 492, 851.

24. Cal. S.P. Col., 1677–1680, nos. 602, 728, 847, 1208.

25. Herbert Jeffreys to Francis Moryson, Apr. 1, 1678, Coventry MSS, LXXVII, 144,
214, 254. On Sir William's alleged affront to the king's Virginia commissioners, see Cal.
S.P. Col., 1677–1680, nos. 171, 186, 188, 189, 190, 191, 193, 194. On Alexander Culpeper's
roles, see grant to Alexander Culpeper, Oct. 25, 1671, Cal. S.P. Dom., 1671, 538; petition of
Alexander Culpeper, [July 27], 1677, certificate of John, Lord Berkeley, Nov. 19, 1677, Cal.
S.P. Col., 1677 1680, nos. 374, 483. Ibid., nos. 505, 506, 511, 512, and n. 26 below, carry the
defense of Berkeley down to its final defeat on Dec. 6, 1677.

try." So said the lieutenant governor, Colonel Herbert Jeffreys, head of the royal commission for Virginia and an officer high in the favor of both king and duke. Another royal commissioner to investigate Virginia government, Major Francis Moryson, added that the Green Spring faction was small in number, though large in malice, "two or three hundred (and not above thirty of them that really espoused his Majesty's interest)." Agreeing with Jeffreys and Moryson (who were backed by the third crown commissioner for Virginia, royal naval captain Sir John Berry), the king and council determined to crush the political power of the Green Spring faction. King Charles recalled Governor Berkeley, revoked Berkeley's acts against the authority of the royal commissioners and of the king in Virginia, rejected the efforts of John, Lord Berkeley, to vindicate his brother, and dismissed from office the men identified by the commissioners as the leading Berkeleans, including Lord Culpeper's kinsman-in-law and land agent, Philip Ludwell. The crown officers then wrote into Lord Culpeper's commission an explicit royal reconfirmation of every act of Lieutenant Governor Jeffreys and his fellow commissioners. All of the commissioners' private recommendations for further royalization were included in Culpeper's instructions.[26]

26. See n. 25 above; Daniel Parke to Williamson, Jan. 30, 1678, *Cal. S.P. Col., 1677–1680*, no. 590; Moryson to Mr. Cooke (Coventry's secretary), May 28, [1678], Coventry MSS, LXXVII, 254; Moryson to Samuel Wiseman, Feb. 25, Mar. 4, 1678, *Cal. S.P. Col., 1677–1680*, nos. 615, 619. Royal condemnation of Berkeley and his diehard supporters is overwhelmingly detailed, *ibid.*, nos. 239, 242, 244, 245, 247, 302, 304, 377, 425, 457, 505–506, 510, 512, 516, 881, 888, 384, 385, 386, 388–448, 509, 523, 579, 887, 908, 909, 910. Particular members of the faction were singled out for especial disgrace. On Edward Hill, see inhabitants of Charles City Co. to Jeffreys, Berry, and Moryson, May 10, 1677, answer of Hill, May [?], 1677, information of Thomas Grendon, Mar. 1678, petition of Hill, June 23, 1680, *ibid.*, nos. 228, 229, 644, 1375. On Thomas Ballard, see Jeffreys to Williamson, June 11, 1677, *ibid.*, no. 293. And on Robert Beverley and the younger Ludwell, see Jeffreys to Moryson [abstract], Dec. 30, 1677, Moryson to Wiseman, Feb. 25, 1678, *ibid.*, nos. 541, 615. The commissioners' proposals appear in their "Narrative of the Rise, Progress and Cessation of the late Rebellion in Virginia," in Samuel Wiseman's Book of Record, 2582, Pepysian Library, Magdalene College, Cambridge University (used by the kind permission of the Librarian). Another manuscript copy appears in C.O. 5/1371, P.R.O. A printed edition, in modernized text and without the marginal references to the county grievances, has been printed in Charles M. Andrews, ed., *Narratives of the Insurrections, 1675–1690* (New York, 1915). See also the "Particular account of how we your Maties Commissioners for the affairs of Virginia have observed and complied with . . . our Instructions," Wiseman, Book of Record, Pepys 2582. For the adoption of the commissioners' suggestions, compare their "Narrative" and their "account" with Lord Culpeper's commission and instructions, *Cal. S.P. Col., 1677–1680*, nos. 866, 881, 932, 1210–1211, 1213, 1215; C.O. 5/1355, 315*ff*; "Some instructions of the Lord Culpeper with his [Lordship's] Answers thereon . . . ," The Papers of Francis, Lord Howard of Effingham, IV, no. 269, Library of Congress, Washington, D.C. (cited by the kind permission of the owner). The similarity between the commissioners' recommendations and Culpeper's instructions may owe something to the chancellor's use of the Virginia commissioners' secretary, Samuel Wiseman, in the composition of legisla-

Despite these unmistakable declarations of royal intent, Lord Culpeper did not disavow the "Caball at Green Spring," which continued to operate under the aegis of Frances Culpeper: "My Lady Berkeley . . . acts still in the same manner as if Her Husband were still living, and she with the rest of the Faction giving out, and abusing my Lord Culpeper in making use of His Lordship's name by telling the people what alteration they shall find at His [Lordship's] arrivall, by this means encouraging their own factious party and driving the rest of the people into despair."[27] This analysis by Lieutenant Governor Jeffreys was unwittingly confirmed by the Secretary of Virginia, Lord Culpeper's in-law Thomas Ludwell, when he protested Colonel Jeffreys's removal of the Berkeleans from office and begged for the colonel's replacement by Lord Culpeper. His kinsfolk expected Thomas, Lord Culpeper, to support them and their Green Spring allies. The king and the duke, however, ordered Governor-General Culpeper to discipline the Green Spring group by adopting the military, centralizing, imperialist methods of Colonel Jeffreys and the commissioners. Since it was impossible to satisfy both his royal masters and his Virginia partisans, it is hardly surprising that Culpeper kept putting off his departure.[28]

While Culpeper delayed, his dilemma deepened. The continued defiance of the royal commissioners by the Green Spring

---

tion and orders for Virginia (Moryson to Blathwayt [?], Jan. 1678, *Cal. S.P. Col., 1677–1680*, no. 562ii).

27. Jeffreys to Coventry, July 7, 1678, Coventry MSS, LXXVIII, 268–270. See also Jeffreys's "Narrative of some Affairs in Virginia since . . . July 1677," *ibid.*, 168. Culpeper was fully informed of the commissioners' proceedings and of the privy council's approval of them (*Cal. S.P. Col., 1677–1680*, nos. 377, 425, 442, 505, 516). He gave way to the salary arrangements whereby Jeffreys collected the governor's salary in Virginia during the governor's absence (*ibid.*, nos. 385, 539). Yet Culpeper supported Lord Berkeley's protests against the summoning of an assembly to consolidate the royal authority (*ibid.*, no. 388). See also Culpeper to Coventry, Dec. 28, 1679, Coventry MSS, LXXVIII, 430–431. Capt. Alexander Culpeper was both the active correspondent of the Berkeleans and Lord Berkeley's investigator at the Colonial Office for Sir William's posthumous, unsuccessful defense (*Cal. S.P. Col., 1677–1680*, nos. 483, 505, 506, 507, and see Jeffreys to Moryson, Apr. 1, 1678, Coventry MSS, LXXVIII, 214, complaining that "all the whole Faction Hold a Strong Correspondence with Capt. Culpeper"). William Sherwood asserted that the irreconcilables were "upheld by the hope of Lord Culpeper doing mighty things for them" (Sherwood to Williamson, Aug. 8, 1678, *Cal. S.P. Col., 1677–1680*, no. 776). Lady Berkeley's hatred of the commissioners is notorious: "Where the women engage, there are no bounds to wrath," as the postillion incident attests. On this alleged affront to the dignity of the Virginia commissioners, see n. 25 above and *Cal. S.P. Col., 1677–1680*, nos. 216, 293, 374.

28. See n. 27 above and, for Ludwell's appointment as secretary of the Virginia council and for the faction's continued opposition to the commissioners, see *Cal. S.P. Col., 1677–1680*, nos. 663, 727, 746, 753, 754, 804, 817, 818, 821. In his letter of Sept. 18, 1678, Moryson drily noted that the faction's actions would demonstrate to the privy council plantations committee "how well His Majesty's orders are obeyed in Virginia" (*ibid.*, no. 804).

party, both in the Virginia council and in the assembly session that met at Green Spring, provoked the king to order the governor-general to further restrict local self-government. In October 1678, for example, "His Majesty, taking notice of the great presumption of said Assembly in calling in question his said authority derived to his said Commissioners," ordered his privy council committee for plantations to vindicate "His Majesty's authority" and to reduce the "said Assembly to a due sense and acknowledgment of their duty and submission towards His Majesty, and such as are commissionated by him." The most important of the ensuing orders to Lord Culpeper was that which extended from Ireland to Virginia the essence of Poynings's Law: crown dictation of provincial legislation. The king intended to draft all colonial laws in England, and he ordered the privy council committee immediately "to prepare a scheme of laws and orders to be transmitted to said Colony of Virginia" with Governor-General Culpeper.[29]

The privy councillors dutifully agreed with the king that the Green Spring assembly's opposition to the king's officers and so to royal authority was "seditious and even tending to rebellion." The formulation of "laws and orders" to end Virginia independence, and their incorporation into Culpeper's commission and instructions, proved to be a tedious business, however. The lords did not even begin this work until mid-December 1678, for they felt that they must await the testimony of the Virginia councillor sent by Lieutenant Governor Jeffreys to convey his recommendations for chastising the opponents of royal rule.[30]

Even though he remained in London, Lord Culpeper had already responded to Colonel Jeffreys's initial paramilitary suggestions. Culpeper then stressed his own economic concerns. The result was that peculiar combination of the forcible and the fiscal that characterized Culpeper's administration but that also, more generally, reflected the two dominant considerations of government in England's developing empire. Culpeper thus readily backed Colonel Jeffreys's plan that a citadel be built at the seat of government in Virginia and that it be garrisoned by regular troops to support royal authority, but Culpeper also insisted on clauses in his commission to protect his proprietary revenues. He asked for assurances that a scheduled naval convoy would be provided for Virginia's tobacco fleet: as Virginia's proprietor, he intended to tax

29. Order of the king-in-council, Oct. 30, 1678, *Cal. S.P. Col.*, *1677–1680*, no. 821.

30. Moryson to [Blathwayt], Dec. 13, 1678, journal of the privy council plantations committee, Dec. 13, 14, 1678, Feb. 6, 1679, *ibid.*, nos. 845, 846, 847, 881.

tobacco exports. He announced his support for a proposed Virginia port bill. The town centers it provided for would facilitate trade and customs collections, he noted, and both governmental centralization and military security would be enhanced by town development, as garrison government in England had long demonstrated.[31]

While Lord Culpeper reacted to authoritarian and economic initiatives from Virginia, the "scheme of laws and orders" to reduce "the arrogancy of the Virginia assembly" was brought to the privy council board and passed. It included a bill that would increase the royal revenue available for use in Virginia and so reduce the executive's financial dependence on the provincial assembly. The king further ordered his governor-general to require the Virginia assembly to approve an act that limited that legislature's authority to one of assent or dissent to executive proposals. That limitation lay at the heart of Poynings's Law as applied in Virginia. The king completed his grant of royal authority to Governor-General Culpeper when he conferred on his viceroy the symbols of royal supremacy: the mace, the sword, the flag, and the communion service of the Church of England.[32]

Equipped at last with all the stuff of sovereignty—military, constitutional, financial, and symbolic—Culpeper was expected to sail for Virginia in February 1679. It was the second week in March, however, before the plantations committee made their initial report "touching Lord Culpeper's Commission and Instructions as Governor of Virginia." Then news of Colonel Jeffreys's death reached London. "His Majesty was very sensible of the loss of Colonel Jeffreys," the more so because of "the absence of my Lord Culpeper [from his government], who will be despatched upon the next opportunity with Instructions . . . requisite for the quiet and Settlement of that Colony." But on April 2, the day after this prediction of his imminent departure, Lord Culpeper was speaking in the house of lords in an effort to obstruct the impeachment of Lord Treasurer Danby and to blunt the attack on the prerogative that the impeachment represented. Until parliament

31. Journal of the privy council plantations committee, Dec. 13, 14, 21, 1678, May 20, 1679, order of the king-in-council, Dec. 20, 1678, *ibid.*, nos. 846, 847, 855, 996, 851. See also n. 24 above.

32. Moryson to Blathwayt, Oct. 25, 1678, *VMHB*, XXIV (1916), 78; order of the king-in-council, Oct. 30, 1678, journal of the privy council plantations committee, Feb. 6, 10, 1679, order of the king-in-council, Mar. 14, 1679, *Cal. S.P. Col., 1677–1680*, nos. 817, 821, 881, 888, 932; warrant to the commissioners of the ordnance, Dec. 10, 1679, *Cal. S.P. Dom., 1679–1680*, 306. For a fuller treatment of these issues, and for manuscript citations, see chapter 8 below.

was dissolved, the crown could not spare Lord Culpeper for Virginia.[33]

In any case, Governor-General Culpeper's instructions were still being revised and were completed only in mid-April. By that time, the opposition in parliament had forced the king to reorganize his privy council and to recall Shaftesbury from the political wilderness to be its president and the senior member of the committee for plantations. But this change came too late to alter the prerogative program Culpeper was to carry out. The laws intended for Virginia passed the seals early in May. Despite a debate in the recast privy council, and notwithstanding the success of the opposition in securing military retrenchment elsewhere, the Virginia military establishment of general staff, surgeon, chaplain, and two companies of infantry was also retained as "being for His Majesty's service and necessary support of that Government." On June 18 the new privy council even accepted Culpeper's request for funds to retain the military engineers of the expeditionary force in Virginia, so that they could plan the Virginia citadel, and to pay the gunsmith and his mates to care for the government's arsenal.[34]

The plantations committee further formalized the military status of imperial officers by agreeing "that all payments made to the Governors and other officers of the Plantations, and for the soldiers maintained there, be transferred from the Exchequer and paid by the Paymaster of the Army upon a general establishment to be settled for that purpose." The colonial governors-general, their general staffs, and their garrisons were thus even more closely identified with English garrison government, as they joined the officer-governors of English jurisdictions, their staffs, and their troops, on the crown's military establishment. Like the domestic garrison commanders, the governors-general overseas found that the amount of their army funding varied according to the size and circumstances of their command. In Barbados, the army estab-

33. Blathwayt to Lord Baltimore, Jan. 1, 1679, Blathwayt Papers, XVII, folder 5, Colonial Williamsburg Foundation, Williamsburg, Va. (hereafter cited as Blathwayt Papers, Williamsburg); order of the king-in-council, Mar. 14, 1679, the king to the council of Virginia, Apr. 1, to Sir Henry Chicheley, Apr. 2, to Culpeper, Sept. 10, 1679, *Cal. S.P. Col., 1677–1680*, nos. 932, 951, 952, 1112; Coventry to Chicheley, Apr. 1, 1679, Coventry MSS, LXXVIII; Sir Robert Southwell to the duke of Ormond, Apr. 12, 1679, HMC, *Ormonde*, N.S., IV, 501–503. Danby took credit for suppressing the Virginia rebellion without having to call on parliament for money (Burnet, *History*, II, 202 n. 4).

34. Journal of the privy council plantations committee, Apr. 14, June 12, 1679, order of the king-in-council, Apr. 16, June 18, 1679, warrant to the lord chancellor, May 7, 1679, memorandum, June 18, 1679, *Cal. S.P. Col., 1677–1680*, nos. 966, 1019, 973, 1022, 985, 1025.

lishment provided for the governor-general's salary. In the ducal proprietary of New York, it supported fort upkeep (and occasional crown subventions helped the duke sustain his garrison). In the Leeward Islands, the governor-general and two eighty-man companies, plus their officers, were paid as part of the English army. In the crucial crown colonies of Jamaica and Virginia, the imposition of a militarized and centralized royal government was carried out by full general staffs—captain general and governor-in-chief, lieutenant general and lieutenant governor, and major general—supported by English army salaries, by funds for fort maintenance, and by two infantry companies, each of one hundred men plus officers. Culpeper's additions of engineering and gunsmithing staffs to his establishment made his military payroll the largest in America. Of course, English army salaries for governors-general and their garrisons increased royal officers' independence of the local elites assembled in provincial legislatures. Captain General Culpeper fully exploited this opportunity for pelf as well as for the protection of the prerogative, thus setting a double precedent that his successors in Virginia would use to the full.[35]

Early in November 1679 the imperial fixer, William Blathwayt, reported that "my Lord Culpeper is at length so far advanced in his final dispatch for Virginia that I do not see what can hinder his departure before the next month." Culpeper's excuses turned out to be as vexatious as they were unforseeable. After a full month of them, King Charles ordered Lord Culpeper acquainted with "the high displeasure His Majesty hath conceived at his delay and neglect of duty, and that his royal intentions are to appoint another Governor for Virginia unless he repair without further delay on board the Oxford frigate." But Culpeper had already missed the ship. He caught up to the *Oxford* at its next port of call, but the wind turned foul. "I am here," Culpeper wrote from Deal on December 14, "in a Readiness in every point, Soldiers, Servants, and Goods, to set Sail with the first offer of a Wind." Instead of wind there came "a Great Fogge." Both the ship bringing Culpeper's paraphernalia from London and the royal yacht carrying his garrison's ammunition from the Tower to the Virginia fleet were delayed for a week. In this brief time, even

35. Journal of the privy council plantations committee, June 27, 1679, order of the king-in-council, June 27, 1679, report of Sir Stephen Fox (the paymaster general) to the king, Oct. 28, 1679, four warrants for payment of companies of foot in Virginia, Oct. 28, Nov. 1, Dec. 1, 1679, the king to Culpeper, Dec. 5, 1679, *ibid.*, nos. 1036, 1038, 1162, 1163, 1164, 1165, 1166, 1172, 1200, 1207; Stephen Saunders Webb, "William Blathwayt, Imperial Fixer: From Popish Plot to Glorious Revolution," *WMQ*, 3d Ser., XXV (1968), 6; minutes of warrants for payments, [Dec.?] 1679, *Cal. S.P. Dom., 1679–1680*, 319.

before the voyage had begun, three of Culpeper's soldiers died in their coffin-like quarters on board ship. The admiralty officials threatened to strip Culpeper of his servants by releasing all those who now protested that they did not want to go to Virginia. "I was never more uneasy or melancholy in my life," Culpeper complained. And he had yet to board ship himself.[36]

Two weeks later, on December 28, his lordship was actually aboard the *Oxford*, recording a fair wind. Before he could finish his letter, however, it had veered foul again. On January 11, 1680, Blathwayt was "sorry to find your Lordship so long detained by contrary winds." Another two weeks had passed when Blathwayt noted that Lord Culpeper still "remains at Deale, intending to sail with the first wind." At last, in the third week of February 1680, Thomas, Lord Culpeper, "now finally left" for Virginia. Seventy-nine days later, "after a most tedious passage full of death, scurvy, and calentures, we are . . . arrived within soundings of Virginia," Culpeper wrote. He had yet to reconcile any of the contending forces he represented: proprietorship, provincialism, and the prerogative.[37]

Herbert Jeffreys: The Professional Soldier Becomes a Royal Governor

The civil wars taught two political lessons, one particular— "imperator bonus idemque robustus miles"—and the other general —"sovereignty and the sword go hand in hand."[38] The English sovereigns' need for strong soldiers through whom to rule produced a class of career military officers who rose to political authority because they had administrative abilities tested on battlefields and in police actions. After the Restoration, these professionals prepared provincial governments for the administrations of grandees such as Carlisle or for exploitations by courtiers such as

36. Blathwayt to Baltimore, Nov. 4, 1679, Blathwayt Papers, XVIII, 1, Williamsburg; order of the king-in-council, Dec. 3, 17, 1679, orders of the privy council, Nov. 28, Dec. 17, 1679, *Cal. S.P. Col., 1677–1680*, nos. 1195, 1201, 1231, 1232; Culpeper to Coventry, Dec. 14, 1679, Coventry MSS, LXXVIII, 421. See also the letter of Dec. 13, 1679, *ibid.*, 419–420.

37. Culpeper to Coventry, Dec. 28, 1679, Coventry MSS, LXXVIII, 430–432; Blathwayt to Culpeper, Jan. 11, to Stapleton, Jan. 25, 1680, Blathwayt Papers, XVII, 1, XXXVII, 2, Williamsburg; Culpeper to [Blathwayt], May 2, 1680, *Cal. S.P. Col., 1677–1680*, no. 1350.

38. "The welfare of the sovereign depends on the strength of his soldiers": John Heath, in his introduction to George [Monck], duke of Albemarle, *Observations upon Military and Political Affairs* (London, 1671), 144.

Culpeper. When the Carlisles and Culpepers left, the professionals picked up the political pieces. Finally, in the last quarter of the seventeenth century, the professionals began to dominate imperial governments. Their predominance persisted for at least half a century.

Herbert Jeffreys's Civil War Seasoning

One of the Stuart sovereigns' swordsmen was Herbert Jeffreys of Hertfordshire. His martial career began at Oxford in 1642. There Charles I commissioned him as a lieutenant in the Comptons' regiment of horse. He fought for a time in the war of petty garrisons that resulted from trying to win England not just city by city, but hamlet by hamlet, and to wring resources out of every one. King Charles "gave *Banbury*, and that Part of the Country, to the Earl of *Northampton*," Jeffreys's colonel. Now governor of Banbury, Northampton "was commanded to raise a Regiment of Horse." The earl in turn assigned to Lieutenant Jeffreys and his troop two Oxfordshire villages as quarters and a recruiting base. Exercising garrison government at its lowest level, Jeffreys and his men tried to parlay physical force into effective sovereignty. They seized territorial control of the villages. They forced "contributions" of crops and livestock, money and men. They substituted royal military authority for the customary rule of local elites. Jeffreys's cavalry coerced the Oxfordshire villagers to obey such governors' commands as this: "Know that unless you bring to me . . . the monthly contribution for six months, you are to expect an unsanctified troop of horse among you, from whom if you hide yourselves, they shall fire your houses without mercy, hang up your bodies wherever they find them, and scare your ghosts." When the captain of Jeffreys's "unsanctified troop of horse" was killed while executing such orders, Lieutenant Jeffreys was promoted to the command.[39]

Captain Jeffreys soon absorbed the royalist doctrine so eloquently stated by his lieutenant, Richard Bulstrode: "The King is singly Sovereign, and no Power on Earth co-ordinate with him: And as Almighty God is the absolute Sovereign of all Princes, so

---

39. Firth, *Cromwell's Army*, 19, 19 n. 2, 28. Compare Apsley's threats and demands to the inhabitants of Barnstaple, in chapter 1 above. See also Sir Richard Bulstrode, *Memoirs and Reflections upon the Reign and Government of King Charles the Ist. and K. Charles the IInd. . . .* (London, 1721), 88–89, 92–93; John Gwyn, *The Military Memoirs of Captain John Gwyn*, in Richard Atkyns, *The Civil War*, ed. Peter Young from *John Gwyn*, ed. Norman Tucker (Hamden, Conn., 1968), 56–57 (hereafter cited as Gwyn, *Military Memoirs*).

imperial Princes (as the Kings of *England* are esteemed) are absolute, next and immediately under God, to whom alone they are accountable."[40] For these royalist officers, the object of the civil war was to deny that contradiction in terms, parliamentary sovereignty. Thus they would prevent chaos, "for there is no longer any Government, where the Inferior incroaches upon the Superior, and confounds the Relations of Kings and Subjects, [as] in that Anarchical Whimsey of imagining that Kings are to govern by Contract, and Subjects to obey accordingly." A Virginia legislature, far from Jeffreys's thoughts in 1642, and an as yet unwritten charter for that English government overseas, were to suffer from his lifelong adherence to this doctrine. On behalf of monarchy, Captain Jeffreys fought, failed, and followed his royal masters into exile.[41]

In France, Herbert Jeffreys joined the staff of James Stuart, duke of York, the soldierly second son of Charles I and a lieutenant general in the army of Louis XIV. With Jeffreys served Richard Nicolls, Thomas Dongan, and Charles Wheeler. James and each of these staff officers afterward applied the combined lessons of English and French civil wars to English and colonial governments. Indeed, France's civil war reinforced their earlier English experience: domestic wars for political authority revolved around fortified towns ruled by military governors. Successful sieges ate up the enemy's army, garrison by garrison, absorbed his territory, province by province, until an advantageous peace conferred the conquests on the victor. The army, these English exiles thus learned, was the indispensable tool of territorial expansion, political authority, and international aggrandizement. They absorbed its leaders' obsession with imperial frontiers. They observed its direction, military and political, by officers serving as governors. They assisted Marshal Turenne in his substitution of modern, centralized, state forces for the old-fashioned, piecemeal pattern of frontier garrisons weakly linked by patrols (a strategy that Sir William Berkeley disastrously continued into the 1670s in Virginia until Herbert Jeffreys displaced him). Centrally directed armed authority was the political weapon of an aggressive state in its reduction of provincial autonomy and aristocratic hegemony. Governors, garrisons, the army of which they were parts, all were to be subject to an absolute commander who sought to impose national values—the

40. Bulstrode, *Memoirs*, 66–67.
41. *Ibid.*

general welfare—on shortsighted provincial populaces and over-powerful provincial elites.[42]

The educational and well-paid French service of Jeffreys and his fellow officer-exiles ended soon after Mazarin's treaty with Cromwell forced James from the French army in 1656. In the following spring his officers had to follow him, for Charles II had concluded an alliance with Spain that promised support for at least the basis of a British royal army. He summoned his subjects to him in Flanders. There they were formed into six skeleton regiments under James Stuart's command. One of these units, some four hundred English "men of quality," became King Charles's own Guards. Captains of these Guards included Herbert Jeffreys, Jonathan Atkins, Charles Wheeler, and other future soldier-administrators of the English empire.[43]

The number of English officers in Flanders increased dramatically with the landing of six thousand Cromwellian troops. They joined Turenne's army to attack the strategic port town of Dunkirk, which was covered by the Spanish army and its English royalist regiments. Despite the duke of York's local success at the Battle of the Dunes—and surely no modern English sovereign has ever had a record of personal combat such as James was compiling—the day was lost. The few survivors of his cavalry Life Guard were the last formed troops to leave the field. Of the allied infantry, only Charles II's foot Guards were enveloped without being broken. The Cromwellian and French lines eddied around the little block of the Guards as they stood fast, "for they were all English," the proud duke exclaimed. Their officers, Captain Jeffreys among them, replied to demands that they surrender, by saying that "they had been posted there by the Duke." They would not move without his command. Their admiring commander reported that two Guards officers were escorted to a nearby hilltop to be shown "that none of our Army was left standing excepting only themselves." Even then the Guards surrendered only their weapons

---

42. William L. Sachse, *The Colonial American in Britain* (Madison, Wis., 1956), 146; A. Lytton Sells, trans., *The Memoirs of James II: His Campaigns as Duke of York, 1652–1660* (Bloomington, Ind., 1962), 64, 98–99, 129, 130, 143, 148, 155, 169, 188, 191, 194, 210, 211, 212, 238, 240, 253, 275 (hereafter cited as *Memoirs of James II*); Albemarle, *Observations*, 7, 9, 12, 119, 130–139, 144; Elton, *Art Military*, 187–190. On the Yorkist context of Jeffreys's career, see S. S. Webb, "Household of James Stuart," *Perspectives in American History*, VIII (1974), 55–80.

43. *Memoirs of James II*, 219, 222, 223, 225n, 226; Firth, "Armies in Flanders," RHS, *Trans.*, N.S., XVII (1903), 67–71; Gwyn, *Military Memoirs*, 86n, 91; Hamilton, *Grenadier Guards*, I, appendix 3.

and themselves, being promised their personal belongings as the reward of their courage.[44]

Most of the Guards were eventually paroled to rejoin the duke's command. They underwent two years of near starvation as the royal fortunes touched bottom. Unable to keep new clothes on his own back, Charles could do nothing for the tattered remnants of his Guards. What little financial allowance the Spanish offered was embezzled, usually before it reached the English officers, nearly always before it got to their men. The Guards "were a tedious time without money by the corruption of the officers, who kept wholly to themselves the route-money due unto us . . . sold the canteen of wine and beer; and likewise sold the bread money; and when they had converted to their own use that little we had to keep life and soul together, in consideration of it gave the soldiers passes to go up and down the country a-begging."[45]

Even after his restoration, Charles was slow to help his regiment. Of the Guards, his officers wrote, there is "scarce left one part of four whom at Dunkirk battle entirely devoted themselves to be sacrificed for our Kings sake. . . . But, having escaped the worst . . . three parts of us perished with a tedious imprisonment and want of bread, and the few remainder here languish as having no allowance to live."[46] The injustice of paying bounties to Cromwellian regiments after the restoration of the monarchy while allowing the king's own Guards to starve in Flanders was so apparent that in August 1660 parliament authorized the addition of the royal regiment to the garrison of Dunkirk—Oliver Cromwell's conquest, now Charles II's possession. Former royalist exiles brought a thousand recruits to Dunkirk to fill the Guards' decimated ranks.[47]

44. *Memoirs of James II*, 264, 266, 269–272; Gwyn, *Military Memoirs*, 89, 91; Firth, "Armies in Flanders," RHS, *Trans.*, N.S., XVII (1903), 77–78, 87–88, 94, 110; Lt. Col. John Davis, *The History of the Second Queen's Royal Regiment, Now the Queen's (Royal West Surrey) Regiment*, 4 vols. (London, 1887–1902), I, 44, 64, 74, 83; Dalton, ed., *English Army Lists*, I, 75, II, 229.

45. Gwyn, *Military Memoirs*, 95; *Memoirs of James II*, 275, 276.

46. Gwyn, *Military Memoirs*, 96.

47. Prominent among the former exiles who now joined the Dunkirk garrison was Major Henry Norwood (see Appendix, no. 35), who had spent some of the Interregnum in Virginia. A notable follower of General Monck, now a Guards officer at Dunkirk, was Captain John Mutlow (no. 90), who would lead a company of the Coldstream Guards (Monck's regiment) to Virginia in 1676–1677. Note also the presence in the Guards at Dunkirk of Robert Needham. He served, both in Dunkirk and in Tangier, as a captain in Lord Rutherford's regiment and then followed a number of the Tangier officers to New York; see Dalton, ed., *English Army Lists*, I, 7, 8, 19, 24, 33, 39, and S.P. 44/2, 14. Alexander Spotswood's father, Robert, served at Dunkirk and at Tangier, where Alexander grew up; see S.P. 44/2, 14; Dalton, ed., *English Army Lists*, I, 195; and, on Alexander Spotswood, Appendix, no.

When the scattered remnants of the royal regiment gathered at Dunkirk and were joined by their recruits, the rest of the garrison was still Cromwellian, in origin if not in allegiance, except for the duke of York's Life Guard and the new governor, that doughty Scots professional soldier Lord Rutherford. "The souldiery here are highly satisfied" with the governor, it was said, "as being a person of such known experience in military affairs, and one that hath ever had a loyal affection to his Majesties service." As they straggled into Dunkirk, battered royalists like Jeffreys made brave efforts at self-discipline, drill, and the defense of the town. As the Guards' numbers approached twelve hundred, and as the Cromwellian officers of the garrison regiments were replaced by royalist officers such as Thomas Dongan and Charles Littleton, the Guards and the garrison began to demonstrate that the public morality and professional militarism of the Cromwellians could be married to the personal debauchery and political autocracy of the royalists. Together, they would beget the police and administrative class of the Restoration.[48]

Dunkirk demonstrated in extreme form both this class's martial methods and its political ends. "The Governor hath used great care and diligence in setting the garrison," it was said. He assigned the troops to quarters in the town and scoured the countryside for food and forage in the worst wartime tradition. "The neighboring parts did for a while refuse to pay contribution," one newspaper correspondent reported, "but since they found that his Lordship sent out parties, and fetch'd in such as refused it, they come in willingly, and pay their obedience to this garison." Housed and fed at the cost of the citizens, the united garrison was now set to work to build a citadel. Some said that it was "raised to secure the haven"; others noted that it was "a place of much importance booth to command the towne, to keepe itt in obedience, and likewisse to defend itt against an enemie." Work on this apparatus of protection and coercion began at five o'clock in the morning in summer and quickly took its toll in morale. Soon the king had to caution the governor to limit leaves, and he noted that "there is of late much drinking and debauching practiced among some of the

206. See also Firth, "Armies in Flanders," RHS, *Trans.*, N.S., XVII (1903), 101; duke of Albemarle to the navy commissioners, Oct. 26, 29, 1660, Capt. Samuel Tittsell to the navy commissioners, Nov. 7, 1660, *Cal. S.P. Dom., 1660–1661*, 323, 325, 354.

48. Gwyn, *Military Memoirs*, 99–100. The evaluation of Gov. Rutherford (Appendix, no. 34) is from the *Mercurius Publicus*, June 20–27, 1661, reprinted in Firth, "Armies in Flanders," RHS, *Trans.*, N.S., XVII (1903), 117. On the condition of King Charles's Guards, see also HMC, *Hodgkin*, 123–125. See Appendix, "Dunkirk," and nos. 43, 149.

Officers and Soldiers in Dunkirk, to the Scandal of the Nation and of his Majesty's Government." King Charles ordered that the guilty officers be cashiered. Still more officers were purged on political grounds, each English plot having its miniature reflection across the Channel.[49]

To strengthen discipline after one of these shake-ups, Lieutenant Colonel Henry Norwood was commissioned in March 1662 as "Deputy Governor of Dunkirk Town and Garrison." Norwood spent the long winter evenings at Dunkirk "drinking and debauching" with his messmates, among them Herbert Jeffreys and John Mutlow. His masterful and exciting tales of his epic Atlantic crossing in 1649 and of the exotic and primitive society of the Old Dominion alerted his fellow officers to the problems of a province where they would afterward serve and with which Norwood himself was still connected. Appointed Virginia's auditor in 1650, Colonel Norwood retained the office until at least 1669, and the crown consulted him about Virginia concerns. Norwood would criticize the high and regressive taxes and the military ineptitude of Sir William Berkeley's regime and deplore the governor's licensing of trade with the very Indians who raided all around the English forts. He would record "injuries done in the Courts through the Governor's passion, age, or weakness," and object to the political hegemony of Berkeley's council clique. Norwood's indictment of Berkeley's proprietarial, provincial, and oligarchical misgovernment was precisely that afterward offered by Nathaniel Bacon and his rebels and that Norwood's messmate Herbert Jeffreys would be dispatched to cure.[50]

49. See the *Mercurius Publicus* articles for June 20–27, 1661, May 9, [1662], and especially Aug. 22–29, Sept. 7, 1661, reprinted in Firth, "Armies in Flanders," RHS, *Trans.*, N.S., XVII (1903), 117–119. See also *The Life of Marmaduke Rawdon of York . . .* , ed. Robert Davies, Publications of the Camden Society, LXXXV (Westminster, 1863), 92–95; S.P. 44/2, 15, 34–35; Rutherford to Nicholas, July 8, 1662, *Cal. S.P. Dom., 1661–1662*, 432; Hamilton, *Grenadier Guards*, I, 90.

50. On Norwood's early career, see P. H. Hardacre, "The Further Adventures of Henry Norwood," *VMHB*, LXVII (1959), 271–272, and Henry Norwood, *A Voyage to Virginia*, in Peter Force, comp., *Tracts and Other Papers Relating Principally to the Origin, Settlement, and Progress of the Colonies in North America, from the Discovery of the Country to the Year 1776*, III (Gloucester, Mass., 1963 [orig. publ. Washington, D.C., 1844]), no. 10. Norwood's commissions as lieutenant colonel and deputy governor of the town and garrison of Dunkirk are in S.P. 44/2, 7–8, 25. Henry Guy addressed "Col. Henry Norwood" on the subject of his Virginia auditorship in 1680 (T. 44/88, 8b–9a, P.R.O.). Auditor General William Blathwayt's report to the treasury commissioners, Oct. 4, 1680, noted Norwood's exercise of the Virginia auditorship in the years 1660 to 1669 (T. 64/88, 26b). See also Berkeley to Col. Richard Nicolls, May 26, 1666, Blathwayt Papers, 81, Henry E. Huntington Library, San Marino, Calif. (cited by permission); Norwood to Williamson, July 17, 1667, *Cal. S.P. Col., 1661–1668*, no. 1532; and chapter 7 below.

Jeffreys, the Guards, and English Garrison Government

Late in the summer of 1662, just before Colonel Norwood sailed from Dunkirk to govern Tangier, Captain Jeffreys and his company were transferred to another of England's overseas possessions, the island of Jersey, the duke of York's former government. The English risings of October 1662, however, led the duke to bring the Guards home from exile at last to help police his current government, the town, garrison, and citadel of Portsmouth. There the duke's deputy governors were Captains Richard Nicolls (afterward of New York) and Sir Philip Honeywood (formerly of Virginia). Captain Jeffreys allegedly led his Guards company in suppressing Presbyterian and Anabaptist meetings in Portsmouth in March 1663 and claimed the fines levied on the dissidents he arrested as the reward of his police work.[51]

Captain Jeffreys left Portsmouth in August 1663 and marched the length of England at the head of three companies of the Guards. They entered York just in time to make the arrests that squelched a rising against royal government. The king also sent commissioners of oyer and terminer to York. These royal commissioners condemned twenty-one persons for treason. Another royal commission purged and remodeled the city corporation, removing five aldermen for parliamentary sympathies. This assertion of the prerogative—military, judicial, and political—threatened the merchant oligarchy's dominance of York almost for the first time in the city's modern history.[52] In the same manner, thirteen years later these same royal regulatory devices—the king's troops and royal judicial and political commissions—would be used again by Herbert Jeffreys against both local rebellion and the hegemony of local elites, this time in Virginia.

Despite the royal regulation of York, rebellion recurred there. Captain Jeffreys expressed his attitude toward traitors by asking the king for their property: as their defeat was his responsibility, so

51. Orders to Lord Rutherford, Aug. 22, Sept. 22, 1662, S.P. 44/2, 31, 36; Hamilton, *Grenadier Guards*, I, 92–93. The duke, as lord admiral, dispatched transports for the transfer of the Guards. See warrant to the duke of York, Aug. 22, 1662, warrant for payment of Jeffreys's company, Sept. 22, 1662, warrant to Rutherford, Sept. 22, 1662, *Cal. S.P. Dom., 1661–1662*, 465, 494, 495; Ranke, *England*, III, 392, 393. On the police operations of Jeffreys and the Guards, see (the not always reliable) Hamilton, I, 90.

52. James J. Cartwright, ed., *The Memoirs of Sir John Reresby, . . . 1634–1689* (London, 1875), 54, 58–59. Cartwright's text has been checked against the modern, standard edition by Andrew Browning (Glasgow, 1936). Variations are indicated by double citations. See also G.C.F. Forster, "York in the Seventeenth Century," *A History of Yorkshire, The City of York* (Oxford, 1961), 179–181; Gee, "Derwentdale Plot," RHS, *Trans.*, 3d Ser., XI (1917), 136.

their fall ought to provide his reward. With his troops, Jeffreys was the city's chief protection against rebel risings. This was no passive role. York had been the principal target of the Derwentdale plotters in August 1663. In October, warned of renewed rebellion, the king ordered "York, or any stronghold to which the disaffected may resort, to be well watched." Captain Jeffreys and the Guardsmen under his command responded vigorously to the king's order: they made hundreds of arrests; they protected the royal courts that condemned the arrested conspirators to prison in Chepstow Castle, the Channel Islands, Tangier, or Jamaica; and they escorted the public executions that embellished York bar with a frieze of severed heads. Nonetheless, in February 1664 Jeffreys and his men were nearly overwhelmed by "the dangerous attempts of seditious conventicles." The king immediately turned to one of the best of his surviving civil war cavalry commanders, Francis, Lord Hawley, now the duke of York's closest military and political aide. Lord Hawley was ordered to ride to Captain Jeffreys's support with two troops of the royal horse Guards, followed by a reinforced regiment of the foot Guards.[53]

The Guards' assertion of royal power in Yorkshire was furthered on August 6, 1665, by the arrival of James, duke of York, fresh from his naval victory over the Dutch off Lowestoft. The king "sent his Royal Highness to York, that he might have an eye upon the Northern Parts," for dispatches from Jeffreys, Carlisle, Gower, and Hawley had warned of a "rising designed by the Phanatics and others of the old Cromwellian and Republican Party." James brought with him additional companies of the Guards to help Captain Jeffreys hold down "the stubborn North."[54]

The royal duke cemented military government onto York to put down political protest. "James was the most complete Royalist

53. Hamilton, *Grenadier Guards*, I, 96. The property of felons reverted to the king. The well-connected applied for it as largesse. See Jeffreys's applications from Dunkirk and York: reference to the lord treasurer of Jeffreys's petition, Mar. 8, 1662, *Cal. S.P. Dom.*, *1661–1662*, 302; reference to the lord treasurer of a petition from Jeffreys and Miles Matthew, May 15, 1663, *ibid.*, *1663–1664*, 138; memorandum for Lord [Arlington], [1670?], *ibid.*, *1670*, 640. On the plot and its suppression, see Gee, "Derwentdale Plot," RHS, *Trans.*, 3d Ser., XI (1917), 134, 140–141, 141n; Sir Thomas Gower's papers concerning the rising, Oct. 12, 1663, Bennet to the duke of Buckingham, Oct. 14, 1663, *Cal. S.P. Dom.*, *1663–1664*, 298, 301; Hamilton, *Grenadier Guards*, I, 101. Lord Hawley's commission of Feb. 5, 1664, is in S.P. 44/20, 3–4, and see Dalton, ed., *English Army Lists*, I, 4, 47.

54. Arthur W. Tedder, *The Navy of the Restoration from the Death of Cromwell to the Treaty of Breda; Its Work, Growth and Influence* (Cambridge, 1916), 45, 51–60, 119–126; S.P. 44/20, 82; [Dicconson], *James the Second*, ed. Clarke, 421–422, also 522; Hawley to Williamson, May 13, 1664, *Cal. S.P. Dom.*, *1663–1664*, 586; Sir Charles Littleton to Hon. Christopher Hatton, from York, Aug. 7, 1665, Add. MSS 29577, 52–52b; Hamilton, *Grenadier Guards*, I, 117; *Memoirs of James II*, 522.

that it is possible to conceive; he regarded rebellion as a crime so heinous as to be past forgiveness, and he not only denied mercy to traitors, but was disinclined to allow justice to persons accused of treason." Yorkists construed any opposition to royal government as treason, and they were extending that government to the colonies. Captain Jeffreys now executed the orders of absolutism's personification, the duke of York, in York, as he had done previously in Oxford, in France and Flanders, in Dunkirk, Jersey, and Portsmouth, and as he would do in command of Virginia after 1676.[55] Meanwhile, the Dutch conflict abroad helped the officers of the royal army to stretch their political sway at home.

Even after the duke of York's departure, Captain Jeffreys stayed on to command three companies of Guards. They protected the city of York against the remote danger of Dutch invaders and the real menace of local rebels. Disaffection to the crown infected even the reformed city corporation. An aggressive officer-governor was needed to assert the prerogative in York. John, Lord Frescheville, had been named commander of York's enlarged garrison during the duke's residence in June 1665. He was commissioned "governor" of York in June 1667, and Captain Jeffreys was appointed his deputy. In fact, Jeffreys relieved the old soldier of most of the burden of garrison government administration.[56]

The commissions of 1667 conferred on the two commanders of York all the military jurisdiction of commanders-in-chief. They controlled both the regular soldiers of the garrison and the city militia of York. Frescheville and Jeffreys were authorized to set the guard of York, to assign the soldiers to quarters in the city, and to police the town with their troops. Their urban authority was summarized by the king's order to the governor or his deputy "to keep the keys of the gates and postern at York . . . and to open and shut the gates as he finds cause, for the King's service, and security of the place." Physical control of the city distinguished the rank of governor from that of other field officers. It was the "holding" or "keeping" of the keys that the York corporate elite objected to in their governors, now and henceforward. As the keeper of York's

55. F. C. Turner, *James II* (New York, 1948), 81.
56. The statement that commissions for "governor" and "deputy governor" were issued in 1667 depends on Hamilton, *Grenadier Guards*, I, 128–129. Frescheville's military commission of Aug. 21, 1665, is calendared in *Cal. S.P. Dom., 1664–1665*, 527. This was renewed and expanded in June 1667, on the same day that Carlisle was commissioned lieutenant general of the north (*ibid.*, 1667, 209). The governor was one of the horse Guards officers sent with their colleague Lord Hawley to garrison York. Frescheville began to march toward the governorship as early as August 1663, with a commission as general of the forces gathered at York to suppress the conventicles (Dalton, ed., *English Army Lists*, I, 4, 35).

keys, Lord Frescheville was addressed as "governor" by the resentful city dignitaries, and Frescheville's and Jeffreys's vigorous civil and military police actions set precedents for their successors in the government of York.[57]

Nevertheless, Frescheville and Jeffreys do not appear to have been "governors" in the fullest sense of that term. They were not appointed civil magistrates. Instead, they requested civil authorization from the sheriff (who was, conveniently enough, himself a fellow officer in the Guards), or from the urban justices of the peace, before they undertook police actions. On the other hand, Yorkshiremen petitioned King Charles to add Captain Jeffreys to the commission of local worthies that examined the grievances against hearth-tax collectors. Tax collection ranked with religious dissidence and political plotting as one of the three major problems of the crown's northern administrators. Jeffreys's involvement in the investigation of these tax grievances says something for his local reputation for fairness and disinterestedness. It broadened his experience of civil administration in a way that was to be particularly appropriate in his Virginia governorship. Yet it was chiefly the military security and political police aspects of governorship that preoccupied Captain Jeffreys for nearly nine years as deputy governor of York. This long exercise of paramilitary authority on behalf of the crown—despite the resentment of the local ruling class—goes far to explain the character of Herbert Jeffreys's subsequent government of Virginia.[58]

The commission that authorized Captain Jeffreys's martial command of York (as well as that which empowered his often-

57. The phrase "to keep the keys" is used in Elton, *Art Military*, 189, 190, to define the governor's authority, and in Frescheville's and Jeffreys's commissions of June 18, 1667, in *Cal. S.P. Dom., 1667*, 209, and in S.P. 44/35A, 10b. See also Browning, ed., *Memoirs of Reresby*, 226, 227.

58. On police actions and relations with the magistracy, see Frescheville to [Williamson], Aug. 2, to Arlington, Aug. 30, 1670, *Cal. S.P. Dom., 1670*, 361, 401; Hamilton, *Grenadier Guards*, I, 90, 91–93, 96; and Dalton, ed., *English Army Lists*, I, 111. See also the activities of Sir Edward Musgrave, captain of the third company of (Wentworth's battalion in) the Guards. Musgrave had served in the Carlisle garrison with Sir Jonathan Atkins (Appendix, no. 5) and John Tongue (no. 195) and was also sheriff of Cumberland in 1665 (Dalton, ed., *English Army Lists*, I, 15). Note too the administration of another Guards captain in command of a garrison town, Captain Bennett at Hull (Hamilton, *Grenadier Guards*, I, 148–149). (This may have been Edward Bennett, son of the secretary of state; see *English Army Lists*, I, 37, 43, 66.) On the other hand, Secretary Arlington's anti-militarism found expression in his refusal to permit Lord Frescheville to enforce the game laws (a usual corollary of gubernatorial control of the city gates), on the grounds that "being a military man, he may exercise authority with more vigour than usual" (William Godolphin to [Williamson], Sept. 12, 1663, *Cal. S.P. Dom., 1663–1664*, 271). On Jeffreys's investigation of the hearth tax collection, see petition of William Harwood, Apr. 11, 1666, *ibid., 1665–1666*, 346, and Abbott, "Conspiracy and Dissent, II," *AHR*, XIV (1908–1909), 701.

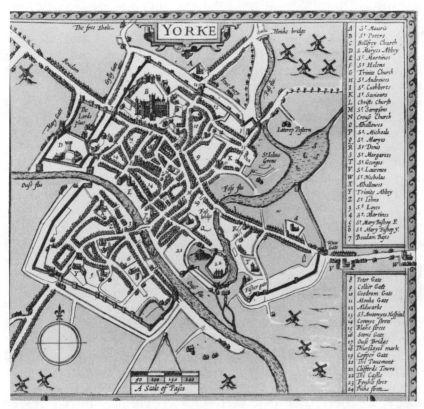

City Plan of "Yorke." From "The West Ridinge of Yorkshire" in 1610, fol. 79v–80r of John Speed's atlas, *The Theatre Of The Empire Of Great Britaine: Presenting An Exact Geography of the Kingdomes of England, Scotland, Ireland and the Isles ajioyning . . .* (London, 1611).

absent superior, the aged Lord Frescheville) was reissued on May 9, 1670. Jeffreys was again "entrusted with the keeping of the Keys of the Gates and Posterns of Our said Citty of York" and authorized to command all forces, both regular and militia, at any time in the city. Now, in addition he could also march these forces out to any part of Yorkshire "to Secure the Peace thereof, as you shall think necessary for our service." Two days after the issue of this commission, sectaries rose in Bristol, London, and Hull to resist enforcement of the Conventicle Act that forbade their meetings. Everywhere these "riots" were put down by military force. In York, Captain Jeffreys and his fellow Guardsmen (including Sir Philip Monckton, the high sheriff) broke up one meeting after another. Jeffreys acted on special orders to march against "Methodists."[59]

Then, on the last day of July 1670, the Quakers, locked out of their meetinghouses, rallied in the streets of York. First, Captain Jeffreys sent his subordinate Captain Blakiston to fetch an alderman to give them "a check for meeting." The Quakers refused to disperse, and Jeffreys had the names of the demonstrators recorded. Next, he called out the main guard to arrest the leaders and jail them in Clifford's Tower. Finally, Jeffreys personally led a raid on the nonconformists' headquarters, where he seized the Quaker register. Listed in the register were the names of five hundred Quaker leaders and teachers in Yorkshire, the locations of their monthly and quarterly meetings, the names of all Quakers who had at any time since 1652 been incarcerated in Clifford's Tower, and the names of the officers and governors who had ordered them imprisoned. Captain Jeffreys sent out his cavalry and dragoons to round up the conventiclers named in the register, not only in the city of York itself, but across the breadth of the shire. King Charles rewarded Captain Jeffreys's zeal with a substantial share of the fines levied on the dissenters and on their organizers, veterans of the Cromwellian army.[60] Once more, and not for the last time, Herbert Jeffreys found power and profit by repressing those who resisted royal government.

---

59. S.P. 44/35A, 10b–11a, 11b–12; Dalton, ed., *English Army Lists*, I, 35, 111. See also n. 60 below.

60. Jeffreys to Frescheville, Aug. 1, 1670, Frescheville to Arlington, Aug. 30, 1670, R. Hodshon to Frescheville, Aug. 29, 1670, *Cal. S.P. Dom., 1670*, 361, 401, 402; warrants granting fines to Jeffreys, Feb. 28, July 26, 1671, *ibid., 1671*, 108, 397. Hamilton, *Grenadier Guards*, I, 150, insists that Jeffreys acted without the magistrates' authorization.

King Louis XIV, the City of London, and the Old Dominion

By October 1672 York was pacified. Captain Jeffreys, and the three companies of Guards he commanded in York, were ordered to attend King Charles. A month later, however, Jeffreys's own company (and presumably their captain) sailed for France, where they rejoined the army of Louis XIV as the cadre of its Royal English Regiment. Jeffreys's company served throughout the third Dutch war in King Louis's army, Europe's premier military machine, once more commanded by Marshal Turenne. It was this army's Royal English Regiment, together with that of Sir John Lanier (governor of Jersey) and the Irish corps led by Colonel Thomas Dongan (until he was reassigned as the duke's governor of New York), that fueled the English opposition's fears that the duke of York would force "popery and the French interest amongst us." "The Duke," his enemies noted, "has been a principall cause of both" by "his constant indeavour to have had an army of English and Irish alwaies in France," quartered within easy march of the Channel coast and ready for instant recall to England. There, his enemies anticipated, the French-trained soldiers would apply the duke's axiom "that there was no way of governing the Parliament but as Cromwell did governe them," with an army.[61]

Jeffreys and his company returned from the French service to guard duty in London in December 1674, and again had to quell English civil disturbances. In August 1675 they and three other companies of the Guards marched against rioting weavers, and Jeffreys arrested the London militia officers who had refused to keep the peace. The powerful, and for some years to come, inseparable mixture of political loyalty and professional discipline—on which Jeffreys and the Guards acted when they suppressed the weavers—was reiterated during the summer of 1676 by their arrest of Cromwellian ex-officers for plotting against the crown.[62]

Their royalism and regularity meant that Guards officers also saw to the discipline of the royal army. In September 1676, for example, Herbert Jeffreys and John Mutlow sat on a court-martial

---

61. Hamilton, *Grenadier Guards*, I, 173–174; Winston S. Churchill, *Marlborough: His Life and Times*, 6 vols. (New York, 1933–1938), I, 99–112; MacKinnon, *Coldstream Guards*, I, 146–147. Jeffreys's company does not appear on the list of those drawn out for the French service (Add. MSS 5752, 204, printed in MacKinnon, *ibid.*, II, 266–267). On the coercive potential of these forces, see Danby's "Memorandums about the Duke of York, etc." (c. Sept. 1679), in Browning, *Danby*, II, esp. 91–92, also I, 256, II, 64.

62. Disposition or quarters of his majesty's forces, 1674, *Cal. S.P. Dom., 1673–1675*, 491; *ibid., 1675–1676*, 250–263; S.R 11/13, 100–101.

as the senior captains of the First and Coldstream Guards, respectively. Acting under the army's articles of war (written by the duke of York), they cashiered an officer who dared disobey the duke of York's deputy governor of Portsmouth. Jeffreys and Mutlow expected their fellow officers to give what they themselves offered: unquestioning obedience to the commands of the king's officers and governors. The personal allegiance and professional expectations of these Guards captains were bounded and shaped by the person and program of James Stuart.[63]

It was the duke who directed the royal reaction to the news that filtered into the imperial capital during the summer of 1676. By September there could be no more doubt: royal government in Virginia had fallen prey to a long-fermented rebellion. On the duke's advice, the king immediately commissioned Jeffreys as lieutenant governor of Virginia and colonel of a Guards-based battalion. Helping this devoted royalist and Yorkist officer to lead the punitive expedition to Virginia were officers representative of the Cromwellian era of armed order. John Mutlow of the Coldstream Guards (Albemarle's old regiment) was named as Colonel Jeffreys's second in command. Captain John Tongue, the earl of Carlisle's muster master, took leave from the earl's service and from the Coldstreamers to become Colonel Jeffreys's chief of staff as quartermaster and provost marshal of the battalion. Senior company grade and noncommissioned officers were drafted from the First and Coldstream Guards, the duke of York's (Admiral's) Regiment, and the Holland Regiment, as were substantial cadres of privates, fully equipped. Other instruments of royal rule, the garrisons of Portsmouth, Plymouth, Hull, Gravesend, Rochester, Landguard Fort, the Tower of London, and Windsor Castle, also sent soldiers to join Jeffreys's command.[64]

63. "Lt. Wm. Morris to . . . the Court Martial," [Sept. 1676], sentence of the court-martial, Sept. 28, 1676, *Cal. S.P. Dom., 1676–1677*, 341, 342.

64. Hamilton, *Grenadier Guards*, I, 197–200, 201–202; MS All Souls, 233; Dalton, ed., *English Army Lists*, I, 186; S.P. 44/29, 166, 167, 169, 173–184, 188, 189; MacKinnon, *Coldstream Guards*, I, 155–156, 159, II, appendix 55, p. 271; commissions to officers of five foot companies for Virginia, Oct. 4–8, 1676, establishment for officers and soldiers sent to Virginia, Oct. 7, 1676, the king to the lords of the admiralty, Oct. 13, to Carlisle and Morpeth, Nov. 7, 1676, *Cal. S.P. Dom., 1676–1677*, 354, 358, 369, 407; *Cal. S.P. Col., 1675–1676*, nos. 1051, 1053–1064, 1074, 1076, 1077, 1080, 1083, 1088–1092, 1104, 1105, 1110–1114, 1117–1119, 1121, 1122, 1130–1132, 1134, 1136, 1139, 1140. See also S. S. Webb, "Household of James Stuart," *Perspectives in American History*, VIII (1974), 68 n. 17, 69 nn. 18, 19, and the Appendix below.

Together, "the Guards and Garrisons" extended across the Atlantic the martial methods of the English executive's garrison government. Garrison government—Colonel and Governor Herbert Jeffreys and his battalion of guardsmen and garrison soldiers, instructed by the duke and by the king—would convert the Old Dominion into a province of empire.

Militant Monarchy: The Arming of the English Executive, 1569–1678

On January 20, 1569/70, the army of the rebel earls fell before the royal harquebusiers of General Lord Hunsdon at the fords of the River Gelt. Garrison government was triumphant in England. On June 30, 1677, the Indian kings of Virginia knelt before the Guards battalion of Colonel Herbert Jeffreys at the Middle Plantation (observed by the equally disciplined and more obviously sullen oligarchs of the Green Spring faction). Garrison government was established in England's overseas empire.

In the century that separated the battle beneath the ruined Roman Wall from the ceremony at the midpoint of the old peninsula stockade, every provincial capital, major seaport, and royal colony, in Britain, Ireland, and America, was affected by the transformation of the medieval military captaincies into modern governorships. Captains became governors as they acquired civil duties. Military governors became responsible to the national executive for provincial peacekeeping as well as for defense. Both civil and military officers, these governors-general were the proconsuls of the first English empire. As such, they laid the monarchical and military foundations of the American political system.

Prerogative politics, "the court working with the mob," rather than outright force, was the usual means by which the English executive imposed its authority on the provinces. Sir George Carey's long political effort to expand the captaincy of Carisbrooke Castle into a governor-generalcy of the Isle of Wight was more typical of the methods that extended Tudor sovereignty into the localities

---

Each part of the *Governors-General* concludes with a "Coda." As the late Sir C. Hubert H. Parry, bt., remarked (Eric Blom, ed., *Grove's Dictionary of Music and Musicians*, 5th ed. [New York, 1954], II, 362), "It is reasonable when all the variations are over to add a passage of sufficient importance to represent the conclusion of the whole set instead of one of the separate component parts." Its materials are those of the Part preceding, and so are not documented anew in the Coda. If the author follows a great example and "occasionally . . . goes so far as to introduce a new feature into the coda," it is nonetheless constructed out of material from the preceding Part, to which the reader is referred.

than was the slaughter of the northern earls' feudal levy by Carey's father, Lord Hunsdon, the first "governor" of Berwick. It did not normally require combat to convince the traditional elites of the futility of overt resistance to the armed state. The presence, sometimes the mere threat, of royal garrisons acting as political police sufficed as the makeweight of paramilitary power. Using it, the governors-general rallied local resources to sustain themselves and to support the national policies they represented in England's provinces.

The military and political dimensions of the Tudors' authoritarian administrative achievement became apparent by contrast with the weak leadership of the early Stuarts. As Sir Ferdinando Gorges found at Plymouth, monarchy's armed force and martial law could not control or direct either town oligarchy or country aristocracy without centralized direction. National will was political morality in monarchy: only respected leadership could excuse physical coercion; only public purpose could justify prerogative power. Whenever monarchy lacked popular ends at home or abroad, the inescapable association of the royal prerogative with military force seemed tyrannical, especially in contrast with local elites' adherence to custom and consent, tradition and legislation.

Tyranny was defined by public opinion, which focused on urban centers and seaports. Towns were the arenas in which the combat of provincial autonomy and central authority was decided. Where opinion, population, wealth, and government came together, there struggled central authority with local, court with country. Both parties realized that control of provincial capitals, ports, and towns dictated the allegiance of England's dependencies and that the loyalty of the provinces, first of those in the British Isles and then of overseas possessions as well, would influence, if not determine, England's own crises of authority. Executive authority was identified with empire. So much was implied by the country opponent of Governor Carey— "if he would needs be a governor, then he should go into the West Indies"—and made plain by the imperial ambition of Captain Gorges, *soi-disant* governor-general of New England. Empire elevated the English executive, potentially before 1654 and actually afterward.

The unity of imperial, Anglo-American politics was reinforced, and the imperial future of England's dependencies determined, by the outcome of the civil wars. The nation would be supreme over the provinces. The same forces, even the same men, determined the triumph of the English state in Scotland as in

Barbados, in Ireland as in Jamaica, in Yorkshire as in Virginia. Everywhere in the empire, the agents of English supremacy were the military governors. As the pressures of the civil wars heightened urban, garrison, and provincial governments' distinctiveness and lent them an executive and military tone, so these conflicts also redefined the relationship of national executive to local oligarchy in terms of governor and council. Civil war also clarified the relationships of rulers to ruled in terms of protection and obedience, defense and taxation, social organization and economic production. The exigencies of civil strife worked alike on royalist and parliamentary military governors. Colonel Hutchinson acted for the parliament in Nottingham. Colonel Apsley commanded for the king in Barnstaple. In both cases the need to channel the men, money, and matériel of the localities to the military and political purposes of a central sovereignty gave institutional shape and ideological definition to the power struggles of the executives with the elites, of the state with the regions. It also imparted a peculiarly "popular" cast to prerogative politics.

"In a constitutional government the fighting-men have the supreme power, and those who possess arms are the citizens." So Aristotle wrote. So the governors-general believed. As a class, they were devoted to the interests and the organization of the armed freemen. That "military virtue is found in the masses" was especially apparent and important in the civil wars (as it was in colonization). A local military commander such as General Massey of Gloucester (and, by nomination, of Jamaica) recruited and commanded armed citizens, "and their voluntary submission was a witness to his moderation."

The moderation of such military executives resulted from their recognition of the limits and the exceptionality of force in politics. The statist symbolism and the physical potential of military force, rather than its actual exercise, were the usual props of a governor-general's political authority. Yet, as outright force determined the civil wars, underlay the Protectorate, and restored the monarchy, so it was the foundation of the imperial ethos and effort that coerced the royalist colonies of Barbados and Virginia, conquered Spanish Jamaica, and reduced all of them to royalist regularity during the Restoration:

And for the last effect
Still keep thy Sword erect:

Besides the force it has to fright
The Spirits of the shady Night,
The same *Arts* that did *gain*
A *Pow'r* must it *maintain*.

The maintenance of authority by the sword, and the related arts of imperial administration, appeared in the English executive's conquest, colonization, and garrison government of Ireland. Resort to force was frequent where the governed were not considered citizens or subjects but rather "natives" or "rebels." Exploitation was intensified in those places where even elites had but limited access to law or legislature. Force and tribute together increased and institutionalized the imperial authority of the English executive in this overseas dominion. The paramilitary political patterns inscribed on Ireland's government by its viceroys—James, duke of Ormond, chief among them—were carried by their subordinates to every overseas colony and to Scotland as well.

The English conquerors and governors of Scotland recognized the illegitimacy of force as the regular rather than the last resort of government. Besides, they could not raise the resources for wholly military rule, because they could not overexploit an agricultural society. Thus they admitted the prudential and administrative necessity of the consent, or at least of the passivity, of the political classes. The English military governors of Scotland anticipated that these constraints would limit their overseas administrations. Lord Broghill thus advised Cromwell not to order Colonel Brayne to impress Scots to people the Jamaica conquest. Rather, the colonel should be authorized to promise free land and political liberties to settlers. Of course, Brayne should also take out a garrison of English regular troops from Scotland and Ireland not only to protect the planters but also to discipline a labor force of convicts, prisoners of war, and indentured servants. These recommendations produced the Protector's orders, under which Brayne and his garrison settled and socialized Jamaica.

A colleague of Brayne and Broghill in the English empire's military government of Scotland, Charles Howard (the earl of Carlisle), sought to balance the imperial constitution between protection and obedience, consultation and compulsion, during his Jamaica administration. Like Brayne, he made political as well as military use of every one of the weapons of garrison government developed in England, applied in Ireland, and reforged in Scotland. These governors-general used the institution of the militia to subordinate the oligarchs who were its officers and to discipline their dependents, the militiamen, as well as to police the province and to defend it. The militia's place of arms, the provincial citadel, became a public works project and the seat of authority. Besides social discipline, physical protection, and public works, all functions of the militia, Brayne and Howard promoted provincial free trade (unhampered by London-merchant-inspired laws), low duties, and naval development. These objectives, practiced in British garrison government, seemed to Brayne and Howard appropriate also in Jamaica to encourage small farmers in their political obedience, food production, and military service, and to discourage oligarchs' political autonomy, economic engrossment, and international pacifism. Such methods had an added imperial merit: they increased the power and the profits of the governors-general.

Their social bias in Scotland and their territorial focus on Jamaica during the Protectorate became controversial when officers such as Carlisle capitalized on their Cromwellian apprenticeships in the garrison governments of the later Stuart empire. Former Cromwellians lacked sympathy for the individualism of cavaliers like Lord Culpeper and for the royalism of Yorkists like Colonel Jeffreys. Besides, these royalists were concerned with an American continental domain, whereas such former Cromwellian proconsuls as Carlisle retained the Cromwellian concentration on the West Indies. Each of these three governors-general also represented a different class of military administrator: grandee, courtier, and professional.

Charles Howard, earl of Carlisle, was a grandee, deriving his offices, titles, and authority immediately from the state. In his origins, the master of Naworth was, by regional as well as by familial ties, an essentially feudal figure. Howard was caught up as a youth by the competing sovereignties of the civil war before he could realize his feudal and familial heritage, however, and his physical survival, as well as his rising social status, became irretrievably associated with state power—military, fiscal, diplomatic, and political. He rose through the wars to become a Cromwellian governor, general, and lord, an agent of the aggressive state. To secure commissions, salaries, and honors from the government for himself and his dependents, Carlisle had to administer national policies. When their paramilitary extremes offended his sensibilities, class or constitutional, he modified these statist assertions,

whether in administering the major generalcy of England's northern counties or the governor-generalcy of Jamaica. Yet Carlisle
commonly accepted and usually applied these nationalist, centralizing, executive measures. Their product was the reduction of
local autonomy and the assimilation of the ruling classes to the
service of the state. Regulated corporations, reduced judicial independence, purged local offices, and limited liberties for the subject left Carlisle freer to concentrate provincial power—military,
naval, and fiscal—in himself as a governor-general. As such, however, he acted for national army, admiralty, and treasury bureaucracies, and so he was increasingly subject to them. Reduced local
self-government and increased national authority made more effective the exchange of protection for obedience. This exchange
justified England's empire, both within the British Isles and overseas, for it promised that imperial government would foster social
stability and enhance physical security. As a mediator of state-
defined stability and security, the earl of Carlisle was a grandee, an
agent of central authority at once "arbitrary" and "popular." He
personified the impact of the armed state on the traditional society.

The courtier Thomas Culpeper, baron of Thoresway, equaled
Carlisle's influence on the society and constitution of the colonies,
if not on those of England and Scotland. Culpeper's advance from
the captaincy of the Isle of Wight to its governorship reflected the
Stuart monarchy's reluctant resort to the paramilitary politics of
the civil wars and Interregnum, as well as the Stuarts' resumption
of the Tudors' administrative methods and jurisdictions. As the
island's governor, Culpeper conveyed the royal demands for an
increase in local revenue to finance further protection (and make
possible further coercion), an essentially imperial demand that finally produced the American Revolution. In monarchy's domestic
progress, however, Lord Culpeper was only a dull tool, unwilling
and inept. His lasting contribution to empire was made in colonial
counsels and councils. Here too Culpeper was a courtier: he served
himself and his king; he did not willingly strengthen the state's
executive, the crown. He used the government he disliked for personal gain. Greed combined with indiscipline to create Culpeper's
contests with the developing bureaucracies of the colonial office,
the treasury, and the armed forces.

Contrast Carlisle's symbiotic relationship with the state with
Culpeper's self-seeking methods. Both the grandee and the courtier were political moderates, but Carlisle's temperance was inspired by the imperatives of class and region, whereas Culpeper's
was in large part produced by petty pecuniary desires and by

laziness. Selfishness and narrowness led Culpeper to public robbery and duplicity. These reprehensible means promoted praise-
worthy ends: a colonial constitution so well balanced between
consultation and coercion, between local legislature and imperial
executive, that it gave structure to a century of provincial growth
and imperial development. There is little evidence that Culpeper
saw beyond his private means to these public ends. He salvaged
some of the provincial legislature's privileges because they enabled
the assembly to grant him cash gifts, not because he held any
principled respect for provincial representation. Yet Culpeper did
preserve the Virginia assembly. He lied to this legislature about the
intentions of the English executive because he wanted to ensure
that the legislature would levy the taxes Culpeper collected for
himself, not to conceal a crown policy he thought unwise or to
win a royal revenue. But these levy laws did support later, more
public-minded governors-general. It is ironic that the courtier Lord
Culpeper, for the most selfish of reasons, did more to produce the
lasting constitutional compromise between imperial authority and
local self-government than did the more statesmanlike grandee,
the earl of Carlisle.

The two aristocratic types of governors-general, the grandee
and the courtier, included members of the gentry segment of the
ruling class as well as the nobility. Lord Culpeper's courtier counterpart was his cousin Sir William Berkeley of Virginia. The earl
of Carlisle shared with Sir Thomas Modyford of Jamaica the patronage of that greatest of grandees, General George Monck, the
duke of Albemarle. That both Modyford and Berkeley were removed from office for defying imperial orders to make peace
lends their careers a somewhat deceptive similarity. Both were
victims of the crown's campaign against colonial autonomy and
so against gubernatorial independence. Each of these executives,
however, embodied a very different administrative era. Berkeley
boasted an antique provincialism and royalism, a pre–civil war
pose. Modyford manifested a modern imperialism and statism, a
Cromwellian concept. The courtier, Berkeley, stumbled over his
incomprehension of the monarchy's transformation from the personal rule of the king to the systematic absolutism of the crown.
The grandee, Modyford, suffered because he clung to Cromwellian
aggression after Albemarle, its surviving spokesman, had died and
after Arlington, its severest critic, had enthroned a mercantilist
policy. Modyford was merely out of step in the countermarch of
mercantile and imperial forces. Berkeley, as his protest against
mercantile acts in 1662 and his resistance to imperial orders in 1677

made clear, could not accept either of the competing ideologies of the postwar empire.

Although Modyford, the son of a merchant, had only recently joined Berkeley, the scion of an ancient house, in the rank of gentleman, their status, like that of the nobles Culpeper and Carlisle, made them, made courtiers and grandees alike, part of the traditional governing elite. Colonel Herbert Jeffreys, however, represented the new class of career administrators and professional soldiers, state-made and self-made men. Lacking the social qualifications for command, officers such as Jeffreys defined their public posture by their professional experience. As a Guards officer and as a servant of the duke of York, Jeffreys embodied the military and absolutist underpinnings of garrison government and imperial ideology.

The patron of Jeffreys and of empire—James, duke of York—was distinguished by administrative genius and political malevolence. James's characteristics were so crucial to Anglo-American history that they demand separate study. They are briefly noticed here, however, both because they finally felled Lord Culpeper and because the social openness that was part of James's political absolutism created a career for Colonel Jeffreys in Oxford, in France and Flanders, York and Virginia. So James elevated Jeffreys to command with the mechanisms that he repeatedly used to substitute professional administrators for noble viceroys. Ultimately, James's most accomplished officer, John Churchill (afterward the first duke of Marlborough) projected James Stuart's principles of officer-administration to effect the empire that James had designed.

As James Stuart's servant and as John Churchill's superior in the Guards, Herbert Jeffreys obeyed the one and anticipated the other when he defined and implemented the military aspects of prerogative politics in England and elsewhere in the empire. Jeffreys learned to look to the king as commander-in-chief and to view the crown as a combination of executive agents. He learned how to direct the royal Guards against provincial autonomy, against oligarchical independence, and against the anarchy threatened by a wide variety of more humble and more numerous dissenters from royal authority, political, religious, and economic. During their nine years at York, Jeffreys and the Guards policed a city and a province, disciplined their oligarchy, and ordered their peoples in the interest of the national executive. In so doing, they practiced the paramilitary politics they afterward applied in Virginia, elements of which were copied first in Jamaica and subsequently in other parts of the empire. Military administrators such as Colonel

Jeffreys built court parties from the most ambitious, efficient, militant, and professional elements of provincial societies, just as they themselves had been plucked from families of the middling sort by social disorder, raised by war to the notice of ministers of state, and promoted by the prince to command, in the king's name, the garrison governments of the English empire.

Shared experience of English garrison government thus linked the imperial administrations of such varied types as Jeffreys, Carlisle, and Culpeper. These men first applied to English metropolitan and provincial governments the principles of military administration laid down in such texts as Governor Elton's *Compleat body of the Art Military*. The governors-general then implemented these principles of garrison government—and the statist ideology implicit in them—in the wider and still socially unformed world of England's American colonies. They thus expressed a classic imperialism, territorially expansive and governmentally direct. They tried to make every county and parish of the empire subordinate to the monarchical executive of the metropolitan state and, in the major royal colonies, they succeeded.

Each of the governors-general thus imposed imperial atop mercantile colonial practices. Mercantilism, the exploitation of staple-producing colonies by the merchant class of the mother country, fostered colonial self-government in exchange for metropolitan control of colonial commerce. Shaftesbureans, mercantile politicians, traded American colonial autonomy for English commercial monopoly. Mercantile practices underlay oligarchical authority both in the provinces and in the metropolis. Imperial officers and institutions supported military monarchy in the realm as they did in the dominions.

To command its provinces overseas and to rally their resources to support monarchy at home, the English executive relied on the officer corps of its army, the agents of its rule throughout the British Isles. To overlay mercantile exchange with imperial authority, to add paramilitary politics to commercial connection, the English executive enlisted not traders but soldiers. Officers—biddable, statist "commissioners" possessed of broad social vision and yet linked to the military and monarchical chain of command —were preferred to merchants—exploitative, individualist, privatist civilians. Like the crown, colonial courtiers (and many ordinary colonists as well) wanted military men, not merchants, to command. Leeward Islanders wrote of the "known Loyalty, Courage, and fidelity, Mixt with military prudence," of their governor-general, Colonel Sir William Stapleton, and they praised his "Vigor and Conduct." The colonies "under his Command being at the least disgust at home [in Europe] little less than Garrisons," the colonists insisted that military merit was "requisite for a Chiefe Commander." The merchant rumored to be their next governor would endanger "the Safety of his Majesties honor, Interest and our Estates by his want of Experience in time of Warr, and in times of peace make [us] miserable by his Interest in Trade."

Whatever their economic interests, Governors-General Carlisle, Culpeper, and Jeffreys all were veterans of garrison government, the paramilitary practices of which were especially functional in socially immature and turbulent frontier societies, colonies in a world of warring empires. These officers thus met social as well as military needs when they carried the centralizing and militarizing aspects of garrison government from the British Isles to England's oddly assorted, hitherto autonomous, colonial settlements and trading stations. By 1681 garrison government had converted the leading colonies into provinces of empire. It tied them to the English executive by a centralized political system, the chain of command, shackled onto the royal colonies and ultimately maintained by force.

Before they led their garrison companies to the command of colonies, military executives often acquired ministerial experience and political exposure by association with the burgeoning imperial bureaucracy. Culpeper and Carlisle, for example, were deeply involved in the debate over the colonial constitution carried on first in the Shaftesbury council and then in the privy council's committee for the plantations. The issue in debate was not a small one. Would colonial governments, and the societies they at once reflected and shaped, be oligarchical, mercantile, and whig, in a word, councilliar? Or would the American provinces be monarchical, imperial, and tory, in a word, executive? Of course, this debate was a subset of the larger contest over the English polity. Therefore, the course of English politics from 1674 to 1678 shaped Carlisle's commission for Jamaica and Culpeper's for Virginia while it defined English political partisanship in the now familiar terms of "whig" and "tory." To this political definition the empire overseas made a notable, but hitherto unnoticed, contribution. Disciplined by English force and governed by English officials, the provinces of empire necessarily took a direct part in English politics by their material and constitutional contributions to both the emerging parties.

The political and military links prescribed by garrison government became the bonds of the first British empire far more effectively and pervasively than those descriptions of commerce called the acts of trade. From being mercantile colonies, nominally regulated by parliamentary acts passed during periods of executive recession, the English dominions became imperial provinces, governed by military executives (the commander-in-chief and his governors-general), their councils (privy and provincial), and a growing class of state servants (bureaucrats and patent officers). Charter and proprietary colonies remained largely outside of this system of direct and directed rule, though affected by it. Their numbers were reduced, however, decade by decade, under the imperial urge early expressed by Sir Ferdinando Gorges. The provincial norm became monarchical, militarized, imperial government. Through garrison government the governors-general consolidated an extensive, externalized, commercial connection and moved toward an intensive, probing, empire in depth. The chief agents of empire were the governors-general. By the hundreds they laid the foundations of the first British empire, and of the American political system derived from it.

PART II Lord of Jamaica:
The English Executive
in the West Indies,
1654–1681

Carolus II.^{dus} D.G. Ang: Sco. Fra : et Hib: Rex
Fidei Defensor. &c.

W.Wissing pinx   J.Vandervaart fec   E.Cooper exc
Cum Privilegio Regis

Charles II. William Wissing's portrait of the king, engraved in mezzotint by John Vandervaart, is from the collection of the author. It is described in John Challoner Smith, *British Mezzotinto Portraits*, III (London, 1880), 1404.

CHAPTER 4

Design for Empire:
Jamaica and the Protectorate

Imperial Conquest and Political Controversy

The conquest and colonization of Jamaica—"the vastest expence and greatest design that was ever made by the English"—was a by-blow. An amphibious force mismanaged by General Robert Venables, whose pen proved mightier in excuse than had his pike in war, and by Admiral William Penn, who served his own greed more readily than his country's good, was bloodily defeated before Santo Domingo. Casting about for easier prey, Penn and Venables turned from the rich capital of well-developed Hispaniola in May 1655 to attack the little Spanish farming communities scattered about the Jamaica savannas. The English invaders outnumbered the Spanish troops on Jamaica twenty-six to one. Naturally, the Spaniards ran away, all the faster because they thought the English force twice as strong as it actually was.[1]

The island was undefended and undeveloped, but possession of Jamaica nonetheless enabled Venables to meet Cromwell's command to conquer, garrison, and govern by martial law an island colony in the Greater Antilles as a base for raids on the American trade and territory of the Spaniards. As a provisioning place—"most fertile in every description of provisions and cattle and tobacco"—and by location, this acquisition was ideally suited for American aggression. The island, the defeated Spanish governor acknowledged, was exactly "what the enemy wants," for it lay short distances upwind of Spain's most valuable territories and

1. "The History and State of Jamaica under the Lord Vaughan with the Alterations of Government that have happened since the appointment of the Earl of Carlisle," Phillips MS 11009, 16, West India Reference Library, Institute of Jamaica, Kingston; Firth, ed., *Narrative of Venables*, 34–35. The Spanish garrison numbered about 300, and the population about 8,000, according to Gov. Don Juan Ramirez's letter to the king of Spain, Jamaica, May 24, 1655, Frank Cundall and Joseph L. Pietersz, [eds.,] *Jamaica under the Spaniards, Abstracted from the Archives of Seville* [by Irene A. Wright] (Kingston, Jamaica, 1919), 52–53. Ramirez estimated the English invasion force at 15,000 men from more than 100 vessels. The English put ashore perhaps 7,000 men from about 38 ships.

athwart their sea routes to Europe. The minimum estimate of the conquest was that of the first English commander of Jamaica, General Venables: "We effected what we were sent about; the fixing of a Colony, tho' we failed in the place."[2]

The "fixing of a Colony" was the distinctive and imperial element in Cromwell's "Western Design." The concept of a permanently settled society as the foundation for military aggression and territorial conquest in the New World distinguished the Protector's project from the hit-and-run raids of the Elizabethans, with which it has so often been equated in its hatred of Spain and of Catholicism. It was the prospect of physical conquest as well as economic gain, the lure of world power and imperial prestige, that led the conqueror of the British Isles to send an army to America "for getting Ground and gaining upon the Dominions and territories" of Spain there.[3]

In such an imperial outpost, the necessarily martial character of garrison government would challenge the essentially civilian ideals of traditional society even more profoundly than it had in the British Isles. Yet, to survive, the settlement needed farms. Farmers naturally demanded a title to the land they worked; so a landed interest appeared. Plantation surpluses conjured up commerce, commerce meant merchants who sought civil courts to pursue their debtors, and merchants added their voices to the demand of the landed classes for civil government to protect their property from military requisition. Men of property sought po-

2. Council for the Indies to the king of Spain, Madrid, Apr. 12, 1658, in Irene A. Wright, "The Spanish Resistance to the English Occupation of Jamaica, 1655–1660," RHS, *Trans.*, 4th Ser., XIII (1930), 139 n. 2–140; "Instructions to Genl. Robert Venables given by His Highness by Advice of his Council . . . ," Add. MSS 11410, 41–45, British Lib.; Firth, ed., *Narrative of Venables*, 47; Arthur P. Watts, *Une Histoire des colonies anglaises aux Antilles (de 1649 à 1660)* (Paris, 1924), 464–469; "History and State of Jamaica under the Lord Vaughan," Phillips MS 11009, 9; Edward Winslow to Thurloe, Mar. 16, 1654, Venables to Thurloe, June 13, 1655, Birch, ed., *Thurloe S.P.*, III, 254, 545.

3. Arthur Percival Newton, *The European Nations in the West Indies, 1493–1688* (London, 1933), 213, equates the Elizabethan and Cromwellian designs. In much less qualified form, so does Gardiner, *Commonwealth and Protectorate*, II, 473–474. See also the statements of C. H. Haring, *The Buccaneers in the West Indies in the XVII Century* (London, 1910), 89, and Richard S. Dunn, *Sugar and Slaves: The Rise of the Planter Class in the English West Indies, 1624–1713* (Chapel Hill, N.C., 1972), 152. Cromwell's imperial intent is apparent in his orders to Venables (see n. 2 above) and in his commission to the commissioners for the expedition, Dec. 9, 1654, in Watts, *Colonies anglaises*, 462–466. His intention was, in its aggressiveness and territorial design, the essence of imperialism; it appears, additionally, *ibid.*, 261, 463. On the background of this intent, see Newton, *European Nations*, esp. 179–180, and 204ff, esp. 210, 214, 223. See also *Cal. S.P. Col., 1675–1676, Addenda, 1574–1674*, nos. 229, 230, 231, 232, which summarize the Protector's reaction to the conquest. See also Granville Penn, *Memorials of the Professional Life and Times of Sir William Penn*, 2 vols. (London, 1833), II, 136–137. Contrast Andrews, *Colonial Period of American History*, III, 5.

litical privilege, legal protection, and social influence in return for the enormous capital investment required to produce a permanent plantation society. Each of these civilian concomitants of settlement undercut military discipline. From the first, observers of the conquered colony noted the incompatibility of private property and public necessity, of independence and obedience. They anticipated the clash of civil rights with military law and the conflict between representative government and the chain of command.[4]

General George Monck and other military imperialists saw Jamaica as a self-provisioning station ship, anchored in enemy waters to shelter and feed England's armed forces for an unceasing war on the commonwealth's West Indian rivals, Spain especially. The dreadnought *Jamaica*, its dependencies, and the warships they serviced were not just

> Ships, but rather Arks of War,
> And beaked Promontories sail'd from far;
> Of floting Islands a new Hatched Nest;
> A Fleet of Worlds, of other Worlds in quest;
> An hideous shole of wood-Leviathans,
> Arm'd with three Tire of brazen Hurricans.[5]

In this view, which was Cromwell's own, all other English possessions were resources on which the English executive could draw to strengthen Jamaica. As the Cromwellian planners posed their imperial equation: "If war must be applied to there [in Jamaica]," the Protectorate was "to collect many assistances from the Severall Colonies; which must here after be brought to understand, that they are to be looked upon as united, and embodied, and that their head and Centre is here."[6]

Scotland and England were not exempt from imperial requi-

4. "Several Considerations to be humbly represented to his Highness the Lord Protector and Council in behalf of the Army in America," July 18, 1655, in Firth, ed., *Narrative of Venables*, 63–65; Birch, ed., *Thurloe S.P.*, III, 497–498, 661; "Proclamation of the Protector relative to Jamaica," *ibid.*, III, 753; "A Journal kept by Coll. William Beeston from his first coming to Jamaica," Add. MSS 12430, 23. See also n. 5 below.

5. Andrew Marvell, "The First Anniversary of the Government under O.C.," lines 357–362; "The Grounds of the undertakinge the Designe of Attemptinge the Kinge of Spaine in the West Indies," from Edward Montagu's notes on the debates in the Protector's council concerning the last Indian expedition, Apr. 20, 1654, in C. H. Firth, ed., *The Clarke Papers: Selections from the Papers of William Clarke . . .*, Vol. III, Publications of the Camden Society, N.S., LXI (London, 1899), 205 (appendix B).

6. Orders of the council of state, Oct. 17, 1655, Feb. 13, July 8, Dec. 16, 1656, Sept. 29, 1657, petition to the council of state, Mar. 25, 1656, *Cal. S.P. Col., 1574–1660*, 431, 437, 444, 452–453, 459, 437–438; Cromwell's proclamation, Mar. 25, 1656, in Frank Cundall, *The Governors of Jamaica in the Seventeenth Century* (London, 1936), xxxii–xxxiii.

sition. Together, they could contribute ten thousand malcontents to man this island expression of a united empire. Transportation would bleed Britain "of the burdens[ome] there by this expedition of the West Indies." Land grants and tax relief would lure experienced planters to Jamaica from Barbados cane lots and Virginia tobacco fields, where they had produced profits for the Dutch. In Jamaica they would apply their skills for the benefit of the "whole commonwealth." Other, godly colonists, called from "poor, cold New England," would lend moral strength and military manpower to the tropical outwork of the war with Antichrist. Although few of them settled in Jamaica, the farmers and sailors of New England did supply the food that kept its garrison alive. Coordinating transportation, migration, and trade for war and conquest, the imperialists hoped to establish a uniform government over the outposts of England's empire. Naturally, such an imperial government would be constructed and administered largely by the Cromwellian army officers who had conquered, united, and now governed the British Isles.[7]

Empire was opposed by London merchants. Alderman Martin Noell and his protégé, Thomas Povey, argued for the merchants that the proposed war with Spain in the West Indies would be self-defeating. The produce of the Spanish colonies was already England's, they said. Englishmen resident in Spain conducted that country's American commerce via Spanish puppets. War would ruin this profitable arrangement. The hated Dutch—"How fit a Title clothes their *Governours*, / Themselves the *Hogs* as all their Subjects *Bores!*"—would seize Spanish trade from English merchants if England were at war with Spain. These mercantilists, however, were diverted from their opposition to the Protector's "Grand Design" by the argument that Spain was too weak to take action in Europe against an attack in the West Indies.[8]

Prospective profits silenced the commercialists' remaining objections to the design. Noell was one of the commissioners

7. See the "Instructions unto Generall Robert Venables . . . upon his expedition to the West Indies": "You have Hereby powre with the advise of the said Commissioners . . . to place Garrisons in any such Places as shall be taken in, and to appoint fit Governors thereof, and to give them Commissions under your hand and seale accordingly, And to slight the said Garrisons, and remove the said Governors . . . " (Firth, ed., *Narrative of Venables*, 114). See also n. 6 above and Maj. Gen. Sedgewick's commission for New Netherlands, Nova Scotia, and Newfoundland. See also *Cal. S.P. Col., 1574–1660*, 9, 424, 426, and *ibid., 1675– 1676, Addenda, 1574–1674*, nos. 202iii, 205–208, 210.

8. Montagu's notes, in Firth, ed., *Clarke Papers*, III, 205, 208. On the contradictions in mercantile opinion, see Andrews, *Colonial Period of American History*, III, 5, 11–12, 30 n. 2. See also Add. MSS 11410, 67a; Firth, ed., *Narrative of Venables*, 10, 109–115.

named to organize the Jamaica expedition, and he had himself and
Povey appointed as the army's provisioning agents. They compounded inefficiency by theft. The food they supplied was both
scantily measured and rotten, and the weapons they procured
were short-counted and outdated. One sample of many: "Instead
of fifteen hundred arms, which Mr. Noel, the Protector's agent,
was directed to ship, they received but one hundred and ninety;
and these for the most part unserviceable." The expedition was
crippled even before it sailed by the profit taking of the Protectorate's war contractors.

These supposedly pacifist merchant-statesmen were prepared
to profit from the spoils of war as well as from spoiled provisions.
Thomas Povey had his brother Richard commissioned as army
commissary. Thomas told him to trade food to the soldiers, whom
Povey had not provisioned, in return for the Spanish plunder of
which he disapproved on principle. Venables's wife contrasted
Povey's and Noell's piety with their greed. They "pretended the
honour of God, and the propagating of the Gospel," she wrote,
"But alas! their intention was self-honour and riches—and so the
design prospered according to their hypocrisy."[9]

They first opposed and then mismanaged the West Indian
expedition, but the merchants argued for the retention of its
conquest nonetheless. They saw Jamaica not as a raider's resort or
as the imperial base for further American conquests, but as an
entrepôt for peaceful trade with the Spanish. The commercialists
were uninterested in the imperial scheme of small farms cultivated
by free, white soldier-settlers, which would feed the armed forces
protecting the island and supply the manpower to extend the English empire. Instead, they promoted large, highly capitalized
plantations tilled by servile labor. These would produce cash crops
—sugar, tobacco, cocoa, and dyewood—to provide freight for
English merchant ships and constitute factorage for the London
merchants and their agents, the island traders. Where militarists
envisioned a warship *Jamaica*, commercialists saw a merchant's
storeship, anchored in peaceful seas, supplying a growing commerce with the Spanish Main. The merchantman *Jamaica*, argued
the commercialists, should be governed by English civil law, aug-

9. For complaints of Noell's cheating in the supply of arms, see the letter sent to Lord
President Lawrence and others of the council of state, Feb. 28 [20?], 1655, in Firth, ed., *Narrative of Venables*, 8; also Penn, *Memorials of William Penn*, 120. See also the Povey-Noell correspondence in Add. MSS 11410, 6–8; Venables to Noell, June 13, to Rowe, June 14, 1655,
in Firth, ed., *Narrative of Venables*, 49–50; "Some Account of General Robert Venables . . .
with . . . the Diary of His Widow Elizabeth . . . ," Chetham Society, *Miscellany*, IV (1871),
28.

mented by the ordinances of an assembly of wealthy trader-planters. The law of England, the law of property rights, and local law as well, must be administered by civilian courts and judges, men of substance. Merchants, if not suitable as governors, ought at least to be the executive's powerful councillors. Merchants agreed with soldiers that uniform government must be imposed on all of England's colonies and centralized in London. But the merchants saw themselves, not the military, as dominant in commercial and colonial, not territorial and imperial, counsels. In their efforts to have colonial trade restricted to themselves, the merchants stressed the lawmaking role of the parliament and rejected the ordinances of the executive.[10]

The acts of trade and navigation were the parliamentary products of this vision, but the English commercialists wanted more direct colonial leverage as well. Their favorite agents of centralization were neither planters nor governors but patent officials appointed in London. Both planters and governors had too large a stake in a given colony's landed, local prosperity to accept English merchants' commercial, metropolitan exploitation. But with patent officials, preferably members of merchant families (the Poveys, for example), in provincial power to thwart the economic localism of planters and governors, the colonies could be fully exploited by English merchants. From these economic appendages of England, Spanish settlements also could be milked. These mercantile objectives were attainable, however, only if civil law ruled and property was thereby made sacred. Government by the propertied and for the propertied must prevail in a peaceable, oligarchical colonial system. Such was the commercialist belief in 1660, and such became the whig dogma in the following decade.[11]

There was not in the seventeenth century—and there would never be—a single English "colonial policy." Each politically influential group or "interest" had its own ideas of how most thoroughly to exploit England's overseas possessions. In time, this convenient equation of personal advantage with national good produced distinct ideologies. The imperial ethos was executive oriented. Contemporaries labeled it "court" at first, and then

10. Thomas Povey, "Register of Letters Relating to the West Indies, 1655–1661" ("Propositions concerning the West Indian Council"), "An Essay . . . for the Regulation of HH's affairs in the West Indies," Add. MSS 11411, 3, 11–12. See especially the classic mercantilist argument, "The State of the Difference . . . between the Merchants and the Planters . . . ," *ibid.*, 3–5.

11. See the correspondence of Noell and Povey with Gov. Searle, *ibid.*, 41b–53.

"tory." It asserted state authority and was regulatory, military, and expansionist in character. It was countered by a "country" credo, afterward called "whig," that was legislative and mercantile, aristocratic and oligarchical, commercial and individualistic, in effect, anti-military and anti-expansionist.

The imperial ideology had a head start in Jamaica. In the seven years that elapsed between the conquest of Jamaica and the establishment of a civil government there, the imperial precepts of the conquerors were indelibly printed on the social fabric of the colony. These precepts summarized England's garrison government experience. Their application was retarded, however, by the mercantile corruption and military disorganization of the 1654 expedition and its subsequent reinforcements. This sequence of disasters demonstrated that the central government of the empire was as yet too immature institutionally to govern effectively overseas. Left largely to their own devices, England's soldiers paid a price in lives that both indicted their superiors at home and dreadfully demonstrated the geographical, psychological, biological, and institutional obstacles to the centralized and militarized empire envisioned by imperial-minded soldiers.

Planting Garrison Government in Jamaica

Massey's Men

Three imperial criteria determined the selection of the commanders for the expedition of 1654: military rank, colonial experience, and political exposure. The first and last were marked attributes of General Edward Massey, the military governor of Gloucester. Massey had commanded several of the officers chosen for the West Indian expedition. Just as his experience in garrison government qualified him for the governor-generalship of Jamaica offered to him in 1661, so his English garrison subordinates received lesser colonial commands. General James Heane, a major of cavalry under Massey in 1645, was governor of Weymouth in 1647. He "died with his sword sheathed in his enemies bowels, not six men standing by him," in the rout at Santo Domingo in 1655. Captain Gregory Butler served as Massey's aide in the West Country until Massey's army was disbanded. Then Butler went out to Barbados, where his combined experience in the army and in America secured him an appointment as one of the advisory commissioners to the 1654 expedition. As long as General Heane lived, Butler loyally supported his former West Country commander. But Butler's drunken behavior at St. Christopher (he fell off a stationary horse in front of the assembled island militia) and on the Jamaica executive commission earned him universal contempt. Even his fellow commissioner, the charitable former governor of Plymouth, Edward Winslow, could say no more of Butler than, "We all persuade ourselves he is very honest; but hope, yea persuade ourselves he will take with the better side in case of differences of judgement." Winslow's own death after the repulse at Hispaniola removed the last restraint from Butler's meddlesome exaggeration of the interservice, political, and personal rivalries of the expedition's leaders.[12]

Yet Butler's intrigues among the elements of a badly divided command were not altogether destructive. For one thing, they aligned him with Colonel Anthony Buller, yet another veteran of General Massey's staff and a former governor of the Scilly Islands. At the end of 1655, Colonel Buller, with Butler's support, persuaded the other officers of the expedition to quarter their regiments on the Jamaica plantations captured from the Spanish. Buller proposed both to deny the growing crops to the enemy and, more important, to form the basis of an English military colony.[13]

From Ireland to Jamaica: Robert Venables and Plantation Policy

Such proposals for military colonization would become commonplace in the American colonies as the influence of officer-governors grew and as they acquired the garrisons they hoped for.

12. On Massey, see chapter 1 above and the citations therein. Firth sketches Heane's career in his introduction to *Narrative of Venables*, xviii. Heane's death is described in Henry Whistler's Journal of the West India Expedition, *ibid.*, 158 (appendix E), and by Francis Barrington, an officer with the expedition, in a letter of July 14, 1655, Historical Manuscripts Commission, *Seventh Report of the Royal Commission on Historical Manuscripts* (London, 1879), Part I, Report and Appendix, 573. Butler's drunkenness was notorious: see Firth, ed., *Narrative of Venables*, 50, 60–61, also 60 n. 1. Butler's support of Heane is recorded in Venables to Lord Fleetwood, Oct. 26, 1655, *ibid.*, 80. Winslow's evaluation of Butler is in his letter to Thurloe, Mar. 16, 1654, Birch, ed., *Thurloe S.P.*, III, 249–251. For Winslow's other services to the Protectorate, see order of the council of state [notations], Dec. 2, 1654, *Cal. S.P. Col., 1574–1660*, 419; for the influence of his "alwaies irresistible" counsel, see Birch, ed., *Thurloe S.P.*, III, 505. On the evils of the divided expedition command, see J. Daniell's letter of June 3, 1655, *ibid.*, 507–508. Butler subsequently sought the governorship of Tortuga, the great buccaneer refuge (order of the council of state, Sept. 26, 1659, *Cal. S.P. Col., 1574–1660*, 477).

13. On Buller, see Firth's introduction to and appendix D of *Narrative of Venables*,

Indeed, the imperial example of Rome had taken flesh already in Elizabeth's and in Cromwell's Irish military "plantations." General Robert Venables had come fresh from commanding England's military conquest and colonial settlement of northern Ireland to lead elements of Cromwell's "army into America for securing and increasing the interests of this Commonwealth in those parts, and for opposing, weakening, and destroying that of the Spaniards."[14]

Venables's adventurous military career stretched back to the beginning of the civil wars. Of an ancient Cheshire family, Venables had sold land to raise troops for the parliamentary cause. He was captured at the battle of Westhoughton in 1642, appeared prominently at the siege of his shire town, and was commissioned governor of the neighboring town of Tarvin in 1645. He left his neighborhood to share in the parliamentarians' conquest of Wales in 1646. Crossing to Ireland in 1649, he became commander-in-chief of all Ulster. In person, he successively governed Belfast, Antrim, and Lisnegarvy. In 1654 he returned to England as the delegate of the army of occupation's council of war, which sought Cromwell's confirmation of their plantations in the conquered kingdom.[15]

Head of a powerful, propertied army corps, Venables was a threat to the Protector: he "was popular in Ireland, had too much Interest there." So he "was sent to be destroy'd not to do Service" in the West Indies. Like General Massey's parliamentarian officers, General Venables was a victim of Cromwell's plan to "rid himself of some persons he could neither securely employ nor safely discard: which end seemed chiefly to influence the managery of the whole business" of the Western Design. Having deliberately manned his expedition with malcontents, the Protector's surprise and anger at the harmful lack of "union of hearts and councils" among the expeditionary leaders seems the height of hypocrisy.[16]

xix–xx, 138; Birch, ed., *Thurloe S.P.*, II, 352; Gardiner, *Commonwealth and Protectorate*, II, 437. The date of this decision is not clear; Agnes M. Whitson, *The Constitutional Development of Jamaica, 1660–1729* (Manchester, 1929), 4, gives it as July.

14. Webb, "Army and Empire," *WMQ*, 3d Ser., XXXIV (1977), 5 n. 6; note 2 above.

15. On Venables's career to 1654, see "Some Account of General Robert Venables," Chetham Soc., *Misc.*, IV (1871), 2–8, 27; Venables to the lord lieutenant of Ireland, Nury, Sept. 22, 1649, *Letters [by Oliver Cromwell and R.V.] from Ireland* . . . (London, 1649); Venables's apology, in George Wilson Bridges, *The Annals of Jamaica*, 2 vols. (London, 1827–1828), I, 393–394.

16. On the politics of Cromwell's appointments, see Venables's own estimation of this threat to the Protector in Firth, ed., *Narrative of Venables*, 88, and especially the document printed in the "Memoir of Colonel Robert Venables," prefaced to Venables's *The Experienced Angler* (London, 1827 [orig. publ. London, 1662]), iii. See also Bridges, *Jamaica Annals*, I, 397 (where tense is silently altered), and Cromwell's protest, Oct. 10, 1655, *Cal. S.P. Col., 1675–1676, Addenda, 1574–1674*, no. 230.

Ireland had taught Venables what Cromwell's machinations, the resulting jealousies among the expeditionary officers, and their failure at Hispaniola all confirmed: the necessity of unity of command. Venables imposed it in Jamaica. He used precedents from his Irish experience to oppose the division of command personified by Cromwell's commissioners. They were, he said, "so many spies" who were set on his actions and on each other. As one field officer with the most intimate Cromwellian connections admitted:

We have in many things acted against common reason, nay, our grandees [the Commissioners] have been [so] slow to action that (altho' stirred up by the coll.) they would not command such business to be done which apparently would have been of great advantage to the army; one thing worse we used, the council ordering anything to be done (which amongst us stands for a law) yet the general, contrary to that council, hath acted as his own will led him; we that are soldiers account this the height of arbitrary power.[17]

Venables's conception of a unified and military executive authority was reiterated during the Spaniards' formal surrender of Jamaica. He demanded that the Spanish commissioners for negotiating the capitulation be "military officers in active service, or the governor, or the maestre de campo [colonel]." He assured them that "if the governor would come in, he should be received and treated with the honors of captain general, and presently return to his tent." When the Spanish governor acceded to General Venables's demand, the sixty-six companies of the English army were drawn up, each beneath its particular color, to do the Spanish executive the military honors that English soldiers considered a governor-general's due. Less politely, the terms the conquerors of Jamaica imposed in 1655 were an exact, military vengeance, being just those that the Spaniards had forced on the puritan English garrison of Providence Island in 1641: terms whose only concession was that the defeated military officers might retain their swords and insignia of rank.[18]

17. Francis Barrington, whose brother was lord of Cromwell's bedchamber and an intimate of the Protector's family, made the assessment from Jamaica in an important letter of July 14, 1655; HMC, *Seventh Report*, Pt. I, 571–575, esp. 573. See also Bridges, *Jamaica Annals*, I, 397, and [Edward Long], *The History of Jamaica. Or, General survey of the antient and modern state of that Island . . .* , 3 vols. (London, 1774), I, 223. Venables's opposition to the commissioners' direction was widely supported by the army, especially after the commissioners checked the soldiers' plundering, for the soldiers "were wont to have Pillage when they took any place by storm in England. . . . Many of them declared that they would never strike stroke more where should be Commissioners to controul the Soldiers" (Firth, ed., *Narrative of Venables*, 17–18).

18. Julian de Castilla, "The English Conquest of Jamaica: An Account of What Hap-

Besides the concepts of unitary command of the armed forces for the conquerors and unconditional surrender of the land by the conquered, General Venables also looked to his experiences with the English army in Ireland for men and for social patterns. Veteran troops from that army of occupation were Venables's prerequisite for attempting further conquests from Spain. His "army" for the Western Design was made up of draftees cast off from the most sluggardly units in England, broken men swept up from London streets, failed farmers from the Leeward Islands, and runaway servants from Barbados. Venables's men had behaved so badly before the walls of Santo Domingo that their general was convinced that they were too cowardly for further service against the Spaniards. The Irish experience, however, suggested a use for broken soldiers. Venables put them to making "plantations" in Jamaica on the same model he had used in Ulster. As the general explained, "If they must not be the men to carry on this design in the field, it may be, they may in the country by planting."[19]

When he ordered a thousand soldiers to cultivate the Spanish plantations, General Venables laid the basis of a new society. Settlement and cultivation now replaced fighting as the primary concern of Venables's council of war. After the Spanish hamlets were occupied, "the army was devided by regiments into severall quarters of the habitable parts of the countrey to plant garrisons." Each garrison was commanded by a field officer, a rank that now acquired added meaning. For the army, it was plant or starve: naval officers refused to send them any more of the scanty provisions stored in their ships. Settlement immobilized the survivors of the army that Cromwell intended for the conquest of the Spanish Main. Venables's argument that planting would create a permanent English presence in the Indies made a virtue of necessity, but the general was justified by events: "A Colony, the work I was sent about, was effected."[20]

---

pened in the Island of Jamaica, from May 20 of the Year 1655 . . . Up to July 3 of the Year 1656," trans. and ed. Irene A. Wright, *Camden Miscellany*, XIII [Camden Society Publications, 3d Ser., XXXIV] (1924), 7, 9, 12; Watts, *Colonies anglaises*, 203–209; Newton, *European Nations*, 190–192.

19. "Memoir," in Venables, *Experienced Angler*, iii–iv; Barrington to [?], July 14, 1655, HMC, *Seventh Report*, Pt. I, 571–572; Bridges, *Jamaica Annals*, I, 385; Venables to Thurloe, June 13, 1655, Barrington to Disbrowe, July 14, 1655, Penn's account of his voyage, Sept. 12, 1655, Sedgewick to the Protector, Nov. 5, 1655, Birch, ed., *Thurloe S.P.*, III, 545, 646, IV, 30, 151–152.

20. Firth, ed., *Narrative of Venables*, 40, 47, 61, 102, 103, 138, 140, 142; "Narrative of the Expedition to San Domingo," in Firth, ed., *Clarke Papers*, III, 59–60; Barrington to [?], July 14, 1655, HMC, *Seventh Report*, Pt. I, 574, Castilla, "English Conquest," trans. and ed. Wright, *Camden Misc.*, XIII (1924), 14n–15; "Oliver P., Commission to Gen. Venables,"

To protect the colony's naval lifeline to England, Venables began to fortify the island's best harbor, Cagway (or, as it became known after 1660, Port Royal). The metropolitan task, common to garrison governments, utterly exhausted him, as it did so many later governors-general. Venables gladly accepted the recommendation of the council of war that he go home to report the needs of the military colony to Cromwell. Before he could depart, however, the general fell into fevered delirium. At the end of June 1655, the unconscious Venables was carried from the island. He recovered at sea, only to be thrown into the Tower on his arrival in London for being absent without leave from his command. Cromwell did not release Venables until he agreed to resign both his command as "General of the English forces sent into America" and also his regimental, governor's, and general's commissions in Ireland. Thus the Protector's Western Design had not only won a colony in the Indies but also secured him a province in Ireland and eliminated a political menace in England—or so he thought. Venables, however, lived to seize Chester for King Charles II in August 1659. The king's captain general, George Monck, commissioned Venables governor of Chester in the spring of 1660. Dismissed for religious nonconformity, Venables fell under suspicion of involvement in the Farnley Wood plot of 1664. This too Venables survived, but barely. He concluded that "the minds of anglers being usually more calm and composed than many others" (especially those of generals and politicians), fishing was the key to an untroubled retirement. He lived until 1687, recording the sensible preferences of the perch for quiet streams and gaining renown as "the experienced angler" with generations that had forgotten his imperial conquest.[21]

General Venables's last act as commander of England's West Indian outpost had been to summon the council of war. There his officers summarized their units' efforts at colonization, planned further plantations, and projected expansion from the Jamaica base. The army council called on the Protector for clothing, tools, and provisions for the island garrison. The officers also asked for

---

Dec. 4, 1654, in Watts, *Colonies anglaises*, 464–466. Venables might "grant commissions to all such commanders, officers and governors of the said army, forces and garrisons; as shall be thought necessary for the command and government of the same." The association of governors with garrisons, territorial control, and the local representation of central authority appears also in Venables's instructions; see especially no. 6, *ibid.*, 468–469.

21. Birch, ed., *Thurloe S.P.*, III, 523, 581–582; Firth, ed., *Narrative of Venables*, 62–63, also 4–5, 32, 40, 45, 47, 56, 67–70; Penn, *Memorials of William Penn*, II, 72–73, 101, 108, 120–123, 127; "Memoir," in Venables, *Experienced Angler*, iv–v, xvii–xviii, xx–xxii; Bar-

laborers from Scotland to be sent to them as servants, in lieu of their arrears of pay. Besides these means to further cultivation, the officers asked Cromwell to confirm their ownership of the regimental plantations, arguing that these would create surplus crops to feed additional attacks on Spain's empire. The military council also asked the Protectorate to guarantee London financial credits for development of the island. They admitted that merchant capitalists would require a political quid pro quo, "a Civil and setled Government" for the colony. The rule of law in the garrison government might be either "such Constitutions and Laws as his Highness shall think fit," or such laws as the Protector authorized the senior officers of the garrison to make. More important to these officers than law, whether made in England or locally, was that Cromwell should commission a single commander and invest him with admiralty authority as well as martial law jurisdiction. The military council also insisted that their proposed governor-general be backed by "a Considerable supply of well disciplin'd, approv'd, and Experienc'd Soldiers, such as have been accustom'd to hardship in Ireland or elsewhere."[22]

Puritan Planters: Fortescue, Holdip, and Sedgewick

Awaiting Cromwell's decision on Jamaica's development was the island's new commander-in-chief, Major General Richard Fortescue. Formerly a colonel of the New Model army and active in the garrison governments and wars of the West, Fortescue had been another of Edward Massey's devoted subordinates. Like his commander, Fortescue supported parliament against the army in 1647. Then, with many other like-minded officers, he was assigned to the Western Design, perhaps as much to remove him from the Protector's path to military dictatorship as to help expand England's empire. In any case, Fortescue was determined to settle Jamaica and so to ensure its permanent possession by En-

rington to [?], July 14, 1655, HMC, *Seventh Report*, Pt. I, 571; Bridges, *Jamaica Annals*, I, 394–395, 396, 402. On Venables's later career, see the "Memoir." Note both Isaac Walton's estimation of *The Experienced Angler*—"the epitome of *Angling*"—and the testimony of its numerous editions—1662, 1668, 1676, 1683, 1825, 1827. See also Watts, "Penn et Venables en Angleterre," in *Colonies anglaises*, 242–248, also 195–196; Penn, *Memorials of William Penn*, II, 136, 140–142; Firth, ed., *Narrative of Venables*, 73ff. On Venables's royalist plotting, see also Underdown, *Royalist Conspiracy*, 308–309. Penn likewise retired to Ireland from the Tower, becoming governor of Kinsale in 1661 and fleet captain to the duke of York in the Dutch war

22. Firth, ed., *Narrative of Venables*, 63–65. Bridges, *Jamaica Annals*, I, 402–404, gives a truncated version.

glishmen. He asked that the Protectorate acknowledge the island's present strategic importance and its commercial potential. Yet Jamaica's prime attraction for General Fortescue was the opportunity it presented him to do God's work in the world. His writings glow with the fusion of religious enthusiasm and national ambition that propelled so many puritans to colonial accomplishment. "We have," the general wrote from Jamaica, "encountered and waded through many hardships and difficulties, but all's nothinge so as we may be instrumental to propagate the gospell. . . . Doubtless God is doinge a greate and strange work. Who would not be forward to have a hand in it? . . . What a desirable and joyful thing would it be, to see many godly men flock and flow in hither. . . . Here they may serve God, their country and themselves."[23]

Fortescue served God, country, and self by investing his own energy and capital and the labor of his regiment in two large plantations. Chief among the officers who supported Fortescue's plantation program was Colonel Richard Holdip. Formerly governor of Surinam, Holdip became one of the expeditionary commissioners and a regimental colonel, commanding the planters recruited on St. Christopher. Whatever their liabilities as soldiers, Holdip's former farmers and escaped servants were effective pioneers. Under the military discipline of this officer with tropical command experience, they rapidly made Colonel Holdip's plantation the best in Jamaica.

For one week following Fortescue's death in October 1655, the commissioners imposed Holdip on the army as president of the council of war and thus as Jamaica's commander-in-chief. The other officers reacted quickly and decisively. They declared themselves to be "the council for the management of the affairs of his highness and the commonwealth in the West Indies." As such, they accused Holdip of embezzling the pay due his troops. They court-martialed their nominal commander, found him guilty, stripped him of military rank, and deported him from Jamaica. Then they broke up Holdip's regiment, taking his land and soldier-planters for themselves. Of course, Holdip's flourishing plantation at Liguanea fell apart; this had been a major object of his degradation and exile. Many of the soldier-adventurers wanted the settlement program to fail, for its success would tie them to pestilential Jamaica. Other officers considered Colonel Holdip "a very ill

---

23. Fortescue to Taylor, Jamaica, July 15, 1656, Birch, ed., *Thurloe S.P.*, III, 651. See also Firth's sketch of Fortescue in his introduction to *Narrative of Venables*, xviii–xix.

member to this army," because he had supported the absolutism of General Venables and because they feared that his administration of Jamaica would confirm his reputation as the tyrant of Surinam. Bored soldiers, idealistic republicans, and conservative believers in councilliar government thus combined to oust Holdip, and they lobbied through London friends against any orders to return him to command in Jamaica.[24]

Holdip was replaced as one of the expeditionary commissioners, and as the chief sponsor of settlement in Jamaica, by Major General Robert Sedgewick. A passenger in the Winthrop fleet of 1630, Sedgewick had settled in Massachusetts as a Charlestown merchant. His martial past, however, was recognized by his appointment as captain of the Boston Artillery Company, commander of Castle Island, and, in 1652, major general of Massachusetts Bay. Cromwell then recruited Major Sedgewick for an attack on the Dutch in New Netherland. Peace with the Dutch delayed this project until the crown took it up in 1664. Instead, Sedgewick captured French settlements in Nova Scotia and Newfoundland. His success there in July 1654 again suggests the imperial unities of the century, forecasting the later attacks by Sir William Phips and General Francis Nicholson. Sedgewick personally reported his success to Cromwell, who sent this veteran soldier-colonist out with a regiment of reinforcements to join "the Southern expedition."[25]

General Sedgewick looked for the expedition on Hispaniola. He found its remains on Jamaica, "in as sad, and deplorable and distracted a condition . . . as ever poor Englishmen were in, the commanders having left them, some sick, and some in indifferent health; the soldiers many dead, their carcasses lying unburied in

24. "An Instrument made at the Council of Jamaica," Oct. 8, 1655, Sedgewick to Cromwell, Nov. 5, 1655, Searle to Cromwell, Nov. 7, 1655, Brayne to Thurloe, Apr. 1657, Birch, ed., *Thurloe S.P.*, III, 71, IV, 151, 156–157, VI, 391. Brayne primed Martin Noell to oppose Holdip's return. See also Goodson to Thurloe, June 25, 1656, *ibid.*, IV, 151. For the probable location of Holdip's plantation, see S.A.G. Taylor, *The Western Design: An Account of Cromwell's Expedition to the Caribbean* (Kingston, Jamaica, 1965), 121. Holdip was succeeded as colonel by Samuel Barry, who, besides becoming a political leader of Jamaica after 1660, also became governor of Surinam, as Holdip had been. The next object of anti-settlement attack was Lt. Col. Henry Archbold, commander and chief planter at Liguanea both before and after 1660. Archbold was Edward D'Oyley's client, however, and the military chief saved his follower at the general court-martial (*ibid.*, 122–123). Taylor's study is distinguished by its clear treatment of local sites and by its effective use of Spanish sources transcribed by Irene A. Wright.

25. Sedgewick managed to capture a Dutch ship in New England waters (order of the council of state, July 19, 1655, *Cal. S.P. Col., 1574–1660*, 426–427). See also order of the council of state, May 9, 1655, *ibid.*, 424; W. Noel Sainsbury's preface, *ibid.*, 1661–1668, xxxiii; "Nova Scotia" in the Appendix below.

the highways, and among bushes. . . . [Those] that were alive, walked like ghosts or dead men, who, as I went through the town, lay groaning and cried out, bread for the Lord's sake."[26] General Fortescue himself died a few days after Sedgewick's arrival. The newcomer thought that the whole army would follow their commander to the grave. Bewildered and enervated on a strange, tropical island, humiliated and sick, the troops would not build shelters for the provisions that lay rotting on the beach, much less take thought for the morrow. "Dig or plant they neither can nor will," Sedgewick reported, "but do rather starve than work." Only his sense of duty, reinforced by fear for his neck if he abandoned his post without Cromwell's leave, drove Sedgewick to join the administration of Admiral Goodson, commander of the naval squadron, and Colonel Edward D'Oyley, the senior surviving army officer. The triumvirs presided over the deliberations of the council of war that took up the Jamaica command following Holdip's ouster in October 1655.[27]

As an experienced colonizer and former merchant, Major Sedgewick had three clear priorities for Jamaica. "There are two things principally enjoined by his highness to the army, fortification and planting." In addition, Sedgewick's commercial experience led him to oppose piracy, even against Spaniards. He thought it disgraceful "that your Highness fleet should follow this old trade of West-Indian cruisers and privateers, to ruin and plunder poor towns, and so leave them." But men joined the armed forces to escape the hoe and the plow. They delighted in privateering, its brutality and its promise of sudden wealth. Not only were the privates addicted to piracy, but the army officers also refused to take orders from Commissioner Sedgewick about privateering—or fortification, plantation, or anything else—and they claimed all the best land for themselves. Sedgewick felt that the authority of these grandees must be overthrown and that the land they claimed must be allocated to planters if the Jamaica garrison was to become a colony.[28]

Sedgewick set out to attract planters to Jamaica. In fact, he

26. Sedgewick to the Protector, Nov. 5, 1655, Birch, ed., *Thurloe S.P.*, IV, 151–152.

27. Goodson to Thurloe, Jan. 24, 1655, *ibid.*, 453; "Coll. Edward D'Oyley's Journal of his proceedings during the time he held the chief Command in the Island of Jamaica (19 Nov. 1655–27 May 1662)," Add. MSS 12423, 2–3; "An Instrument made at the Council of Jamaica," Oct. 8, 1655, Birch, ed., *Thurloe S.P.*, IV, 71. The author of the "History and Present State of Jamaica under the Lord Vaughan" (Phillips MS 11009, 13) states that D'Oyley actually commanded during the six months from Fortescue's death to Brayne's arrival.

28. Sedgewick to the Protector, Nov. 5, 1655, Birch, ed., *Thurloe S.P.*, IV, 152–155; Long, *Jamaica*, I, 254, 248–250.

had probably inspired Cromwell's scheme to populate the conquered island with New Englanders. The council of war, now presided over by Colonel D'Oyley, refused to permit the major to leave Jamaica to recruit settlers in person. Sedgewick therefore dispatched Captain Daniel Gookin to summon the godly from Massachusetts Bay. With Gookin, Sedgewick sent the Protector's proclamation promising settlers free transportation to the island and also land, livestock, and the rights of Englishmen. While Jamaica's reputation as a pesthole populated by turbulent soldiers and menaced by "skulking Negroes and Spaniards" deterred immigrants from New England, Sedgewick's widespread publication of the Protector's offer nonetheless brought sudden and substantial results. In March 1656 Governor Stokes of Nevis announced that most of that overcrowded island's people would follow him to Jamaica to dwell in Cromwell's promised land. Some fourteen hundred colonists made the journey with their governor. The Protector was so pleased with Sedgewick's work that he made him commander-in-chief of "the army in America." The recipient of this honor was less than happy about it. When he heard of his appointment, Sedgewick said "that he was undone . . . that much was expected, but little probability to have much done; so [he] fell sick, and in a few dayes died." He was buried twelve days after receiving his commission. Once again the government of Jamaica returned to the council of war, dominated by Colonel D'Oyley.[29]

Garrison Government, from Scotland to Jamaica: William Brayne

In January 1657, six months after Sedgewick's death, Major General William Brayne arrived to take command—not just of Jamaica, but of military matters in all America. Such was the reach of the imperial design Cromwell focused on Jamaica. A veteran of the Cromwellian conquest of Scotland, a protégé of Monck and Broghill, and governor of Inverlochy, Brayne had requisitioned men and money from Scotland for the Western Design for a year

29. On the army council's restraint of Sedgewick, see Add. MSS 12423, 3b. See also Stokes to Sedgewick, Mar. 12, 1656, Goodson to the Protector, Oct. 18, 1656, Birch, ed., *Thurloe S.P.*, IV, 500, 602; names of the committee for the business of Jamaica, Sept. 26, 1655, *Cal. S.P. Col., 1574–1660*, 430. For the Gookin mission, see Gookin to Thurloe, Boston, Jan. 24, 1655, May 1, Sept. 24, 1656, Birch, ed., *Thurloe S.P.*, IV, 449, V, 6–7, 146–148; order of the council of state, Sept. 26, 1655, *Cal. S.P. Col., 1574–1660*, 429–430; Watts, *Colonies anglaises*, 299–300, 341; Long, *Jamaica*, I, 258, 261–262. Cromwell's proclamation pointing out that "those who remove thither will be under the immediate protection of this State," Oct. 10, 1655, is in *Cal. S.P. Col., 1675–1676, Addenda, 1574–1674*, no. 229, and that

before he embarked twelve hundred picked troops with him for Jamaica.

More than two hundred of these veterans drowned on the coast of Ulster, victims of the first of the winter storms that wracked this, the major reinforcement of the Jamaica garrison, and watered down its influence on the island's future. The surviving vessels of Brayne's convoy were pounded by a second storm in the Bay of Biscay. The general's own ship suddenly blew out her mizzen and became unmanageable. To balance the ship, the crew cut away the spritsail. Without sails to check her roll, the ship threatened to capsize. To reduce tophamper, the sailors hacked off the main-topmast. To lower the center of gravity, they pushed the ship's boat overside and prepared to heave over the guns. The storm abated before the armament was jettisoned, but the crippled vessel made a slow passage and had to put into Barbados for water. Brayne took advantage of the stop to recruit experienced planters, over the protests of the Barbados establishment. Then the general sailed for Jamaica, hoping that the merchant ships with his troops aboard, which he had not seen since the storm broke, would somehow follow him. One by one, they straggled into the harbor at Cagway and dumped their shaken soldiers onto Jamaica's undeveloped shore.[30]

These veterans of Cromwell's military consolidation of the British Isles were the intended agents of empire abroad and the first respectable regiments committed to the Western Design. Many of their predecessors were miserable drafts from raw recruit regi-

---

of Mar. 1656, for Gookin's use, is reproduced in Cundall, *Governors of Jamaica*, opp. xxxii. The accession of some 1,500 settlers to Jamaica from Nevis, their settlement at Port Morant, and the immediate death of two-thirds of them, probably from malaria, is narrated by Cundall, *Historic Jamaica* (London, 1915), 237–242 (largely from Long, *Jamaica*, I, 261, 263–266), and by Taylor, *Western Design*, 115–119. On D'Oyley's succession, see Sedgewick to D'Oyley, May 12, 1656, Goodson to Thurloe, June 7, 1656, D'Oyley to the Protector, June 20, 1656, Birch, ed., *Thurloe S.P.*, V, 12–13, 96, IV, 138.

30. Brayne to the Protector, Jamaica, Jan. 9, 1657, the Protector to the chief commanders in America, June 17, 1656, Birch, ed., *Thurloe S.P.*, V, 770, IV, 103; order of the council of state, May 15, 1656, instructions for Brayne, June 5, 1656, *Cal. S.P. Col., 1574–1660*, 440–441, 442. Brayne was paid £1,000 cash to undertake the command, and his Scots troops also received their arrears (Birch, ed., *Thurloe S.P.*, VI, 424). His part in Scots recruitment is noted, *ibid.*, III, 497–498, and, more forcefully, in Cromwell's orders to the council of Scotland, *ibid.*, IV, 129–130. On the latter, see also chapter 2 above. Monck's organization of the expedition is recorded in his letters to Cromwell and to Thurloe, June 10, Aug. 5, 19, 26, Sept. 2, 9, 1656, *ibid.*, IV, 103, 277, 323, 348, 375, 396. The expedition embarked on Oct. 4, 1656 (*ibid.*, IV, 474). See also Brayne to Cromwell and to Thurloe, Dec. 1, 1656, to Cromwell, Jan. 9, 1657, *ibid.*, IV, 668, V, 770–771. Martin Noell arranged transportation for the expedition at £5 10s. per man for 1,200 men; see order of the council of state, May 22, 1656, *Cal. S.P. Col., 1574–1660*, 441. See also the "History and State of Jamaica under the Lord Vaughan," Phillips MS 11009, 14.

ments, the offscourings of London slums, driven by force into overcrowded transports where fever reduced whatever hardihood they might once have had. The quality of the colonial recruits was even worse. They were the refuse of the Caribbees, islands that were "the Dunghill wharone England doth cast forth its rubidg." Such colonials were "only bold to do mischief, not to be commanded as Souldiers, nor to be kept in any civil order." Both the Jamaicans' fighting spirit and their determination to survive grew dramatically with the infusion of Brayne's veterans into the garrison community. The general also allowed "all the troublesome and unusefull officers to goe for England." In the absence of those commanders who had opposed planting, "the soldiers go cheerfully to work." The surviving officers, particularly the picked leaders of Brayne's reinforcements and the staff built up by Colonel D'Oyley during his presidencies, became Jamaica's officer-planter elite.[31]

In addition to fresh leadership and raised morale, Brayne's expedition also brought out to Jamaica the material requisites of garrison survival: provisions, tools, and the Western Design's first serviceable weapons. Brayne applied all of these resources to promote planting. For example, he sent veteran companies from Ireland and Scotland to the new settlements at Port Morant as "a guard for the planters that came [from Nevis] with Colonel Stokes; for should they receive any baffle by the enemy, it would discourage others from adventuring hither on the like account." Brayne also laid out a fort and armed it with cannon to command the port and secure the settlement.[32]

An experienced garrison governor, General Brayne concerned himself with more than just military security for agricultural settlements. He also applied to the organization of an overseas empire other lessons learned in the English conquest of Britain. Noting the obstructionism of provincial elites in Ireland, Scotland, and Barbados, Brayne asked that an English receiver and auditor be assigned to each colony. English officials would ensure that local revenues were spent on fortifications, administration, and settlement. In particular, imperial officials could insist on the transfer of poor planters and time-expired servants from overpopulated

31. Firth, ed., *Narrative of Venables*, 30, 146; Brayne to Monck, Jan. 8, 1657, Firth, ed., *Clarke Papers*, III, 86. See also Monck to Thurloe, Aug. 5, 1656, Brayne to the Protector, Jan. 9, 1657, Birch, ed., *Thurloe S.P.*, IV, 277, V, 770.

32. Brayne to the Protector, Jan. 9, 1657, to Thurloe, Mar. 12, Apr., 1657, Birch, ed., *Thurloe S.P.*, V, 770, VI, 110, 391. The cost of Brayne's supplies was enormous. see orders of the council of state, May 15, 29, 1656, instructions for Brayne, June 5, 1656, *Cal. S.P. Col., 1574–1660*, 440–442.

older settlements to the Protectorate's own province, Jamaica. While advocating fiscal centralization, garrison government, and an imperial bureaucracy to forward self-supporting colonies of small farmers, Brayne further anticipated later governors-general by stressing the advantages of free trade to colonial development. He deplored mercantile exclusiveness as a self-defeating policy of international provocation and economic isolation.[33]

To carry out his imperial policies, General Brayne ended the divisions of command that had hampered Jamaican development. He ignored the commissioners, dismissed the council of war, and found in Admiral Goodson a naval commander who would co-operate with the army and fight the Spaniards, rather than the reverse. Brayne's good relations with the naval officers on his station had been the basis of his successful administration of iso-lated Inverlochy. It was equally essential to his Jamaica efforts, as the governor-general indicated when he made sole command of Jamaica's troops, naval forces, civil government, and trade the precondition of his further service in the colony. He warned Crom-well's secretary that "if the old way of commissioners be resolved on, I shall humbly beg, that I may have liberty to return for England; for in the small experience I have had, I find there will nothing be done but bandying of factions, and spending time in debates." Brayne got his way. His administration established the supremacy of the commander-in-chief, not just in Jamaica, but, by precedent, in all colonies administered by the English govern-ment. Brayne had secured for American governors-general all the powers accorded garrison governors in the British Isles. These powers were multiplied to a level approaching absolutism by the distance of his province from the imperial capital.[34]

General Brayne used his enhanced executive authority both to end the enervating factionalism of the Jamaica command and to surmount the stupendous bungling and corruption of the Protec-torate's West India design. More than five thousand lives and more than one million pounds sterling had been invested in Jamaica before Brayne brought the colony through its "starving time" to achieve his objectives: "plantation, fortification, annoying the enemy."[35]

33. On the garrison experience Brayne gained at Inverlochy, see chapter 1 above and Brayne to Thurloe, Jan. 10, 1657, Birch, ed., *Thurloe S.P.*, V, 778–779. See also Brayne to the Protector, Mar. 12, 1657, *ibid.*, VI, 110; Long, *Jamaica*, I, 265.

34. Brayne to Thurloe, Apr. 1657, Birch, ed., *Thurloe S.P.*, VI, 391; Egerton MSS 2395, 283.

35. On monetary investment in Jamaica, see T[homas] P[ovey] to "Edw. Doily, Gov-ernor of Jamaica," n.d., Add. MSS 11411, 87b–88. The human cost, certainly high, can only

Brayne's plans developed the Protector's commands. The officers of Jamaica's garrison were ordered to expand their own plantations, guard those of the growing number of civilians, and build warehouses for plantation produce. They were also to fortify a citadel at Cagway, from whose harbor English warships would sail "to strive with the Spaniards for the mastery of all these seas." Brayne centered a Jamaican metropolis on this citadel, a metropolis he designed as a colonial combination of his own military settlement at Inverlochy and the garrisoned market towns and seaports of England. Next to the fortress that terminated and guarded the Cagway peninsula, Brayne built his own "general's house," the army's warehouses, and the naval base. He protected the whole complex with a wall across the base of the peninsula and batteries of cannon to protect its shores, but Brayne left room for the growing number of civilian residences, shops, taverns, and warehouses. The result was the town renamed Port Royal in 1660. Once the inland agricultural settlements had been cultivated, the Cagway citadel built, and a commercial city founded, General Brayne could write to his patron, General Monck, that Jamaica had the requisites of garrison government. "The country is healthfull and fruitfull, as any in the Spanish quarters, situated in the eye of the Indies, haveing safe and defenceable harbours." Most im-

be estimated. Some 2,500 troops were enlisted in England for the expedition. Between 3,000 and 4,000 additional men were enrolled at Barbados. Perhaps 1,200 more came from the Leeward Islands. Taking into account the "sea regiment," the force that attacked Hispaniola totaled between 8,000 and 9,000 men. It lost at least 1,000 men there. Contemporary estimates of the number of men landed on Jamaica in May 1655 range from 6,551 to 7,000. Only about 2,700 of the original army were still alive the following February, about 2,531 in July. By September 1656 that number had fallen to 2,355. The lessening rate of mortality attests to the "seasoning" of the survivors. This led to the extraordinary importance that colonial planners attached to holding the survivors in Jamaica. But death was the dominant fact in Cromwellian Jamaica. "God is rending us in pieces," Brayne wrote. The clearest mortality records are the provision rolls appearing in Add. MSS 12423, fols. 7b–8b, 18, 23b. They were padded, however. See the commander-in-chief's proclamation, July 26, 1656, *ibid.*, fol. 117b. For the original numbers of the expedition, see also Firth's introduction to *Narrative of Venables*, xvii–xviii, xxiv–xxxii; Cundall, *Governors of Jamaica*, xxxiv, xl; and Winslow to Thurloe, Barbados, Mar. 30, 1655, Birch, ed., *Thurloe S.P.*, III, 325. In a letter to the king of Spain, Feb. 28, 1658, Don Pedro Zapata, the governor of Cartagena, estimated English losses to disease and war at between 6,000 and 8,000 men (Cundall and Pietersz, [eds.,] *Jamaica under the Spaniards*, 70, 71). A Spanish Jamaican, the lieutenant general, reported 2,500 English killed and 6,000 dead from disease in the period 1655–1657 (*ibid.*, 83). See also Long, *Jamaica*, I, 250n. Taylor, *Western Design*, 92, estimates the total loss at 5,000 men, which agrees with my calculations from the musters. Dunn moves beyond the military figures to repeat the estimate that "12,000 Englishmen came to Jamaica in the first six years, yet the population of the colony in 1661 was only 3,470" (*Sugar and Slaves*, 153). The brief account [census], [Dec. 1661], in *Cal. S.P. Col., 1661–1668*, no. 204, breaks this figure down into 2,956 white men, women, and children and 514 blacks, which makes the English loss even greater, but the degree to which the floating population of buccaneers was counted is not clear.

portant, "wee have heare about 5000 men well armed, and I hope well resolved."[36]

The soldiers' spirits starved with their bodies in the spring of 1657. In March, Brayne's troops took from the storehouses the last of the provisions he had brought from England. By mid-April the governor-general had to admit that "our present condition is sad, neither fleet nor land forces having any provisions." All the troops, except for plantation laborers, were dispersed to hunt in jungle and savanna for subsistence. Their discipline was ruined, but their hunger was unassuaged. Suddenly, unexpectedly, in the last days of April ships from England made port with supplies. The crisis had passed. The garrison would live until crops came in from the new plantations. But Brayne would not. Reporting the colony's reprieve, he asked for his own immediate recall. He felt "so great a decay by this climate both in my body and intellectuals, that I fear I shall scarce be so long capable to serve in this place." On the second of September 1657, Lieutenant General William Brayne died.[37]

Edward D'Oyley:
Founder, General, and Governor of Jamaica

Brayne left orders appointing "Colonel Edward D'Oyley commander in chief both by sea and land . . . in these parts of America, in as full and ample manner as I myself had the same."[38]

36. The Protector to Fortescue, n.d., to the chief commanders in America, June 17, 1656, Brayne to Thurloe, Apr. 1657, Birch, ed., *Thurloe S.P.*, IV, 633, 103, 391; chapter 1 above. The limits and necessity of protection were apparent in the location of Gov. Stokes's farmers from the Leewards. They settled at Port Morant, the easternmost point of the island, in part because the Spaniards had destroyed all (i.e., at least 16) of the English villages west of Brayne's headquarters at Villa la Vega; Ysassi (the Spanish governor of Jamaica) to Albuquerque, July 9, Aug. 29, 1657, Cundall and Pietersz, [eds.,] *Jamaica under the Spaniards*, 56, 60. Ysassi's objective was to force his English enemy "to retire to his forts and prevent him from doing any planting or benefiting from what planting he has already done." See *ibid.*, 60, 61, 62, 63. On the state of the island and of the fortifications at Cagway, see Brayne to Monck, Cagway, Jan. 8, 1657, Firth, ed., *Clarke Papers*, III, 86. The Spanish governor estimated the total English population at 4,000 in July 1657 (Cundall and Pietersz, [eds.,] *Jamaica under the Spaniards*, 55, 57). But in the same month his chief lieutenant reported 3,000 English infantry and 3,000 settlers. Allowing for 1,000 women and children, this estimate coincides with Brayne's report, as does the governor of Cartagena's statement of Feb. 28, 1658, that "the enemy's people now in the Island, including soldiers, negroes and women are from five to six thousand souls" (see n. 35 above).

37. Brayne to the Protector, Apr. 18, to Thurloe, Apr. 1657, D'Oyley to the Protector, Sept. 12, 1657, Birch, ed., *Thurloe S.P.*, VI, 110, 211–212, 236, 512; "History and State of Jamaica under the Lord Vaughan," Phillips MS 11009, 14.

38. Brayne to D'Oyley, Aug. 27, 1657, Birch, ed., *Thurloe S.P.*, VI, 483.

Thus, for the third time, D'Oyley was called to the Jamaica command. This time he governed the island for five years, guiding it toward the permanent plantation and sustained economic growth that converted the conquest into a colony. D'Oyley's defense of the island kept it English until the Restoration made it a royal colony and made the king of England "Lord of Jamaica."

D'Oyley had been born into a Wiltshire Puritan family in 1617. In an age when the most distant relationships of blood or marriage created worldly ties, that D'Oyley's mother was a Nicholas conferred on him a most useful relation to the future royal secretary of state, Sir Edward Nicholas. When the civil wars broke out, D'Oyley abandoned his professional education at the Inns of Court to join the parliamentary forces. 'Twas "time to leave the Books in dust, / And oyl th' unused Armour's rust." He returned to England from his command in Ireland when Cromwell became Protector. Shortly thereafter D'Oyley was sent to the West Indies as lieutenant colonel of General Venables's own regiment.[39]

On their arrival in the West Indies, Venables named his second in command colonel of the regiment raised in Barbados. Despite the notoriety of his "Barbarians" and the disasters that overtook the expedition, Colonel D'Oyley avoided all the labels of faction or ineptitude that contemporaries pasted onto most of his colleagues. He was courageous, a stern disciplinarian, impersonal and moderate in the army's factional disputes, cool and realistic in his command decisions. D'Oyley was self-contained. He was so discreet as to seem ungenerous. Taught the high price of principle during the civil wars, D'Oyley shared the political amorality of the wartime younger generation who survived to dominate the Restoration.

As the army squabbled and rotted in Jamaica, Colonel D'Oyley quickly became the only officer widely acceptable to the dominant "interests" in the Western Design: the impressed planters of the Caribbees, who found fresh farmsteads on D'Oyley's regimental plantation; the plantation-minded commissioners, who, like D'Oyley, saw settlement as the foundation of colonial society; the aggressive soldiers and sailors, who valued D'Oyley's military leadership and the base he provided for their attacks on the Spaniards; the London merchants, with whom D'Oyley had profitable

39. Cundall, *Governors of Jamaica*, 1–2; D'Oyley to Nicholas, Sept. 11, 1660, Mar. [?], 1661, *Cal. S.P. Col., 1574–1660*, 489, *ibid., 1661–1668*, no. 61; D'Oyley to the Protector, June 1656, Birch, ed., *Thurloe S.P.*, V, 138; Firth's introduction to *Narrative of Venables*, xxvii, also 116, 121; "A particular list of the names of the persons . . . under the command of General Venables," Dec. 1654, *Cal. S.P. Col., 1675–1676, Addenda, 1574–1674*, no. 212. The poetry is from Marvell's "Horatian Ode," lines 5–6.

relations; and the colonial counselors of the Protectorate, who were impressed with D'Oyley's successes, settlement especially. This last was largely the work of the West Indian planters who made up D'Oyley's own regiment. Their loyalty to their colonel was the military root of his political power, and their agricultural experience produced plantations for D'Oyley and themselves. As farmers, they were the basis of Jamaica's social and agricultural development; as soldiers, they helped D'Oyley to win the victories essential to English survival on Jamaica.[40]

The Formative Year, 1655–1656

D'Oyley's first term in command of Jamaica followed Penn's and Venables's departure in mid-July 1655. D'Oyley became one of the civil commissioners in October, and in November, president of the governing council of war. As commissioners Admiral Goodson and Major Sedgewick informed the Protector, "the command of the army naturally fell upon col. Doyley" by seniority. They insisted that he was "the most capable and best suited for the employ."[41]

D'Oyley's journal of proceedings "during the time he held the chief command in the Island of Jamaica (19 Nov. 1655–27 M[a]y 1662)," is a unique record of a colony's beginnings. It highlights the military strictures clamped on the government of this, institutionally the most significant conquest of the nascent empire. In the other Cromwellian colonial conquests of the Interregnum, the political power of the conquerors was limited by articles of surrender. In Barbados and Virginia these agreements preserved civil and representative government. In Virginia the articles of surrender explicitly erased all reference to the fact of conquest, so as to foreclose imposition of the absolute power of government that conquest legally conferred. Thus, only in Jamaica prior to Charles II's restoration, and only in Tangier and Jamaica immediately after it, was the new imperialism able to govern

40. The sources of this assessment are largely those for D'Oyley's administration, given below, but note in addition that he alone of the major officers escaped criticism in the accounts of the expedition printed by Firth. See D'Oyley's circumspect letter to the disgraced Gen. Venables, July 12, 1656, Firth, ed., *Narrative of Venables*, 28. His relations with Noell and Povey were of the best, as evidenced by his correspondence with the latter, n.d., Dec. 18, 1657, Mar. 28, 1658, n.d., also Thomas to Richard Povey, n.d., Add. MSS 11411, 21, 48, 61, 87b–88, 17a–18.

41. Sedgewick to the Protector, Nov. 5, 1655, Goodson and Sedgewick to the Protector, Jan. 24, 1656, Birch, ed., *Thurloe S.P.*, IV, 152–154, 455; "History and State of Jamaica under the Lord Vaughan," Phillips MS 11009, 13.

freely. Institutionally, Jamaica was tabula rasa. Colonel D'Oyley etched it deeply with the attitudes typical of military governors.[42]

In D'Oyley's second council meeting as president, he began to adopt the trappings of command. These were especially important in an age when appearances indicated rank and when force was the prerequisite of obedience. The council of war authorized Colonel D'Oyley to set a table at his headquarters. There he might entertain his subordinates, visitors of rank, and his followers. A life guard of cavalry was recruited to protect and dignify the president's person and to lend force to his commands. The impact of the horsemen was all the greater since they were the only mounted troops in a garrison that had been terrorized by Spanish lancers at Hispaniola and because the English army's own police were horsemen. The council also ordered stockaded houses built for the president and his guards. These headquarters buildings were located at the town of Villa la Vega, the former Spanish capital (later St. Jago), now surrounded by the quarters of three of the four garrison regiments. Here D'Oyley built an inland, agricultural capital and stronghold as an alternative to the citadel at the port of Cagway.[43]

At Villa la Vega the English commander-in-chief sketched out provincial headquarters on the familiar British model of the garrisoned town. Within a walled central square stood D'Oyley's fortified house and the barracks of his immediate guard. This, in addition to his mounted life guard, consisted of two companies of infantry (the usual English town garrison that in the Restoration

42. D'Oyley's "Journal," Add. MSS 12423. In the matter of the sovereign rights conferred on the English executive by conquest, the classic rule is that laid down by Sir Edward Coke in "Calvin's Case" in 1608 (T. B. Howell, comp., *Cobbett's Complete Collection of State Trials and Proceedings for High Treason . . .* , II [London, 1812], 639–640). This decision acknowledged that the prerogative had an unrestricted sway in conquered Christian countries such as Jamaica. Even without this precedent, all English authorities agreed that this was the case in Jamaica. The later cases are discussed in Whitson, *Constitutional Development of Jamaica*, esp. 13–17. For the cases of New York and of Jamaica under Lynch, and for colonies in general under the rule of conquest, see Webb, "Francis Nicholson," *WMQ*, 3d Ser., XXIII (1966), 522 and n. 14.

43. Orders of the Jamaica council of war, Nov. 20, 1655, Dec. 3, 1657, Add. MSS 12423, 2–2b, 42b. D'Oyley's citadel is detailed in Domingo Rodriquez de Vera to Albuquerque, July 24, 1657, Cundall and Pietersz, [eds.,] *Jamaica under the Spaniards*, 58. See the Spanish Map III of Cagwaya Harbour, reproduced *ibid.*, opp. 104. The subsequent Map IV shows a more developed fort on the point (Cagway or Port Royal). By 1675 governors again resided in Villa la Vega, according to Cundall, *Historic Jamaica*, 47–48. Cundall also shows (pp. 112, 115) that the two-residence system continued at least until 1693, as befit the government's double orientation toward planting and toward the endless war at sea. For the location and relation of these places to the island, see especially Edward Slaney's map of 1678 in the *Blathwayt Atlas*, John Carter Brown Library, Providence, R.I. (no. 36 in the facsimile edition edited by Jeannette C. Black [Providence, R.I., 1970]). See the map on p. 277.

became the standard military support for commanders-in-chief of Jamaica and for governors-general in Virginia, the Leeward Islands, New York, and New England as well). The companies were mustered nightly and drawn on for the town watch, main guard, and sentries usual in a garrison government. In addition, a troop of D'Oyley's cavalry rode out each night to patrol the adjacent countryside. The central square of D'Oyley's capital also contained a magazine of weapons, a storehouse, and a church, all designed to prop up social order.[44]

Thus protected, President D'Oyley endeavored to make his military colony permanent. He joined Admiral Goodson and Commissioner Sedgewick in issuing orders for construction of forts and storehouses, with the aims of stimulating settlement and trade and of protecting persons and goods. He issued land patents and provided tools with which to clear and cultivate the grants. His own troops did most of the planting. The sites they located, cleared, cultivated, and protected, determined seventeenth-century Jamaica settlement.[45]

Protection was the prerequisite of settlement. The Spaniards and their former slaves waged guerrilla war against the English invaders for five years. Twice the Spaniards put invading armies ashore on the north side of the island. Against all such perils President D'Oyley organized surprisingly effective defenses. No one who had witnessed the navy's bungled landings on Hispaniola or observed its ships rotting at anchor in Cagway harbor, or who had watched the English troops run at Hispaniola and die in their own filth in Jamaica, could have foreseen the efficiency of English naval scouting, the endurance and tenacity of the combat patrols D'Oyley sent inland, or the success of D'Oyley's own amphibious operations against Spanish invaders.[46]

As he won physical security, D'Oyley was able to establish

44. The arrangement of the guards, which, except for the cavalry patrol, was duplicated at Cagway, was reported to the Spanish governor on the basis of interrogations of prisoners from the garrison (Cundall and Pietersz, [eds.,] *Jamaica under the Spaniards*, 81). Compare the like arrangements of the garrison towns in England, discussed in Part I above.

45. D'Oyley's "Journal," Add. MSS 12423, 2b–3; D'Oyley to Thurloe, Mar. 12, 1656, Goodson and Sedgewick to the Protector, Mar. 12, 1656, Birch, ed., *Thurloe S.P.*, IV, 602–603, 601.

46. The chief Spanish source on the conquest and the first year of the resistance is Capt. Julian de Castilla's account of the period from May 20, 1655, to July 3, 1656, translated and edited by Irene A. Wright as "English Conquest of Jamaica," *Camden Misc.*, XIII (1924), esp. 10–11, 13, 18–19, 22n, 23–26. See also Barrington to [?], July 14, 1655, HMC, *Seventh Report*, Pt. I, 574–575, and Firth, ed., *Narrative of Venables*, 45–46. Wright, "Spanish Resistance," RHS, *Trans.*, 4th Ser., XIII (1930), 117–147, picks up the story where Castilla stopped and uses the materials published as Cundall and Pietersz, [eds.,] *Jamaica under the Spaniards*. On the Spanish resistance, see also n. 36 above.

forms of government and to impose them on the patterns of settlement he also dictated. To a degree unprecedented in the history of English colonization in America, Jamaica was a planned society. Its distinctive character was set by the institution of the army, whose corporate identity and discipline lent shape and force to the social concept of the general good. Military organization was the means by which an army executive enforced his social priorities. So molded, Jamaica's influence on the rest of the empire, both direct and by example, was profound.

Characteristic episodes of D'Oyley's administration give dimension to his accomplishments. Nothing, however, short of reading the journal he kept in his own hand, can convey a full impression of the terrific weight of daily administrative tasks that he bore, often without even the help of a clerk. By January 1656 D'Oyley had doubled the army's rations and still had food to spare for the troops he put to work on the citadel. He fed their courage with liquor and nourished their souls with sermons. Their officers nonetheless told the commander-in-chief that they and their men were "discouraged by their Great Mortality and Continual Sickness that utterly disables them from either performing any public service for the Commonwealth, or to plant for their subsistence here." D'Oyley put the morale problem more bluntly. The officers, he wrote, deafened him with a "continual clamour of home, home."[47]

Although many of them hated the island and despised planting, D'Oyley's officers nevertheless gave him the authority to relocate their regiments at will, which he used to set most of the troops to farming. All houses outside the new plantation quarters were burned, if the Spaniards had not already destroyed them. Thus, D'Oyley checked scattered, undisciplined settlement. He issued more tools as they came in from old England. Food arrived from New England, paid for with the cattle hides collected by the hunters D'Oyley had sent out. Tools and food promoted planting and so, by reducing hunting, permitted the increase of the cattle herds. The result, as President D'Oyley reported in March 1656, was that "our condition (as to health) is very good, considering where we are, and that our private soldiers drink nothing but water: . . . our soldiers are fully occupied either in fortifying,

47. A list of Jamaica's needs is in Egerton MS 2395, 135–136. For D'Oyley's administrative tasks, see the eloquent evidence of his "Journal," Add. MSS 12423, which includes (at 3b) the petition of his officers, Jan. 4, 1655, to "Edw. D'Oyley, Commander in Chief of the Army." See also Sedgewick to Thurloe, Mar. 12, 1656, Birch, ed., *Thurloe S.P.*, IV, 605, and n. 48 below.

planting or guarding, of which planting is the most grevious, and performed with so much unwillingness."[48]

Plantation labor became dangerous as well as onerous when Spanish raiders emerged from their mountain retreats. The ambush of English hunters, stragglers, patrols, and convoys was unending. Raids were signaled by smoke from flaming fields or from the burning blockhouses that were supposed to protect isolated soldier-planters from the artilleryless Spaniards. A Spanish officer pithily explained the whole English expansion into the countryside and the reaction of the former owners: "Hunger urged them forth and our people killed them." Still, the retaliation of a conquered people was familiar to Cromwell's veterans, and their repressive tactics well rehearsed. By the summer of 1657 D'Oyley's hunting dogs, counter ambushes, mounted patrols, and renegade guides had finally put down the attacks that until that time had seriously disrupted English expansion to the west and inland of Villa la Vega. Subsequently, the English patrols began to picket their horses at night and to sleep undisturbed by guerrillas, even in the hills and jungles.[49]

Both the tragedy of expropriation and its familiarity to the old English soldiers appear in the comment of one of D'Oyley's subordinates. Lieutenant Colonel John Daniell reported to his brother, then a garrison governor in Scotland, that the Spanish settlers "are fled scattering to the mountains, saying, they were all born here, have no acquaintance of friends in Spain to relieve them, and so [are] resolved rather to die here than to beg there, which will put us to some trouble to expell them; like your tories in Ireland, or moss troopers in Scotland" (or, Daniell might have added, like your Indians in Virginia and New England), "who may mischief our stragglers, but dare not face the smallest party, [they] will keep us waking to mind our duty as soldiers, and humble us before God, that he give us not into their hands."[50]

More menacing to successful settlement than Spanish raiders

48. Note the increasing elaboration of form and the fuller attendance at meetings of the council of war, marks of increasing institutional maturity, Jan. 18, 1656, Add. MSS 12423, 4b. See also order by the president, Feb. 7, 1656, minute of the council of war, *ibid.*, fol. 6; D'Oyley to Thurloe, Mar. 12, 1656, Birch, ed., *Thurloe S.P.*, IV, 602.

49. See the Spanish sources cited in nn. 36 and 46 above, especially Castilla.

50. J. Daniell to [Col. William Daniell], Birch, ed., *Thurloe S.P.*, III, 505–506. J. Daniell, like Venables, was a Cheshire man. He was one of D'Oyley's most successful officers at both farming and fighting and, afterward, one of Cromwell's major generals. His brother, William, was governor of St. Johnson's, Scotland. See also Wright, "Spanish Resistance," RHS, *Trans.*, 4th Ser., XIII (1930), 127–128.

were undisciplined English troops. Despite a death penalty for the offense, they went on wastefully killing both cattle and horses for hides. D'Oyley finally curtailed the practice by enslaving unlicensed hunters. Even when confined to the plantations and protected there, the soldiers were at best lazy planters. Two hours of field work in the morning and two more in the afternoon seemed to them too much. Moreover, the men resisted laboring on the regimental plantations, knowing that their officers claimed to own the land. The soldiers also despised the inferior rations given them and resented being denied a share of the prizes brought in by the fleet.[51]

In April 1656 a regiment of these disgruntled soldiers refused to march into the fields. Colonel D'Oyley personally led out his provost marshals to put down the revolt. To D'Oyley the episode epitomized the difficulty in commanding soldiers to be farmers. "We cannot yet make our soldiers sensible of their condition," he explained, "nor without much severity [make them] plant so much as provision for themselves. We have forced them to work for fear of hunger." The morale of these military colonists also suffered from tropical heat, illness, and insects, and from a feeling of uselessness and isolation—of doing "our nation no service." Yet D'Oyley was sure that his garrison's duty to England lay in developing Jamaica. He determined to persevere. "I was not borne for myself," he wrote, "but for my nation."[52]

Plantation, Protection, and Prerogative, 1656

D'Oyley's own resolve, and his prior successes against both English mutineers and Spanish attackers, made him resent the brief interlude of Major General Sedgewick's command. Hostility to Sedgewick was widespread. Only his untimely death prevented a rising against him by both officers and privates, a coup that had

51. Minute of the council of war, Mar. 19, 1656, Add. MSS 12423, 9. See also D'Oyley's general orders, nos. 1, 4, 7, dated June–Sept. 1656, minutes of the council of war, Feb. 14, Apr. 11, Oct. 20, 1656, *ibid.*, 114b–115b, 6b, 11b, 28; Goodson to Thurloe, June 25, 1656, Birch, ed., *Thurloe S.P.*, V, 151. On the soldiers' workday, see the Spanish observation in Cundall and Pietersz, [eds.,] *Jamaica under the Spaniards*, 57. In the spring of 1656 the commissioners and the council of war promised pay, garden plots, and then 30-acre allotments for those soldiers who would farm the land (Taylor, *Western Design*, 93–94). See also Taylor's account from Spanish sources of one of the more successful Spanish ambushes on the trails to Villa la Vega (pp. 103–107, 110).

52. D'Oyley to Thurloe, Apr. 18, to the Protector, June 20, 1656, Birch, ed., *Thurloe S.P.*, IV, 711, V, 138; minutes of the council of war, Apr. 3, 1656, Add. MSS 12423, 11; Taylor, *Western Design*, 69–70.

been previously pointed at President D'Oyley. "One considerable person told me," D'Oyley recalled, "that if I would not let him go for England, he would make mutinies. . . . I precautioned him not to try how far my power extended, nor give me cause to show severity, which in such case I would adventure." Colonel D'Oyley was as firm as his word. His first act on resuming power in June 1656 was to execute the leader of the plotters.[53]

"Again elected to supply the public charge," D'Oyley reported, "I have a great deal of trouble, being commander in chief, commissioner, judge advocate, and treasurer; all of which if I did not undertake, things must of necessity run to confusion." D'Oyley asked Cromwell for orders and for a commission "as commander in chief of the forces, or governor." "I am already so," he pointed out, "by election [of the council of war], succession [to Fortescue, Brayne, and Sedgewick], and confirmation of the commissioners." Colonel D'Oyley had, he wrote, "endured the sour, and would gladly see if any sweet came from it."[54]

Not waiting for English confirmation of his authority, D'Oyley continued his program of Jamaica's agricultural development. His encouragement of planting received an ironic tribute when farming units announced that they could spare no men for patrols. "Debate about laying out and appointing Severall proportions of Land for the use of the severall Regiments of the Army to settle upon, and plant in," continued through the summer of 1656. Not until October did the council of officers finally agree on the boundaries of the six regimental plantations. Each plantation encompassed an area where a regiment was already quartered and farming. D'Oyley's council reserved additional plantation areas around the "quarters" for the expansion of these military settlements. The areas were declared off limits to the civilian planters who were trickling into Jamaica. This was the conclusion of the process whereby "the first plantations begun" in Jamaica were established "according to the Quarters assigned to the Severall

53. Sedgewick to D'Oyley, May 12, 1656, D'Oyley to Thurloe, June 20, 1656, Birch, ed., *Thurloe S.P.*, V, 12–13, 139, 138. There is no clear link between D'Oyley and the officers who organized a rising against Sedgewick, an attempt for which D'Oyley and the army council had Maj. Throckmorton executed after Sedgewick's death (Goodson to Thurloe, June 25, 1656, letter from Jamaica, Sept. 25, 1656, *ibid.*, 131–132, 374). For the rash of officer politics in this period, see, e.g., the president and council to Goodson, June 17, 1656, *ibid.*, 127. (The similarity of army government in Jamaica with that in modern underdeveloped countries is striking. For a general view, see chap. 4 of Gavin Kennedy, *The Military in the Third World* [New York, 1974].) There is a discussion of the conspiracy as an episode of the contest between the pro- and anti-plantation officers in Taylor, *Western Design*, 120–123, reflecting Long, *Jamaica*, I, 259.
54. See nn. 52 and 53 above.

Regiments." Despite the slackness of individual soldiers, the island's best plantations were made by officers using martial labor.[55]

As "quarters" became the Jamaican term for "settlement," betokening the military roots of plantation, so the colonial use of "provost marshal" for "sheriff" suggested that the army underlay the government. Officers willing to develop the garrison government into a provincial regime were described by D'Oyley as the "cordially and well-affected men in the army." He helped them to acquire and cultivate the plantations that produced their restoration-era fortunes and so provided the foundation for their continuing influence in imperial politics and society. Nevertheless, the commander-in-chief met almost universal officer opposition to his demand that the troops who labored on the land must also share in its ownership. The officers were determined that if the soldiers "must plant, they should plant only as their servants." Instead, D'Oyley proclaimed a "property in lands to the private soldiers."[56]

By the time, six years after this proclamation, that the governor-general left his Jamaica command, the success of D'Oyley's plantation policy was clear. Then, in 1662, the six regimental quarters accounted for two-thirds of the cultivated acreage on the island and, with the two garrisoned towns, included all but three of the colony's settlements. "The most secure and the richest province of Jamaica" was that occupied by D'Oyley's own regiment (which, on D'Oyley's departure, became that of Colonel Thomas Lynch, afterward twice governor of the colony). The largest remaining settlement was Stokes's Nevis plantation at Port Morant. There 120 of Port Morant's total population of 511 settlers were the garrison soldiers, placed by Brayne and sustained by D'Oyley, and who now divided their duty between fields and fort. Two additional army outposts marked the conquest of the eastern savannas in 1658, Anaya (the "Old [Spanish] Harbor" district) and Guadibocoa ("Clarendon"). In each settlement, soldiers still in arms in 1662 constituted at least a third of the white male population. Many others were soldiers discharged from the ranks in the six previous years because of their success at farming or their desire to hunt.[57]

55. Minutes of the council of war, June 24, Aug. 20, Oct. 3, 13, 1656, Add. MSS 12423, 15, 22b–23, 26, 26b; minutes of the committee of foreign plantations, Jan. 10, 1660, considerations, Egerton MS 2395, 289, 283; Birch, ed., *Thurloe S.P.*, V, 152; Taylor, *Western Design*, 122–124.

56. See n. 55 above and n. 58 below.

57. The estimate of the particular plantation success of D'Oyley's own regiment is Sir Charles Littleton's, in C.O. 138/1, 22. Littleton also identified the several settlements as

The social result of D'Oyley's policy of privates' proprietorship was relatively densely populated settlements—fully farmed and self-provisioning, capable of self-defense by a disciplined militia of small planters, many of them veterans, and further protected and disciplined by garrisons of regular troops. These redcoats guarded each settlement's executive officer and its arms depot and enforced the orders of the governor-general. Four skeleton regiments were stationed in the Jamaica settlements, and the island commander kept up a full troop of cavalry as his life guard, the elite corps of the colony for the rest of the century. The field grade officers of these five units constituted most of D'Oyley's council, even after 1660. The four regimental colonel-councillors were still the chief planters in their respective quarters (or "parishes," as they were by then labeled) as late as 1671.[58]

Governor-General D'Oyley had built a military executive into colonial society. The chief executive made his military subordinates the masters of landed estates, and they served as his major political supporters and institutional administrators in both the central executive council and in their several local communities. To construct such a relationship with local leaders was the continuing aim of imperial executives. Its realization, however imperfect, was the basis of Governor-General D'Oyley's present power in Jamaica and the foundation of colonial "court parties" in the coming generation. One of D'Oyley's favorite officers explained this court calculus of land and loyalty, economics and empire: "My proportion of land (His Highness confirmeth it) I hope in a few years to make it worth unto me a 1,000*l.* sterling per annum. This island is a gallant island. . . . It will produce as good a trade as any island in America." If successfully settled, this officer-planter concluded, Jamaica would also be the best possible base for continuing the attack on Spain in America.[59]

"Regiments," the majority of whose field officers were those of the old army. Compare Cundall, *Historic Jamaica*, esp. 236, where similar success stories for the army's officer-planters are related, parish by parish, to Sir Thomas Modyford's analysis (C.O. 138/1, 36) of the population, produce, and militancy of the original settlements. Compare also the instructions for expanding D'Oyley's pattern of development, beginning with clause no. 16 of Lord Windsor's instructions, C.O. 138/1, 17.

58. The censuses of 1661 and 1662 are in the appendix to *Journals of the House of Assembly of Jamaica, 1663–1686*, 14 vols. (Jamaica, 1811–1829), I; Taylor, *Western Design*, 205; Watts, *Colonies anglaises*, 483; "Brief account," [Dec. 1661], *Cal. S.P. Col., 1661–1668*, no. 204. For the future of the commanders, see their plantations and production noted on the 1671 maps of Jamaica, in Black, ed., *Blathwayt Atlas*, nos. 33, 35; the discussion of St. John's Parish (Guanaboa quarter), in Dunn, *Sugar and Slaves*, 171, 176 (which reflects our Apr. 1968 discussion in Williamsburg); the analysis of landholding in chapter 5 below.

59. Barrington to [?], July 14, 1655, HMC, *Seventh Report*, Pt. I, 575. See also Long, *Jamaica*, I, 267–269, 272.

Governor-General D'Oyley
and Provincial Jamaica, 1657–1660

The survival of English settlement on Jamaica, much less the use of Jamaica as a fortified base against Spanish America, was by no means assured. The island colony depended upon the material support and continuing direction of the English executive. By October 1656, however, D'Oyley began to think that he would never even receive orders from England. He complained to Secretary Thurloe that the army's condition was "not at all worse, only it appears to us so, by our so long not hearing from you. Now it is above eight months . . . since we have had no one letter from England; we are almost afraid we are forgot." If D'Oyley was "almost afraid," most others had altogether despaired of support from home. The Protectorate committee for Jamaica finally recognized, as one of its members put it, that colonists were like little children in the dark; they needed constant, visible support. The English authorities dispatched General Brayne with supplies and reinforcements. As has been noted, he arrived in December 1656, added to D'Oyley's plantation promotion a vigorous and successful recruitment of settlers from the overpopulated Caribbees, and died in September 1657, having ordered D'Oyley to succeed him as "Commander in Chief of all his Highness Forces in America."[60]

D'Oyley obeyed, "tho' with much unwillingness." He complained that command of the Jamaica forces by land and sea was "a burden too heavy for me to bear." The difficulty of leading a discontented and unpaid army, without fresh orders and additional authority from England, depressed him. Yet he could "bless God I have the advantage of the affection of the people here, beyond any that ever yet commanded, and a spirit of my own not to sink under the weight of unreasonable discontents." Nevertheless, the new commander-in-chief asked for an early relief from the task that his duty compelled him to take up. "Honors and riches," D'Oyley wrote to his military patron, General Charles Fleetwood, "are not the things I aim at. . . . A good name and a competent livelihood is all I desire upon earth, and eternal life in heaven. And of statesmen and great commanders I fear few there be, that will find it." Perhaps these were undiplomatic words to address to a great general and public figure, but they coincided with the char-

---

60. D'Oyley to Thurloe, Oct. 6, 1656, Birch, ed., *Thurloe S.P.*, V, 476; "considerations for the more convenient supplying HH's affairs in the West Indies," Add. MSS 11411, 10–11, Brayne to D'Oyley, Aug. 27, 1657, Birch, ed., *Thurloe S.P.*, VI, 483. See also Brayne's letters of Jan. 9, 10, 1657, *ibid.*, V, 770, 778, and, on settlement, n. 29, above.

acter of this forthright man. They explain D'Oyley's continuing desire "to sequester myself from this tempestuous and trouble-some world." Still, D'Oyley's relief was five years in coming. As he himself predicted, few commanders could be found willing to sacrifice their health and reputation on the island altar to the ambition of Oliver Cromwell. Moreover, such English authorities as that imperial figure General Monck were alive to Jamaica's need for the strong leader that D'Oyley had proved himself to be.[61]

Once he was addressed by the English authorities as "gover-nor," in recognition of his combined civil and military authority, D'Oyley moved from defense of England's conquest to renewed assault on Spanish territory. Reinforced from England by two frigates under the redoubtable Captain Christopher Myngs, the governor organized a raid on Cuba. This expedition began to gar-ner the plunder that capitalized Jamaica's development and pro-moted D'Oyley's dual plantation policy whereby soldier-settlers as well as officer-grandees prospered directly from the privateers. London merchants and their island factors, whose immediate con-cern was trade—primarily with Spain and its colonies—rather than the development of Jamaica, pointed out the multiple eco-nomic waste of using laborers—who could have been raising crops for export to England—to man the ships that attacked and destroyed Spanish vessels, ports, and settlements—the source of additional exports—and thus aroused unprofitable antagonisms in Europe. In the end, however, the leading raiders invested their Spanish plunder in their Jamaica plantations. So they manifested the symbiotic relation between privateering and planting. This first raid brought another benefit to Jamaica by giving command experience to two of D'Oyley's regimental captains, Henry Mor-gan and Thomas Lynch, his eventual successors as governors and generals of Jamaica.[62]

Governor-General D'Oyley himself further divided the is-

61. D'Oyley to the Protector, Sept. 12, 1657, Birch, ed., *Thurloe S.P.*, VI, 512, also 513. On what D'Oyley called "the plainness and freedom of my expressions" and his "natural uncourtly habit," see his letter to the council of state, Feb. 27, 1658, *ibid.*, 833. See also D'Oyley to the Protector, June 20, 1656, Monck to Thurloe, Dec. 8, 1657, *ibid.*, V, 138, VI, 664.

62. For the title "governor," see Add. MSS 11410, 143, and Add. MSS 11411, 21, 87b. Orders were henceforward issued in D'Oyley's name as commander-in-chief of all his highness's forces in America, rather than, as previously, under the signatures of the council of war or its president (Add. MSS 12423, 35–36). See also the "History and Present State of Jamaica under the Lord Vaughan," Phillips MS 11009, 14. The raid on Cuba increased D'Oyley's defensive capabilities by adding captured Spanish cannon to the Cagway for-tifications (Taylor, *Western Design*, 131–134). See Haring, *Buccaneers*, on this raid (pp. 92–95), on plunder as colonial capital (p. 98), and on D'Oyley's accomplishments as governor-general (pp. 96–97). Note the assertion by Cornelius Burrough to [the secretary to the ad-

land's future between planting and privateering. In 1657 he invited the English buccaneers of Tortuga to settle at Cagway and join the English navy's attacks on Spanish ships and cities. When, following Charles II's restoration, the English navy decayed and almost disappeared from West Indian waters, the buccaneers remained in Jamaica, augmented by several hundred former soldiers from the regiments of the Western Design. These privateers became the province's own naval force, a major part of the island colony's unique military strength. For decades after Cromwell's death, they executed his imperial legacy and protected his conquest. Perhaps the privateers were the key to Jamaica's survival in the face of unremitting Spanish hostility. Certainly they were a forceful presence in its politics and society during the first decade of the Restoration.[63]

The pervasiveness of the privateering influence was described by the island's historian, the perspicacious Edward Long (himself the descendant of D'Oyley's chief aide, Captain Samuel Long). He noted that the buccaneers shielded Jamaica from Spanish raids by their patrols and their presence and stimulated its trade by pumping Spanish plunder into the island's commerce. Most important, however, the privateer fleet's need for enormous quantities of food underlay the prosperity of hundreds of peasant proprietors. These were the ex-privates who farmed ten- to thirty-acre plots on the plains around Villa la Vega, the quarters of their old regiments, and sold their produce, largely for privateer provisions, in Port Royal's (Cagway's) frenetic markets. These former private soldiers were the foundation of the island militia—just as their less rooted colleagues manned the privateer sloops. The militia was the second element in this island's unparalleled military prowess. These soldiers and their small landholdings, like the sailors and their port, were the objects of the military governor's solicitude. To create such a martial population on farms and in ports became a leading social goal of almost every governor-general in the empire.[64]

---

miralty commissioners], Jamaica, June 9, 1659, that "Planting prospers exceedingly well; forwarded much by Capt. Myng's late success. 'Not a man on the island but can say he hath reaped a benefit by that action.' . . . Believes the General mentioned in his letter 400,000l.; a great deal scattered amongst them" (*Cal. S.P. Col.*, *1675–1676, Addenda, 1574–1674*, no. 319).

63. See Haring, *Buccaneers*, 116–117, 122, on some of the interrelationships of Jamaica and Tortuga. The history of the latter settlement, to 1640, is discussed in Arthur Percival Newton, *The Colonising Activities of the English Puritans: The Last Phase of the Elizabethan Struggle with Spain*, Yale Historical Publications, Miscellany, I (New Haven, Conn., 1914). See also Bridges, *Jamaica Annals*, I, 407–409.

64. Long's analysis is in *Jamaica*, I, 281–283.

The downfall of both the peasants and the buccaneers was a direct result of the Treaty of Madrid in 1670. This big-planter, London-merchant agreement, by making peace with Spain in America, severely prejudiced the former privates of the Protectorate, whether privateers or pioneers. The old soldiers' buccaneering was immediately outlawed and eventually suppressed. Thus their mixed farms, the produce of which had provisioned the privateers, slowly lost their major market. Displacing sailors and smallholders, the mercantilist policy realized at Madrid accelerated the conversion of Jamaican agriculture into a highly capitalized, large-unit, commercial machine, in which slave labor produced abundant sugar and social disaster and from which English ships took bulk cargoes and left Jamaica's sloops to rot.[65]

In the meantime, however, Governor-General D'Oyley spent years building up Jamaican population, agriculture, and commerce. To meet the mercantile strictures of the first navigation act, he certified that the hides, tobacco, dyewoods, and cloves shipped from Jamaica for London were all grown on the island. While much of this produce was actually Spanish plunder, an increasing proportion of it was what the governor-general testified it to be: the produce of English plantations. In July 1657 D'Oyley was able to report that the army had more acres in crops than had ever been cultivated in the European history of the island. To increase his force of farmers, he sent recruiters to Bermuda, Nevis, and St. Christopher with orders not to let their governors obstruct emigration to Jamaica. When the chiefs of the older, civilian colonies objected, the Protectorate backed up Governor D'Oyley's immigrant enlistment. The governor of Barbados was warned that he must "complement the Commander in Chief in Jamaica and offer your best assistance . . . for his Highness looks upon Jamaica as the principal Situation at present of his Honour and Interest in the Indies."[66]

D'Oyley protected that honor and interest by assaulting the Spanish invaders assembling in Jamaica's jungles. Having learned of the Spanish buildup late in October 1657, the governor-general

---

65. For the mercantile counterargument, usually associated with William Beeston, see Dunn, *Sugar and Slaves*, 150, 176–177. Also see Dunn, *passim*, on the social catastrophe of the island society.

66. Add. MSS 12423, 36b, 37; Taylor, *Western Design*, 125, 205; Watts, *Colonies anglaises*, 351n; Burrough to [the secretary to the admiralty commissioners], Nov. 28, 1658, *Cal. S.P. Col., 1675–1676*, no. 308. If D'Oyley's claim was correct, the Spanish cultivation must have been very small, for as late as Oct. 1662 the English had planted less than 3,000 acres. The warning was conveyed by Thomas Povey to Daniel Searle, Jan. 8, 1658, Add. MSS 11411, 54b–55.

embarked a picked force on a week-long sail around the east end of Jamaica. He landed with 350 men at Ocho Rios on the island's north shore. They fought their way through the Spaniards' jungle ambush and stormed the enemy's stockade. While some of D'Oyley's redcoats ran right up to the wooden walls and fired at the defenders through gaps between the logs, others hacked open a breach. When the English axemen broke through the palisade, the Spanish garrison fled over the far side of the fort, down into the sea. They left behind 120 dead, uncounted wounded, and all the military stores they had so tediously smuggled in from Hispaniola and Cuba. D'Oyley's men scoured the beaches for surviving Spaniards, assuming that their former slaves would have little mercy on those who fled into the woods. While this assumption was wrong, the fierce little fight, followed by a series of successful patrol actions on land and sea, disarmed the guerrillas and confined them to the mountains of west central Jamaica. The victory ended the Spanish raids overland from northside bases against English plantations on the fertile south side of the island. Governor-General D'Oyley had won time for his planters to dig their roots into Jamaican soil and for himself to solidify his own political control of an evolving English provincial society.[67]

On his return from military victory at Ocho Rios, the English commander extended his civil authority: he created a system of administrative and judicial commissioners in the settlements. D'Oyley ordered the commissioners to prevent anyone from leaving Jamaica without his approval and to confiscate abandoned, unimproved, or excessive land grants. The governor also appointed surveyors to stake out all grants, and so assist the commissioners. Subsequently, D'Oyley added civil causes and misdemeanors to the jurisdiction of the commissioners' courts. "The General," as he was addressed, and as his successors would be titled after him,

67. The Spanish instructions clearly pointed out the English weaknesses (Birch, ed., *Thurloe S.P.*, VI, 54). D'Oyley's dispatch on the battle of the Charreras, Feb. 3, 1657, was printed in London in 1658, by Cromwell's order, as *A Narrative of the Great "Success" God hath been pleased to give His Highness Forces in Jamaica against the King of Spain's Forces . . . As it was Communicated in a Letter from the Governour of Jamaica.* Copies are in the British Library, the John Carter Brown Library, Providence, R.I., and the Harvard College Library, Cambridge, Mass. (photostat). D'Oyley was delighted that the captured Spanish commissary book tallied with the munitions he took, testifying to the totality of his victory. The Spanish accounts of the action are in Cundall and Pietersz, [eds.,] *Jamaica under the Spaniards*, 64–65, 68, and the Spanish background is narrated by Taylor, *Western Design*, 146–153. See Taylor also for the dates of the action (p. 159n) and for additional Spanish reports (pp. 158–164). See also Watts, *Colonies anglaises*, 319, 327, 343, 362, and Long, *Jamaica*, I, 227. Wright, "Spanish Resistance," RHS, *Trans.*, 4th Ser., XIII (1930), 129–137, describes D'Oyley's offensive, culminating with the battle at the Rio Nuevo.

reserved all major civil and criminal actions for judgment by his court-martial.[68]

In February 1658 Governor-General D'Oyley finally received from Cromwell the long-promised cash with which to pay for stone fortifications. He also got extra rations, which released men from planting food crops to patrol the island and to build military installations. "And it was high time" that he was supplied, D'Oyley exclaimed, for "our ships were going to shift for themselves and our land-forces altogether destitute." The governor-general warned that even with the new supplies the prospect was poor for improving the lot of the troops. He would have to take most of his effective men from their plantations when the Spaniards attacked in force, always provided that he could find shoes for his men to march in. He asked for the margin of survival that still more provisions from England would provide. Better yet, he thought, would be money with which to buy the superior (the un-Poveyed) produce of New England. Even with the scanty resources he had received, however, D'Oyley declared that he would fortify the harbor and send out his ships "to prevent the enemies landing and obstructing their trade."[69]

The governor-general's ships did not "prevent the enemies landing." On May 8, 1658, the long-expected Spanish flotilla slipped by the English patrols and put ashore thirty companies of regular, but rather scruffy, infantry at the Bay of the Rio Nuevo, the midpoint of Jamaica's north side. Twelve days later, however,

68. D'Oyley's orders of Nov. 10, 1657, Add. MSS 12423, 40b. D'Oyley's surveyor general, John Man, also commanded the Cagway fortress (Cundall, *Governors of Jamaica*, 7).

69. D'Oyley to the council of state, Feb. 27, to Thurloe, Feb. 28, 1658, Birch, ed., *Thurloe S.P.*, VI, 833, 834. For his issuance of the fortification money and reorganization of the army in Feb. 1658, see Add. MSS 12423, 45. Some additional resources accrued to the commander-in-chief when Capt. Myng brought captured Dutch ships (seized at Barbados) to Jamaica for D'Oyley to condemn (report of commissioners of the admiralty, July 31, 1658, *Cal. S.P. Col., 1574–1660*, 467). Even at the lowest ebb of English naval strength before 1660, D'Oyley seems to have commanded four warships on the Jamaica station. Double that number was usual, and the official establishment was six frigates. The official establishment, with the frigates' use by D'Oyley, is detailed in Leo Francis Stock, ed., *Proceedings and Debates of the British Parliaments Respecting North America*, Vol. I, *1542–1688* (Washington, D.C., 1924), 265–267, and Arthur W. Tedder, *The Navy of the Restoration* (Cambridge, 1914), 14. While even D'Oyley suffered somewhat from the usual interservice rivalries (Haring, *Buccaneers*, 98–100), no other governor overseas in the 17th century ever enjoyed such splendid naval support. Compared with the piteous plaints of Restoration governors-general for a ketch or a single fifth rate, D'Oyley's complaints of naval deficiencies testify to the imperial effectiveness of the Protectorate navy. For a negative view of the Jamaica squadron, however, see Andrews, *Colonial Period of American History*, III, 26–27. The crucial importance of provisions from New England and the Leeward Islands to the Jamaica garrison's survival is also testified to by Spanish observers; see Cundall and Pietersz, [eds.,] *Jamaica under the Spaniards*, 70.

before the Spaniards were able to secure their beachhead fully, D'Oyley's scouting squadron discovered them. After skirmishing inconclusively with three Spanish ships, the English squadron hovered off the bay while one of their number sailed around the island to alert their general, who immediately called together his council of war. The council advised him to attack the Spaniards before they could finish their fortifications. D'Oyley ordered up 750 men from the plantations, requisitioned a shipload of shoes for them, seized three more merchant ships, crammed them with the troops, and sailed for the Rio Nuevo to fulfill the Spanish fear that their English enemy "as master of the sea . . . will throw troops on me, as he does, whenever it may suit him."[70]

On the morning of June 22, the little English expedition came to anchor. They found that in the month since their landing, the Spanish troops had thrown up a fort on a high bluff overlooking the beach. There the invaders had been joined by the Spanish governor of Jamaica and his guerrillas. On the beach itself the English saw two Spanish companies drawn up to dispute their landing. In the face of cannon fire from the fort and musketry from the beach, the English waded ashore, drove the Spaniards off the beach, and killed both of the enemy's company commanders and twenty-three of their men. Within the hour, the rest of the English troops landed, despite the continuing Spanish cannonade. The capture of this defended beach offset the cowardly performance of many of these same English troops at Hispaniola. Seasoning, by combat, by weather, and by D'Oyley's discipline, had won a beachhead, but that was all. The English tried all day, but could not reach the Spanish fort with their ships' guns, much less silence the Spanish artillery or open a breach in the enemy's walls. D'Oyley's troops also faced a river of unknown depth, which barred them from the foot of the fortified bluff. Finally, to his surprise and dismay, D'Oyley discovered that the Spanish defenders outnumbered his English attackers.[71]

70. D'Oyley received ample warning of the Spanish invasion from his ships on the coasts of Cuba; Add. MSS 12423, 41b, 45–45b. In Mar. 1658 D'Oyley had ordered the patroling ships into the routine that discovered the Spanish landing; ibid., 47. The naval action is described in Cundall and Pietersz, [eds.,] Jamaica under the Spaniards, 74, 75, 77. See also ibid., 75, and orders to the firemaster and grenade manufacturer, and orders requisitioning shoes and ships, May 3–26, 1658, Add. MSS 12423, 49.

71. The author of the "History and Present State of Jamaica under the Lord Vaughan," Phillips MS 11009, 16, estimated the Spanish force at between 1,000 and 1,200 and the English at 600 men. In fact, the numbers were almost equal: about 700 men to each side. The muster of the accompanying Mexican forces—31 companies, 557 officers and men—is in Cundall and Pietersz, [eds.,] Jamaica under the Spaniards, 69–70. Their untrained and mongrel state is insisted on (p. 82). The Spanish governor, Ysassi, added perhaps 200 guerrillas to this

Seemingly "at a stand how to attempt them," the English officers spent a day in polite, but apparently fruitless, parley with the Spanish governor. Meanwhile, D'Oyley's men secretly assembled scaling ladders and filled hand grenades. Before dawn on June 24, the English governor-general sent part of his squadron down the bay to feint a landing on the far side of the fortress. At the same time, he led his men into the jungle, crossed the Rio Nuevo upstream of the fort, toiled up the back of the bluff, and beat up a Spanish work party. Then the English sat down and had a drink. Advancing again, they came in sight of the fort and found, "to our exceeding joy," that it was not finished on the land side to the same height as it was to the seaward. "Without any further dispute," the English charged into the Spanish musketry. They were led by D'Oyley himself, dressed for the occasion in his best and brightest clothes. His gallant behavior was answered both by officers and "soldiers with a silent cheerful obedience." The redcoats rallied at the angles of the bastions, tossed their grenades into the fort, climbed its projecting walls, and, in fifteen minutes of fighting, mastered the fortress. They drove the Spanish troops over the seawalls and followed them down the face of the bluff. The demoralized Spaniards were trapped on the beach between the pursuing infantry and the English sailors, who, "seeing them run along the rocks, came out with their boats, and killed many of them."[72]

Some three hundred Spanish troops perished, nearly half their total number. Another hundred were captured, including the six Spanish captains whom D'Oyley sent home to give body to his modest report. With prisoners and report, the governor-general also dispatched a dozen captured company colors and the royal standard of Spain. He noted that the remainder of the Spanish force were scattered. He "supposed [they] will not know how to live in wild woods and rocks." After his men leveled the Spanish works, buried about thirty English dead, and carried off an equal number of wounded, D'Oyley sailed for Cagway. There the captured Spanish ordnance and stores of war helped to fit out his own fortress. Even more important than the captured matériel was the heightened English morale. It sprang, as D'Oyley said, out of yet

---

force. The dates given here are those used by the English—10 days earlier than the Spanish reckoning.

72. The best account of the action is D'Oyley to Thurloe, July 12, 1658, Birch, ed., *Thurloe S.P.*, VII, 260–262. See also D'Oyley's military patron, Charles Fleetwood, to Henry Cromwell, Oct. 5, 1658, and Downing to Goodson, *ibid.*, 423, 55.

another of the victories that had "exceedingly endeared us to one another since we came here."[73]

D'Oyley's was a triumph small in size, but it was decisive to Jamaica's English future because it revived imperial sentiment in England and practically ended Spanish efforts to recapture the island. The Spanish never again put troops ashore on Jamaica. As the Englishmen's knowledge of the country grew, they capitalized still further on their command of the sea to raid the remaining Spanish camps and to cut Spanish communications. The conquerors also benefited from the shifting allegiance of the Spaniards' former slaves. Finally, led by the blacks, the English marched across the island for the first time. Under Colonel Edward Tyson, the English redcoats and their black allies destroyed the base camp of the Spanish guerrillas and captured their last supply ship. Within two years after their defeat at Rio Nuevo, the last remnants of the Spanish garrison were driven from Jamaica forever.[74]

Meanwhile, in English opinion D'Oyley's victory displaced the memories of the humiliating defeat at Hispaniola, which had so dampened support for the Western Design and its Jamaica base. Additionally, this well-publicized triumph of English imperial arms—which Cromwell ordered published—helped to offset the loss of imperial impetus caused by his death soon thereafter. Their Jamaica exploit showed that the prowess of his redcoats was not altogether dependent upon Oliver Cromwell. Perhaps the empire that he had envisioned and that they had conquered would not pass away with him. General George Monck, now the leading imperialist, responded to D'Oyley's victory from his occupation headquarters in Scotland. "Truly," he wrote, "it was very considerable to us at this time. God give us hearts to be thankfull to him for it."[75]

73. The Spanish commander acknowledged that 300 of his men were killed on the spot, many wounded, and that only 230 of his entire force survived, scattered and starving because their supplies had been wiped out. He thought that the English had landed almost three times as many men as they had (Cundall and Pietersz, [eds.,] *Jamaica under the Spaniards*, 79, also 93). See also Cundall, *Historic Jamaica*, 284–288, and the map and physical description of the Rio Nuevo battlefield in Taylor, *Western Design*, 166, 169.

74. "History and Present State of Jamaica under the Lord Vaughan," Phillips MS 11009, fol. 16; Capt. William Dalyson to Robert Blackborne, Jan. 31, 1660, *Cal. S.P. Col., 1675–1676, Addenda, 1574–1674*, no. 331. On the Spanish evacuation, May 3, 1660, see Cundall and Pictersz, [eds.,] *Jamaica under the Spaniards*, 98–102; Taylor, *Western Design*, chap. 17; Wright, "Spanish Resistance," RHS, *Trans.*, 4th Ser., XIII (1930), 143–146. Taylor, *Western Design*, 144–145, 167, notes that the victories of the English fleet against the Spanish off the European coast prevented the organization of a major expedition to retake Jamaica. (On those victories, see also Andrew Marvell, "On the Victory Obtained by Blake.")

75. Monck to Thurloe, Oct. 12, 1658, Birch, ed., *Thurloe S.P.*, VII, 435.

Military victory once again led Governor D'Oyley to a signal advance in plantation policy: the link between successful protection and the growth of population was obvious. The strategy of the Spanish guerrillas had been to prevent planting, obstruct settlement, and even halt hunting by all but large units. The Spanish governor warned at the time of the conquest that "if the enemy begin to gather fruit and profit by the Island," they could permanently populate Jamaica as a base from which they would dominate the Greater Antilles. Having countered the Spaniards' strategy, Governor-General D'Oyley fulfilled their prophecy. The officer he sent to recruit settlers from Virginia was told to assure them that "they may settle where they please." If settlers did not want land in the army quarters, D'Oyley promised to grant them lands elsewhere and to build and arm forts to protect the new settlements. He could point to the example of Port Morant, where three hundred of the surviving settlers from Nevis farmed 464 acres around their fort. Their palisade mounted ten guns and housed an overstrength company of redcoats to protect the planters from human enemies (though not from the far more lethal fever).[76]

The success of D'Oyley's policy of feeding his garrison from the plantations they protected was acknowledged by despairing Spanish observers. In the year following D'Oyley's decisive victory at Rio Nuevo, his enemies reported that the English governor-general had built up a force of fifty-five hundred fighting men, of whom six hundred were mounted. By 1659 he had made most of those soldiers into "husbandmen who are cultivating and reaping the products of the land," both the land that they cleared and the old Spanish fields. The English troops and civilian settlers, according to the Spaniards, produced food grains (including maize) and such cash crops as cocoa, pimento, tobacco, and cotton. They had taken over the Spanish sugar works and supplied them with cane from Spanish fields as well as from new clearings. The soldier-settlers also harvested Jamaica's woodland riches: brazilwood, red ebony, and ship timber. The English herded cattle and horses—both stocks built up from Spanish herds—as well as driving pigs. Whether military or civilian in origin, all these farmers and herds-

76. Guerrilla strategy is discussed in the governor of Cartagena to the king of Spain, Feb. 28, 1658, Cundall and Pietersz, [eds.,] *Jamaica under the Spaniards*, 71. See also *ibid*., 60, 94. See D'Oyley's instructions for Capt. Francis Emperor, Cagway, June 23, 1658, Add. MSS 12423, 52. Founded during Brayne's brief tenure of command and used as a base by D'Oyley during his expedition to Rio Nuevo, the Port Morant garrison settlement was described by the Spanish governor, Aug. 16, 1658, in Cundall and Pietersz, [eds.,] *Jamaica under the Spaniards*, 82.

men were also "exercised in the use of arms so as to turn to them when they have to defend themselves."[77]

Besides the growing inland capital, Villa la Vega, the port town of Cagway, and the hamlet at Passage Fort, the Spanish counted seven major English "plantations and pens with strongholds." Six of these were the original regimental quarters, each with its "governor," the regiment's senior field officer. They were located on the savannas north and west of Villa la Vega and, east of it, adjacent to Passage Fort. Garrisoned settlements also dotted the southeastern coast of the island, from the Old Harbor to Port Morant, home of the Nevis emigrants. Each was located where isolated plains or the valleys that lie between the foothills of the Blue Mountains come down to the sea.[78]

To those who would join these settlements or make their own, D'Oyley pledged that, save for militia musters and for defense of the island against invasion, they would be exempt from military duty. Such assurances were the planters' profits from an imperial victory—a victory that, as it relieved the planters from garrison service, bound them to obey the government which had won the land and now protected them. Of equal political portent was D'Oyley's promise that, save for a small quitrent, settlers on Jamaica were "to have no other taxation laid upon them except what they shall consent to by their deputies for the defence of the Island." Although he was in absolute command of Jamaica—and thereby found ways to get around this concession to the principle of representative government—D'Oyley felt that he had to promise prospective colonists representation in order to attract them to Jamaica from dominions with relatively popular legislatures. The accuracy of D'Oyley's perception afterward prevented even absolutist Stuart monarchs from resuming the legislative privilege.[79]

77. Burrough to [the secretary to the admiralty commissioners], Nov. 28, 1658, *Cal. S.P. Col., 1675–1676, Addenda, 1574–1674*, no. 308. See also n. 78 below.

78. The English settlements were named by the Spanish governor (Cundall and Pietersz, [eds.,] *Jamaica under the Spaniards*, 84). They may be located by comparison of the contemporary Spanish maps reproduced *ibid.*, chap. 4, with the English ones of about 20 years later, especially Edward Slaney's (1678) and F. Lamb's, in Black, ed., *Blathwayt Atlas*, nos. 33, 34. More efficiently, consult the excellent sketch maps in Taylor, *Western Design*, esp. opp. 49, and see Taylor on the quarters at Bridge Pen, La Puente, and Los Angeles (pp. 57, 71). See also the reconstructed map of "Jamaica in 1655–1661," in Cundall, *Historic Jamaica*, 7. On Guanaboa quarter under its "governor," Col. Tyson (executed for conspiracy against "Captain General" D'Oyley in Aug. 1660), see Tyson's correspondence in Cundall and Pietersz, [eds.,] *Jamaica under the Spaniards*, 94–95. For the allocation of regimental plantation quarters in Oct. 1656, see n. 55 above.

79. "Power and protection draweth legeance": Coke's opinion, in Howell, comp., *State Trials*, II, 623. See also D'Oyley's instructions for Emperor, Add. MSS 12423, 52. Note in these instructions the reiterated identifications of government with defense. As long as the

By 1660, at least half of Jamaica's people were civilian settlers from England's older colonies. To attract these experienced planters and their human capital of servants and slaves—"the wealth of Planters and the seed of Plantations"—D'Oyley had had to promise that only their representatives would levy taxes, but tax legislation was all that he conceded. Administration by legislators or under civil law was, in his opinion, "debauched." He alone made social policy during Jamaica's formative period, and he enforced his decisions with his armed forces.[80]

Once D'Oyley was sure that Jamaica had a future, he tried to shape it. He began with privateering. He demanded that the sea rovers secure licenses from him, and he ordered his frigates to capture unlicensed privateers. He then organized Jamaica's ships of war, both public and private, for systematic attacks on Spanish commerce. These raids culminated in D'Oyley's dramatic attempt to ambush the Spanish plate fleet. It failed by just the few hours that the governor's main force took from the ambush to refill their water butts. D'Oyley could only warn the English authorities of the approach of the treasure ships he had seen from his own vessel. "It was a strange tantalizing to us to be in the midst of millions," he wrote, "and not able to venture for it without manifest indiscretion and ruin; but we are something comforted with the hopes you will meet them from home." Clearly, Colonel D'Oyley shared his men's privateering urge.[81]

Yet the governor-general also paved peaceable roads to prosperity. He formed convoys to protect Jamaica's growing commerce and freighted these fleets with crops that he repeatedly insisted were Jamaican in origin. He tried to control cutting of the island's dyewoods, and his patrols turned from chasing guerrillas to pursue the hide hunters who continued to destroy livestock. He insisted on conservation of Jamaica's natural resources as the basis of its participation in imperial commerce. D'Oyley further encouraged this commerce by judging merchants' disputes and establishing markets. At the same time, he encouraged artisans and tradesmen by price fixing and licensing. Edward D'Oyley not only ordered the first ship built on Jamaica but also was her chief

---

Spaniards retained any force in the bush, however, D'Oyley thought that immigration was endangered (Dalyson to Blackborne, Jan. 31, 1660, D'Oyley to the commissioners of the admiralty, Feb. 1, 1660, *Cal. S.P. Col., 1675–1676, Addenda, 1574–1674*, nos. 331, 332.

80. "A Briefe Survey of Jamaica," Egerton MS 2395, 609–610; minute of the committee for foreign plantations, Jan. 10, 1660, *ibid.*, 290; D'Oyley to the commissioners of the admiralty, June 1, 1660, *Cal. S.P. Col., 1574–1660*, 480.

81. Add. MSS 12423, 64–64b, 67, 83b; D'Oyley to Thurloe, Nov. 30, 1658, Birch, ed., *Thurloe S.P.*, VII, 539–540. For a sketch of this operation, see Haring, *Buccaneers*, 97.

owner, and he provided most of her cargo of (Guatemalan) indigo. The good ship *Edward* sailed from Jamaica in July 1660, bound for the port of London and the Povey warehouse.[82]

Despite the loss of dignity that trading entailed, the governor-general had to play the merchant (as did his successors in many colonies) because he had not received any of his military salary for several years. No civil salary was allocated for Jamaica's chief executive before 1660. D'Oyley's financial stress was increased by Jamaican prices, which were triple those paid in London, he complained. The traditional officer swindle of collecting pay for dead and imaginary privates was unrewarding when the English government paid no one. Although promoted to lieutenant general's rank and pay, D'Oyley still had to compromise his gentility—and his executive principles—by engaging in trade. The result was a profitable union of the officer and the trader in D'Oyley's person, presaging the pragmatic adjustment that all governors-general made to the weakness of the central government they represented and to the strength of the profit motive they shared.[83]

Profit required protection, the imperial obligation. Providing protection continued to be General D'Oyley's chief preoccupation, as it would be that of so many English military executives after him. D'Oyley reminded his subordinates that the Protector himself had promised settlers "the assistance of his forces here, for their defence, and protection, against the natives of the Country, and other Enemies." If he were properly to protect the conquest and promote its settlement, however, Jamaica's population must be increased. Whether soldiers or settlers, "our great want is men," wrote the governor-general. Again he asked that British political prisoners be sent to Jamaica to serve the army's officers in lieu of their salaries. "We lessen every day," D'Oyley explained, "and are in the midst of many enemies; and the planting we have hopefully begun will fall to nothing" without more people. Shipments of laborers would encourage the military leaders of colonization to remain in Jamaica, as well as increase the island's population. Again, Governor-General D'Oyley promised to protect the people he longed for. "I have made two handsome garrisons or forts," he wrote from the Cagway citadel, "and am making

82. Add. MSS 12423, 80b, 81b, 48, 66b, 67b, 82b, 83, 86, 91b. Cargo invoice, wage statement, ship construction costs, and receipts for the *Edward* are in the Blathwayt Papers, Huntington Lib.

83. D'Oyley to the commissioners of the navy, June 1, 1660, *Cal. S.P. Col.*, *1574–1660*, 480–481. See the parallel cases of Col. Richard Nicolls of New York and Sir William Berkeley of Virginia, in the Blathwayt Papers, Huntington Lib.

the third and chief, which is for the security of this harbour, and indeed for the reputation of our country."[84]

Reputation aside, the physical survival of the new society still depended upon the occupying army. In August 1660 part of that army rose in revolt against their lieutenant general, the governor. D'Oyley said that some of the troops had been corrupted by civilians who, "not being under the Military Power have traitorously and seditiously dared to infuse into the soldiers principles of liberty and freedom from my authority." Indeed, the discontented officers and men of the Guanaboa regiment and quarter asserted that "they would live no more as an Army." Instead, they "declared they would have the Island settled in Colonies," that they would "make constables and civil officers." While jealousy of the governor-general was rife, there was more than spite in this protest. Much of political sentiment in the army was "country," even republican, and it was tinctured with social leveling. The governor-general was a social conservative, a believer in executive authority, a grandee in the Protector's army. His views anticipated the monarchical and "court" convictions that warred with republican and "country" principles in Restoration Jamaica. It was principally the death of the Protector himself, however, that led Jamaica's would-be civilians to question the validity of D'Oyley's continued military government. But because the governor-general was responsible for Jamaica's well-being, he felt justified in ruling. As D'Oyley put it, "the loss of this place will inevitably fall on me if I should neglect to take sure course." The governor-general moved quickly to save himself and his authority. First he seized a ship anchored in the harbor, to be used for his escape "if he saw things grow desperate." Then he summoned the loyal officers to meet in a court-martial and mustered his own reliable regiment to back his court's expected condemnation of the rebel officers. The governor-general's troops surrounded the dissidents' headquarters and "persuaded" the men there to give up their leaders, Colonels Raymond and Tyson. D'Oyley had them taken out and shot.[85]

From Cromwellian Conquest to Royal Colony, 1660–1662

Despite this absolute military defeat of his political opponents, Governor-General D'Oyley's authority quickly declined.

84. D'Oyley to Lt. Col. Francis Mercer, Oct. 1, 1656, Add. MSS 12423, 116; Brayne to the Protector, Jan. 9, 1656, D'Oyley to Thurloe, Nov. 1, 1658, Birch, ed., *Thurloe S.P.*, V, 770, VII, 499; instructions to Maj. Wilbrahm, Sept. 12, 1659, Add. MSS 12423, 70b, also 64, 66b, 78b, 81, 86.

85. Order for establishing a court-martial, Aug. 1, 1660, Add. MSS 12423, 93b; Taylor,

He could not prevent his regiment from plundering the rebel colonels' townhouses and plantations. On the civil side, the governor feared that appeals from his decisions might be carried to some new, perhaps hostile, authority in England. He therefore stopped hearing merchant disputes in his court-martial. Temporarily, he also ceased to grant lands or to promote settlement. A new government in England might disallow his grants and oust the settlers. If the new regime were that of the exiled Charles II, the king might even fulfill his promise to return Jamaica to his royal ally, the king of Spain. Beset by doubts about his own authority and the future of Jamaica, D'Oyley reduced his role to peacekeeping.[86]

As a caretaker governor-general, D'Oyley passively reflected the shifts of English authority. As his commercial partner, civil functionary, and military subordinate, Captain Cornelius Burrough, wrote: "We are just like you at home; when we heard of the Lord Protector's death we proclaimed his son, when we heard of his being turned out we proclaimed a Parliament, and now own a Committee of Safety." In June 1660 D'Oyley himself assured the commissioners of the admiralty that although he did not know who held executive power in England, he would unquestioningly obey the sovereign authority.[87]

At least the governor-general of Jamaica was sure that there would be an admiralty office, whatever the form of government. The admiralty had been his chief link with the restored commonwealth in 1659. It was the admiralty, under the duke of York, that would first grant royal authority to D'Oyley. The governor-general's confidence in military bureaucracy carried over to the agencies of war and colonial affairs, and to the treasury as well. One lesson of the civil wars had been the constancy of these agents of executive authority. Another lesson was that neither the names

Western Design, 196–197. See also D'Oyley's statement, June 12, 1660, that "if any mischance should befal this place, it may redound to my discredit" (Add. MSS 12423, 90b). A yet more sanguinary account, in which D'Oyley is portrayed as personally leading his life guard to the defeat of the rebels, "after a stout resistance," is in Long, *Jamaica*, I, 281. There are indications that the incident had roots in the conflict of the socially conservative— "Presbyterian," or Masseyan—convictions of the D'Oyley group with the more radical republican army feelings of the Raymond-Tyson faction. Hints of the latter are in Cundall, *Governors of Jamaica*, 5–6, and Add. MSS 12423, 93b–94. For a variant story, see Taylor, *Western Design*, 197–199. On Tyson and the Guanaboa quarter, see n. 78 above.

86. Beeston, "Journal," Add. MSS 12430, 23b; statement by Gen. D'Oyley, Jan. 3, 1660, Blathwayt Papers, Huntington Lib. On Charles II's alliance with Spain, see Thornton, *West-India Policy*, 68.

87. Burrough to Blackborne, Jan. 19, 1660, *Cal. S.P. Col., 1675–1676, Addenda, 1574–1674*, no. 326; D'Oyley to the commissioners of the navy, June 1, 1660, *Cal. S.P. Col., 1574–1660*, 480.

of the agencies nor the form of executive authority mattered as much as the chief executive's power to command both the armed forces and the civil service. The alliance of the military and the bureaucracy with the executive in the interest of social peace and stability underlay the growing strength of the English executive in the coming generation.[88]

Until General Monck, at the head of the army, decided that public order demanded the acceptance of Charles II as the chief of state, the authority of the governor-general of Jamaica's garrison government rested on the force of Edward D'Oyley's personality, on the martial discipline he had repeatedly enforced on his soldier-settlers, on the habit of subordination produced by the length of his regime (now approaching five years), and on the success of the effort to apply to Jamaica the classical dictum that it was "not . . . the Custome for Foreign Dominions to discompose their own Governments by taking notice of Reports" of upheavals at home. Rather, it was hoped that provincial governments would preserve the peace "according to their present grounds, until they shall receive other Directions from the Supremacy." These directions were slow in coming. Successive English authorities in these turbulent years were too concerned with saving themselves to take the time to alter Jamaica's distant government.[89]

Still, the news that came to Jamaica a few days after the suppression of the August 1660 mutiny upset the provincial army of the Protectorate much more than had the alterations of authority between army and parliament in England during the preceding year. Charles II was restored. Would the new king give Cromwell's conquest to Spain? Would he make it the private domain of some hungry courtier returned with him from long years of exile? If the king kept the island, what form of government would he confer on it? All of Governor-General D'Oyley's acts might be repudiated. The Jamaica executive waited vainly for word of his fate, and the island's. On March 6, 1661, D'Oyley wrote that he had "hoped that long ere this the further pleasure of his Majesty or his privy Council could have been made known to us And the Governor here had been impowered to act accordingly, but the deferring such advertisement hath caused several distrac-

88. Besides n. 87, see Blathwayt Papers, Huntington Lib.; declaration of parliament (read Sept. 1659), Add. MSS 12423, 75; house of commons proceedings, July 30, 1659, Stock, ed., *Proceedings of British Parliaments*, I, 265–267; Taylor, *Western Design*, 202; Thornton, *West-India Policy*, 44.

89. Povey and Noell to Searle, London, Apr. 30, 1659, Povey to "Gen. D'Oyley, Governor of Jamaica," Add. MSS 11411, 84, 21–23a.

tions in the Army and people." For eleven months after he proclaimed the monarchy's restoration, General D'Oyley had to grasp at legal straws to support his authority and to justify killing those who called his government illegal. He feared all the while that "after all my services, I be paid with an accusation of acting arbitrarily." Like so many of his successors, the governor-general sought (and ultimately secured) the protection of the sovereign's pardon for his illegal or extralegal executive actions.[90]

Jamaicans wondered if their colony had an English future, but certitude concerning it prevailed in London. After all, King Charles had at least implicitly approved the West Indian expedition of 1654 when he was consulted in exile by General Venables and Admiral Penn. Even after the king's restoration, Cromwellian sponsors of the expedition still composed much of the English executive. They were especially powerful in matters of trade and empire. Led by former Cromwellians, the king-in-council on December 5, 1660, rejected the Spanish demand for Jamaica's return.[91]

As this decision to keep Cromwell's conquest suggests, too much is made of 1660 as a meaningful date in imperial and mercantile policy. While the head of state was changed, many of the old regime's policymakers, administrators, and their colonial programs remained. From George Monck, now the duke of Albemarle, the king's captain general and the senior member of the privy council committee for Jamaica, down to Thomas Povey, a member of the royal council for foreign plantations, the imperial and mercantile sponsors of the Western Design continued to support its Jamaican offspring. Naturally, the new council for foreign

90. Add. MSS 12423, 103; D'Oyley to the council of state, Feb. 27, 1657, Birch, ed., *Thurloe S.P.*, VI, 834; Beeston, "Journal," Add. MSS 12430, 15. D'Oyley received a pardon for having been "compelled to inflict punishments upon mutinous and seditious persons to prevent anarchy, but being then without the formality of a Commission" (petition of D'Oyley, Apr. [?], 1664, warrant for a pardon, Apr. [?], 1664, *Cal. S.P. Col., 1661–1668*, nos. 703, 705). On the significance of this pardon, and for other cases, see S. S. Webb, "Blathwayt," *WMQ*, 3d Ser., XXV (1968), 19–20, XXVI (1969), 390–391. D'Oyley based his continuing authority on the royal proclamation that sustained the powers of the Commonwealth officers until further notice, and on two sets of instructions to royal naval captains ordering them to obey D'Oyley as the commander-in-chief of Jamaica (Add. MSS 12423, 95, 105). On the possible sale of Jamaica and the weakness of imperial administration and policy that this implied in the Clarendon era, and for two years thereafter, see Thornton, *West-India Policy*, 14–15. See also n. 91 below.

91. Why Charles II approved of the expedition is a question complicated by the deviousness of the politics and diplomacy of the exiled court. See, e.g., Penn, *Memorials of William Penn*, II, 14–16, 27; Long, *Jamaica*, I, 241–242; Underdown, *Royalist Conspiracy*, 125, 308–309 (who doubts Clarendon, *History*, Bk. XV, No. 6); Gardiner, *Commonwealth and Protectorate*, III, 214–217.

plantations was charged with continuing the Protectorate's policies of colonial centralization and uniformity.[92]

Given this continuity of personnel and purpose, plans for
developing Jamaica advanced almost without interruption from
before Cromwell's death in September 1658 until a royal decision
was reached regarding the D'Oyley government in January 1661.
In fact, the analysis and advice first put forward by the colonial
committee of the Protectorate in June 1657 was precisely that
finally adopted by the crown. "As yet Jamaica looks only like a
great garrison, and rather an Army than a Colony," the committee
had commented. The committee agreed that this "great garrison"
must be developed, for it was in "the Interest of your Highness
and this Commonwealth to support Jamaica as your principal fort
and Settlement in the West Indies." The methods recommended
by the Protectorate committee—and adopted by the crown—to
achieve colonial growth in Jamaica were those suggested by the
island's successive military governors, Edward D'Oyley in particular. These were, first, the English government's public promise of protection and support for Jamaica. This would attract
merchant and planter investment in the colony. Second, colonization could be assured by converting the soldiers into planters. To
settle their garrison on the land, the Jamaica governors-general
called for payment of the army's arrears of salary in the form of
servants, tools, provisions, and clothes. Once equipped to plant,
the seasoned veterans must be denied permission to leave the

92. Albemarle was the senior member of the privy council committee that advocated
the retention of Jamaica by the crown and the extension of D'Oyley's command; see proceedings of the privy council, Oct. 17, Nov. 30, Dec. 6, 1660, W. L. Grant and James Munro,
eds., *Acts of the Privy Council of England, Colonial Series [1613–1783]*, 6 vols. (1908–1912;
repr. Nendeln, Liechtenstein, 1966), I, nos. 491, 500, 501. Povey's "white paper" on Jamaica,
as commissioned by the committee, is in Egerton MS 2395, 301–302. See also the lucid
statement on the Jamaica debate in Whitson, *Constitutional Development of Jamaica*, 8–9,
13–14, and the sources cited therein. As early as Sept. 1660, Charles II assured the leading
merchants on Jamaica that he would retain the island and would commission Sir Edward
Massey governor (Beer, ed., *Diary of Evelyn*, entry of Sept. 27, 1660). For institutional and
policy continuity, see the register of the new council for foreign plantations, in C.O. 1/14,
59, cited in Thornton, *West-India Policy*, 10. See Thornton, 6–7, on the influence of Povey.
Col. Venables (son of the conqueror of Jamaica), Noell, and Povey all were members of the
council for foreign plantations's select committee for Jamaica. The latter two had been
members of the Jamaica committee established in 1656 (together with Tobias Bridge, whose
imperial influence certainly did not fade in 1660, and such Anglo-American worthies as
Stephen Winthrop) (Watts, *Colonies anglaises*, 448). As a clerk of the privy council, Povey
dominated the select committee, and so found acceptance for his proposals. He furthered
organization of a colonial bureaucracy, centered on himself, by securing appointment as receiver general of the American revenues (grant to Povey, Sept. 20, 1661, *Cal. S.P. Col.,
1661–1668*, no. 173). The post was inherited by Povey's protégé, William Blathwayt. See
also the minutes of the council for foreign plantations, Jan. 7, 14–25, 1661, *ibid.*, nos. 3, 5.

island. Of course, D'Oyley had already employed these means to settle many of his men. His Whitehall superiors endorsed another of his practices when they recommended that the most obedient remnant of the troops be made into a "standing militia" of a thousand men—horse, foot, and dragoons. This force would be subject to the governor as commander-in-chief.[93]

The paramilitary political implication of this last proposal was soon made explicit. The Protectorate committee concluded that the responsibilities of military commander and civil governor should continue to be merged in the person of a governor-general. Such a merger had become standard practice in the garrison governments of dependencies in the British Isles, whether towns, islands, or subordinate kingdoms. In Jamaica, as in British garrison governments, the attempt to divide civil and military powers between commissioners and commander had failed. The general commanding the settlement's garrison had parlayed military power into civil authority and therefore had been accorded the additional title of "governor." Jamaican experience, and the British garrison government precedents it reflected, combined with the menace of the conquered colony's dangerous neighbors and the difficulties posed by its distance from England to convince the committee that the island's governor-general must be absolute, that he must command both civilians and the military on land and on sea. He must be an honest, popular officer, concerned to preserve his honor and that of the empire. Only such an honorable man would refrain from the abuse of his absolute power. Only such a well-known soldier could attract and secure settlers, the substance of empire, "it being impossible that any good can be effected in America without people."[94]

93. Thomas Povey to "Edw. Doily, esq. Governor of Jamaica," n.d., to Richard Povey, n.d., Add. MSS 11411, 87b–88, 17–18; "Abstract of a Report of October 12th and 29th, 165–," Blathwayt Papers, XLI, no. 1, Williamsburg. There was a hiatus in planning for Jamaica during the few months of the restored Commonwealth. On Charles II's attitudes toward the Spanish demand that he sell them Jamaica (and Dunkirk) or be attacked, see the implications of Keith Feiling, British Foreign Policy, 1660–1672 (London, 1930), 38–39. See Feiling also on Spain's fading hopes of recovering Jamaica by negotiation (pp. 172–173) and on the final Spanish concession of English possession (p. 326). Bridge, Noell, and Winthrop to Cromwell, June 2, [1657], Egerton MS 2395, 123.

94. "Considerations about the Peopling and Settling the Island Jamaica," report of the Jamaica committee, Oct. 17, 1658, Egerton MS 2395, fols. 283, 158; chapter 1 above. Although the governor-general was to be omnipotent, he was not expected to be omnicompetent. Functionaries of all sorts, from secretaries to ministers, were to be appointed by the English executive and sent out to assist in the government. The report thus recommended both an imperial, military executive and mercantile, civilian patentees, reflecting the split between army officers and merchants in the committee that wrote it. See Thornton's surprised remark that D'Oyley's "Commission is rather an oddment, its civil and military

To protect the people, reinforce the governor-general's authority, and symbolize the permanence of England's occupation, the committee recommended completion of the citadel commanding Jamaica's chief port and capital, Cagway, now renamed Port Royal. Where generals governed, the citadel manifested their authority. So it would in Jamaica. The committee echoed the colony commanders' argument that "the building the fort is absolutely needful to secure the island of Jamaica and encourage people to come into it." Fort Charles would symbolize the predominant, military element of imperialism.[95]

Indeed, the island's strategic location and the demonstrated willingness of its soldier-colonists to defend it were the imperial characteristics that finally persuaded the crown to retain Jamaica. Then, too, the army was as useful in Jamaica as it would be dangerous at home. Like the red-coated garrison of Dunkirk (which the crown dispatched to preserve a client state in Portugal and to create an imperial base in Tangier), the English garrison of Jamaica represented one of the major classes of Englishmen driven by the civil wars to people an empire. Soldiers in Iberia and in Africa, sailors and settlers in the West Indies, servants in Virginia, refugee republicans and regicides in New England—all of these men, displaced from the traditional society and disciplined to modern military and political purpose in Cromwell's army, were important elements in the growing imperial population.[96]

If the Cromwellian army's island conquest was to be a royal colony, and the conquering troops its inhabitants and garrison, clearly their general must be the king's governor of Jamaica. The obviousness of this choice was increased when Lieutenant General D'Oyley revealed that he was a cousin of Charles II's secretary of state. In January 1661 the king's committee for foreign plantations had only to ask "whether in the next Commission it may be necessary to style Doilie Lt. Genll. or Governor"? The crown

---

strands closely interwoven" (*West-India Policy*, 45). Such was the long-standing tendency of garrison government. See Egerton MS 2395, 283. See also nn. 95, 96, below.

95. To n. 94 above, add the minutes of the council for foreign plantations, Jan. 30, 1661, and D'Oyley's instructions as governor, Feb. [?], 1661, *Cal. S.P. Col., 1661–1668*, nos. 12, 22. Fort Charles not only survived the Port Royal earthquake of 1692, the fire of 1703, and the hurricane of 1722, but was improved after each of these disasters to protect what "became by far the most important British base in the Caribbean," and still stands. On the fort and the port, see Michael Pawson and David Buissert, *Port Royal, Jamaica* (Oxford, 1975), *passim* and 125. On the great naval expansion, see Ruth A. Bourne, *Queen Anne's Navy in the West Indies* (New Haven, Conn., 1939). I am indebted to Dr. Bourne not only for her published work on the West Indies but also for her illuminating correspondence and for manuscript copies of her more recent work on a variety of Anglo-American topics.

96. D'Oyley to Nicholas, Sept. 11, 1660, *Cal. S.P. Col., 1574–1660*, 489.

committee concluded that Edward D'Oyley should be "Governor and Captn. Genll." On February 8, 1661, King Charles recognized Edward D'Oyley's "ability . . . fidelity and experience" in a royal commission and instructions to him as governor-general of Jamaica. While D'Oyley was denied the title "captain general"— presumably for the same civilian constitutional reasons that were applied by Clarendon and Southampton to deny even the name of "governor" to the earl of Carlisle in his title town or to Lord Culpeper on the Isle of Wight—he nevertheless received royal authority for what he already practiced: "to bee the Governor in and uppon our said Island (and to do all things appertaining thereto)." The paramilitary forms of garrison government evolved by the Tudor executives and spread over the British Isles by the pressure of civil war had leaped to Jamaica, spurred by the orders of a military dictator. Garrison government was now recognized by the restored monarchy as the preferred mechanism for ruling the expanding English empire. Exalting executive authority, garrison government became the imperial norm. To that norm the Stuart sovereignty would also reduce the older, institutionally independent colonies, if it could.[97]

The crown's success was manifest in that the royal orders of 1661 to Jamaica's military executive helped to shape the administration of the English empire at least until the nineteenth century. Governor-General D'Oyley's commission and instructions were the vehicles that carried the imperial policies of the Protectorate forward into the counsels of the Restoration and beyond. Although these important constitutional documents of the old empire have been ignored by modern students of royal commissions, British

97. As an alternative to D'Oyley, the Jamaica committee considered only Gen. Massey, the parliamentary and royal governor of Gloucester under whose command so many of the Jamaica officers had served. See *DNB*, s.v. "Massey," chapter 1 above, and n. 92 above. The presence on the four-man subcommittee of Albemarle (Monck), who had long appreciated D'Oyley's military virtues, and Nicholas, who could testify to D'Oyley's social respectability, must have counted strongly in the governor's favor. See *Privy Council, Col. Ser.*, I, no. 491, and Thornton, *West-India Policy*, 43. The joining of the title "general" with that of "governor" had substantial meaning. The English royal authorities argued that "general" with its implication of the involvement of the governor's command in the military chain of command, clearly indicated the high degree of "dependency" they sought to impose on the colonies. The king's designate and representative, the governor-general, was to subordinate the colonies to the government of the crown. See objections against Lord Willoughby, July 16, 1660, *Cal. S.P. Col., 1574–1660*, 483; minute of the Jamaica committee, Jan. 10, 1660, Egerton MS 2395, 289. D'Oyley's commission, Feb. 8, 1661, and his instructions, Feb. [?], 1661, are in Add. MSS 12428, 6–9b, 8b–13b, in C.O. 138/1, 3b–5, 6–10, and are calendared in *Cal. S.P. Col., 1661–1668*, nos. 20, 22. Note the parallel use of the title for the Virginia chief executive by this committee and the implications of its first denial to Sir William Berkeley, discussed in chapter 7 below.

officials did take all of the articles of D'Oyley's instructions as precedents in writing subsequent colonial constitutions. Edward D'Oyley's orders defined England's empire.[98]

Their preamble asserted that "the defence, security and good Government" of Jamaica required and justified royal government. Royal government, D'Oyley's commission continued, was designed to secure the "orderly peaceable conduct and preservation of the Several Soldiers planters and other Inhabitants there residing." Charged with defending Jamaica and with preserving the colony's civil peace, the governor-general was given three legal bases for his authority: the royal commission and instructions; "such good just and reasonable Customes and Constitutions as are exercised and settled in our other Colonies . . . provided they be not repugnant to our Laws of England"; and his own discretion. Although the island executive himself combined civil and military authority, these powers were otherwise constitutionally separate. Thus, with the advice of a quorum of his advisory council, the governor was to establish civil courts of law. In keeping with his military role, however, the chief executive alone had the power to "muster command and discipline all the Military forces of the said Island . . . and to fight kill slay repress and subdue all such as shall in a hostile or mutinous manner by Insurrection or Invasion disturb the peace or attempt the surprise of our said Island of Jamaica." In such cases—as if power of life and death were not enough—the governor-general was also authorized to "put in execution the Laws martial," but only upon soldiers. (Governors evaded this limitation, if such it was intended to be, by calling out all able-bodied men as the militia, and so subjecting them to martial law.) The extent of military compulsion also appeared in orders to the governor to draft soldiers and settlers, servants and slaves, in order to complete the citadel at Port Royal as the seat of executive authority.[99]

In addition to defending the island and administering justice, both military and civil, the governor was to regulate Jamaica's economy. He was instructed to license craftsmen and tradesmen, encourage merchants, prevent monopoly, and so to protect "the Buyer who becomes necessitous and impoverished where Trade is

98. Abstract of the "Commissions and Instructions formerly and at this time given to the *Governors* . . . 1740," Add. MSS 30372. Leonard Woods Labaree, *Royal Instructions to British Colonial Governors, 1670–1776* (New York and London, 1935), prints no text dating before 1670.

99. D'Oyley's commission, Feb. 8, 1661, Add. MSS 12428, 6b; his instructions, *ibid.*, 10b, and in C.O. 138/1, 4–8. See also Blathwayt Papers, Huntington Lib.

not duely and prudently regulated." Commercial encouragement and consumer protection were important enough, but land underlay the economy. The governor-general controlled its distribution. His control of this, the island's chief resource, together with his power to regulate trade and his military mandates, went far to provide the royal military governor with more political ammunition in his province than patronage and revenue provided his kingly commander-in-chief in England. In an underdeveloped agricultural economy, great power belonged to the governor, who not only granted land to individuals but also appointed the surveyors. In addition, the governor retained the right to resume control of undeveloped plots and those that he deemed were being held for speculative purposes.[100]

The social implications of the governor's military, judicial, and economic authority were made more explicit by requiring him to use all his power to enforce high morality on officeholders, to suppress popular drunkenness and debauchery, and to encourage the establishment and authority of the Church of England throughout his government. Social and religious regularity should stabilize the new society. To give this stability the indispensable support of the soldier-settlers, D'Oyley was ordered not to permit anyone mustered as a soldier to depart the island without leave from him. Finally, the crown recognized the executive discretion essential to distant and endangered settlements when it authorized the governor to take any action that would protect his command or promote its settlement, provided he had consulted five of his councillors.

As this proviso points out, the governor was not to rule alone, unassisted and unchecked. "For the better Administration of Justice and Management of Affairs" in Jamaica, the governor was ordered to organize a council of twelve persons to assist him in civil affairs. Should the military governor proclaim martial law in effect, he was required to convene a dozen officers to administer military discipline. In practice, these officers turned out to be the same individuals who constituted the council of state.[101]

The identity of military officers and civilian authorities in the provincial council was anticipated by the definition of the council's constituency in the governor-general's instructions. Eleven of his (nominally) civil councillors were to be selected by as many of the army officers, planters, and inhabitants "as by your best and

100. See n. 99 above.
101. On the role of governors' councils, see chapter 1 above.

most equal contrivance may be admitted thereunto whether at one or several places." Just as the Tudor officer-governors of Calais and Tournai, and the soldiers who commanded the garrison governments of the civil wars and Interregnum, had been checked or supported by centrally authorized councils of garrison officers and local leaders, so the authority of governors-general overseas after 1660 was limited. Another check on that authority came in the form of patent officers of the central government, who sat ex officio in the council. In the case of Jamaica, the twelfth member of the council was to be the royally appointed secretary of state for the island.[102]

Although General D'Oyley had been named as the restored king's governor of Jamaica, no one in the colony knew it officially, and many persons denied D'Oyley's authority because the royal orders composed in the summer of 1660 and signed the following February did not reach Jamaica until June 1661. To be sure, the duke of York had ordered the royal naval captains who brought the news of the restoration to Jamaica to subordinate themselves to the "governor" there. D'Oyley tried further to authenticate his position as the royal representative by ordering officers and planters to sign an instrument "declaring their obedience and subjection to his Majesty," but so far as Jamaicans knew, his majesty had yet to recognize Edward D'Oyley as his governor. A newcomer to the colony described the result of this communications failure—the truncated government of 1660. Jamaicans, wrote William Beeston, "were still as an Army but without Pay. Commanded by Gen. D'Oyley . . . the Govmt. was only by a Court Martial held once a month at St. Jago and what disputes Genl. D'Oyley heard and decided himself who lived very mean and private."[103]

D'Oyley declined public display because more than six months had passed since he had proclaimed Charles II as king, but he had still not received a royal commission. By January 1661 his soldiers again began to "speak reproachfully and rebelliously."

102. See n. 99 above. Richard Povey's commission as secretary of state and as commissary and steward general is the first item in the Jamaica Entry Book (C.O. 138/1, 1–2b), antedating D'Oyley's commission by almost a month (commission to Povey, Jan. 10, 1661, *Cal. S.P. Col., 1661–1668*, no. 4).

103. Beeston, "Journal," Add. MSS 12430, 23. See instructions from the commissioners of the admiralty to Capts. Thomas Wilkes and John Wilgresse, May 21, 1660, and instrument dated Aug. 18, 1660, Add. MSS 12423, 95, 92, and 95b; "Edw. D'Oyley Genl in Chief in America to all Govrs of Islands, Capts of Ships, officers and soldiers under his command," Feb. 5, 1661, D'Oyley to Nicholas, Mar. [?], 1661, *Cal. S.P. Col., 1661–1668*, nos. 17, 61. Haring, *Buccaneers*, 100, also cites S.P. Spain/44, 318.

In March, D'Oyley executed two of these "rebels" in order to preserve discipline. He feared that he had murdered them. During the Protectorate he had limited liquor licenses—wine and spirits were already the bulk of Jamaica's imports—to those who contributed to settlement by developing plantations or importing laborers. Now merchants challenged his authority to enforce his regulations. He stopped doing so. Demoralization doubled the social disorganization and indiscipline caused by this reduction in government authority. The rumor grew that no royal government had been established for Jamaica because King Charles had given the island back to Spain. Planting decayed, debauchery increased, and D'Oyley declined to judge civil disputes. Chaos ensued. Apparently, only the strong hand of the commander-in-chief had held the young colony together. [104]

As garrison government collapsed in Jamaica, a royal naval vessel dropped anchor off the citadel on June 2, 1661. The *Rosebush* brought the king's commission to "Colonel Edward D'Oyley" as governor of Jamaica. D'Oyley immediately published the commission and sent out the provost marshal to the quarters with warrants for the election of the councillors, mostly the field officers of his council of war and his own staff officers, as it turned out. Backed by the crown's commission and his councillors, Governor D'Oyley reimposed his regulation of the liquor traffic and levied the taxes on liquor imports that became his government's major revenue. Turning to his garrison, the governor ordered new uniforms issued, the first part of King Charles's "gift" to the army in lieu of pay. This donation was designed, as governors-general had recommended, to set up the seasoned soldiers as planters. Money and sugar mills followed the clothes, as did the last provisions from the army warehouses. [105]

104. Capt. Wilkes to the commissioners of the navy, Mar. 26, 1661, *Cal. S.P. Col., 1661–1668*, no. 57; Add. MSS 12423, 103–103b. D'Oyley's letter to Nicholas, Mar. 1662, is in C.O. 1/15, 37, and calendared in *Cal. S.P. Col., 1661–1668*, no. 61. See also "The Relation of Coll. Doyley . . . to the Lord Chancellor," and D'Oyley's statement of Jan. 3, 1660, Add. MSS 11410, 21–22, 485; Beeston, "Journal," Add. MSS 12430, 15. D'Oyley stopped patenting land, which he had previously done by his sole order, written "at the General's house," by his personal secretary. See the sample patent of Jan. 12, 1661, in Bridges, *Jamaica Annals*, I, 426.

105. D'Oyley's proclamation, June 5, 1661, Add. MSS 12423, 106. All the councillors held military rank of captain or higher. More than half of them had been active in D'Oyley's previous administration. See orders of the governor and council of Jamaica, June 18, July 2–3, 1661, *Cal. S.P. Col., 1661–1668*, nos. 108, 123. Tools, milling equipment, clothing, and fishing tackle were included in the distribution (minutes of the council for foreign plantations, Apr. 15, 29, 1661, orders of the governor and council of Jamaica, July 2–3, 1661, *ibid.*, nos. 70 71, 73, 123). See also orders of the governor and council of Jamaica, June 18, July 15, 1661, *ibid.*, nos. 108, 131, and Add. MSS 12423, 109.

The accelerated conversion of soldiers into planters, the proclamation of peace, the growth of civilian and mercantile populations, in short, the declaration of a plantation future for Jamaica required more complex social regulation than had been necessary for a wartime garrison conducting subsistence agriculture. Acting under the royal commission, Governor-General D'Oyley and his council quickly copied Barbados's rigid regulation of servants. Terms of service (and punitive additions to those terms for disobedience, fornication, and bastardy) were decreed by ordinance. To this labor code the Jamaica executive added new penalties for absence without leave and for theft. The governor-general also provided for the certification, sale, and manufacture of this disciplined labor's produce. He proclaimed the times and places of public markets, and he regulated prices and wages, weights and measures. No one was to enter, leave, or do business on the island without the governor-general's license. D'Oyley even became Jamaica's social worker, personally arranging marriage settlements and awarding poor relief. Under royal authority he had now increased the social and economic scope of his command without lessening its martial and executive characteristics.[106]

The council, ostensibly a civilian element in Jamaica's new crown constitution, did little to limit the martial and executive authority of the colony's commander-in-chief. When his old army subordinates, assembled as his civil council, presumed to challenge the governor's independent actions, he rebuffed their interference. D'Oyley "could not forget he had been a General, though it was for the rebels." He also reminded his subordinates that he now ruled by the king's commission, not theirs. These authoritarian assertions would be repeated by D'Oyley's successors in Jamaica and by the governors-general of other imperial outposts.[107]

Military principles and personnel also pervaded the supposedly civil courts established by the governor and his council of

106. On trade and labor regulation, see orders of the governor and council of Jamaica, June 18, Aug. 27, Oct. 8, Nov. 15, 1661, Jan. 16, 1662, proclamations of Gov. D'Oyley, July 3, 1661, orders of the governor of Jamaica, July 3, 1661, proclamation of the governor and council, Aug. 20, 1661, *Cal. S.P. Col., 1661–1668*, nos. 123, 169, 176, 182, 215, 124, 125, 159, 164. On servants, see also Barrington to [?], July 14, 1655, HMC, *Seventh Report*, Pt. I, 572. On the class war in Barbados, see Dunn, *Sugar and Slaves*, 69, 257.

107. D'Oyley is quoted by Cundall, *Governors of Jamaica*, 8, and in narrative of events, June 14, 1661, *Cal. S.P. Col., 1661–1668*, no. 106. See nn. 102 and 105 above on the councillors. On the dominance of military attitudes, see the narrative of events, June 14, 1661, minutes of the council of Jamaica, Apr. 16, 1662, *Cal. S.P. Col., 1661–1668*, nos. 106, 283, and nn. 108 and 109, below.

state. D'Oyley named those councillors who had been his regimental colonels to be the judges of the courts that replaced the regimental courts-martial. These colonel-councillors also dominated the council of state, which succeeded the general's court-martial as the supreme court of the colony. Despite the continued control of justice by military men—officers who, as their commander remarked of himself, were "ignorant of the law"—the very creation of civil courts "pleased the trading people." The soldier-planters, however, were restive under the new, nominally civilian, regime. They "could not forbear talking even to Mutiny. For that [at] the first Quarter Sessions which was July 2 [1661] one of them was hanged to let them see the Law could do as much as a Court Martial." The identity of judges and justice under civil and military government was thus harshly demonstrated. The new system paid its administrators better, however, for the general, turned governor and chief judge, split the liquor tax revenue with his colonels, now the councillors and assistant judges. By contrast, D'Oyley neglected the royal patent officials, "because they were not officers of his own making." As one civilian merchant complained, "Gen. D'Oyley . . . had indeed no respect to any either planters or Traders but those who had been of the Army."[108]

Many of these veterans were still privateers and still the cutting edge of English imperialist aggression against Spain in America. Despite his proclamation of the king's peace with Spain, Governor-General D'Oyley continued to command sea rovers and to share in the proceeds of their Spanish prizes. Pushed by his men and by his desire for profit, D'Oyley had quickly decided that the peace with Spain did not apply "to this side of the line."[109]

Quick profit attracted D'Oyley all the more because, by November 1661, he had heard that he would be recalled, or, as King Charles politely insisted, General D'Oyley had urgent private business to look after at home. The general's successor in the

108. Minutes of the council of Jamaica, Apr. 16, 1662, *Cal. S.P. Col., 1661–1668*, no. 283. See Beeston, "Journal," Add. MSS 12430, 24b, on the succession of the civil to the martial law. Civil disturbances—all termed "mutinies" by D'Oyley and other officer-governors—continued. There were casualties among the governor's defenders, as well as executions of the "mutineers"; see, e.g., proclamation of the governor and council of Jamaica, Aug. 13, 1661, *Cal. S.P. Col., 1661–1668*, no. 157.

109. D'Oyley's decision to war on Spain is noted in his letter to Nicholas, Mar. [?], 1661, *Cal. S.P. Col., 1661–1668*, no. 61. See also petition of Col. Guy Molesworth to the king, [May 30], 1663, petition of officers and mariners, Dec. 2, 1663, the king to D'Oyley, Jan. 19, 1664, note of seizure of a ship and confiscation of goods by D'Oyley, 1664?, *ibid.*, nos. 461, 594, 641, 643.

government arrived on August 11, 1662. He brusquely refused to permit D'Oyley to remain in Jamaica. On September 10, 1662, Edward D'Oyley sailed from Jamaica into obscurity. He, more than any other man, had won Jamaica for the English and had shaped its garrison government—the imperial polity pioneered by that colony in England's American empire.[110]

110. Report of the council for foreign plantations to the king, July [?], 1661, the king to the governor and council of Jamaica, July 18, 1661, *ibid.*, nos. 132, 133; Beeston, "Journal," Add. MSS 12430, 25–25b. The departure of D'Oyley's kinsman, Sir Edward Nicholas, from the secretaryship of state in Oct. 1662 (see Pepys, *Diary*, III, 226 [entry of Oct. 16, 1662], 226 n. 2) was followed by the governor's recall, but the decision to appoint Windsor dated to July 1661. See the praise of D'Oyley by that enemy of governors and critic of the military, Edward Long (Long, *Jamaica*, I, 284–285).

CHAPTER 5

Courtiers and Professionals, Grandees and Aristocrats

Edward D'Oyley, the first governor-general of Jamaica, arrived in England in the winter of 1662, after a voyage of epic length punctuated with near disasters. Lord Chancellor Clarendon immediately asked him to report on Jamaica's problems and prospects. D'Oyley saw more of the former than of the latter, but many of the Jamaican problems he complained of were colonial commonplaces. When the former governor-general lamented the "many insolent Miscarriages" of royal naval captains and objected to the home authorities' "Crying up Merchants and Trade and their being heard and countenanced against the Governour," he pointed to the powerful rivals of every provincial executive.[1]

Naval officers possessed their own entrenched bureaucracy at home and met a profound military need in the colonies. These attributes gave political power to ship captains, just as they strengthened army governors. Few colonial planters or English merchants could resist opportunities to make these rival military representatives of the central government neutralize each other. Such opportunities were frequent, for interservice jealousy was bitter and pervasive. Yet D'Oyley himself always recognized that naval strength was essential to empire.[2]

Merchants, too, found bureaucratic supporters as they sought mercantile dominion in the empire and strove to subordinate military priorities to commercial concerns. Despite his anger at what seemed to him merchant selfishness, D'Oyley also acknowledged the necessity of trade—its customs revenue, the seamen it trained, and the ships it financed and freighted—to imperial government

---

1. "The Relation of Col. D'Oyley upon his returne from Jamaica to the Lord Chancellor," Add. MSS 11410, 13, 14, British Library, and copy in the Bodleian Library, MS Rawlinson, A 347.
2. "Without shipping, this Place appears to mee of noe use to the Comonwealth": D'Oyley to the commissioners of the admiralty, June 1, 1660, C.O. 1/14, no. 7, P.R.O. (noted in Thornton, *West-India Policy*, 42).

and seaborne empire.[3] Even "a garrison place" such as Jamaica required people and planting, and General D'Oyley admitted that every privateering expedition lured men from the island, caused the loss of the crops they abandoned, sacrificed commerce, and so drove many Jamaicans to settle in Virginia.

D'Oyley himself was unsure whether the privateers' destruction of trade with Spanish America and their distraction of Jamaicans from planting were offset by the privateers' contribution of Spanish plunder and military might to the colony. He was convinced nevertheless that his counsels were surer than those of sailors or traders. He grumbled to Clarendon that these seaborne rivals of governors-general unfairly biased the deliberations of imperial government: they sailed home to plead their selfish cases while provincial commanders were duty-bound to distant colonies. The governor-general insisted to the lord chancellor that the appointment of capable army officers as governors—and the grant to those governors-general of full power over both navy officers and merchants—was requisite to the exploitation of Jamaica's chief assets, its magnificent harbor and strategic location for war or for trade with the Spanish Indies.[4]

A "Young Lord" Uses Garrison Government

Edward D'Oyley conceded that his recommendation had already been carried out, at least in part, by the appointment as governor-general of "a person of Honor [that is, a nobleman] to give Reputation" to Jamaica. Thomas, Lord Windsor, like D'Oyley, was a veteran of the civil wars, though a royalist and ten years D'Oyley's junior. His background and career characterized the Restoration's officers and governors. As Thomas Hickman, the future governor-general had served as a captain of royalist cavalry in the first civil war, had become a lieutenant colonel of horse in the second, and had been distinguished at Naseby. When the cause of monarchy was lost, the young royalist colonel compounded with the parliament for his estates and seemingly settled down to improve the navigation of the Salwarpe. He was implicated, however, in the royalist rising planned for March 8, 1655. That day's

3. D'Oyley supported the government of Jamaica in part by taxing trade and ships. See Add. MSS 12428, 25; C.O. 139/1, 1, 4; *Cal. S.P. Col., 1675–1676,* no. 332; Whitson, *Constitutional Development of Jamaica,* 21.

4. *Cal. S.P. Col., 1661–1668,* no. 578; "Relation of Col. D'Oyley," Add. MSS 11410, 11–15.

events led to the death or transportation to the colonies of many of his colleagues. Undaunted, Hickman backed Charles Littleton (afterward his deputy and successor in the Jamaica command) in the Worcestershire royalist outbreak of 1658. Two years later, when Monck's legions restored the monarchy, the captain general named Colonel Hickman to a command in a regiment grown famous under Major General James Berry. It had patrolled the borders of Wales and Scotland, repressed royalist risings, and was a military police force in the West when its new captain joined it. Now titled "the Royal Regiment," so that "the soldiery may see . . . the affection that his Sacred Majesty hath for the army," it was not disbanded until December 1660.[5]

Hickman, a royalist captain commanding an ex-Cromwellian company, was now created Baron Windsor, named lord lieutenant of Worcestershire, and ordered to secure the county for the king. With his deputy lieutenants, among them Charles Littleton, Windsor kept "very strict eyes over all the Fanatic party." He issued orders "to disarm divers at least to search for arms in the houses." He drilled the Worcestershire militia, and also raised "80 or 90 volunteer Troopers without charge to the County, which and if I should find anything to beg would give me confidence to ask the king." Such military and political service in support of the crown, especially Windsor's activity against "the Presbyterian Parsons" in the election of 1660, won him a royal pension and gave him a claim to the profitable government of Jamaica in place of the Presbyterian nominee, the former parliamentary general who was now the royal governor of Gloucester, Sir Edward Massey. Six days before Windsor's commission as governor-general of Jamaica was signed, Thomas Povey described his lordship as "a gent of great Reputation here, and of handsome fortune which he is willing to improve."[6]

Windsor's reputation may have been as much a figment of Povey's imagination as his lordship's wealth was, but improvement of the latter immediately and tangibly followed the Jamaica

5. *Cal. S.P. Col., 1661–1668*, nos. 135, 145; "Relation of Col. D'Oyley," Add. MSS 11410, 14; Cundall, *Governors of Jamaica*, 15; S.P. 44/29, 2, P.R.O.; Underdown, *Royalist Conspiracy*, 143, 156, 160, 273 n. 31; Firth and Davies, *Regimental History*, xxxvi, 240, 244, 245, 246, 251, 253, 715; Stock, ed., *Proceedings of British Parliaments*, I, 247–263; Gardiner, *Commonwealth and Protectorate*, III, 344–346, IV, 34, 53; Berry and Lee, *A Cromwellian Major General: James Berry, passim.*

6. S.P. 44/20, n.p., 44/164, 154–155; Littleton to Christopher Hatton, Aug. 24, 31, [1661], Add. MSS 29577, 23b, 25; Windsor to Hatton, Sept. 19, Mar. 28, 1660, Add. MSS 29550, 361, 351, Mar. 4, 1661, Add. MSS 29551, 118b, Thomas to William Povey, Add. MSS 11411, 33. See also Beer, ed., *Diary of Evelyn*, entry of Sept. 26, 1660.

commission. The new imperial rule—"that every Governour, shall have his Commission reviewed . . . and renewed in one form"— had as its corollary that "the several Governors [are] to be paid their allowances from hence . . . that their dependency be immediately and altogether from His Highness, and that they may be the better brought to be accountable here for their Governments." Windsor quickly collected his first year's salary of £2,000 from the English exchequer. This fund was supposed to purchase his equipment and pay for his transport. The duke of York, however, as lord high admiral, supplied the governor-general with a frigate to carry him to his command and to use for trade and privateering. The duke also ordered the navy to transport the indentured servants whom Windsor, Littleton, and the earls of Clarendon and Carlisle sent out to develop the extensive lands that Windsor would grant them. Cromwell's territorial conquest would profit both the governor-general and his imperial associates.[7]

Together, the imperialist dukes of York and Albemarle, the royalist bureaucrats Clarendon and Nicholas, and the proto-whig mercantilists Thomas Povey and Anthony Ashley Cooper (Shaftesbury) composed Windsor's commissions and instructions for the government of Jamaica. A colony won by conquest, Jamaica legally had no government save that dictated by the conquering state. Only specific royal concessions gave the islanders any vestige of civil liberty, personal property, or representative government. Yet, like Cromwell and his lieutenant general, Edward D'Oyley, King Charles, or rather the officers of the crown who drew up Lord Windsor's instructions, made substantial political concessions in order to retain and to attract settlers. Thus Lord Windsor was authorized to grant Jamaicans both a legislature and the civil rights of Englishmen. The actual extent of these constitutional concessions would be long debated between the Jamaicans and the English executive. Not until 1728 would the islanders win conclusive royal recognition of their right to representative government. In this struggle the royal governors were racked between the adamant autonomy of the islanders they governed and the absolutist assertions of the crown they served.[8]

7. "Overtures touching the Council to be erected for foreign plantations," Egerton MS 2395, 271; Littleton to Hatton, Oct. 8, [1661], Add. MSS 29577, 29. Windsor recalled that he did not profit from the frigate and wished the governor of Guernsey better luck with his naval vessel (Windsor to Hatton, Jan. 10, 1671, Add. MSS 29553, 364). See also the king to the duke of York, Mar. 24, Apr. 7, 1662, S.P. 44/3, 32, 35; Latham and Matthews, eds., *Diary of Pepys*, III, 52, 62–63 (entries of Mar. 25, Apr. 10, 1662), 52 n. 3, 63 n. 1; and *Cal. S.P. Col., 1661–1668*, nos. 135, 145.

8. *Privy Council, Col. Ser.*, I, nos. 491, 500, 522; *Cal. S.P. Col., 1661–1668*, nos. 145, 259. These groups were also much involved in organizing the continued supply of the

The imperial planners recognized that Lord Windsor would have peculiar problems in establishing royal government in Jamaica. The Cromwellian army there had been "kept on foot." Therefore, Windsor would have to repeat on a larger scale in Jamaica the royalizing work he had done with Berry's regiment in England. That meant, in effect, disbanding most of the troops, yet winning the loyalty of a sufficient number of them "to make good the Forts against an Enemy, and his Authority against mutinies, or Conspiracies, which may be stirred up at so great changes . . . at his first entrance upon his Command." To meet mutiny, the governor-general's instructions extended his power of martial law even beyond that given General D'Oyley. Lord Windsor might try by court-martial "all notorious offenders," however he defined them and whether or not they were enlisted in the armed forces. In addition to maintaining a small standing army to put down local rebellion, Windsor was to arm every plantation and all "Christian servants." He was to make sure that his militia were "trained up in military discipline." The select committee was confident that such a disciplined militia in such an ordered polity, backed by a garrison of D'Oyley's seasoned regulars and commanded by a governor-general, would be able to beat off any invasion by the riffraff European soldiery sent overseas. As Jamaica was England's "frontier plantation in America, and thereby the more exposed to . . . attempts from the Spaniard," an unusually efficient militia always remained one of the colony's most marked characteristics. Its backbone of Cromwellian veterans helped make it so, as Windsor's old commander, Captain General Monck, duke of Albemarle, had planned. With the rest of the privy council's select committee for plantations, Albemarle ordered Windsor to make every effort to retain the Cromwellians as militiamen and planters by giving them the royal gift of clothing and agricultural tools. The

Jamaica colony by the English government. See the report on supplies needed for Jamaica, by Nicholas, Albemarle, and Annesley, Oct. 18, 1660, *ibid.*, *1675–1676, Addenda, 1574–1674*, 490, and following orders and considerations. A legislature was authorized by clause 14 of Windsor's instructions (Add. MSS 12428, 18–18b [C.O. 138/1, 18, numbers that clause as 20]). In his proclamation of Dec. 14, 1661, the king promised civil rights to prospective Jamaica settlers (Add. MSS 12428, 19–19b). Both concessions were noted in Windsor's Barbados declaration, [July 11], 1662, *Cal. S.P. Col., 1661–1668*, no. 324. The legislative branch was not provided for in Windsor's commission and was only permitted, not enjoined, in the governor-general's instructions (*ibid.*, nos. 145, 259). The king limited the political elements in his appeal to settlers (Dec. 14, 1661, *ibid.*, nos. 195, 196): English citizenship was granted, obedience to Windsor and his successors was demanded. On the discretionary authority of the crown, see Whitson, *Constitutional Development of Jamaica*, 14–17.

governor-general was also to assure his soldier-colonists that their produce would be exempt from customs duties for seven years.[9]

When he reached Jamaica in August 1662, Windsor found some sixteen hundred of the old army still in arms. Word of his avarice had preceded him. So much did the "old Soldiers" fear that the governor's greed would tempt him to tax their plantations, their produce, and their plunder that they "were like to Mutiny." Windsor quickly imprisoned "some of the most noted of them." He raised a troop of cavalry to mount guard day and night at the Port Royal fort, and he made that citadel his residence. "Yet still the old Soldiers murmur and threaten to relinquish their Plantations." So the governor-general proclaimed martial law. Now absolute in his government, Windsor declared war on the Spanish Indies, in part for personal profit and in part to draw off the Cromwellians to man the privateers. But he blamed the hostilities on the Spaniards' refusal to trade. The illogic of declaring war to secure trade did not deter enlistments against the hated Spaniards. Between twelve and thirteen hundred of "the Soldiers being poor and wanting Conveniences to settle . . . gladly embrac'd this opportunity" to join the expedition that Windsor organized around the redoubtable Captain Christopher Myngs and his *Centurion.* Myng's fleet carried the troops off to attack St. Jago in Cuba.[10]

In their absence the governor-general rapidly organized a loyal militia. Lord Windsor's followers staffed the new Port Royal regiment; his lordship commanded it himself. Just two weeks after the fleet's departure the governor-general mustered the citadel's regiment, "Completely Officer'd and Armed." He commissioned Sir Charles Littleton as colonel of the second regiment and recruited other royalists to command two additional regiments. All the surviving Cromwellian colonels were isolated as the officers of a fifth regiment. Having secured a four-to-one military advantage, the governor-general distributed the king's gift. Of course, most

9. [Thomas Povey], "Overtures for the better providing for Jamaica," June 1, 1661, Egerton MS 2395, 301; commission to Lord Windsor, Aug. 2, 1661, Add. MSS 12428, 15b–16; clause 9 of the commission, *ibid.*, 17b, also C.O. 138/1, 9–10; "Considerations about the Peopling and Settling the Island Jamaica," Egerton MS 2395, 283; *Cal. S.P. Col., 1661–1668*, no. 281; additional instructions for Thomas, Lord Windsor, Apr. 23, 1662, Add. MSS 11410, 149, calendared in *Cal. S.P. Col., 1661–1668*, no. 287; clause 10 of Windsor's instructions, Add. MSS 12428, 18.

10. Beeston, "Journal," Add. MSS 12430, 25b; "History and Present State of Jamaica under the Lord Vaughan," Phillips MS 11009, 17, West India Reference Lib. D'Oyley had estimated the number of Cromwellian exiles at 2,000 (D'Oyley to Nicholas, Sept. 11, 1660, *Cal. S.P. Col., 1574–1660*, 489). The total white male population was only about 2,458 (*ibid., 1661–1668*, no. 204). For the attack on the Spaniards, see *ibid.*, no. 364 (Sept. 12,

of its designed recipients were serving in the fleet off Cuba. Their share did not leave Lord Windsor's coffers. With the small fraction of the original donation that he actually dispersed, his lordship grossly favored 88 men. These included D'Oyley's bodyguards, the senior surviving Cromwellian officers, and the old army's military technicians: artillerymen, gunsmiths, and engineers. Windsor had bought up the headquarters corps of the old army. These were the troops most experienced in government and most valuable to it. The favored officers and guards each received at least four shares of the bounty, while those of the ordinary soldiers who received anything got a little over one share apiece. But only 450 of some 1,600 soldiers still in arms received any of the royal bounty. Nearly 900 disbanded veterans, including many of the solid small land-holders, received none of the royal reward intended as compensation for their years of combat with hunger, disease, Spaniards, and the land.[11]

While he dealt out some of the king's gift to the palace guard of the old regime, the governor-general also convened his council. Together, governor and council passed ordinances for disciplining servants and slaves. They set commodity prices as the basis of a barter system of exchange. No sooner was the economic legislation promulgated than the fleet returned from the raid on Cuba. On October 22, 1662, its ships anchored close to the Port Royal fortress. There they unloaded the plunder taken from St. Jago and its hinterland, and from the seven ships captured in its harbor. Lord Windsor took his cut and six days later sailed for England.[12]

This officer-governor had spent just ten weeks in his command. He had hardly exercised his civil powers. He had neither convened law courts nor called an assembly. Those actions would

1662). The additional instructions authorizing it were given to Windsor when he left England (C.O. 138/1, 19, also *Cal. S.P. Col., 1661–1668*, no. 278). No one assumed that the Spaniards would admit English traders to their colonies. War was therefore expected. For the shifting English policies in this matter, see the excellent third chapter of Thornton, *West-India Policy*.

11. Beeston, "Journal," Add. MSS 12430, 26; "An Acct. of the Officers and Soldiers of The Militia of Jamaica raised by Order of His Excellency Thomas Ld Windsor," Add. MSS 11410, 8. These numbered 53 officers and 2,030 men (*Cal. S.P. Col., 1661–1668*, lxxi, no. 397). Windsor assumed that the incorrigible soldiers would go with the fleet while he dealt out the king's bounty to those with an interest in planting (Add. MSS 11410, 5b). The value of the king's "gift" is estimated at £20,000, in "History and Present State of Jamaica under the Lord Vaughan," Phillips MS 11009, 17. Thornton's figure is £21,200, in *West-India Policy*, 48, 48 n. 1. As little as £12,274 was actually distributed; see Long, *Jamaica*, I, 614.

12. Beeston, "Journal," Add. MSS 12430, 26; "The Condition of the Island of Jamaica at the Lord Windsor's departure being 28 October 1662," Add. MSS 11410, 5b. The history of the St. Jago expedition is in Haring, *Buccaneers*, 104–106. Windsor read to the council his leave to depart, Oct. 24, 1662, *Cal. S.P. Col., 1661–1668*, no. 375.

have bespoken due process, deliberation, and consultation. Windsor preferred personal military rule. It prevented political interference with his profitable plundering. The governor-general boasted of constituting civil courts and appointing civil officers, but he had not let them function. He argued that he had established the rule of law in Jamaica, but his only "laws" were ordinances passed by a council he appointed, not acts passed by an elected legislature. As soon as he had pocketed the profits inherent in the personal rule of a buccaneering colony, and had realized that continued residence threatened his health, Lord Windsor abandoned his government. As one indignant imperial bureaucrat concluded, "My Lord Windsor's being come home from Jamaica unlooked-for . . . makes us think that these young Lords are not fit to do any service abroad."[13]

A Yorkist Courtier in Jamaica

The imperial service in Jamaica was now headed by Lord Windsor's deputy, Sir Charles Littleton. Only nineteen when he took arms on behalf of Charles I in 1648, Littleton went into exile when the king was killed and became cupbearer to his son Charles II (just as the young Edmund Andros served Charles's sister). Thereafter, royal favor never failed Littleton. He earned it. After he served in the French army as a member of the household of James, duke of York, Littleton followed the royal duke into Flanders. Of the fighting there, the duke wrote, "A mettled page of mine, one Litleton, charg'd so home, that he was taken." That "mettled" spirit also carried Littleton through desperate days of service at Dunkirk, and it won him the notice of his colleagues in that garrison, among them Colonel Richard Nicolls, afterward conqueror of New York, and Major Henry Norwood, of Virginia,

13. See Windsor's instructions, Add. MSS 12428, esp. clauses 4, 5, 12–14. Windsor had busied himself granting Jamaica lands, presumably for a price, even before he left England (*Cal. S.P. Col., 1661–1668*, no. 217). For Windsor's self-proclaimed accomplishments, see "Jamaica at the Lord Windsor's departure," Add. MSS 11410, 5b, calendared in *Cal. S.P. Col., 1661–1668*, no. 379, also see no. 638. Windsor sought for himself 400 acres of waterfront adjacent to the fort and ferry rights in the harbor (*ibid.*, no. 447). On the relation of Windsor's declining profits to his departure, see Beeston, "Journal," Add. MSS 12430, 26. Windsor's intention to stay only briefly in Jamaica was indicated by his last-minute instruction permitting him to return to England as soon as the new Jamaica government was settled (C.O. 138/1, 20, calendared in *Cal. S.P. Col., 1661–1668*, no. 294). Pepys, who disapproved of Windsor's conduct on Jamaica and his return to England, did record that, "by his men," Windsor "hath raced a fort of the King of Spain's upon Cuba, which is considerable, or said to be so, for his honour." See Latham and Matthews, eds., *Diary of Pepys*, IV, 41, 54–55, 94 (entries of Feb. 13, 23, Apr. 3, 1663).

Tangier, and Gloucester fame. In addition, Littleton was deeply engaged in a number of the royalist conspiracies of the later 1650s, serving with Thomas Hickman (Lord Windsor) among others. The young officer's experience with professional militarism and political absolutism under Marshal Turenne and James Stuart, together with his futile struggles against Cromwell's major generals, taught Littleton the political potential of militarization and centralization and the social utility of the military and absolutist principles of unity, popularity, and protectiveness. His career in garrison government—in Dunkirk, Jamaica, York, Harwich, Sheerness, and the Netherlands—exemplified these lessons.[14]

On October 28, 1662, Sir Charles Littleton took command of Jamaica. He was as popular as a garrison governor as he had been as a field officer in Flanders and in Worcestershire. "The people were generally easy to be governed," Sir Charles found, for he had enough political sense to realize that Jamaicans were best ordered "rather by persuasion than severity." He also benefited from Windsor's strategy for dealing with the Cromwellian military colonists. "The Attempts . . . upon the Spaniards and Privateering had let out the many ill humours," Littleton wrote, "and those that remained were in ways of thriving and by that made Peaceable and Industrious."[15]

Littleton continued to use freebooting to bleed Jamaica of its incorrigible warriors as well as to forward his military objectives. He licensed privateers in spite of the official peace with Spain. When his administration was just a month old, he authorized a raid on the Spanish Main. "Forceful trade" he called it, "which I have hopes will do his Majesty and our Nation some honour and service." As had Windsor, Littleton organized the expedition around the Jamaica station ship, the *Centurion*, and provided a landing force of troops under ex-Cromwellian officers. Their objective was the Spanish city of Campeche on the Yucatan Peninsula. While this force was at sea, Littleton dispatched a second

14. *Memoirs of James II*, 279; S. S. Webb, "Household of James Stuart," *PAH*, VIII (1974), 55–80; Underdown, *Royalist Conspiracy*, 129–131, 154–155. Note that Littleton corresponded with Nicolls in Flanders and spoke of him familiarly to Christopher (afterward Viscount) Hatton, just as Lord Windsor spoke to the same correspondent of Littleton himself (*Hatton Family Correspondence*, I, 13, 15). See also Dalton, ed., *English Army Lists*, I, 50, 50 n. 1.

15. Cundall, *Governors of Jamaica*, 16–17; Dalton, ed., *English Army Lists*, I, 50, 50 n. 1; Littleton to Hatton, July 3, 1657, and, from Breda, Apr. 22, 1660, Add. MSS 29577, 1, 34. Littleton acted as chancellor for Windsor even before the latter was commissioned, seeing Windsor's commission through the seals, and he was sworn in when the Jamaica council met on Sept. 5, 1662 (*Cal. S.P. Col., 1661–1668*, nos. 146, 364). Littleton read his commis-

expedition to seize the pirate port at Tortuga, so as to complete his dominion over the sea rovers.[16]

Between naval excursions, Sir Charles absorbed the military energies of his people by replacing the crumbling earthworks of Port Royal with a cut-stone citadel, Fort Charles. He supervised frequent militia drills, and he personally inspected each militia-man's weapons. To insure that his Jamaican army would be warned of any need to use these arms, Littleton subsidized spies in the Spanish strongholds of Puerto Rico and Santo Domingo.[17]

Notwithstanding his continuous military activity and despite his royalist allegiance, Sir Charles personally, and without parti-sanship, encouraged planting as the basis of the colony's future strength. Despite royalist remonstrances, the deputy governor confirmed the Cromwellian officers' possession of miles of cacao walks. When his brother Constantine died, Governor Littleton entrusted the management of his Jamaica plantation (which he hoped would be a patrimony for his younger children) to Captain Samuel Long, former secretary to Cromwell's commissioners for Jamaica and Governor-General D'Oyley's admiring subordinate. Littleton would set the seal of his approval on the soldier-planters by leaving the government in the custody of Colonel Thomas Lynch, the president of the council, who had qualified for political responsibility in Jamaica first as a Cromwellian captain and then as a staff officer under Edward D'Oyley's command.[18] Thus Littleton deserves the credit not only for confirming their conquest to the Cromwellians but also for effectively incorporating the former officers of the Protector's American army into the power structure of royal government in Jamaica. In that colony, these veterans served out their lives: they built a plantation society on the basis of their military achievements. The Cromwellian captains imparted a military cast to every aspect of island existence. Jamaica's uniquely powerful militia, for example, was founded on the soldier-farmers and soldier-servants of the "quarters," while the colony's own

---

sion to the council, thus taking command, on Oct. 28, 1662 (*ibid.*, no. 375). See also "A Brief Acct. of the State of Jamaica by Sir Charles Littleton . . . to the Lord Chancellor," Add. MSS 11410, and, as quoted, C.O. 138/1, 23. Littleton felt secure enough to dismiss Windsor's cavalry bodyguard and to stop nightly patrols (*Cal. S.P. Col., 1661–1668*, no. 375). See also Littleton to Hatton, Jan. 13, 1663, Add. MSS 29557, 37.

16. On the Campeche and Tortuga expeditions, see Beeston, "Journal," Add. MSS 12430, 26b–27; Haring, *Buccaneers*, 107–109; "History and Present State of Jamaica under the Lord Vaughan," Phillips MS 11009, 17; *Cal. S.P. Col., 1661–1668*, no. 390.

17. Beeston, "Journal," Add. MSS 12430, 16, 26b; *Cal. S.P. Col., 1661–1668*, nos. 411, 384, 360.

18. Cundall, *Governors of Jamaica*, 18; Littleton to Hatton, Jan. 13, 1663, Oct. 2, 1683, Add. MSS 29577, 36b, 549b; "History and Present State of Jamaica under the Lord Vaughan," Phillips MS 11009, 18.

navy was largely made up of their brethren in arms, turned buccaneers and logwood cutters. Many units of both the land and sea
forces were commanded by the regimental officers of the old army.
These veteran commanders also became the majority of the colonial council, the leading assemblymen, and for twenty-five years
to come their leader, Thomas Lynch, was as often as not the
commander-in-chief of England's first imperial conquest.

When Sir Charles Littleton set out to reconcile the soldiers of
the Protector to the rule of the king, Jamaica was still, as it "had
been hitherto governed in a Military Way, and barely had the face
of a Civil Power." After Littleton confirmed the soldier-planters
in their share of the land and government and satisfied the soldier-
privateers with adventure and booty, he began to exercise the
powers of civil government neglected by Lord Windsor. With
the advice of his council, Sir Charles called for elections to the
colony's first assembly.[19]

The assembly met in January 1664. It marked out the issues
and boundaries of Jamaica's Restoration politics. On the one hand,
Littleton, like future governors-general, strongly expressed imperial concerns. A voice for these concerns in the assembly was
assured by the provost marshal, Colonel Thomas Lynch. The
returning officer for the Jamaica precincts, Lynch acted in the
royal executive's interest. On the other hand, Jamaica planters and
merchants sought to control the legislature and to assert its authority in Jamaican government. They sought to dominate the
island and to insure the island's autonomy within the empire. The
first elections gave these self-governing views a champion in Captain Samuel Long. Even during his service under the Cromwellian
commissioners and with Governor-General D'Oyley, Long had
represented the republicanism widespread in the ranks of Jamaica's
conquerors. His legislative loyalties were enhanced when he became the first speaker of the Jamaica assembly. He was supported
in his opposition to monarchical authority by his colleagues in the
Port Royal delegation, the merchants William Beeston and Robert
Byndloss. These three men would lead the island oligarchy for a
generation to come. They immediately secured a legislative presence in provincial government by insisting on assembly control of
the levy, issue, and audit of all funds raised by taxation. Such
funds, they asserted, were for "the public service of this Island."
They made no mention of the king's service, or England's. Moving
earlier and more decisively than did the members of the parliament

19 Samuel Long's Narrative, Add. MSS 12420, 18b, Beeston, "Journal," Add. MSS
12430, 29; [Sir Thomas Lynch], "The Constitution of Assemblys in Jamaica," Add. MSS
12428, 25; Whitson, Constitutional Development of Jamaica, 22.

itself, the Jamaica assemblymen asserted that taxes might be raised only by legislative consent, that tax receipts could be issued only by assembly appropriations, that these tax funds were to be applied by treasurers approved by the legislators, and that the assembly had a right to audit the treasurers' accounts.[20]

For years to come, the crown remained unaware of this attack on its fiscal prerogatives. Following Clarendon's fall in 1667, fluctuations in the structure and membership of the supervisory committees for the colonies distracted the English executive from colonial developments. In any case, viceroys deliberately downplayed legislative activity in their reports, lest they irritate the crown and lead to politically troublesome orders. Here the military character of the imperial executive hampered the prerogative's advance, for the governors-general secured the largest part of their profits from their military commands. They were paid as royal army officers, and they embezzled the pay of their soldiers. As provincial commanders-in-chief, or as vice admirals, governors-general received large shares of the captures made by the private men-of-war and by the naval station ships based in their governments. Privateers paid the governors-general for giving out licenses, for neglecting to collect royal dues on plunder, and for granting official permission to sell stolen goods. Thus enriched, Jamaica's military executives could afford to preserve the island's political peace by acquiescing in the assembly's financial aggression. Governors-general elsewhere did likewise. Only after the crown decided in 1670 that trade with Spain and its colonies was more profitable than plundering them did it deny executives a share of piratical loot. Loss of loot finally led the viceroys to make the fiscal and legislative reports that awoke the crown to its losses. Not until the tide of imperial centralization rose to its full height in 1675, however, was the viceroy ordered to reduce the assembly's pecuniary powers. But by then it was too late for the crown to regain the complete control of taxation and expenditure exercised by D'Oyley and Windsor, by Littleton until he convened the Jamaica assembly, and by Governor Modyford, who largely avoided meeting the assembly.[21]

20. Whitson, *Constitutional Development of Jamaica*, 22–23, 27; *Cal. S.P. Col., 1661–1668*, nos. 573, 580, 604, 837, 838; C.O. 139/1, 43, 46; Lynch, "Constitution," Add. MSS 12428, 25.

21. "This money is the devil," as one governor-general remarked. Its sources were as varied as the roots of evil. Occasional bonanzas were realized from pirates' goods, escheats, legal prize shares, and seizures under the acts of trade. For governors-general, however, company and staff command pay, deductions, dead pays, fortification grants, and other military allowances were both the most steady and the most substantial forms of income. The best sources on this subject are Auditor General William Blathwayt's Letter Books, T. 64/88, 64/89, P.R.O. But see also Add. MSS 22616, 28076, among other Add. MSS vol-

The assembly of January 1664 went beyond the writing of revenue bills. It passed some forty measures to regulate planting, hunting, and morals, as well as the island militia, the units of local government, and the law courts. The close of the session inspired drunken dinners of mutual congratulation and witnessed the deputy governor's signature to "a Body of Laws as good as could be expected from such young Statesmen."[22]

While some Jamaicans made laws, others destroyed Spanish Campeche. The raiders first looted and then burned the town, tore down its walls, removed the cannon, blew up the fortress, and stripped the neighboring plantations. Then the Jamaicans carried off their plunder in the fourteen ships they had seized in Campeche's harbor, and brought home to Port Royal both Spanish riches and fear of Spanish retaliation.

Sir Charles Littleton hurried completion of Fort Charles. He was assisted both by the Spanish booty and by the timber and military stores shipped out to Jamaica by Lord Windsor and his colleagues at the board of ordnance. Littleton felt that the completion of the fortress was the greatest accomplishment of his administration, sure to win the approval of his commander-in-chief, the king. As had every previous Jamaica executive, the deputy governor pointed out that the island's chief asset was its strategic location. Therefore, fortification of the chief harbor should be the government's first priority. Littleton was so convinced of this truth that he advanced £500 from his own purse to finance military construction. The manning of this vital citadel, Sir Charles said, ought not to be entrusted to the Port Royal militia. Instead, in terms typical of governors-general, he asked the crown for a garrison of regulars. He also urged that they be specially equipped for wilderness warfare, since, as he tried to persuade the English board of ordnance, pikes and firelocks were useless in field and forest fighting. Long pikes were unwieldy in the woods; firelocks kindled the dry fields. Colonial troops must have flintlock firearms instead, Littleton insisted.[23]

umes. The very similar situation of New York's governors in the mid-18th century is described by Beverly McAnear, *The Income of the Colonial Governors of British North America* (New York, 1967), and in my review of his volume, in *WMQ*, 3d Ser., XXVI (1969), 308–309. For the relations of Jamaica executives with the privateers, see Haring, *Buccaneers*, 73.

22. Cundall, *Governors of Jamaica*, 19; Beeston, "Journal," Add. MSS 12430, 29. Frederick G. Spurdle, *Early West Indian Government* (privately printed, n.d.), 27, 57–58, asserts that Littleton did not sign these laws and that this early legislative activity (militia regulation, for example) was designed to strengthen executive authority, not to reduce or confine it.

23. Beeston, "Journal," Add. MSS 12430, 28; Littleton to Hatton, Jan. 13, 1663, Add.

For all his substantial military and civil achievements, and his notable acquisition of wealth, Sir Charles Littleton suffered from the usual liabilities of deputy and lieutenant governors–general, and in November 1663 he asked to be recalled. Littleton had no salary himself, and he had to share the profits of office with Lord Windsor. Moreover, he resented the neglect of his command by the English government. For one thing, the naval reinforcements promised to Littleton in England had still not arrived in the five months after he assumed the Jamaica command. Their absence symbolized another of Littleton's worries. King Charles was increasingly opposed to that use of naval force most profitable to the Jamaican executive: attacks on Spanish ships and colonies. The new secretary of state, Sir Henry Bennett, had returned from Spain complaining of the strain that aggressive Jamaicans put on England's diplomatic relations with Madrid and on Anglo-Spanish trade. Through Bennett, the king ordered Littleton to stop raiding the Spanish Indies. These attacks, the secretary reminded Sir Charles, both angered Spain and drained Jamaica of needed men. Governor Littleton received these letters in August 1663. He prepared to call in the privateers—and with them much of his income and most of his naval strength. Then the anti-Spanish secretary of state, William Coventry, countermanded the orders. Naturally, Sir Charles took advantage of the confusion to keep his profitable clients at sea, but he knew that the future of privateering was uncertain at best.[24]

At once rebuked for his hatred of Spain and thwarted in his determination to protect Jamaica, Littleton felt his personal griefs all the more. He had found the island a "melancholy place" and "terrible sick." Ill himself, Littleton saw his brother Constantine die in December 1662. Meanwhile, Lady Littleton suffered from the shock of exile. She wrote that "the town of St. Jago is very pleasantly situated, but the country is much in disorder, and looks wild." She complained that "our greatest want is good company." Loneliness and wilderness intensified the pains of heat prostration, fever, dysentery, and childbirth. Not even the arrival of "a pretty little boy" strengthened Katherine Littleton's will to live: "I am so

---

MSS 29577, 37; "A Brief Acct. by Sir Charles Littleton," Add. MSS 11410, 15b–16, 17; *Cal. S.P. Col., 1661–1668*, nos. 530, 566; C.O. 138/1, 22–23. As Littleton reported, even "the ways are narrow, and full of thick Wood." That firepower would predominate in American "grounds woods and ruftes" long had been apparent to thoughtful military commentators; see J. Frederick Fausz and Jon Kukla, eds., "A Letter of Advice to the Governor of Virginia, 1624," *WMQ*, 3d Ser., XXXIV (1977), 122.

24. The king (by Nicholas, but countersigned by Bennett) to Littleton, Apr. 28, 1663, *Cal. S.P. Col., 1661–1668*, no. 443; also see nos. 441, 442, 449, 524, 530, 531, 535, 566, 571, 645, 648, 650; Littleton to Hatton, Jan. 13, 1663, Add. MSS 29577, 37.

dull with being continually sick that I could hardly divert myself with anything." After his lady's death, Sir Charles, who "knew not how to covet for anything so much as for her sake," found his precarious profits utterly unenticing. In May 1664, as soon as Sir Charles received the king's leave to be absent from his command, he sailed for England.[25]

The Western Design in the Restoration

Modyford and Monck Rule Jamaica

A month after Littleton left the island, Captain General and Governor-in-Chief Sir Thomas Modyford brought to Jamaica his dreams of imperial conquest. Governor-General Modyford commanded under the aegis of his cousin, George Monck, the military author of the Restoration who had become the king's captain general and the duke of Albemarle. Followed by Modyford, Monck had entered the civil wars as a royalist officer but then had joined the victorious parliamentary forces. Monck, like his protégé, next partook of power under the Protectorate, before supporting Charles II's restoration. Monck was the dominant minister of the Restoration's first decade, at least in matters military and imperial. His position became apparent in his support of the Western Design after 1654, but until he arranged the appointment of Modyford to the command of Jamaica a decade later, the West Indian barometer of Anglo-American politics fluctuated widely. At one extreme were the colonial autonomy and commercial values of the Cardinal's Cap clique. At the other were the English-oriented plans of Thomas Modyford and the imperial goals of his cousin the captain general. The fluctuating fortunes of General Monck and of imperialism first dictated Modyford's 1654 triumph—the development of the Western Design and the arrival in Barbados of the imperial expedition—and then permitted his political eclipse, once the expedition sailed for Hispaniola and Jamaica. By 1657 Modyford had to use London merchant interest to secure the orders that protected him from the vendettas of Barbarian factions and the jealousy of Governor Daniel Searle. General Monck's reapplication of the martial authority of the English executive to colonial affairs, however, finally enabled Colonel Modyford to

25. Littleton to Hatton, Jan. 13, Feb. 26, 1663, Add. MSS 29577, 36–36b, 38–39b; K[atherine, Lady] Lyttleton, to Hatton, Sept. 3, 1662, Add. MSS 29550, 440.

overcome Barbados provincialism and to become governor of the island under the council of state in 1659, first royal governor and then speaker of the Barbados assembly after the Restoration in 1660, and then, in 1664, successively, baronet, captain general, and governor-in-chief of Jamaica.[26]

There had been some question whether "the General" (as Modyford called Monck even after he was created duke of Albemarle), could secure the Jamaica command for his kinsman. After Sir Edward Massey took his Presbyterian influence back to his old government of Gloucester, rather than out to Jamaica, a series of noblemen, beginning with Lord Windsor, vied for the governor-generalship. As soon as Windsor's deputy, Sir Charles Littleton, asked to be recalled, the old royalist soldier Colonel Edward Morgan was named deputy to the earl of Marlborough, James Ley, the prospective governor-general of Jamaica. Either the earl declined or the duke prevailed, as Albemarle was apt to do in military appointments. On February 15, 1664, King Charles commissioned Thomas Modyford governor-general of Jamaica and created him baronet. Neither paper power nor titled status, however, was as essential to Modyford's authority in a province primarily peopled by Cromwellian veterans, as was "the Lord General's recommendation, who once before sent the fittest and worthiest man in the world" (Colonel William Brayne) to command England's conquest.[27]

26. A letter from Mr. Muddiford, June 20, 1655 (no. 1), commissioners for the southern expedition to Cromwell, Mar. 7, 1654, Birch, ed., *Thurloe S.P.*, III, 565–566, 203–204. The degree to which the Barbados legislature was an assembly of the elite is seen in Modyford's lost election of 1655, by a vote of 20–19, recorded, *ibid.*, 622, and commented on by Dunn, *Sugar and Slaves*, 93 n. 12. For the Cardinal's Cap clique and their struggle with Searle, see Thomas Povey's letterbook, Add. MSS 11411, and especially Thomas to William Povey, Jan. 4, 1658, to Searle, Mar. 27, 1658, Searle to T. Povey, May 10, 1658, Add. MSS 11411, 51b–53, 58–60, 71–72. See also Harlow, *Barbados*, 119–125, 129*ff*, and esp. 81*ff*, for a superlative discussion of this period. See also the petition of Modyford to Cromwell, Aug. 1653, Searle to the council of state, Sept. 19, 1653, appointment of Modyford to the Barbados council, Jan. 14, 1654 (no. 1), extract of a letter from Barbados, May 6, 1660, *Cal. S.P. Col., 1654–1660*, 406–407, 408, 413, 479; *ibid., 1661–1668*, no. 40; Latham and Matthews, eds., *Diary of Pepys*, I, 183 (June 23, 1660). On Modyford's government of Barbados and royal approval of it, see the king to Modyford, Nov. 1660, *Cal. S.P. Col., 1654–1660*, 492. The basis of Modyford's government in his military command, and the disbandment of his regiment as the first act of Modyford's successor, are recorded in the minutes of the Barbados council, Dec. 11, 1660, *ibid.*, 494. Modyford's reelection as speaker appears *ibid., 1661–1668*, no. 141. See also Harlow, *Barbados*, 125–127. On p. 128, *ibid.*, Harlow notes that on May 16, 1660, Monck secured a royal pardon for Modyford (for acting under the usurpers) and procured an order in council against trying Modyford for treason in Barbados (p. 134). See also *Cal. S.P. Col., 1661–1668*, nos. 1, 6, and *Privy Council, Col. Ser.*, I, no. 509. Modyford acknowledged that Monck had made him governor of Barbados (*Cal. S.P. Col., 1661–1668*, no. 6). Cundall, *Governors of Jamaica*, 21, states that Albemarle's (i.e., Monck's) influence secured Modyford's speakership.

27. Memorial of Morgan to Bennett, [1663?], *Cal. S.P. Col., 1661–1668*, no. 601. Mor-

Modyford and Monck, baronet and duke in an era whose leaders looked longingly back to government by aristocracy, were also captain generals in a troubled time when force remained the foundation of authority. These military grandees now applied in Jamaica the four-tined plan of imperial development they had evolved over the previous decade. Its watchwords were population and protection, planting and privateering.

"The chief want there will be men and women," General Monck had written of Jamaica in 1657, and Colonel Modyford had already attempted to settle planters there. The cousins also speculated together in the slave trade. Not surprisingly, Modyford and his partner, Peter Colleton (also Monck's kinsman), were named as the Royal African Company's factors in Barbados, and the king ordered Sir Thomas to protect the company's operations in Jamaica. In the meantime, Albemarle named Modyford to promote emigration from Barbados to Carolina, of which the duke was a proprietor. When their involvement in Jamaica deepened, Albemarle assured Modyford that he might offer prospective settlers in his island government the same free land, free religion, and free trade that he had been told to promise emigrants to Carolina. As a result of these sustained efforts at recruitment, Modyford reported, at least 400 people would sail with him from Barbados to Jamaica when he took up the command, and 1,200 more would follow within the year.[28]

The colonial captain general was better than his word. More than 600 Barbadians preceded him to Jamaica. When Sir Thomas landed on June 4, 1664, his own retinue numbered 80, and 200 additional emigrants followed him ashore. To increase island population was the greatest of Modyford's many achievements in Jamaica. General D'Oyley had kept alive some 2,500 soldiers and had added 400 to 500 settlers to them. In the four years of their government, Lord Windsor and Sir Charles Littleton presided over an addition of about 2,000 persons. To these 5,000 Jamaicans,

gan's commission as deputy governor of Jamaica, Jan. 18, 1664, is in the secretary at war's military affairs entry book, S.P. 44/20, 7. Thornton, *West-India Policy*, 61, states that the earl of Craven was also interested in the command. On Albemarle's recommendation, see Sir Thomas Lynch to Bennett, May 25, 1664, *Cal. S.P. Col., 1661–1668*, no. 744. Brayne had been Monck's protégé in Scotland before assuming the Jamaica command; see chapter 1 above. The king announced Modyford's appointment in a letter to him, Jan. 11[?], 1664, calendared in *ibid.*, no. 635, from C.O. 1/18, no. 7.

28. Monck to Thurloe, July 28, Dec. 8, 1657, Birch, ed., *Thurloe S.P.*, VI, 424, 664, reflecting Modyford's dispatches; Harlow, *Barbados*, 132, 132 n. 1. On slaving, see clause 19 of Modyford's instructions, C.O. 138/1, 34, and *Cal. S.P. Col., 1661–1668*, nos. 417, 689,

Modyford quickly added 987 settlers from Barbados and took in 400 English refugees from Dutch-conquered Surinam. He made little further gain in peopling his government until the close of the second Dutch war. Subsequently, a degree of peace, and the stable military government that Captain General Modyford imposed on Jamaica, helped to triple the number of island inhabitants by 1670.[29]

To add ten thousand colonists to his underpopulated yet turbulent outpost of England's empire, "circled in with Enemy's Country," Sir Thomas had to reconcile the claims of garrison government with the political privileges required for plantation prosperity. The need for physical security and political stability, met by garrison government, competed with the need to encourage plantation investment, met by protecting private property and by securing the political privileges of the propertied class. The rivalry between security and liberty was anticipated in Modyford's instructions, but their bias toward order appeared in the royal endorsement. King Charles wrote that the object of royal authority in the island province was to insure "the orderly and peaceable conduct and Preservation of all our Subjects, as well Planters and Soldiers, as other Inhabitants there residing."[30]

To preserve the peace, the governor-general of Jamaica was to choose and dismiss the members of his council. This, then, was an advisory and administrative body, wholly at the governor-general's command. With any six of these assistants, he could legislate for the Jamaicans, tax them, and even alter the form of their provincial government. Free of constitutional limitations, Sir Thomas was also unbound by custom or by civil law courts. He could personally suspend civil law and impose martial authority at any time. Moreover, the governor-general was instructed to write the military law himself. (He quickly did so. The result cataloged for imperial use the social and institutional dicta of the military. Modyford combined the royal code, composed by the duke of

---

693. For concessions and emigration, see *ibid.*, nos. 83, 547, 649, 559, 687, 744, 784, and Beeston, "Journal," Add. MSS 12430, 29b.

29. In 1670 the population of Jamaica numbered 15,198, according to a survey of inhabitants by parish, C.O. 138/1, 61–76, calendared in *Cal. S.P. Col., 1669–1674*, no. 270. This was a substantial increase over Modyford's estimate of 4,205 in 1664 (Cundall, *Governors of Jamaica*, 23). Note that Modyford's first instruction was to give the governor of Barbados the English executive's orders to encourage emigration to Jamaica, a procedure first suggested by Modyford in 1654 and practiced by him in 1655 (*ibid.*, 29). See also Thornton, *West-India Policy*, 60–61.

30. "The Governor of Jamaica's Answer to Inquiries" and Modyford's proposals, received Sept. 28, 1670, C.O. 138/1, 136, 138; Modyford's commission and instructions, C.O. 138/1, 27. The proposals are also calendared in *Cal. S.P. Col., 1661–1668*, no. 629.

York for England's Guards and Garrisons, and the older ukases of his cousin the captain general, with Cromwell's favorite military forms, as copied from Gustavus Adolphus.) In addition to his military authority over the island colony, Sir Thomas received commensurate power "in all Marine causes and matters" as vice admiral to the duke of York, who was the lord high admiral of the empire as well as of England. Governor-General Modyford was given the material substance as well as the paper commission of military authority. The king granted English military salaries to the garrison government's general staff—the captain general and governor-in-chief, the lieutenant general and lieutenant governor, and the major general, who was the chief organizer and drillmaster of the provincial militia—and to "such a number of Soldiers, both horse and foot, as shall be requisite for the Guard of your [that is, the generals'] persons, and the Public Magazine of Arms or Ammunition." The viceroy had been given a miniature of the king's own Guards and Garrisons. With it, he was expected to uphold provincial garrison government as royal authority was upheld in England.[31]

Modyford's military might was obvious, yet the civilian government that was so often alleged to be essential for economic development was also officially provided for (although much neglected by General Modyford in practice). The king gave the governor-general and his council permission to summon an assembly elected by the freeholders. The legislators might consent to the bills offered by the executive, "according to the usage and custom of our other Plantations." Sir Thomas, however, had a more exalted conception of the place of the legislature in the colonial constitution than these royal instructions implied. The island assembly was "an Humble Model of our high Court of Parliament," he wrote. In it, the governor-general acted "as his Majesty's Commissioner." His council took part "as representing the Lords House," while the representatives of the freeholders were "chosen as the Commons in England." But Governor-General Modyford never let this parliamentary concept interfere with his

31. Modyford's commission and instructions, C.O. 138/1, 24, 25, 29, 33; an establishment for Jamaica from Dec. 25, 1663, by Southampton, Albemarle, Arlington, *ibid.*, 35. It is not recorded that Modyford spent this money on his cavalry guard or on his armed household of 400 persons. The Jamaica general staff was shackled to the military chain of command. See the secretary at war's military entry book, S.P. 44/20, 6–7, 20, 195, for this, and for the duke's martial code. For its application to Jamaica, as in "Articles and Military Laws set forth by his Excellency Sir Thomas Modyford Kt. and Baronet Governor General of His Majestys Island of Jamaica and Vice Admiral to His Royal Highness the Duke of York . . . ," see Add. MSS 12429, 72b–75b.

practical control of the colony. In his seven years as governor-general, he convened, briefly, only one assembly, and never called another. Modyford ended his administration with the casual observation that "there is no assembly in being—nor that I know urgent occasion for any."[32]

Jamaica's first assembly, summoned by Sir Charles Littleton and largely influenced by the provost marshal, Colonel Thomas Lynch, was in session under Lynch's presidency when the advance guard of the Modyford migration arrived from Barbados, led by Lieutenant General Edward Morgan. The very existence of this old guard assembly was an affront to the new regime. Worse, the assembly, warned of Sir Thomas Modyford's approach, had just resolved that the executive might not legislate without its participation. To insure that participation, the assembly's speaker, Captain Samuel Long, had moved to assert legislative control of taxation. He told the Jamaicans that English tax farmers were enriched and Barbados planters impoverished by the 4.5 percent duty on island exports that, he alleged, had been King Charles's reward for commissioning Sir Thomas Modyford governor of Barbados. Modyford might try to pay for his new commission or to purchase further royal favor by sending taxes paid by Jamaicans to the English exchequer. Alarmed by Long, the Jamaica assemblymen insisted that taxation without their consent was illegal. Then they refused to levy taxes in the king's name lest he misappropriate them (the Jamaicans had been told that the 4.5 percent duty designed for Barbados's government had been spent on the king's mistresses). What taxes the assembly did authorize it appropriated "for the use of the island." These levies were to be collected, disbursed, and accounted for by officers of the assembly, headed by their treasurer, Speaker Long. Incensed by the assembly's attempt to defend Jamaica's old order from the royal prerogative and from his commanding officer, the governor-general, Lieutenant General Morgan dissolved the assembly as soon as he landed.[33]

Despite the dissolution, Captain Long continued as treasurer. He refused to issue any of the tax revenue to either Morgan or Modyford until an assembly so appropriated it. Thus Governor-General Modyford was forced to convene an assembly, but he did not do it until five months after his arrival. His political use of the

32. Modyford's commission, the governor's answers, C.O. 138/1, 27, 96.

33. Beeston, "Journal," Add. MSS 12430, 29; Whitson, *Constitutional Development of Jamaica*, 23–24, 24–26, citing C.O. 139/1, 41–42; *Cal. S.P. Col., 1661–1668*, nos. 826, 837.

interval is evident in the election of some new settlers to the assembly and the equivalent reduction in the number of ex-army grandees. Sir Thomas Whetstone, "a malicious, beggarly, debauched fellow," was "chosen Speaker of the house to replace Captain Long, more by the desire or rather the order of the General than the election of the Gentlemen." The new assembly first repealed all the acts of its predecessor; then it levied an excise on liquor and appropriated it to the use of the king's government, on the governor-general's warrant. After reenacting laws to regulate slaves, servants, and hunters, prices, fees, and credit, crops and transport, religion and the militia, Modyford's packed house called on their patron to bring Treasurer Long to book for high treason.

Speaker Whetstone alleged that Long had led an assembly that met illegally in the absence of Deputy Governor Littleton, that Long had sought to monopolize legislative power by excluding the royal executive, and that Long had usurped the king's fiscal prerogative, "which is the chief flower of his Crown—being the ornament of peace and the sinews of war." Treasurer Long's denial of money to the viceroy was said to be the first step toward rebellion. Not for the last time, a governor-general stripped Samuel Long of all his offices and jailed him. With the leader of the opposition defanged, his trial for treason was deferred to the next session of the assembly.[34]

There would be no next session. Modyford's abuse of the assembly had united the civilian representatives with those of the old army against him. In particular, the attack on Long had consolidated the interests of newly established merchant-planters like William Beeston with those of the old army officers, led by Colonel Thomas Lynch. A formed opposition to the court party meant that the assembly's remaining "business went on but like Bells rung by Boys all jarring." A "splendid dinner provided with Wine and Music" to soothe legislative sensibilities ended in drunken duels and the death of an assemblyman. His death presaged that of the assembly itself. Modyford immediately prorogued the legislature, and his repeated prorogations kept it from meeting until, in October 1665, he no longer cared to delude the colonists that they

34. Lynch contrasted the new legislators' poverty with the army grandees' ample estates (Lynch to Bennett, Feb. 12, 1665, *Cal. S.P. Col., 1661–1668*, no. 934). His comparison is partly borne out by the 1670 parish lists. Modyford extended representation to two new constituencies; of the six parishes, only two were represented by their greatest landlords, Maj. Richard Hope and Col. Thomas Freeman, both officers of the old army. According to C.O. 138/1, 61, 65, Freeman held 1,309.5 acres in St. Thomas, and Hope (here titled lieutenant colonel), 1,497 acres. Cundall, *Governors of Jamaica*, 23, says that the number of electoral districts was reduced.

had a voice in Jamaica government. He dissolved the assembly. He never called another.[35]

Having eliminated the assembly, Governor-General Modyford legislated through proclamations that he issued with his council. Yet even the council contained politicians independent of his authority—the royal patentees. The most powerful patent officer was Colonel Thomas Lynch, formerly General D'Oyley's chief of staff and still president of the council, chief justice, and holder of a royal patent as provost marshal. As marshal, Lynch was a military supersheriff for the whole colony, an obvious obstacle to Modyford's intended political monopoly. Modyford protested that the provost marshal's office was "only fit for an army," where it had indeed originated. He asked that "our Duke," Albemarle, eliminate it. Provost Marshal Lynch, however, was closely linked to the royal secretary of state, Sir Henry Bennett (soon to become the earl of Arlington), who was the leading proponent of a pro-Spanish and anti-military, pro-mercantile and European-oriented colonial policy. In other words, he was the chief opponent of the Cromwellian, Spanish-hating, American-focused imperial program sponsored by England's captain general, the duke of Albemarle, and executed by the captain general of Jamaica, Sir Thomas Modyford. Arlington protected Lynch, partly to frustrate Albemarle and the imperialists, but also to build a peace party subset in Jamaica. To do this, Arlington relied on Lynch as the head of the planter party within the old army in Jamaica and, after 1664, as the leader of the planter party's merchant allies. Thus Anglo-American political rivalries saved Lynch's position but pushed him into a lifelong struggle with "the faction of the Modyfords." To reduce Lynch's power, Sir Thomas Modyford declared that no man could be both provost marshal and chief justice, that is, both policeman and judge. With fine impartiality, he dismissed Colonel Lynch from both offices. Lynch immediately sailed for England and did not return to Jamaica until Arlington sent him back to arrest Modyford, replace him as governor, and reverse his policies.[36]

Modyford's policies were personal aggrandizement and imperial aggression. Both depended on the absolute authority that he and his family now wielded for six eventful years. The governor-general himself took Lynch's place as chief justice, "for want of a

35. For the activities of the assembly session, see n. 34 above; Beeston, "Journal," Add. MSS 12430, 29–30b; and *Cal. S.P. Col., 1661–1668*, nos. 836, 837, 838, 882, 1063.

36. Beeston, "Journal," Add. MSS 12430, 30b; *Cal. S.P. Col., 1661–1668*, nos. 785, 1085; the king to Modyford, Mar. 30, 1670, Egerton MS 2395, 469; C.O. 138/1, 98.

better lawyer," as he modestly explained. He commissioned his brother Sir James Modyford, the lieutenant general and lieutenant governor, as a councillor, chief judge of the vice admiralty court, and customs collector. Another kinsman and councillor, Colonel Robert Byndloss, was commissioned as captain of Fort Charles and governor of Port Royal. The governor-general's son John further extended his father's command by acting as Jamaica's major general until succeeded by his brother Thomas, who was yet another Modyford councillor-colonel. Having staffed his garrison government, its council, city, citadel, courts, and militia, with his family, Governor-General Modyford sought the support of the "privateer party," the aggressive, anti-planter, imperialist element of the old army. With the privateers, the governor set out to make Jamaica what in 1655 he had predicted it would become: the scourge of Spain; the center of English empire in the Indies; the platform that would so elevate the Modyfords that none would stand between them and the sun in the world of the Western Design.[37]

Modyford was an imperialist. No other word can describe the governor-general of an English colony who self-consciously modeled himself on the provincial commanders of the Roman Empire. Modyford claimed proconsular independence in his command, and he pressed this Roman model on the king's councillors. The only way to administer the empire, Modyford wrote, was to commission "a Prudent and Loyal person for the Government and then trust him with that Commission which the wise Romans gave their Generals, videat ne Insula nostra Jamaica aliquid detrimenti a accipiat." Such advice was seconded in Whitehall by England's captain general, the duke of Albemarle, and by the lord high admiral, the duke of York, both of whom also searched the history of imperial Rome for lessons in empire building and administration. While the dukes reserved ultimate power to themselves and their prince, they recognized the limits that the Atlantic placed on their immediate command of England's overseas provinces. "This vast distance and uncertainty of advice," as Modyford called it, reinforced the subordinate officer's citation of imperial precedent for his independent authority. Jamaica's governor-general pointed to "the Romans giving such large powers even in Italy at their own Doors so well did they understand the rule of trusting him that was on the place who clearly sees what cannot be imagined by

37. Lynch to Bennett, Feb. 12, 1665, Cal. S.P. Col., 1661–1668, no. 934, also see nos. 935, 1085; Whitson, Constitutional Development of Jamaica, 35–36.

much wiser men at so great a distance." Modyford's claim to proconsular discretion caused no controversy so long as he, Albemarle, and York, provincial military and naval chiefs, all had the power to act on their agreements. One such imperial premise was that the sword of English empire in the Indies was Jamaica's provincial navy, its savage seamen, and its Cromwellian captains. When death and disfavor struck down the imperially minded dukes, however, the governor-general's independence created a crisis in Anglo-Spanish diplomacy, imperial administration, and Anglo-American politics that could only be resolved by his arrest and degradation.[38]

Martial Society and Imperial Politics

The forces of the Western Design had no sooner seized Jamaica from the Spaniards and established the garrisoned harbor settlement that became Port Royal than they sailed from their island base to attack the enemy at sea and to raid his ports. At the end of General D'Oyley's administration, some fifteen hundred ex-soldiers manned the Port Royal fleet. When Sir Thomas Modyford took command as governor, general, and admiral, these soldiers-turned-seamen crewed some thirty private men-of-war. Most of these were sloops of fifteen or sixteen tons burden, each with two, three, or four guns and twenty-five to forty men. The larger privateer vessels were ketches of about forty tons, six guns, and forty to sixty men. Occasionally, the privateers manned a ship, which they called a frigate, and which typically displaced fifty tons, had a few more crewmen than tons, and carried ten or a dozen cannon. Only the fleet's flagship or a royal man-of-war on the Jamaica station exceeded one hundred tons in size, had that many men in crew, or mounted as many as twenty guns. A small force this, to terrify half a hemisphere, vex the statesmen of Europe, make and break the careers of viceroys and admirals, English and Spanish.[39]

38. These and subsequent citations of Roman imperial precedent and practice by English imperialists are all ignored in Richard Koebner's sketchy and denigrating treatment of English imperialism in *Empire* (New York, 1965), 61–68. But see "Conditions by Sir Thomas Modyford for strengthening His Majesty's Interest in the West Indies," C.O. 138/1, 137, and Latham and Matthews, eds., *Diary of Pepys*, IV, 217 (July 4, 1663). Pepys was appalled that an English privy councillor did not know the meaning of "S.P.Q.R." on a tapestry of Rome in the duke of York's chambers. Pepys associated knowledge of imperial antiquity with scholarship functional for English officials. Modyford explained that the passage from Jamaica to England, or vice versa, required about three months, and an additional three months were needed just to get an order out of England's faction-ridden bureaucracy.

39. *Cal. S.P. Col., 1661–1668*, nos. 12, 744, 786. These particulars are digested from "A

The privateers were supposed to disappear when the restored Stuart dynasty resumed its traditional peace with Spain in 1660. Secretary Bennett made sure that King Charles ordered Modyford to recall the privateers, revoke their commissions, and hang recalcitrant raiders. Modyford was to sponsor peaceful trade in place of privateering. Even before he left Barbados for Jamaica, Sir Thomas sent emissaries to the Spanish viceroys. One week after he took over his new command, he forbade further attacks on the Spaniards, and he sent the proclamation home to satisfy Secretary Bennett. At the same time, the governor-general voiced the military apprehension and imperial ambition that drove him to subvert the secretary's plans for peaceful commerce. If he actually stripped the privateers of their English commissions, Modyford wrote, they would go over to the French. Modyford had served for three years as councillor and colonel under Lord Willoughby, a governor-general whose daily discourse was that France alone menaced England's imperial future in the Indies, and, in particular, that only the French could capture Jamaica from its English conquerors. To alienate fifteen hundred buccaneers and so force them to take French commissions and orders seemed insane to Jamaica's governor-general. Since he lacked royal naval ships to discipline the sea rovers, Sir Thomas concluded that Jamaica could choose between harboring the privateers and being attacked by them.[40]

This, the utter incompatability of Bennett's policy of peace and Modyford's imperial aggressiveness, produced the governor-general's declaration to the secretary of state that he could not enforce the severe anti-privateer policy enjoined by his instructions. Ten days later Jamaica's commander appealed to England's captain general for the money and materials required to complete the citadel at Port Royal, and so to dominate the privateers, in part at least, by establishing physical control of the harbor and city. At the same time, the governor-general assured the privateers that his pro-Spanish proclamations were mere window dressing. He gave substance to his assurances by buying a Spanish prize. Modyford's personal profit joined the imperialists' aggressive policy, to favor privateering.[41]

"On the 27th of February 1665[/6] Sir Thomas Modyford

List of the Ships Under the Command of Admiral Morgan," C.O. 138/1, 105. They agree with the usual rule for 17th-century ships: one man per ton and 10 of each per cannon.

40. Modyford's instructions, no. 70, C.O. 138/1, 30, the king to Modyford, June 15, 1664, S.P. 44/17, 41, Cal. S.P. Col., 1661–1668, nos. 578, 744, 746, 767, 786.

41. Albemarle's response dated May 30, 1665, was acknowledged on Mar. 1, 1666. See Thornton, West-India Policy, 93–94, and Cal. S.P. Col., 1661–1668, no. 785, also nos. 786, 976. On the strengthening of Fort Charles, see the diagrams in C.O. 138/2, 1–2, and the discussion in Pawson and Buisseret, Port Royal, 37–38.

Caused a War against the Spaniards to be Solemnly Proclaimed by beat of drum." Sir Thomas knew that Arlington's (i.e., Bennett's) friendship for Spain made the issuing of commissions against its American commerce and colonies highly dangerous. He told Arlington that Albemarle had authorized this attack on Spain, but he also pointed out that he had issued all commissions in his own name. Thus the English authorities might deny all knowledge of his actions when negotiating with the Spanish. Modyford also begged Albemarle to protect him. The captain general assured his subordinate that, in spite of a pending treaty with Spain, the protection of Jamaica took priority. If island security required it, Albemarle wrote, Modyford might continue to commission privateers against Spain. More than that, the captain general helped obtain the implicit approval of the crown for his kinsman's course.[42]

Acting on Modyford's commission, the privateers first captured the old puritan headquarters of Providence Island, lost to the Spanish for a generation. Modyford had called on Albemarle to procure a governor and garrison to hold the island as a base of current operations against the Nicaraguan coast and as a staging point for a future grand design against the Spanish Main. There followed Sir James Modyford's royal commission as lieutenant governor of Providence Island, under the command of the captain general of Jamaica. This commission was official approval of the privateering policy that had recovered an early outpost of the English empire.[43]

The war with Spain further militarized Governor-General Modyford's administration. He proclaimed long periods of martial

42. "A Narrative of Sir Thomas Modyford," Aug. 23, 1670, *Cal. S.P. Col., 1669–1674*, no. 103, stresses the crown's formal submission of military considerations concerning the West Indies to the captain general, Albemarle; Albemarle's grant of discretion regarding the use of privateers to his Jamaica subordinate, Modyford; his approval of the use made of this grant to commission the rovers; and his declaration that the peace of 1667 did not extend to the West Indies. Modyford summed up the chain of command by saying that he received "letters from Lord Arlington, [informing Modyford] that from the Lord General he should receive his Majesty's directions touching the privateers, and also letters from the Lord Chancellor to the same purpose." The mercantilists of the peace party were washing their hands of responsibility for imperial aggression. As Thornton writes in *West-India Policy*, 99 n. 2: "Arlington may genuinely have considered that Jamaica, a military garrison, was in the Lord-General's 'department,' at least to begin with." The Jamaica captain general quotes his English counterpart as writing, "and for your giving commissions to the privateers I think you have done pursuant to your own instructions and orders sent you" (*Cal. S.P. Col., 1669–1674*, no. 103). See also *ibid., 1661–1668*, nos. 1144, 1147, 1216, 1263, 1264, 1276, 1327. The evidence for Albemarle's permission is discussed by Thornton, 93–94, 98–100. For the proclamation, see Beeston, "Journal," Add. MSS 12430, 31b–32.

43. Sir James Modyford's Providence commission, Nov. 10, 1666, is in S.P. 44/20, 134A.

law, during which he conscripted labor and requisitioned materials from the plantations to improve the forts and batteries that protected Port Royal by land and sea. Thus the "law marshal" directed the colony's politics and economy, but it also reshaped civil law and administration. Together, the governor-general and his councillor-officers, who were bound by martial law to obey him, decreed a reorganization of the Jamaica judiciary: the councillor-colonels would preside in county or precinct courts, and the governor-general would act as chief justice of the supreme court. They ordered all persons to accept the governor-general's commissions to civil or military office, if offered, and to be bound by the discipline that those commissions imposed. The governor-general and his council of state and war extended martial law from soldiers in pay to the whole of the militia. Then they made a public example of the first soldier who disobeyed an order by torturing him on the garrison parade at the inland capital, St. Jago de la Vega.[44]

Modyford's development of martial law during 1667 was wholly to the taste of the old soldiers of the garrison. Calling themselves "the conquerors of the land," they also controlled large portions of the council, the courts, and the militia. To the power of their plural offices they were accustomed to add the authority of martial law, to "keep up their own boundless tyrannical power under pretence of carefulness." Martial law reached far down into the structure of society. Officer-grandees used it to compel small planters (and their servants or slaves) to do all of the local militia regiment's share of labor on the forts. The ensuing neglect of their crops forced small landholders into debt. To pay these debts, they had to "sell their plantations to their lords and masters."[45]

One group of these "lords and masters" were the ranking officers resident in St. John Parish, originally the Guanaboa military quarter of Colonels Buller, Barrington, Tyson, and Burrough. Every one of the officers who ruled St. John Parish in 1667 was a veteran of the conquering army and had carried his rank into Jamaica's militia (most of whose members were these officers' former soldiers). John Cope was a relative of General D'Oyley and had been a field officer and a member of D'Oyley's council. Now Cope was lieutenant colonel of General Modyford's own guards

44. *Cal. S.P. Col., 1661–1668*, nos. 1702, 1703, 1810, 1861.
45. John Style to Sec. William Morrice, Jan. 14, 1669, *Cal. S.P. Col., 1669–1674*, no. 7. The republican Style family was associated with Arlington (see Harlow, *Barbados*) and led the opposition in Jamaica to rule by the governor-general and his council, particularly to the taxes they levied without legislative consent. See *Cal. S.P. Col., 1661–1668*, no. 1792 (all parts), and *ibid., 1669–1674*, no. 7.

and a councillor who owned 683 acres in St. John Parish. Major Thomas Ayscough had transferred his rank from the Cromwellian infantry to Modyford's regiment of cavalry, the island's military elite corps. The major was judge of the court of common pleas and held 880 acres in St. John. Two of Modyford's captains of the guards, Whitgift Alymer (one of the Guanaboa regiment's original officers) and Richard Oldfield, owned, respectively, 294 and 330 acres in the parish. Cromwellian captains who commanded in Modyford's militia included John Laugher and R. Nelson (former captain of Governor-General D'Oyley's own cavalry escort). They owned 204 and 1,300 acres, respectively, in St. John. The parish landlord class was small. Only eighty-three of almost one thousand inhabitants owned any land in St. John. Most of these few landlords owned less than 200 acres, indeed, thirty-two of them owned less than 100 acres. But all the officers were among the upper half of the landlord class, and two-thirds of these former Cromwellians were among the richest sixth of the parish's landed class. These owners of 500 acres or more, besides Cope, Ayscough, and Nelson, were the lieutenant general, Sir James Modyford (1,000 acres); Lieutenant Richard Nelson (984); Elizabeth and Captain George Reid (927, 1,403), both members of the conquest family; and three men not of the military establishment—John Style (the chief enemy of the military colonists and, with 3,200 acres, the greatest landlord of the parish), William Bragg (950), and Jonathan Cock (1,403).[46]

While St. John Parish exhibited an especially high degree of economic and political dominance by officers of the old army, a similar situation prevailed in every parish based on army quarters. For example, in St. Andrew Parish—the Liguanea quarter (which surrounded Port Royal)—two of the four largest landholders were Colonel and Councillor Henry Archbold (2,030 acres) and Lieutenant Colonel Richard Hope (1,497 and 907 acres), both of whom had been field officers in the quarter's founding regiment and who had brought their families out from England in 1658. In the same

46. *Cal. S.P. Col., 1669–1674*, nos. 7, 8; "Survey of St. John Parish," and "A List of the Trained Bands June 1670," C.O. 138/1, 74–75, 106. St. John lay on the upper reaches of the Rio Montano, now Rio Cobre, and the Black River. See the maps in C.O. 138/3, and in Black, ed., *Blathwayt Atlas*, nos. 33–36. On the origins and early history of the Guanaboa quarter, see Taylor, *Western Design*, esp. 36, and Cundall, *Historic Jamaica*, 123–129. On the personnel, see the sources cited in chapter 4 above. Note that the St. John military oligarchy was more extensive than Style's list indicates. Col. Cope's brother-in-law, Col. Thomas Freeman, represented the parish in the assembly (although most of his lands were in St. Thomas Parish). Francis Price and Richard Guy were influential officer-politicians identified with the parish. Alymer rose to be a colonel and assemblyman.

parish, Firemaster Nicholas Leine (643 acres) and Captain William Vallett (220 acres) were veterans of General D'Oyley's garrison. There were forty-six Jamaican estates of 1,000 acres or more in 1670. More than one in four were owned by officers of the old army. The absence of complete records for the army officers is compounded by the lacunae in the land records, but the degree of army ownership is remarkably high for this time: that is, sixteen years after the conquest; ten years after the Restoration (which had led to Windsor's vast land grants to absentees such as Clarendon, Carlisle, and King Charles); and five years after the Modyfords took 30,000 acres to themselves and disposed of an additional 270,000 acres. The old army influence was even more apparent in privateering and in the possession of patent places, two economic alternatives to land as the basis of wealth and power in Jamaica.[47]

As for the privateers, war with Spain and fear of French or Dutch attack put a premium on a militarily disciplined and physically fortified colonial community and on that community's fighting men, the buccaneers who manned Jamaica's navy. Seamen also constituted one-third of the Port Royal militia, whose ranks were completed with artisans, shopkeepers, laborers, and others who lived off the privateers. The captain general of Jamaica thought that the sea rovers brought to Jamaica's metropolis such an increase of military strength as was in itself sufficient excuse for fighting the Spaniards. He wanted to retain at least a thousand of the buccaneers in pay, if only "to keep up a military Spirit in that People which when they are reduced to no other militia, then dull trained Bands, will flag and come to nothing."

Admittedly, the buccaneers were not model subjects, but Modyford used martial law to discipline privateers as well as planters. The general's guards and the provost marshal's men policed the streets of the port while the privateers drank and drabbed away their plunder. These military patrols locked up unusually riotous revelers in the guardhouse overnight. Sir Thomas remarked that the most notorious offenders against public order were the officers of the old army, "who from strict saints are turned the most debauched devils." If they drank more deeply than the governor-general's own cronies, they must have been sodden indeed. There was a licensed tavern for every ten men in Port Royal. The island's arable land was dotted with sugar mills,

47. In addition to Cols. Archbold, Cope, and Thomas Ballard (St. Katherine, 2,391 acres), all formerly members of D'Oyley's council. Lt. Col. Hope and Maj. Thomas Fuller (St. Katherine, St. Dorothy, and St. John) were amply landed officers of the old army who sat on Modyford's council in 1669. See n. 42 above and *Cal. S.P. Col., 1669–1674*, no. 148.

each distilling rum from its waste molasses. Modyford remarked that Spanish visitors "wondered much at the sickness of our people, until they knew of the strength of their drinks, but then wondered more that they were not all dead." When not dead drunk, the inhabitants were as notorious for fighting one another as for slaughtering Spaniards. The garrison of Port Royal spent far more time in police work than in defense.[48]

Port Royal's garrison government, police, and protection were all the more essential, for the buccaneers' headquarters had become "the storehouse or treasury of the West Indies." "Bags and cakes of gold, wedges and pigs of silver, pistol[e]s, pieces of eight . . . with store of wrought plate, jewels, rich pearl necklaces and . . . of pearls unsorted and undrilled several bushels," shared the royal government's Port Royal warehouses with the more mundane yet even more valuable produce of the Indies, indigo in particular. The governors-general exercised an economic as well as a military command over Jamaica's port city. Sir Thomas Modyford himself collected the royal warehouse rents. His brother and lieutenant, acting as chief judge of the admiralty court, declared the plunder that filled the government sheds to be legal prize, and so a legitimate part of English commerce. Of the prize goods, 10 percent was collected for the king, as commander-in-chief, and was supposedly applied by his governor-general to Jamaica fortification. An additional fifteenth was taken by Sir Thomas as vice admiral (in the name of his chief, the duke of York, the lord high admiral of the dominions). No convincing account of the 16⅔ percent of the buccaneers' loot thus ostensibly reserved for the crown was ever made, and how much additional plunder went to Modyford will never be known. The governor-general admitted to receiving only £500 in "presents" from the privateers. The Spaniards alleged that Modyford's share of a single raid on Nicaragua was worth more than £2,400. There were at least five other major cities sacked during Modyford's governor-generalship, as well as innumerable ships captured. Sir Thomas profited from them all. Not only did he collect dues for king and duke, fees for commissions, rents for warehouses, and "presents" for unspecified services, but from the time he declared war on Spain in 1665, he also took

48. *Cal. S.P. Col., 1661–1668*, nos. 1085, 1132, 1264, 1383, 1448, 1456; proposals of Sir Thomas Modyford, C.O. 138/1, 40. Note that fees for tavern licenses were a significant part of the executive's income. For a horrified account of Jamaican debauchery, see Style to [Arlington], Jan. 4, 1670, *Cal. S.P. Col., 1669–1674*, no. 138. See also Haring, *Buccaneers*, 77–78, the duelists on James Moxon's map of Jamaica, 1677, in Black, ed., *Blathwayt Atlas*, no. 36, and the lists (of 44 victuallers, vintners, and tavern keepers, 1664–1692, and of 20 taverns) in Pawson and Buisseret, *Port Royal*, 184–185, appendix 12.

an admiral's share of the privateers' plunder. Modyford undertook to guarantee his gain by writing into the buccaneers' commissions a proviso that all prizes must be brought to Port Royal for condemnation and sale under his government.[49]

Modyford had staked his own future, if not Jamaica's, on continued war with Spain. When unofficial news of the Anglo-Spanish peace reached Jamaica in December 1667 (eight months after it was concluded in Europe), the governor-general announced that he would not comply until officially ordered to do so. He was not so ordered. Apprehensive of Spanish attack—he had heard of Spain's refusal to admit any English right to Jamaica—the governor-general sent Henry Morgan to raid Cuba for intelligence. Morgan duly turned up evidence that the Spanish were mobilizing against Jamaica. He immediately sacked Puerto Principe as a profitable preventative measure. Jamaica's admirals knew what every swordsman knows: the best defense is a good attack.

In May 1668, Modyford ordered Morgan and four hundred Jamaicans to attack Puerto Bello. This Atlantic terminus of the Panama portage was ostensibly one of the bases of the anticipated assault on Jamaica. Morgan's men stormed the harbor fort, locked its garrison into the powder magazine, and blew up men, fort, and munitions. Stunned, the people of Puerto Bello submitted to weeks of robbery and rape. Spanish soldiers marched across the Isthmus from Panama City to recapture Puerto Bello. They were ambushed by the Jamaicans within sight of their goal. The invaders then leisurely loaded 250,000 pieces of eight into ships already ballasted with the cannon from Puerto Bello's defenses. After a pleasant sojourn on an isolated Cuban beach to divide the loot, Morgan's fleet sailed into Port Royal in August 1668. They received an understandably warm welcome.

Well paid in Jamaica, Sir Thomas Modyford feared English reaction to this exploit. He had deliberately broken his king's new peace with Spain, a peace beloved of powerful London merchants

49. H[enry] Slingsby, "Account of the Profits to Sir Thomas Modyford as Governor of Jamaica," C.O. 138/1, 134. Slingsby was Modyford's agent, an officer of cavalry, gentleman of the bedchamber to Charles II, and, from 1674, lieutenant governor of Portsmouth to the duke of York (Dalton, ed., *English Army Lists*, I, 4, 178, 298, 308). On the credit side of the governor-general's ledger Slingsby noted £1,000 per annum salary, £900 commission fees and presents from privateers, and plantation interests. According to Slingsby, Modyford had spent the (lord high admiral's) 1/15 of prizes (£700) on fortifications, as well as £2,500 of his own money. The king owed the governor-general £1,800, but even if this amount were paid to him, Slingsby added, Modyford's estate in Europe would total only £10,700. See also *Cal. S.P. Col., 1661–1668*, nos. 1076, 1144(II); *ibid., 1669–1674*, no. 103; Haring, *Buccaneers*, 73.

and a leading minister, the earl of Arlington. Governor-General Modyford was, however, fully and correctly confident of the captain general's favor and protection.[50] Sir Thomas's interest at court and his authority on the island were further reinforced by the frigate *Oxford*, sent by the leading English imperialists, the lord admiral, York, and the captain general, Albemarle, "to countenance the war with the Spaniards." Modyford's request for a man-of-war to discipline the privateers, given his promise that his government would maintain the vessel and pay her crew's wages, was approved by both dukes. Sir Thomas then had the ship drydocked at his own expense and sheathed in metal to resist the teredo worm. Not since Sir Ferdinando Gorges of Plymouth Fort prepared to coerce the New Englanders had a governor-general launched so fine a flagship, but she carried a cargo of English duplicity to Port Royal. Arlington had pledged peace with Spain; King Charles agreed. Albemarle and York wanted war with Spain in the Indies; King Charles agreed. A divided court reflected opposed mercantile and imperial forces in the society it headed. It also permitted the autonomy (and the amorality) of the governors-general. Greed, duty, or patrons might direct the imperial executives. All three, Modyford said, dictated his continual attacks on his Spanish neighbors.[51]

In obedience to his orders, and in the tradition of garrison government, Governor-General Modyford's first and last consid-

50. Albemarle's renewal of Modyford's discretionary power in Feb. 1668, following the peace with Spain, confirmed the Jamaican captain general's confidence (Modyford to Albemarle, Dec. 28, 1667, *Cal. S.P. Col., 1661–1668*, no. 1652). It seems that Modyford did eventually see a copy of the treaty, but he reminded Arlington on July 6, 1670, that the Spanish would admit "no Peace in the Indies . . . for they always use us, as in a Condition of War . . . and therefore as I have often hinted to the late Lord General it is their endeavor to defeat this Colony . . . [so that] they may be Masters of the Sea, and so impede our Trade . . . but on shore we fear them not, and do hope in time (for the preservation of our Plantations) to fix the War in their Country" (C.O. 138/1, 43). Modyford's unwillingness to abandon his strategy of preemptive strikes until Spain renounced its claim to Jamaica is detailed in his letters to Albemarle, Oct. 1, 1668, *Cal. S.P. Col., 1661–1668*, nos. 1850, 1851. The raid is recounted in the "information of Adm. Henry Morgan and his officers . . . given in to the Lt. Gen. of Port Royal by command of his excellency," Sept. 7, 1668, *ibid.*, no. 1838, where the number of Spanish defenders is magnified to 1,030 men, the relieving force to 3,000 men, and the ransom exacted is reduced to 100,000 pieces of eight. See also *ibid.*, 1863. The Spanish ambassador cited English merchant bills from Jamaica to prove that in plate alone, "the share of every soldier" was £80, "whence it may be guessed what quantity the officers, Governor, and their confidants had" (*ibid., 1669–1674*, no. 1). See also Arlington to Modyford, Mar. 16, 1666, *ibid., 1661–1668*, no. 1150. Note that the secretary was already freezing out the Modyfords from military offices and allowances (see *ibid.*, nos. 1718, 1845, 1863, and Beeston, "Journal," Add. MSS 12430, 32b), and they were trying to buy Sec. Williamson's favor instead (*Cal. S.P. Col., 1661–1668*, nos. 1864, 1865).

51. Albemarle to York, Mar. 12, 1668, petition of Charles Modyford to the king, June 1668, *Cal. S.P. Col., 1661–1668*, nos. 1711, 1776.

erations were the security of his command. The king could only occasionally spare money, men, or ships from England for Jamaica's defense, but the privateers were "1,500 of the best men in the world," their admiral noted. Man for fighting man, they have had few equals. The Spanish sailors they attacked often boasted beforehand that they would hoist the Jamaican sloops aboard as ship's boats and sail away unscathed. The garrisons of the Spanish cities regularly outnumbered their conquerors two or three to one. The privateers would be equally formidable foes of Jamaica, its commander warned, if they were ousted from Port Royal. If forced to find government commissions (which were all that stood between the privateers and piracy) and ports of refuge, relaxation, and market, from the Portuguese, Dutch, or French, the privateers would perforce obey their orders to attack the English. This, said Modyford, "we must prevent or perish."[52]

The savage Anglo-French war that broke out in the summer of 1666 sharpened Modyford's anxiety to reinforce the privateers' allegiance to Jamaica. Without such a naval force, the English settlers on St. Christopher were wiped out by the French. And four hundred refugees from Montserrat reminded the Jamaicans of the value of their seamen's accomplishments, both in clearing the French from the waters around Jamaica and in adding the Huguenot privateers to their ranks. As long as they were based in Port Royal, the privateers' self-interest made them amenable to Vice Admiral Modyford's orders to patrol Jamaica's coast and to collect useful military intelligence for him from the far reaches of the Caribbean. He used taxes on privateer plunder to fortify Port Royal and to build up his armory at St. Jago de la Vega. In an age when naval auxiliaries were a realistic concept, Jamaica's commander-in-chief could increase his government's naval might by encouraging his irregular forces to invest their profits in strengthening their ships. The twenty-five fine brass cannon that Morgan's men had brought in from Puerto Bello went a long way toward creating more uniform and more powerful batteries aboard the ships of Jamaica's navy. Paradoxically, peace would reduce island security by weakening the privateers. As they asked Modyford, "Will [peace] pay for new sails or rigging?" And the privateers advanced the empire: they were Modyford's amphibious striking force that, as Puerto Bello proved, terrorized Jamaica's eternal enemy, the Spaniards; their attacks on their French rivals protected Jamaica for a decade from the growing menace of the French; and they encouraged the

52. *Ibid.*, nos. 1085, 1138, 1142, 1144, 1147, 1209, 1264, 1265.

"high and military spirit" of their Jamaican compatriots. All in all, it was the activity of the privateers that underlay the governor-general's belief that the Western Design would be realized.[53]

Equal to the military benefits of the war on the Spanish colonies were the economic gains that accrued to Jamaica. Modyford and his colonists used Spanish plunder to capitalize the development of this colony conquered from Spain. The money was there for the taking. Everywhere, Modyford gloated, his men found the Spaniards "very weak and very wealthy," an irresistible combination. Spanish crops, cloth, tools, and slaves all passed directly from the privateers to the planters. In many cases these were the same men. Privateering also provided the specie, tropical produce, hides, and tallow "whereby the men of New England are invited to bring in their provisions" so that more Jamaican acres could be devoted to "the sweet negociation of Sugar." Trade in privateer plunder also attracted "many merchants to reside at Port Royal." These men were valuable additions to the colony's stock of ambition, administrative talent, and commercial connections with other English provinces. They marketed the island's growing agricultural output. And privateering even increased the planting population. At least Modyford asserted that the lure of privateering drew "down yearly many an hundred of English, French and Dutch, many of whom turn planters."[54]

The mercantilists for whom Arlington spoke, and a like-minded and growing group of the wealthiest Jamaica planters and merchants, rejected all Modyford's arguments. Instead they insisted that the privateer crews drew off potential plantation laborers and that privateer plunder was a tax on peaceful commerce. They argued that the profits of peaceful commerce with Spain and its colonies would vastly exceed the value of privateers' plunder and that the costs would be far less in lives and money. In June of 1669, having persuaded the members of the Triple Alliance that resistance to France in Europe required the preservation of Spanish imperial integrity and prosperity in America, Secretary Arlington,

53. *Ibid.*, nos. 1138 (which repeats Modyford's sentiments in C.O. 138/1, 40), 1283, 1456, 1537; Modyford to Ashley, July 6, 1670, C.O. 138/1, 49–50.

54. Modyford to Albemarle, Mar. 1, June 8, 1666, *Cal. S.P. Col., 1661–1668*, nos. 1142, 1213; Modyford to the Spanish ambassador, June 15, 1669, C.O. 138/1, 41. The governor-general elsewhere noted that a soldier-settler was the Jamaican norm in any case: "Being both a Souldier and a Planter . . . is the general Profession of all the Gentlemen of this Island" (C.O. 138/1, 132). Of Modyford's three examples of privateer–planters, however, only a Cromwellian captain, Richard Guy, appears as a major landholder, with 753 acres in St. John Parish. Modyford's choice as captain of the *Oxford*, Edward Collier, held 1,020 acres in Clarendon Parish (C.O. 138/1, 71, 76).

in the king's name, ordered General Modyford to proclaim peace with Spain.[55]

The Jamaica governor-general duly revoked his commissions against Spanish shipping (he had never authorized, in writing, attacks on Spanish towns), but he nonetheless permitted the privateers to use Port Royal as before. The same French menace that inspired the secretary of state's diplomacy persuaded the governor-general to preserve his privateers as a force in being. "If the peace with France were immortal," Modyford wrote Arlington, "or if that warlike Prince had no design this way, I should be little concerned at the lawless motions of these privateers." Lasting peace, however, was as unlikely as French aggression was certain. Therefore, "it troubles me to be driven to that saddest error of all Governments to act so imprudently as in this most active age to weaken ourselves and strengthen our enemies" by driving the privateers out of Port Royal and into the arms of the French.[56]

Panama

It was not French aggression, however, but a dying reflex of Spanish imperial authority that impelled Governor-General Modyford, once again and finally, to defy Secretary Arlington's orders and English mercantilist opinion. As Sir Thomas penned his defense of privateering, the Spanish queen's cedula of April 20, 1669, was en route to her governors in the Indies. It ordered attacks on any and all English possessions "beyond the line." In the autumn these orders were followed to the West Indies by a Spanish fleet, the intended vehicle of an assault on Jamaica. Modyford's spies reported the Spanish intention to blockade eastern Jamaica and thus cut off the island's communications and commerce with England. More ominous to English empire than Spanish enmity was the death of the duke of Albemarle, the champion of militant Jamaicans, he "that only befriended us." The unhappy coincidence of the captain general's death and "this war, our making a blind

---

55. Arlington to Modyford, June 12, 1670, C.O. 138/1, 42. Feiling, *British Foreign Policy*, 275–280, notes that the guarantee of Feb. 1669 applied to Spanish territory in any part of the world. This, then, was the direct impetus for Arlington's letter of June 12, which ordered Modyford to forbear land fighting. Thornton, *West-India Policy*, 108, notes that the king, followed by York and Rupert, was simultaneously negotiating an anti-Spanish pact with the French.

56. See Beeston, "Journal," Add. MSS 12430, 32b; Style to [Arlington], Jan. 4, 1670, Modyford's narrative, Aug. 23, 1669, *Cal. S.P. Col., 1669–1674*, nos. 138, 103.

peace, no frigates, nor orders coming," gave the colonists "cruel apprehensions and makes us remiss."[57]

Apprehensions became reality in June 1670. The Spanish raided the isolated plantations of Jamaica's north side, destroying them and carrying off the survivors as prisoners. Jamaica's governor-general rallied the privateers in Port Royal. Under the martial law he proclaimed, Modyford protected the seamen from their merchant creditors and from the civil courts, conscripted slaves to strengthen Jamaica's land defenses, and called up the planter-militia to man them. As the privateers reorganized and the Spanish retreated, Modyford learned of the cedula. On June 29, 1670, the governor-general's council endorsed his exercise of his military authority and his citation of the "general welfare" clause of his commission to justify recommissioning Henry Morgan as admiral. Modyford ordered Morgan to lead Jamaica's navy against Spanish ships and against the ports from which the attack on Jamaica had been launched. Writing to Lord Ashley (a request that he succeed Albemarle as the protector of Jamaica and of its governor-general), Modyford proudly described his military reprisal as "a fond rash Action, for a petty Governor without Money to make and entertain a War with the richest, and not long since the powerfulest Prince of Europe."[58]

Admiral Morgan had no sooner sailed from Port Royal to begin this "fond rash Action" with his thirty-six ships and their 1,846 men than Modyford received Arlington's dispatch reporting the imminence of a worldwide peace with Spain. The treaty would bring enormous commercial advantage to England, the secretary said, but Spain had yet to sign it. Arlington now admitted that the privateers were a useful threat to compel Spanish compliance with the treaty, but he feared that any extraordinary buccaneer outrage might drive the Spaniards into refusing it. Arlington therefore ordered Sir Thomas "that in what State soever the Privateers are, at the Receipt of this Letter, you keep them so till we have a final Answer from Spain . . . with this Condition only, . . . that you

57. Commission of War by the Spaniards against the English in the West Indies, C.O. 138/1, 46. The inaccurate endorsement, "Spanish Commission against the Privateers," suggests the bias of Arlington and the mercantilists. And see n. 58 below.

58. See Modyford to Arlington, July 6, 30, Aug. 9, 1670, declaration of war by Modyford and his council against the Spaniards in the West Indies, June 29, 1670, Modyford to Ashley, July 6, 1670, C.O. 138/1, 44–50. (Some of these are calendared as Cal. S.P. Col., 1669–1674, nos. 207, 209, 211, 212.) Modyford recognized the political danger to himself from Arlington's influence. There was widespread expectation of the governor-general's fall and replacement (by the earl of Carlisle); see Cal. S.P. Col., 1669–1674, nos. 172, 227. Modyford himself told Arlington "how great my Distractions were at the frequent Advices of your Lordships displeasure against me." (Aug. 20, 1670, C.O. 138/1, 52).

oblige them to forbear all hostilities at Land." That condition specifically prohibited Modyford's plan to raid the Spanish ports. Modyford recalled Morgan to read it.[59]

The two admirals rejected these orders and agreed to attack every Spanish city the privateers could reach, and their reach would realize the fondest dreams of an ancient enmity. Modyford himself had commanded in the war against Spain in the Indies since 1654, and that war was a century old. The governor-general could conceive of no other policy compatible with empire. Peace with Spain would permit the mercantilists to sell Jamaica and abandon England's imperial future. Jamaica's commander would sabotage that peace if he could. Sir Thomas pled necessity as an excuse for sacking Spanish cities: necessity knows no law; much less would it recognize instructions from a pro-Spanish secretary of state. Modyford pointed out that his government had been attacked, its plantations burned, its people killed or captured, and its English commerce curtailed, while the privateer vessels that could have protected the island rotted in outlying cays because of a purported peace with the inveterate Spanish enemy. French viceroys, Modyford recalled, had been deposed by their colonists for refusing to counterattack against Spanish raiders. Sir Thomas said he feared for his life—not to mention the authority of his royal office—if he failed to retaliate. And an attack was psychologically vital: it would sustain his people's military pride and prowess while it doubled the enemy's fear, "reputation doing many times more in military affairs then force."[60]

The raid also offered the governor-general an opportunity to reorganize his striking force. As the price of his commissions, he demanded that the privateers submit "to Martial Law and a stricter Discipline than those rugged fellows could ever yet be brought to." The authorizations had to endorse the sacking of Spanish cities, however, for Jamaica's seamen supplied "ships, Armes, ammunition, and provisions on their own charge," and they expected plunder in return. "As the late Lord General that great Master of War adviseth the soldier," Modyford explained, so Jamaica's privateers "look on the Enemy as the surest pay and it cannot be imagined or expected by any rational man that those

59. A list of the ships under the command of Adm. Morgan is in C.O. 138/1, 105. The expanded account of Modyford to Arlington, Oct. 31, 1670, is calendared in *Cal. S.P. Col., 1669–1674*, no. 310. See also Arlington to Modyford, June 12, 1670, C.O. 138/1, 42.

60. Modyford to Arlington, Aug. 20, Sept. 20, 1670, C.O. 138/1, 51–53, 54, calendared in *Cal. S.P. Col., 1669–1674*, nos. 237, 264; "Considerations from Sir Thomas Modyford which moved him to give his consent for fitting the privateers of Jamaica against the Spaniards," C.O. 138/1, 136.

should be under so much Command as Soldiers under their Prince's care and pay are." In short, the governor-general and vice admiral of Jamaica had unleashed his seadogs before Arlington's orders arrived. He could not call them home unfed, nor did he want to.[61]

Modyford ordered Morgan to sack the ports from which Jamaica had been attacked. More than that, the governor-general told his admiral to garrison the capital of Cuba as the metropolis of a new province in England's empire. Whenever he could not hold a city, Morgan was "to destroy and burn and leave it a wilderness, putting the men slaves to the sword and sending the women slaves hither to be sold for the account of his fleet." So the Spanish had treated Jamaica's plantations and their slaves. Reciprocity was the rule of revenge with regard to whites as well: Modyford ordered Morgan to give the Spaniards whatever quarter they had given the English; he knew that this was to be no quarter at all. With savage irony the governor-general concluded that he offered his humane concession "to make all people sensible of his moderation and good nature and his inaptitude and loathness to spill the blood of man."[62]

Modyford's mockery of "moderation" and his compulsion to slay the Spaniards were fueled by an imperial design, not by the need to revenge the raid on his garrison government or to prevent further raids on Jamaica, for both revenge and prevention had been served before Morgan sailed. First, Modyford knew that the Spanish settlements were "not sufficiently stored with People to hurt us," whatever orders the queen of Spain might send out. Then, in September and October 1670, a fleet commanded by Captain Edward Collier had destroyed the Spanish ships that had raided Jamaica. Finally, their home ports, Santa Marta and Rio de la Hacha (on what is today the coast of Colombia) had been plundered. Modyford found in these successes excuses again to attempt the Western Design. Thirty-eight of the captured Spaniards were "examined" in Jamaica. Two of them were persuaded to swear that the people of Cartagena had been "in arms offensive against the English." Modyford used this testimony to justify a raid on that city, which he had sought to destroy since 1654. The Spanish prisoners also testified that the president of Panama had commissioned ships to attack the English. Governor-General Modyford ordered appropriate retaliation. To determine it, Admiral Morgan's

61. Considerations from Sir Thomas Modyford, commission and instructions from Modyford to Morgan, June 29–July 2, 1670, C.O. 138/1, 136–137, 47–49, *Cal. S.P. Col., 1669–1674*, nos. 211, 212, 226.
    62. *Ibid.*, 212.

captains met in council of war on December 2, 1670. They resolved that "it stands most for the good of Jamaica and safety of us
all to take Panama."[63]

As the first step toward enacting Modyford's sixteen-year-
old plans for an imperial offensive, the privateers again occupied
Providence Island. They achieved the original strategic purpose of
the puritan stronghold: they used it as a base from which to storm
the Spanish forts on the Charges River. This opened the trail to
Panama. There followed the privateers' epic march across the
Isthmus: ten days of hunger, ambush, and all the hazards of the
jungle. Twelve hundred Jamaicans emerged from the mountains
on January 17, 1671. On the plain of Panama they were met by a
Spanish force twice their size. Morgan's men broke through the
Spanish ranks and swarmed over the city walls, only to watch
helplessly as Panama burned, fired by its fleeing garrison. After the
ashes cooled, the site of the greatest city in Spanish America was
utterly looted and laid waste. It was never rebuilt. For twenty-
eight days its surviving population was tortured by the buccaneers. They extorted at least £30,000 from the Spaniards. In
mid-February, Morgan's men withdrew over the Isthmus and on
March 6 sailed for Port Royal. There they arrived during April,
divided their loot, and, on the last day of May 1671 received the
official thanks of Governor-General Modyford and his council of
state and war.[64]

Sir Thomas Lynch and the
Evolution of the Imperial Constitution

Coup and Purge: The Seizure of a Garrison Government

Giving the privateers his approval as commander-in-chief and
taking an admiral's share of the Panama plunder were very nearly
Sir Thomas Modyford's last official acts. His dispatches of August

63. Modyford's answer to inquiries, C.O. 138/1, 96, Modyford to Arlington, Oct. 31,
1670, Cal. S.P. Col., 1669–1674, no. 310, also see no. 359. By Dec. 18, Modyford had twice
sent copies of the Treaty of Madrid after Morgan, so that he would "do nothing that might
prevent the accomplishment of his Majesty's peaceable intentions. . . ." The first vessel returned without finding the admiral. If the second ship did catch up with the expedition, not
a difficult task, no one thought fit to acknowledge its embarrassing message.

64. Morgan's deposition of Apr. 1671 and William Fogg's "Relation of Panama," Apr.
4, 1671, C.O. 138/1, 120–128, and Beeston, "Journal," Add. MSS 12430, 32b–33, are the
basis for this narrative.

1670 reached London in October. The moment that Arlington read that the privateers were loose again, he nominated Colonel Thomas Lynch as Modyford's replacement. The colonel was no sooner knighted and instructed than in June 1671 the news of Panama set London agog. "Such an action had not been done since the famous *Drake*," one member of the council for foreign plantations exclaimed. Courtiers took a less favorable view. Sir Thomas Modyford's disobedience to his orders was the aspect of the exploit that impressed Whitehall. Modyford's son Charles was instantly locked up in the Tower as surety for his father's appearance there.[65]

King Charles ordered Sir Thomas Lynch and the captain of his naval convoy to sail immediately for Jamaica. There they were to arrest Sir Thomas Modyford and ship him home a prisoner to answer to the king "for the many hostilities and depradations committed upon the Countrys and Subjects of our Good brother the Catholic King in America without Warrant or Authority from Us." But Colonel Lynch was warned not to move against his predecessor until he controlled Fort Charles and had secured the loyalty of at least a bodyguard from the island regiments. The captain of the frigate, appropriately named the *Assistance*, was to cover the new governor from the harbor. He was ordered not to step ashore himself, lest he be captured, until Lynch had arrested Modyford. If "any accident befall the person of Sir Thomas Lynch," or even if he was opposed, the captain of the *Assistance* was to attack the islanders "with his utmost force, and particularly by burning, sinking, and destroying the Privateers."[66]

Sir Thomas Lynch landed from the *Assistance* in Port Royal on June 25, 1671. He read his commission and then took to his bed in the house of the very man he had come to arrest, for "the gout had seized him in a terrible manner." From this unlikely vantage point the lieutenant governor planned the coup that would capture his host, Sir Thomas Modyford. The ex-governor-general dwelt amidst his "family" of four hundred persons, in a town peopled

65. Order of the council for foreign plantations, Oct. 5, 1670, *Cal. S.P. Col., 1669–1674*, no. 287; revocation of Modyford's commission, Jan. 4, 1671, Lynch's commission and instructions, Jan. 5, 1671, king's order of Feb. 28, 1671 (requiring Modyford to surrender his command, forts, and places of strength and then to come home to report), C.O. 138/1, 85*ff*; warrants for the arrest and detention of Charles Modyford, May 16, 1671, *Cal. S.P. Col., 1669–1674*, nos. 528–530. Modyford's formal reports on Panama reached the council of foreign plantations, of which Evelyn was a member, on June 29. Evelyn's reaction is recorded in Beer, ed., *Diary of Evelyn*, Aug. 19, 1671.

66. Arrest orders are in the king to the duke of York, Mar. 1671, S.P. 44/24 (Secret Letters and Warrants), 48, and in Private Instructions to Sir Thomas Lynch, n.d., *ibid.*, 49–50.

by many of his fifteen hundred privateer allies. The seamen were cowed, however, partly by the news of peace, more by the presence of the *Assistance*. Neither they nor Modyford's household retainers were as politically puissant as the Port Royal Regiment, however, for it made up the governor's guards and the citadel's garrison. Sir Thomas Lynch quickly commissioned himself as this regiment's colonel. He named his protégé, William Beeston, as its major. Lynch also appointed his followers to most of the company captaincies. Modyford's men were not universally disgraced, but they now held less than one-third of the regiment's commissions. A veteran of the army that had conquered and colonized Jamaica, Lynch had calculated these public changes of command with care, "knowing how much it takes amongst this sort of people." Now he could count on the loyalty of the six files of the regiment on duty in Fort Charles, at the seaward end of the city. He made equally sure of the guards posted at the redoubt and gate in the landward wall across the Port Royal peninsula. Anchored offshore, between the fort and the wall, was the *Assistance*. With one battery, she commanded the narrow spit of land on which the town was built; with the other, her captain was prepared to sweep the harbor.[67]

Then word arrived of Charles Modyford's arrest in London, as a hostage for his father's appearance. Sir Thomas Lynch heard the news first, for he took the usual garrison governor's precaution of interviewing all arrivals before permitting them the freedom of the town. Lynch immediately jailed the messenger, proclaimed martial law, posted guards over every boat in Port Royal, and ordered the outlying militia units to station pickets to prevent anyone sailing from the island's outports. Then Lynch ordered units from the inland regiments to reinforce him in Port Royal. Selected companies commanded by Lynch's old army colleagues marched on the capital, yet Sir Thomas Modyford still seemed to suspect nothing when, early on the morning of August 12, he was told that an urgent order from the king awaited him aboard the *Assistance*. He arrived at the waterside to find Sir Thomas Lynch awaiting him, guarded by a picked company of uniformed militia under the command of Lynch's ally from the D'Oyley days, Colonel Thomas Freeman. Modyford tried to draw back, but he was somehow "tricked" into taking his own boat out to the *Assistance*. He came aboard to find the ship's crew in arms, headed by Vice Admiral Lynch. Modyford's boat crew was told to shove off

67. See n. 68.

or be sunk. As Modyford's men rowed away, Sir Thomas Lynch read to "the late General" the king's order for his arrest. Modyford was immediately locked up and not allowed ashore again, even to part from his dying younger son. The former captain general of Jamaica had fallen as he had governed, by the hand of power. As Lynch wrote, he had made Modyford "a prisoner by surprise and kept him so by force."[68]

Before sunset of that same day, Lynch revoked Modyford's commissions to the privateers. As soon as his predecessor was well on his way to England, locked in a merchantman's cabin under a constant naval guard, the new commander-in-chief of Jamaica offered to pardon every privateer who submitted to his authority. He ordered the captain of the *Assistance* to capture and burn the ships of those who refused the offer. Then Sir James Modyford, brother and lieutenant of the deposed governor-general, boldly used his authority as a judge of the admiralty to free one outlawed rover. Lynch reversed the decision, hung the pirate, dismissed Modyford from the admiralty bench, and suspended him from the council as well. King Charles himself, not noted for squeamishness about judicial murders in support of royal authority, told his lieutenant in Jamaica that this execution violated every rule of justice. Court gossip, however, held that "Lynch has given good satisfaction here in all that he had done." Despite various noblemen's aspirations to govern Jamaica, "the King likes so well of Sir T[homas] Ly[nch] that he will not think yet of sending another." King Charles showed that liking when he confirmed Sir Thomas Lynch's removal of Sir James Modyford and of the entire Modyford family faction from every office they held in Jamaica, civil and military.[69]

Ruthless use of his military authority, authorized by explicit

68. Beeston, "Journal," Add. MSS 12430, 33; Littleton to Hatton, Sept. 6, 1671, Add. MSS 29577, 89; Lynch to Sandwich, Aug. 20, to Arlington, June 27, 1671, Add. MSS 11410, 185, 189–190, 182; Lynch to Arlington, July 2, Aug. 20, 1671, Modyford to [Arlington], [Nov.] 17, 1671, *Cal. S.P. Col., 1669–1674*, nos. 580, 604, 655. Lynch promoted Freeman to colonel's rank, commissioned him chief justice of the common pleas, assisted his son in his purchase of the deputy secretaryship from Povey, and admitted Robert Freeman to the council—all of which exemplifies the utility of patronage in tying an island magnate and his family both to the governor's party and to the imperial interest. See C.O. 138/1, 6, 23, and *Cal. S.P. Col., 1669–1674*, no. 604(I). Lynch to the king, n.d., Add. MSS 11410, 269.

69. Lynch to Arlington, Aug. 22, 1671, *Cal. S.P. Col., 1669–1674*, no. 609; Lynch's strict orders to the officers of the guard, Aug. 14, 1671, Add. MSS 12430, 20–21; Lynch to Littleton, Mar. 5, 1672, Add. MSS 11410, 243; Lynch to Slingsby, Oct. 9, 1672, *Cal. S.P. Col., 1669–1674*, no. 945. On the simultaneous arrest of Modyford and pardon to the privateers, see *ibid.*, nos. 602, 604. King Charles's formal reprimand (no. 1024) upset Lynch, but the duke of York expressed his satisfaction with his vice admiral's action (Lynch to Williamson, Dec. 15, 1671, Aug. 12, 1673, to Worsley, Aug. 12, 1673, *ibid.*, nos. 691, 1129,

royal orders and backed by the king's approval, enabled Lynch to execute his instructions "to a title." He put down the Modyfords' privateering and ended Jamaica's war with Spain. It was with reluctance, however, that Lynch obeyed the royal order to complete the ruin of the Modyford regime by arresting its renowned admiral, Henry Morgan, and sending him as a prisoner to England. Not only was Morgan Lynch's father-in-law, and ill, but a principle of command also underlay the new executive's objections to the arrest of Admiral Morgan. He pointed out to the royal authorities that Morgan had acted under the orders of a governor-general, which he "nor no subject can or ought to dispute." As Jamaica's commander-in-chief, Lynch argued that "if obedience should be a crime, it would occasion disputes and disobedience, especially in these remote colonys." Certainly, no one in Jamaica now presumed to disobey that old soldier Sir Thomas Lynch, even if he were only a lieutenant governor-general. His forceful acts might not make him loved, Lynch acknowledged, but even "those that envy or hate me most must confess, the Kings Power and authority is so established here that the least of his servants . . . will be revered and His Majesty's Commands readily obeyed."[70]

Sir Thomas Lynch Balances Jamaica's Constitution

The royal commands to the new viceroy alarmed elements of the London merchant community. They feared the growth of royal authority anywhere in the empire—and they warned their Jamaica correspondents that it meant increased taxation. The merchants "buzzed in the People's Ears that his Majesty, as Lord of this Island, may impose what Taxes he pleaseth." They wrote that the king's courtiers claimed Jamaica had been "conquered at the charge of the State, and so no consent of the freeholders is necessary to tax." Taxation without representation, these merchants said, signaled the court's intent to impose "an Arbitrary Government, which . . . English Men abhorrs."

This abhorrence was expressed by the Modyford faction. They had turned libertarian as soon as they were out of office. They now insisted that the king must be brought to admit that Jamaica was part of the realm and that therefore "he holds himself obliged to protect his good Subjects there, in their Possessions and

1130). The court talk was repeated by Littleton to Hatton, Nov. 28, 1671, and n.d., Add. MSS 29577, 95b, 98.
    70. Lynch to Littleton, Mar. 5, 1672, to Sandwich, Aug. 20, 1671, to Arlington, Mar. 29, Apr. 3, 1672, Add. MSS 11410, 243, 246, 185, 262–263, 271.

Estates, and in their lives and just Liberties as fully and as amply"
as he did his other English subjects. The king should promise not
to tax the property of Jamaicans "without the consent of the Major
part of the Representatives of the freeholders of that his Island,
according to the usual manner (by his Royal Writs) assembled."
Finally, King Charles ought to confirm the acts of Modyford's
(only) assembly and return them to the colony to serve as its
fundamental law.[71]

   This, Sir Thomas Modyford's last-minute bid for popularity
with Jamaica's planters (and perhaps for the favor of the newly
elevated earl of Shaftesbury), heightened his successor's difficulties
in shouldering the yoke of Anglo-American politics. Sir Thomas
Lynch was a royal executive, not an aristocrat or a merchant. He
possessed "his Majesty's Authority, and represents his person and
is solely enabled to govern by his Commission." Yet Shaftesbury
was entering on his period of great influence in Anglo-American
politics, and his effort to hedge the royal prerogative with the
political privileges of the propertied ruling class found a primitive
expression in an instruction to Lynch. "Without good cause," the
Jamaican executive was "not to augment or diminish the number
or suspend any of the present Members of the Council." Some of
these councillors were Sir Thomas Lynch's former colleagues
from the old army, but others were allied with "the faction of the
Modyfords," led by Sir James Modyford and by Admiral Morgan.
Practically dependent on the councillors for regional administration, Lynch admitted what Shaftesbury insisted on, that the provincial executive was obliged "to consult his own Council in all
affairs of Moment, for they are what the King's Council and house
of lords are in England." The lieutenant governor also felt politically compelled to recognize the legislative authority of an assembly, that is, his council and the nineteen legislators elected by the
717 Jamaican landlords from among their own number. These
were but a tiny fragment of the 15,198 island inhabitants, yet the
unrepresentative character of the Jamaica assembly only confirmed
that it was what Lynch called it, "a kind of Parliament." Lynch
explained that the assembly was fundamental to Jamaica's constitution because "the people here look on it as a privilege and their
Magna Carta, that they shall be governed according to their Municipal Laws and those of England, and not have anything im-

71. Modyford to Arlington, Sept. 20, 1670, C.O. 138/1, 54. Modyford's "Propositions
for the speedy settling of Jamaica" are *ibid.*, 59.

posed on them but by their own Consents, as the Barbados and the Cariby Islands have."[72]

Sir Thomas Lynch came out to govern at a time of political assertion by the parliamentary classes, led in the American provinces, as in England, by Shaftesbury. Nonetheless, as a veteran of civil war and garrison government in the British Isles, and as a leader of the army that conquered and colonized Jamaica, obsessed with his realization that "this is a Frontier Colony and remote," Colonel Lynch was determined to exercise his military authority to protect and order his government. He requisitioned material and conscripted labor to complete the citadel of Fort Charles. He regularized the garrison it drew from the Port Royal Regiment, and he used his newly commissioned major general, James Bannister, both to enforce the militia act and to recruit new companies from among the settlers Bannister brought in from Surinam. Fleeing from their colony, conceded to the Dutch in return for New York, the vanguard of Bannister's settlers, led by the major general himself, had landed on Jamaica just in time to back Lynch's seizure of Modyford.

The new commander returned the favor by granting land to four hundred of these seasoned colonists. This was an auspicious beginning for Lynch's plan to limit land grants to cultivators, to take strict surveys, and to require quitrents. Reverting to General D'Oyley's policy of soldier settlement, Colonel Lynch argued that an increased small planter population would strengthen the militia, intensify cultivation, and increase production. All evidence shows that he was right. By 1673 the island population had risen to 17,272. "During the time of his Government," a contemporary wrote, "many ships were loaded with the natural produce of the

72. While Lynch's correspondents were politically varied, they had two common characteristics: they were not friends of Modyford and, as Lynch wrote (to Sir John Trevor, Mar. 9, 1672, C.O. 138/1, 250), they were "those who I know have particular care of and affection to His Majesty's Service and interest in these remote Countrys." Col. Lynch's military experience was especially valued in light of French aggressiveness and the threat of Spanish revenge; see Willoughby to [Povey], Sept. 24, 1670, Egerton MS 2395, 270. Lynch described the Jamaican political institutions in his "State," C.O. 138/2, 4–38. Note here, as in Modyford's case, the extensive political influence of Barbados on the colonial constitution. Dunn, *Sugar and Slaves*, records the influence in Jamaica of Barbados's economic model. M. Eugene Sirmans, *Colonial South Carolina: A Political History, 1663–1763* (Chapel Hill, N.C., 1966), discusses Barbadian influence on many aspects of Carolina life, and Winthrop D. Jordan, *White Over Black: American Attitudes Toward the Negro, 1550–1812* (Chapel Hill, N.C., 1968), documents the influence in the continental colonies of slavery as organized by the English in Barbados. Such unities of imperial history should be generally observed.

Island, before it never one, and in the end of his Government land was risen to four times the value it had been in the beginning."[73]

"Peace and an easy government," Sir Thomas Lynch said of his command, "will in a short time make it a most flourishing Country." In his first public speech in Jamaica, Lynch promised "an easy government" when he refuted rumors that a great lord was coming out as governor-general of Jamaica to tax the colonists by royal fiat. The king, his lieutenant said, "intended himself to be their Governor as well as their Sovereign Lord and Proprietor." He "was so far from abandoning them to be a Prey to any particular person" that he had constituted "in England a just and honorable Councell to take care of their Interest." Not only was the new council for foreign plantations to speak for the colonies to the crown, but Lynch also assured both present and potential Jamaicans that they might speak for themselves through their assemblies, for the king had "commanded me to lay no imposition" upon the islanders except by their own consent.[74]

Having thus begun his administration by rejecting taxation without representation, the lieutenant governor issued writs on December 1, 1671, for the election of "two of the most Sufficient and discreet freeholders" from each parish, save his own bailiwick, the old St. Jago regimental quarter, now St. Katherine parish. To this, his capital district, Lynch gave three representatives. The delegates of the freeholders may not have been altogether "discreet." Some of them accused Lynch of managing the election by his manipulation of districts and by the advantages he gave some candidates by commissioning them to military and civil office. The assemblymen were certainly "sufficient," however. Of the nineteen assemblymen-elect, fourteen appear in the "survey" of 1670, and two of the unlisted members were Port Royal's representatives and among its richest merchants. Even with the landless merchants included, the legislators possessed estates averaging 879 acres each. This compares rather favorably with the average Jamaica plantation of 260 acres. Indeed, only three assemblymen owned plantations as small as that, and two of these three held plural offices, that is, they were bureaucrats. Ten assemblymen used military titles. Six others were judges of common pleas. In February 1675 Sir Thomas Lynch called these island oligarchs into session.[75]

73. C.O. 138/2, 7–11. Bannister to [Arlington], Aug. 14, 1671, Lynch to Sandwich, Oct. 14, 1671, *Cal. S.P. Col., 1669–1674*, nos. 600, 640; "History and Present State of Jamaica under the Lord Vaughan," Phillips MS 11009, 21; Dunn, *Sugar and Slaves*, 155.

74. Lynch to Arlington, June 27, Dec. 17, 1671, Add. MSS 11410, 180–182, 215.

75. *Cal. S.P. Col., 1669–1674*, no. 669, gives the date and C.O. 138/1, 119, provides the

The lieutenant governor expected that to avoid a tax on their crops, the planter-legislators would oppose a grant of revenue to the royal government. He let it be known, however, that no laws would pass until the assembly authorized some form of taxation. Thus, even before the assembly met, the lines of political combat were drawn. Lynch wryly reported to Jamaica's former commander-in-chief, Sir Charles Littleton, that the islanders, like Englishmen at home, had matured politically in the decade since Sir Charles had won tax laws from the colony's first assembly. He had met, Lynch told Littleton, "a very representative of your Parliament that is an Assembly, a People naturally as Jealous of their own Interests and as careful not to promote those of the King or Public as any Popular Harengeur with you."[76]

To secure the interest of "the King or Public" from the assembly, the lieutenant governor adopted standard executive tactics. He nominated as speaker his old army associate, the anti-Modyford leader, Captain Samuel Long, and imprisoned those who had identified themselves as an opposition when they charged that the lieutenant governor had managed the election. After coercion, compromise. When he had weakened the opposition, Lynch offered to allow the assembly to examine the accounts if they approved a royal revenue. The assemblymen responded by raising £1,800 to repair Fort Charles. Lynch's quid pro quo was his signature to an act declaring the laws of England in force in Jamaica. Together, the lieutenant governor and the assembly then revised the local code written by Modyford's legislature. The lieutenant governor thus admitted a legitimate role in government for the provincial legislature and, more particularly, accepted English common and local law in Jamaica. These concessions to civil law and local lawmakers were necessary, Lynch said, "not so much for governing the people here, who are very respective to authority, as for encouraging others to come."[77]

By these statutes and schemes—to use peace with Spain to promote population growth and plantation expansion—Sir Thomas

---

language of the writs. An outline of Lynch's system of representation, including the provost marshal's returns, is in *Cal. S.P. Col., 1669–1674*, nos. 604, 662, 726. The members' landholdings appear in the 1670 survey (C.O. 138/1, 61*ff*), and their civil offices are listed in Lynch's "State" (C.O. 138/2, 23). Whitson, *Constitutional Development of Jamaica*, 41–43, clearly summarizes the alterations in assembly composition under Lynch's command.

76. Lynch to Littleton, Jan. 28, 1672, *Cal. S.P. Col., 1669–1674*, no. 743; Lynch to Sir Robert Murray, Mar. 2, 1672, Add. MSS 11410, 239.

77. Minutes of the council of Jamaica, Feb. 1, 5, 7, 8, 16, May 11–14, 1672, Lynch to Arlington, Mar. 2, 1672, Nov. 29, 1671, 34 acts of the assembly of Jamaica, May 14, 1672, Lynch to the council for foreign plantations, Mar. 10, July 5, 1672, *Cal. S.P. Col., 1669–1674*, nos. 747, 752, 761, 827, 773, 663, 829, 777, 885.

Lynch and the assembly raised the representative and civilian part of the colonial constitution toward equality with its authoritarian and military foundations. The new harmony was symbolized in the concluding law of Lynch's first assembly: the legalization of the old army holiday of May 10 as "Conquest Day." Similarly, law and force were allied in assembly acts that regulated the militia and reinforced the executive's military prerogative. The assembly also adopted past executive actions: it made several orders of the governor-and-council part of statute law, and it endorsed the table of fees for appointive officers. Thus the assembly helped to yoke the conquered colony's military executive and orders to a plantation province's civilian system of representation and legislation. Officers had become planters as well. Soldiers were also settlers. And privateers had turned turtle hunters, logwood cutters, and coastwise shippers. In the interstices of this military society, merchants and immigrants had found places. They filled out the social structure, the leadership of which was summarized in the assembly composed of the governor, his council, and the representatives of the old army's grandees, the civilian planters, and the cosmopolitan merchants.

Under Sir Thomas Lynch, the Jamaican polity thus acquired a mature form. This achievement was not immediately apparent, however. From 1674 to 1677, islanders of country or republican vision were spurred by their English counterparts to advance the claims of the oligarchy to rule through the assembly. After 1678 the crown retaliated by trying to eliminate the assembly and so to crush the island autonomy it proclaimed. In 1681, however, the social reality which was summarized in the balanced constitution that Lieutenant Governor Lynch had fostered and defended was royally recognized by his appointment as Jamaica's captain general. Finally, in 1689, after Governor-General Lynch's death in 1684 had been followed by a renewed royalist resurgence in Jamaica, William III explicitly reaffirmed and extended to the whole of England's American empire Sir Thomas Lynch's Jamaican constitution.[78]

78. See chapter 6 below, and S. S. Webb, "Blathwayt: 1689–1717," WMQ, 3d Ser., XXVI (1969), 376.

The Military Executive: Lynch at War, 1672–1674

Lynch's recognition of civil authority was merely balanced against—it did not replace or reduce—the martial elements in the government of the conquered colony. Major General Bannister had backed Lynch against Modyford and had reorganized the militia. Lynch assigned another veteran commander, Colonel John Cope ("a very good officer" in Lynch's experienced estimation), to take military and civil charge of the 350 former redcoats who hacked out the new settlements of Jamaica's north side. Lynch made these men part of Jamaica's militia. Their captains, who were Lynch's military appointees and Colonel-Councillor Cope's subordinates, represented the North Side in the assembly. That Lynch continued the Cromwellian colonial program of population, plantation, and protection (in peacetime, imperial conquest and privateering had to be laid aside) was clear when he incorporated these military men and their settlement on an exposed sea frontier into both the military and civil institutions of the older society. In so strengthening Jamaica's martial tradition and reinforcing its strategic location, Lynch expressed a defensive version of the imperialist argument. "There is no place so fit to be well manned, planted, and fortified," as Jamaica, Lynch concluded, "for awing or defending the Spaniard, strengthening trade, and preventing designs of French or Dutch."[79]

Imperialists and mercantilists alike now agreed on Jamaica's importance: "Whether, therefore, we regard interests of State or trade, it will be found our main interest to mind the planting, settling, and increasing its inhabitants." But English merchants in Spain warned that once again Spanish warships and troops had assembled to attack England's frontier colony in the West Indies. Sir Thomas Lynch reacted with stiffened militia discipline and rebuilt defenses. The colonial commander called his council of war into session. They amended the militia act (the assembly's effort to define the crown's military authority) and, without either assembly approval or royal confirmation, enforced it in the altered form. Lynch thus acted domestically and defensively on his own authority, as delegated by the crown and assented to by his council of war. He was restrained offensively, however, by the tightened royal rein on viceroys. As he reminded his council, he would share

79. Lynch's "State," C.O. 138/2, 7, 10; D'Oyley's Journal, Add. MSS 12423, 34b, 74; Lynch to Williamson, Jan. 13, 1672, Add. MSS 11410, 225b; summary of advantages to the crown from the planting of Jamaica, 1670?, Cal. S.P. Col., 1669–1674, no. 375.

Sir Thomas Modyford's cell in the Tower if he attacked the Spaniards without the king's express command.[80]

That command came six months later. In July 1672, confronted by the hostility of all of England's imperial rivals, the council for foreign plantations approved Sir Thomas Lynch's plans to attack the enemies of Jamaica: the imperialist French, the monopolistic Spaniards, and the commercial Dutch. The Jamaica commander was officially authorized to use the royal navy to protect the logwood trade (the felling of dyewood in nominally Spanish territory), the occupation to which Lynch had converted the poorer privateers. The English exchequer would pay Lynch's bills for supplying from Jamaica the royal warships necessary to shield island commerce with England from the French. And the crown promised to rotate relief ships yearly for Vice Admiral Lynch's squadron. He was ordered to use his strengthened fleet and reorganized militia to attack Dutch Curaçao.

These welcome orders arrived aboard a special dispatch vessel sent to warn Jamaica's commander-in-chief that the Dutch and Spanish intended a joint attack on the English island. Whitehall testified to its belief in the warning by hastening out two frigates to reinforce Lynch's squadron. The king's councillors also assured Sir Thomas that they understood his alarm at the growth of French power in the West Indies. The staff of the colonial office added their recognition that the colonies had become constituents of the European balance of power. Admiralty, privy council, and secretariat all agreed with Dr. Benjamin Worsley's observation to Lynch "that they should ere long find it as great an affair of state to balance power in the West Indies, as it is now amongst Princes in Christendom."[81]

From the moment that the king's ketch *Eaglet* arrived early in March 1673, Sir Thomas strove to meet the threat of imminent invasion. He sent fast scout ships to windward, embargoed all other shipping, and converted three small vessels into fireships, the guided missiles of their day. On land, the colonial commander called up enough troops to insure an ample garrison for Port Royal around the clock. He posted cavalry pickets as lookouts and dispatch riders, and he assigned defensive positions to the inland

80. Minutes of a council of war, Nov. 9, 1671, Lynch to Arlington, Dec. 17, 1671, *ibid.*, 650, 697.

81. Council for foreign plantations to the king, July 2, 1672, minutes of the council of Jamaica, July 2, 1672, Lynch to the council for foreign plantations, July 5, to Capt. John Wentworth, Sept. 8, to [Slingsby], Nov. 5, 1672, Worsley to Lynch, Nov. 2, 30, 1672, council for foreign plantations to Lynch, Nov. 2, 1672, *ibid.*, nos. 879, 881, 885, 921, 954, 952, 975, 952 (I).

militia regiments. After convening his council of war, Sir Thomas proclaimed martial law and commandeered slaves by the hundred to work on coastal defenses.[82]

The cost of these defensive measures forced the beleaguered lieutenant governor to call the assembly into session. The assemblymen refused Lynch's request for new moneys, complaining that he had exceeded his powers as commander-in-chief by conscripting their slaves to work on the forts. They implied that if "the general" chose to rule by martial law, he could not expect legislative assistance. Lynch thought their arguments so "insolent" that he dissolved the assembly and ordered the officer-assemblymen back to their military posts. The Jamaicans' obstructive, "countrified," and provincial refusal to tax themselves in their own defense and in the face of invasion ended Sir Thomas Lynch's sympathy for Jamaica's "shadow of a Parliament." He feared that the Anglo-American union of the anti-monarchical party would infect all the assemblies "with malignant spirits, which are not to be conjured down by reason." Lynch now thought that only "an absolute power" unlimited by any need to consult legislature or law could discipline assembly resistance to government, for that was incited from England by the arguments of the parliamentary opposition to the crown. Anti-prerogative arguments, Lynch noted, were being systematically spread among Jamaicans by their factors, the London merchant allies of Shaftesbury.[83]

Yet, despite the assembly's obstructionism, Sir Thomas remained convinced that periodic assemblies were necessary to the colonial constitution. At least in peacetime, he observed, Englishmen would only be ruled by law, and in the colonies that law must be "rather formed to the particular usage of these parts, than assimilated to the laws of England." Insolent, ungrateful, they undoubtedly were, but assemblymen were essential from time to time to give local form to English law. The English authorities, Lynch insisted, must limit their review of these local laws to the question of whether or not "these laws preserve his Majesty's prerogative and sufficiently improve his revenue, but of the rest they are hardly competent judges." Even in a military emergency, then, Lynch defended the necessity and integrity of local legislation by governor, council, and representatives; he opposed the meddlesome amendments of English merchants; and he scorned

82. Minutes of the council of Jamaica, Mar. 11, 21, 1673, Lynch to the council for foreign plantations, Apr. 4, 1673, *ibid.*, nos. 1047, 1055, 1062.

83. Minutes of the council of Jamaica, May 9–12, 1673, Lynch to Worsley, May 15, July 8, 1673, *ibid.*, nos. 1089, 1090, 1115.

the impossible strictures imposed by bureaucratic ignorance. Sir Thomas Lynch thus struck a chord echoed for a century to come by the governors-general of England's American provinces.[84]

At the height of the invasion scare, Sir Thomas's authority was undermined by renewed rumors that noble courtiers were seeking appointment as Jamaica's governor-general. Lynch venomously wished them already in Jamaica. An aristocrat could not feed himself on his salary, Lynch said, and a fop would carry into ruin even those colonists—the privateering faction—who wanted a weak and greedy viceroy. "Young colonies are made or ruined by their Governors." Lynch admitted that he was not courtier enough to flatter some at court, or sufficiently cultivated to impress others, for he had "been always brought up in the noise and tumults of war." The old soldier was just the commander the colony required at this juncture, however. His tenure would last out the war, for hungry nobles waited to succeed Sir Thomas Lynch until the wearying war was succeeded by a profitable peace.[85]

When the invasion scare ended in January 1674, Lynch ended martial law, and he had to face the assembly again because the council for foreign plantations, after months of nit-picking consideration, had failed to revise, accept, or return the Jamaican laws he had passed two years before. Since the council had not acted within the two-year term imposed on unconfirmed laws, Lynch now found himself in peacetime without statutes to administer, even without a salary. Forced to recall the assembly to renew the laws, Lynch did his utmost to insure its obedience to him as commander-in-chief of the colony. Ignoring the Shaftesbury council's instructions to the contrary, Lynch ordered every officer in Jamaica, civil and military, to take the oaths of allegiance and supremacy to the king—and to himself as the king's representative —or be summarily dismissed. "The General" thus struck from public life the "factious people" who had obstructed his will in the previous summer's assembly.[86]

Most of the wealthy officers who had constituted Lynch's first assembly were once more returned, and one of the Port Royal merchants was replaced by William Beeston, whom Lynch had promoted to lieutenant colonel of the city regiment. The assem-

84. Lynch to Worsley, Aug. 12, 1673, ibid., no. 1130.
85. Lynch to Worsley, Apr. 6, 1673, ibid., no. 1066, and C.O. 1/30, no. 9.
86. Minutes of the council of Jamaica, Jan. 15, Feb. 18, 1674, Cal. S.P. Col., 1669–1674, nos. 1206, 1223.

blymen were duly respectful of the lieutenant governor. They quickly passed the revenue act (which taxed merchants' imports, not planters' land). They moved the supreme court from Port Royal, the privateering capital, to Sir Thomas's planter capital at St. Jago. They acted to preserve the cattle ranches and small planters whom Lynch valued, and they provided for additional fortifications.

Notwithstanding their obedience to the executive, the legislators also imparted new definition and dignity to the assembly itself. For the first time, Jamaican legislators adopted a committee system to draft legislation. They kept themselves to their work by fining absentees. They established a more stable, less executive-dominated legislative future when they wrote a statute that defined electoral districts. More efficient, more conscientious, and more secure than their predecessors, the assemblymen of 1674 systematically reviewed previous local legislation. Again, they claimed whatever elements they wanted out of English law. They rearranged the composition and jurisdiction of the Jamaica courts and held that these courts could administer both the English common law and colonial codes. Jamaica's legislators reflected the particular concerns of frontier planters by the special attention they devoted to laws that regulated labor, livestock, land, transportation, and credit. Passed by the council and by the lieutenant governor, the code of 1674 quickly became a vehicle of provincial identity as well as legal utility for Jamaica's planter class. After seven years and many vicissitudes, Sir Thomas Lynch would at last secure the crown's confirmation of a corpus of colonial law—a constitution based on this assembly's output.[87]

The Vagaries of Lord Vaughan

In the eventful interim, Lynch's influence was applied in England, not in Jamaica. With the news of peace on June 6, 1674, came word that Lynch's commission as lieutenant governor had been superseded by the appointment of a governor-general, John, Lord Vaughan. Vaughan's visit to Jamaica both fulfilled Sir Thomas's warning that "assemblies are apt to be refractory," and disappointed his expectation that they would now be "restrained by an absolute power such as (he supposes) the King will confer

87. Jamaica laws, Feb. 1674, minutes of the council of Jamaica, Mar. 14, 1674, *ibid.*, nos. 1241, 1242.

on the nobleman he sends Governor, that his authority and interest be established betimes." Lynch had expected the earl of Carlisle to come out empowered as a viceroy. Instead, Lord Vaughan came out bound by Shaftesburean restrictions on his executive authority. Vaughan did not object, for he was, at least ostensibly, a parliamentarian. Certainly, he was no friend either to imperial sovereignty or to Stuart sovereigns. In any case, Lord Vaughan's political principles were at the service of his monetary greed. His lordship actually admitted as much to the king and council: "To me its not quam dure but quam bene" that mattered. Because he picked their pockets, Vaughan alienated the Jamaicans, in spite of his encouragement of their provincial autonomy. The harm thus done to executive authority was doubled when Vaughan's support for "country" principles in Jamaica stimulated assembly assertiveness. This legislative aggression provoked the prerogative coup that Lynch had predicted four years previously—the crown's orders to the earl of Carlisle to impose Poynings's Law on dissident Jamaica.[88]

In using an interval of international peace to weaken monarchy and strengthen oligarchy, Vaughan was true to the purposes of his patrons, Shaftesbury and the council for foreign plantations. Indeed, the destruction of executive authority was the object of the alterations made in the Jamaica constitution by the Shaftesbury council when they wrote Vaughan's orders as governor-general. The orders to the governor-general were the foundation of every royal colony's constitution: "The source of the Government is the Captain General's Commission and Instructions by which he is fully enabled and directed how to Govern." As Locke explained, his employers (Shaftesbury and the council) intended to strengthen the aristocratic element in Jamaica's constitution against the monarchical one, that is, "to prevent the great inconvenience of the Council being too much at the Governor's devotion," and to make the councillors able to "restrain or amend" the viceroy's actions. To further enhance the authority of provincial leaders, the Shaftes-

88. Beeston, "Journal," Add. MSS 12430, 34; Lynch to Worsley, July 8, 1673, *Cal. S.P. Col., 1669–1674*, no. 1115; Lynch to Blathwayt, May 10, 1683, Blathwayt Papers, XXIV, 1, Williamsburg; chapter 2 above. The Shaftesbury council's nomination in England of the Jamaican governor-general's council is a suggestive instance of the limits intended for the executive. See the draft commission to the earl of Carlisle, by Shaftesbury, Gorges, Hickman, Wynch, Slingsby, and Waller, Mar. 23, 1674, C.O. 138/1, 171–177. See more particularly those instructions drafted by the Shaftesbury council that exalted the power of the council and decreased that of the governor-general (C.O. 138/1, 177–185). They are endorsed "Mr. Locke delivered the foregoing Draughts . . . sealed up to Mr. Bridgeman for the Earl of Arlington 27 March 1674" (C.O. 138/1, 187).

bury council not only authorized Lord Vaughan to summon a legislative assembly, they practically compelled him to call it into session by their refusal to consider or confirm the permanent revenue act passed by Sir Thomas Lynch's legislature. Thus they left Vaughan dependent on a new assembly act for his salary. By their failure to review Lynch's acts, the Shaftesbury council also forced Vaughan to go to the assembly for laws to regulate labor, administer justice, and, as Vaughan thought, to defend the colony. His lordship preferred military authority granted to the executive by the legislature's militia act to that conferred on him by his royal commission as captain general. Vaughan even admitted, after some argument, the assembly's authority to define his military and judicial jurisdiction as the duke of York's vice admiral.[89]

The debility of Captain General Vaughan's command was forecast when the Jamaica convoy in which he sailed was scattered and its military storeship, the *Jamaica Merchant*, was wrecked. Twenty bronze cannon destined for the Port Royal citadel were lost in the wreck, and the great quantity of ammunition and small arms sent by the crown for the protection of the colony was severely damaged. Vaughan himself landed unscathed from the frigate *Foresight* on the evening of March 13, 1675. Four days later

89. The country party's alteration of Jamaica's constitution dated from the earl of Carlisle's nomination to the government, Jan. 23, 1674, C.O. 1/31, 30. His commission and instructions were drafted in Mar. (*ibid.*, 77–78, 84–86, C.O. 138/1, 177–185), and adapted for Vaughan by Apr. 3, 1674 (C.O. 138/1, 1–11, 12–26). On the constitutional centrality of these orders, see C.O. 138/2, 46. Locke's letter to Arlington, Jan. 7, 1673, is in C.O. 1/31, 2, where the full paragraph reads: "2. It would prevent the great inconveniences, that would follow upon the Council's being too much at the Governors devotion which they are like to be, when depending upon his pleasure, whereby making up one Obedient Vote they serve only to confirm and justify any Errors and miscarriages he may fall into; but are not likely to restrain or amend them which is their proper business." Contemporary observers of the island constitution stressed that Vaughan's "Commission named his Councellors directed his calling Assemblys . . . who were to be deemed Representatives of the People to make Laws" (Add. MSS 12428, 25b–26). See also a courtier's comment that the council's prestige and power to "Vex and disturb the Governour" depended upon their "immediate Nomination from his Majesty" (Add. MSS 12429, 80b). Williamson afterward speculated that these orders were the Shaftesbury council's deliberate sabotage of the prerogative (notes by Williamson, Oct. 30, 1677, *Cal. S.P. Dom., 1677–1678*, 433). On this issue, see chapter 2 above; on the limitations, see especially, C.O. 138/1, 188, and C.O. 138/3, 3, summarized in *Cal. S.P. Col., 1669–1674*, nos. 1197, 1251, 1252, 1386, 1392, 1398, 1423. The military powers are commented on by Sir Jonathan Atkins, Dec. 1673, *ibid.*, 1184. Vaughan's instructions retained strictures provoked by Modyford's conduct: clause 46 forbade retaliation against the Spaniards; clause 48 limited the governor-general's power to declare war. The motivation was explained by Coventry to Vaughan, Dec. 31, 1674, Feb. 3, 1675, Add. MSS 25120, 45, 65–66. The secretary said that reprisals must be a last resort, "all Wars in those parts being extremely prejudicial to the settling of that Plantation." In any case, "the Circumstances of time is to be considered as well as the Justice of the cause" before war was declared in the Indies.

he accepted his council's advice to call an assembly. By consenting to meet the legislature before he could identify a court party and redistribute island offices to them, Vaughan insured that the assembly would be little beholden to him. Influence would lie with the "privateer faction" of the new lieutenant general and lieutenant governor, Sir Henry Morgan, and with the "planter party," the old army-new merchant faction led by the displaced commander-in-chief, Sir Thomas Lynch. Still holding the office of provost marshal, Lynch controlled the election returns.[90]

Led by such veteran officials as Lynch and Morgan, the island's established factions dominated the assembly that met on April 26. For the first time, however, neither of these factions was commanded by the governor. Rather, Vaughan's appointments only strengthened the two extant groups. For example, Vaughan named former governor-general Sir Thomas Modyford (now released from the Tower and transformed by imprisonment from an absolutist executive into a self-styled spokesman of the rights of Englishmen) as the island's chief justice. Sir Thomas's son Charles had been commissioned while in England to the politically potent surveyor generalship. The "faction of the Modyfords" was back in business. But they were more concerned to revenge themselves on Sir Thomas Lynch, Modyford's captor and successor, and to attack Lynch's merchant and planter partisans than to support the new governor. Vaughan further strengthened the privateering faction by commissioning Sir Henry Morgan as governor of Port Royal and chief judge of the admiralty court. The latter appointment, Morgan himself admitted, had little to do with law. "The office of Judge Admiral was not given me for my understanding of the business better than others," the buccaneer wrote, for "I left the schools too young to be a great proficient in either that or other laws, and have been much more used to the pike than the book." A pike pushed by Morgan could do more than any book to compel privateers to pay off the new administration. Without keeping a single weapon in his own hands, however, Vaughan could not control his subalterns.[91]

90. *Cal. S.P. Col., 1675–1676*, nos. 467, 471, 484; Add. MSS 12430, 34. On the powers of the provost marshal and other royal patentees, see C.O. 138/2, 20–21, 67. See also C.O. 138/3, 26, where the governor was ordered to permit patentees the free enjoyment of their offices. For the case of the receiver general and the other patentees, see *ibid.*, 109–119, and n. 91 below. The correspondence is in *Cal. S.P. Col., 1669–1674*, no. 1394; *ibid., 1675–1676*, nos. 484, 514; Coventry to Vaughan, July 28, 1675, July 31, 1676, Add. MSS 25120, 47–49, 84. See also Whitson, *Constitutional Development of Jamaica*, 73–74.

91. The commission to Charles Modyford, by the king, witnessed by Vaughan, is in C.O. 138/2, 48–49. This and other appointments are noted in *Cal. S.P. Col., 1675–1676*,

The conclave of island interests that assembled at St. Jago in late April and early May 1675 showed its freedom from the new governor-general's influence by choosing its own speaker without any nomination from Lord Vaughan. They reelected Samuel Long, Sir Thomas Lynch's nominee in 1672 and his ally since their shared staff service under General D'Oyley. In his own right, Long spoke for the republican element among the conquerors. Like D'Oyley and Lynch, Long boasted both legal training and military service in the cause of parliament. This combination produced colonial politicians who married force with law in defiance of traditional thought, which stereotyped such a union as contradictory or impossible. They found the military camp as compatible with their legalistic and legislative ideas as the court of law. The cliché "inter armes leges silent" had not prevented Colonel Lynch from appointing Captain Long as Jamaica's chief justice. Now, as speaker of the assembly in 1675, Long "asked or desired nothing but his rights and privileges as an Englishman and [declared] that he ought to have [them] and would not be contented with less." The historian Edward Long, who shared his ancestor's opinions, boldly explained the significance of Speaker Long's resistance to imperial authority: "To these jarring principles of the royalist and the republican we are to attribute a large share of these intestine feuds and continual duels for which [Jamaica] was so remarkably distinguished many years after it fell into English hands."[92]

Lord Vaughan was as unwilling as he was unqualified to duel with such Jamaica republicans as Speaker Long. What the speaker demanded, the governor-general fostered: legislative "free speech, free access and freedom from arrest." The speaker's first ruling asserted the assembly's authority over its members' qualifications, discipline, and rules of debate. Vaughan did not just accept the displacement of Jamaica's royal executive from assembly influence, he actually instructed Speaker Long in legislative procedures,

---

nos. 496, 514, 515, 800. For Morgan's admission, see *ibid.*, *1677–1680*, no. 1304 (commented on *ibid.*, p. li). Contemporary comments are by Locke, *ibid.*, *1669–1674*, no. 1197; [Nevill], Add. MSS 12429, 81; and Beeston, Add. MSS 12430, 34. Morgan's brother-in-law, Robert Byndloss, and William Beeston were the other admiralty judges.

92. The composition and complexion of the assembly are outlined in *Cal. S.P. Col.*, *1675–1676*, nos. 536–538, 554. At least 50% of Lynch's last assembly were reelected, including all of the officers of the old army (*ibid.*, *1669–1674*, nos. 747, 761, 1089, 1223). Vaughan was not utterly without representation in the assembly, having procured the election of his personal physician, Dr. Thomas Trapham (Cundall, *Governors of Jamaica*, 78). On Samuel Long, see especially Whitson, *Constitutional Development of Jamaica*, 44, 45, 49–50. Also, *Cal. S.P. Col.*, *1669–1674*, no. 1344; *ibid.*, *1677–1680*, nos. 1511, 1522; Firth, ed., *Narrative of Venables*, 66, 97; Taylor, *Western Design*, 223–224; E. Long, *Jamaica*, I, 299. Samuel Long was also Vaughan's assistant in chancery (C.O. 138/2, 68).

first in the parliamentary forms of reading bills. Then the speaker complained that the governor-general's care to sign acts in private would shield him from assembly pressure. Vaughan replied that if the legislators wished to coerce "the general," they had only to present him the bills that cropped the prerogative before they offered those measures that supported the government. Speaker Long thereupon withheld the revenue bill until the governor signed all the others offered him, including a declaration that the laws of England were in force in Jamaica, a declaration designed to destroy the royal right to determine what was law in the crown colony. Moreover, far from strengthening the royal executive, the revenue act appropriated all moneys it raised to colonial use. Speaker Long erased from the measure the very name of the king. As Vaughan told an English member of parliament, he considered the assembly "the figure of your Parliament." He had done his best to make it so, at high cost to the royal prerogative.[93]

The Jamaica assembly's use of Shaftesbury's anti-prerogative program combined with Shaftesburean assaults on executive authority in England to incite a court counterattack. A committee of prerogative-minded privy councillors displaced the Shaftesbury council for foreign plantations just one week after Vaughan sailed out to make Jamaica into a "country" polity. When the lords of the privy council plantations committee learned that the assembly claimed the laws of England for the colony, they thought it "a thing that may be of very evil consequence for the security of the place. For the laws of England favour not any guards or standing forces." Besides the danger to the military essence of garrison government in an enforcement of English law, the crown councillors also resented the colonists' threat to their own executive authority, for "the statutes here have taken away the power and authority of the Council Board." The island's declaratory act also associated representation with taxation, and it asserted islanders' rights to jury trial and to writs of habeas corpus. "Considering the remoteness of that frontier place," to concede such claims "might leave all in confusion if everything that is law in England should at the demand of every subject there be strictly put in execution."[94]

The privy councillors also observed that it was "instructions"

93. Minutes and acts of the assembly of Jamaica, Apr. 26–May 15, Apr. 26, 1675, minutes of the council, May 3–8, 11–15, 1675, *Cal. S.P. Col., 1675–1676*, nos. 537, 538, 548, 554. See especially the assembly journal for May 13–15, *ibid.*, 217–218. See also Vaughan to Col. George Legge (governor of Portsmouth), May 23, 1675, HMC, *Dartmouth*, I, 25; C.O. 139/1, 43–53, 140/3, 613–639; Add. MSS 12428, 26b; Long, *Jamaica*, I, 17.

94. The lords of the committee to Vaughan, Aug. 11, 1675, C.O. 138/3, 28.

by the English opponents of royal authority that had led the Jamaicans to try to write into their constitution the progress of the English parliament in the past generation and the hopes of the country party for the political future. "The Government there," the privy councillors complained, carried on "according to [Shaftesbury's] Instructions from hence hath a great if not too much Conformity with the practice of this Kingdom." Opposition politics as well as English law must be purged from the overseas provinces, the king's councillors concluded. In their place, a constitution should be imposed that would subject the province to Charles II's "imperial crown."[95]

Since it was axiomatic that "force governs law," the privy council paid particular attention to the law allocating force among government agencies as it considered a less liberal constitution for Jamaica. The privy council made it clear that the crown did not object to assembly militia acts per se. While they must not claim to confer on the crown the military authority it possessed inherently as well as by act of parliament, colonial acts could help to reinforce the crown's control of colonial troops. Nowhere was this control more crucial than in the case of Jamaica's red-coated regiments, for nowhere else in England's empire was a provincial militia so powerful, militarily and politically, or a province itself in greater danger. Commanded by a royally commissioned general staff, led by colonels hardened in civil war and colonial conquest, inspired by Cromwellian tradition, and disciplined by weekly drills and by months of martial law, the Jamaican units were "not inferior to regular troops." Indeed, as they had proved against the Spaniards and the Dutch, and would prove against the French, these militant colonists could beat European regulars in open combat.[96]

Jamaican soldiers took pride in being "more subject to Martial Laws" than were ordinary militia. They pointed to the garrison government of their chief seaport as an example of the authority to their rulers and the security gained for themselves as a result of their "martial spirit." Uniformed in their traditional red coats with blue facings, the ten companies of the Port Royal Regiment took turns standing guard in the city citadel, Fort Charles. There they

95. *Ibid.*, and see additional privy council reactions, *ibid.*, 88 and C.O. 138/2, 129. See also *Cal. S.P. Col., 1669–1674*, nos. 1410, 1412, and *ibid., 1675–1676*, no. 1002, for hints of the changing climate of Anglo-Jamaican politics.

96. The usefulness of militia acts to the prerogative is noted by Spurdle, *Early West Indian Government*, 58, and Long, *Jamaica*, I, 123. On the Jamaican soldier-settlers' repulse of Spaniards, see chapter 4 above, on their successful resistance to French invasion, see Beeston to Blathwayt, Aug. 7, 1694, Mar. 15, 1695, Blathwayt Papers XXI, 3, Williamsburg.

were commanded by the fort's full-time governor, the cavalier colonel Theodore Cary, who was assisted by a staff of artillerymen and storekeepers. At daybreak and dusk, the Port Royal companies, like their English garrison counterparts, changed the guard on the parade. The company on guard, as in garrisoned towns at home, were the town police, serving "instead of Constables and Watches to keep the Streets quiet at night." They swept the sodden seamen and their drunken doxies into "the Pen" for morning actions by the Port Royal parish court, five of whose seven justices were also captains of the Port Royal Regiment. Each captain drilled his company on the Port Royal Parade once a week, commanded it on guard, executed the orders of the field officers at the regiment's monthly drill day, and sat as a judge of the regimental court-martial. The Jamaica assembly asserted that "no Militia in your Majesty's Islands undergo the like Military duty as Your Majesty's Subjects in Jamaica as is evident to all men that ever set foot in Port Royal which cannot be distinguished from a Garrison either in Peace or War but by their not being paid for their Service."[97]

Companies of the inland infantry regiments of the Jamaica militia served also as the slave patrol. This duty was salaried by the assembly, alarmed at the major rising of the blacks of St. Mary Parish in 1676. The growth of slave numbers and the decline in white population worsened the odds in the militia's continual combat against runaways and rebels. Therefore, "besides the Command that the title implies," Jamaica's major general acted as "Commissary General of the Musters, which is a place absolutely necessary . . . for the strict observing that the proportions of Whites be kept up according to the Law in which consists a great part of the security of our Lives. . . . the Number of men in Arms there being all Whites above Sixteen Years of Age that are one Month resident." The immigration, enlistment, and exercise of white fighting men all were the major general's responsibilities. As the next governor-general of Jamaica, the earl of Carlisle remarked, with only 4,526 white militiamen to hold down some 50,000 blacks, it was just as well that the young planters were "very hardy and much delighted in arms." That delight was depicted by the elaborate trophies of arms that both James Moxon,

---

97. [Nevill] to [Carlisle], n.d., Add. MSS 12429, 82b; *Cal. S.P. Col., 1677–1680*, nos. 1370(II, III), 1371, 1651; *ibid., 1681–1685*, no. 13; C.O. 138/2, 113–116. The fiscal, commercial, and military dominion of the fortified and garrisoned port city over the colony appears in the statistics of population and taxation compiled by Dunn, *Sugar and Slaves*, 179–187. The assembly's address is in Add. MSS 12429, 95n.

in 1677, and Edward Slaney, in 1678, placed on their maps of this militant province as its characteristic symbols.[98]

The militia cavalry also saw regular service. The regiment of horse was commanded in chief by the governor-general whom it protected: "A Squadron of the Governor's own Troops . . . does Mount every Sunday to wait on the Governor's Coach to Church." The cavalry regiment's six troops, each made up of forty-five to eighty mounted men, did more than ceremonial work. For example, a slaver who landed a cargo of blacks in violation of the Royal African Company's monopoly complained that he "was pursued in a most barbarous and Hostile manner by several of the Governor's own Troopers and at the Ferry . . . over the River with several Red Coat Soldiers arm'd to seize the said Negroes."[99]

The memory of a red-coated past, as well as present pride in the uniformed forces, appeared in an act of Governor-General Vaughan's first legislature. The act again proclaimed May 10 as Conquest Day, a celebration of the Cromwellian capture of the colony in 1655. The act was subsequently disallowed by the king-in-council "as too much reflecting on the circumstances of those times and of that conquest which rather seems to have been made in opposition to his Majesty." A Cromwellian military holiday insulted Stuart monarchy, but a more direct military threat to the royal prerogative was posed by the new militia bill. Vaughan insisted that the bill make clear that the king's representative "may in all things and upon all occasions and emergencies act as Captain-General and Governor-in-Chief, according to all the powers and commands given unto him by his Majesty's commission." Speaker

98. The battle with the blacks is recorded in C.O. 138/3, 253; Cundall, *Governors of Jamaica*, 80–81; *Cal. S.P. Col., 1675–1676*, nos. 820, 822; *ibid., 1677–1680*, xlv, nos. 402, 477; and Add. MSS 12429, 76, 77. On the major general's command of the militia and enforcement of the militia act, see C.O. 138/2, 7, 8–11, and Add. MSS 12429, 84. The duty was similar to that of Virginia's Maj. Gen. Smith (*Cal. S.P. Col., 1677–1680*, no. 1600), and was compared with that of English provincial muster masters, such as Gen. Carlisle's Capt. Tongue of Cumberland and Virginia service. Gov.-Gen. Carlisle wrote that white males were already 205 short of the legal and prudential requirement that they number 1/10 of the black population. His arming of servants only filled the ranks emptied by those who left the colony when their time expired. Thus Carlisle, like every other officer-governor, stressed the military and social necessity of encouraging family settlement by whites, and so of promoting small farms and discouraging large plantations. This social attitude was part and parcel of the pro-military and anti-planter policy that the Jamaica elite pleaded against Carlisle. See his letter to Coventry, Sept. 15, 1679, C.O. 138/3, 333–335, calendared in *Cal. S.P. Col., 1677–1680*, no. 118, and see no. 1370. The maps cited are reproduced in Black, ed., *Blathwayt Atlas*, nos. 34, 36.

99. The cavalry were recompensed for the high cost of their equipment by legislative exemption from other public service and by pay for patrolling, see Add. MSS 12429, 95b, 119b.

Long objected that such a proviso made the king's commission the supreme law of the colony. By enacting it, the colony's own assembly would consent to the royal effort to monopolize power in the provinces through expansion of the governor-general's military authority. Vaughan truthfully assured the assembly that such was not *his* intention, and they finally accepted a clause admitting that "nothing in this [act] contained abridge the Governor's power, but he to act according to his Commission and His Majesty's Instructions."[100]

Citing this militia act (and so recalling it to the crown's consideration), Governor-General Vaughan revoked Sir Henry Morgan's commissions as lieutenant general, governor of Port Royal, and colonel of the politically powerful Port Royal Regiment. Morgan had not given Vaughan enough privateer plunder. Vaughan's action against Morgan outraged King Charles, when Morgan's appeal reached him. Not only did the king have a personal liking for the old buccaneer, but his royal prerogatives as imperial commander-in-chief were also infringed upon by Vaughan's action. The governor-general was told that "his Majesty will not endure that a Lieutenant General by his Commission shall be left out of all power Military and Civil and others put in who were never approved by him." Sir Henry was informed of the king's sentiments and received the royal orders for his restoration to command. These orders also reminded the lieutenant governor that he was Captain General Vaughan's subordinate. Morgan was ordered to make any further complaints to his immediate superior, the governor-general. Only if they were ignored might the lieutenant general appeal up the chain of command to the sovereign. Like the model officers of Elton's *Art Military*, Morgan was further warned to keep to the letter of his commission in the presence of his superior, the garrison governor: to those who held them, royal commissions were as much instruments of hierarchical and imperial discipline as enhancements of individual and provincial power. After he obeyed the king's command to restore Morgan as lieutenant general, the governor-general of Jamaica therefore tried to justify his earlier actions: he exposed Morgan's dealings with the privateers. The tactic backfired. The king was furious that his orders against privateering had been disobeyed, but he censured both his Jamaica generals. "The king intendeth to make a Planta-

100. The act is in C.O. 138/2, 137, and its disallowance is in C.O. 138/3, 145. See also *Cal. S.P. Col., 1675–1676*, nos. 530, 747, 926; Whitson, *Constitutional Development of Jamaica*, 58, 59 (but see p. 64); C.O. 138/2, 139.

tion of Jamaica and not a Christian Algiers," Vaughan was sternly reminded, and his recall became a certainty.[101]

Lord Vaughan was a lame duck executive when in April 1677 he summoned an assertive assembly to reenact the expiring laws of 1675. There followed the "disorders which begott a change in the government." That is, this session's political results confirmed the crown's military decision to remove Vaughan from his command, and the assembly's excesses excused the privy council's prior determination to destroy the assembly—and so squelch parliamentary politics in Jamaica. Like the parliaments and politics of Virginia, Ireland, and England in the same year, the 1677 session of the Jamaica assembly simultaneously illustrated and intensified the crisis of the seventeenth-century imperial constitution.[102]

Jamaica's unconfirmed local laws were about to expire, yet privy council pressure meant that the colony's legislature might not be assembled. The islanders therefore feared that, "for the future, they might be forc'd to live under such [laws] only as the King's Royal Pleasure should appoint them." And it seemed that those laws would also be administered by creatures of the crown, rather than local leaders, for Governor-General Vaughan now dismissed the admiralty judges, including Robert Byndloss, the brains of the privateering faction, and he dismissed Sir Thomas

101. Note Morgan's instructions and Vaughan's weakness in C.O. 138/2, 82; Beeston's remarks, Add. MSS 12430, 34; Vaughan to Legge, May 23, 1675, HMC, *Dartmouth*, I, 25; and Vaughan to Southwell, Jan. 28, 1676, C.O. 138/3, 35–36. Note also Vaughan's disparagement of peace with Spain in the Indies, C.O. 138/3, 35, 122–123, 126, 218. The attack on Morgan is in Vaughan's letter to the lords of the committee, May 3, 1676. See C.O. 138/3, 53, 62–67, 95–104, 140. Morgan's denials are in *Cal. S.P. Col., 1675–1676*, no. 807, and see no. 823. The other documents are calendared *ibid.*, nos. 657, 673, 703, 912, 913, 916, 998, 1006, and see *ibid., 1677–1680*, no. 1370. See also Thornton, *West-India Policy*, 219–220, 222; Coventry to Vaughan, July 30, 1675, June 8, 1676, to Morgan, Aug. 24, 1675, to Vaughan and Morgan, Mar. 29, 1676, Add. MSS 25120, 52, 74–78, 57–58, 69–73.

102. Add. MSS 12429, 81, 83b; Add. MSS 12430, 34b; *Cal. S.P. Col., 1675–1676*, no. 1154; Ralph Palmer to Viscount Fermangh, Jan. 27, 1713, HMC, *Seventh Report*, Pt. I, 508; *Cal. S.P. Col., 1677–1680*, no. 172. See also *ibid., 1675–1676*, nos. 799, 926, 927, 1002, 1094; Whitson, *Constitutional Development of Jamaica*, 59–60; Egerton MS 2395, 523–524. On the "disorders," see Blathwayt to Carlisle, Oct. 20, 1679, Blathwayt Papers, XXII, 2, Williamsburg. Despite this statement and those of modern commentators, it appears that the decision to eliminate the assembly antedated the actions of the Apr.-June session of 1677. The lords acted on Apr. 30, 1677, months before they knew of the assembly acts; see *Cal. S.P. Col., 1677–1680*, nos. 200, 226. These were considered (in relation to Vaughan's code of 1675) in Sept. and Oct. 1677. They did stimulate refinements in the new model: see *ibid.*, nos. 206, 412, 480. More important, the assembly's acts were leading examples of the "late Stubborn Carriage in the Plantations [which] will occasion a Stricter enquiry [into] their Comportments then hath been hither to made" (Add. MSS 25120, 121). Assembly defiance of the imperial prerogative reinforced the royal determination not to let Jamaica follow in "the footsteps of New England" (Southwell to Ormond, Nov. 20, 1677, enclosing the new model in the form of laws intended for Jamaica," HMC, *Ormonde*, N.S., IV, 386).

Modyford from the post of chief justice. The legal insecurity that
followed the ouster of the Jamaican judges and the lapse of local
law was "the main spur to disloyalty," that is, to the all-out attack
on the royal prerogative and the exaltation of its own laws by the
endangered assembly when, in April 1677, Vaughan allowed it to
meet to pass his salary.

The local leaders immediately reenacted the 1675 law that
declared the laws of England in force in Jamaica, or at least such
laws as the legislators chose. They repassed the militia law, but
they excised the clause that preserved the executive's military
authority as the king's captain general in Jamaica. They went on to
declare that the island assembly was a high court capable of reversing the decisions of the prerogative courts. The assembly then
annulled a decision of the governor-general's court of oyer and
terminer, authorized a writ of habeas corpus for a prisoner condemned to death by that court, ordered the provost marshal not to
execute the court's sentence, and referred the case to a court of the
assembly's own creation. This was a legislative attack on the prerogative of justice unparalleled since "the parliament pretended to
sovereignty" a generation earlier. Shocked at last into the realization that he would never receive from the assembly even the salary
for which he had sacrificed so much of the king's authority, Lord
Vaughan protected the royal prerogative of justice by having the
convict hung and by dissolving the assembly in June 1677.[103]

Within twenty hours after Lord Vaughan dissolved the assembly, he learned unofficially that he would be replaced as governor-
general by the earl of Carlisle. Vaughan immediately called his
council back into session and secured its advice and consent for the
election of another assembly to meet in September. In the autumn,
all was harmony. The governor signed almost every act the legislature offered him, including one for a "present" of £1,300 (which
brought his official income for a term of four years to more than
£24,000, as contrasted to Lynch's £6,800 for more than three

103. Add. MSS 12429, 81b–82, 86. The opposition of the factional chiefs and former
governors led Vaughan to conclude that "His Majesty's interest cannot be secured here but
by a Governor whose dependence is only from England, and who has no private interests in
Jamaica" (*Cal. S.P. Col., 1677–1680*, no. 270). On Vaughan's replacement of Modyford by
Long, who was an ally of Lynch, see *ibid., 1675–1676*, no. 1154. On the habeas corpus order
(an act which even the assembly ultimately admitted was "not justifiable in the manner")
and on other legislative aggression, see: Add. MSS 12429, 84, 97–97b, 105b; Add. MSS
12430, 34b; Coventry to Vaughan, Nov. 21, 1677, Add. MSS 25120, 118; Papers of the Earl
of Carlisle Relating to Jamaica, Sloan MS 2724, 211, British Library; *Cal. S.P. Col., 1677–
1680*, no. 365; Cundall, *Governors of Jamaica*, 83–84.

years' service). Bribed by the assembly and resentful of his successor, Vaughan then reacted to the "certain news that the earl of
Carlisle was coming Governor" by vetoing the assembly's revenue measure. He doubly disapproved of a bill that would both
offend the court (to which he must now return) by its appropriation of all revenues to the public use of the island (as defined by the
assembly) and that would also provide a salary for that aggressive
executive, the earl of Carlisle.[104]

In March 1678 Lord Vaughan convened his last council. He
complained of poverty, although "he had redeemed his estate and
amassed wealth by the government of Jamaica." He bewailed his
failing health, although he would live another thirty-six years.
He announced he was leaving Jamaica, although the king had
ordered him to remain at his post until relieved by Jamaica's new
commander-in-chief. On March 14 Vaughan sailed for England,
"leaving the Island, Sir Henry Morgan his Successor and the Lord
Carlisle without any revenue," but faced instead with the most
profound constitutional crisis in the young colony's history. The
privy council's "new model" constitution for Jamaica would confirm the provincial elite's worst fears of imperial absolutism. The
struggle over it would be a decisive event in the formation of
Anglo-American government.[105]

---

104. Add. MSS 12430, 35. Coventry's formal letter of May 31 probably arrived in
mid-Sept., but news of Vaughan's recall was public by Aug., as evidenced by Sec.
Beckford's request to Sec. Williamson for a recommendation to Carlisle, *Cal. S.P. Col.,
1677–1680*, no. 375. On the subsequent session and the preparations for Vaughan's departure and Carlisle's arrival, see *ibid.*, nos. 395, 398, 402, 412, 477, 544, 622.

105. See n. 104 and, on Vaughan's plunder, see HMC, *Seventh Report*, Pt. I, 508. Add.
MSS 12429, 85b, lists annual official payments to Vaughan of £1,200 "in England," £2,000
"from the country's establishment," £1,000 from quitrents, £1,200–1,300 in naturalization fees—a total of salary and fee income of £5,500 per annum. Others estimated Vaughan's
yearly income at double this figure, and the incident of Martin's gold purse suggests why.
Coventry to Vaughan, Nov. 21, 1677, Add. MSS 25120, 118, conveyed the king's refusal
of Vaughan's request for leave.

CHAPTER 6

Absolutism versus Autonomy, 1678–1681

The Epitome of Garrison Government: 1678

On July 19, 1678, a new captain general and governor-in-chief of Jamaica's garrison government landed at Port Royal, under orders to carry out an imperial counterrevolution. The earl of Carlisle was the ideal island executive—a military aristocrat—as envisioned by Jamaica's first governor-general. "A person of Honour" was required "both to give Reputation to the place" and "to head the people." So Governor-General D'Oyley (and other commentators) had written. The new governor-general was an earl of ancient family, but Carlisle was also an officer of vast experience in garrison government. He was paid an English army salary to command Jamaica, and he drew funds from the royal exchequer to strengthen his seat of authority, Jamaica's citadel. Hurried out to Jamaica "upon the expectation of war" with France, Carlisle's naval strength was bolstered by the frigate *Jersey* and by two additional armed vessels. Their cargoes included twenty "great guns" and £3,762 5s. 4d. worth of munitions for the governor-general's provincial fortress and domestic garrisons.[1]

1. "Hurried" is a relative concept. Carlisle's commission and instructions were completed on Feb. 4 (*Cal. S.P. Col., 1677–1680*, no. 596) and approved by the king-in-council on Feb. 15 (*ibid.*, no. 600). Carlisle was expected in Deal as early as Apr. 24 (Richard Watts to Williamson, Apr. 24, 26, *Cal. S.P. Dom., 1678*, 132, 134) but "at last" took his leave of the king on Apr. 27 (*Cal. S.P. Col., 1677–1680*, no. 693). He sailed from Deal on May 8 (*Cal. S.P. Dom., 1678*, 163) but stopped on May 15 in Plymouth to tour the new citadel (*ibid.*, 177). His ship anchored in Port Royal on July 18 (*Cal. S.P. Col., 1677–1680*, no. 770). He noted that "my departure [was] much pressed upon the expectation of war" (C.O. 138/3, 279, P.R.O.). See also Bryan Edwards, *The History, Civil and Commercial, of the British Colonies in the West Indies*, 3 vols. (London, 1801), I, 267, and Thornton, *West-India Policy*, 242 n. 1. On the need for a "person of honour," see "Relation of Col. D'Oyley," Add. MSS 11410, 14. See also Richard Forster to Williamson, July 13, 1666, *Cal. S.P. Dom., 1665–1666*, 530. Carlisle's army pay included £2,500 as captain general, from Sept. 1677 (*ibid., 1677–1678*, 535, also at *Cal. S.P. Col., 1677–1680*, no. 544), and £600 for fortifications (*ibid.*, no. 1569). The policy was not a new one: see Egerton MS 2395, 485–486. It was also extended to the Leeward Islands, New York, and Virginia on the account of the Guards and Garrisons: see *Cal. S.P. Col., 1677–1680*, nos. 1036–1038, and Webb, "Blathwayt: Popish Plot to Glorious Revolution," *WMQ*, 3d Ser., XXV (1968), 6 n. 10. Further military

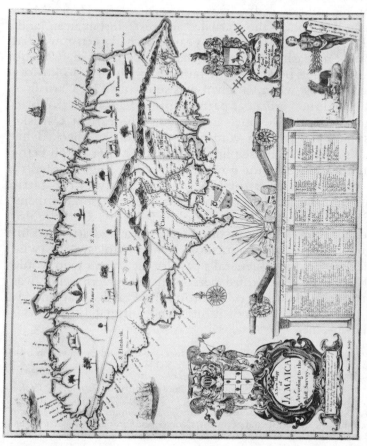

"Jamaica." James Moxon's 1677 revision of Major John Man's map, Number 36 of *The Blathwayt Atlas*, ed. Jeannette D. Black (Providence, R.I., 1970, 1975), reproduced through the courtesy of the John Carter Brown Library. See Stephen Saunders Webb, review of *The Blathwayt Atlas, William and Mary Quarterly*, 3d Ser., XXXV (1978), 159–162.

To elaborate and execute his orders, the governor-general included on his military staff a lieutenant general, Sir Henry Morgan. Morgan had upheld the Carlisle "interest" in Jamaican land, loot, and lucrative office for many years. He had been rewarded with field rank in Carlisle's English infantry regiment in 1673 and was named Carlisle's lieutenant for Jamaica in January 1674. Morgan retained the post when Vaughan was substituted for Carlisle in April, and he led the "privateer party" during Vaughan's troubled term. When Morgan's colonel and patron, the earl of Carlisle, finally assumed the Jamaica command in 1678, he checked his subordinate's infamous indiscipline by making Major Ralph Fetherstone (another officer of the governor-general's English infantry regiment) captain lieutenant of Morgan's company in the garrison. Carlisle left the administration of his own garrison company to an officer of the First Guards, John Tolderny. Carlisle also commissioned Tolderny as a justice of the peace and arranged his marriage to the sister of a councillor, Hender Molesworth (who commanded the governor-general's cavalry escort and who would command Jamaica). The "third person in the government" was the new major general, the ubiquitous Sir Francis Watson. He became a councillor, colonel of militia, and, ultimately, Jamaica's commander-in-chief.[2]

---

payments were made in the form of exchequer allowances for arms and for munitions from the office of the ordnance (C.O. 138/3, 165–168, 175–176; *Cal. S.P. Col.*, *1677–1680*, nos. 479, 496, 643).

2. The staff and company commissions for Jamaica are listed in Dalton, ed., *English Army Lists*, I, 224. See also *ibid.*, 135, 195, and S.P. 44/29, 235, 237, P.R.O., where these commissions appear together with: Carlisle's commissions as commander and governor of the city, town, and castle of Carlisle and of the forts, forces, and fortifications thereunto belonging, and as captain of a garrison company (S.P. 44/29, 239, 240); the (second) duke of Albemarle's commission as colonel of the queen's regiment of cavalry, which he resigned prior to becoming governor-general of Jamaica (*ibid.*, 253); Littleton's commission to execute martial law at Bruges (*ibid.*, 273); and Culpeper's commission as governor-general of Virginia (*ibid.*, 294–295), where he succeeded Herbert Jeffreys, who was named captain of the king's company of the 1st Foot Guards (*ibid.*, 296). All of these commissions were issued within weeks of one another. All granted further powers to governors-general of American colonies. Only one was issued in response to foreign war. The pervasiveness of peacetime garrison government is here powerfully presented. The major general of Jamaica, Sir Francis Watson, had served as Carlisle's subordinate when both were Cromwellian officers (Sloan MS 2724, 243), and he had also served under Carlisle's brother, Sir Philip Howard (afterward named governor-general of Jamaica), in the household cavalry (*Cal. S.P. Dom.*, *1663–1664*, 168). Watson's commission as major general is in *Cal. S.P. Col.*, *1677–1680*, no. 573. Carlisle granted his major generals extensive lands and plural offices in their colonial command. Watson became president of the council and acting governor, ruling under martial law, in Mar. 1689 (Sloan MS 2724, 246, 253). See Watson's precedential services in English garrison governments in chapter 2 above. For Carlisle's further recruitment of his Jamaica military household from his lieutenant generalcy of the northern counties, see William to Daniel Fleming, Feb. 19, 1678, HMC, *Le Fleming*, 143. For the local appointments of the garrison officers, see *Cal. S.P. Col.*, *1677–1680*, no. 1371, and Sloan MS 2724, 246, 253.

Besides his general staff and munitions, Carlisle's naval convoy carried two companies of regular infantry to help him impose on Jamaica the colony's new law code, "brought ready out of England according to the Constitution of Ireland." At the height of his struggle with the Jamaica assembly to establish this "Irish model," Poynings's Law, the governor-general explained that "the Companies were essentially necessary to the present State of the Government." The garrison company's first duty was to guard the governor-general's person and to make visible his authority in the province. To this end, Carlisle's own company was stationed at St. Jago de la Vega, the inland capital and the earl's favorite residence. There they did sentry duty at the town gates and adjacent river crossings, and at the governor-general's house (which was also a major magazine of small arms). Besides escort and sentry duty, this company was also used by the governor-general as a police force in the capital area. Its captain was commissioned by Carlisle as a justice of the peace to ensure that military and civil authority united. Lieutenant General Morgan's company was quartered in Port Royal. There the general governed the city, and his company bolstered the guard of the citadel, served as the marines on board royal naval vessels and on the Jamaican auxiliaries, and also escorted members of the general staff.[3]

The political impact and military efficiency of the garrison varied with political tensions in the province and with threats of foreign invasion. Other variables were the commanders' care for their companies and whether or not the soldiers were paid. Even when there was cash to pay the companies, the standard English subsistence of sixpence per day would buy a redcoat just one quart of beer in Port Royal. Therefore, in peacetime Carlisle and Morgan had to let their lieutenants license many of the men to work for wages. On ceremonial occasions officers filled the ranks of the companies with locals hired for the purpose. These sunshine soldiers were paid with the regulars' salaries. Otherwise, the officers retained their furloughed men's money for themselves. In emergencies Carlisle recalled the redcoats to the ranks and recruited time-expired servants to bring the companies up to full strength.

3. The warrant to the captain general of Jamaica to beat the drums for 200 men is in S.P. 44/29, 230, also *Cal. S.P. Col., 1677–1680*, no. 570. The challenge of unreconstructed Cromwellians and defiant dissenters, familiar to Carlisle from his commands in the north of England, was compounded in Jamaica by the continued transportation of Scots conventiclers to the island (*Cal. S.P. Dom., 1678*, 340). Compare chapter 2 above. Carlisle's statement is in his letter to the lords of the committee, Feb. 23, 1680, C.O. 138/3, 392. The disposition and duty of the companies are detailed in Add. MSS 12429, 119b; Sloan MS 2724, 33a; C.O. 138/4, 42–43; *Cal. S.P. Col., 1681–1685*, nos. 16, 158; and n. 17 below.

The ex-servants, "after their experience of duty," were "daily importunate for their discharge." They occasionally won that discharge by sentence of court-martial—more often by death from physical neglect or even starvation. The wealthy captain general himself complained that the crown's delay in paying him "very much aggravates my private wants," but non-payment of their pittances made "the poor soldiers life uneasy in their quarters and occasions many of their deaths." Without their wages, the men could not pay rent and board to the taverners and householders who quartered them. The economic cost of the garrison added to Jamaicans' political uncertainty: were these troops "designed for their protection against a foreign foe or for their own suppression by the King"?[4]

Thus English force bred provincial fear even as the governor-general came ashore to "the Solemnity of the Artillery from the forts and Ships" and took the salute of the Port Royal Regiment "drawn up to receive him." Carlisle called the councillors together and read them his commission. Unlike Lord Vaughan's commission, Carlisle's named no councillors. Instead it specified that he might suspend any councillor at will and deny suspended councillors the right to run for the assembly, and that he need not inform the councillors of his instructions or consult them about appointments to office. Carlisle closed the first meeting of his council by suspending every one of its members who had voted against the clause in the militia act "saving" the crown's military prerogative. As he acted on his commission from the king, Governor-General Carlisle's troops landed.[5]

Mindful of King Charles's personal warning that war with France was likely, Carlisle met his purged council on the morning after his landing, praised Sir Henry Morgan's new fortifications, and sent out his frigates on patrol to recover the cannon lost when Vaughan came out. He then discussed with his council the legislative and statutory aspects of the new constitution. It eliminated the legislative initiative of the Jamaica assembly, forbade it to amend the king's bills sent out from England, and included for the as-

4. Carlisle to Coventry, Sept. 15, 1679, Feb. 23, 1680, to lords of the committee, Feb. 23, 1680, C.O. 138/3, 337–338, 386–387, 392*ff*; Carlisle to commissioners of the treasury, Aug. 19, 1684, Blathwayt Papers, Huntington Lib.; Sloan MS 2724, 15b–16a, 62a, 104, 108, 109, 148a, 152a; Thornton, *West-India Policy*, 251.

5. Beeston, "Journal," Add. MSS 12430, 36b. Carlisle's commission as captain general and governor-in-chief, Mar. 1, 1678, and his instructions are in C.O. 138/3, 198–210, 216–241. The powers regarding councillors were less than Carlisle had asked. He wanted to be able to nominate as well as to remove councillors, since he saw special need to replace those who had voted against the saving clause of the militia act (*ibid.*, 159, 164).

sembly's acceptance a code of laws headed by a militia act that clarified provincial duties but wholly exempted the crown's military prerogative from local limitation. The "old standers and officers of Cromwell's army" among the councillors instantly objected to this "saving" clause. Led by Samuel Long (now elevated to the council by Lynch's "interest" at court), the veteran councillors again argued that the clause made everything in the king's commission and instructions—instructions to which they were no longer privy—the supreme law of the island. The proposed militia act substituted the crown's military prerogative for civil law and custom as the basis of colonial government.[6]

The councillors and governor-general agreed only that the assembly must be summoned to consider (Carlisle said "accept") this militia bill and the rest of the code of laws that the king-in-council had culled from the statutes of 1675. The representatives' consent remained a part—and their only part—of the "new model" of legislation. The "new model" specified that, henceforward, bills drafted by the governor and council were to be sent to the king-in-council for amendment. Then the bills would be returned to Jamaica for assembly consent or rejection, but not amendment.[7]

The likelihood of obtaining that consent diminished when Carlisle dismissed the councillors without having applied to them and their followers the patronage whip that might have ensured an obedient assembly. Then, just prior to the assembly meeting in September 1678, the news of a general peace in Europe reached Jamaica. For a crucial year, peace drastically reduced the military threat to Jamaica and thus lessened the islanders' willingness to render obedience to the crown in return for its protection. Peace also reduced the governor-general's opportunities to make political use of his military patronage and to apply martial law to control political activity.[8]

Far from forcing the new law code on the assembly, Carlisle presented to the September session an opening speech that argued against the new model of legislation as much as it did for it. The governor-general told the legislators that his authority as well as theirs was severely limited by the new legislative method. He said that he had joined others of the privy council committee on the colonies to oppose this "restraint that both he and we lie under in

6. There are contrasting accounts of this episode by Speaker Beeston, Add. MSS 12430, 36b, and Long, *Jamaica*, I, 198. Carlisle reported the council objections to Coventry, July 18, Aug. 14, 1678, Edwards, *British Colonies*, I, 262–263, and C.O. 138/3, 245.

7. C.O. 138/3, 82–83; Add. MSS 12429, 87; C.O. 1/43, no. 185, fol. 370b.

8. See n. 6 above, n. 19 below, and chapter 5 above.

the new Laws he brought over." Carlisle insisted, and of course the assembly agreed, that the transfer of deliberative power to the king-in-council from the governor, council, and representatives of Jamaica eliminated the local knowledge, adaptability, and responsiveness required in the laws of societies so young, mutable, and distant as the colonies. The laws now sent over from England needed amendment to meet the changed circumstances of the three years since they had been drafted. Moreover, liberty to do some rewording might make such laws as the militia act locally acceptable, but, as Carlisle complained, "I have no power to make any alteration which I might have done both to their satisfaction and the preservation of the King's right." The difficulty of communication between Jamaica and England increased the need for legislative flexibility, Carlisle observed. Even if the crown acted immediately on the draft laws sent to it by the governor and council, it would still be six months before the governor-general could hope to have his proposed laws returned to him for approval by the local assembly. In short, Carlisle found the new model unworkable. And he let the assembly know it. He also assured the Jamaicans "that he had always been accounted a Man of Property and was in nothing more affected than to do good to this place and come with an intent so to do and therefore would not by his Power lead us into inconvenience or our Posterity."9

The governor-general had neither used the absolute authority of his commission nor employed his military might to coerce the colonists to assent to the new model. He promised that, as a matter of principle, he would not do so. But, also as a matter of principle, he insisted that they must obey the royal commands. "Disputing them was next of kin to those in Virginia," Carlisle admonished the assembly. Jamaicans were well informed of the military occupation of that rebellious province and the royal reduction of its defiant assembly's authority. On the other hand, that many Englishmen opposed monarchical might encouraged the Jamaicans to resist the new model of crown-imposed law. "Popular dis-

9. The assembly journals are in C.O. 139/1, 195–206. See also the remarks of Speaker Beeston (in Add. MSS 12430, 36b); Beeston was nominated by Carlisle on Morgan's recommendation (C.O. 138/3, 250). Carlisle's speech to the assembly is quoted from the summary in Add. MSS 12429, 86b–87b. The accuracy of these notes is seen in the identical language used by the earl himself in his letter to Coventry, Aug. 14, 1678, C.O. 138/3, 245. Note also the identical objections repeated in this letter and in those of Oct. 24 to [Coventry] and to the lords of the committee, and to the latter on Nov. 15, 1678, *ibid.*, 245–246, 270–272, 273, 280, calendared in *Cal. S.P. Col., 1677–1680*, nos. 779, 815, 832. For anticipations of Carlisle's difficulties in applying Poynings's Law to Jamaica, see the comments of those who applied it in Ireland (Southwell to Ormond, Nov. 20, 1677, HMC, *Ormonde*, N.S., IV, 386).

courses prevail here as well as in England," the earl of Carlisle observed. Caught between the court's commands and their own country convictions, the assembly announced that "they would consent to wear chains but would not by any act of theirs impose them on their posterity." That is, they would dutifully obey the imperial crown, but they would never endorse the proposed laws. Carlisle replied with a proposition. If the assembly would provide him with the money and men that government required, he would take their case to the crown. The assembly agreed. Thus, in the autumn of 1678, the governor-general sent his major general, Sir Francis Watson, to England to plead before the king and council for the traditional autonomy of colonial governments and against the rising tide of imperial centralization.[10]

Plots and Plans: The Privy Council
Debates the Imperial Polity, 1679

When Watson arrived in London, he found that the Popish Plot had distracted the crown from imperial affairs. Titus Oates's revelations obsessed everyone "from his Majesty to the Constable." Not until February 1679 did the privy councillors demonstrate their imperialist determination to uphold the new model. They extended it to Virginia, recommended a royal veto of the most recent revenue act from Jamaica (because it admitted assembly fiscal authority), and advised the king to reject the amendments that Jamaica's governor-general proposed to the crown's militia bill. "There is nothing . . . which your Majesty can depart from without the greatest prejudice to your Royal Authority," the council insisted, for "the sole Supreme Government, command, and disposition of the Militia is the undoubted Right of Your Majesty within all your Majesty's Dominions." The governor-

10. In addition to the sources cited above on the conduct of the assembly, see especially: "A Breviate of what passed in the Assembly . . . to Mr Blathwayt Esqr this To be shewd no body," Egerton MS 2395, 576; Long, *Jamaica*, I, 202–206; Edwards, *British Colonies*, I, 263–265, 268; *Cal. S.P. Col.*, *1677–1680*, nos. 786, 794, 807, 814, 1648. The king's determination is voiced in Coventry's letter to Atkins, Nov. 21, 1677, Add. MSS 25120, 120. Carlisle's estimate of the "popular" nature of the reaction is in a letter to Coventry, Sept. 10, 1678, C.O. 138/3, 249, calendared in *Cal. S.P. Col.*, *1677–1680*, no. 794. On the bargain, see: *ibid.*, nos. 807, 814, 827, 832–833, 1030, 1096, 1648; Edwards, *British Colonies*, I, 264–265; Add. MSS 12429, 96; Blathwayt to Carlisle, May 31, 1679, Blathwayt Papers, XXII, 1, Williamsburg. The governor was as good as his word, writing to the lords on Oct. 24 and Nov. 15, 1678, C.O. 138/3, 270–272, 273.

general must retain this unfettered military prerogative "as essential to the trust Your Majesty has reposed in him."[11]

Finally, at the end of May 1679, King Charles himself found time to preside at a meeting given over to the Jamaica issue. He heard a debate colored by the interplay of imperial regulation and domestic politics. To defuse the opposition, the king had recently named the earl of Shaftesbury to be lord president of the privy council and of its plantations committee. Naturally, the country leader wanted to restore the dominion of aristocracy and assembly in Jamaica. This champion of parliamentary government by the propertied ruling class was just as alarmed as his Jamaica clients at the clause of the militia bill that provided that "the Governor may upon occasion or Emergencies as Commander in Chief" ignore every legislative limit upon the prerogative. Not only did it make the royal governor-general an absolute executive in the province, but worse, it also implied that the monarch would rule by his military discretion at home. The earl of Shaftesbury likewise agreed with the Jamaican country party that the royal executive would "divert" tax revenues unless the moneys were appropriated to specific uses by the legislature, issued by its treasurer, and accounted for by legislative audit. The lord president further believed that the new model of legislation was too inflexible for a changeable and remote colony. A convinced mercantilist, concerned for the commercial growth of the colonies, politically and financially involved with London sugar refiners, and the great defender of the rights of men of property against the rule of the royal prerogative, Shaftesbury warned "that the new Regulation would drive away the Planters who claimed the rights of Englishmen and would not be governed as the Irish."[12]

11. Coventry to Carlisle, Nov. 17, 1678, Mar. 29, 1679 (n.s.), Add. MSS 25120, 132, 138–139. Blathwayt told Carlisle, Dec. 6, 1678, that the lords of the committee had been unable to meet since Oct. 30. Blathwayt's reports of the rumored replacement of Williamson by Sunderland and of Coventry by Temple (the former accurate) emphasized the pressures against the crown's forward policy in the empire, Feb. 29, 1679, Blathwayt Papers, XXII, 2, Williamsburg. See also Cal. S.P. Col., 1677–1680, nos. 827, 830, 832, and Add. MSS 12430, 37. Order of the king-in-council, Feb. 21, 1679, C.O. 138/3, 258, but the possibility of rewording this order was held open, ibid., 260. See Blathwayt to Carlisle, Jan. 23, 1679, Carlisle to Blathwayt, Apr. 20, June 10, 1679, Blathwayt Papers, XXII, 1, 2, Williamsburg.

12. Official minutes are in Add. MSS 12429, 88–92b, unofficial ones in Blathwayt to Carlisle, May 31, 1679, Blathwayt Papers, XXII, 1, Williamsburg. Calendars are in Cal. S.P. Col., 1677–1680, nos. 1001, 1009; Edwards, British Colonies, I, 275–278; Privy Council, Col. Ser., I, 1274, 1275. The meeting itself was a political event, for by it King Charles honored his pledge to abandon cabinet deliberations "and bring all business into the Privy Council," where the leaders of the opposition were now seated. Fortescue suggests (Cal. S.P. Col., 1677–1680, xlvi) that Halifax led the council minority, which may well be so, but Shaftes-

Shaftesbury showed that Jamaica's planters were correct to count on the support of England's country party, but he and they found that monarchists were a majority both in the plantations committee and in the full privy council. The central issue was force. Proponents of the prerogative reminded King Charles that even English law conceded to the sovereign "the Sole Supream Government Command and disposition of the Militia and all forces by Sea and Land and of all forts and places of strength within all your Majesty's Realm and dominions." A provincial assembly therefore had no basis in law from which to protest the crown's military monopoly. As for the secondary issue of taxation, the assembly's suggestion that the king or his representative would misuse tax moneys was undutiful. It was ungrateful as well, considering how much the king spent on imperial defense. As for the argument that the dominion's great distance from England made provincial autonomy imperative, the privy councillors replied that the governor-general and his council of state and war had ample emergency powers to deal with difficulties not anticipated by English authorities. To allegations of rigidity they replied that "the Inhabitants have free Access to make Complaints" to the Jamaica executive. Such a reply only furthered colonial fears of gubernatorial absolutism, but the lords insisted that, however powerful he was locally, the governor-general would not misbehave because under the new model he "is now more than [ever] become accountable to your Majesty of all his most Important deliberations and Actions."[13]

Increased accountability to the crown was precisely Carlisle's objection to the new model. Likewise, the governor-general's reduced accountability to the assembly underlay its dislike of the new model. Reduction of all provincial autonomy, whether executive or legislative, and the direct imposition of crown commands on both, was the essence of the new imperialism. The courtier lords of the privy council alleged that imperial centralization was defensive, that the colonial elites, like their English allies, had tried to use legislatures "to grasp all power as well as that of a deliberative voice in making Laws," that the legislative leaders had pre-

---

bury had been named lord president on Apr. 22, 1679 (*ibid.*, no. 977). See also Edward Raymond Turner, "The Privy Council of 1679," *EHR*, XXX (1915), 251–270. On Shaftesbury's attitudes, see C.O. 138/3, 293, 294–305.

13. The lords also gave the disputed clause of the militia bill priority: see C.O. 138/3, 297; *Cal. S.P. Col., 1677–1680*, no. 840; Edwards, *British Colonies*, I, 275. On taxation, see C.O. 138/3, 297–298, and on the balance of distance from England by the royal executive's power, and of that power by gubernatorial accountability to the crown, see *ibid.*, 298–299, 301, and Edwards, I, 277.

tended to privileges not their due, and that "they have thereby entrenched upon your Majesty's Prerogative and exceeded the bounds of duty and loyalty." The councillors advised their king that his firmness in resisting the island assembly's usurpation of "a power which they have thus abused and to which they have no pretentions of right" would define the crown's future force in the empire. "Your Majesty's resolutions in this case," the privy councillors warned, "are likely to be the measures of respect and obedience to your Royal Commands in other Colonies."[14]

Faced with so forceful an argument, and one so favorable both to his increasing absolutism at home and to his hardening determination that his colonial subjects also "are not to govern themselves, but to be governed by him," King Charles agreed that he must "put a restraint upon these enormities" of the opposition overseas and at home. The king's determination to substitute his prerogative for legislative privilege was increased, and the unity of Anglo-American politics was reemphasized, when the English merchants trading to Jamaica, instead of "petitioning the King to restore [the colonists] to their former method of Government, as they had fair opportunity of doing . . . on the contrary applied themselves to the Parliament endeavoring to have Jamaica annexed to the Crown and their rights as they call them settled by Act of Parliament." The ancient alliance of the country party and the city merchants was as evident—and their joint concern for colonies as investment opportunities and for colonial constitutions as England's political experiments was as strong—as it had been on the eve of the civil wars. Like their anti-monarchical predecessors, Shaftesbury's country party and their merchant allies still relied on parliament and hated the crown. The country party's need for colonial profits and its involvement in Anglo-American politics meant that, once again, between 1679 and 1681, colonial autonomy helped to sustain English liberty.[15]

King Charles showed his enmity to both autonomy and lib-

14. C.O. 138/3, 300, 301–302. See the alternate formulation, that the colonists had "never had any other right to Assemblies than by permission of the Governors and that only Temporary and for probation" (Add. MSS 12429, 91b). Calendars are in *Cal. S.P. Col., 1677–1680*, nos. 954, 1009; *Privy Council, Col. Ser.*, I, 1274; Edwards, *British Colonies*, I, 276–277, 278. Small wonder the whigs asserted that Danby (in the Tower) and York (in exile) still directed crown policy.

15. Coventry to Atkins, Nov. 21, 1677, Add. MSS 25120, 120; C.O. 138/3, 301; Blathwayt to Carlisle, May 31, 1679, Blathwayt Papers, XXII, 1, Williamsburg, in which also observe Blathwayt's suggestive running together of "sedition," "assembly," "merchants," and "parliament."

erty at the conclusion of his privy council's debate. The king ordered his governor-general to call another assembly and to offer them one more chance to accept the new model and the laws he had prepared. "In case of refusal," the king accepted his council's advice to confer on Carlisle "such powers as formerly given unto Colonel D'Oyley Your first Governor of Jamaica and since to other Governors." That is, the governor-general could base his rule upon "the Laws of England, where the different nature and constitution of that colony may conveniently permit the same." He could take the advice of his council. Or the viceroy might do whatever he considered "necessary and proper for the good Government of that Plantation." In short, the island elite could either accept the king's new model, which permitted them to ratify or reject laws, or they would lose the rule of law altogether.[16]

The governor-general as well as the assembly was to be disciplined for his continued independence of the lords of the privy council plantations committee. Carlisle was ordered to enforce the policy that he had repeatedly and publicly criticized. On the advice of the privy council committee, the king rejected the draft legislation that Carlisle had sent home for royal approval, as required by the new model, for these proposed measures seemed less protective of the prerogative than the versions sent out with the earl. The committee of the council went on to protest that Carlisle, like other autonomous provincial executives, had failed to supply them with enough information about the colony to permit them to make policy for it: "His Majesty hardly knew the Laws or the men by which his Plantations were governed." The lords now required legislative journals, quarterly reports from all royal colonial councils and secretaries, and continual correspondence from the governors-general. The resulting imperial information made centralized government possible. The reporting system thereby established lasted as long as the empire itself. The privy councillors already knew enough to label Carlisle's revenue act "mean" in amount, "distrustful" of royal intent, and ludicrously limited in duration. They took it as evidence that "no good can be expected" from the assembly, and they hoped Carlisle had not called it back into session before their orders arrived. Those orders admonished

16. *Cal. S.P. Col., 1677–1680*, nos. 954, 960–962, 1011 (which is the third personal letter from King Charles to the earl of Carlisle as governor-general of Jamaica, an unprecedentedly direct involvement of the king in colonial correspondence), 1009; Edwards, *British Colonies*, I, 272–278; C.O. 138/3, 304, which recognizes that D'Oyley's administration had provided "the first principles of Jamaica government" (Add. MSS 12429, 97).

Carlisle to either pass the new model or revert to the government of General D'Oyley, which the privy councillors conceived to be wholly military.[17]

The Military Prerogative in Jamaican Practice and Imperial Politics, 1679–1680

By the time the privy councillors' dispatch reached Jamaica, the governor-general had decreed martial law, but he had also recalled the assembly. To summon the assembly, Carlisle had exercised the emergency clause of his commission, which permitted him to convene the legislature so that it could raise money in case of invasion or insurrection. Wanting money, Carlisle apprehended invasion. The governor-general took advantage of a series of incidents that began when a French ship exchanged cannon fire with Fort Charles on July 3, 1679. When, at dusk on the seventh, a French fleet was sighted off the harbor, the governor-general rode in from St. Jago de la Vega to be at the head of the Jamaican forces. They had assembled under arms in Port Royal before daybreak on the eighth. He convened the council of war and proclaimed martial law. In the meantime, however, he sent word to the home government that he expected no trouble with the French, for they had carefully informed him that they intended to harass the Spanish. Nevertheless, Carlisle did not let the Jamaicans relax. Instead, "the whole of the inhabitants, soldiers and slaves, were set to work to increase the fortifications," the governor-general wrote, "I being very glad of the opportunity of carrying on work which would otherwise have gone forward very slowly"—and he was happier still of the excuse to solicit money from the assembly.[18]

The earl suspended the law martial just prior to the meeting of the assembly on August 19, 1679. Miffed at Carlisle's multi-

17. Add. MSS 12429, 92b, 98b, 99b, 97; Blathwayt to Carlisle, May 31, 1679, Blathwayt Papers, XXII, 1, Williamsburg; lords to Carlisle, May 31, 1679, Jan. 14, 16, 1680, C.O. 138/3, 313–316, 334–337, 348; Cal. S.P. Col., 1677–1680, xlviii, nos. 954, 960, 1011, 1012, 1117 (where Carlisle insisted that the provisions so objected to by the lords had been written in by Long after the bills left the governor and council), 1141. On the new system of reports, see, in addition to the lords' letters to Carlisle, their directives to the governor and council collectively, to the secretary, and to the clerk of the assembly, C.O. 138/3, 352–356. Note the important principle, enunciated by Williamson, Feb. 16, 1678, that the king would receive information primarily from and announce his orders through the governors of localities, in England as in the colonies, Cal. S.P. Dom., 1677–1678, 651.

18. Carlisle to Coventry, July 10, Aug. 13, 1679, C.O. 138/3, 320–323, 324–325, calendared in Cal. S.P. Col., 1677–1680, nos. 1059, 1094.

plied favors to the Morgan men, the Modyford faction played up Jamaica's version of the Popish Plot. The Modyfords alleged that King Charles had sold the colony to Louis XIV and that the French fleet now anchored off the island had come to take possession of the Catholic king's purchase. Then the anxious assemblymen learned of the king's order to the governor-general: offer the new model of legislation for the assembly's approval; failing that, govern by decree and by force. The assembly was startled by the royal resolution, "so much contrary to their expectation" of the Popish Plot's promotion of Anglo-American legislative pretensions. Desperate for a delay, they passed the revenue bill for which they had been summoned, but they limited it to six-month salaries for "the three generals" and a grant for fortifications. Moreover, they secretly resolved that Carlisle's acceptance of this act admitted their right to raise, appropriate, and account for taxes. Publicly, the island elite petitioned the governor-general to prorogue them so that the military officers, who were a majority in both houses, could be recalled first to the council of war and then "be disperst to their Commands to . . . secure the Island and Consider this great Business."[19]

On August 28, 1679, the governor-general accepted the revenue bill, knowing full well that its short term would infuriate the privy council committee. He then dismissed the legislature, "and the same day a Council of War was held at St. Jago to settle the Army in case of an Attack in known Orders, Rendezvous and Posts." Carlisle capitalized on his vast command experience and on his expertise in the political and military uses of militia to reorganize his forty-five hundred officers and men in eight regiments. He personally took command of the island cavalry regiment and rode at the head of its senior troop. The governor-general also made himself colonel of Jamaica's brigade of foot guards. He

19. Carlisle to Coventry, July 10, Aug. 30, 1679 (read July 10, 1680), Sept. 15, 1679, C.O. 138/3, 320–323, 331–338, 382–384. Carlisle had not violated his instructions, as the lords thought, by authorizing a new assembly election. He merely met the prorogued body, which he subsequently prorogued again to Dec. 1679. On this body's summons and sessions, see *Cal. S.P. Col., 1677–1680*, nos. 1059, 1096, 1097, 1098, 1101, 1103–1105, 1107, 1117, 1118, 1140. On the rumor of the French threat, see also *ibid.*, no. 1097. For parliament's resentment of sales of imperial possessions, see Julian S. Corbett, *England in the Mediterranean: A Study of the Rise and Influence of British Power Within the Straits, 1603–1713*, 2 vols. (London, 1904), II, 108. News of the plot was rife in Jamaica by Feb. 18, 1679 (n.s.), *Cal. S.P. Col., 1677–1680*, no. 894. On the conclusion of the session, see also Edwards, *British Colonies*, I, 280–282, and Add. MSS 12430, 38. Even in May 1680, more than five months after Governor-General Carlisle had purged the opposition assemblymen from office, 15 of the 32 members of the assembly dissolved on Dec. 1, 1679, had captain's rank or higher in the militia, while 9 of the 14 councillors were colonels. See *Cal. S.P. Col., 1677–1680*, nos. 1095, 1107, 1370, 1371.

commissioned Lieutenant General Morgan and Major General Watson to command a regiment of infantry each. Four councillor-colonels—three of whom had come to Jamaica as officers of Cromwell's conquering army—led the remaining regiments of foot soldiers.[20]

The general staff and the field grade officers met as the governor-general's council of war. There they received general orders and accepted articles of war copied by Carlisle from those issued in England by the captain general of the forces. These orders and articles they passed on to their subordinates at regimental courts-martial. Thus instructed and disciplined, the Jamaican troops were not only drilled in the latest formations, both for cavalry and infantry, but also exercised with their snaphance muskets, modern weapons in comparison with the antique matchlocks of many English units. While the veteran field officers trained their men, the three generals' chief duty was to coordinate the island regiments in defense of the province. The governor-general's hard-pressed secretary complained, "I am now a Secretary of War, much labour, but no money." He added, however, that the "whole business" of the viceroy's staff "now is the life of Artillery men, continually entertained with Drum or Trumpet which we are much delighted in, from the hopes we have of giving our Attackers warm entertainment." The secretary of war reflected the governor-general's assurance: the Jamaicans could defeat any invader, if their ammunition held out.[21]

The military crisis excused Carlisle's resort to martial law, but it did not disguise the uncertainties of his position. He faced passive but persistent political resistance in the colony. He read of political upheaval at home. He had been censured by the privy council's plantations committee for his failure to enforce a program that would reduce his own autonomy as governor-general as well as that of the island's assembly. Carlisle's tenure was ques-

20. Carlisle released the assembly because he could not see how to make the Jamaican legislators accept the system of Poynings's Law without at least some verbal changes in the militia act and a reduction of the term of the revenue act from perpetuity, *Cal. S.P. Col., 1677–1680*, no. 1030. On the militia reorganizations, see: *ibid.*, nos. 1370, 1371; Watson to Carlisle, Sept. 30, 1680, Sloan MS 2724, 242b; and, especially, the "State of Jamaica," C.O. 138/3, 437–439. Cols. Thomas Freeman, Thomas Fuller, and John Cope were among the conquerors. Compare Carlisle's own service as a Cromwellian officer and his experience in the political use of militia, in chapter 2 above. The great increase in the island's military strength both in men and weapons can be measured by comparison of the text with Littleton's report, C.O. 139/1, 232.

21. In addition to n. 20 see *Cal. S.P. Col., 1677–1680*, nos. 1122, 1466; C.O. 138/3, 331, 335; Rowland Powell to William Blathwayt, St. Jago de la Vega, Sept. 16, 1679, Blathwayt Papers, XXVII, 2, Williamsburg.

tionable, and his command was apparently in peril, physical as well as political. Military opportunity and political need, and a desire for quick profit, inspired Carlisle to follow Sir Thomas Modyford's example. At the height of the invasion scare, Carlisle took public command of the privateers.[22]

Carlisle argued that, as vice admiral, he had to draw the privateers' allegiance away from the French. He also accepted the Modyford-Morgan position that in the absence of a substantial squadron of English warships, the buccaneers were Jamaica's navy, essential to island defense. There were flaws in the admiral's argument. The royal frigates under his command were formidable enough to persuade the privateers to enter their plunder in the Port Royal customhouse. That they had plunder to enter suggests that the privateers were not on the defensive, but the governor-general winked at their raids because he collected at least a third of the loot for himself as the price of legitimizing it. Undaunted by Carlisle's rake-off, the privateers sacked the Spanish storage hulk and indigo storehouses at Honduras.[23]

That this "trade," as Carlisle called it, was seized from the Spanish allies of his king, bothered Carlisle not at all. He had been engaged in attacks on the Spanish Indies for a quarter-century, since he helped to organize the Western Design. Despite King Charles's clear and repeated orders about the need to conciliate Spain in the Indies, and despite the king's decision that Jamaica's own best interest lay in eliminating its destructive privateers, the governor-general even permitted the buccaneers anchored in Port Royal to organize an attack on Puerto Bello and the South Sea commerce of Spain. He felt justified in this warlike act because the Spanish seized and confiscated every English ship they could catch, regardless of its destination, cargo, or character. If the

22. Add. MSS 12430, 37b–38b; Add. MSS 12429, 107; *Cal. S.P. Col., 1677–1680*, nos. 1117–1118.

23. Carlisle to Coventry, Oct. 24, 1678, Feb. 18, 1679, C.O. 138/3, 283, 290, calendared in *Cal. S.P. Col., 1677–1680*, nos. 815, 894. Carlisle's desire to increase the white population and so multiply Jamaica's military strength also led to his request that men disbanded from English regiments (following the French war scare and under pressure from the country party) be sent to Jamaica and given land. Later governors-general were more successful with similar requests, which were patterned partly on Carlisle's experience of sending Cromwellian soldier-settlers to Jamaica from Scotland and which, in authority's view, counterbalanced the continued transportation of political criminals to the colony. See also *Cal. S.P. Col., 1677–1680*, no. 1002, and chapter 2 above on military manpower and the army as the instrument of settlement, and for Carlisle's comparable command as a vice admiral in his English government. Eyewitness accounts of Carlisle's direction of privateers are offered in Add. MSS 12429 by Long (113) and Beeston (124). On Carlisle's relations with the pirates, see also C.O. 138/3, 367–369 and Add. MSS 12429, 108b, 110, 112b–113, 116–118, 119, 122, 123b–124.

Spanish protested the governor-general's continuation of militant Jamaica's traditional "trade," they would add little to the crown censure that Carlisle anticipated in any case for his support of the Jamaica garrison government's autonomy. A cushion of Spanish money would soften the blow of a recall. In war and in hatred of Spain, as well as in paramilitary politics, Carlisle was, as his enemies said, still a Cromwellian.[24]

On October 27, 1679, Jamaica's commander-in-chief ordered the regimental colors cased. Thus he signaled the revival of civil authority in the province. On the next day, the assembly met. In it, the Lynch party predominated, under the joint guidance of the speaker, "Colonel" Beeston, and "Captain" Long of the council. The assembly majority again refused to accept the new model of legislation. They repeated that "they will submit to wear but never to make chains." The Jamaica officer elite, incorporated as the assembly of a conquered colony, were devoted equally to civilian political principles and to paramilitary governmental practice. They knew that the military prerogative was essential for the protection and government of their island outpost of empire, but they did not think that the practice of the crown's military authority need conflict with the political privileges that the country party at home, and its Jamaica representative, Lord Vaughan, had assured them were their English birthright.[25]

The assembly acknowledged (in an address written by Samuel Long) that the central issue of their constitutional controversy with the crown during the last five years was their refusal to agree to a royal amendment to the militia bill. The amendment insisted

24. See Add. MSS 12429, 120b, confirmed by Blathwayt to Carlisle, Dec. 22, 1679, Blathwayt Papers, XXII, 2, Williamsburg, regarding Carlisle's desire to retaliate against Spanish depredations. The king's personal letter to his governor-general, Mar. 29, 1680, ordering him to convert the privateers to planting is in *Cal. S.P. Col., 1677–1680*, no. 950. In his first letter home following receipt of the privy council censure, Carlisle asked for leave to return to England (Carlisle to Blathwayt, Sept. 15, 1679, Blathwayt Papers, XXII, 2, Williamsburg).

25. On casing the colors, see C.O. 138/2, 139. Carlisle's account of the assembly, its address to him and objections to the laws, are briefly calendared in *Cal. S.P. Col., 1677–1680*, nos. 1188 (I–III), 1189, and Edwards, *British Colonies*, I, 267ff. Long, *Jamaica*, I, 206–213, prints "abstracts" of the assembly minutes and addresses, which illuminate his (and his ancestor's) attitudes. Long's continued use of his Cromwellian military title and evidence of his position as "a man of very great influence upon the assembly," whose members esteemed him as "the Patron of their Rights and Privileges as Englishmen," appear in Add. MSS 12429, 105, and *Cal. S.P. Col., 1677–1680*, nos. 794, 1188, 1512. See also *ibid.*, no. 1199; Carlisle's correspondence to Coventry, Oct. 24, 1678 (read in committee, Apr. 5, 1679), Dec. 1, 1679, and to the lords of the committee, Sept. 15, Nov. 23, 1679, C.O. 138/3, 278, 365, 374; and *Journals*, I, 55–56.

on by the crown authorized the viceroy to act "in all things" and "upon all occasions" as "Captain General and Governor in Chief" according to "all the Power and Authorities given unto him by his Majesty's Commission," regardless of any restraint in statute law. Such a clause, the Jamaicans argued, did away with civil government and the rule of civil law. It would return the island constitution to its state prior to Sir Charles Littleton's administration, that is, to the rule "of an Army which until that time was deemed the Supreme Authority." Such exaltation of martial law was imprudent, the legislators pointed out: civil forms, by protecting property, had produced provincial prosperity. Moreover, the assembly asserted, unlimited military government was unnecessary: traditionally, and under the assembly's original militia act, "on any apprehension of danger, the General with his council of officers have power to put the law martial on foot for what time they please, and to command us in our own persons, our servants, negroes, horses, even all that we have, to his majesty's service."[26]

To prove their point, the members of the assembly recalled that every governor-general since the establishment of royal government had exemplified "the strength of his majesty's commission" by exercising full military authority over the island. The assembly cited Sir Thomas Modyford's military government in 1665 and 1666, when he had strengthened Fort Charles by the forced labor of the planters and their slaves. His successor, Sir Thomas Lynch, the assemblymen noted, had built Fort James under martial law and had added other works. "In the Lord Vaughan's time," the legislators wrote, "tho there was no probability of War yet we wanted no trial of his power also in the Militia and our Obedience to it," for the governor-general had called up the militia to man ships in pursuit of pirates and interlopers. Under Lieutenant General Morgan, the islanders remembered, "we were again put under Martial Law in which time Fort Rupert Fort Carlisle and a new line at Fort James were built." Most recently, the Jamaicans concluded, under Captain General Carlisle's

---

26. Add. MSS 12429, 93, 93b, 94, 98, briefly calendared in *Cal. S.P. Col., 1677–1680*, no. 1188 (II), and printed in Edwards, *British Colonies*, I, 286–295. The lords agreed that the military prerogative was the heart of the constitutional struggle (*Cal. S.P. Col., 1677–1680*, no. 840), but the court ultimately concluded that the parliament had given the king such sweeping military powers that they needed no reiteration by a colonial assembly (*ibid.*, no. 1238). Carlisle dealt with the address point by point, noting, for example, that the assembly's assertion that D'Oyley's had been a wholly military government was false, for Sir Thomas Lynch had himself enjoyed a jury trial, with Robert Byndloss as foreman (Carlisle to lords of the committee, Nov. 23, 1679, C.O. 138/3, 365–366, calendared in *Cal. S.P. Col., 1677–1680*, no. 1188; Edwards, *British Colonies*, I, 285).

military government they had built Fort Morgan and its battery and constructed further defenses for Fort James—"all which fortifications are substantially built with Stone and Brick wholly at the Charge or Labour of the Country." By their submission to military law and requisitions, by their self-taxation for defense, and by daily martial display and guard duty, the Jamaicans claimed to demonstrate their deference to the military character of "your Majesty's Governors, the Militia having always waited on them to Church, in their progresses, and all public Occasions." Finally, the Jamaicans vaunted their "Military duty" done for the imperial crown: Port Royal was, as they were fond of repeating, largely guarded by militia, but it could not "be distinguished from a Garrison either in Peace or War."[27]

The assembly devoted nearly as much space in its address to the fundamental constitutional question of military power, its bounds and command, as to all other issues combined. As for the most provocative of these, the omission of the king's name from their revenue bill, the assembly somewhat disingenuously suggested that it was the inclusion of his majesty's name that would have been novel. The governor issued all moneys by his warrant, and the bulk of the revenue was consumed by his salary and that of his general staff. Therefore, legislative appropriation was hardly a real issue either, according to the assembly. To them, the essential fiscal problem was the repeated royal demand for a perpetual revenue. Quite properly, the legislators were obsessed with "a fear that if they . . . make it perpetual, they should be assembled no more, but governed by Governor and Council, as they were in Coll. Doyley's time . . . and some part of Sir Charles Littleton's."[28]

---

27. On Modyford, see Add. MSS 12429, 95, and Edwards, *British Colonies*, I, 288. Carlisle denied what he took to be the assembly's contention that Lynch's entire administration had been by martial law, noting that although the council order for military rule was a standing one, its exercise by Lynch was periodic (Carlisle to the lords, Nov. 23, 1679, C.O. 138/3, 366, calendared in *Cal. S.P. Col., 1677–1680*, no. 1188; Edwards, *British Colonies*, I, 289). Note that fort names were the colony's military honors to imperial commanders. Carlisle agreed that the work claimed by the assembly had been done, but he pointed out the legislators' intent to appropriate the government's regular revenues to pay for that work, i.e., £1,228 of the £1,500 impost. His own accounts of fortification are in Sloan MS 2724, 70b–71, and those of ordnance are in *Cal. S.P. Col., 1677–1680*, nos. 1119, 1120.

28. In Add. MSS 12429, folios 93b–95b and part of 99b are devoted to the military question, folios 96–98b to the others. In the printed version, Edwards, *British Colonies*, I, pp. 287–289 and part of 294 are given over to the prerogatives of physical power, and pp. 289–293 to all other issues, such as finance. See also C.O. 138/3, 144–145, and C.O. 1/43, 371. The disingenuousness appears in Samuel Long's previous omissions of the king's name from Jamaica legislation. This deliberate and repeated act of resistance to the assertion of royal authority in Jamaica took place during the republican Long's assembly clerkship

To balance the executive's authority by that of the legislature and of the civil law was the assembly's objective. Thus the limited scope of the statutes sent out by the king-in-council was almost as alarming to the Jamaicans as was their legislature's diminished authority. None of the laws of England was allowed to them, the Jamaicans protested, yet the law "was the medium between the king and people." It alone could limit the discretion of the executive. It was on behalf of the law, the assembly explained, that they had ordered their speaker to support the chief justice's writ of habeas corpus in the case of a man condemned by an executive court. The assemblymen summed up the limits on laws and legislative bodies that appeared in Carlisle's commission, and the concomitant increase in executive authority, by their complaint that the governor-general, as "Chancellor . . . and Admiral joyned with his Military authority lodges so great a power in him that being united and Executed in one person makes him Totum in toto and Totum in qualibet parte So that he may at any time Invalidate anything done under his own Commission." That is, the governor-general's imperial authority was without legal limit—absolute. The provincial legislators were left to "hope their Lordships intend not that we are to be Govern'd as an Army the Governor be impowered to Lay any Tax by himself and Council." After all, the assemblymen asserted, the king had divested himself and his council of the authority to tax without the consent of a representative body. The colonists questioned the king's power to confer on his governor-general and council in Jamaica authority that he did not possess in England. [29]

By pointing out that the crown's power in the dominions was greater than it was in England itself, the Jamaica assemblymen exposed the issue that made their cause that of Shaftesbury and the country party, and that made the authority of the governor-general the concern of York, of Danby, of the court, and even of King

---

(Long, *Jamaica*, I, 96). The parallels between his career and that of Robert Beverley in Virginia recur. The assembly's fears appear in Add. MSS 12429, 96, and are summarized by Carlisle to Coventry, Oct. 24, 1678, C.O. 138/3, 281.

29. Other cases in point were the governor-general's revocation of a clerk's patent, leading Beeston to argue that "therefore no man's Freehold in [the] whole Island is Safe," and the imprisonment of Heane for words spoken against Carlisle: see Add. MSS 12429, 123a, and S.P. 44/62, 349. The assembly also complained of the subservience of the council under Carlisle's commission. This appears in the council's address, Add. MSS 12429, 100–101; Edwards, *British Colonies*, I, 295–297. The lonely resistance by Councillor-Captain Samuel Long seems to be the exception that proves the rule (*ibid.*, 282–283, and *Cal. S.P. Col.*, *1677–1680*, no. 1189). The executive's limitless authority, greater than in England, is exclaimed over, and concluding pleas against military rule are made, in Add. MSS 12429, 98, 99b, Edwards, *British Colonies*, I, 293, 294, and note 47 below.

Charles himself. To the degree that the king could unfetter his military prerogative and decrease legislative authority in the colony, he could set an imperial precedent for the degradation of the parliament and for the assertion in England of his own authority as commander-in-chief. The struggle over Jamaica's constitution attracted the attention of both court and country leaders in England because it exposed the absolutist potential and the danger to legislative and legal authority inherent in what became known as the "standing army issue."

Contemporaries stressed that the crown would do away with representative institutions if it could tax by military requisition. On September 15, 1679, Carlisle warned the imperial authorities that the Jamaica legislators and their London merchant allies planned to carry this issue to the house of commons, "who as it is reported here, are about making an Act to punish any levying of money but by consent of Parliament but whether they may include the Plantations I know not." That the Jamaicans were correctly informed of country intent was borne out when the commons voted, on December 17, 1680 (simultaneously with learning of Jamaican charges against Carlisle's attacks on legislative authority), that the "illegal exaction of money from the subject should be high treason." Carlisle pointed out to his peers on the privy council that, faced with such threats of impeachment, none of them would collect taxes without legislative authorization. It was public knowledge that certain Port Royal merchants, in touch with their London counterparts, had determined not to pay any such levy. They would force the executive to confiscate their property instead, and so provide the occasion for a petition to parliament against forcible seizure of the subject's goods. The Jamaicans intended to charge the royal executive, before a hostile house of commons, with taxation by military force and without representation.[30]

"Fair means of persuasion having failed" to convince the assembly to accept the new model, the governor-general dismissed the leader of the opposition, Captain Samuel Long, from his posts as councillor, colonel, and chief justice. Then Carlisle arrested and

30. Carlisle to Coventry, Sept. 15, 1679, and to lords of the committee, Feb. 23, 1680, C.O. 138/3, 334, 390–391, calendared in *Cal. S.P. Col., 1677–1680*, nos. 1118, 1302; Ogg, *Charles II*, 605, quoting *Commons Journals*, IX, 682; Whitson, *Constitutional Development of Jamaica*, 94, 95–96. The king's growing personal interest in the imperial issues raised in Jamaica appears in his three personal letters to Carlisle and in his participation in the May 1679 debate.

imprisoned Long on a charge of high treason for having erased the king's name from the 1675 revenue act. He denied Long's application for a writ of habeas corpus and announced that Long would be sent to England for trial. To avoid similar treatment, Speaker Beeston and five other leading legislative opponents of the new model promised the governor-general that they would appear before the king-in-council to answer Carlisle's charges against them. They would have to tell the king himself why they and the assembly had refused to obey his order to adopt the new model and why they had rejected every one of the twenty-five acts offered them by his majesty's command. The earl of Carlisle expected that these provincial leaders would "receive those reasons as sufficient inducements for their obedience in England which they will not be persuaded to admit of in Jamaica."[31]

To the arrest of their leader and the threat of English trials for Jamaica opponents of royal policies, the assembly replied with an address which demanded that the governor-general attack the privateers "with the two frigates and the two companies of foot maintained by the King with that object." Even without such an address by the assembly—designed to alert the commercial and political supporters of the Spanish alliance, and the king himself, to a Jamaica executive's support of privateering—Sir Thomas Modyford had been removed from the government and consigned to the Tower for countenancing the buccaneers. By its address, the assembly sought to ensure like punishment for the earl of Carlisle.[32]

Carlisle quickly counterattacked. He summoned the assemblymen to his presence on December 1, 1679, called them "Fools Asses Beggars Cowards and many other appellations," and dissolved the legislature. The governor-general then asked each councillor and ex-assemblyman individually—"most of them being in military trusts," as it was noted with disciplinary reference both to obedience and to patronage—if he would swear to "submit to this form of government which his majesty hath been pleased to order

31. Add. MSS 12429, 104b, 105b–106, 121; Add. MSS 12430, 39; *Cal. S.P. Col., 1677–1680*, nos. 1188, 1189, 1302, 1345; Edwards, *British Colonies*, I, 282–283; Carlisle to the lords of the committee, Feb. 23, 1680, C.O. 138/3, 389–390. Carlisle also proposed that the size of future assemblies be halved to facilitate executive control. See Long, *Jamaica*, I, 200, on the governor-general's intent "to punish such stubborn disobedience, by sending the leaders of them prisoners to England to be dealt with there by his Majesty as disaffected and rebellious to government."

32. Add. MSS 12429, 110; Add. MSS 12430, 39; *Cal. S.P. Col., 1677–1680*, nos. 950, 1094, 1188 (III); Blathwayt to Watson, July 6, 1680, Blathwayt Papers, XXVII, 4, Williamsburg.

for this island of Jamaica." Some members followed Long and
Beeston in declaring that, while they always obeyed the king's
commands—the most radical said that they obeyed only the king's
"lawful" commands—the only oaths commanded by law were
those of allegiance and supremacy, that they had taken those, and
that they would swear no others. The governor-general replied
that "such as would not obey his Majesty under this form of
Government were not fit to bear an Office either Military or
Civil." Thereupon he purged Beeston, and the Lynch party in
general, from all public office.[33]

The earl of Carlisle asked his own followers only if they
would obey the king, without reference to the new model. Their
assent saved their offices. The continued loyalty of Carlisle's clients, long after he had left the government, and their repeated use
of his principles of military government, even after the earl himself had died, suggest that such political purgation and party building as Carlisle now undertook at the crisis of his administration
might have produced a constitutional settlement to the crown's
taste, if it had been applied at the outset of the earl's administration. But by the time the king's repeated personal orders finally
convinced Carlisle of the crown's determination to impose the
new model, the Jamaicans and their English merchant and country
allies had entrenched themselves in principled opposition to it.
They had armed themselves with the weapons of the Exchange
and Westminster while the crown had been temporarily weakened
by the combined crises of Popish Plot and Exclusion. As the
governor-general told the secretary of state, "your disorders at
home leave us in great uncertainties."[34]

The need to resolve these uncertainties for himself, combined

33. The testimony of the principals is as follows: Beeston, Add. MSS 12430, 39, and
Add. MSS 12429, 122b*ff*; Long, *ibid.*, 111–112; Bathurst, *ibid.*, 118; Beckford, *ibid.*, 120;
Carlisle, *ibid.*, 107b, 108; C.O. 138/3, 282; Edwards, *British Colonies*, I, 269.

34. The governor-general had applied the test first to the council, in Oct. 1678, *Cal.
S.P. Col., 1677–1680*, no. 815. See also *ibid.*, nos. 1188, 1189, 1199, and Edwards, *British
Colonies*, I, 282*ff*. For the rhetoric that has covered the issues of test and purge, see Long,
Jamaica, I, 11. Carlisle spoke of the effect upon himself of repetition of the royal orders
(Add. MSS 12429, 105). On his precedential remodeling of the Scots judiciary, see chapter 2
above. The replacement of Judge (and Col.) Barry, son of the Cromwellian commander, a
leader of opposition to the new royal model, and a follower of Lynch, by Morgan's deputy,
Col. Theodore Cary ("Coll. in the late King's Army"), epitomizes the nature and antiquity
of Jamaica's political divisions as well as Carlisle's ultimate choice between them (Add.
MSS 12429, 108; *Cal. S.P. Col., 1677–1680*, no. 1303). Carlisle's removal of Lynch's appointee, Long, from the chief justiceship, and his appointment of Byndloss, the leader of the
Morgan faction, and Lynch's subsequent reversal of this show the clarity and duration of
partisan divisions in island politics (*ibid.*, 28; Add. MSS 12429, 115). On transatlantic "disorders," see Carlisle to Coventry, Feb. 23, 1680, C.O. 138/3, 386.

with the deterioration of his English political position and the
deepening bitterness of the Jamaica constitutional struggle, convinced Carlisle that he would have to carry home his charges
against the opposition. Having from his first speech to the assembly in 1678 promised to sail home if necessary to settle the
government, Carlisle was now more certain than ever that only if
he applied his personal influence with the king and council during
their interrogation of the Jamaicans could he encourage "some
compliance on both sides" and so promote a constitutional settlement. As soon as Major General Watson returned from England
with the king's verbal leave to the governor-general to depart
from his post, Lieutenant General Morgan was named to command in place of his "Patroon and General," and on May 7, 1680,
the earl of Carlisle sailed from Port Royal.[35]

The Exclusion Crisis
and the Imperial Constitution, 1680–1681

Contemporaries saw in Carlisle's homecoming an attempt to
parlay the politics of the Exclusion Crisis into a lifetime grant of
Jamaica's government for himself and a reversion of it to his
second son, Frederick. So he had procured the command of the
city of Carlisle for himself and for his heir, Lord Morpeth, by
supporting the challenged crown six years before. A sea of difficulties lay between the earl of Carlisle and another garrison government for his family. In the passage home, the earl's ship was
separated from its convoy in a storm, dismasted, and finally found
(by the ship carrying the assemblymen whom Carlisle had ordered to England) three and a half months out of Jamaica, drifting
off the Scilly Isles, without food and almost without water. When
the weakened earl finally reached England, he had to face the personal hostility of the Jamaican merchant-planter-politicians and
their English country party counterparts, well financed from colonial coffers to attack the continued government of Jamaica by an
absolutist governor-general and privateer admiral.

Both Carlisle's quest to make Jamaica the overseas equivalent

35. *Cal. S.P. Col., 1677–1680,* no. 1096; Carlisle to Blathwayt, Sept. 15, 1679,
Blathwayt Papers, XXII, 2, Williamsburg. Carlisle's claim to verbal leave is in *Cal. S.P.
Col., 1677–1680,* no. 1344. Morgan's relations with Carlisle appear in their correspondence
for 1680 (Sloan MS 2724, 198, 236) and in Watson to Blathwayt, July 16, 1680, Blathwayt
Papers, XXVII, 4, Williamsburg.

of his title town and Jamaica's constitutional crisis were resolved in a series of spasms. Each was set off by a major political event of the frantic months of parliamentary pressure and crown concession, of parliamentary dissolution and royalist counterrevolution, that marked the end of the Exclusion Crisis.[36] The extended and repeated attention that the king and his council devoted to Jamaica's constitution in the nine months that followed the return of Carlisle and the court to London on September 9, 1680, is remarkable in itself, and it is telling testimony that the Jamaica controversy had become a widely watched barometer of Anglo-American politics. The hearings of the governor-general's charges against Samuel Long took place in mid-September. Long's countercharges were heard by the king-in-council during January 1681. These charges were defused in March by the dissolution of Long's intended auditory, the Oxford Parliament. In June and July 1681 the privy council worked out a final compromise of the imperial issues raised by the Jamaica case. This compromise struck a lasting constitutional balance between the crown and the province. The contest personified by Captain Samuel Long and Charles Howard, earl of Carlisle, produced the great imperial settlement of 1681 that was applied throughout England's American empire and outlasted it.[37]

Physical as well as political factors shaped the privy council's hearings of Governor-General Carlisle's charges against former Chief Justice Long. The earl's gout, always inflamed by the dehydrating diet and debilitating lassitude of a long sea voyage, had crippled him after his four months' passage from Jamaica. Physically, Carlisle was hardly able to present his case against Long and wholly unable to press it. It would not be pressed without him. Beset by Popish Plot and Exclusion Crisis, King Charles tried to avoid the appearance of absolutism. Instead the king relied upon his servants to act against the opposition, "His Regality being only to give the Laws and to keep the Peace." At first, hearings on Jamaica were adjourned until Carlisle could attend, but with increasing frequency they were held without him.[38]

36. On Carlisle's hopes for the government, see especially Sir Charles Littleton to Viscount Hatton, Sept. 14, 1680, Add. MSS 29577, 287. See also Add. MSS 12429, 114, 115b; Add. MSS 12430, 39b; Sloan MS 2724, 60, 227; Add. MSS 11410, 260b–261; C.O. 138/3, 482.

37. Littleton to Hatton, Sept. 9, 1680, Add. MSS 29577, 285b; Jenkins to Godolphin, Sept. 16, 1680, to Carlisle, June 24, 1681, S.P. 44/62, 72–73, 186; Add. MSS 12429, 116b; Blathwayt to Stapleton, Jan. 25, 1680, Blathwayt Papers, XXXVII, 3, Williamsburg; *Cal. S.P. Col., 1677–1680*, nos. 1501, 1503, 1509, 1512, 1540, 1550, 1561, 1571–1572; Edwards, *British Colonies*, I, 307–319.

38. *Cal. S.P. Col., 1677–1680*, xlv, nos. 1345, 1514, 1517, 1645; Jenkins to Godolphin,

Carlisle's case against Long—the crown's case against representative government in Jamaica—was further prejudiced by the threat of civil war. The sovereign claims of the Jamaica legislature, its appeal to the law against the prerogative, and its confident reliance on the support of a majority of the English parliament against the crown, all were responses to that parliamentary assertiveness that reminded observers of 1641. Fearing renewed civil war, the court and the country contested for the crucial support of the moderates. In parliament the greatest "trimmer," the earl of Halifax, supported the court by his powerful opposition to the exclusion of the duke of York from the succession. Within the privy council and its colonial committee, however, Halifax supported Jamaica's ex-chief justice, Samuel Long. In the case of both the imperial succession and the provincial legislature, Halifax's activity was important to the winning side, if not decisive by itself. His choice of causes was even more influential. Halifax signaled the moderates' inclination, both in England and elsewhere in the empire, to uphold the balanced sovereignty both of the king-in-council and of the king-in-parliament, rather than to sustain either monarchical or legislative government exclusively.[39]

The symbolic weight of the Long case in the politics of the period was emphasized by Carlisle's charges against him. Speaker Long had erased the king's name from the revenue bill. Chief Justice Long had issued a writ of habeas corpus for a defendant condemned to death by a prerogative court, and he had procured a legislative order to the king's provost marshal to obey that writ. Councillor-Colonel Long had refused to obey the orders of the governor-general. On the contrary, he had organized the opposition to the crown's attempt to apply Poynings's Law to Jamaica. Republican soldier "Captain" Long had spread "Seditious Insinuations among the People" that "Twas against Justice and against Law for his Majesty to make any alteration of our Constitutions We had so long lived under or put us under any other form than

---

Sept. 18, 1680, to Sir Edward Phillips, Apr. 28, 1681, S.P. 44/62, 76, 154; *Cal. S.P. Dom., 1680*, 25.

39. Blathwayt to Carlisle, Dec. 22, 1679, Blathwayt Papers, XXII, 2, Williamsburg; Add. MSS 12429, 118; Jenkins to Godolphin (for the king's attention), Sept. 23, 1680, S.P. 44/62, 87, and *passim*, esp. 79, 117–118, 145, 154, most of which are calendared in *Cal. S.P. Dom., 1680*, as are the indictment of the duke as a Catholic recusant and the promise of Shaftesbury's supporters to find York guilty although he appeared sword in hand at the head of his Guards (p. 44), and the preoccupation of the privy council with Plot and Exclusion through the whole of the Jamaica hearings (pp. 40, 62). See J. P. Kenyon, *Robert Spencer, Earl of Sunderland* (London, 1958), 56, 58–59, who notes Halifax's prestige at this time (pp. 48, 55, 59–60). See also Burnet, *History*, I, 281 n. 1; Foxcroft, *Halifax*, I, 225–228; Dorothy Lane Poole, ed., "Some Unpublished Letters of George Savile, Lord Halifax . . . ," *EHR*, XXVI (1911), 538–539.

what is truly agreeable to that of England, which by our Birth-rights we ought to enjoy." The contest between colonial self-government and the civil law, upheld by the elected legislature, and garrison government and the martial law, justified by the royal prerogative, could not be made clearer.[40]

In defense of local autonomy, statute law, and legislative privilege, Long used "the rights of Englishmen" as his weapon against the executive. Long claimed that no legally admissible evidence existed to prove that he had erased the king's name. He contended that his assembly's interference with the prerogative court of the governor-general was a necessary response to an illegal assault on the liberty of the subject. He insisted that, as a subject, he could constitutionally consult about the new model with his representatives in the assembly, regardless of the governor-general's prohibition.

Long's defense of civil liberty was unyielding; his counter-attack against the prerogative reached republican heights. His erasure of the royal name from the revenue bill, Long asserted, was by order of the assembly. Therefore, the issue was not his lèse majesté but the legislature's right to appropriate the taxes of their constituents to the public's use rather than to the king's. The king's own orders were unlawful, Long insisted, for the new model contravened Englishmen's right to representation, and the planters were Englishmen both by birth and by parliamentary recognition (not, note, because the king had proclaimed them so in 1662). Only lawful commands need be obeyed. Therefore, Long told the king-in-council, neither he nor any other member of the Jamaican opposition had been either seditious when they argued against the new model or criminal because they had dis-obeyed the orders of the king and his governor-general to accept this unlawful constitution. "Such Arguements" as Long's, the horrified Secretary Jenkins exclaimed, were those with which "mutinies and Seditions used to be maintained withall. In a word, he is a man that hath some skill in Law (he was Chief Justice in Jamaica) but seems to have little of good affection to the government."[41]

40. Sloan MS 2724, 211–212; *Cal. S.P. Col., 1677–1680*, nos. 1509, 1512; Add. MSS 12429, 105–106; Edwards, *British Colonies*, I, 307–308; the earl of Carlisle's charge against Col. Long, Rec'd, Sept. 16, 1680, S.P. 44/62, 72. Contrast this argument with Richard S. Dunn's contention that "the big Jamaica sugar planters were anxious to co-operate with Charles II" ("Imperial Pressures on Massachusetts and Jamaica, 1675–1700," in Alison Gilbert Olson and Richard Maxwell Brown, eds., *Anglo-American Political Relations* [New Brunswick, N.J., 1970], 61).

41. Jenkins to Godolphin, Sept. 16, 1680, S.P. 44/62, 72–73. A less assertive version of

The king's ministers were angered by Long's legalisms, offended by his legislative loyalties, and alarmed by his correspondence with the English opponents of the crown. They could not resist either Long or his allies, however, when the crown's chief witness and prosecutor, the earl of Carlisle, was too ill to testify, when the effective spokesman in parliament for the hereditary succession, the earl of Halifax, made two consecutive and widely noted appearances (one at the full privy council and another at its plantations committee) to countenance Long, and when the defendant himself let it be known that he would appeal any royal action against him to the parliament. Secretary Jenkins wryly recorded the results: "My Lords will report tomorrow to the Council . . . that Long and his bail are to be discharged of their Recognizances, this I fear may be some disadvantage to my Lord of Carlisle and matter of great triumph to this man when he returns to the Island."[42]

The "triumph" of the Jamaican champion of representative government depended on the meeting of a parliament hostile to the prerogative. It was the conjuncture of Long's particular case and the parliamentary crisis that impelled the privy councillors to ask whether the king possessed the absolute authority as the conqueror of Jamaica on which the new model was legally based. If not, the councillors sought constitutional precedents to justify an imperial compromise. King Charles, who was personally attending the meetings of what was called "the Jamaica committee," added to it the lord chief justice, Francis North. The king asked North whether by the royal proclamation that Lord Windsor had published in 1662, or otherwise, the king had limited his power to alter utterly and at will the forms of his government in Jamaica. As the debate continued during the fall and winter of 1680 and 1681, other questions went to North: Were the revenue acts of D'Oyley and Littleton still in force? Did the laws of England extend to the island colony? Money for the king and some substitute for English law for the colonists were the elements of the constitutional compromise that the privy council committee at last ordered Chief Justice North to work out with "the Jamaica gentlemen." The Jamaicans then petitioned the king to accept their compromise with North. The king referred this petition to the privy council committee for Jamaica. It then met daily for a full week to refine a constitutional settlement for the colony. At the end of October,

---

this defense appears in *Cal. S.P. Col.*, *1677–1680*, no. 1509. See also *ibid.*, no. 1512, and Add. MSS 12429, 119.

42. Jenkins to Godolphin, Sept. 18, 1680, S.P. 44/62, 76.

the councillors announced that King Charles would again authorize legislation in Jamaica by the governor-general, council, and
assembly. In return, his majesty expected a long-term revenue act.
The taxes it authorized would be collected by the royal receiver
general and issued by the royal governor's warrant. The king
agreed, however, that the assembly might specify the general use
to which the king could put these revenues. He also agreed to
spend the moneys to support his government in Jamaica. To
ensure that both these terms were met, the assembly might audit
the accounts. As a final concession, in return for taxes sufficient to
relieve his English exchequer of all Jamaica costs, the king promised that for whatever term of more than seven years for which the
assembly granted the revenue, he would confirm Lynch's 1675
code of laws, as amended by the privy council. Although the king
still refused to grant the colonists access to the laws of England, he
would confirm an act that established civil courts in the colony
and conferred on them power to administer local laws to protect
planter property, even from English creditors and the Royal African Company. The king would insist that the assembly's militia
act recognize his governor-general's military authority and admiralty jurisdiction, but he would approve a stringent statute against
privateering, the only viceregal abuse of his prerogative that King
Charles recognized as having occurred.[43]

No sooner had he promised these legislative and fiscal con-

43. The course of the inquiry can be followed in *Cal. S.P. Col., 1677–1680*, nos. 1540,
1550–1552, 1559, 1561–1562, 1566–1572, 1612, and Edwards, *British Colonies*, I, 310–316.
The crucial nature of the king's 1662 proclamation by Windsor was ultimately agreed to by
all parties and became a constitutional substitute for a royal charter in Jamaica (*ibid.*, I, 171–
174, 248; Long, *Jamaica*, I, 212, 217–218). The constant parliamentary pressure on the ministers of the crown is apparent throughout the Jamaica debate. Even North was under threat
of an impeachment (voted Nov. 24) for authorizing the king's proclamation against petitions for the meeting of parliament (Kenyon, *Sunderland*, 67; Ogg, *Charles II*, 604; *Commons
Journals*, IX, 662). See North's views on the government of dependencies as illustrated in his
correspondence, in Samuel Weldon Singer, ed., *The Correspondence of Henry Hyde, Earl of
Clarendon, and of his brother Lawrence Hyde, Earl of Rochester* (London, 1828), I, 183–187:
"And it is not unreasonable that a conquered nation should receive laws at the pleasure of
the king alone." North admitted that the dependence of taxation on representation, together
with the factor of distance, set practical limits on the exercise of the conqueror's legislative
authority. North's correspondence points out that the crown's Irish legislation in the 1680s
raised the same dissidence as the royal attempt to impose the Irish constitution on Jamaica.
He suggested the imperial remedies that were applied throughout the empire: the crown
must assert its authority, encourage Englishmen, and establish the Church of England in the
dependency, a church reformed by law, not rebellion, preaching obedience to a king accountable to none but God. Whitson (*Constitutional Development of Jamaica*, 107–108) argues
from the silence of the judges on the question of the crown's power to revoke the Jamaica
constitution that the colony's resistance "succeeded because the law officers could not find
legal support for the policy of the Crown." The influence of the Jamaica lobby in this crisis
again exemplifies Lynch's observation to Lord Cornbury: "I myself have found an interest

cessions (while retaining his legal and military authority) than King Charles's undiminished determination to rule as well as reign in the province was reinforced and unleashed by the defeat of the Exclusion Bill on November 15, 1680. Royal orders had been written to subject all provincial legislatures and garrison governors to increased imperial supervision. The king limited the damage to the prerogative potential in his restoration of provincial legislatures by commanding that all future local laws must be passed without limit of time and sent home within three months of passage for his confirmation or disallowance. While the laws were royally reviewed at home, the viceroy who had approved them in the colony and sent them to the sovereign (or else lost a year's salary) was to stay at his post. Governors-general who left their commands, as Carlisle had, without formal written leave from the king-in-council would be, and henceforward were, dismissed from the government. Governors-general were to reside in their provinces, the commander-in-chief ordered, and protect his prerogative as well as his people.[44]

These restrictions reflected King Charles's displeasure with his general staff in Jamaica. They had failed to carry out his orders to govern solely through the prerogative. Instead, they had abused the prerogative to promote piracy. The king penalized the errant general staff by eliminating his military financing of garrison government in Jamaica. Thus he also exercised the economy necessary to royal government if it was to escape paying the political price that parliament had placed on tax bills. By suspending most of his military expenditures in the province, King Charles also made the Jamaica assembly and their constituents feel the fiscal weight he had carried for their protection and pacification. On the same day that the king restored the Jamaica assembly, he disbanded his two companies of infantry in the island garrison, ended his allowance for Jamaica fortification, and stopped the English military salaries of the colony's general staff. King Charles had reduced his contribution to garrison government in Jamaica to ships, ammunition, and orders.[45]

---

here [in Jamaica] gives me more money and credit in Europe than any Lands of double the value in England" (Add. MSS 11410, 258).

44. Edwards, *British Colonies*, I, 317–319; powers of Nov. 3, 1680, C.O. 138/3, 444–446; instructions, *ibid.*, 448–454. The king also authorized the Jamaica assembly to write a clause into the revenue act denying any salary to nonresident governors (C.O. 138/4, 24).

45. It was expected that the apparatus of garrison government would be maintained in Port Royal, St. Jago, and elsewhere, but that the cost would be transferred wholly to the Jamaica taxpayers, who were to pay the salaries of the captain and lieutenant generals and the captain of Fort Charles, and for all fortification (some of which had been subsidized by

The reduction of the royal military presence and the degradation of the three generals encouraged Long and the Jamaica legislators in England in their intention to secure orders—either from king or parliament—to weaken the royal executive politically as well as to rejuvenate the assembly. Indeed, the island elite intended to make their assembly more powerful than it had been even under Lord Vaughan. One way to do this was to act at court to convict the current provincial general staff for their neglect of planting and their promotion of privateering, both against royal orders. Alternatively, accusations of absolutism against the king's Jamaica generals might produce parliamentary pressure to reduce the general staff's political authority. The king's new alliance with Spain (which condemned privateering) and the parliament's revival of the Exclusion Bill (which attacked absolutism) offered Long and the Jamaicans opportunities on both fronts to malign Governor-General Carlisle and his subordinates. And if the generals could not be impeached, at least they might be replaced by executives more sympathetic to Jamaica's oligarchs.[46]

Testifying to the privy council committee on plantations, Long pictured himself as the leader of the planter party. As such, he claimed, he had been persecuted by the privateer chieftains, Generals Carlisle and Morgan. Long implied that it was because he had "never been an encourager, but rather the contrary of privateering," that he had been arrested by Carlisle. Long noted that his application for a writ of habeas corpus had been denied by Carlisle's appointee as chief justice, Robert Byndloss, chief counsel of the privateer party. His "violent exile" from Jamaica, Long alleged, was punishment for his opposition to piracy, a deliberate act of "terror to His Majesty's subjects in the Island." Long and his supporters said that such actions, encouraged by the absolutism of the new model, were forcing Jamaica's wealthiest merchants and planters to flee to England where they could have the protection of known statute law.

The Jamaica lobby insisted that the king redress their griev-

the king) (Lynch's instructions as captain general and governor-in-chief, Sept. 8, 1681, C.O. 138/4, 38). The recommendation of the lords of the committee for the elimination of the offices of lieutenant general and major general (July 28, 1681, *ibid.*, 3), while approved, did not take permanent effect, although Gens. Morgan and Watson were reduced to councillor status. The orders of the king in council to eliminate the military financing of Jamaica and to restore its legislature's authority, both dated Nov. 3, 1680, are in C.O. 138/3, 441–442, 447–454, and are calendared in *Cal. S.P. Col., 1677–1680*, nos. 1569, 1570.

46. The treaty of July 10, 1680, which was limited to Europe in its operation, is discussed in Feiling, *British Foreign Policy*, 598–599, 602. See also Ogg, *Charles II*, 594, and Kenyon, *Sunderland*, 46.

ances by reinforcing local law against the provincial executive with a promise never again to eliminate the assembly. They also requested again what the king had just denied them—permission to use English law in Jamaica. The Jamaicans also asked the king to allow appeals from the island courts to English judges. They demanded that the king command his governor-general to put down piracy. They asked the king to pare the governor's military power. They requested a royal order to the provincial executive to share his judicial jurisdiction in chancery, church, and admiralty, with the council. The Jamaicans asked King Charles to permit councillors suspended by the governor to seek election to the assembly. And finally, the assemblymen asked to be allowed to formalize their English political connections by levying taxes to support lobbyists in London.[47]

English political change allowed the crown to reject the islanders' impudent assault on its legal, judicial, military, and legislative prerogative. On the eve of parliament's Christmas recess (during which the king began to change the ministry, and after which he announced he would make none of the concessions demanded by the parliament), the lords of the committee rejected the whig substance of every one of the Jamaica lobby's proposals. Jamaicans might appeal substantial cases to England, the king's councillors said, but not to any court other than the king-in-council. The assembly might levy limited funds for an agent, the lords allowed, if the governor-general were informed in advance of any complaint to be made about him by that agent. The privy council would permit no reduction of the governor-general's legal authority, civil or military. On the contrary, it took special care that the new commission to the governor reaffirmed his power to discipline the colonists, by martial law if necessary. The king empowered his viceroy to enlist every Jamaican in the colony's armed forces and even to march or ship them "from one place to another for the resisting and withstanding of all Enemys, Pirates and Rebells both at Land and Sea, and to transport such forces to

47. Blathwayt to Watson, July 6, 1680, to Powell, Dec. 11, 1680, Blathwayt Papers, XXVII, 3, 4, Williamsburg, and Blathwayt to Carlisle, with enclosures, Nov. 29, 1680, C.O. 138/3, 476–479; Petition of Jamaica Planters, rec'd Oct. 28, 1680, Carlisle's answer, Sloan MS 2724, 215–217. Long subsequently changed his story to charge that Carlisle, as chancellor, was guilty of denying him the rights of an Englishman (Add. MSS 12429, 104b). The original complaint is in *Cal. S.P. Col., 1677–1680*, no. 1345 (IV). See also *ibid.*, nos. 1560, 1575, 1588. Morgan concluded that the protests of the Jamaica country party against the governors-general had "risen more from their ambition to be popular than their zeal for his Majesty's service, valuing themselves from the frequent obstruction they often give it. God forgive 'em, I do . . . " (to Jenkins, Apr. 9, 1681, C.O. 138/3, 481).

any of Our Plantations in America . . . to execute Martial Law in time of War or insurrection and to have all power as Captain General." As for the governor-general's council of state and war, the king's commission provided that "no Counsellor suspended shall be capable of public office" of any kind. Any councillor who crossed the garrison governor would be cut off from public life.[48]

Thus the king categorically denied the island elite's demands for increased local autonomy, the rule of law, and the reduction of the prerogative. He demonstrated the political puissance that underlay his imperial authority by dissolving parliament on January 18, 1681. Long and company had lost their campaign against regal authority in Jamaica. Still, they might win a change of viceroys, securing the soldier-planter Sir Thomas Lynch in place of the privateering earl of Carlisle. To link corruption with Carlisle's staff and piracy with his government, Long charged that the governor-general had imposed an illegal test oath on the assembly, ousted judges, fired customs officers, and promoted a mint—all in the interests of the "old trade" of privateering, all in opposition to legitimate commerce and plantation agriculture.[49]

In reply, the governor-general simply asserted that his imposition of the test and his purge of officeholders, judges included, were required to secure Jamaican consent to the new model constitution and to enforce obedience to royal government. He denied that he had supported extortioners; the island courts were open to sue them, he said. Carlisle denied that he had fired the opponents of privateering per se from public office; he had, he explained, dismissed them for quarreling with their superiors. A mere discussion of minting, even of pirate gold, was not actionable, Carlisle contended. He had not encouraged privateers, the governor-general concluded, except to come in and plant in Jamaica, as he had been ordered to do.[50]

The Jamaicans countered with circumstantial, but convincing, depositions in support of each charge. They added that, besides injuring their trade, the earl's practice of passing pirate plunder through the customs as legal goods deprived the king and duke of their shares of what should have been condemned as prize goods. It was odd for Long and company to show concern for royal income, odder still for Carlisle to take a leaf from Long's lawbook

---

48. *Cal. S.P. Col., 1677–1680*, no. 1618, 1622; the lords of the committee (Clarendon, Bath, and Jenkins), report, Dec. 18, 1680, C.O. 138/3, 456–459. The resulting instructions are in C.O. 138/4, 5, 10–11, 34.

49. The charges are in Add. MSS 12429, 106b–107b.

50. Carlisle's reply, *ibid.*, 107b–110.

by attacking the legal competence of the evidence against him. He pointed out that these charges and depositions were allegations, implications, and hearsay statements, uncorroborated, unsigned, and unsworn to. The governor-general pointed out that, at most, the depositions merely proved his words or that someone had used his name, but, he argued, they did not legally prove his personal complicity in privateering.[51]

The Spanish ambassador added to the charges against Carlisle: pirates had used Port Royal as the base for their raid on the Spanish city of Puerto Bello and the Spanish commerce of the South Sea. Carlisle denied any knowledge of the plans of English seamen who passed through his government on their own occasions. Next, the Spanish ambassador charged that the governor-general admitted to the Jamaica customhouse goods stolen from Spanish subjects. Carlisle replied that, so far as he knew, goods entering the island ports were the property of English subjects. He observed (for the benefit of the English privy council) that these goods were exchanged in accordance with England's acts of trade. The offensive fact to Spain, Carlisle concluded, was not the alleged illegality of Jamaican trade, but rather that England had any trade at all in the Americas.[52]

Legally, Governor-General Carlisle's case was as flawless as ex-Chief Justice Long's. The law that protected both of them from crown prosecution, however, saved neither of them from royal displeasure. King Charles denied Long any of the rewards that this enemy of royal government demanded for exposing Carlisle's

51. Depositions, *ibid.*, 111b–124. Blathwayt's statement that Long would bring charges against Carlisle both in privy council and parliament was made to Powell, Dec. 11, 1680, Blathwayt Papers, XXVII, 3, Williamsburg. The charges are not recorded as fully as the text suggests, but Carlisle gave them body by replying more to their intent and to their implications than to the bare accusations. The accuracy of his reading is confirmed by the depositions of the Jamaicans and the assessments of the chief of the colonial bureaucracy, William Blathwayt. The charge (of nonpayment) is in Add. MSS 12429, 116b, 124, to which Carlisle's legalistic reply appears in Sloan MS 2724, 215a–217. See also Littleton to Hatton, Sept. 14, 1680, Add. MSS 29577, 287, and Add. MSS 12429, 122.

52. Carlisle's replies are in Add. MSS 12429, 107b–110; Sloan MS 2724, 215–217. Morgan, exclaiming "how by a malicious confederacy his Excellency the Earl of Carlisle and my self have unduly been exposed and falsely scandalized in the matter of countenancing Pirates and privateers," innocently inquired whether the king's government had extirpated highway robbers in England (Morgan to Jenkins, Apr. 9, 1681, C.O. 138/3, 480–481). Carlisle had taken care to get his councillor's testimony ("signed at the Council Board in my presence, 21 May 1680") that the lack of force and plain law to regulate the privateers combined with Spanish provocations to limit the governor-general's actions. See the council of Jamaica to the lords of the committee, May 20, 1680 (read Sept. 10, 1680), *ibid.*, 407–409. Carlisle's response to the charges of the Spanish ambassador was read to the lords of the committee, Sept. 21, 1680, C.O. 138/3, 431–433. See also *Cal. S.P. Col., 1677–1680*, nos. 1497, 1498, 1516, 1517.

dealings with the privateers. He even refused to issue the protection Long asked for against the revenge of "the privateer faction" in Jamaica. Nonetheless, the king was offended by his governor-general's abuse of the royal prerogative to protect the privateers. The earl of Carlisle had publicly disobeyed his king's command to suppress privateering. As the crown's colonial secretary, William Blathwayt, summed up the royal reaction, "Colonel Long and several other Planters of Jamaica have presented a Complaint to the Council against my Lord of Carlisle, chiefly for having encouraged the Privateers and the circumstances have been so made out that although his Lordship is not charged with it by the King yet [it] is likely that neither his Lordship nor Sir H. Morgan [the lieutenant governor-general] will be long continued in the government."[53]

Blathwayt's estimate, made at the end of January 1681, was a little premature, for during the spring the political climate changed. It was growing weather for the prerogative. King Charles dismissed the Oxford Parliament, and "the recalcitrant Opposition were dispersed in all directions as if a gust of wind had suddenly scattered all the leaves from a tree." Captain Samuel Long and his colleagues were blown back to Jamaica, downcast at their failure to reduce the prerogative of Jamaican governors-general but delighted at their restoration of even a limited legislative authority for the island assembly. The Jamaicans were happy to accept limited concessions because the crown's campaign against corporate political privilege was accelerating again, first in English jurisdictions and then in the overseas provinces of the empire, as the likelihood lessened that King Charles would ever recall privilege's protector, the parliament. The country party in Jamaica were correspondingly "careful of exposing themselves to another voyage" to face the king and council. Excessive opposition might risk what local legislative authority they had managed to recover. Jamaicans would accept the compromise offered by the crown: they would give a royal revenue; they would get a local law code.[54]

53. *Cal. S.P. Col., 1681–1685*, nos. 11–12; Blathwayt to Stapleton, Jan. 25, 1681, Blathwayt Papers, XXXVII, 3, Williamsburg.

54. Blathwayt to Stapleton, Apr. 3, 1681, Blathwayt Papers, XXXVII, 3, Williamsburg; *Cal. S.P. Col., 1681–1685*, nos. 100, 118; Ogg, *Charles II*, 614, 616, 619; Kenyon, *Sunderland*, 75; Haley, *Shaftesbury*. In light of his catalog of every other possible setback to the prerogative, it is notable that historian Edward Long did not record any result of his ancestor's attack on Carlisle (*Jamaica*, I, 202) and admits (219–220) that no guarantee of rule by law was given Jamaica until 1728, when permanent laws were confirmed by the crown

Meanwhile, the king was prevented from acting on his resentment against Carlisle for "having Encouraged the Privateers" by the earl's parliamentary service to the prerogative: Carlisle not only protected that archroyalist, the duke of Ormond, the lord lieutenant and governor-general of Ireland, from an impeachment based on Shaftesbury's allegations of an "Irish Plot," he even engineered a counteraccusation against Shaftesbury himself. After the dissolution of parliament, royal fear of civil war demanded that the earl be dispatched to his garrison at Carlisle to repair its fortifications, restock its magazine from the Berwick depot, and use its garrison (and the militia under the earl's command as lieutenant general) to police the Border and put down "seditious and dangerous people." The king had to be considerate of this politically and militarily powerful governor-general.[55]

The crown resolved its dilemma—how to keep Carlisle's goodwill in England and yet transfer his authority in Jamaica to another officer—by a polite letter to the aging, ailing earl. At the end of June 1681, Secretary Jenkins wrote that the king had concluded, after a cabinet discussion of Jamaica, "that He finds the presence of a Governour upon the place to be necessary for His Service, and therefore would be glad that your health would permit you to return, as soon as His Majesty's Service requires it, to that place . . . and desires to know from your Lordship what disposition you find yourself to be, as to the undertaking that voyage."[56]

The earl's ill health alone may have dictated the answer. It appeared in the decision of the privy council on July 5, 1681, that if Sir Thomas Lynch did not demand the military pay of his rank, he was to be commissioned captain general and governor-in-chief of Jamaica. Thus it was that the crown replaced one Cromwellian army officer turned royal governor-general with another in the command of Cromwell's conquest, Jamaica. Once again, Governor-General Lynch sailed to the island colony to repress one half of the island's military heritage, privateering, and encourage instead the other half, plantations centered on the conquering army's quarters. Sir Thomas Lynch's qualifying experiences and

in return for a permanent revenue granted to it. See also Edwards, *British Colonies*, I, 180-181.

55. Sloan MS 2724, 96, 98, 113, 141; HMC, *Le Fleming*, 192; *Cal. S.P. Dom., 1680*, 139. Carlisle's continued power in England and patronage in Jamaica is indicated in *Cal. S.P. Col., 1681–1685*, no. 125.

56. *Cal. S.P. Col., 1681–1685*, no. 125; Jenkins to Carlisle, June 24, 1681, S.P. 44/62, 186. Carlisle was now 52 years old and would die Feb. 24, 1685 (*DNB*, s.v. "Howard, Charles").

his institutional tools were those of garrison government. Garrison government was the executive arm of the imperial system. Garrison government, in the empire at large as well as in England and in Jamaica, was the paramilitary political creation of English civil strife. It was revived during the Restoration to provide political discipline and to support social stability. It was applied both to the British kingdoms and to the royal provinces overseas. As the international struggle for empire intensified after 1676, garrison government was made more functional in the next quarter-century than it had been at any time since the civil wars.[57]

57. *Cal. S.P. Col., 1681–1685*, no. 161. Narcissus Luttrell, *A Brief Historical Relation of State Affairs from September 1678 to April 1714*, I (Oxford, 1857), 77, noticed the recall of Morgan and his replacement by Lynch, as well as Carlisle's recall, under the date Apr. 25, 1681, and said that Charles II's bastard, the duke of Grafton (Arlington's son-in-law), would succeed Carlisle. Blathwayt did not announce the actual change (to Sir John Werden, requesting York's secretary to ask the duke to grant a vice admiral's commission to Lynch) until July 15, 1681, C.O. 138/3, 484. Lynch's commission and instructions, Aug. 6, Sept. 8, 1681, were identical to Carlisle's except for an additional power (the nomination of councillors) and a renewed authority (to call assemblies and to legislate by governor, council, and assembly). See C.O. 138/4, 1–15, 17–39.

From Conquest to Constitution: Garrison Government in Jamaica, 1655–1681

After the conquest of Jamaica in 1655, English statesmen saw that it would soon be "an affair of state to balance power in the West Indies as it is now amongst Princes in Christendom." By conquering the American colony of a European rival, England had fully entered the imperial scene. Henceforward, its colonies on four continents would be subject to the European power balance.

For the next century, even England's settlements in the Americas lacked social self-sufficiency, economic independence, and military capability. They clung to English identity and culture. They accepted English rules and rulers, military and civil. They paid psychological tribute to English government, English strength, and English social values. And they were exploited by the English economy. This imperial connection both defined colonial dependence and strengthened the English executive, for it employed the state's military officers, stimulated its bureaucratic development, and elevated its political aspirations. The executive had to recognize and to respond to the social tensions inherent in the empire's physical expansion and economic growth by its repeated choices between the needs of peasant proprietors and those of planter oligarchs, between the spatial greed of power-hungry soldiers and sailors and the monetary motives of garnering merchant-capitalists. The militarist program created an empire of new provinces, enhanced prestige, and unpaid bills. The mercantilist strivings generated the customs revenue that fueled the growth of the state, but the pacifism abroad and individualism at home of men made rich by overseas trade challenged imperial autarchy and executive authority. From the moment that Oliver Cromwell ordered a military expedition to the West Indies and that Povey and Noell undertook its material supply, imperialist-mercantilist rivalries focused on Jamaica.

As the embodiment of the English executive and the conqueror of Jamaica, Oliver Cromwell defined the island province's commanding place in England's empire: the American base of English aggression against Spain's possessions (despite mercantile desires for peaceful commerce) would be a military "plantation" (systematically opposed to oligarchical social norms). Jamaica exemplified imperial values for all of English America, because its own institutions and ideas were offshoots of the Cromwellian dictatorship in England, of its military governments of Ireland and Scotland, and even of the Protector's favorite bits of England overseas, the puritan colonies conquered from the natives in North America.

English veterans all, General Edward Massey's officers from the garrison government of Gloucester were distinguished in Jamaica by their allied attentions to military plantation and garrison self-sufficiency. They sought a socially regulated, godly society. Collectively, they composed a councilliar check on powerful commanders-in-chief, whether provincial garrison governors or the Protector himself. Menaces to the dictatorship of Oliver Cromwell at home, these "presbyterian" officers were nonetheless apt agents of England's empire overseas.

Such an officer was General Robert Venables. He brought to Jamaica "plantation" methods and military priorities from the conquest and colonization of Ireland. On Anglo-Irish models, Venables's garrison began a citadel, a seaport, and settlements. To these elements of plantation, Major General Robert Sedgewick added English reinforcements for the Caribbean war with Spain and his own American experience of imperial conquest and provincial development. As Massachusetts's major general, Sedgewick had begun England's attack on Dutch New Netherlands and French Acadia. As Jamaica's commander, he inaugurated the economic exchanges between New England and Jamaica that underlay the prosperity of the older colonies and provided for the survival of the new province. Acting on his New England experience, Sedgewick laid the bait of liberty and property to lure emigrants from both Britain and America to Jamaica.

Sedgewick's plan to stimulate migration by an offer of English liberty and free land to newcomers was also that proposed for Jamaica by the Cromwellian military governors of Scotland. One of them, Colonel William Brayne, succeeded Sedgewick in command of Jamaica. Brayne had served in the conquest of Scotland with another former New England officer, George Fenwick. There they helped to implement a prerogative-oriented political system and military-agrarian social priorities. For all their differences of scale, the conceptual and the physical similarities of the citadel societies that Brayne and Fenwick commanded—Saybrook in Connecticut and Berwick in England; Leith, Edinburgh, or Inverlochy in Scotland; Cagway in Jamaica—bespoke the unities of garrison government throughout England's empire.

The military merits of Brayne's battalion brought garrison government to Jamaica, provided disciplined guards for the expanding settlements and raised martial morale in the dispirited old army. To fence, root, and cultivate garrison government, however, was the work of the province's first governor-general, Edward D'Oyley. Like his predecessors, D'Oyley recorded imperial identities. The Spanish guerrillas he defeated were "like your tories in Ireland or moss troopers in Scotland": both were the resistance movements of imperial England's victims. Likewise D'Oyley replicated British imperial institutions in America: he made military plantation on the Irish model the development plan for Jamaica, England's "principal fort and Settlement in the West Indies." The society D'Oyley shaped to such punitive and plantation patterns became the American exemplar of imperialism: a source of soldier-planter population (and political sedition) for Virginia; a spring of garrison government ideas (and tropical imports) for New York; a training ground of officer-administrators (and a trove of pirate plunder) for England itself.

At the basis of Jamaican society lay the six original regimental quarters or plantations. These centers of subsequent settlement were worked by privates turned farmers, policed by provost marshals, protected by cavalry patrols and by privateers' ships, and commanded by the regimental field officers. These planter-colonels composed the council of war, which advised the governor-general. Despite these officers' ambition, avarice, and autarchy and the army's councilliar tradition, Governor-General D'Oyley's government was distinguished by his devotion to the economic interests of the private peasant proprietors and by his military discipline of Jamaica's grandees, the officer-planters. He drove both planters and peasants to cultivate the land. He maintained control over both, and defended the colony, by reorganizing the army as a militia and in garrisons. Finally, D'Oyley's guidance of this Cromwellian community assured its physical survival in Jamaica and promoted its political acceptance by the restored royal regime in England. Thus D'Oyley preserved in America a working garrison government as a source of imperial precedents, social, economic, political, and, over all, military.

D'Oyley's administration demonstrated the martial essence of English imperialism. His defeat of the surviving Spanish soldiers and settlers at Ocho Rios concluded the conquest of the colony. His defense of the English conquest from Spanish invasion at the Rio Nuevo was the first of many Jamaican rebuffs to England's European rivals for American empire. Such territorial combats were the elements of imperial wars. They contrasted with the traditional form of English military intervention in America, raids on commercial shipping. Following England's aggression in Jamaica, however, amphibious operations came to characterize the European struggle for American possessions. Subsequent English invasions of Curaçao and New Netherlands incited Dutch retaliation against Virginia and New York. French assaults on New England and Jamaica were answered by the English on the St. Lawrence and in the Leeward Islands. Like the exchanges with Spain, these repeated hostilities were the inevitable result of England's physical expansion into areas actually occupied, not merely claimed, by European powers.

The outcome of such imperial actions was determined as much by popular morale as by material factors. This was apparent both in the willingness of D'Oyley's men to fight off the Spanish and in the English elation at the colonists' victory. Psychological victories as well as physical triumphs were the prerequisites of plantation expansion and population growth. The sequence of military victory and settlement extension, as D'Oyley demonstrated, cleared the way for the physical growth and, finally, the political pruning of a stable provincial society. Territorial conquest and military discipline also implied the forcible dispossession of Spanish settlers and the arbitrary execution of English dissidents. Such were the physical manifestations, constructive and destructive, of imperial expansion and garrison government.

Fighting and hanging were also part of the reflexive response of garrison governments, overseas as at home, to the turbulent transitions of the English executive. Jamaican reactions to the fall of the Protectorate, the rump's relapse, the short-lived army councils and committees of safety, and, finally, to the restoration of the monarchy were early examples of compulsive provincial adaptation to metropolitan political change. Such reaction remained the rule of Anglo-American politics until the American Revolution.

In the crisis of 1660, what afterward developed into the prevalent pattern of English imperial governance in America was defined in Jamaica. The restored royal regime confirmed Cromwell's paramilitary administration of the conquered colony. Jamaica's distance, frontier status, and lack of traditional society, and its obvious and utter dependence on continued military plantation and administration, together commanded a readier royal approval of the Cromwellian system of provincial control than did similar examples in England. As with administrators, so with agencies: just as it was unable to dispense with the leadership exemplified by Governor-General D'Oyley in Jamaica, so the English executive recognized by royal commission the martial absolutism that D'Oyley had made the norm of the overseas executive. To D'Oyley's adaptation of Cromwellian military government and settlement, the Jamaica committee of the privy council added all of the moral, social, political, and economic prerogatives that the crown claimed in England and would exercise in the dominions.

Well-wishers to the prerogative as well as its enemies, courtiers and militant imperialists as well as commonwealthmen and pacifist mercantilists, sat on the Jamaica committee of the privy council. It oversaw the replacement of a highly professional officer, Edward D'Oyley, as governor-general of Jamaica by an especially calculating courtier, Lord Windsor. Commonwealthmen such as Cooper and Povey provided for an elected provincial legislature and statute law in Windsor's instructions, but the realization of such privileges in the colony was long delayed. Jamaica was a society of soldiers and commands, not civilians and laws. Not until 1728 was the debate concluded that stemmed from the libertarian aspects of Windsor's orders. During Windsor's own administration all questions about the scope of the English executive's absolutism were repressed by his exploitation of his military colonists, mostly to raid Spanish towns, but also to man a palace guard and urban police force.

Windsor's deputy, Sir Charles Littleton, added "popularity" to prerogative power: he allowed the planters as much legislative representation and as many civil courts as were permitted them by the crown. Such recognition of consultative and judicial roles for the officer class diversified, but did not diminish, military influence in the colony. Jamaica, as it "had been hitherto," was still "governed in a Military Way, and barely had the face of a Civil Power." "The face of a Civil Power" did offer the provincial ruling class mechanisms of political self-expression and local authority. The Jamaica planter elite, and their English oligarchical allies, agreed that their economic class should exercise substantial provincial authority, regardless of the more-than-royal prerogatives of the governor-general. The assembly was recognized in the island and at home as the agency of elite authority.

Assembly assertiveness and local legal privilege, especially when leavened with old army republicanism, were inadmissable to the author of the royal restoration, England's premier militarist and imperialist. That grandee on a great scale, General George Monck, the duke of Albemarle, Charles II's captain general, patronized Sir Thomas Modyford as one who would emulate him in Jamaica. Like his patron, Modyford employed military authority to widen executive influence and so to stabilize the turbulent society of the young colony. Like Monck also, Modyford raised his own family's stature by making them the agents of the imperial state's armed sovereignty. Asserting paramilitary executive power in Jamaica, Governor-General Modyford locked up Speaker Long, dissolved the assembly, packed the council and the courts with his sons, kinsmen, and cronies, and suspended the civil law. He mounted a life guard and promoted privateering. As captain general and vice admiral, he ruled by martial law, citing Roman proconsular precedents. So long as he held power, Sir Thomas Modyford praised, but did not permit, parliamentary privileges for the provincial assembly. He boasted of the islanders' rights as Englishmen even as he violated them.

Without metropolitan English assistance, no faction of local "country" leaders could resist the governor-general's absolute authority, much less end his administration. But the political opponents of Sir Thomas Modyford's military and familial rule were protected by that enemy of Albemarle and of imperialism, the earl of Arlington. This friend of Spain and of mercantilism ultimately ousted Modyford and replaced the chief of the privateer party and everlasting enemy of Spain with Colonel Thomas Lynch, an agent of the plantation party and an enemy of privateering. Modyford thereupon converted to liberalism. Thus he returned to Jamaican public life under the unlikely auspices of Lynch's successor, Lord Vaughan, a creature of Shaftesbury and a parliamentarian and mercantilist. Modyford's marvelous costume changes all had one meaning: in Jamaica, as elsewhere in the empire, English politics and personalities determined the careers of American governors-general.

The case was also reversed. There were implications for England itself in provincial garrison governments. For example, every imperial trait of Modyford's regime offended an element of mercantile opinion. Military government, territorial ambition, raids and privateering, all produced plunder with which to capitalize provincial development and promote intercolonial trade independent of metropolitan merchant-capitalists. The mercantilists stressed civilian administration on behalf of London's trader-investors. They called for the restraint of imperial aggression in the interest of European commercial exchange. The death of Albemarle and the rise of Arlington placed ministerial weight on the side of mercantilism. At precisely that moment, the imperial imperatives built into Jamaica's garrison government, including its hostile relationship to Spanish America, produced the Panama expedition. This recapitulation of Elizabethan and Cromwellian anti-Spanish traditions forecast England's eighteenth-century imperial expansion in America.

The Panama expedition epitomized garrison government's aggressive imperial character. The arrest of the governor-general responsible for that expedition demonstrated garrison government's coercive domestic side. Colonel Lynch seized command of Jamaica when he mastered the Port Royal Regiment and so subjected the island colony's port city and citadel to his authority. His influence with the plantation militias conferred control of the countryside on Lynch. His naval convoy cowed the privateers. The new military executive's arrest and deportation of "the late General" and the overthrow of his regime depended upon such authoritarian techniques as censorship, passport control, martial law, political proscription, and finally, judicial murder.

Although Colonel Lynch's military coup negated all the legal "rights of Englishmen," his subsequent administration gave more scope to the rule of local law, and so more responsibility to the local legislature, than had those of all his predecessors put together. The resulting union of military tradition and legislative development was symbolized when Lynch's assembly enacted "Conquest Day" as a holiday, and when the acts, drafted by this military executive and his oligarchical assembly and ultimately approved by the king-in-council, became Jamaica's fundamental laws. This method of legislation became one of the major mechanisms of the imperial constitution: the overseas provinces were linked to the imperial executive both by royal commands obeyed in the colonies and by the crown's review and acceptance of provincial legislation. Orders and laws alike, however, were mediated between metropolis and province, between court and country, by the imperial executive personified in the governor-general: "young colonies are made or ruined by their Governors."

The governor-generals' compromises between authority and autonomy, and the competition of the provincial legislatures with the imperial executive, both reflected English political divisions. These divisions also prevented either imperialists or mercantilists from freely imposing their principles on the provinces, although the duration of monarchy as contrasted with the periodicity of parliament worked in favor of the imperialists, the party of executive authority. Given executive endurance amidst the distractions of English public life, the predominant provincial political figure remained the governor-general. Changing governors-general changed the provincial government. Colonel Lynch's recall and Lord Vaughan's arrival made this fact only too apparent in Jamaica. Vaughan's personal weakness, as much as his parliamentary principles, made him an appropriate agent of Shaftesbury's anti-monarchical instructions. What English parliamentarians signaled via Vaughan, their provincial correspondents enacted: veteran republicans led the Jamaica assembly to extreme positions of local autonomy, legislative authority, and the rule of statute law. Their language drew on the revolution of 1641. It was not exceeded in the revolution of 1776.

Such republican, localist, libertarian, civilian terms were antithetical to a cosmopolitan, coercive, military empire. Indeed, the "first British empire" had been born out of the Cromwellian reaction to the social disorder that followed 1641 and to the republican inability to check that chaos. This empire was killed by the republican revival called the American Revolution. The existence of empire in the intervening century and a quarter was posited on the prevalence of executive authority, an authority based on force as much as on law, on compulsion as well as on consent. It was monarchical far more than it was parliamentary. Thus the reaction of the imperial crown against republicanism in Shaftesbury's English parliament or in Vaughan's Jamaican assemblies—a republicanism that made legislative control of the armed forces of the state its first demand—was to reduce legislative power, pack the law courts, and arrest the leading enemies of the executive. "Force governs law."

Jamaicans feared that "for the future, they might be forc'd to live under such [laws] only as the King's Royal Pleasure should appoint them." Local law was negated and military force rein-stated in its place by the earl of Carlisle's orders as captain general and governor-in-chief of Jamaica. Carlisle arrived, together with alarms of war with France, in a convoy carrying two companies of regular infantry and munitions for the garrison. He was accom-panied by a military staff paid on the English army establishment, and he appointed these army officers as civil magistrates in Jamaica (a widespread garrison government practice). All these military resources had a political purpose: to quell resistance to the applica-tion to Jamaica of Poynings's Law—"the Constitution of Ireland."

The executive's monopoly of force did dampen assembly de-bate about its loss of initiative under Poynings's Law. Carlisle's garrison prevented any such outbreaks of country wrath at the "new model" as the plant cutting in Virginia. The governor-general discovered, however, that the passive obedience he de-manded could not be usefully distinguished from the passive disobedience he received. The unanimous opposition of the pro-vincial governing class to the political absolutism proposed by the new model forced Carlisle to govern by the unaided military prerogative. He knew from his service as a Cromwellian military administrator in Scotland and England that military government could not be long sustained without the fiscal, administrative, and social support of a critical mass of the local elite. The governor-general also realized that the crown's attack on provincial au-tonomy was as much a check on his own independence as it was on that of the assembly. Jamaica's circumstances of distance from England, rapid growth, and novel environment all rendered direct, absolute, and ill-informed government from the metropolis offen-sive to Carlisle's administrative common sense. Such government also offended the social sensibilities of a grandee of Carlisle's stature, an economic individualist, a social conservative, "a Man of Property and . . . Posterity." Himself opposed to the Irish new model, Carlisle nonetheless prescribed colonial obedience to it as a matter of political principle. And, pragmatically, due obedience would be the best backing for petitions to King Charles about his plan's impracticality, Carlisle contended. The governor-general himself sent such a petition to his commander-in-chief, seeking to recover the large measure of autonomy traditional in provincial garrison governments. Like Gloucester in the civil war, Jamaica during the Restoration had been "a branch almost divided from the main stock," and Carlisle echoed his predecessors' point that provincial "distance from the fountaine of power had derived upon the Trustee a more free command, and made way for the perfect work of a souldier both in councel and action, which is the way to make such commands both active and prosperous."

Carlisle continued Jamaica's garrison government in a predominantly prerogative mode, but with occasional legislative assemblies, while he awaited the result of his request that the commander-in-chief restore the provincial political structure. The governor-general's tactics were copied by the island assemblymen. They accepted the governor-general's martial administration, but they also asked members of the English parliament to legislate restoration of the provincial legislature's authority. Stalemate ensued, as much because of the rivalry of crown and parliament for imperial influence as because of their disagreement over the respective power of provincial proconsuls and legislatures. Officers of the crown resented that the Jamaica lobby, rather than "petitioning the king to restore them to their former method of Government as they had fair opportunity of doing," on the contrary "applied themselves to the Parliament." The partisans of parliament insisted that military command was a function of aristocracy and that public finance also should be controlled by representatives of the ruling class. They feared (with good reason) that what the crown could do in Jamaica it might attempt in England.

The king and council claimed for their colonial counterparts an exclusive military prerogative unbound by law, and tax revenues without the restrictions of legislative appropriation. The court reiterated its prerogative position by extending Poynings's Law from Ireland and Jamaica to Virginia. The crown began to coordinate its garrison governments overseas by systematic collection of imperial information, and royal officers gave centralized control a rationale by raising alarms of war with France. But the country party countered each of these imperial initiatives. They tried to have Jamaicans' provincial "rights as they call them settled by Act of Parliament." They planned a provincial tax strike. They lent ideological meaning to these and other measures of resistance to imperial authority by concocting a transatlantic propaganda campaign, the Popish Plot.

Directed from England, the Jamaica assemblymen broadcast the Popish Plot and passed secret resolutions that reaffirmed provincial fiscal authority. The governor-general responded by using a passing French fleet as the occasion to declare martial law and reorganize Jamaica's militia—and in the process disciplined most of the assemblymen. Like their English superiors and advisers, both the provincial party of authority and that of autonomy had moved to extremes. The governor-general's martial law covered his seizure of private property. His acts as vice admiral led to a renewal of privateers' plundering abroad and their debauchery in Port Royal. Speaker Samuel Long led the assembly to opposite excesses. It composed crippling legal limits on the governor-general's military and admiralty authority and repeated its refusals to support the government with taxation. Carlisle counterattacked by first insulting the assemblymen and then dissolving the assembly itself. He put a political test oath to each of the ex-members and ousted from every "Office either Military or Civil" all those who would not promise to obey the king's commands unconditionally. This partisan purge consolidated the control of public office by the governor-general's military subordinates and political allies, and in garrison government these were almost identical groups. Indeed the purge created a court party. Viceregal politicians more skillful than Carlisle (such as Culpeper of Virginia) built such parties at the beginning of their administrations. Not having used the legislative prerogatives of his post to take control of the assembly at the outset, however, Governor-General Carlisle had perforce relied on his military authority to destroy the legislature. Now he also deployed the imperial legal prerogative: he reimposed martial law, announced his own control of local legislation, and reported that the crown had denied English law to the colony. The colony's country partisans correctly concluded "that we are to be Govern'd as an Army."

The loss of the local legislature and the civil law, the assertion of armed executive authority, meant military dictatorship, immediately in English provinces overseas potentially in the kingdom itself. Empire-wide issues of taxation, representation, and law, of requisition authority, and empire, all were apparent in the Jamaica case. In 1680 it was transferred to the metropolis for a final decision. To secure a settlement of the imperial constitution, the Jamaica assembly had accelerated its approach to parliament. The island executive then arrested the assembly's leader and sent him home to be tried for treason before the king-in-council. Other prominent assemblymen were dispatched as unwilling witnesses. The governor-general himself came to England as prosecutor. The ensuing parliamentary debate and privy council deliberations produced the constitution of the "old empire." This was the Anglo-American outcome of the Exclusion Crisis.

From November 1680 until July 1681, two cycles of legislative-legal assertion and executive-absolutist reaction ordered the process of constitution-making. The first cycle began when Governor-General Carlisle's charges of treason against Speaker Long were lost. Carlisle was too ill to prosecute them effectively. Then the earl of Halifax brought the weight of moderate parliamentary opinion to bear on Long's behalf. The crown required the support of that opinion to prevent passage of an act excluding the duke of York from the throne. Pressed by essential parliamentary allies, King Charles agreed to compromise the crown's claims overseas. He would restore the provincial assembly's legislative initiative in return for a long-term local revenue to be disposed of by his governor-general. He would approve permanent provincial laws and permit their application by locally constituted courts, if the assembly admitted the military prerogative of the king's governor-general to be without limit (save for privateering, which King Charles wanted quashed).

The defeat of the Exclusion Bill unleashed the first phase of the royal reaction in Anglo-American politics. To ensure that the legislation he allowed the assembly to write did not encroach on his prerogative, King Charles ordered his governor-general to send all bills to him in council for review and, if necessary, amendment or veto. To ensure that in this as in other matters the viceroy did his duty to king and colony, King Charles ordered his representative to reside constantly in his government. To reduce the cost of this closer supervision, that is, to remove what had been a subsidy to ungrateful provincials and undutiful generals, King Charles disbanded his garrison companies. It seemed that he might recall Carlisle as well. Grandees, like courtiers, had proved to be governors-general more expensive than compliant.

Emboldened both by the king's legislative concession and his criticism of the governor-general, Speaker Long and the Jamaica lobby began the second cycle of constitutional discussion. After a particular criticism of Carlisle's connivance with the privateers, Long launched a general attack on the royal governor-general's prerogative powers, judicial and legislative as well as military. Long sought in 1681 what whigs thereafter aspired to at fifteen-year intervals, the Shaftesbury program of 1674: oligarchical, commercial, self-governing, colonial.

King Charles rejected these whig demands as soon as he had decided to dissolve the Exclusion Parliament. The king then concluded the imperial constitutional settlement by issuing to the governor-general of Jamaica a new commission and instructions.

Its terms were afterward repeated for each royal colony. Essentially, the king refused to reduce his representative's prerogatives. That there would be no royal reconsideration was assured by the king's dissolution of the Oxford Parliament and by the widespread understanding that he intended it to have no successor. Without a parliamentary forum, the whigs' imperial influence was decisively diminished.

The crown's unchallenged control of the nation's provinces meant that the king's commission of 1681 to Sir Thomas Lynch, as captain general and governor-in-chief of Jamaica, did more than promote a former Cromwellian army officer and an experienced American executive. It declared the island's political future, and the empire's. It was fortunate, therefore, that the king's commission to Lynch embodied that veteran's wise observation that neither the libertarian and legislative chaos of the Shaftesbury-Vaughan period nor the military and executive tyranny of the York-Danby-Carlisle era were practical or proper ways to govern provinces of England's empire. Instead, King Charles's commission to Colonel Lynch fairly summarized the political lessons learned in a quarter-century of English administration of Jamaica. The king's commission largely subjected this Cromwellian conquest turned royal dominion to the orders of a military executive, but it also admitted that the laws of the local legislature had a regular role in provincial government overseas. The whip hand in Jamaican government remained the governor-general's, but garrison government now formally permitted what it never long denied in practice: local leaders' share in provincial administration, legislation, and adjudication. So balanced between executive and elite personnel, military and civil forms, the Jamaica model became the norm for royal colonies. Sir Thomas Lynch's orders embodied the imperial constitution of 1681.

This constitution did not authorize or anticipate "self-government." It was designed, as Lynch wrote of Jamaica, to ensure that "the King's power and authority is so well established here that the least of his servants . . . will be revered and His Majesty's Commands readily obeyed." Given English motives for empire, many of these commands would be politically authoritarian and economically exploitative. After James II's absolutist aberrations, however, and because of the military coup against him, which spread across the empire in 1688 and 1689, the settlement of 1681 was restored as the institutional framework of provincial order and imperial defense. Created out of Tudor traditions by the reaction against the chaos of England's civil wars, expanded by the English executive's experience in the Cromwellian conquest of the British Isles and by the needs of England's overseas plantations for protection and direction, garrison government, as described in the royal commissions of 1681, became the institutional structure of the first English empire.

PART III   Coercion and Constitution:
The Old Dominion and the
Definition of English Empire
in North America, 1676–1683

Jacobus Secundus Dei Gratia Anglia, Scotia, Francia, et Hibernia, Rex, &c.

James II. Nicholas de Largillierre's portrait of the king, engraved in mezzotint by John Smith, is from the collection of the author. See John Challoner Smith, *British Mezzotinto Portraits*, III (London, 1880), 1185.

CHAPTER 7

The Imposition of Royal Government on Virginia, 1676–1678

Rebellion and Reaction

On April Fool's Day, 1676, the governor of Virginia, Sir William Berkeley, assured his English superiors that his forces could check ten times the number of Indians then raiding Virginia's frontiers. Yet he admitted that these Indians had recently killed thirty-six settlers on the Rappahannock River frontier. Sir William casually added that within the colony there had recently been two "mutinies" against his government's high taxes. Both the lack of defense and the high cost of government reflected Berkeley's senility and his councillors' dishonesty. Within the month the discredited Berkelean system collapsed into civil war.[1]

The roots of conflict—social and physical insecurity—had been manifest in Virginia under Sir William Berkeley for nearly thirty years before they erupted in Bacon's rebellion. The Berkelean monopoly of Indian trade seemed to blind the government to the native menace and the farmers' fears. Military insecurity, by sea as well as by land, characterized a corrupt, oppressive, hated provincial government. So respectable a figure as Colonel Henry Norwood had reported these Berkelean inadequacies and abuses to the crown as early as 1667. The whitewashing skill of Thomas Ludwell, secretary of Virginia, and the court influence of the Berkeley family had conspired with the crown's obsession with domestic security to block royal reform of Virginia's administration. Over the subsequent decade, however, the royal search for security recast the paramilitary machinery of garrison government that finally ousted Berkeley and imposed imperial authority on the Old Dominion.[2]

1. Berkeley to [Sir Joseph Williamson], and to [Thomas] Ludwell, *Cal. S.P. Col., 1675–1676, Addenda, 1574–1674,* nos 858, 859 See also *ibid.,* 906, 909, 962, 1019, C.O. 5/1355, 269, P.R.O.

2. For a thoroughgoing anticipation, in the years 1644 to 1647, of the issues of Virginia society and politics in the Restoration years of the Berkeley regime, see William Waller Hen-

By the time Virginia revolted in April 1676, another English institutional development besides the revitalization of garrison government also promoted imperialism. An executive committee of the privy council for plantations had surplanted the mercantilist council of foreign plantations. Two significant events marked the replacement of Shaftesbury's council by that of the crown. The first was a renewed attack on Massachusetts's chartered independence. The second was the substitution, in the government of Jamaica, of the earl of Carlisle and an autocratic commission for Lord Vaughan and his parliamentary proclivities. In the third great American province, the king's privy councillors suspected that Virginia's governor, Sir William Berkeley, was no champion of crown control. He had not answered English questionnaires. The royal advisers also saw evidence of Berkeley's executive incapacity in the resistance of growing numbers of Virginians to Berkeley's clique of irresponsible officeholders. The few recent English royal appointees in Virginia reported that this resistance was justified. Thus the king's councillors were warned of Berkeley's autonomy and provincialism, as well as of his misgovernment. Their increasing suspicions received sudden, sad confirmation in the news of Bacon's rebellion.[3]

Berkeley's superiors thought that his independence of their orders and advice underlay the rebellion. As one of them explained, "For more than ten years altogether there has not been from some places any communication between His [Majesty's] Governors and His Ministers," which "has lately produced a Rebellion and other unhappy effects." "The uproars of Virginia have been so Stupendious," Secretary of State Sir Henry Coventry

ing, ed., *The Statutes at Large; Being a Collection of All the Laws of Virginia, from the First Session of the Legislature, in the Year 1619*, 13 vols. (Richmond, New York, and Philadelphia, 1809–1823), I, 235*ff.* Norwood's protest is discussed in chapter 3 above.

3. The plantations committee to Berkeley, Apr. 14, 1676, Samuel Wiseman's Book of Record, Pepys Library no. 2582, Magdalene College, Cambridge, used by the kind permission of the Librarian (also see *Cal. S.P. Col., 1675–1676, Addenda, 1574–1674*, nos. 879, 880). This is presumably Sir John Berry's copy of Wiseman's "three large Books (one for each Commissioner)" (C.O. 5/1355, 247). Another copy is C.O. 3/1371, but the fuller Pepys manuscript has been preferred here. On Berkeley's lack of response, see also the council committee to the commissioners for Virginia, Sept. 28, 1676, Pepys no. 2582, and *Cal. S.P. Col., 1675–1676, Addenda, 1574–1674*, nos. 460, 648, 884. His original instructions, Sept. 12, 1662, to give a "state" of the colony yearly, are in S.P. 44/4, 716, P.R.O., and in C.O. 5/1354, 279. The (unanswered) letter of Apr. 14, 1676, noted the appointment of this select committee, including the earl of Carlisle, dominated by strangers to Berkeley. The committee pointed out that Berkeley's last report was dated June 20, 1671, and that "the condition of Colonies is subject to many changes." They asked for a full state of Virginia (C.O. 5/1355, 47–52). See also *ibid.*, 53–54, and the reiteration of this demand, Oct. 13, 1676, *ibid.*, 114. For the testimony of Giles Bland, see *ibid.*, 557, 698, 897, 922; Egerton MS 2395, 555; and nn. 20–23 below.

noted, "but what hath most disturbed his Majesty and Councill hath been the little or no account we have received from any interested in his Majesties affairs there." Not until Sir William Berkeley's letter of June 3 and Councillor Philip Ludwell's letter of June 28 finally reached London together on September 3, 1676, did any Berkelean report the "mutiny" that had begun the previous April. Only when he was surprised by the arrival of a royal expedition commanded by his replacement did Sir William Berkeley at last recognize and admit "my supposed crime and neglect of my duty" in failing to communicate with Whitehall. The governor's silence gave the crown no option but to accept the Baconian argument that the king had been kept from knowledge of the misgovernment and the ill-defense of his subjects in Virginia by a weak governor and his official oligarchy of excessive taxers and extortioners, "spungers," "unworthy favourites," and "juggling parasites."[4]

To replace the aged governor and his corrupt coterie, to put down the rebels, to find out what was going on in Virginia so that the crown could govern there, and then to impose imperial garrison government on the hitherto autonomous colony, the king chose tried instruments of his authority. Experienced military administrators were organized as a royal commission of enquiry. The royal determination to rule as well as reign in the Old Dominion was further expressed by the collection of a naval squadron, the recruitment of a regiment, and the king's selection of a military policeman, Colonel Herbert Jeffreys, as Virginia's governor. Colonel Jeffreys would command both the province and these freshly organized armed forces.[5]

The new governor brought to Virginia the techniques of gar-

4. William Blathwayt to Col. William Stapleton, Jan. 25, 1680, Blathwayt Papers, XXXVII, 2, Williamsburg. (The censure of Berkeley's associates is complained of by Thomas Ludwell to [Williamson], Nov. 9, 1676, *Cal. S.P. Col., 1675–1676*, no. 1123, and to Sir Henry Coventry, Coventry MS, LXXVII, 301–302, Longleat House, Warminster, Wiltshire, cited by the kind permission of the Marquess of Bath, from microfilm in the Library of Congress.) Coventry to Berkeley, Nov. 15, 1676, Add. MSS 25120, 94, and Berkeley's reply, Feb. 2, 1677, Coventry MS, LXXVII, 350. For the Baconian complaints, see *ibid.*, 442, 444, 445, and for the crown's crediting of them, see Coventry's minute of the privy council meeting, Aug. 22, 1676, *ibid.*, [188], and the instructions to the commissioners, Pepys no. 2582. See also *Cal. S.P. Col., 1675–1676, Addenda, 1574–1674*, nos. 940, 964, 1010, 1031, 1050, 1099, and Egerton MS 2395, 545–553.

5. Council minute, Aug. 22, 1676, Coventry MS, LXXVII, 187; *Cal. S.P. Col., 1675–1676*, no. 1032, 1036, 1041, 1118. The identification of army rank and garrison governorships appears notably in the royal order making each of Col. Jeffreys's five company captains commander-in-chief of Virginia and of the regiment in succession to Jeffreys (C.O. 5/1355, 89). See under "Virginia" in the Appendix for these captains' military and adminis trative careers.

rison government that he had learned in English towns. He led Guards to the Old Dominion as he had to York, on the same political errand. Judicial powers were once again added to military force when the king named Colonel Jeffreys and his fellow royal commissioners part of a panel of judges of oyer and terminer. That is, the judges might hear and determine, according to whatever law they thought applicable, all cases of opposition to royal authority or of harm done to his majesty's subjects.[6] In 1676 in Virginia, as in 1662 in York, the king's military forces and a royal political commission were combined under Herbert Jeffreys's command to depose local leaders who resisted royal commands. Once again, the crown's military and judicial power produced political change, reduced the strength of a provincial oligarchy, and increased that of the central government.

Such results required strong royal representatives. Colonel Jeffreys's fellow commissioners and judges were splendid selections. Francis Moryson was a civil war veteran and a former governor of Virginia. Sir John Berry, a distinguished veteran of the Dutch Wars, had long been a commander in American waters and had repeatedly investigated colonial problems for the privy council. Both officers combined military with colonial experience, as most royal executives in America did by 1676. Captain Berry's imperial experience would not be brought to bear on Virginia until 1676. Prior to that date Major Moryson remained royal government's chief Virginia agent.

Francis Moryson:
From Royalism to Imperialism

After serving in the Oxford garrison, Major Francis Moryson had fled to Virginia in August 1649. There he prospered as a protégé of Sir William Berkeley. The old governor died after the royal commissioners, among them "Colonel" Moryson, officially exposed his debility. The governor's brother, John, Lord Berkeley, accused Moryson of virtual murder. "With an angry voice and a Berkelean look," his lordship "fell upon me," Moryson wrote, "taxing me with ingratitude, loading me with more obligations from his brother, than the whole family had done to the whole

6. For Jeffreys's service in York, see chapter 3 above, and for his parallel commissions in 1676, see Pepys no. 2582, or C.O. 5/1371, generally, and the specific citations in nn. 32 and 43–49 below.

world; and indeed, spoke of me as if I had been a servant (and that a mean one too) in the family, and not an honour of it." Lord Berkeley had reason for his bitterness, but Colonel Moryson had recognized a larger obligation that compelled him to censure his patron. In the distance that separated personal loyalty from state duty lay the measure of Moryson's imperial career.[7]

When he set out for exile in Virginia in 1649, Francis Moryson had risen to major—that especially administrative rank—in the army of Charles I. "The bloody and bitter stroke of the king's assassination" drove Moryson to Virginia, together with such notables as Majors Henry Norwood and Richard Fox. They were part of that cargo of talented officer-executives that crammed the *Virginia Merchant* for her nightmare passage: dismastment, dismantlement, starvation, marooning, cannibalism were the lot of the *Merchant*'s passengers and crew. Major Moryson survived them all to join his brother, Captain Richard Moryson, whom Charles I had commissioned commander of the fort at Point Comfort. The major must have been disappointed, as his brother had been, to find that there was no fort at Point Comfort. The major's chagrin was all the greater because the (nonexistent) Virginia command was a Stuart sovereign's recompense to the royalist Moryson family for their loss of the offices of master general of the royal ordnance and president of Munster. As seasoned military and colonial administrators, however, the Morysons turned their attention to making what they could of the government of Virginia.[8]

Shortly after his brother's arrival, Captain Richard Moryson left Virginia, perhaps with Major Norwood on that voyage of loyalty to Breda to invite Charles II to join his officers in Virginia. Sir William Berkeley then commissioned Francis Moryson captain

7. Moryson to T. Ludwell, Nov. 28, 1677, printed in John Burk, *The History of Virginia, from Its First Settlement to the Present Day*, 4 vols. (Petersburg, Va., 1804–1816), II, 266.

8. Henry Norwood, *A Voyage to Virginia. By Colonel Norwood* (n.p., n.d.), in Peter Force, ed., *Tracts and Other Papers, Relating Principally to the Origin, Settlement, and Progress of the Colonies in North America . . .*, 4 vols. (Washington, D.C., 1836–1844), III, no. 10, 3; Underdown, *Royalist Conspiracy*, 13–14; the will of Sir Richard Morison, *VMHB*, XX (1912), 70–71; Moryson to Clarendon, [1655], New-York Historical Society, *Collections* (1869), 109. The Morysons' Virginia appointments are noted in Hening, ed., *Statutes*, I, 320, 360. The captaincy is authorized and reserved to royal nomination in Berkeley's instructions [of Aug. 9, 1641], paragraphs 8 and 13, C.O. 5/1354, 227, 230; *VMHB*, II (1894–1895), 284. See also Robert A. Brock, "Virginia, 1606–1689," in Justin Winsor, ed., *Narrative and Critical History of America*, III (Cambridge, Mass., 1884), 148, and Norwood, *Voyage to Virginia*, in Force, ed., *Tracts*, III, no. 10, 4, and as quoted in William Maxwell, ed., *The Virginia Historical Register . . . .*, I (1849), 137. See alternatively the copy in the Lambeth Palace Library, no. 754.

of Point Comfort. Long afterward Major Moryson admitted that the fort at Point Comfort "hath been a Castle only in the Air these 30 years." That did not keep him from accepting a solid salary as fort captain, or from collecting port dues for castle maintenance (dues whose value was estimated in 1661 at sixty thousand pounds of tobacco). To add to Moryson's profits, these duties were increased by taxes on passing ships, levied in munitions and in fees per ton and per passenger. Thus Francis Moryson particularly prospered from the fraudulent fort finance that was one of the chief "grievances" he later reported to the king as a cause of Bacon's rebellion. By Governor Berkeley's favor, Major Moryson also acquired land, collected escheats, and was awarded the profits of justice. In addition, he managed Virginia's finances on behalf of Major Norwood, the absentee treasurer of Virginia.[9]

Although favored by the royalists Berkeley and Norwood, Moryson remained in authority and grew in power under the republicans. In December 1656 he became speaker of the house of burgesses. He signed the burgesses' reconfirmation of their 1652 agreement with the parliamentary commissioners. This treaty specified that the burgesses, as the representatives of the people, were Virginia's chief governmental agency. When, in March 1660, the burgesses elected Sir William Berkeley governor of the colony, Berkeley appointed Moryson one of his council. Together, the assembly and the governor selected Francis Moryson to act as governor during Berkeley's absence in England, from April 1661 to October 1662.[10]

The acting governor renewed his royalist credentials. "Colo-

9. Maxwell, ed., *Va. Hist. Register*, 121–122, 126, 127, 128, 131, 137; Norwood, *Voyage to Virginia*, in Force, ed., *Tracts*, III, no. 10, 49–50; Moryson to Clarendon, [1665], N.-Y. Hist. Soc., *Colls.*, II (1869), 122; Philip Alexander Bruce, *Institutional History of Virginia in the Seventeenth Century: An Inquiry into the Religious, Moral, Educational, Legal, Military, and Political Condition of the People . . .* , 2 vols. (New York, 1910), II, 247. On the history of this fort, see *ibid.*, 135–149. See also, Hening, ed., *Statutes*, II, 9, 134–135; *VMHB*, VIII (1900–1901), 38. Moryson gave up these dues to the governor in 1656, while he was speaker of the assembly (Hening, ed., *Statutes*, I, 423) and secured a salary (as did Maj. Charles Norwood, clerk of the assembly [*ibid.*, 424]). This assignment to the governor was continued to Berkeley in Mar. 1660, when the assembly appointed him governor and was restored to Moryson during his governorship (*ibid.*, I, 543, II, 134–135). On the escheats, see *ibid.*, II, 56–57. For the profits of justice, see *ibid.*, 13, and on the treasury, *VMHB*, VIII (1900–1901), 167; Burk, *History of Virginia*, II, xli–xlii, xliii, liii–liv. See also David S. Lovejoy, "Virginia's Charter and Bacon's Rebellion 1675–1676," in Olson and Brown, eds., *Anglo-American Political Relations, 1675–1775*, 43.

10. On Moryson's speakership, see Hening, ed., *Statutes*, I, 403, 424, 426, 428; Burk, *History of Virginia*, I, 114, 116–117. On Moryson's council appointment, see Hening, ed., *Statutes*, I, 526, 528–529n, 530–531, 544, 545; Burk, *History of Virginia*, I, 116–117; *VMHB*, III (1895–1896), 133. See also *ibid.*, VIII (1900–1901), 108. On the governorship, Apr. 30, 1661, to Oct. 9, 1662, see *ibid.*, 167; XIV (1906–1907), 195–196; and nn. 11–12 below.

nel" Moryson, as he was titled from his governorship, used his command of the colony, his training as a lawyer, and his refreshed royalist convictions to write a Restoration settlement into the laws of Virginia, much as his model, Chancellor Clarendon, was doing in England. In March 1662, under Moryson's direction, the Virginia assembly eliminated "all unnecessary acts and chiefly such as might keep in memory our inforced deviation from his majesties obedience." A Virginian summarized Moryson's work: "By these Laws, the Church of England was confirmed the established Religion, the Charge of the Government sustained, Trade and Manufactures were encouraged, a Town projected, and all the Indian Affairs settled." Moryson showed his vision by legislating the Indians' protection from—and their subordination to—the colonists in the very terms he would use again as a royal commissioner in the treaty of 1677. He appreciated the political power of religious conformity and boasted of his law establishing the church to that noted churchman Chancellor Clarendon. For the support of government (that is, to pay the salaries of governors and fort commanders such as himself), Moryson won reenactment of the famous duty of two shillings per hogshead of tobacco exported, and he obtained a new levy for the port duty on ships.[11]

Colonel Moryson had practically rewritten Virginia's law, but he did even more to restore the authority of the executive in Virginia and to reduce the powers acquired by the legislature during the Commonwealth and Protectorate periods. He wrested the power of appointment from the assembly and returned it to

11. For the legislation of the "Grand Assembly Held at James City March the 23d 1661–2," see Hening, ed., *Statutes*, II, 41–148. Moryson and the clerk, Henry Randolph, were appointed a committee to revise "all the acts." The dimensions of the clerk's contribution are unknown, but Moryson's notable influence was reemphasized by his review of the laws before the privy council and by his readoption of some of them as a royal commissioner. The quoted phrase, *ibid.*, 42, is felicitously used by Richard L. Morton, *Colonial Virginia*, 2 vols. (Chapel Hill, N.C., 1960), I, 189–190. See also the orders of Gov. Moryson and Speaker Robert Winn, Hening, ed., *Statutes*, II, 149–162. For the degree of Moryson's dominance, see esp. *ibid.*, 156. Beverley's summary is in his *History*, ed. Wright, 66–68. The Indian legislation is in Hening, ed., *Statutes*, II, 138–143. The connection between it and the treaty of 1677 is noted by Wilcomb E. Washburn, *The Governor and the Rebel: A History of Bacon's Rebellion in Virginia* (Chapel Hill, N.C., 1957), 135. Note that the code provided for a college to educate Virginians for the ministry (Hening, ed., *Statutes*, II, 25, 30–31; Beverley, *History*, ed. Wright, 66–67) and fully anticipated the other accomplishments of the Nicholson regime (Webb, "Nicholson," *WMQ*, 3d Ser., XXIII [1966], 532–534). Moryson's political intent in establishing religion is noted not only to Clarendon (N.-Y. Hist. Soc., *Colls.*, II [1869], 112), but also in his approval of the military chaplain's "preaching to the country the doctrine of obedience" in 1677, for which see J. R. Tanner, ed., *A Descriptive Catalogue of the Naval Manuscripts in the Pepysian Library* . . . (London, 1923), IV, 511. On the financial measures, see Hening, ed., *Statutes*, II, 99, 136–137, 177–178; Beverley, *History*, ed. Wright, 67.

the governor and council. Commissions to surveyors, county clerks, justices of the peace, and sheriffs could be sources and tools of power for either a republican legislature or a royalist executive. Moryson made such appointments the basis for building an oligarchy of officials that became the Berkelean plural executive. Equally important in lessening legislative authority was Moryson's successful insistence that the assembly recognize the crown as an intrinsic, even the dominant, element of the colony's constitution. When Virginians accepted royal authority, they consented to provincial status in the English empire.[12]

The logic of empire quickly took Colonel Moryson from Virginia to England. His law code concluded with a clause seeking royal confirmation. Moryson knew that besides the crown's legal sanction, Virginia required imperial economic regulation and physical protection. He reached Whitehall in 1663 as Virginia's agent to the crown, succeeding Sir William Berkeley. For a dozen years in the imperial court and capital, Moryson witnessed the crown's growing determination both to reduce the autonomy of provincial elites and to suppress recurrent popular turbulence. During this period, Moryson himself shifted from being a Virginia agent to being a royal commissioner, a sea change that shocked the unreconstructed Berkelean oligarchs who still thought of Moryson as one of themselves.[13]

Francis Moryson's devotion to his family and to its lovely property, the ancient precincts of Bishops Waltham, underlay the Virginia agent's deepening friendships with members of the expanding royal bureaucracy. The ties of person, profession, and property sustained the growth of social stability, personified by the king and effected by the crown. Moryson's association with an expanding national executive and with an increasing social stability in England contrasted with Sir William Berkeley's adherence to an antique provincialism in isolated, socially underdeveloped Virginia. Different environments dictated the widening distance between their understandings of the growing power of imperial authority and the potential limitations of colonial self-government. Sir William remained a royalist of 1641 and 1661, personally loyal to King Charles but never apprehending that new reality, "the

12. Hening, ed., *Statutes*, II, 58–59, 63–66, 69–70, 76. On sheriffs, see *ibid.*, 78. Note also the induction of ministers by the governor, *ibid.*, 46; land grants by the governor and council, *ibid.*, 95, and Burk's generalization, in *History of Virginia*, II, 147–148.

13. Moryson's license from the governor to depart Virginia, Mar. 26, 1663, and his recommendation from Berkeley, *Cal. S.P. Col., 1661–1668*, nos. 428, 429. See also *ibid.*, 973–974, 1937, 1194, 1231; *ibid.*, *1669–1674*, no. 195; and the representation of the governor and council, Mar. 28, 1663, Egerton MS 2395, 360–361.

imperial crown of England." Colonel Moryson was gradually converted into an imperialist supporter of an almost absolute executive, symbolized by the king. In 1676 the monarchist Moryson insisted that Virginia's chief desire was "to be assured of the perpetual immediate dependence" of the colony on the crown. Certainly the Berkeleans did not agree with what Moryson meant by this. They did not even understand it.[14]

Agency and Charter, Proprietorship and Empire

The centralization of Anglo-American relations, which had eluded Berkeley and impressed Moryson, affected Virginia when the colonial elite sought royal protection against the proprietary claims of Lords Culpeper and Arlington. The Virginians succeeded in exciting imperialist ministers, principally the duke of York, to rebuff the proprietors, but only at the cost of their own political autonomy.

The issue was raised in February 1672, while Lord Culpeper was a paid member of the Shaftesbury council for foreign plantations and the earl of Arlington was secretary of state. They combined the ancient family interest of the Culpepers in Virginia with Arlington's political clout to secure from King Charles a grant of all land in Virginia for thirty-one years and the patronage of every office dealing with land. The resulting threat to colonial property was equaled by the danger of political anarchy. The provincial assembly insisted that the proprietary grant, if effected, would strip the Virginia government "of those just powers and authorities by which this Colony hath hitherto been kept in peace and tranquility, and all men's rights and properties duly administered and preserved unto them." The assemblymen told the king that, in attacking their jurisdiction, the proprietors' patronage power also reduced the royal authority that underlay all government. To preserve the crown's titular authority in Virginia and their own actual sway, the provincial governor, council, and burgesses sent the colony's major general, Robert Smith, and its secretary of state, Thomas Ludwell, to join the established agent of Virginia, Colonel Moryson, in England. The three agents requested a royal charter to preserve their privileges and their property in June 1675.

14. The quality of Bishops Waltham was noted during a personal visit. Moryson himself testified to his domestic attachments, and his relations with the members of the imperial secretariat also appear in his correspondence (Coventry MS, LXXVII).

In October 1675 the attorney and solicitor generals reported that it would "not only be for His Majesty's Service but for the increase of the Trade and Growth of the plantation of Virginia" if the king would grant the Virginians ten concessions by letters patent.[15]

The ensuing document was summarized by the agents as a royal ratification of "the power and Authority of the Grand Assembly." The Virginia assembly was defined as the "Governor, Council, and Burgesses" meeting and acting together. The only check on this assembly's authority would be the king's veto of its laws. This check, the agents hastened to note, was really a double veto, for the crown-appointed governor would also presumably protect the king's prerogative with his negative voice. Each of the Virginia agents was a member of the ruling council of the colony, and, except for the royal disallowance of laws, what they now asked King Charles to confirm by charter was the Virginia constitution as they and their assembly colleagues had formulated it in 1662. "Consider," they wrote, "that no alterations of the present Virginia government is at all desired, but earnestly that the same may be established and confirmed by his Majesty's Charter." For a moment it seemed as if Charles II would indeed formalize and legalize the old order in Virginia. In November 1675 the king-in-council ordered a bill prepared for passage under the great seal. The charter thereupon disappeared into the Whitehall warren for the winter.[16]

15. *Privy Council, Col. Ser.*, I, no. 1029; Coventry MS, LXXVII, 319; C.O. 5/1355, 34; Hening, ed., *Statutes*, II, 312; Morton, *Colonial Virginia*, I, 209. On the antiquity of the Culpeper family interest, see "The Names of the Adventurers for Virginia . . . 1620," in Burk, *History of Virginia*, I, 340–341. On Maj. Gen. Smith's career in support of the Virginia executive, see *VMHB*, I (1893–1894), 432; *Cal. S.P. Col., 1675–1676, Addenda, 1574–1674*, no. 602, and chapter 8 below. The most recent discussion of the Virginia agency is Lovejoy, "Virginia's Charter and Bacon's Rebellion," in Olson and Brown, eds., *Anglo-American Political Relations, 1675–1775*, which did not use the Coventry MS on which the present narrative is based or the entry book, C.O. 5/1355, which, cited below, reproduces some of the material in the Coventry MS and is itself calendared with a notable fidelity but with varying completeness in the *Cal. S.P. Col.* For the law officers' report to the privy council, Oct. 11–12, 1675, see Coventry MS, LXXVII, 191. See also Moryson's explanation of each clause of the proposed charter, *ibid.*, 46–48, largely reproduced in Burk, *History of Virginia*, II, appendix, xlvi–l. See also the reference and report, *Cal. S.P. Col., 1675–1676, Addenda, 1574–1674*, no. 603, 696–697; C.O. 5/1355, 38–39, 40–42, 43–46.

16. Coventry MS, LXXVII, 29b; C.O. 5/1355, 37; Burk, *History of Virginia*, lii, no. 2. Note that the assembly agents thus conceded as a matter of common sense the "double veto" that the burgesses resisted so violently during the government of Lord Howard of Effingham. Report and order to prepare, Nov. 19, 1675, Coventry MS, LXXVII, 23–24; C.O. 5/1355, 46–47.

Lord Culpeper tried to keep the Virginia charter closeted in Whitehall. He was "resolutely determined to hinder our composure," the agents complained. Culpeper first blocked the sale of the proprietorship to the Virginians, a sale that had been agreed to by his partner, the earl of Arlington. Then he refused to follow Arlington's example and surrender to the king his political claims in Virginia. Instead Culpeper sought and secured a reversion to the Virginia governorship on the death or recall of Sir William Berkeley. While the agents correctly thought that Culpeper sought the titular governorship only to protect his proprietary profit and that he had no intention of actually going out to head the government, they feared that if his lordship had to go out to Virginia, he would govern by force and not by law. The record of Culpeper's administration of the Isle of Wight amply supported their apprehensions.[17]

While Lord Culpeper delayed the charter's passage, the king and his ministers began to realize that the self-government legitimated by the proposed Virginia charter challenged all English interests in the province, public and imperial as well as private and proprietary. As the year 1676 came on, Francis Moryson repeatedly had to assure King Charles that the Virginia assembly wanted only "a confirmation of our just rights and privileges." They did not seek "such power from him as may here after Jostle with the Royal Prerogative." Such assurances were obscured by the loud alarms of the English colonists' great war with the Indians. The autonomous colonial governments seemed incapable of defending the king's American subjects, territories, trade, and customs. The colonists needed protection by the crown. That meant the assertion of the prerogative in the colonies. The Virginia agents could only insist again and again that, in the case of the Old Dominion, passage of the pending charter would inspire their compatriots to defend the property and the liberties it confirmed to them.[18]

17. Burk, *History of Virginia*, II, appendix, xxxiii–xliii, esp. xli–xlii, liv. Note that Burk dates these meetings in Apr. 1674. They occurred a year later. The agents to Coventry, n.d., Coventry MS, LXXVII, 29. On Culpeper's Isle of Wight regime, see chapter 3 above.

18. Moryson's explanation is in Coventry MS, LXXVII, 46, and similarly in Burk, *History of Virginia*, II, appendix, xlvi–l. The stages of the charter negotiation and the document's progress are summarized in *Cal. S.P. Col., 1675–1676, Addenda, 1574–1674*, no. 834, 835. On the spreading Indian war, see Berkeley to Coventry, Feb. 16, 1676, Coventry MS, LXXVII, 56, and Berkeley to Coventry, Apr. 1, 1676, in which Berkeley responded to Secretary Ludwell's warning that his failure to communicate with the ministry was being criticized. The governor was so out of touch with the secular, protective, imperial concerns

Yet, when May bloomed, the charter still had not passed the seals. The agents discovered that the lord chancellor (Heneage, Baron Finch) had been listening to assertions that charter privileges would exempt Virginia from the acts of trade. The agents accurately labeled this objection "of no great weight." The charter had already been amended twice to ensure that the acts of trade would continue to bind Virginia. The lord chancellor's objections had delayed the passage of the charter another month, however, and that delay was fatal to Virginia's hopes of political autonomy. On the last day of May 1676, the chancellor was ordered not to pass the Virginia charter.[19]

Autonomy Ended

The Virginia charter was forever lost because it was now recognized in England that the elite the charter would confirm in political power had failed to govern effectively. The secretary of state, Sir Joseph Williamson, had received letters from the collector of customs in Virginia, Giles Bland, who reported not only that Sir William Berkeley's government had failed to protect the king's subjects in Virginia from Indian raiders but also that it had provoked a rebellion by its military feebleness and its political corruption. In letters to Williamson and to other ministers, Bland noted with alarm that the rising was "led by persons of quality"— not by the ragtag and bobtail who had headed the earlier attacks on the Berkeleans.[20]

---

of the new generation of ministers that he could only offer the comment that King Philip's war was a divine judgment on the New Englanders—the king's enemies, those rebels and murderers of the blessed Charles I. Such royalist piety was not helpful in planning a practical response to the security crisis of the English colonies, as became apparent when the war reached Berkeley's own government. See the privy council order of Apr. 18–19, 1676, which followed Moryson's and Ludwell's representation to Coventry on Apr. 15, Coventry MS, LXXVII, 70, 74; Burk, *History of Virginia*, II, xxxiv, lvii–lx; C.O. 5/1355, 55–56.

19. Moryson and Ludwell to Coventry, May 8, 1676, Coventry MS, LXXVII, 83b; *Cal. S.P. Col., 1675–1676, Addenda, 1574–1674*, nos. 892–893; C.O. 5/1355, 56.

20. The Bland story began to break on May 30 when the petition of Mrs. Sarah Bland on behalf of her son Giles, the royal collector, was read to the privy council (C.O. 5/1355, 57–58). The attack on Secretary Ludwell, agent of the Virginia government, and on the Berkelean clique itself, as well as the appeal for the intervention of the crown in Virginia's un-English, arbitrary, violent, and injurious judicial system, all were of great potential impact on the charter negotiations, as was noted by Ludwell, *ibid.*, 59–64. See also *ibid.*, 65–67,

Giles Bland's Accusations

Bland's warnings were reinforced by every one of the scanty and scattered reports that reached the crown in the summer and autumn of 1676. His analysis of the Virginia situation became that of the English executive. Bland reiterated what Colonel Norwood had reported a decade before—that Virginians were angered by the high and inequitable taxes levied by the assembly and by the assembly elite's corrupt consumption of these tax revenues. Bland described the symptoms of the sick system: unbuilt or ineffective forts, expensive and apparently ineffective agencies to England, and "the main cause of those tumults"—the "not timely suppressing the Incursions of those formidable savages," savages supplied with arms by Governor Berkeley's Indian traders. Like Norwood, Bland blamed military failure, fiscal corruption, and judicial injustice on Sir William Berkeley.[21]

The obviousness of Bland's conclusion impressed all the counsels of the crown in 1676. It seemed "to be very unlikely that the Authority and power, Lodged in the Aged Governor and his divided Council," could regain control of the rebellious colonists.

---

and the long debate that ensued in the privy council committee, *ibid.*, 67. On Bland, see also *VMHB*, XX (1912), 238–239, 242, 350–354; *ibid.*, XXI (1913), 127–135; Tanner, ed., *Pepysian Manuscripts*, IV, cxvii, 378, 417, 430; *Cal. S.P. Col., 1675–1676, Addenda, 1574–1674*, nos. 698, 897, 922, 934, 942, 949–951, 980; Washburn, *Bacon's Rebellion*, 92–93. Bland's letter to Secretary Williamson, Apr. 28, 1676, and the enclosed "State of Virginia," were received in June (*VMHB*, XX [1912], 352–357; *Cal. S.P. Col., 1675–1676, Addenda, 1574–1674*, nos. 906, 907). By June 19, Ludwell's correspondence from Virginia was in Secretary Coventry's hands (*ibid.*, no. 942; Washburn, *The Effect of Bacon's Rebellion on Government in England and Virginia, United States National Museum Bulletin 225*, Paper 17 [Washington, D.C., 1962]). See also Bland to his kinsman, Thomas Povey, July 8, [1676], received Aug. 28, [1676], Egerton MS 2395, 555.

21. Norwood's relation is printed in *VMHB*, XXI (1913), 123–125. Its existence flatly contradicts Washburn, *Bacon's Rebellion*, 158, who says "there is not a shred of responsible evidence to support this supposed charge," i.e., "that after the restoration of Charles II the governor gradually became oppressive, greedy, and corrupt." Norwood's credentials, for which see chapter 3 above and Bernard Bailyn, "Politics and Social Structure in Virginia," in James Morton Smith, ed., *Seventeenth-Century America: Essays in Colonial History* (Chapel Hill, N.C., 1959), 101 n. 29, on "the Berkeley-Norwood connection," were as respectable as Berkeley's own. Indeed, Berkeley himself recommended to [Clarendon,] Mar. 30, 1663 (Egerton MS 2395, 362–364), that "Cozen Norwood" be appointed to investigate Virginia and "report to His Majesty what a growing Empire he has here, in which all the Plantations in the West Indies begin to centre." Norwood's observations of "the governor's passion, age, or weakness," were unsparing. See the identification of this material as Norwood's and its dating at July 17, 1667, in *Cal. S.P. Col., 1661–1668*, no. 1532. See also the confirmation of Bland noted in Coventry MS, LXXVII, 325, and even by Washburn, *Bacon's Rebellion*, 187 n. 63.

Moreover, the Indian enemy would take advantage of "these disorders in the government, which already wants that reverence that should enable it to protect itself and the public." Royal assistance was essential both to reform and to strengthen Virginia government. Bland was not writing just against the Berkeleans or for an English executive. He was a political moderate, and he particularly wanted a royal declaration to the Virginians "enlarging their liberty," protecting their property, lowering the salaries of their burgesses, enforcing better fiscal accounting, and equalizing taxes by shifting from a poll to a land levy. A land tax, Bland concluded, would also force engrossers to open their unused land holdings to settlement.[22]

Bland's recommendations for tax policy got a sympathetic hearing at Whitehall, for they would increase both the royal revenue and the small planter population. More planters meant a stronger Virginia military and greater productive capacity. Reduced salaries for assemblymen would promote government economy. More important, such a recommendation catered to the royal ministerial prejudice against self-important, self-serving, and self-governing legislators. The English executive's burgeoning desire for effective, disciplined provincial government meant that Bland's report of the debility of the Berkeley regime led to royal repression of Virginia's political liberties, instead of motivating the political concessions he desired. The custom collector's letters, powerfully authenticated by Indian attacks and by Bacon's rebellion, had made clear to the crown its fiscal stake and therefore its political investment in effective Virginia government. The £100,000 sterling that the king received from the customs on Virginia tobacco was the measure of his independence of the English parliament. Bland convinced the crown that its tobacco revenue "must hold or be diminished according to the security, peace, and prosperity of this place."[23]

22. Bland to Mr. Charles Berne, Apr. 20, 1676, Burk, History of Virginia, II, 247–249. On "land lopers," see also the eloquent denunciation in "Virginia's Deploured Condition," Massachusetts Historical Society, Collections, 4th Ser., IX (1871), 164. Gov. Thomas Notley of Maryland also supported Bland's position against the Berkeleans (Cal. S.P. Col., 1677–1680, 12, 263; William Hand Browne, ed., Archives of Maryland, V [Baltimore, 1887], 153–154).

23. As the author of "Virginia's Deploured Condition" (William Sherwood, so Washburn notes, in Bacon's Rebellion, 171–172), Mass. Hist. Soc., Colls., 4th Ser., IX (1871), 176, put it, "unless his sacred Majesty do speedily send a considerable supply of men, Armes, Ammunition and provision," Virginia will be lost either to the Indians or the rebels. The fiscal and political effect of the loss of tobacco revenue in forcing the king to meet a hostile parliament is detailed by Washburn, Effect of Bacon's Rebellion, U.S. National Museum Bulletin 225, 147–149.

Bland's letters ruined the rationale for passing the Virginia charter. The case for the confirmation of the assembly system had been the agents' assertion that it "by 50 years experience hath been found A Government most easy to the people and advantageous to the Crown. For in all that time there hath not been one law complain'd of, burdensome to the one or prejudicial to the Prerogative of the other." Moreover, Moryson had argued that the Virginia constitution was "in a humble subordination representing and agreeing to the English monarchy." He asserted that the Virginians themselves "ever have been heartily affectionate and loyal to the monarchy of England." Bland asserted, however, that Virginians were now rebelling against both local law and the provincial government and that the Virginia constitution, far from being compatible with the English executive either in form or in interest, had endangered the crown's finances by fostering a legislative tyranny. The assembly system, inefficient in all but corruption, might even drive the outraged people to seek independence from England. Alarmed at last into looking at Virginia, the king's ministers discovered that the assembly elite had misused their local autonomy and abused their privileges of self-government, and that the proposed charter would perpetuate this disastrous system.[24]

The crown's worst fears were further confirmed, and the agents' strongest arguments more deeply debased, when Sir William Berkeley finally got around to reporting the previous April's rising. "A Young fellow one Bacon," Sir William wrote, had "infused into the People the great charge and uselessness of the forts which our Assembly had most wisely founded to resist the Enemies." Then "a monstrous number of the basest of the People declared for him in less than ten days in all parts of the Country." Berkeley concluded that "this Rebellion is more formidable because it has no ground and is not against any particular Person but the whole Assembly." With the whole structure of government under attack, the crown could not confirm it by charter. The relative political independence previously exercised by the Virginia assembly seemed unjustified in the lurid light cast by unquenched Indian war and domestic rebellion.[25]

24. Coventry MS, LXXVII, 48; Burk, *History of Virginia*, II, appendix, xlix–lii.
25. Berkeley to Coventry, June 3, 1676, Coventry MS, LXXVII, 103.

Sir William Berkeley's Failure

Governor Berkeley himself reported that the assembly was making decisions that, in the crown's estimation and in garrison government practice, ought to have been the governor's. The aged Sir William Berkeley was not the powerful paramilitary figure suggested by English precedent or required by American circumstance. The elderly governor admitted to Secretary Coventry that "I am so over wearied with riding into all parts of the Country to stop this violent Rebellion *that I am not able to support myself at this Age six months longer and therefore on my knees I beg his sacred majesty would send a more Vigorous Governor.*"[26]

Not only must the new executive be *"more Vigorous"* personally, he must also be institutionally stronger. In particular, royal officials agreed that Berkeley's replacement must possess the martial powers and military backing that had become the essence of garrison government since Sir William had come out to Virginia on the eve of the civil wars. Neither the title "captain general" nor its operative authority—the power to declare and execute martial law—had been given Sir William. First issued in 1641 and refreshed in 1650 and 1662, Berkeley's authority was defined at just those times when the military power of the Stuart sovereigns—and of their governors—was at low ebb. Berkeley was sent out to Virginia with limitations on his executive authority like those that had so confined Sir Ferdinando Gorges in Plymouth. Berkeley was twice reappointed, first by a king in exile and then under the civilian dispensation of Chancellor Clarendon. His lack of authority made Sir William Berkeley more nearly a presiding councillor in Virginia than the commander of a province. Unable to act apart from councillors named in the same royal commission as himself, Berkeley was supported neither by martial authority nor by the physical backing of a citadel and regular guards. Occasionally he mustered unofficial forces—"some Servants which we kept at our own charges as Garrison Soldiers." Following the servant conspiracy of 1663, the assembly raised twenty men as a guard for themselves, and they protected the governor as part of the assembly. Essentially, however, Sir William was militarily powerless himself, and yet, even when rebellion overspread the colony in 1676, he did not seek the support of the English executive, in either a supply of arms or a grant of authority. Berkeley's was a deliberately, determinedly, and to the eye of imperialists, a provocatively provincial government. Instead of appealing to his royal

26. *Ibid.* (italics in original document).

master for help in supporting the royal prerogative in Virginia, Berkeley answered the anxious queries of the crown by referring the English ministers back to the Virginia agents in England.[27]

The agents duly reported "to his Majesty the defect of Sir W. Berkeley his Authority in point of War." Concerned to find that Sir William's "powers are very defective in the Military part," the king's cabinet concluded that the governor ought to "have a commission as other Generals have during the War." Such commissions provided that governors commissioned as captains general might raise, arm, discipline, and employ military forces and that they might proclaim and execute martial law during invasions or insurrections. Governors-general could order their troops to kill invaders or rebels, or they might have their enemies executed following summary courts-martial.[28]

The constitution of a governor-general for Virginia alarmed

27. The 1641 instructions are printed in *VMHB*, II (1894), 281–288. The commission of June 3, 1650, and the instructions of Sept. 12, 1662, are in Coventry MS, LXXVII, and, with the precedential instructions to Sir Francis Wyatt, in C.O. 5/1354, 218–223, 224–241, 243–252, 270–280; S.P. 44/4, 62–72. On Gorges, see chapter 1 above. Sir William Berkeley only began to call himself "governor and captain general of Virginia" on May 20, 1676 (*ibid.*, 77, 151), a title, as it seems in Berkeley's case, of martial necessity, not royal authority. Coventry to Berkeley, July 14, 1676, Add. MSS 25130, 89, noted that, "your Agent here having acquainted his Majesty that your powers are very defective in the Military part," the king had ordered a military commission for Berkeley as large "as any other Governor hath," but it was not sent; see n. 28 above. If the title was based at all in legal process, it was from Berkeley's election by the Interregnum assembly (Hening, ed., *Statutes*, I, 530). The title "captain-general" was not confirmed by the crown, however, in keeping with the civilian policy of 1660; see chapter 3 above. The "Garrison Soldiers" were referred to by Berkeley in Apr. 1663 (Egerton MS 2395, 365), and the assembly guard was authorized in Sept. following (Hening, ed., *Statutes*, II, 200).

28. July 22, 1676, at the committee of foreign affairs (the "cabinet" of the text), Coventry MS, LXXVII, 150; Coventry to Berkeley, July 14, 1676, Add. MSS 25120, 89. It is apparent, however, from the remarks of Coventry (n. 27 above), Moryson (C.O. 5/1371, 6–12, quoted by Washburn, *Effect of Bacon's Rebellion, U.S. National Museum Bulletin 225*, 141), and of the other royal commissioners (Pepys no. 2582), that no martial commission was sent to Sir William Berkeley and that, therefore, Colonel Jeffreys was the first Virginia royal governor to have military power "as ample in that part as any other Governor hath," another indication of the constitutional divide that separated the Berkeley regime from subsequent administrations. Washburn, *Bacon's Rebellion*, 89, 91, 232 n. 29, however, terms Berkeley "captain general" and justifies his martial courts and executions by reference to Culpeper's actions in repressing plant cutters. Berkeley ceased to term himself "captain general" as soon as the royal commissioners arrived. They pointed out to him that, while the law of necessity had justified his summary court-martial proceedings in time of actual hostilities, he had no authority from the king that could do so in peacetime (Moryson to T. Ludwell, Nov. 28, 1677, Burk, *History of Virginia*, II, 266). The crown subsequently voided all Berkeley's arbitrary actions that occurred after the end of hostilities (nn. 54, 62, below). See also the following chapter and Hening, ed., *Statutes*, II, 545–556, esp. 547–548. The effective power of captains general in this period is detailed in S.P. 44/29, 171, 380; S.P. 44/44, 1, 26–27; and S.P. 44/164, 27. In contrast to Berkeley, Culpeper possessed these powers in the fullest measure, by clause 14 of his commission (C.O. 5/1355, 320–321).

the agents of the Virginia assembly, especially when it became clear that the crown would apply its military authority directly, not through the old governor and the council, but rather by a specially commissioned and thoroughly experienced English garrison governor, backed by substantial numbers of English regular troops. The crown would forcibly impose its authority on the colony. That an armed prerogative would physically as well as constitutionally counterbalance the hitherto unchallenged rule of the local elite became all too clear to the assembly's agents when the cabinet not only chose a governor-general but also erased from the draft Virginia charter all royal recognition of the assembly. Henceforward "the power of the Assembly would be only in instructions" to the governor-general, the agents lamented. The assembly would not exist, except when called into session by the governor-general. Destruction of the assembly's autonomous existence made the alternative, military mechanism of garrison government especially menacing to the continued authority of the provincial elite.[29]

Militarizing the Executive

During the late summer and autumn of 1676, the crown organized a punitive expedition to Virginia. The Restoration executive now applied to Virginia's subordination a decade's experience in the use of regular forces to command provinces. In July 1676 it was proposed that Sir John Berry convey a military commission to the governor of Virginia and enforce it with his frigate (Francis Moryson had reminded the royal officials that naval supremacy was vital to control of the Chesapeake colony). Next, as many regular troops as Berry's ship could carry were added to the force intended for the pacification of Virginia. Dispatch of the vessel was delayed, however, to permit the receipt of further intelligence. Each report from Virginia was more alarming than its predecessor. The ministry soon concluded that parchment authority, plus a single ship and a few soldiers, would not supply the deficiencies of the silent, some said senile, old governor. As Sir William finally said of himself, "No seasonable showers or dews can recover a withered root."[30]

29. Hening, ed., *Statutes*, II, 540–541, 542.
30. Admiralty Journal, June 26, 1676, gives the first official intimation of the coming expedition (Tanner, ed., *Pepysian Manuscripts*, IV, 323 and n.). The preparation of ordnance supplies by Sir Thomas Chicheley is detailed in C.O. 5/1355, 68–77. On Berkeley's silence as leading to his censure and to the appointment of commissioners, see *Cal. S.P. Col.*,

On August 22 the cabinet, meeting under the presidency of the duke of York, ordered "Sir W. Berkeley to be recalled." The ministers of the crown had concluded that Berkeley was "totally unsuitable for the execution of so weighty a charge as the management of the king's affairs." They retained enough memory of Sir William's "long and faithful service," however, to wish to avoid his public disgrace. In a mistaken decision, never afterwards repeated, the cabinet permitted the governor to retain his title. They added that he was not to exercise any authority after his successor arrived in Virginia. It would be difficult to dissociate office and authority, however, particularly since the governor's removal was phrased in the polite terms usual on such occasions. Berkeley was recalled by "a letter from his Majesty taking notice of his great Age, And the desire he himself hath made to be eased . . . and giving him leave to come to England."[31]

"A Lieutenant Governor" was "to be constituted in his Place," the royal ministers decided. Their first nominees to the king were the veteran Sir Henry Chicheley, who was in Virginia, and Major Thomas Fairfax. Their patrons, respectively, were Secretary Williamson and the duke of Ormond. Both of these imperial officials sat in the cabinet, which quickly decided that whatever officer was finally named to the post, his military power must be made unquestionable, as Berkeley's obviously had not been. The cabinet hoped Bacon would now "surrender his Commission [as general] considering that his Majesty hath sent one from hence to command in Chief etc." Then the new executive could condemn Bacon under martial law. As a military executive, the lieutenant governor could deal with the remaining rebels quickly by using his powers to pardon traitors immediately or to condemn them summarily.[32]

1675–1676, Addenda, 1574–1674, no. 1041; the statement of the privy councillors, C.O. 5/1355, 78–79; and his own recognition, quoted on p. 331 above.

31. "Virginia Despatch," Aug. 22, 1676, "present His Royal Highness, the Lord Treasurer, the Duke of Ormond, Sir W. [Coventry]," Coventry MS, LXXVII, 187b–188; "Instructions Given at the Committee for Foreign Affairs Sept. 1, 1676, Concerning Virginia," *ibid.*, 195; memorial to Coventry, *ibid.*, 297–298. See also *ibid.*, 336, sec. 2.

32. Many of the orders, appointments, power, etc., previously decided upon are summarized in the minutes for Sept. 29, 1676, C.O. 5/1355, 79–81. See also Coventry's undated cabinet minute on Berkeley's leave, Chicheley's and Fairfax's appointments, and the clause of martial law, Coventry MS, LXXVII, 272. On Fairfax's service under the duke of Ormond, and as a courtier and political manager, see HMC, *Ormonde*, and W. D. Christie, ed., *Letters Addressed from London to Sir Joseph Williamson* . . . , Camden Society, XXXVIII (London, 1874); Beer, ed., *Diary of Evelyn* ("a soldier, a traveller, an excellent musician, a good-natured, well-bred gentleman"), and Dalton, ed., *English Army Lists*, I, 192, 219, 244, on his career in the Guards (where he received a captaincy on the departure of the Virginia expedition), as colonel of a regiment, and as governor of Limerick as a major general. On Sir Henry

The military power given the new royal executive of Virginia was only the first and most direct part of the crown's attack on provincial autonomy. The cabinet council also agreed to pass a charter for Virginia, which not only erased all royal recognition of the old assembly order in Virginia but also excised every political authority from the surviving proprietary grants. Denying both provincial and proprietary power, the amended Virginia charter effected an "immediate dependence upon the Crown of England" in a fashion more stark and more effective than the Virginia assembly and its agents expected or desired. Instead of confirming "the authority formerly placed in that government," the charter announced the direct rule of the crown in the colony through the enhanced executive power of a royal governor-general. This military executive's provincial power was further extended by his judicial authority, which was far greater than Berkeley's had been. Besides conferring full original and appellate jurisdiction upon its new governor (sitting with his newly subordinated council), the crown made its representative the president of an extraordinary commission of oyer and terminer. All significant judicial decisions were to be reviewed by the king and council. In short, the crown had accepted enough of the Virginia agents' argument that the colony was "an extension" of England to justify it in imposing on Virginia the martial and monarchical government already stapled onto the British kingdoms, Ireland preeminently, and onto several overseas provinces, Jamaica in particular.[33]

If nothing else had done so, the decision to impose garrison government on Virginia doomed Sir William Berkeley. He admitted that he knew none of the new breed of ministers who favored imperialist and militarist political policies in England and in her empire. Berkeley had repeatedly declined to respond to their queries about his government, even during the rebellion, when his response was seen not just as essential to imperial planning but as vital to the very preservation of Virginia "from the cruelty

---

Chicheley's civil war record as lieutenant colonel to that famous officer-governor, Sir Richard Willis, and for his Virginia commissions, including those of lieutenant general and deputy governor, see Dalton, ed., *English Army Lists*, I, 163, 171, 259; S.P. 44/35A, 85b, 86; and S.P. 44/31, 125. The argument concerning Bacon's commission indicates that the cabinet gave some credence to Bacon's argument that he had been commissioned by Berkeley and so, by delegation, by the king (*Cal. S.P. Col., 1675–1676, Addenda, 1574–1674*, no. 969).

33. Coventry MS, LXXVII, 190, 279, 293, 319; Burk, *History of Virginia*, II, appendix, lxi–lxii; Hening, ed., *Statutes*, II, 531–533; warrant to prepare the charter, Sept. 9, 1676, *Cal. S.P. Col., 1675–1676, Addenda, 1574–1674*, no. 447; letters made patent, Oct. 10, 28, 1676, entered in Samuel Wiseman's Book of Record, Pepys no. 2582; *Cal. S.P. Col., 1675–1676, Addenda, 1574–1674*, no. 1066; and, dated Sept. 9, C.O. 5/1355, 94–96.

of the Indians and the rebellion of the Vulgar." The duke of York himself had recommended to his brother the king that he immediately recall Berkeley. On September 1, 1676, the duke added that Sir William ought to cease "meddling" in the government of Virginia the instant his successor arrived. Even Lady Berkeley, then in England, explicitly acknowledged that Sir William was subject to the result: the royal and "absolute Commands on him immediately after the arrival of your Majesty's fleet in Virginia to go on board some ship bound for England." What was clear in England would nonetheless be resisted by Sir William, his Lady, and their partisans in Virginia.[34]

Imperial Force

That Sir William Berkeley would resist a royal order was wholly unexpected, but the troops who finally forced him from office seemed essential in any case to restore the king's peace in the province. A report reached London on October 13 that "Bacon and his officers" had driven Governor Berkeley, some of the council, "and most of the better sort" of Virginians from the mainland. The rebels had imprisoned Sir Henry Chicheley, the report continued, and had appointed an admiral and formed a fleet around a thirty-gun flagship. The Baconian "commander-in-chief for the northern parts" was riding at the head of 250 horsemen into Maryland "to kindle the fire there."[35]

The royal response was militarily impressive. Within four days the admiralty secretary, Samuel Pepys, reported that his preparations to concentrate 1,077 men for the Virginia battalion were well advanced. Already 250 of the Guards were on board transports in the Thames. Veterans from the garrisons of Plymouth and Portsmouth, Hull and Landguard Fort, were at sea en route to the Tower, whence they would be rowed down to Long Reach, the rendezvous of the growing Virginia squadron. Other detachments of regulars from the Windsor, Rochester, Dover, Gravesend, and

34. Berkeley to Coventry, Apr. 1, 1676: "I have out lived the knowledge acquaintance and memory of all the Kings counsel but yourself and my Brother . . . he is now out of England" (Coventry MS, LXXVII, n.p., but ca. fol. 60). The instructions ending Berkeley's authority were given at the committee for foreign affairs, ibid., 195. For Lady Berkeley's admission, see ibid., 307, 308. The "Letter to recall Sir Wm. Berkeley," "to order you to repair into this our Kingdom of England," Nov. 5, 1676, is in C.O. 5/1355, 127.

35. T. Ludwell to Coventry, Oct. 5, 1676, John Goode's deposition, Jan. 10, 1677, Ludwell to Coventry, Oct. 13, 1676, Coventry MS, LXXVII, 231, 347, 254.

Sheerness garrisons were on their march toward the Tower. There Captain John Tongue, on leave from mustering the earl of Carlisle's militia, organized the garrison detachments into companies and assigned them to transports.[36]

Sir John Berry

These eight ships, with a convoy of four men-of-war, were commanded by Sir John Berry. Indeed, in the navy's view, the whole operation was "Sir John Berry's expedition to put down the rising in Virginia." In Berry's rise to this command, the royalization of the Restoration navy and the development of its imperial role were both summarized.[37]

The son of an Anglican clergyman deprived of his living and despoiled of his property for his royalism, Berry spent a decade at sea (and in Spanish jails) until, in 1663, his father's friends got him a petty officer's appointment in the royal navy. When Berry's service took him to Jamaica, Sir Thomas Modyford commissioned him lieutenant of the ketch *Swallow*. Fierce fighting won him command of the *Swallow* in September 1665. Berry sailed from the Jamaica station to success against the Dutch in the English Channel. This service attracted the attention of the duke of Albemarle (patron of Berry's patron, Modyford) and of Prince Rupert. Together they secured Berry's promotion to captain in 1666—another accomplishment of the campaign to replace with royalists the naval officers of the Interregnum.[38]

Early in 1667 Berry, in the *Coronation*, led the fleet carrying the Barbados Regiment to the West Indies. There he requisitioned merchant ships to form the squadron that launched the attacks on the French and the Caribs led by those noted governors-general Tobias Bridge, William Stapleton, and Edmund Andros, then the field officers of the Barbados Regiment. Berry's notable victory in Nevis Roads on May 10, 1667, over a combined Dutch and French fleet of double his squadron's strength, not only saved Nevis from invasion but also preserved the young English empire's hold on the Lesser Antilles.[39]

36. Pepys to Coventry, Oct. 17, 1676, *ibid.*, 256.

37. Tanner, ed., *Pepysian Manuscripts*, III, xxv–xxvi. Berry's part in the organization of the expedition is detailed *ibid.*, IV, index, and esp. 357, 370–371, 374.

38. John Charnock, *Biographia Navalis; or, Impartial memoirs of the lives and characters of officers of the navy of Great Britain . . .* , 6 vols. (London, 1794–1798), I, 143–156; J. K. Laughton, *DNB*, s.v. "Berry, Sir John," does not mention Berry's Virginia service.

39. *Cal. S.P. Col., 1661–1668*, nos. 1477, 1488, 1773, record Berry's actions off Nevis, while *ibid.*, nos. 1524, 1880, note his combined operations with the Barbados Regiment.

Having risen in the royal service and acquired experience of the empire, Berry found fame and favor at the battle of Sole Bay. There, in May 1672, "captain Berry observing his royal highness the duke of York very hard pressed, left his station and came in to his relief, where the service proved so hot, that in less than two hours he had no fewer than one-hundred-and-twenty men killed, as many more wounded, and his ship scarcely able to float; upon this he was towed out of the line, stopped his leaks, and fell into station again in an hour." Charles II knighted Berry immediately after the battle, added to his naval commands company captaincies in the marines, in Vane's regiment, and in the Holland Regiment (where Berry served with a half-dozen officers who afterward were commanders in America), and commissioned Sir John governor of Deal.[40]

Sir John Berry's last commission before being dispatched to Virginia was a voyage to investigate the struggle between the fishermen-settlers of Newfoundland and their would-be rulers. "Its my opinion that his majesty will never have a Regulation of this fishery unless a Governor be settled," Sir John wrote, "for here . . . he that is strongest treads down the weaker." His recommendations that the local elite of merchants and sea captains, and their English backers, be restrained in their exactions from the commons (who, Berry said, both supported themselves and profited England) were adopted by the crown in August 1676, and the royal naval officers commanding the annual convoy to Newfoundland were made the governors of the island. Sir John had exhibited social paternalism, political authoritarianism, and professional skill in his imperial missions. These qualities, and his high standing with the duke of York, underlay his commissions of October 1676 to command the Virginia squadron and to serve on the royal commission of investigation. Likewise, Berry's attitudes, experience, and connections helped dictate both the commission's anti-oligarchical conclusions about Virginia and the imperial authorities' favorable reception of these findings.[41]

40. Charnock, *Biographia Navalis*, 149–150; Dalton, ed., *English Army Lists*, I, 122, 154, 322, II, 26, III, 128; *Cal. S.P. Dom., 1673*, 577; S.P. 44/63, 43, 45; S.P. 44/43, 248 (in which regiment Francis Nicholson [Appendix, no. 31] was then an ensign); S.P. 44/69, 142. Berry's command at Solebay was the subject of Van de Velde's great painting *The Resolution in a Gale.*

41. *Cal. S. P. Col., 1675–1676, Addenda, 1574–1674*, 163, nos. 628, 665, 666, 731, 744, 769; Berry to Coventry, July 24, Sept. 12, 1675, Coventry MS, LXXVI, LXXVII. See Berry's call for "regularity . . . under Government," *Cal. S.P. Col., 1675–1676, Addenda, 1574–1674*, nos. 731, 769, and *ibid.*, nos. 870, 882, 1015, 1121, 1294, 1300, 1510, 1536; *ibid.*,

Royal Commanders, Commissioners, and Reforms

As October ended, Bacon's victory seemed complete. The pace of repressive preparations accelerated. Even King Charles was shocked from his relaxed detachment and became "very earnest for the sending away of the forces to Virginia." On October 20 the cabinet discussed the whole range of expeditionary needs and purposes. These ranged from the odd and the minute (the provision of "swine's feathers," anti-cavalry spears for defense of the king's infantry against Bacon's rumored horsemen), through straightforward military organization (nominating officers and assigning them to companies that were named after their parent regiments and that marched under the standards of the king and the duke of York), to such important imperial questions as the possibility of sending the Virginia battalion and its commissioner-commanders on to assert imperial authority in New England after Virginia was subdued.[42]

Finally the cabinet faced the question of just who would command the subjugation of Virginia and the remodeling of its government. Early in September, the cabinet had concluded that a captain of the Guards, Herbert Jeffreys, would command whatever troops were sent to Virginia. As the month wore on, the news grew worse, the expedition was enlarged, and the ministry expanded Jeffreys's authority. He was empowered to commission his own subaltern officers and was authorized to use those officers and their troops to execute martial law in Virginia. On October 3 the cabinet decided that Jeffreys was to be the expeditionary commander-in-chief. This military appointment was naturally followed, on November 5, 1676, by a privy council order to commission Colonel Jeffreys as the king's "Lieutenant Governor pro interim till he send a Governor."[43]

1677–1680, 215. Tanner, ed., Pepysian Manuscripts, III, 239, 353, 361, IV, 374, 382–383; Cal. S.P. Col., 1675–1676, Addenda, 1574–1674, nos. 744, 1051, 1036, 1041, 1049–1051. See also Coventry's minute of Aug. 22, 1676, on the royal confidence in Berry's experience, in Coventry MS, LXXVII, 98b. His commission of Oct. 3, 1676, is in C.O. 5/1355, 121.

42. Tanner, ed., Pepysian Manuscripts, III, 279–280, 283–284, 294, 299, 304–305, 310, ibid., IV, passim, and especially 358, 362, 366n, for the buildup of a force of 1,130 privates and noncommissioned officers; minute, committee for foreign affairs, Friday, Oct. 20, 1676, Coventry MS, LXXVII, 260. See also the order from the cabinet meeting of Nov. 2, Cal. S.P. Col., 1675–1676, Addenda, 1574–1674, no. 1074. See the draft instructions to the royal commissioners to observe the trade of New England in violation of the Acts of Trade, the connivance of the charter governments therein, and the political grievances and divisions of the New Englanders, Coventry MS, LXXVII, 273.

43. The public announcement of Jeffreys's appointment was delayed by the redefinition of his position. Between entries dated Sept. 29 and Oct. 3, Robert Southwell noted

In an emergency, the imperial executive had resorted once again to the appointment of a veteran military administrator. Once again a professional would replace a titled figure, an obedient lieutenant governor would displace an errant governor-general, and the crown would order its lieutenant to use military force to quell provincial disorder. Colonel Jeffreys's expedition to Virginia and his forcible removal of Sir William Berkeley was very like Colonel Lynch's mission to Jamaica and his capture of Sir Thomas Modyford. A part of each mission was the professional executive's purge of the provincial elite—the Green Spring faction in Virginia and the privateer party in Jamaica. Another shared objective was the officer-governor's repression of popular, anti-authoritarian groups —the Baconians in Virginia and the buccaneers in Jamaica. Such double repression was required because both Berkeley and Modyford not only had failed to control the provincial populace but also had rejected royal orders to discipline their personal followers into conformity with imperial policies. The old colonial elites defended assembly autonomy in Virginia and privateer autonomy in Jamaica. They thus identified themselves as the localist leaders that the crown intended to topple in every province of the empire. Undisciplined, autarchical, both the aristocrat Berkeley and the grandee Modyford were cast down by the armed agents of state power.

Like "Colonel" Lynch in Jamaica, "Colonel" Jeffreys (as he was also titled on becoming a garrison governor) in Virginia combined the civil and military powers of the English executive. This authoritarian union was the essence of the paramilitary imperial political system that had been introduced into English America with the conquest of Jamaica but that was only now imposed on Virginia. As lieutenant governor, Colonel Jeffreys was authorized "to hang, pardon, proclaime Pardons, etc." Secretary Coventry was ordered to write into Lieutenant Governor Jeffreys's commission a "clause of Martial Law." Attached to that commission were

---

"that Colonel Jeffreys was appointed Lieutenant Governor instead of Sir Henry Chicheley, and commissioner instead of Major Fairfax," which is exactly how it ultimately worked out (C.O. 5/1355, 81). On Oct. 3, however, the king and council noted Jeffreys's appointment, as "Governor and Captain General there, also appointing Capt. Robert Walter and the said Jeffries to execute Martial Law," and named Berry, Moryson, and Jeffreys as commissioners to investigate the grievances that had caused the rebellion, as had been noted previously (ibid., 78, 81). Later in the same meeting, Sec. Coventry was ordered to prepare Jeffreys's commission as "Lieutenant Governor." In like manner, Berkeley was first ordered to leave, then allowed to pardon the rebels and to name a deputy governor. While the crown's intent was clear—Berkeley was to be replaced by the more powerful Jeffreys—this sort of muddle was never cleared up. The old governor made use of it to retain his authority for months after his replacement arrived (ibid., 82).

"the Articles of War." Both civilian subjects and military servants were thus subjected to the absolute authority of the king's representative. The armed instruments of Colonel Jeffreys's monarchical, martial authority—a royal naval squadron and its convoy of troopships laden with elements of the imperial crown's Guards and Garrisons—assembled in the late autumn of 1676 at the mouth of the Thames, under the command of Sir John Berry, who, with Colonel Herbert Jeffreys and Colonel Francis Moryson, had been named to a royal commission to investigate Virginia's polity.[44]

The royal commissioners were instructed by the crown that the "divisions," "distractions," and "disorders" of Virginia had been "occasioned by diverse Grievances." "By reason of the great

44. The cabinet decision on Jeffreys's military instructions, and the draft instructions, are in Coventry MS, LXXVII, 260, 281–282, 288–289; see also *Cal. S.P. Col., 1675–1676, Addenda, 1574–1674*, no. 1074. The official appointment was dated Sept. 20 or 29, 1676, but, like so many of the dates in this hectic autumn, this was repeatedly altered (here predated), to provide seniority to various officers (*Privy Council, Col. Ser.*, I, no. 1094–1095; Coventry MS, LXXVII, 298b; *Cal. S.P. Col., 1675–1676, Addenda, 1574–1674*, no. 1109, and n. 41 above). The commission itself is dated Nov. 9, 1676, C.O. 5/1355, 86–90. The need for a vigorous paramilitary governor also dictated the replacement of Chicheley (*Cal. S.P. Col., 1675–1676, Addenda, 1574–1674*, no. 1110). This decision was followed by the summary recall of Sir William Berkeley (*ibid.*, no. 1118). Washburn concludes that Berkeley was not unconditionally recalled and that the royal commissioners were subject to him, by assuming that "lieutenant governor" refers to Sir William (*Governor and the Rebel*, 95, 100–101). In every case after Nov. 6, 1676, "lieutenant governor" refers to Colonel Jeffreys, as the above citations and the commissions in Wiseman make explicit: see Pepys no. 2582; n. 43 above; and the king's commission, ordering Berkeley "with all possible speed, [to] return into England," replacing him with "a Lieutenant Governor of Our Colony," "hereby constitut[ing] and appoint[ing] him the said Herbert Jeffreys Lieutenant Governor of our Colony and Plantation of Virginia aforesaid," and conferring on him, from the time of Berkeley's departure, all "authorities belonging to the office of Governor of Our said plantation and of Captain General of our Forces" of or in Virginia, C.O. 5/1355, 87; *VMHB*, XIV (1906–1907), 356, 357. Likewise, Washburn (*Governor and the Rebel*, 94–95) argues that the commissioners exceeded their authority, because they were to be "assistant to Our Lieutenant Governor or Commander in chief there" whom he assumes to be Berkeley but who was Jeffreys (see n. 43 above). In any case, the commissioners' authorization to investigate and recommend reforms not only of grievances but of "*all other matters, things and causes which have occassioned the said late divisions, distractions and disorders,*" gave them a power of political investigation that they used to great effect (C.O. 5/1355, 84, italics in original). Jeffreys also stressed the royal commissioners power of "*redress*" (*ibid.*, 148). Before the commissioners were reinstructed on Oct. 3 (C.O. 5/1355, 83*ff*), Jeffreys replaced Fairfax as commissioner (*Cal. S.P. Col., 1675–1676, Addenda, 1574–1674*, nos. 1049, 1050) because Jeffreys had been appointed commander-in-chief, Oct. 21, 1676 (*ibid.*, no. 1074). This latter appointment could not now be given Fairfax because the expansion of the expeditionary force led to the commissioning of officers senior to him as company commanders. While Jeffreys was made the colony's commander-in-chief, he could not be made governor-in-chief, for that appointment was vested by letters patent in Lord Culpeper, formally effective from the moment of Berkeley's recall (MS All Souls 254, Bodleian Library; *VMHB*, XXVI [1918], 393). One other factor, besides experience, rank, availability, and the duke's favor, must have played a part in Jeffreys's appointment: his brother John Jeffreys was the greatest tobacco merchant in England and an alderman of the City of London with excellent connections at court (*Cal. S.P. Col., 1681–1685*, no. 5).

distance of the said Plantation" from England, the instructions asserted, the king's "good subjects" of Virginia had not been able to report the injuries done them. Thus royal redress had been delayed. Now, however, Charles II had appointed political commissioners to discover in Virginia and report to him "all such Grievances and Pressures" suffered by "our Loving Subjects within the Plantation." The king's commissioners were authorized either to alleviate these grievances on the spot or to suggest to the crown royal remedies for the ills of Virginia.[45]

Although, nominally, the crown and its commissioners were going to investigate the Virginia situation, both were already sure what and who had incited Bacon's rebellion. The proximate cause was the Indian war. Therefore the commissioners were ordered to help the king's "Lieutenant Governor or Commander in Chief," Colonel Jeffreys, make peace with the Indians. Then the commissioners could expose to royal rebuke the provincial officials whom the crown held responsible for the domestic discontent that had converted an Indian raid into a civil war. The king particularly commanded the commissioners to investigate the behavior of Sir William Berkeley, "our then governor of that our Colony." More broadly, the crown told its commissioners to discover "wherein their hath been any failure . . . and by whose neglect and willful fault," but it had already concluded that the greed of Virginia's assemblymen was the most obvious "willful fault." The commissioners were told to help Lieutenant Governor Jeffreys reduce burgess salaries. The English investigators were also to examine the councillors' "capacity and disposition." The rebellion had discredited councilliar government. Jeffreys, Berry, and Moryson had also to overhaul the governmental tools of force, especially the militia. In particular, they were to ascertain the "quality, disposition and capacity of the Officers." Finally, the commissioners were to review the Virginia statutes and send them, with their advice for alteration, to the king.[46]

An imperial analysis of provincial government was embodied

45. "Instructions to Our Commissioners for Our Colony of Virginia," Nov. 9, 1676, Pepys no. 2582. An earlier version, dated Oct. 3, is in C.O. 5/1355, 83–85. A crucial clause of that version is quoted in n. 41 above. The later version, here dated Nov. 11, 1676, is in C.O. 5/1355, 209–210, 222–229.

46. The use to be made of the assembly is noted in the instructions to the commissioners, Nov. 9, 1676, Pepys no. 2582; to Berkeley via the commissioners, Oct. 13, 1676, C.O. 5/1355, 111–114; and to Jeffreys, Nov. 11, 1676, ibid., 122. The privy council's plantations committee investigated the performance of each of these instructions on the commissioners' return to England. They gave particular attention to the quality of the councillors and the revision of the laws (C.O. 5/1355, 209–210, 222–229).

in the crown's orders to its commissioners. It was distinguished by detailed attention to the legislative, judicial, and military instruments of local authority. Equal stress was placed on the quality of the local elite that manned these institutions. The crown's determination to dominate the province's institutions and its elite reflected centralizing lessons learned in the English civil wars and in the subsequent restoration of royal authority. Garrison government now would impart a monarchical and metropolitan—an imperial—element to Virginia's constitution and society.

To be sure that they understood the crown's intentions, the commissioners submitted an interpretation of their instructions. They understood that, initially, they were "to reduce the mislead people to obedience." This was to be done in two stages: the defeat of the rebels and the execution of Bacon were to be followed by the grant of royal clemency to all who submitted to the king's authority. Next, the commissioners were to discover, and either suggest to the king or impose themselves, whatever measures were required to redress Virginians' political grievances, "first of such as arise from the Governour, separate from the council, 2nd of those wherein he is enjoined with them." Finally, "all misdemeanours of Commissioned officers of the Crown" were to be identified by the commissioners and redressed immediately or referred to the king.[47]

The commissioners acknowledged that to deal with grievances imposed by the governor, the council, and the colonial officers, they must reform the assembly. To begin with, the chief agent of the Virginia assembly's oppressive authority was to be displaced from the legislature. "It is necessary," the commissioners noted, "that [Governor Berkeley] sets not in the Assembly," except at the opening and closing ceremonies, for "his constant being there much retards business at all times but now tis more unfit." The removal of Governor Berkeley from the assembly chair was designed not only to destroy the hegemony of his faction but also to be the first step toward a balance of the constitutional elements of governor, council, and burgesses. The commissioners thereby intended to establish the political presence of the crown in the colony. The governor's authority was to be made independent of the assembly and so increased in the province, but because his power was now derived from the crown, the governor's previous independence of Whitehall was to be eliminated. His councillors were to be demoted from their former status as the governor's

47. Coventry MS, LXXVII, 336.

constitutional colleagues in a plural executive. Instead, the royal commissioners were to subordinate the colonial councillors to the governor as his advisors, staff, and magistrates. No longer named in the commission of government with the governor, the councillors would be nominated to the crown by the new governor and named only in the governor's private instructions from the king. Berkeley's councillors would be suspended by the governor and dismissed by the king unless they demonstrated responsiveness and respect to the crown and its Virginia viceroy. In the future, the commissioners noted, councillors' administrative credentials and their devotion to the crown would be much more closely reviewed by the imperial secretariat and by the privy council's plantations committee than those of the Berkelean councillors had been.[48]

The assembly, which these councillors had dominated, was also to be downgraded, disciplined, and directed by the royal commissioners. They summarized their orders: the assembly was to meet less often; for shorter sessions; at a lower per diem salary. The commissioners were to make sure that the provincial legislative product was sent home to be reviewed and revised by the crown. Indeed, some crucial laws were being composed by the crown, and these were to be imposed on the provincial assembly by the royal commissioners. Other reformist laws were supposed to emerge from the assembly's response to the popular grievances collected and presented to the local legislators by the commissioners. Thus legislative initiative was to pass up to the crown and down to the burgesses. The former legislative authority of the council was thereby lessened and the functions of the three assembly elements separated. The royal governor, the provincial council, and the elected burgesses were thus to be exposed to royal supervision. The long-term result of the royal reform ordered in 1676 was increased authority for the more clearly defined lower house. This result was overshadowed for almost two generations to come, however, by greater executive control of both the council and burgesses.

In short, the royal commissioners acknowledged their orders to reform by disintegrating the old unitary assembly system of provincial government. The crown justified its transformation of the provincial constitution on the grounds that the injustice, corruption, and military inefficiency of antiquated and unqualified assembly chieftains had driven the people to revolt. As the king told his commissioners, they must convince the Virginians "that

48. Compare Pepys no. 2582 to the instructions to the king's lieutenant and governor-in-chief, Jan. 27, 1682 (*VMHB*, XXVI [1918], 393*ff*).

as We are and ever will be severe in punishing such as shall will-
fully violate our Laws and Royal Authority, and shall presume to
Encourage or Abet Tumults and Rebellions, So shall We be no less
indulgent to the just Complaints of Our oppressed people, and as
soon as informed of their Grievances direct proportionable re-
dresses for them, and take such resentment upon the Authors and
continuers of them as the Quality of the Offence shall require—
and this you may let them know was the chief cause of Our
sending you thither."[49] The commissioners knew that the crown
had identified the "authors and continuers" of the grievances of
"Our oppressed people" as the former governor and his associates
in power, the Berkeleans. The Baconians were those who acted
"to Encourage or Abet Tumults and Rebellions." The crown was
determined to crush both misgovernors and rebels and to replace
them by authentic and direct royal rule in the public interest of the
empire.[50]

Imperial aggression against Virginia's autonomy finally passed
from planning to performance on November 14, 1676, when the
latest bad news from the battered colony forced the king to
summon his cabinet into an emergency session. On their advice,
King Charles ordered Sir John Berry to set sail the next day for
Virginia in the *Bristol*, taking with him Colonel Moryson. Colonel
Jeffreys remained in London to send down to the transports the
last infantry units, five hundred of the Guards who had helped
police the capital until the last possible moment. He completed
this task by November 18. On that day the yacht *Merlin* sailed
from Greenwich carrying "Colonel Jeffreys, commander-in-chief
of the forces going to Virginia." They met the convoy in the
Downs on November 25. Ten days later the whole expedition had
cleared the coasts of England en route to Virginia, completing the
most speedy military dispatch of the seventeenth century.[51]

49. The quoted material is clause no. 6 of the king's instructions to the royal commissioners, Nov. 9, 1676, Pepys no. 2582. See also n. 27 above and the additional instructions to
Berkeley and to Jeffreys, Oct. 13, Nov. 11, 1676, C.O. 5/1355, 111–114, to call an assembly
that would meet once every two years, instead of yearly, that would sit for no more than
fourteen days, that would be composed of members elected by freeholders only, and that
would receive a reduced salary. These instructions were published for all Virginians to read
in the king's pardon to the rebels, *ibid.*, 131–132.

50. With his usual quickness, Sec. Thomas Ludwell was the first of the Berkeleans to
perceive "the frowns of the ministers" (Williamson to Ludwell, Dec. 31, 1677, *Cal. S.P.
Col., 1677–1680*, no. 543; see also *ibid.*, 663). The quoted phrase is from Ludwell to Coventry, Nov. 21, 1676, Coventry MS, LXXVII, 299. For Berkeley's receipt of censure, see
Coventry to Berkeley, Nov. 15, 1676, Add. MSS 25120, 82. On Sir William's hostile reception in England, see chapter 3 above; Berkeley to Coventry, Feb. 2, 1677, Add. MSS 25120,
350; the remarks of the chancellor, in Burk, *History of Virginia*, II, appendix; and n. 62 below.

51. Tanner, ed., *Pepysian Manuscripts*, III, 319–320, 321–322, 324–325, 328–329, 331,

After a voyage of two months, Sir John Berry anchored the *Bristol* in the James River on January 29, 1677. His ship was cleared for action against the rebels. He hastily landed seventy redcoats—all the troops he had on board—and hurried them to Sir William Berkeley's defense. With them he sent a letter reporting that seven more ships carrying an additional royal commissioner and a thousand more troops were close at hand to help Sir William reconquer the colony. Berkeley replied that he had already quelled the rebellion and that he had no housing, no food, and no use for the king's troops or, he implied, for the king's commissioners.[52]

Berkeley's Resistance

Sir William, Lady Berkeley, and their cronies soon made it clear that they wanted no royal influence in Virginia save that which had previously legitimized their regime. They defied every royal command, whether directly addressed to Sir William or conveyed to him by the commissioners. The aged governor refused to surrender Virginia's government to the king's appointee, despite explicit royal commands. Secretary of State Coventry had warned Sir William that the king "hath wrote a Letter to you calling you hither . . . and hath given a Commission to Col. Jeffries to act in your stead under the title of Lieutenant Governor, which Letter and Commission will be delivered and shewed you by Colonel Jeffries himself *upon which his Majestie expects your return hither, and that he should from that time act in your Stead.*" Berkeley's council backed his refusal to obey the royal injunction.

---

339. *Ibid.*, 345–346, notes the unusual formal investigation as to why the convoy captain had failed to sail Dec. 2, suggesting the seriousness with which this convulsive effort was undertaken by the officials of the crown. See also *Cal. S.P. Col., 1675–1676, Addenda, 1574–1674,* nos. 1060, 1064. The material support for this imperial venture received special attention from Lord Treasurer Danby, despite the low state of the exchequer (Tanner, ed., *Pepysian Manuscripts,* III, 296, IV, 356; Coventry MS, LXXVII, 256). Berry and his men received six months' pay in advance for this difficult service (Tanner, ed., *Pepysian Manuscripts,* IV, 349; see also *ibid.*, 355, III, 306). The treasury also supplied Sir John with £500 for contingencies (*ibid.*, III, 312, IV, 377). The commissioners collectively received contingency funds in the amount of £1,500 (*Cal. S.P. Col., 1675–1676, Addenda, 1574–1674,* no. 1043). And Col. Jeffreys received an additional contingency fund as commander-in-chief (*ibid.*, no. 1063). Extraordinary care was also taken for both the original supply and the replenishment of the land forces (Tanner, ed., *Pepysian Manuscripts,* III, 301, 302–303, 307[2], 308–309, 310, 314, 315–316, 411, 416, 435, 458; *Cal. S.P. Col., 1675–1676, Addenda, 1574–1674,* nos. 1053, 1057, 1058, 1062, 1114). Contrast this evidence of forethought and care with Washburn's argument in *Effect of Bacon's Rebellion, U.S. National Museum Bulletin 225,* 141.

52. Berry to Berkeley, Jan. 29, 1677, the commissioners to the secretaries of state, Feb. 2, 1677, and Berkeley to Berry and Moryson, Feb. 9, 1677, Pepys no. 2582.

Sir William then refused to issue the royal pardon to the people of Virginia for their rebellion, since the king's pardon would end all excuses for the Berkeleans' continuing campaign of vengeance. While he denied the king's clemency to his enemies, Berkeley nonetheless accepted a royal pardon for his own unlawful acts and for those of his supporters during the rebellion.[53]

Against express royal commands, Sir William and his friends continued to plunder and kill. Berkeley aimed "thoroughly to heale himself before he car'd to staunch the bleeding gashes of this woefully lacerated Country," the commissioners complained. "In spite of Law, and contrary to his Majesties most gracious act of Forgiveness and Restitution," they noted, Sir William Berkeley was "making and treating men as Delinquents . . . seizing their Estates, Cattle, Servants and carrying off their Tobacco, marking the Hoggsheads with the Broad Arrow head, and afterwards altering it to his own private mark calling this 'securing it to the Kings use.'" The old governor's program of revenge went beyond confiscation to terror, "Hanging and intending to Hang upon this Rebellion, more than ever Suffer'd Death for the Horrid Murder" of King Charles I. The royal commissioners told King Charles II that the panic-stricken planters were ready to abandon their crops and their homes and to flee Virginia.[54]

When the royal commissioners arrived in Virginia, Sir William had already summoned his local chieftains to Green Spring under the rubric of "the General Assembly of Virginia." The commissioners hoped this would be "the *healing Assembly.*" They presented the legislators with the king's call to redress the grievances of the people: decrease taxes; lower assemblymen's salaries,

53. *Ibid.*; Berry and Moryson to Berkeley, Feb. 8, 1677, Moryson to Berkeley, Feb. 11, 1677, and reply, n.d., the commissioners to Berkeley, Feb. 13, 1677, *ibid.*; Coventry to Berkeley, Nov. 15, 1676, endorsed, "This letter was read and approved by his Majesty Nov. 14, 1676," Add. MSS 25120, 94 (italics mine); the council of state of Virginia to Herbert Jeffreys, Feb. 12, 1677, Jeffreys to Berkeley, Feb. 14, 1677, the commissioners to Coventry, Feb. 14, 1677, a pardon to the governor and assembly, Oct. 28, [1676], Pepys no. 2582. Note Berkeley's own acknowledgment of his summons home and his promise to depart "with all the hast the miserable Condition of my affaires will permit me, and shall gladly obey his sacred Maty gracious direction of leaving the Government in my absence in a Person's hands of so worthy character" ("To the Rt Honble Herbert Jeffreys Esqr. his Mate Lieut. Govern. Feb. 12th 1676–77," Coventry MS, LXXVII, 396). See the king's orders in this matter quoted in n. 44 and cited in n. 34 above. Note also the statement of the privy councillors, Dec. 4, 1679, "that although Sir. Wm. Berkeley did remain actual Governor three months after the arrival of Coll. Jeffries yet the same was contrary to Your Majesty's orders, as appears by Your Royal Letters unto him," C.O. 5/1355, 370. The pardons to Berkeley and to the rebels generally are in C.O. 5/1355, 91–93, 129*ff*.

54. Berry to Berkeley, Jan. 29, 1677, commissioners to assembly, Mar. 13, 1677, and to Coventry, Apr. 5, 13, 1677, Pepys no. 2582. See the crown condemnation of Berkeley's seizures in C.O. 5/1355, 180–197, 276–278; Burk, *History of Virginia*, II, 266.

liquor bills, and secretarial costs; make peace with the Indians; reorganize the militia to defend the country; reform unjust laws; and, finally, forbid further recriminations about the rebellion, which, after all, had been caused in part by the assembly's failure to take such actions previously.[55]

Rather than try to obey the king's commands to conciliate the country, the assembly supported Sir William and his faction. After all, to redress these grievances the assembled Berkeleans would have had to admit their past misgovernment. Instead they insisted that "the Ground of this Rebellion has not proceeded from any fault in the Government but rather from the Lewd dispositions of some persons of desperate fortunes lately sprung up amongst us." This jibed rather ill with the old governor's admission that, of fifteen thousand men in Virginia, not five hundred remained loyal to his government. Berkeley and the assembly showed their contempt for the people's opinion and for the royal command when they denied amnesty to sixty-two individuals by name and condemned unnamed thousands under general descriptions. As Colonel Jeffreys justly observed, the assembly, "instead of making an Act of oblivion [ordered by the king] have made a Statute of Remembrance; to last and intail trouble, from one Generation to another."[56]

Rebuffed by the assembly, the royal commissioners again approached Sir William Berkeley. Even if he would not give up the government or enact the royal pardon, would he, they asked, submit to some of the king's other instructions? To help them protect the frontier, would Berkeley make peace with the Indians and reform the militia? He would not. Nor would he try to halt his followers' looting and thus assist the commissioners to pacify the older parts of the colony. In fact, Sir William roundly declared that

55. The irregular election of the assembly of Apr. 1677 was noted in June by the privy council plantations committee, C.O. 5/1355, 138, 142. Its Berkelean composition is detailed by Wertenbaker, *Virginia under the Stuarts*, 205–206.

56. In a letter of Apr. 13 the commissioners noted that Berkeley "keeps such a Brow upon his Council and the Assembly, that whatever he approves or dislikes, proposes or persuades is only done and complyed with," implying that Berkeley desired and, perhaps, ordered, assembly opposition to the royal commands. Philip Ludwell to Coventry, Apr. 14, 1677, C.O. 5/1355, 152–155, is a most eloquent, bitter, and ironic attempt, quoted in the text, to insist that the fault of the rebellion lay in the masses who rebelled, not in the Berkelean administration that they rebelled against, and so to reverse the royal assumption. Sec. Coventry and the privy council, however, stressed the vindictiveness of the Green Spring assembly in their detailed analysis of Berkeley's and the assembly's acts in contempt of the royal pardon, *ibid.*, 156–160. The text of the acts is *ibid.*, 162–163. The privy council report, which led to the royal veto of those acts and the substitution of laws written by the crown for enactment in Virginia, is *ibid.*, 222–229. Hening, ed., *Statutes*, II, 366–380, 383, 395; Jeffreys to Coventry, May 4, 1677, Coventry MS, LXXVII, 44b.

he knew nothing of any plundering of "rebels," when at that very moment the captain of Berkeley's guard swore to the royal commissioners that he continued to confiscate property on Sir William's orders. The scale of Berkelean sequestrations was large. The evidence of the governor's connivance in his followers' rapacity and of his share in their profits was overwhelming. It is probably kinder to the old man to call him a thief than a dotard.[57]

Balked by Berkeley in their efforts to comply with the royal instructions, the commissioners condemned his "politique, selfish partiality." Sir William replied that Colonel Jeffreys was his deputy governor, not the king's lieutenant governor. Berkeley insisted that the king's commands to him to "repair to the throne to report on His Maties [Majesty's] Gov't" left him free to stay as long as he liked in Virginia. And when he chose to go home, Berkeley threatened to "returne to my Government" (as soon as he had spoken to the king) and prosecute all those who supported those "right honorable" commissioners.[58]

When the ministers of the crown in England learned that Governor Berkeley had abused their intended kindness in leaving him his title and in recalling him to England rather than summarily removing him from office, they ordered Colonel Jeffreys to send Sir William home on the next ship, by force if necessary. The king issued these harsh commands, Secretary Coventry told Berkeley, because his majesty "hath very little hopes that the people of Virginia shall be brought to a right sense of their duty to obey their Governors when the Governors themselves will not obey the King."[59]

Before these orders reached Virginia, however, Herbert Jeffreys had at last lost his patience: after three months of Berkeley's public, calculated insults to himself, to his royal commission, and to his orders from the king, Jeffreys declared himself governor and captain general of Virginia on April 7, 1677. Jeffreys not only ousted the aged governor but also threatened every member of the old regime. He promised to purge "all scandalous, aggressive, incapable, disaffected persons . . . in all places of public trust and authority"; to regulate, reform, and redress the "apparent abuses,

57. Berkeley to commissioners, Feb. 13, 1677, commissioners to Berkeley and reply, Mar. 6, 7, 1677, commissioners to Berkeley, Mar. 21, 1677, Pepys no. 2582, to which and to all subsequent communications, Berkeley did not reply until he had left the colony.

58. Commissioners to Coventry, Mar. 27, 1677, Pepys no. 2582; Jeffreys to Coventry, May 4, 1677, Coventry MS, LXXVIII, 44–45. For Berkeley's own admission that Jeffreys was indeed the king's lieutenant, see n. 53 above.

59. Coventry's "cabinet" notes, Coventry MS, LXXVII, 448–449; Coventry to Berkeley, May 15, 1677, quoted by Washburn, Governor and the Rebel, 138.

aggressions, excesses, and defaults" in the county courts; and even to examine "the lives, licence, abilities and qualifications of the Clergy here" and to suspend scandalous ministers, under his special commission from the bishop of London. Finally, the captain general vowed to attack Virginia's Indian enemies, if they refused to make peace. These pledges to clean the stables of Berkelean misgovernment both condemned Sir William's maladministration and menaced his underlings. Berkeley immediately resisted these royalist reforms, and his followers carried the fight into the coming decade.[60]

Berkeley protested that Jeffreys's "irresistable desire to rule this country" had led him to oust the lawful governor. The hurt old man cried out to his successor that in "your declaration you say that His Majesty out of the knowledge of my inability to Govern did surrogate so able a man as Colonel Jeffreys to supply my defects. I wish from my heart Colonel Jeffreys were so well known to the King and Council as Sir William Berkeley is, for then the difference would be quickly decided." And he signed himself, "William Berkeley Governor of Virginia till his most sacred Majesty shall please to determine otherwise of me." Actually, Colonel Jeffreys had simply quoted the words of his commission, which stated that the king recognized both Berkeley's infirmities and Jeffreys's abilities, and had therefore decided to relieve Sir William and appoint Herbert Jeffreys to command Virginia.[61]

What Berkeley made of this proclamation is pathetic testimony to the old man's low estate at the close of a long and significant career. Poor, bedridden, impotent, humiliated, Berkeley's dream of a prosperous, self-sufficient arcadian England-in-America lay in ruins around him. His claim to popularity had been revealed by the rebellion to be merely a stage set, propped up before his failing eyes by his demanding young wife and his greedy, irresponsible courtiers. At his departure, bonfires burned in celebration. Yet Sir William Berkeley still could not admit to himself that the royal commissioners represented any larger interest than their personal aggrandizement. If they really reflected the royal

60. "A Declaration By His Maty's Governor and Captain General of Virginia, April 27 [sic]1677," C.O. 5/1355, 145–149. Jeffreys's and the commissioners' bypassing of the Berkelean county officials is complained of ibid., 231. On the growing English interest in church discipline in the colonies, see also ibid., 150, and n. 11 above.

61. Berkeley to Jeffreys, Apr. 7, 1677, Jeffreys to Coventry, June 11, 1677, Coventry MS, LXXVII, 34, 45. The language of Jeffreys's commission to which Sir William so bitterly objected was suggested by Berkeley's own plea to Coventry to dispatch "a more vigorous Governor" to replace him (June 3, 1676, ibid., LXXVII, 103).

wishes, then the (heretofore) comfortably distant sovereign whom Berkeley worshipped had damned him. Faced at last with that horrible fact, Governor Berkeley took to his bed on landing in England and died from "grief of mind."[62]

The Assembly Attacked

Berkeley was dead, but his faction fought on in Virginia against every act of the intrusive royal authority. By doing so, the Green Spring cabal kept alive in the minds of the king's ministers the urge to assert direct royal rule and repress local authorities in the Old Dominion, despite the distractions of the Popish Plot hysteria. Spurred by Berkelean defiance, by the like provocation from Jamaica's privateers, planters, and merchants, and by the evasions of puritan Massachusetts, the crown substituted imperial government for colonial autonomy in less than a decade. Virginia inspired as well as exemplified much of the content of this imperial advance.[63]

To impose imperial authority, Colonel Jeffreys had to negate the provincialism of the Virginia oligarchs. Most of the councillors were poor props for royal authority, for they had been appointed to serve Berkeley's "Private By-ends (not His Majesties interest or service)." Colonel Jeffreys quickly suspended three councillors for having administered Bacon's oath to the people. James Bray defied Governor Jeffreys's suspension. He appealed to the council for readmission, asking them to reassert their former control of their own membership "in Defence of the Rights Priviledges and Honor of the King's Council of State in this Country." The governor forbade the council to act on the petition. In reaction, Coun-

62. Berkeley to Jeffreys, Apr. 7, 1677, *ibid.*, 78, 34b; Moryson to [T.] Ludwell, Nov. 28, 1677, printed in Burk, *History of Virginia*, II, 267. On the royal censure of Berkeley, the privy council's confirmation of the commissioners' actions against Sir William and his supporters (despite the lobbying of Lord Berkeley), and the subsequent disgrace of the family, see *Cal. S.P. Col., 1677–1680*, nos. 302, 304, 384ff, 511, 512, 516, 523; and also, *ibid.*, nos. 239, 242, 244–247, 377, 425, 448, 619, 881, 887, 908–910; S.P. 44/68, 102; C.O. 5/1355, 209, 211, 212–213, 230–240, wherein the king-in-council dismissed Berkeley's defense, composed by Alexander Culpeper for Lord Berkeley; the severe letter of Sec. Jenkins to Lord Berkeley, July 25, 1682, and his lordship's dismay at the prejudice the king had acquired toward Berkeley and his family, S.P. 44/68, 102; and n. 54 above. As Sir Henry Chicheley complained, the royal decisions were "altogether in favour of the Rebels . . . as though they were the people only in the right and Sir William Berkeley and his party in the wrong" (Chicheley to Culpeper, July 13, 1679, Coventry MS, LXXVIII, 396–397). See also, Spencer to Coventry, July 14, 1679, *ibid.*, 398.

63. Coventry to Jeffreys, Dec. 5, 1678, Add. MSS, 25120, 136.

cillor Thomas Ballard behaved himself "with much contempt, insolence and falsehood towards me," Jeffreys wrote. He thereupon suspended Ballard from the council and also ousted Philip Ludwell, the leading Berkelean, both without the consent of the other councillors.[64]

Faced with councilliar obstinacy, the lieutenant governor successfully sought from the crown sole control over his council's membership, just as the king constituted the privy council. Jeffreys duly received the right of nomination as well as the power to suspend councillors without the consent of their colleagues. In addition, his English superiors ordered the Virginia viceroy to reduce the councillors' tax exemptions and salaries. The governor obeyed. He also responded to popular protest against the oligarchs by excluding councillors from county courts.[65]

Outraged, the Berkelean councillors led the legislative protest when Governor Jeffreys suspended enforcement of the Green Spring assembly's acts against the former Baconian rebels. Philip Ludwell complained that Colonel Jeffreys "was a worse rebel than Bacon for he had not broke any Laws and that Pitiful fellow Jeffreys had." The royal governor had asserted the prerogative to effect the royal pardon, and he had negated provincial laws to do it. As Ludwell said, "if every Pitiful fellow that Came in Governor to Virginia might break the Lawes of the Country as this had done the[ir] Posterity would be Ruined." Certainly, the power lost to the crown by the fathers would be denied by it to their sons. Ludwell recognized and expressed the precarious position of provincial elites and the fragility of the local law through which they ruled, in the face of imperial garrison government.[66]

Ultimately, Philip Ludwell appealed to the general assembly against the governor. He was supported by the council majority organized by his brother, Secretary Thomas Ludwell. "Thus," the governor noted, "they Endeavour to Avoid his Majestyes Authority and Preferr the Assembly here." Jeffreys directed his coun-

64. Commissioners to Coventry, Apr. 13, 1677, Pepys no. 2582; Jeffreys to Coventry, June 11, 1677, Coventry MS, LXXVIII, 64–65. See also "a coppie of Mr. James Brayes first address," ibid., 85, and the order of the general court [council], Sept. 6, 1677, ibid., 85.

65. Cal. S.P. Col., 1677–1680, no. 888; Hening, ed., Statutes, II, 391–392; the commissioners' reply to the grievances of Westmoreland County, no. 7, Pepys no. 2582. But see Hening, ed., Statutes, II, 390, for the Green Spring assembly's declaration that councillors might sit in any county court.

66. Jeffreys to Coventry, May 4, 1677, Coventry MS, LXXVIII, 44b; governor's and commissioners' orders regarding personal grievances, Pepys no. 2582. Ludwell's remarks are quoted from the depositions of John Seyers, Nov. 24, 1677, and of [John Throckmorton,] n.d., and [Jeffreys,] "A Narrative of Some Affairs of Virginia," [July 1678], Coventry MS, LXXVIII, 134, 135, 168–170.

ter appeal to the king and council in England. They were insulted by Ludwell's preference of the assembly to themselves and offended by the assembly's power to hear appeals. The king and his council added Thomas Ludwell to the list of ousted Virginia councillors, eliminated appeals from the provincial council to the assembly, and imposed on the assembly a law against sedition so stringent that it was a quarter-century before any councillor dared to imitate Philip Ludwell's abuse of a royal executive. Ludwell's challenge to royal judicial supremacy would not recur for a century. The council of colonial Virginia would never again be as powerful as it had been under Berkeley. Over the twenty-year period that began with Jeffreys's assault on their independence, the councillors' authority was reduced until they were "at the Devotion of the Governor . . . ready instruments to advise, act, or execute, not only what he expressly desires, but whatsoever . . . they imagine will serve and please him, be Governor who will."[67]

Facing an English military governor and a crown determined to support him, the dissident councillors sought local support from lesser but like-minded oligarchs among the burgesses. Governor Jeffreys put it strongly: "This Crossgrained faction Value the Power and Laws of a few Ignorant Planters met in an Assembly for this Government to be of greater Authority than his most Sacred Majesty and his Council." In Jeffreys's opinion, the burgesses as well as the councillors would have to be tamed before he could "vindicate my self against these insolencies offered to His Majesties Authority through me."[68] The crown agreed with its governor. Under royal pressure, in Virginia as in other colonies, successive governors stripped so much power from the lower house of the assembly that nearly sixty years passed before the burgesses made up the political ground lost to the prerogative between 1677 and 1687.

The royal commissioners of 1677 were instrumental in the imperial executive's assault on provincial legislative authority. When the Green Spring assembly refused to implement the royal pardon and passed acts of attainder instead, the royal commissioners recommended that the king veto these acts, initiate an act

63. [Jeffreys,] "Narrative," to Coventry, Apr. 2, 1678, *ibid.*, 168–170, 216–218, 268–270; *Cal. S.P. Col., 1677–1680*, no. 888. But see the conflicting statements in *VMHB*, XVIII (1910), 23–24. The death of Sec. Ludwell, Jeffreys's appointment of the courtier Daniel Parke to replace him, and the lieutenant governor's seizure of the seal from Philip Ludwell are noted *ibid.*, IX (1901–1902), 307. On the continued decline of the council, see Henry Hartwell, James Blair, and Edward Chilton, *The Present State of Virginia and the College*, ed. Hunter Dickinson Farish (Williamsburg, Va., 1940), 23–26.

68. Jeffreys to [Coventry], Apr. 2, July 4, 1678, Coventry MS, LXXVIII, 214, 270.

of oblivion himself in the colonial assembly, and revise the Virginia statutes. Beginning with his veto of the Green Spring assembly's act of attainder, the first royal disallowance of a Virginia statute, Charles II followed all of his commissioners' suggestions to make his legislative prerogative felt in the Virginia assembly.[69]

To execute the king's orders to investigate the Virginia assembly's proceedings, the royal commissioners subpoenaed the legislative records held by Robert Beverley, clerk of the assembly and the bitterest partisan of the Green Spring faction. Beverley persuaded the burgesses to protest the seizure and to demand from the crown "satisfaction that they may be Assured no such Violations of their Priviledges shall be offered for the future." Governor Jeffreys replied that the crown commissioners' call for the legislative records was backed by the royal prerogative and that the king might well repeat that order. For his part, Jeffreys said, "I will not presume by any Act of mine to prescribe [to] his Majesty in cases of that nature." Undeterred by the governor's warning and unimpressed by his example, the assembly sent their remonstrance to the king. "See their Insolence in Calling to Question his Majesty's power to us Given," Commissioner Jeffreys exclaimed. Charles II took personal offense at this questioning of his prerogative. He told his privy council to find means "for bringing said Assembly to a due sense and acknowledgement of their duty and submission towards His Majesty, and such as are commissionated by him." To begin with, King Charles ordered his councillors to prepare a code of laws and a form of government to be imposed on Virginia by royal authority. He also directed his viceroy to chastise the assembly in general, to single out for marks of royal displeasure the particular authors of the remonstrance, and to impose on the assembly the acts of oblivion and taxation that had been written in England by royal officials.[70]

While these drastic directives were being composed in England, Governor Jeffreys read to the Virginia assembly King Charles's condemnation of Sir William Berkeley's tampering with

69. Commissioners to [Thomas] Watkins, Mar. 27, Berry's and Moryson's recommendations, July 28, 1677, and the commissioners' fifth instruction, Pepys no. 2582; Hening, ed., *Statutes*, II, 398–399.

70. The commissioners were authorized to "send for such persons, papers and Records as may be useful to you" (C.O. 5/1355, 85). Burgesses to Jeffreys and reply, Oct. 23, 1677, Jeffreys to Coventry, Feb. 11, 1678, "observations upon the insolent carriage and behaviour of Robert Beverley," Coventry MS, LXXVIII, 123, 124, 207, 321; *Cal. S.P. Col., 1677–1680*, nos. 453, 817, 821; Moryson to Blathwayt, Oct. 25, 1678, on the protest that will give the lords "a prospect of the arrogancy of Virginia Assemblies," *VMHB*, XXIV (1916), 78, and *ibid.*, 79–80.

the royal pardon. He proclaimed the king's veto of the assembly acts that had supported Berkeley. As soon as the assembly adjourned, the governor removed the assembly's clerk, Robert Beverley, from all his offices and disbarred him. Then Colonel Jeffreys arrested both Beverley and Philip Ludwell and threatened to send these leaders of the Green Spring faction home to be tried for treason by the privy council. He delayed this draconian step only because he was about to try the political effect of a wholesale purge of the faction from customs collectorships and militia commands.[71]

Protection and Obedience: Garrison Government and Social Stability

The governor's arrest of his opponents and his reorganization of the militia were only a few of the incidents in his repeated resort to force and to the instruments of force to repress or to disarm dissidents in Virginia. This was Colonel Jeffreys's natural response to opposition for he was a veteran of civil and foreign wars and of political police service. He had been commissioned governor and commander-in-chief of Virginia precisely because of this military experience. Four naval vessels, eight merchant auxiliaries, and a battalion of more than a thousand regular troops, stiffened with strong cadres from the royal Guards and led by picked Guards officers of extensive political as well as military experience, gave Colonel Jeffreys the formidable political muscle that enabled him to impose imperial authority on the province over the determined opposition of its ruling elite. Over the next three years, however, Colonel Jeffreys had to replace his regular garrison with cheaper surrogates: the use of martial law and the deployment of rangers instead of regulars on the frontiers; a reorganized militia and the substitution of militia cavalry patrols for red-coated county garrisons.[72]

71. Coventry's "cabinet" minutes, Coventry MS, LXXVII, 499; Jeffreys to Coventry Feb. 11, 17, 1678, Apr. 2, Aug. 7, 1678, and to Moryson, Mar. 31, 1678, Thomas Ludwell to Coventry, Apr. 17, 1678, *ibid.*, LXXVIII, 206, 207, 209b, 215, 216b, 283b; Hening, ed., *Statutes*, II, 366, 373, 377, 408–409, 410–412, 413; Francis Moryson to [Samuel Wiseman], Feb. 25, 1678, *VMHB*, XXIII (1915), 300–301.

72. *Cal. S.P. Col., 1675–1676, Addenda, 1574–1674*, no. 1074; C.O. 1/43, 185, 371; S.P. 44/29, 173–189. The ships of war were the *Bristol*, 4th rate (Berry's flagship), and the *Rose* (of Boston renown) and the *Dartmouth*, 5th rates. The *Deptford*, ketch, was to satisfy the ministry's hunger for information on the Virginia situation and was ordered to return to

The taxation necessary to support even this paramilitary garrison government could serve social purposes as well. Colonel Jeffreys and his fellow crown commissioners proposed to tax all landholdings larger than a thousand acres. This levy was designed to discourage land engrossment and speculation, to increase the small farmer population, and to consolidate settlement. Thus the property stranglehold of the old elite would be broken, the number of the militia would expand, settlements would be made more defensible, and the tax base for support of royal government would be widened. But, the three commissioners warned, taxation, rationalization, and popularization of landholdings would never be "liked of by those great Engrossers of land there; if done it must be effected by his Majesty's immediate Commands." Once again, the royal commissioners insisted that social reform and state security required reduction of local self-government. The imperial crown must remedy what the provincial elite would not. [73]

This land-based social and military program would be written into imperial orders and essayed by governors-general for half a century to come, in every royal province. It was implemented in part by Governor Jeffreys, even though his tour of duty in Virginia was brief and he himself was fever-stricken. [74]

The military merits of garrison government in Virginia were immediately tested. Contrast Berkeley's military failure in 1676 and the response of Jeffreys two years later to the same sorts of emergencies. In March 1678 the dreaded Seneca appeared in the upcountry. The news "put all our frontiers in a fever." The local Algonquian tribes again prepared for war with the Iroquois on one side and the whites on the other. But the new administration

---

England with dispatches as soon as possible. Eight merchantmen were hired as troop-transports and, if necessary, naval auxiliaries. As Coventry explained on Oct. 2, 1676, "His majesty is sending away 1000 men with good Officers. I hope it may turne the Tide before it is become too strong for us" (Coventry MS, LXXXIV, 47–48, quoted by Washburn, *Effect of Bacon's Rebellion*, 147). See also Dalton, ed., *English Army Lists*, I, 186; *Cal. S. P. Col., 1675–1676, Addenda, 1574–1674*, no. 1088. On the selection of the officers, see nn. 42–44 above.

73. Berry and Moryson, "A true and Faithful account . . . ," July 24, 1677, memorandum of the commissioners, Mar. 5, 1677, Pepys no. 2582. For the need to apply quitrent revenue to the support of a garrison, see the commissioners' comment on Accomac grievance no. 5 and the discussion in the following chapter. On land engrossment and the need to impose social reform by reducing the political freedom of the locally powerful, see also the commissioner's comment on James City County grievance no. 10, Warwick's no. 2, and Isle of Wight's no. 14, Pepys no. 2582. Compare the commissioners' proposals and Irish garrison-government practice discussed in chapter 1 above.

74. The degree of adoption is apparent in a comparison of the commissioners' recommendations (above) and the instructions given Col. Jeffreys's successors (*VMHB*, XXVI [1918], 393*ff*). Minute of the committee of foreign affairs, July 12, 1676, Coventry MS, LXXVIII, 160; Coventry to Berkeley, July 14, 1676, Add. MSS, 25120, 89.

had learned from Bacon's rebellion that if the settlers were attacked, "it would hazard new disorders amongst us." Fortunately, Governor Jeffreys had just recovered from "the fever," for to frontier alarms were added those of war with France and of a French fleet loose in the West Indies, ready to bring that war to America. To add domestic danger to the Indian and French menaces, reports came from Carolina's Albemarle settlements "of some Mutineers in Armes there"—some of them escaped Baconians—who threatened to carry their insurrection into Virginia. [75]

Colonel Jeffreys responded to all these dangers. He ordered out the Southside militia to prevent the Baconian exiles (who were leading the Albemarle insurrection) from getting back into Virginia, "least the fire bursting there might set us in A flame." He dealt as firmly with the rebels still in Virginia, sending a company of his regiment "to the Lower parts of James River, to Keep in Awe some of the Late Rebels who were then somewhat Mutinous." Although the king recalled most of his Guards from Virginia to meet the growing political crisis in England, Colonel Jeffreys retained not only his own bodyguards but also the engineer, commissary, and gunners of the expeditionary force to direct construction of coastal forts against the French threat. In sum, Jeffreys "put the Country into the best Posture of Defence I can Possibly." [76]

Defense demanded that the governor turn his attention inland to meet the Indian emergency on the western and northern frontiers. "For securing the Frontiers from further mischiefs," he sent out Indian scouts allied to Virginia by his peace treaty. He backed them with a force of two hundred mounted rangers that he had gotten the assembly to authorize. Here was a direct application of the mobile frontier defense taught by Marshal Turenne to Colonel Jeffreys. Here was a rapid response to the calls of Virginia's frontiersmen for protective patrols, calls that Governor Berkeley had failed to answer. Moreover, Jeffreys found a sufficient number of councillor and upper-class allies to replace all the Berkeleans as commanders of Virginia's frontiers. [77]

Just two weeks after Colonel Jeffreys organized Virginia's

75. Jeffreys to Coventry, Dec. 30, 1677, Aug. 7, 1678, and n.d., Thomas Ludwell to Coventry, Mar. 15, 1678, Coventry MS, LXXVIII, 164, 208, 283, 292. Note that Ludwell was in England in the years 1674 to 1677.

76. Jeffreys to Coventry, Feb. 11, Apr. 2, 1678, *ibid.*, 206b, 218.

77. Thomas Ludwell to Coventry, Apr. 17, June 28, 1678, Jeffreys to Coventry, July 4, Aug. 7, 1678, *ibid.*, 226, 264, 269b, 283.

defenses, two hundred Indian raiders attacked the outlying plantations in Henrico County. There the flames of Bacon's rebellion had been lit by a like raid and by Governor Berkeley's refusal to respond to it. Colonel Jeffreys immediately marched "to their relief with some of my own Redcoats and a considerable number of Horse to give encouragement to those poor distress'd people; So that when I am joyn'd with them, I doubt not (by God's help) but to clear these parts of these perfidious Heathen." The governor was as good as his word. The massacres of 1676 were not repeated. Neither was their offspring, rebellion. Colonel Jeffreys had reestablished the reciprocal relationship between government protection and popular obedience by, as he said, "preserving this country from foreigne Invasions or Intestine Troubles."[78]

Arms and Authority

Faced with external invasion and internal rebellion, no one in Virginia denied the lesson taught by Colonel Jeffreys: the political supremacy of force. "One Arnold" had told the royal commissioners that monarchs "had no Right but what they got by Conquest and the Sword." Ironically proving his point, the commissioners hung him in chains. Beginning thus with the Baconian rebels, Colonel Jeffreys, his fellow commissioners, and the battalion of royal troops that executed their orders (and their enemies), disciplined each element of Virginia's population in turn.

The native inhabitants next learned what England's executives had concluded fifteen years before—that "force, with ceremony, governs all." Colonel Jeffreys summoned the native leaders to sign a peace treaty at the Middle Plantation. There he displayed the military instruments of English dominion: "the Camp in Tents, with my Regiment drawn out in Arms, and so celebrated with this good work the Day of His Majesty's most happy Birth and Restoration." Forced to their knees before the red-coated representatives of royal authority, the natives kissed the treaty. Then "the Field Pieces were discharged several rounds, with Volleys of small shot," and "Fireworks and Loud Acclamations of Joy all over the Camp" proclaimed King Charles II's nativity, his monarchy, and his imperial sovereignty over Virginia.[79]

78. Jeffreys to Coventry, Dec. 30, 1677, [Aug. 27, 1678], Thomas Ludwell to Coventry, Aug. 3, 1678, [Jeffreys,] "Narrative," ibid., 293, 161, 281, 169.
79. Commissioners to Williamson, Mar. 27, 1677, Jeffreys to Coventry, May 4, June 11,

Not only Virginia's rebellious populace and its hostile natives but also its autonomous oligarchs were repeatedly impressed with the physical force that underlay the assertion of royal authority in Virginia after 1676. During Colonel Jeffreys's administration, the council, general court, and assembly all met at the Middle Plantation, headquarters of his regiment. When first the old governor, Sir William Berkeley, and then his Green Spring counselors, resisted Colonel Jeffreys's imposition of monarchical government, "the Souldiers said Hang the Governor and God damn these Councellours."[80] Outraged, the provincial elite had to knuckle under nonetheless to the agents and orders of the imperial state, if only because the concentration of power manifest in the royal regiment and its supporting fleet was at least ten times the size of any force Virginians themselves mustered in the seventeenth century. A disparity in physical power tilted the balance of provincial politics away from the local elite and toward the king's military governor, away from colonial autonomy and toward the imperial authority that, rooted in the reality of ever more powerful English arms and institutions, grew unchecked for half a century to come.

1677, *ibid.*, LXXVIII, 45, 64–64b. Royal discussion and approval of the treaty is entered in C.O. 5/1355, 198–200.

80. Minutes of proceedings on board the *Bristol*, July 16, 1677, Pepys no. 2582. See the parallel case of Col. Hutchinson's administration in chapter 1 above. Note also that Jeffreys declared that any attempt to sue one of his subordinates, without his permission, was an encroachment on the prerogative (*VMHB*, VIII [1900–1901], 187). This was an officer-executive's usual protection of his men from the civil magistracy. The royal executives expected obedience and support in return.

CHAPTER 8

The Reluctant Dragon: Thomas Culpeper and the Constitution of the Empire

Court and Country in Virginia

On August 26, 1678, King Charles II was in the royal strong-hold of Windsor Castle, signing military commissions. Among them was one to Thomas, Lord Culpeper, as "Our Lieutenant and Governor General of Our Colony and Dominion of Virginia." Then the king commissioned Governor-General Culpeper's predecessor in the Virginia command, Colonel Herbert Jeffreys, as captain and colonel of the king's company in the senior regiment of the royal foot Guards. The imperial commander-in-chief had ordered the changing of the guard in Virginia's garrison government.[1]

Colonel Jeffreys did not live to exercise his new commission as the senior captain of infantry in the royal army, his reward for using the sword of state to mortice the direct rule of the crown onto its only American continental province. Despite Jeffreys's premature death, his actions and recommendations, and those of his fellow royal commissioners, had permanently altered the imperial constitution. Within Virginia they had effected a new balance of political power, one that would prevail for more than fifty years.[2]

Jeffreys, and his colleagues in the royal commission for Vir-

1. Culpeper's and Jeffreys's commissions are registered in Dalton, ed., *English Army Lists*, I, 243. Culpeper's commission of Dec. 6, 1679, is entered in full in C.O. 5/1355, 313–326, P.R.O. It summarized, elaborated, and added to powers of government that he already held by virtue of the Virginia proprietorship (1672) and his patent as governor for life, June 21, 1675 (C.O. 5/1355, 299–303). It reiterated his obligation to enforce the acts of trade (duly sworn to by Culpeper in July 1677) and formalized the military jurisdiction conferred in Aug. 1678. For the circumstances of the earlier authorizations, see chapter 3 above.

2. Susanna Jeffreys to Sec. Coventry, Dec. 23, 1678, council of Virginia to Coventry, Dec. 31, 1678, Sir Henry Chicheley to the king, Jan. 1, 1679, Coventry MS, LXXVIII, 295, 297, 329.

ginia, Francis Moryson and Sir John Berry, had attacked and begun to remodel the assembly system of government. Specifically, they had diminished the political and social predominance of the councillors who managed that system, the leading members of the Green Spring faction. At the lower level of the assembly, Colonel Jeffreys encouraged local leaders to challenge Green Spring nominees in burgess elections, and he sought to introduce English procedures into the house to give these new men (and himself) a larger voice in assembly deliberations. To prune the upper branch of the assembly, the officer-governor had begun to purge the Green Spring partisans from the council and to make the councillors the agents of the executive, not his equals. He did so in obedience to the royal orders that Berkeley and his Green Spring associates had resisted. Thirty years of English neglect and Berkelean autonomy had led to the social debacle of 1676 and left Colonel Jeffreys the task of imposing direct monarchical government on Virginia to prevent rebellion's recurrence. To do so, he had first struck down the self-misgovernment of the Green Spring elite. He had now to create an indigenous courtier class who would administer Virginia's counties for the imperial crown.[3]

Although the Green Spring faction understood that the new royal authority menaced their hard-won provincial supremacy, their rivals—county leaders who aspired to provincial status (and who were patronized by Colonel Jeffreys)—together with Lord Culpeper's clients and agents and royal patent officers, all found place and profit in identification with royal, English rule.[4]

Clients, climbers, and patentees became courtiers. They embraced the new imperialism; they responded to the reality of royal power in Virginia that was represented by Colonel Jeffreys's regiment of Guards encamped at Middle Plantation. It was as a place of arms that the site of Williamsburg took on the political importance that would make it the capital of Virginia. Garrison government in the colonies reflected the English institutional maturity that had also produced bureaucracies of state and treasury. Military government, imperial secretariat, and royal exchequer each produced patent places for Virginia leaders. Subject both to the governor-general and to crown superiors in England, these officers

3. On the military methods and the specific reforms of Jeffreys's political program, see the previous chapter and C.O. 5/1355, 270–271, 304.

4. See Culpeper's instructions, articles 18ff, and especially nos. 18–20, 25, 28, 29, C.O. 5/1355, 332ff. Note the privy council committee's recognition of the alienation of the degraded Berkeleans in C.O. 5/1355, 269. The commissions of 1679 (1678 Old Style) to those dominant figures of the Culpeper administration, Auditor Nathaniel Bacon, Sr., and Sec. Nicholas Spencer, are in the addenda to C.O. 1/34.

"Virginia." Manuscript by Augustine Herrman, c. 1677, Number 17 of *The Blathwayt Atlas*, ed. Jeannette D. Black (Providence, R.I., 1970, 1975), reproduced by the permission of the John Carter Brown Library. Note the expressive exaggeration of the rivers, the keys to Virginia in the seventeenth century, and see Black, *Commentary*, *ibid.*, II, 109–118.

became the heart of a "court party" whose members identified their personal and political advantage with support of the royal prerogative in Virginia. Theirs was a positive, imperialist attitude toward the politics of force and its instruments: guards, rangers, garrisons, naval patrols. As courtiers, they hoped to share in the command of this imperial apparatus of military force. Thereby they could both display their loyalty to the crown and secure their internal political control of Virginia.[5]

The leading members of this court party benefited from Colonel Jeffreys's transformation of the colonial council. Subordinated to the viceroy, the council became less powerful as an institution, but its individual members increased in stature through their new roles as regional agents of the prerogative. While the crown considered the Berkeley council to have been illegitimate because Sir William had "omitted" to present the members' names to the king for royal confirmation, royal appointment enhanced the status of their successors and tied them to the net of Anglo-American institutions.[6]

By its discipline of the colonial council, the crown created a "court" party, but when it broke down the monolithic Berkelean assembly of burgesses-council-governor into its components, the crown also incited a "country" opposition. Because the crown coopted both the council and the governor into the imperial executive, the Berkelean leadership found that their remaining political power and what was left of Virginia's self-government were both linked to the authority of the burgesses (or "assembly," as the lower house now came to be called), the scope of its laws, and the independence of the courts that applied them. Thus the political aggression of the imperial executive drove the Green Spring faction into a posture more legislative, legalistic, and libertarian than

5. Paramilitary politics depended upon the use made of the extraordinarily full martial authority conferred on Capt. Gen. Culpeper by King Charles's personal decision, contained in commission clauses 14, 15, and 22–24 (C.O. 5/1355, 320–321, 325–326), and delegated by the governor-general to his administrators.

6. The altered composition of the council was accomplished by the repeated degradation of Philip Ludwell; the ouster of Ballard and Bray following their suspension by Jeffreys; the non-elevation of the ranking Berkelean burgesses, Beverley and Hill; Culpeper's promotion of three courtiers from the burgesses; and his appointment of Spencer to the council presidency. Culpeper's commission (like Carlisle's) barred suspended councillors from assuming assembly seats (C.O. 5/1355, 319), although he did not enforce the prohibition. On the illegitimacy of Berkeley's councillors, see C.O. 5/1355, 261. The situation was remedied by clause 12 of Culpeper's commission (C.O. 5/1355, 319–320), whereby all the governor's council nominations were subject to royal disallowance and all seats at the council board open to direct royal appointment, as well as by the instruction to Culpeper (C.O. 5/1355, 329) that facilitated the royal review of the governor's nominees by requiring him to detail their qualifications to the crown.

that they had espoused in their days of power. Acquiring political principles, they became Virginia's country party.[7]

The Berkelean elite in Virginia had resembled the Modyford faction in Jamaica. Both were sternly repressive of local dissidence, personally loyal to their patron, the local potentate, and nominally royalists because the king seemed to sanction their power. They suddenly turned libertarian, anti-gubernatorial, and anti-monarchical when the imperial executive dispatched a military viceroy to check their sway. Quickly adopting new political principles, the Green Spring faction became the leaders of Virginia's country party, just as the Modyfords had taken command of its Jamaica counterpart. Yet, in each colony, the assertion of imperial authority also stimulated English loyalties and executive allegiances in those ambitious planters who had been previously denied power by the old elites. For every Ludwell or Long deprived of his personal fiefdom in a frontier society and so driven to oppose intrusive central authority, there was a Byrd or a Beeston who acquired a governmental place in a maturing society and so lent his local influence to the English imperial order.

One result of the division of provincial elites was the appearance of Anglo-American political sophistication. The strife of court and country came to the colonies as the rival leadership groups in Virginia, as in Jamaica, identified with their correspondents in England, whether whig merchants and aristocrats—the oligarchy—or tory bureaucrats and militarists—the imperialists. Like the royalists of the London militia lieutenancy, for example, the new Virginia courtier-councillor militia colonels were "generally men of considerable Estates and all of them of great Loyalty. They are entirely affected first to the King, wishing him and his power greater than they are and secondly to the Church in its present Constitution, wishing the Splendor and beauty of it may never be stained or diminished." The royal bureaucratic and orthodox religious devotion displayed, for example, in the correspondence of Virginia's auditor, Nathaniel Bacon, Sr., with treasury officials in England, contrasted with that of Virginia's country partisans who were "inveigled by letters" from whig, outport, merchant factors in England to produce popular pro-legislative petitions and

7. The fullest, clearest, and most recent definition of these 17th-century political polarities is Perez Zagorin's *The Court and the Country: The Beginning of the English Revolution* (New York, 1970). I have suggested the usefulness of this definition for American colonial politics in a review in *WMQ*, 3d Ser., XXVIII (1971), 129–133. Zagorin describes the conflict of court and country as a *political* one, "among the governing and wealthy members of the society, divided by their attachment or hostility to the operation of the authority and prerogative power of the crown" (*Court and Country*, 56). So it was in Virginia.

extremely anti-executive political bills. Finally, the English whigs persuaded their colonial correspondents to undertake armed resistance to the court, beginning with the plant cutting of 1682. Therefore, Lord Culpeper would be caught between court and country in Virginia as much as he had been in England. Dextrous as ever, he took advantage of the opposed forces of the new Anglo-American politics to balance his instructions from the crown with his political moderation (and monetary greed). Thus he was able to mediate an imperial compromise between the court's prerogative aggression and the country's provincial resistance.[8]

Imperial Impositions on Virginia's Constitution

The prerogative pole of the Culpeper period was his lordship's first commission and instructions, dated in their final form December 6, 1679. They were permeated with the conclusion that English imperialists drew from Bacon's rebellion and Berkeley's defiance: "That the late sedition in Virginia did arise only from the Supreme authority and independent power of the Assembly." The royal reply to "the arrogancy of Virginia Assemblies" was contained in the orders to Lord Culpeper as the king's "Lieutenant and Governor General." The title was that of the royal viceroy in Ireland. For the first time conferred on an American executive, it bespoke the imperial intention to reduce Virginia to Irish subservience. Acting on the Irish example in writing Culpeper's orders, the crown elevated to the level of constitutional principle the recommendation of Colonel Jeffreys and the royal commissioners that the king dictate laws to the Virginia assembly. In effect, the crown applied to Virginia the Irish legislative model, Poynings's Law.[9]

8. David Allen, "The Role of the London Trained Bands in the Exclusion Crisis," *EHR*, LXXXVII (1972), 289. Culpeper's analysis is in his letter to Blathwayt, Mar. 20, 1683, Blathwayt Papers, XVII, 2, Williamsburg, and his further representation of Sept. 20, 1683, Effingham Papers, IV, and C.O. 5/1356, 150–151, 156. See also the broadcast of English political pamphlets in the colonies, referred to by Blathwayt and Randolph.

9. The development of Culpeper's commission immediately followed the privy council plantations committee's discussion and acceptance of Jeffreys's, Berry's, and Moryson's report on the first stage of royalization in Virginia, on Nov. 29, and Dec. 5, 1677 (C.O. 5/1355, 229, 230). It was May 1678 before the cabinet considered the Culpeper proposals (C.O. 5/1355, 260). Then it refused to act in the absence of Danby. Only in August were Culpeper's proposals partly incorporated in the draft instructions. It was Dec. 20, 1678, before the Carlisle precedent was extended to Culpeper's military establishment. Not until

Culpeper's commission made it clear why Sir Edward Poynings's act of 1495 was still seen as "one of the precious jewels of his Majesty's imperial diadem." Now in Virginia, as in Ireland (and in Jamaica), when the king thought local legislation necessary, he would send a bill to his governor-general together with orders to summon an assembly. The assembly might accept or reject, but not amend, the royal bill. If the king's governor and council thought local legislation necessary, they were to draft bills for royal revision and approval. Once amended and accepted, these drafts would be returned to the governor as royal bills for assembly enactment. The new style of legislative authority—"Be it Enacted by the Kings most Excellent Majesty, by and with the consent of the General Assembly"—epitomized the expansion of the royal prerogative in Virginia under the new imperial dispensation.[10]

The degraded assembly was not to meet except when summoned by royal command. Then its session was to be as short as possible, and its members' salaries minimal. The governor-general might call an assembly on his own authority only when invasion or insurrection required extraordinary taxation. The ordinary cost of government was to be met by permanent revenues, appropriated to the king's use and issued by the governor's warrant. Legislative appropriation and expenditure of tax revenue were forbidden as "derogatory to Our Right of Sovereignty." Bills for perpetual taxes, to be spent by the executive for its support, were

---

Mar. 14, 1679, did the draft of Culpeper's orders, which now also followed Carlisle's "in relation to the making of Laws and other fundamental parts of the Government under your Majesty," reach the king-in-council (C.O. 5/1355, 262–263, 266). The commission and instructions were essentially completed in Apr. 1679 (C.O. 5/1355, 312), but the revenue act had yet to be written. Then, in August, the chill of the Popish Plot resulted in permission to Culpeper to impose the new settlement or not at his discretion (C.O. 5/1355, 364). Although the king signed Culpeper's commission as governor-general at the end of the month (Dalton, ed., *English Army Lists*, I, 243), his lordship's orders were not finally sealed until Dec. 6, 1679 (C.O. 5/1355, 313, 326). On "Sedition" and the assembly, see Blathwayt to Carlisle, the excised draft of May 31, 1679, Blathwayt Papers, XXII, 1, Williamsburg. Moryson pointed to assembly arrogance in his letter to Blathwayt, Oct. 25, 1678, printed in *VMIIB*, XXIV (1916), 78. On the title of royal "Lieutenant," see Add. MSS 30372, 2.

10. Bagwell, *Ireland under the Stuarts*, 67. Sir Edward Poynings himself had not only governed Ireland for the crown but, as governor of Tournai, had done much to crystallize the governor-council system of royal military rule. See C. G. Cruickshank, *The English Occupation of Tournai, 1513–1519* (Oxford, 1971), 13–14, 40–42, 45–46. I am indebted to Wallace MacCaffrey for calling my attention to this work. This system in turn derived from the military government of the garrison towns of Calais and Berwick, and became widespread in England two generations after Tournai reverted to the French. The crucial legislative clause, the fifth of Culpeper's commission, is in C.O. 5/1355, 315–316. The method is explained in articles 23 and 24 of Culpeper's instructions, and the enacting style is given in article 30 (C.O. 5/1355, 334–335, 336).

the first royal offerings to the assembly of Virginia (and that of Jamaica), under the Poynings model.[11]

Deprived of regular meetings, denied the legislative initiative and authority even to amend legislation, and virtually stripped of the power of the purse, the affected assemblies could hardly have been expected to agree to their degradation, except that the crown's legal prerogative could be used to reduce the assemblies' will to resist the "new model" of legislation. In return for permanent royal revenues enacted by the Irish legislative method, the king offered to confirm the provinces' entire law codes as permanent parts of the proposed constitutional revision. Furthermore, because the crown had begun to snap the legal whip of its power to confirm, suspend, or veto colonial legislation—it had disallowed the Virginia acts of 1677 and had revised Jamaica's 1675 statutes—it could meaningfully threaten to deny the rule of local law to the provinces as well as promise to confirm it in return for permanent imperial revenues.[12]

Among the Virginia laws vetoed by King Charles were those authorizing judicial appeals to the assembly. The royal veto (and Lord Culpeper's orders) proclaimed the crown's monopoly of judicial power. The crown transferred the whole appellate jurisdiction from the joint committee of the council and burgesses in the general assembly of Virginia to the king and privy council in England. The substitution of the king for the assembly as the supreme judicial power was the clearest possible sign of the altered current of constitutional authority. It marked the beginning of the appellate system that lasted as long as the old empire itself. As the provincial symbol of this, "Our Supreme and Immediate Authority," the king commanded his viceroy to order "that all Writs be issued in Our Royal name throughout Our said Colony and Dominion notwithstanding any former usage to the contrary."[13]

11. The Dec. 6, 1679, version of Culpeper's commission, which was intended for publication, authorized assembly meetings "as hath been formerly practised" (C.O. 5/1355, 315). Because such meetings could only enact taxes to meet military emergencies, however, legislative activity was effectively prohibited (C.O. 5/1355, 316). In Culpeper's private instructions, he was explicitly forbidden to meet the legislature without the royal command (article 23, C.O. 5/1355, 334). The requisite permission was granted in the 6th clause of the commission and in the 24th instruction (C.O. 5/1355, 316, 335).

12. The royal restriction on assembly meetings and the crown's power to suspend the operation of provincial law were prefigured in the orders to Chicheley, Aug. 6, 1679, not to call an assembly and to suspend the operation of certain acts of the previous session (C.O. 5/1355, 359). The governor was to read to the legislature the royal assent or dissent to each assembly act, repeatedly demonstrating the royal censorial power.

13. Appeals are dealt with in Culpeper's commission, C.O. 5/1355, 349, and see Add.

Just as fortunate politically for the crown's imperial intent as its legal prerogative was its provincial appointive power, which was greatest in just those martial institutions that were essential to sustain local authority. The Green Spring group's first complaint against Colonel Jeffreys was that he removed them from militia posts. These Berkeleans were especially bitter at the loss of the frontier commands, which deprived them of the profits of fortification, garrison command and supply, and trade with the Indians. The governor-general's absolute authority over military posts was confirmed in Culpeper's commission. He was especially admonished to exercise these powers in regard to frontier commanders, for it was on the frontier that the military feebleness of the Berkeley regime had first and fatally appeared.[14] The king commissioned Lord Culpeper captain general, with "full power and authority" to raise, arm, command, and employ "all persons whatsoever" resident in Virginia against "all enemies both at Sea and Land" in "any of Our Plantations in America." In exercise of the crown's military prerogative, Captain General Culpeper might not only "execute Martial Law," killing or sparing prisoners "at your discretion," but also, as one comprehensive clause put it, "do, all and every other thing which to a Captain General doth, or of right ought to belong, as fully and amply as any Our Captains General do or have usually done." Subsidiary clauses conferred on the captain general power to appoint and dismiss Virginia military officers and to fortify towns, citadels, and frontier posts. The governor-general's military establishment included a salaried general staff with himself at its head, a surgeon, a chaplain, two hundred regular troops plus their officers, and an ample magazine of small arms, artillery, ammunition, and accoutrements stored at the Middle Plantation.[15]

The governor-general's military mandates, men, and munitions composed the royal reaction to the popular grievances about physical security that had come together in Bacon's revolt and that now received particular royal redress. Thus the king ordered his governor-general to see that the militia were armed, drilled, and provided with ammunition. The Moryson-Jeffreys Indian treaty was to be observed, and trade with the natives made less exclusive, as a means of reducing Indian hostility and frontier jealousy. The

MSS 30372, 7b. On the form of writs, see Culpeper's instruction 68, C.O. 5/1355, 353–354. See also C.O. 5/1355, 270.

14. C.O. 5/1355, 337.

15. Culpeper's commission, clause 14, C.O. 5/1355, 320. For the subsidiary clauses, see pp. 356–358.

popular demand for towns naturally suggested to veteran garrison governors such as Jeffreys and Culpeper the establishment in Virginia of a metropolitan government centered on a garrisoned citadel. Lord Culpeper had seconded Colonel Jeffreys's recommendation to that effect. The king now ordered Culpeper to rebuild and to fortify Jamestown as Virginia's "Metropolis." Culpeper's military staff included an engineer, specifically appointed to design the citadel. His lordship sought royal supplies for the proposed strong point, and he secured the king's orders to the assembly to provide material assistance for a fort at the colonial capital "whereby the king may be safe from Rebellion, his customs more secure . . . and the country less liable to Invasions." The crown hoped that in addition to a fortified capital, new regional centers would be established that would focus governmental authority, increase military security, and promote provincial profit. In pursuance of this plan, King Charles ordered Lord Culpeper to encourage the assembly to pass a law establishing a town on each of the great rivers.[16]

The Moderation of Thomas, Lord Culpeper

The suggestion that the Virginia legislature write the citadel and town laws, rather than merely receive royal bills, left far more initiative to the assembly than the Poynings model prescribed. This crucial concession was owing to the anti-executive crisis of the Popish Plot. It had delayed the dispatch of Governor-General Culpeper, whose parliamentary voice and vote were important to the crown. Culpeper's moderate counsels, which cautioned the ministry against immediately enforcing its anti-legislative program in the provinces when parliament was so resurgent at home, were timely and respected. Under these circumstances, Culpeper got King Charles's personal permission to suspend the publication of his commission for six months. He also received royal authority to apply his instructions at his discretion—in compliance with the shifting tides of Anglo-American politics. At a moment of monarchical confidence, the earl of Carlisle had been sent out to Jamaica without such latitude; however, news of the Jamaica elite's resis-

---

16. C.O. 5/1355, 259–260, 267–268, 272, 323–333, 335, 336, 337, 338, 345–347. The governor's troop requests and citadel establishment suggestion are in C.O. 5/1355, 258, 259. Note the exact parallel of the latter with Surveyor Thomas Phillips's recommendations for Ireland, HMC, *Dartmouth*, I, 122, 125, and see chapter 1 above.

tance to the Irish model of government, and of their intent to appeal to parliament, followed Culpeper to Virginia. Jamaican defiance depended on, as it encouraged, the growth of the anti-prerogative party, of parliamentary self-confidence, and of the crown's consequent indecision.[17]

At this crucial moment in Anglo-American politics, Culpeper arrived in Virginia. In May 1680, he faced a Green Spring faction motivated like the parliamentary party in Jamaica, similarly supported by elements of the English opposition, and, like the country party in England's parliament and Jamaica's legislature, in control of the Virginia assembly. Culpeper was able to understand the country party's concerns because he was himself a political moderate. He sought, as he said, to "preserve Unity else Faction and France will destroy us all." In the interest of national unity, the baron of Thoresway (like the earl of Carlisle) opposed both the extremes of Shaftesburean republicanism, on the one hand, and the Francophile absolutism of the duke of York, on the other. Not surprisingly, after he arrived in Virginia, Culpeper decided that the motives of the country party there were not as disreputable as English courtiers—such as the Yorkist commissioners and the Danbyite privy councillors—had insisted. Culpeper suggested that Virginia had been "seen through a mist" from Whitehall.[18]

Beset by extremist political pressures but possessed of moderate political principles, and desperate for the personal proprietary profits inherent in a compromise political solution, Lord Culpeper told no one in Virginia the extent of his orders for the reformation of the Berkelean order. Instead, as the basis of his executive authority, he published only his patent of 1675 as governor for life in succession to Sir William Berkeley. He then summoned the assembly and presented them with three royal bills—for oblivion, naturalization, and taxation—and the royal request for town legislation.[19]

17. The royal order to Culpeper, Aug. 6, 1679 (C.O. 5/1355, 364, 404), is commented on by his lordship (C.O. 5/1355, 334), and in a letter to Blathwayt, Mar. 20, 1683, who replied in May that, after all, the new commission then given Culpeper "may be said to be the only one since the other has not been made public" (Blathwayt Papers, XVII, 2, Williamsburg). The timidity of the government, encouraged by the Plot and by the absence of Danby and York (Robert Southwell to Ormond, Mar. 8, 22, 1679, HMC, *Ormonde*, N.S., IV, 498–500), together with the extended consideration of Culpeper's orders during the crisis, can be appreciated through the comments and chronology in n. 9 above. On the Jamaica situation and Culpeper's understanding of it, see Blathwayt's letter to him of Apr. 5, 1680, Blathwayt Papers, XVII, 1, Williamsburg.

18. Culpeper to Blathwayt, June 15, [1680], *ibid.*, C.O. 5/1355, 385. On the circumstances of Culpeper's passage to Virginia, see chapter 3 above.

19. Hening, ed., *Statutes*, II, 565–567; *Cal. S.P. Col., 1681–1685*, no. 319; H. R. Mc-

Culpeper began the session by flattering the legislators, assuring them that he had convened them because he wanted their advice and information about the colony. Of course, restricted by his new commission, Culpeper could not himself convene the assembly. This session met by the king's command, as Culpeper implied when he admitted that the king had ordered him "to tender" the assembly the three bills written in England. The bill of oblivion pardoned all the excesses of the Baconian troubles, but penalized any future disrespect to officers commissioned by the king. The second act provided for the naturalization of aliens (Culpeper neglected to mention that it shifted the power of denization from the assembly to the governor or that it provided substantial fees to both the governor and the secretary). "The third," Culpeper went on, "is an additional act about the two shillings per hogshead etc. which must necessarily improve that Revenue by preventing frauds and abuses in the payment thereof." With such a disingenuous description the governor proposed to allocate to the crown, perpetually, Virginia's chief provincial tax.[20]

Continuing his speech, the governor-general gave as much attention to the single issue of housing and feeding the Virginia garrison as he had to the three royal acts that, by their crown composition and imposition, if not their content, reshaped the provincial government. This balance of concern was characteristic of garrison government, where troops were at least as important as law. In governments based on garrisons, in royal provinces everywhere in the empire, the billeting of the king's garrisons in subjects' homes was a major grievance. So it had been in Virginia for three and a half years, since the arrival of the royal troops. Householders, both in the counties around the capital and in the Southside sites of the Carolina border garrisons, begged for rent and board payments. The king had ordered much of this military debt discharged even before the assembly's petition for recompense reached London. The governor-general reported to the assembly that he had assigned the leading justices of the peace (now members of the house of burgesses) to make payments in the capital region and that he had personally paid off the gunners and settled their quartering bills. He promised to pay the Southsiders

---

Ilwaine, ed., *Journals of the House of Burgesses of Virginia, 1659/60–1693* (Richmond, Va., 1914), 147–149.

20. The act of oblivion is in Hening, ed., *Statutes*, II, 458–464, and that of naturalization (providing fees of £2 to the governor and 10s. to the issuing officer for each letter of denization), *ibid.*, 464–465.

out of his own salary if the English treasury delayed remissions. Moreover, Culpeper told the burgesses that, in the future, the king had promised to maintain the Virginia garrison on the English army establishment, asking only that the colonists offer continued credit for the soldiers' quarters. Of this burden, Culpeper promised, "I shall ease you of one half for I will pay the Quarters of my own Company punctually my self." The captain general of Virginia attributed much of his legislative success in this assembly to his thoroughgoing settlement of the problems of maintaining a regular garrison in the Old Dominion. Two particularly influential political factors were the cash payments to many voters by the governor-general's burgess agents and the physical presence of the troops. The garrison companies were red-coated reminders that, as Sir William Berkeley had warned Nathaniel Bacon and found out himself, "kings have long arms, both to reward and punish."[21]

Finally, the governor requested assembly action to establish towns, increase the price of tobacco, and moderate the poll tax. He invited the burgesses' opinions of the Indian policies of the royal commissioners. He called for the traditional presentation of local grievances. Culpeper concluded his long address by requiring the assembly to respond quickly to all his charges, for "I am bound up by Instructions on Report of the Late Commissioners to admit you to sit but a few days." As Culpeper afterward admitted, he found personal and political advantage in blaming this anti-legislative limit on the crown and its commissioners. He had no concern for the resulting erosion of colonial allegiance. "I thought it more for the Kings service," the governor explained, "that this Dislike should come from England than from me," especially if he might thereby win assembly approval for the revenue act that would supply his salary.[22]

The governor's soft soap could not conceal the roughness of

21. Culpeper had made payment of the quarters part of his initial proposal for the government (C.O. 5/1355, 261). For quartering as a major grievance in other garrison governments, see also Ossory to Ormond, Sept. 20, 1679, HMC, *Ormonde*, N.S., V, 211. Complaints from Isle of Wight, Nansemond, York, and James City counties, and certificates by Maj. Mutlow, Capt. Morice, and Lieut. Tongue (C.O. 5/1355, 360–361) that the debts complained of were indeed due, proved "that his Majesty's subjects and soldiers of and in this Colony are equally distressed" by the delay in payment. For Culpeper's estimate of the political importance of the garrison issue, see C.O. 5/1355, 384. The burgesses' response to his "Noble care therein" is recorded in McIlwaine, ed., *Journals of Burgesses, 1659/60–1693*, 138, 139. Berkeley is quoted from his declaration, May 29, [1676], Mass. Hist. Soc., *Colls.*, 4th Ser., IX (1871), 180.

22. See the version of "Instructions to Lord Culpeper Together With an Account of his Lordships Compliance therewith" in Vol. IV of the Papers of Francis, Baron Howard of Effingham, deposited in the Library of Congress, cited by kind permission of the owner.

the royal proposals. The act of oblivion was bad enough from the standpoint of self-government, for it initiated the new style of legislative authority whereby the king enacted the bill and the assembly only consented. The act was even worse from the partisan position of the Green Spring elite, for it dated the end of Bacon's rebellion and granted pardons for that insurrection in terms designed to check the Berkeley faction's continuing confiscation of their opponents' property. It made public in the province the royal condemnation of Sir William Berkeley's partisan exercise of power in Virginia after Colonel Jeffreys's arrival. The act of oblivion also established penalties for just the sort of insults the Green Spring group had offered to the colonel and to his and the king's authority. "A Safeguard to Tyranny," some country members termed the act. Nonetheless, the assembly passed it, as well as the naturalization act, without alteration.[23]

The burgesses reserved their wrath for the revenue bill, which was the most menacing to provincial self-government of the three royal measures. The bill proclaimed the permanence of the recently imposed imperial system of garrison government. "Whereas there is a greate and continuall charge required for the maintenance of the governor and severall other officers and persons as alsoe for the fort and fortifycations, besides many other contingent expences, absolutely necessary for the support of the government of this colony," the king declared, the Virginia tax on exported tobacco and the fort duties assessed on ships were to be collected forever for his use and applied by his governor-general to the support of the government of his colony of Virginia. Being as much "in acknowledgement of Our Royal Dignity [as for] the better carrying on our Service and support of Our Government in those parts," this grant symbolized as well as supported the sovereignty of the crown in Virginia. Previously, government revenue in Virginia derived from a provincial statute of 1662. It did not mention the king's title. It provided that none of the revenue resulting from the act was to be issued except by order of the assembly. In contrast to Virginia's 1662 act, the royal measure of 1679 was drafted by the privy council committee for plantations and approved by the king-in-council; it appropriated Virginia

23. Hening, ed., *Statutes*, II, 458–464, 464–465; Beverley, *History of Virginia*, ed. Wright, nos. 117, 118, pp. 87, 88. The legality of court decisions in Berkeley's last months was confirmed even though these were based upon the authority of a nameless "person or persons pretending or assuming the name, title, authority and dignity of governour of the said colony, though not legally so," and on the power of a council likewise unqualified (Hening, ed., *Statutes*, II, 463). See also n. 6 above, on the council, and *Cal. S.P. Col., 1677–1680*, no. 1205.

revenues to the king; and it contained no provision for assembly issue or accounting. Indeed, disbursement was by the governor-general, and audit did not even have to be performed by Virginians. The king had just vetoed the Green Spring assembly's attempt to restrict provincial officeholding to those who had been resident in the colony for at least three years. Charles II had then appointed an aspiring English civil servant, William Blathwayt, to audit the imperial revenues that the new bill would authorize. In short, the revenue bill declared the independence of the royal, English, imperial executive from those of the Virginia elite who assembled as burgesses. They utterly rejected it. On the bill's first reading, not a burgess spoke on its behalf.[24]

The governor-general immediately organized a court party in the lower house. He promised three leading burgesses, Isaac Allerton, Matthew Kemp, and John Page, immediate privileges as councillors and nominations to the first council vacancies if they would organize burgess support for the revenue bill. Culpeper here applied to Virginia the standard English court practice: the crown's spokesmen in the lower house were promised seats in the upper chamber. Thus converted to the court, the three burgesses also received the governor's astute political advice and his patronage. Allerton, Kemp, and Page received militia commands and customs collectorships for themselves and their followers. When the revenue bill came to its second reading, it was only three votes short of passage.[25]

When he heard of the bill's second failure, the governor-general personally intervened in the debate. He summoned the burgesses to attend him at the courthouse. His scarifying speech was, as the legislators afterward admitted, "imprinted in the apprehentions and memory of every individuall member." Lord Culpeper warned the Virginians that the continued existence of the assembly depended on their abandoning legislative arrogance and submitting to the royal commands. He asserted that the king, as the governor of governors, could claim the revenue even under the act of 1662. Culpeper observed that the 1662 act did not restrict the royal use of the money to Virginia and pointed to the

24. Hening, ed., *Statutes*, II, 390, 466; T. 64/88, 2, 4–8, 10b, 19a–20b, P.R.O.; Blathwayt to treasury commissioners, Oct. 4, 1680, T. 64/88, 26a–27b; July 6, 1680, H. R. McIlwaine, ed., *Legislative Journals of the Council of Colonial Virginia*, 3 vols. (Richmond, Va., 1918), I, 10; McIlwaine, ed., *Journals of Burgesses, 1659/60–1693*, 123, 125, 126, 128.

25. McIlwaine, ed., *Legislative Journals of the Council*, I, 6; Culpeper's report on his patronage of Allerton in his "Account," Effingham Papers, IV, and the case of the like promotion of Lawrence Hyde, described to Culpeper by Blathwayt, Aug. 28, 1680, Blathwayt Papers, XVII, 1, Williamsburg.

clause in the act before them that limited tax expenditures to the support of government in Virginia. He recalled that " 'twas with noe Small difficulty I did in your behalves and in Some Sort my Owne too (for my intrest is considerable) obtaine the inserting those words" assigning the king's Virginia revenue to provincial use. Both Culpeper's interest and the assembly's would also suffer by the king's appointment of an English auditor. Therefore, if the assembly passed the revenue act, Culpeper promised to support their petition to the king to continue the practice whereby the governor named a Virginian to audit the colonial accounts. On the other hand, if the assembly refused to pass the royal revenue bill, the governor-general warned them that an angry monarch might choose to collect in cash the arrears of quitrents on their lands, arrears that had built up over many years. King Charles might learn of the fiscal power that remained in the assembly by its assessment of the poll tax and (as he afterwards did) move to eliminate it. Someone might advise the king to veto as harmful to his customs the cessation of tobacco planting so anxiously sought by the assemblymen. Culpeper urged the burgesses to consider the price of resistance to the royal revenue bill, "then reflect if it be *tanti* for you not to concurr, in a thing" that "the King on Mature debate in Councell judges his owne and will soe use it and that more frely then if this Act past." The burgesses retired to their house, reread the governor-general's speech, and passed the king's revenue bill.[26]

The triumphant governor-general reported in Cæsarean mode: "I have called An Assembly, passed the three Acts, and done effectually all I came for." With characteristic lack of candor, Culpeper did not explain that to get the revenue act passed by the burgesses he had conceded additional clauses (such being contrary to his instructions) to exempt Virginia shipowners from fort duties and to repeal the act of 1662. He also neglected to tell his English superiors that he had permitted the assembly to levy and appropriate additional funds by its own orders, rather than consigning all taxes to the king to be spent by his governor-general for the public (as Culpeper's instructions required). He did not now admit, and he afterwards denied, that he had encouraged the assembly to hope for royal approval of a law for a cessation of tobacco planting, even though it would damage the customs receipts and so violate his instructions. That law encouraged the establishment of towns and diverse manufactures, both of which

26. McIlwaine, ed., *Journals of Burgesses, 1659/60–1693*, 129–131.

some English authorities considered destructive of English trade and both of which, in England, Culpeper had promised to oppose. In return for these concessions, he had asked for, and had been given by the burgesses, £650 out of the tobacco tax revenues, even though this money was no longer theirs to appropriate or his to accept.[27]

The Politics of Garrison Government

The day after the governor-general adjourned the assembly, he paid his political debts by elevating to the council two burgesses, militia colonels Matthew Kemp and John Page. Their council careers would be characterized by political use of the tools of force forged by Colonel Jeffreys and confirmed in Captain General Culpeper's commission. The new councillors continued Jeffreys's attempt to integrate English soldiers and military methods with the colony's traditional frontier forces.

The first privy council meeting that included Page and Kemp produced a request that the governor-general order regular troops to form part of each of the five frontier garrisons. This Culpeper was the more willing to do because, even before he arrived in Virginia, he had anticipated that a growing garrison of regular soldiers would supply frontier patrols. Their English officers would eliminate the need for Bacon-like bashaws of the borders whose military and political authority had made them practically independent of the provincial government. Only one of the old-style regional commands survived both Culpeper's predilection for soldierly subordination and the councillor-militia colonels' unwillingness to share military power and Indian trade with non-councillors. On the Southside border, where the danger from rebel and renegade Englishmen was substantial and the Indian trade small, Culpeper agreed to appoint Colonel Joseph Bridger to lead the garrisons stationed by Jeffreys. The governor-general explained that he had "not done so in other parts there being no persons living thereabouts fitting to be entrusted with so great a power that may more endanger the peace of the Country" than not.[28]

The shortage of colonial resources, not only men but materi-

---

27. Culpeper to Blathwayt, July 8, 1680 (received Sept. 4, 1680), Blathwayt Papers, XVII, 1, Williamsburg; *Cal. S.P. Col., 1677–1680*, no. 1350; *ibid., 1681–1685*, no. 1208; "Gift of the Assembly of Virginia to my Lord Culpeper," June 8, 1680, and Henry Guy to Blathwayt, Mar. 10, 1681, Blathwayt Papers, BB no. 3, 9, Huntington Lib.

28. McIlwaine, ed., *Legislative Journals of the Council*, 6, 9; *VMHB*, XXVI (1918), 42–43;

als, dominated the captain general's and his council's discussion of the central citadel and the coastal fortifications proposed by Colonel Jeffreys and mandated by Culpeper's instructions. As for the citadel, Lord Culpeper wrote that "the Country is at present so poor," the debts incurred by the government in the suppression of the recent rebellion so great, and the burden of the frontier defense so excessive, that he could not ask the assembly for an additional military appropriation. Moreover, legislative fear of a citadel's menace to colonial liberty led Culpeper to fear that proposing "it might have interfered with the passing of the Act of the Revenue." Finally, without ample funds, no secure citadel could be built. "A poor one is worse than none," the captain general noted, if only because of the temptation it would offer would-be rebels. Taking the advice of his council (of war) about coastal defense, the governor-general insisted that the multiplicity of landing places made fortification against invasion meaningless. The scattered anchorages of the merchantmen made the protection of only one port for shipping pointless. Besides, and to Culpeper most important, the crown had ordered that the basic cost of fortification be met from the quitrent revenue. But this resource, Culpeper insisted, was still his by proprietorial right. The colonial council, on the other hand, wanted to obey the royal command to put the quitrents to public, military use. Whatever the right of the conflict over the quitrents, it could be settled only by expropriating Lord Culpeper. [29]

In the meantime, although deprived of forts (and so of construction contracts), the council remained interested in expanding the crown's military assistance program. They first reported to the governor-general "how absolutely necessary it is for the peace and safety of this his Majesty's Country so full of great Bays and waters that the Dominion of the Sea Should be preserved (almost of equal concern if not superiour to any reasonable land force)." They asked the governor-general to repeat his request to the king to keep a royal naval vessel constantly on the Virginia station. The councillors noted with gratitude the presence of one of Culpeper's convoy, "which small sea force if formerly allowed had in all

---

Culpeper to Coventry, May 2, 1680, C.O. 5/1355, 378–379, and the quoted passage from C.O. 5/1355, 337. See also Culpeper's somewhat different story in *Cal. S.P. Col., 1681–1685*, no. 319.

29. C.O. 5/1355, 340, 335, 361–364; C.O. 5/1356, 136, 140–141.

30. H. R. McIlwaine, ed., *Executive Journals of the Council of Colonial Virginia*, I (*June 11, 1680–June 22, 1699*) (Richmond, Va., 1925), 6–7. C.O. 5/1355, 258, contains the governor-general's previous request for a station ship.

probability prevented the late Rebellion, and is the most effectual means we can propose to prevent the like or any other disorders for the future." The tactical lessons of Bacon's rebellion and of the punitive expedition were as well remembered as their political impact.[30]

The last surviving unit of that expedition, Sir Henry Chicheley's company, was the subject of a special council report. The company was little drilled, seldom mustered, rarely paid, and never exchanged with other English troops as garrison practice required. The deputy governor's redcoats thus slowly merged with the planter population. Commanded, if that is not too strong a word, by the "weak and crazy" Chicheley and his quarrelsome subordinates, the company lost the discipline that distinguished regulars. After four years in Virginia, these troops, the council complained, "instead of being a guard and Safety to this Colony as, (by his Majesty's gracious favor), was first intended, they have by their long stay and ill behaviour not only been totally useless, but dangerous and the greatest of their Terrors." Governor-General Culpeper's council of war called for the rotation home of Chicheley's men and their replacement by fresh troops, a practice never made effective in the colonies. There troops long in residence became husbands and householders or laborers and vagabonds. In response to his council's complaint, the governor-general of Virginia threatened to dismiss Chicheley's lieutenant and ensign from the royal service if they did not reform. Chicheley himself Culpeper wrote off as "that Lump, that Mass of Dullness, that worse than Nothing." Culpeper did not desire his lieutenant general's death (for such a wish was a sin), but he lamented its delay. Meanwhile, the governor-general ordered one-third of Chicheley's men to serve in the frontier garrisons and dispersed the remainder of the company to quarters in troublesome Gloucester County. He then transferred some of his personal guards to replace Chicheley's sentries at the magazine at the Middle Plantation.[31]

This arms depot was a particular focus of the intense military concern of Culpeper's councillors. All of them were veterans of civil war in the colony. All had witnessed armed political repres-

31. N. Spencer to Sec. [Sunderland], Aug. 20, 1680, *VMHB*, XXV (1917), 147; *Cal. S.P. Col., 1677–1680*, no. 1486; C.O. 5/1355, 396–397, received Dec. 9, 1680. On independent companies in garrison, see chapter 1 above; Webb, "Blathwayt," *WMQ*, 3d Ser., XXV (1968), 20; and Ormond to Sir William Temple, Sept. 20, 1680, Carte, *Ormond*, V, 146. Culpeper's character of Chicheley is from the letter to Blathwayt, Mar. 20, 1683, Blathwayt Papers, XVII, 2, Williamsburg.

sion by the royal army. All wanted to increase their share of paramilitary power. Therefore the councillors requested that the governor-general secure the consent of Charles II, as imperial commander-in-chief, for the administration of the magazine by a committee of the council. This body would succeed Lieutenant William Morice of the royal Guards. He had just resigned as commissary of the stores to go home and testify to Virginia's military needs. The council request led to the appointment of Colonel Page as the colonial equivalent of general of the ordnance, a post in which he would serve royal government well in Virginia's impending civil strife.[32]

Culpeper had, as he thought, left England itself on the verge of civil war. Colonial fears of English conflict were so strong in the summer of 1680 that ships from America hesitated to make port in Bristol, or even in London, lest these cities be once again in the hands of rebels against the king. Culpeper's fear of being out of play when "the cards come to shuffling," together with his apprehensions about the "seasoning" that had slain Colonel Jeffreys and ridden Sir William Berkeley's declining years with recurrent hells of fever, drove him from Virginia less than four months after his arrival.[33]

"I design to step to New England till the Seasoning be over," Culpeper wrote in mid-June 1680, but the governor-general delayed his departure for New England in order to make last-minute military dispositions. He had to guard the government of Virginia from its subjects as well as to protect those subjects from a recurrence of Seneca raids. Culpeper was preoccupied as well with the collection of the newly authorized tobacco tax and of the quitrents, both of which he intended to convert to his own use. To levy the former tax, the governor appointed naval officers. To get

32. C.O. 5/1355, 338, 341; McIlwaine, ed., *Executive Journals of the Council*, I, 12, 13, 25, 38. The embezzlement of military supplies and weapons from the Middle Plantation magazine was on such a large scale and involved Virginia politicians of sufficient importance that Culpeper did not want to investigate it (C.O. 5/1355, 133). Thus in graft, as in politics, the army influenced Virginia. See also, Spencer to Blathwayt, Aug. 12, 1682, and Bacon to Blathwayt, Aug. 26, 1682, Blathwayt Papers, XVI, 1, and XIII, 1, Williamsburg.

33. "Had Charles died at any time in 1679 there would probably have been a revolution" (Ogg, *Charles II*, II, 591). See also *ibid.*, 595, 612, 614, 632; Blathwayt's anxious comments to Culpeper in 1680 on the king's health, Blathwayt Papers, XVII, 1, Williamsburg, and more particularly, Blathwayt to Culpeper, Apr. 5, 1680, Culpeper to Blathwayt, June 15, [1680], *ibid.*, 1; J. R. Jones, *The First Whigs: The Politics of the Exclusion Crisis, 1678–1683* (London, 1961), 58, 66, 113–114, 180. On seasoning, fear, and Culpeper's departure see W[illiam] B[yrd] to Daniel Horsmanden, Aug. 8, 1690, *VMHB*, XXVI (1918), 392; C. Baltimore to Blathwayt, June 8, 1680, Blathwayt Papers, XVIII, 1, Williamsburg; and N. Spencer to the secretary of state, Aug. 20, 1680, *VMHB*, XXV (1917), 146–147. Culpeper's ship cleared the capes of the Chesapeake, Aug. 11, 1680 (*ibid.*, XXVI [1918], 42).

the latter, he recommissioned a slate of sheriffs. He ordered them to make immediate rent collections and to begin the interminable process of compiling a rent roll of every landholding in Virginia. These intrusions of the executive's military, political, and fiscal authority into every county and plantation in the province were followed by the governor-general and council's political and judicial review of the membership and proceedings of each of the county courts.[34]

This deployment of the agencies of "an empire in depth" kept Culpeper in the colony until the middle of August 1680. Then he read to the council the king's permission for him to return to England and set off to make the journey by way of New England.

Lord Culpeper and the Imperial Constitution, 1680–1681

After he abandoned one storm-tossed ship in the shoals off Cape Cod and another in Belhaven, a seasick Lord Culpeper tarried in Ireland. Meanwhile, in England, the future of the empire wavered between reiterated imperialist intentions, on the one side, and parliamentary pressures and debilitating fiscal weakness, on the other. The issue was still undecided by the autumn of 1680, when the colonial events of the year past were considered by the crown. The imposition of the new Irish model had been resisted by the Jamaica assembly and only halfheartedly pressed on them by the earl of Carlisle. Lord Culpeper had not implemented these anti-legislative methods fully or openly in Virginia. To provincial resistance and proconsular reluctance were added such English setbacks to the prerogative as the fall of its most effective proponent, the earl of Danby, and the exile of absolutism's exemplar, the duke of York. Finally, during the summer of 1680, the popularity of the petitions that asked King Charles to assemble the parliament convinced imperial observers that the new colonial constitutions, while sound in centralizing principle, were a tactical error in Anglo-American politics. Now that royal governors-general had criticized the imposition of an Irish status on transatlantic prov-

34. Culpeper to Blathwayt, June 15, [1680], Blathwayt to Randolph, Aug. 20, 1680, Blathwayt Papers, XVII, 1, I, 4, Williamsburg. The summer was quiet. Sec. Spencer thought this was owing to the guards and garrisons (*Cal. S.P. Col., 1677–1680*, no. 1434). Culpeper's arrangements are noted *ibid.*, 1473, 1474, *ibid.*, *1681–1685*, no. 319, and in McIlwaine, ed., *Executive Journals of the Council*, I, 10.

inces, and colonial elites were prepared to take their legislatures' cases to a new and anti-monarchical parliament, the crown's counselors became "sensible of the great inconveniences that have arisen from grasping too great a power without due advice; matters of Power and Government by new ways and forms being not rashly to be propos'd nor easily brought to pass, Excentricall motions often meeting with an Icarian fate."[35]

The king had bitten off more than he could chew. In November 1680, just as the commons majority reemphasized that it would pass no money bills until the king agreed to renounce his brother's succession to the throne, King Charles announced that he would reestablish the Jamaica assembly if it passed a permanent revenue act like that adopted in Virginia. The crown had decided to adopt Culpeper's compromise (although it was not until July 1681 that it formalized this decision in new instructions to Virginia's governor-general). The Virginia-Jamaica settlement would be the imperial constitutional norm of the coming century: the colonists would retain a substantial part of their legislative privileges by paying most of the direct costs of a strengthened royal executive.[36]

The establishment of permanent funds, at the disposal of the executive but authorized by provincial legislatures, under the influence of colonial court parties, marked imperialism's advance toward politics and beyond militarism. The new orders to the governor-general of Virginia would also specify other elements of the crown's newly acquired political mode of provincial control: the imperial review of provincial records, whether legislative, judicial, or financial, that informed and effected the executive's near monopoly of political patronage. In Culpeper's new instruc-

35. For the Jamaica case, see chapter 3 above, and *Cal. S.P. Col., 1677–1680*, nos. 1540, 1559–1561, 1570–1572. See also Blathwayt to Randolph, Aug. 20, 1680, Blathwayt Papers, I, 4, Williamsburg. Note the parallel delay in the *quo warranto* proceedings against the Massachusetts Charter (Jones, *First Whigs*, 169).

36. On the constitutional settlement, see Blathwayt to Powell, Nov. 9, 1680, and to Stapleton, Dec. 18, 1680, Blathwayt Papers, XXVII, 3, XXXVII, 3, Williamsburg. On the acceptance of the body of the Virginia revenue bill, the allowance of an amendment repealing the act of 1662, and the item veto of the amendment exempting Virginia shipowners, see *Cal. S.P. Col., 1677–1680*, nos. 1530, 1541, 1542. It was July 5, 1681, however, before the privy council plantations committee "agreed that the same power for making laws that has been given to other *Governors* be conferred on Lord Culpeper" (*ibid., 1681–1685*, no. 161, italics mine). The use of Virginia as the new constitutional norm appeared immediately, however, in the speech of Gov.-Gen. Sir Thomas Lynch to the Jamaica assembly (Add. MSS 12429, 136), which also repeated the imperial equation: submission to and dependence upon the king would produce protection for the colony and promote the public good. Lynch told the assembly that the king was now determined to be even stronger in his dominions overseas than in his realm at home.

tions, for example, the crown demanded from the council and the secretary quarterly journals of government proceedings. It required assembly clerks to send both legislative journals and laws for royal review. The governor was ordered to report which colonial offices should remain at his disposal and which should be in the king's gift. Most important to Lord Culpeper's imperial future was an order that he (like other provincial executives) was to see to it that the colonial auditor and treasurer submitted to Auditor General Blathwayt all Virginia's public accounts, from those of the province down to those of every parish.[37]

From 1680 on, not only did the governors-general face regular imperial review of their political acts, patronage, and profits, but, because both court and country anticipated civil war throughout the empire, the proconsuls were also sternly reminded of their military obligation to man their posts until relieved. While Governors-General Carlisle and Culpeper were en route to London, another AWOL officer, Sir John Lanier, arrived at court from his government of Jersey. In a startling show of real anger, King Charles demanded to know how Lanier (and other army officers whom he paid to command overseas) dared come to his court without leave. On November 3, 1680, as if to balance somewhat that day's introduction of the exclusion bill into the commons and the restoration of assemblies in the colonies, the king commanded that henceforth no commander-in-chief of governments overseas might return to England without a written order from the king-in-council. Culpeper was publicly informed that this order applied to him when, in April 1681, he finally attended the privy council's plantation committee. Moreover, his appearance at Whitehall was made the occasion of their lordships' proposal that governors-general not be paid during any absence from their commands.[38]

Royal Reaction

These calculated rebukes to Lord Culpeper were early episodes in the crown's accelerating purge of whigs and moderates from "the Court and Army." By dissolving the Oxford parliament, the king eliminated the legislative forum of the opposition

37. C.O. 5/1355, 390; Cal. S.P. Col., 1677–1680, nos. 1541, 1636.

38. Sir Charles Littleton to Christopher, Lord Hatton, July 23, 1681, Add. MSS 29577, 359. The order in council ordering Lanier back to his government is dated July 28, 1681, based on the order to governors of plantations against absence without leave of Nov. 3 previous (MS All Souls 211, Bodleian Lib.) Cal. S.P. Col., 1677–1680, no. 1573, and journal of the privy council committee for plantations, Apr. 16, 1681, ibid., 1681–1685, no. 82.

and so called the whig bluff of civil war. King Charles's decisive political action was supported by a well-publicized display of the royal army. As soon as the king dismissed the parliament at Oxford, the Guards appeared in force in the university, along the Oxford-London road, and in the capital itself. Armed royal authority could displace legislative politics everywhere in the empire if overseas revenues—French subsidies, established Barbadian and Virginian customs revenues, and potential tax proceeds from Virginia, Jamaica, New York, and even New England—either amplified royal resources or prevented drains on the crown's English exchequer. If imperial resources could make parliamentary taxes unnecessary, then the enemies of royal authority would be permanently denied their legislative base. That which colonial legislators feared came to pass first in England with the dissolution of the Oxford parliament. Unimpeded by this oligarchical and aristocratic assembly, the imperial executive resumed its attack on the legislative, judicial, and corporate institutions of self-government in both the realm and the dominions.[39]

Alert to the coming political storm but unsure of its direction, the cautious Lord Culpeper had stayed in Ireland, avoiding alike political declarations and royal reactions, until after the parliamentary dissolution of January 1681. He should have stayed away longer, for he exposed his anti-prerogative politics by appearing late in April in London at the treason trial of Edward Fitzharris. The trial itself began the crown's campaign to recapture from the whigs the use of the courts and of judicial murder as political weapons. Culpeper's presence at the trial appeared to be part of the social support for the defense organized by peers opposed to the court. To this appearance, inappropriate enough for an officer of the crown, was added Lord Culpeper's painful implication in the duke of Monmouth's western "progress," a recruiting tour that laid the basis for the rebellion of 1685. At Tunbridge Wells, attending the bastard duke, the governor-general of Virginia "was thrice knocked down and they say his skull broke" by a tory lawyer infuriated at Culpeper's support of Monmouth's treasonable activity.[40]

39. Littleton to Hatton, July 19, Aug. 2, 1681, Add. MSS 29577, 353, 363–364; Jones, *First Whigs*, 175, 177, 180, 181. Note the whigs' adoption of Ludwell (Virginia) and Long (Jamaica) in Dec. 1680, as witnesses to the crown's absolutist intent (Blathwayt to [Stapleton], Dec. 16, 1680, Blathwayt Papers, XXXVII, 3, Williamsburg). On the issue of executive militarism, see Jones, *First Whigs*, 169, 195; Ogg, *Charles II*, II, 614, and Southwell's memorandum on public affairs, Apr. 19, 1679, HMC, *Ormonde*, N.S., IV, xix.

40. *Cal. S.P. Col.*, 1677–1680, no. 1617; Littleton to Hatton, Aug. 9, 1681, Add. MSS 29577, 365.

Perhaps it was not happenstance that, on the day after Culpeper's defense of Monmouth became the talk of London, the privy council's committee for plantations acted on Auditor General Blathwayt's report that Culpeper had failed to account for the Virginia quitrents. The committee recommended to the king that these rents be taken from his lordship and applied to the support of royal government in Virginia. In the following week, the full privy council censured his lordship's failure to account for the king's revenue in Virginia and insisted that the treasury appoint a deputy auditor for Virginia, on Blathwayt's nomination. The lords rejected the Virginia assembly's petition for appointment of an auditor by the governor. Culpeper's opposition to the imperial audit and auditor extended the scope of his conflict with centralized royal authority. In June and in September, his lordship made his incompatibility with imperialism even more apparent by buying out the remaining proprietorial claims to Virginia. By becoming sole proprietor, Culpeper isolated himself in opposition to the royal assertion—identified with the imperial initiative of James, duke of York—that the king had previously resumed to himself all the proprietorial rights and revenues in Virginia. The crown sought to apply these profits to strengthen its provincial government, especially by constructing a citadel. Culpeper, however, was now prepared to claim the entire contents of the colonial treasury for himself. The paradox of a proprietor presuming to act as an agent of the prerogative had never been more apparent.[41]

Culpeper had picked a bad time to reemphasize the conflict between centralized crown control and private proprietorial profit. William Blathwayt was the author of the royal order to Governor Culpeper to accept an imperial audit of Virginia's accounts. He noted that this order evidenced an executive efficiency and political assertiveness in regard to the overseas provinces that reflected the prerogative's "good aspect at home." The auditor general was heartened, as he told at least one governor-general, by the king's punishment of offenders against the royal dignity, by Charles II's

41. Report, Feb. 18, 1681, T. 64/88, 37b; order of the king-in-council, Aug. 17, 1681, on report of the committee for plantations, Aug. 16, T. 64/88, 48. Note also the committee's prior disapproval of (1) the style of Virginia laws passed by Culpeper, (2) the law for towns, and (3) Culpeper's permitting the assembly to issue orders defining the duties of sheriffs, bounding parishes, and disposing of money (*Cal. S.P. Col., 1681–1685*, no. 161). On the audit and auditor, see the king to Culpeper, Oct. 1, 1681, *VMHB*, XXV (1917), 241. On the order of Aug. 16, see C.O. 5/1355, 404–405, and *Cal. S.P. Col., 1681–1685*, nos. 202, 203, 241. On the reacquisition and use of the proprietorial dues, see the Arlington-Culpeper deed, Sept. 10, [1682], Hening, ed., *Statutes*, II, 578–583; clause 47 of Culpeper's instructions, printed in *VMHB*, XXVII (1919), 332 333; and his theft of the quitrents, Bacon to Blathwayt, Aug. 26, 1682, Blathwayt Papers, XIII, 1, Williamsburg.

unwavering support of those who defended the operation of his prerogative, and by the royal decision not to recall parliament. The king was acting on his warning to his opponents at Oxford: "I will not yield, nor will I be bullied. . . . I have law and reason and all right-thinking men on my side; I have the Church and nothing will ever separate us." As the king's lord lieutenant and governor-general in Ireland had advised him, "You are put to defend and vindicate your royal authority at home which must be effected before you can employ it abroad with any probability of success."[42] Now that the king had championed his own cause at home, he would order his Virginia viceroy, Lord Culpeper, to advance his imperial authority overseas.

Government Recommendations

The king's lieutenant and captain general in Virginia, physically beaten, publicly censured, and subjected to tories, appeared before the plantations committee in mid–October 1681. Compelled to demonstrate his imperial orthodoxy, he made proposals for the more forceful, united, and profitable government of Virginia and the other continental colonies.

Culpeper's proposals exemplified the economic basis of politics but they also envisioned extra-economic, military, imperial power. He asked for full and punctual payment of the garrison companies in Virginia. Besides the security that well-paid troops afforded government, the governor-general pointed out that their maintenance profited many poor people in the troubled regions where the soldiers lived. The governor-general recognized the intimate connection between the king's peace, force, and economics in other ways than by this trickle-down theory of garrison pay. As poverty was the root of rebelliousness in Virginia, so Lord Culpeper sought to lessen civil unrest by increasing planter profit. He therefore asked the crown's approval of the act for towns. Towns, he said, would create centers of local consumption and so diversify Virginia's economy. As for the staple crop, Culpeper stressed the potential of the Russian market (perhaps this suggestion was another product of his long association with the ambassador to Russia, the earl of Carlisle). Culpeper also discussed with the privy council committee the assembly's petition that the to-

42. Blathwayt to Stapleton, Sept. 2, 1681, Blathwayt Papers, XXXVII, 3, Williamsburg; Ogg, *Charles II*, II, 618–619; Ormond to the king, July 22, 1681, Carte, *Ormond*, V, 160.

bacco surplus be lessened through a joint cessation of planting by Virginia and Maryland.[43]

Imperial defense, even more than the tobacco trade, required political coordination of the empire's provinces. Virginia's governor-general called for "uniting all his Majesty's subjects in America" to produce military security. A centralized American military command, he asserted, could resist foreign invasions and Indian raids, and would suppress colonial rebellions as well. To produce a united military force in America, Culpeper advised that the crown dictate the proportions and forms of the several provincial contributions. The governor-general thus advocated the quota system of imperial military requisitions that was put into operation under William III. Culpeper saw himself in command of a centralized imperial system. Repression of American Indian wars and the ensuing intercolonial unrest, he said, should be the responsibility of the king's lieutenant in Virginia. Thus the governor-general of Virginia had planted the seed of the system whereby his successors ultimately became the commanders-in-chief of British North America.[44]

When the privy councillors responded to Culpeper's concern for his garrison by noting that there was treasury pressure to cut back the imperial military establishment, the governor-general replied that Virginia had been repeatedly "ruined," and was still threatened, by Indian invasion. This external menace intensified the domestic discontent, political and economic, that seethed within Virginia and on its borders with Maryland and North Carolina. Defeated rebels from Virginia escaped to "the north part of Carolina which hath always been dangerous to Virginia," Culpeper explained, it "being the resort of the scum and refuse of America, and as yet (almost) without the face of Government." Maryland, at the same time, was on the verge of religious war. Troublesome neighbors on every frontier multiplied the turmoil that poverty bred in Virginia. A garrison, Culpeper insisted, was essential to public peace. As the governor-general reminded the privy councillors, "There hath been a Rebellion there already (which as little a force as this would in all probability have prevented)." A garri-

43. C.O. 5/1355, 405–407, in *Cal. S.P. Col., 1681–1685*, no. 260, and, in a very abbreviated form, in *VMHB*, XXV (1917), 368. See in addition, for the crown reaction to the town proposals, *ibid.*, XXVI (1918), 43, 45; on soldiers' payment, *ibid.*, 48, MS All Souls 225; on the causal relation of poverty and civil disturbance, *Cal. S.P. Col., 1681–1685*, no. 267 and nn. 45, 46, below; and, on the tobacco trade with Russia, *Cal. S.P. Col., 1681–1685*, p. 156, nos. 326, 329, and *VMHB*, XXVI (1918), 16–17.

44. C.O. 5/1355, 405–407.

son was costly, he admitted, but it was not nearly so expensive as the repression of Bacon's rebellion. Distance from England made police actions "five times more chargeable than at home," Culpeper commented. The crown's cost would have been larger yet, he noted, had European powers chosen to weaken England by supporting the rebellion of its colonists. As Culpeper recalled, the royal commissioners recommended that a garrison be kept up in Virginia because they "wisely foresaw" this alarming potential of imperial rivalry, one that was eventually realized and that cost England much of her American empire. Both royal profit (for the crown received more income from the tobacco customs than from all other plantation sources combined), Culpeper testified, and the crown's duty to protect its subjects and to preserve the peace of the colony, required a garrison in Virginia.[45]

Despite anticipated revolt in Virginia and the recommendation of his council's plantations committee that the king retain two complete companies of regular troops in Virginia and pay them fully, King Charles personally refused to continue to support a garrison there. The army establishment was being cut everywhere overseas in order to concentrate at home military resources sufficient to crush the revolt expected at James Stuart's accession. Virginia was not exempted. The army salaries of the colony's general staff—captain general, lieutenant general, and major general—were to be stopped immediately. The pay of the garrison would cease a month later, at Christmas 1681. These dates were afterwards extended briefly for "the Governor and other General Officers" and until June 1, 1682, for the garrison companies. Unless the Virginia government was able to find funds to pay the companies by that time, they were then to be disbanded. For five years the Old Dominion had been the most martial of the royal colonies. Now Virginia's military executive was partially disarmed. But the changes that garrison government had imposed on the colony's constitution, political attitudes, and ruling class could not be reversed.[46]

45. *Cal. S.P. Col., 1681–1685*, nos. 259, 267; *VMHB*, XXV (1917), 369–370. Culpeper to the privy council committee for plantations, Oct. 25, 1681, C.O. 5/1355, 407–409; *Cal. S.P. Col., 1681–1685*, no. 268 (summarized in *VMHB*, XXV [1917], 369), and nos. 267, 275, 277, 319. See C.O. 5/1355, 351, for Culpeper's alarming estimate of the Tuscarora numbers and the Seneca intent. On Maryland, see C.O. 5/1355, 341, 406–407, 408, and *Cal. S.P. Col., 1681–1685*, pp. 92–94, nos. 184–185, 195, 260.

46. *Cal. S.P. Col., 1681–1685*, no. 275; report of the privy council committee for plantations, Oct. 31, 1681, C.O. 5/1356, 1–2, *VMHB*, XXV (1917), 371, C.O. 5/1355, 410; orders of the king-in-council, Nov. 22, 1681, Jan. 16, 1682, C.O. 5/1356, 2, 9–10; *Cal. S.P.*

Imperial Resolutions

So much was clear in Culpeper's redrafted commission and instructions. Completed by the end of January 1682, this revision copied its constitutional clauses from the orders just written for Sir Thomas Lynch's government of Jamaica. In both documents, the assembly was conceded powers of legislative initiative and amendment. Culpeper's commission provided that laws were to be made "in manner and form as is now practiced in Virginia," that is, by "the Governor, Council, and Assembly." The tripartite division designedly emphasized the legislative authority of the imperial executive, so recently achieved in Virginia. Executive influence in both houses of the assembly was reemphasized by what Culpeper considered to be the crucial political clauses of his new instructions: first, the governor might suspend the councillors, or, as he put it, place them "in Purgatory on my suspension" until the king restored or dismissed them, and, second, the base of Virginia's political nation was limited by restricting the burgess franchise to "freeholders as being more agreeable to the custom of England to which you are as near as conveniently you can to conform yourself." A smaller electorate, fewer elections, and shorter sessions combined within a decade to produce a house of burgesses more stable in its membership and more responsive to English imperial initiatives than was the house Culpeper had inherited.[47]

English suzerainty was the theme of orders for the Erastian church as well as for the assembly. The authority of the bishop of

---

Col., 1681–1685, no. 229, 300; T. 64/88, 75b; the king (by Jenkins) to the [senior councillors of Virginia], Nov. 30, 1681, MS All Souls 225; McIlwaine, ed., *Journals of Burgesses, 1659/60–1693*, 167–168.

47. The drafting process began with Blathwayt's letter to Culpeper, Oct. 31, 1681, demanding a "state" of Virginia, civil, military, and fiscal (C.O. 5/1356, 1). The results were the commission, which was dated Jan. 27, 1682, but not sealed until Nov. 27, 1682 (C.O. 5/1356, 15–29). The delay was owing in large part to Culpeper's refusal to pay the fees (C.O. 5/1356, 90). The instructions were dated Jan. 27, 1682 (C.O. 5/1356, 30–61). A printed version of the latter is in *VMHB*, XXVII (1919), 337*ff.* The crucial legislative clauses are nos. 7 and 9 of the commission and no. 11 of the instructions (C.O. 5/1356, 18–19, 33). Those dealing with councillors are nos. 6 and 8 of the commission (C.O. 5/1356, 18, 19). On the qualifications of electors, see instructions nos. 8 and 34 (C.O. 5/1356, 32, 40), all in *VMHB*, XXVI (1918), 395, XXVII (1919), 329. Culpeper's whig tendencies emerged in his assessment of the royal dismissal of councillors as "disenfranchisement," that is, the deprivation of a class right, and by his feeling that the royal limitation of the franchise "barred the free Liberty of choosing whom they think can best represent them" (Culpeper to Blathwayt, Mar. 20, 1683, Blathwayt Papers, XXVII, 2, Williamsburg). The same political position was apparent in Culpeper's devotion to the rule of law (instruction no. 37, C.O. 5/1356, 40–41), in his assessment of it as "being of the greatest consequence imaginable," and in his insistence that the instruction had been "pursued most exactly and precisely with all possible tenderness during my whole Government" (C.O. 5/1356, 131).

London was formally introduced into Virginia's government to promote the subordination of colonial clergy, doctrine, and ritual to English prelates, practices, and political needs. The governor was given power to impose clergymen on the Virginia vestries. King Charles had boasted, "I have the Church," to support royal sovereignty. He now ordered Lord Culpeper to strengthen that prop of his prerogative in his Virginia province. As Culpeper's councillors and his successor made clear, courtiers esteemed the church, even in its feeble colonial form, as an instrument of social discipline. In Canterbury religion, as in London economics and Whitehall politics, the position of the new court party in Virginia was simply a provincial reflection of English loyalties.[48]

Some of the loyalist recommendations for Virginia by Colonel Jeffreys and his fellow royal commissioners were as yet unrealized, but they were again insisted on in Culpeper's new orders. The governor-general was ordered to substitute an excise duty for the poll tax. He was ordered to reform the militia and to send an account of the revised system (right down to the name of every soldier) to the commander-in-chief, King Charles, for his information and approval. He was ordered to make sure that the magazine was kept up and its contents accounted for. To the positive prerogative powers of tax finance and military organization were added the negative ones of censure, removal, and redress. The governor-general was ordered to publicize the royal repeal of the remaining Green Spring legislation, to announce the royal redress of the popular grievances against Green Spring rule (as reported by the commissioners), and to remove officials implicated in arbitrary judicial practices, embezzlement of munitions, deficient military training, or the engrossment of land. Moreover, the governor-general was ordered to continue the royal assault on the authority of the provincial assembly, shortening its sessions, lowering its salaries, and "declaring the Right of Your Majesty and the Officers to Public Records." Thus the royal representative was told both to gain access to the assembly's own reports of its actions and to censure the legislators for objecting to the royal commissioners' seizure of these records. Finally, Culpeper was

48. Clauses 24, 25, 54, 55, of Culpeper's instructions, C.O. 5/1356, 36–37, 46–47, and *VMHB*, XXVII (1919), 326–327, 334. Culpeper was quick to recognize the patronage potential of the 76 or 77 Virginia clerical posts (*Cal. S.P. Col., 1681–1685*, p. 155), but he assessed the impossibility of the task of social regulation when he recorded the failure of morality because of the people's desire "to comfort themselves after their hard labour" and clerical acquiescence therein (*ibid.*, no. 1272, and C.O. 5/1356, 172–174), and despite exemplary (and politically meaningful) efforts at church support by Sec. Spencer. See also Culpeper's comment on his instructions, C.O. 5/1355, 331.

ordered once again to remove appellate jurisdiction from the assembly to the king, according to Colonel Jeffreys's example.[49]

Country Rebellion

Captain General Culpeper's orders summarized the extension of imperial authority to Virginia during the five years following the rebellion of 1676. This imposition of direct, English, military and monarchical rule had largely displaced the old provincial elite, the Green Spring faction, from the upper reaches of Virginia's government. Incited to hostility by their reduction in status, the faction had retreated to the lower house of the assembly. There, as the leaders of the country party, they now organized a last-ditch resistance to the imperial settlement of 1681.

The diehard provincials were led by Robert Beverley, clerk of the Virginia assembly, head of the Green Spring faction, and chief of the colony's country party. The official reports agree that "the premier Ministre Monseigneur Beverley" was anxious for an assembly-authorized cessation of tobacco planting to raise the price of the staple crop and that he organized popular petitions for the meeting of the assembly to enact that cessation. The "importunate motions of the over-active clerk" were identical to the petitioning techniques used previously by the country party in England during the Exclusion Crisis. In Virginia as in England, opposition leaders tried to force the executive to summon the legislature so that it could enact a "country" measure. And in both cases, the frustrated country extremists finally fomented a revolt against the unresponsive royal government. Petitioning—which in England had produced the political labels "petitioners" and "abhorrers," labels that soon became "whig" and "tory"—was suggested to Virginia's country leadership by merchant spokesmen of the English opposition. The court assumed that, in Virginia as in England during the 1670s and 1680s, resort to revolt would inevitably follow petitioners' efforts to coerce the crown as

49. The clauses and supporting documents, grouped in the order they are discussed in the text, are: nos. 31, 32, C.O. 5/1356, 39–40, and *VMHB*, XXVII (1919), 328; no. 80, C.O. 5/1356, 59–60, and *VMHB*, XXVIII (1920), 46 (see also *Cal. S.P. Col., 1681–1685*, nos. 321–322); nos. 26–28, 39, 41, 45, 46, C.O. 5/1356, 38–39, 41, 43–44, and *VMHB*, XXVII (1919), 327–328, 330, 331, 332; nos. 35 and 36, C.O. 5/1356, 40, and *VMHB*, XXVII (1919), 329; C.O. 5/1356, 4–5, 10–11, on the right to records and the reporting requirement; and clauses 64 and 70, C.O. 5/1356, 49, 52–53, and *VMHB*, XXVIII (1920), 13, 16. See also *Cal. S.P. Col., 1681–1685*, no. 371.

it had during the 1630s and 1640s. As Secretary Jenkins asked, "What was there in the beginning and progress of the last War, more designing against Lawful Authority than popular Petitions"? Courtiers recognized that successful petitions would strengthen legislatures and thereby create either a "debased Monarchy or a New Cast Republic." In the end would come another civil war. Fear of civil strife discredited Beverley at court. The fact of riots tarnished his country legislative program in Virginia. So it was in England with Shaftesbury, his whig assertions, and his assassination plots. Unlike the unflappable Charles II, however, the interim Virginia executive, Sir Henry Chicheley, was a feeble, Berkelean figure, unprepared to offer an imperial resistance to provincial clamor.[50]

Beverley, the Burgesses, and Plant Cutting

The popularity of the petitions and the danger of civil war were impressed on Chicheley, the aged deputy governor, by Robert Beverley, his colleague from the Berkeley era. The Green Spring and country chief prevailed on "the easiness of an inclining Governor" to persuade Chicheley to issue writs for the election of the burgesses. Summoning the assembly into an April session, Chicheley not only disobeyed his orders—to consult his council before he summoned an assembly—but also contravened the council's proclamation that had postponed any assembly before November of 1682, when the governor-general was expected. Infirm of purpose and person, Sir Henry was the more inclined to listen to Beverley's advice that he respond to the petitions because he had not received a single royal order about the government since Culpeper's departure almost two years previously. Chicheley was especially upset because the crown had failed to respond to the 1680 assembly's plea for permission to stop tobacco planting for a time. Imperial neglect thus helped Beverley convince Sir Henry Chicheley that he could save Virginia from renewed rebellion first by acceding to the petitioners' request for an assembly and then by acquiescing in that assembly's act for a cessation of planting.[51]

50. Chicheley to the king, and to Jenkins, May 8, 1682, *Cal. S.P. Col., 1681–1685*, 117–118, C.O. 5/1356, 65–66 (received June 14, 1682); the council's state of Virginia, May 4, 1683, *Cal. S.P. Col., 1681–1685*, no. 1063; Hening, ed., *Statutes*, II, 562. Jenkins's condemnation of petitioning is in S.P. 44/62, 43–44. See also n. 8 above.

51. Chicheley to Jenkins, Aug. 10, 1682, mentions, and does not deny, Beverley's alleged influence on him. Instead, the deputy governor proclaimed, in good Berkelean fashion, that Beverley's behavior in Bacon's rebellion had been far better than that of some of

"Big with expectation to enact a cessation," the assembly arrived in Jamestown in the third week of April 1682, only to be told that Sir Henry Chicheley had received royal orders not to call an assembly before November 10. The assembled burgesses cautioned the deputy governor and the council (whose courtier majority was demanding that Chicheley not swear in the assemblymen) that failure to open the legislative session would be physically dangerous and economically destructive. Virginians were pressed by poverty and scared by the Indians, especially since it was rumored that "the Souldiers are forthwith to be disbanded, and consequently the garrisons well settled for the security of the Country dismantled." The people expected the assembly not only to ameliorate the tobacco depression but also to provide for a continued military presence. (This last was what the crown had assumed the assembly would have to do when royal support for the Virginia garrison was discontinued.) Therefore, and in return for being sworn in, the burgesses promised a tax bill to support the garrison. This was a promise particularly tempting to a deputy governor whose only salary was his captain's pay. Alternating carrot and stick, the legislators also reminded Sir Henry that "if the soldiers should be disbanded, and not receive their full pay, and arrears," they would growl. The potential mutiny of the garrison, warned the burgesses, "if added to the dissatisfaction of the Country in general by the thus breaking up of this Assembly, might prove of dangerous, and irrecoverable Consequence to this Countrey and his Majesties interests therein." In brief, if Sir Henry Chicheley and the council dismissed the assembly, the burgesses threatened to incite a rebellion by both subjects and soldiers that would ruin both the provincial government and the royal revenue.[52]

Equally fearful of rebellion and anxious for military support, the deputy governor and the councillors swore in the burgesses

---

the councillors who now denounced him (*Cal. S.P. Col., 1681–1685*, no. 649). For the king's instructions to Chicheley about the assembly, Jan. 20, 1682, see *ibid.*, nos. 370, 371. The council's statement is in C.O. 5/1356, 177. Chicheley rejoined, "I thought that the Council was a body whose advice might be asked or not at discretion." His position on the legislative summons is further documented in McIlwaine, ed., *Journals of Burgesses, 1659/60–1693*, 165; McIlwaine, ed., *Executive Journals of the Council*, I, 15–16; and Chicheley to Sir Thomas Chicheley, June 12, 1682, C.O. 5/1356, 66–69, and *VMHB*, XXVIII (1920), 119. See also Baltimore to Jenkins, May 18, 1682, *Cal. S.P. Col., 1681–1685*, no. 507.

52. The king to Chicheley, Jan. 21, 1682, C.O. 5/1356, 11–12; McIlwaine, ed., *Journals of Burgesses, 1659/60–1693*, 158–159, 162. Chicheley had the governor's usual political advantage over his council in that his instructions from the king were largely secret from them and so they did not know what they could safely oppose him in (council to plantations committee, May 4, 1683, C.O. 5/1356, 176–178; *Cal. S.P. Col., 1681–1685*, no. 1063).

and asked them to make good their promise of a tax bill to keep the garrison on foot. Instead the lower house demanded that the council join them in hearing judicial appeals on the old, assembly basis. To repeated inquiries by the deputy governor, the burgesses replied that they were proceeding with the garrison supply bill. In fact, they were composing a cessation law. After being hood-winked for a week by burgess dissimulation, the council at last persuaded the reluctant Chicheley that he must obey the royal orders not to permit the assembly to sit until after Governor-General Culpeper arrived. On learning that they were to be sent home, the burgesses voted to publish the journal that their clerk and tactician Robert Beverley had written as their campaign document. The burgesses left Jamestown prepared to carry out their threats against the government: they would use their journal to incite public riot and military mutiny.[53]

Four days after the assembly broke up, that is, as soon as the burgesses got home and read their journal to public meetings, pent-up provincial hostilities overflowed the channels of public order. Remembering their recent rebellion, encouraged by their burgesses, "the sick brained people . . . uneasy under the low and mean price of tobacco . . . grown out of esteem by the over great quantities yearly made, the which to lessen, on May day [1682] a Rabble made a May Sport, to dance from plantation to plantation, to cut up Tobacco Plants. This humour wildly begun, spreads it self, with great celerity, and the disorder immediately grew so high, to threaten the whole Country." The garrison, stationed in Virginia to suppress just this sort of disorder, suddenly became itself untrustworthy: "To agravate those disorders, we have met with little less extremes from his Majesty's two foot Companies of soldiers grown rusty for want of Action, uneasy to be disbanded . . . , and in this Exigency of our disorders by the plant Cutters the mutinous tempers of the Soldiers makes our affairs most unpleasant and hazardous."[54]

53. Chicheley to Jenkins, May 8, 1682, *VMHB*, XXVIII (1920), 119, C.O. 5/1356, 67–68; McIlwaine, ed., *Journals of Burgesses, 1659/60–1693*, 167, 168. On the session, see Chicheley to his brother, June 12, 1682, *Cal. S.P. Col., 1681–1685*, no. 550. See also *ibid.*, no. 495; Chicheley to Jenkins, and Spencer to Jenkins, May 8, 1682, C.O. 5/1356, 68, 69, and on its conclusion, see McIlwaine, ed., *Journals of Burgesses, 1659/60–1693*, 169, and McIlwaine, ed., *Executive Journals of the Council*, I, 17, 41; and Hening, ed., *Statutes*, III, 548. See also Chicheley to Jenkins, May 8, 1682, C.O. 5/1356, 68.

54. Spencer to Blathwayt, May 29, 1682, and Blathwayt's unsurprised endorsement, "the Soldiers disorderly at disbandment," Blathwayt Papers, XVI, 1, Williamsburg. See chapters 2 and 3 above for English parallels.

Councilliar Repression

To repress plant cutting and mutiny alike, the new court party majority on the council effectively applied their ample experience in quelling riot and rebellion. Led by the analytical and ruthless secretary of state, Nicholas Spencer, the councillors met at the Middle Plantation. This, the site of Williamsburg, had been the headquarters of Virginia's garrison government since Colonel Jeffreys encamped his regiment of Guards and established a provincial armory there in 1677. The councillors dispersed most of the troops by promising them a favorable rate of exchange in their pay. Having lured the redcoats from the vicinity of the magazine, the council then disarmed them, save for nine reliable soldiers retained as a bodyguard for the deputy governor. The council then ordered the disbanded troops either to reinforce the frontier garrisons or to go to England.[55]

Simultaneously, the council ordered Colonel Matthew Kemp to ride at the head of his militia cavalry into Gloucester County. Gloucester was Robert Beverley's home and the heart of the riots. Colonel Kemp was ordered to find the plant cutters and "forthwith to suppress them by force of Arms." Kemp and his cavalry quickly caught a party of cutters at their work of destruction and captured twenty-two of them. Then he rode on to act "with what hurt he could" against other rioters.[56]

The most important and decisive task of repression was assigned to "the faithful and courageous execution thereof by Major General Smith." Acting on "the vigorous advice given by Mr. Secretary Spencer," the council ordered the major general to ar-

55. Spencer to Blathwayt, Aug. 12, 1682, Blathwayt Papers, XVI, 1, Williamsburg. Baltimore considered Sec. Spencer, not Dep. Gov. Chicheley, as the effective head of the government, as well as of the court party, in Virginia (*Cal. S.P. Col., 1681–1685*, no. 507; see also, *ibid.*, no. 532). On the councillors' actions toward the garrison, see the minutes of their meetings at the Middle Plantation, May 3, 7, June 21, McIlwaine, ed., *Executive Journals of the Council*, I, 18, 19, 25; Spencer to Jenkins, May 8, 28, June 7, 1682, C.O. 5/1356, 70–72; *Cal. S.P. Col., 1681–1685*, nos. 495, 524, 546; Chicheley to Jenkins, May 30, 1682, *ibid.*, no. 531; affidavit of Spencer and Bacon, Sept. 20, 1682, Blathwayt Papers, Huntington Lib.; and Spencer, Bacon, and Ludwell's statement, May 10, 1683, T. 64/88, 117. The money necessary to complete the disbandment did not arrive until June 9, 1682, so that the menace of mutiny haunted the council during the height of the riots ("Warrant for the disbandment of the Forces," June 22, 1684, Effingham Papers, III). At the disbandment, the military staff still included a surgeon, chaplain, engineer, gunsmith and two of his mates, and a master gunner, in addition to 200 privates and their officers, both commissioned and 16 noncommissioned.

56. McIlwaine, ed., *Executive Journals of the Council*, I, 17–18; Culpeper's further representation, Sept. 20, 1683, Effingham Papers, IV. Quotation from the Blathwayt Papers, Huntington Lib., version of Chicheley to the king, May 8, 1682. For more detail, see Sec. Spencer to Sec. Jenkins, May 8, 1682, C.O. 5/1356, 69–74.

rest Robert Beverley. The councillors possessed no legal evidence against the leader of the opposition party. They issued no formal warrant for his apprehension. They never made a specific charge against him. Nonetheless, the major general and his troopers took Beverley from his home, transferred him to a cabin on board the aptly named ship, the *Duke of York*, stationed an armed guard over their prisoner, and rendered him incommunicado. When they seized Robert Beverley, the leader of the opposition, the council courtiers repeated an action taken by Colonel Jeffreys. They followed his forceful example again when they ordered Colonel Kemp to take the assembly records from Beverley. The council even authorized Kemp to use force in his search for evidence of the assembly clerk's complicity in the plant cutting. This search for evidence was a matter of life and death. As Governor-General Culpeper commented afterward, the council intended to hang Beverley if they could justify doing so. Culpeper himself did execute other leaders of the rioting. To justify the death of those who had defied the government, the councillors saw to it that "his Majesty's Deputy Governor declared the cutting of plants to be rebellion against the Crown and Dignity of our Sovereign Lord the King, and peace and welfare of his Majesty's Dominions."[57]

This stark assertion of the prerogative—for no law penalized plant cutting—marked the height but not the end of the courtiers' campaign of social and political repression. This continued for more than a year, as did the imprisonment or restraint of Robert Beverley. His long incarceration and the subsequent government actions against him prevented Beverley from actively leading the country party for three and a half years. In that time, the courtiers consolidated a grip on the government of Virginia that later enabled them to ride out unscathed even the storms of the Glorious Revolution. To keep the leader of the opposition out of circulation,

57. Culpeper's further representation, C.O. 5/1356, 155–156. See Maj. Gen. Smith's petition for his arrears on the English army establishment for general officers in Virginia. The crown took the occasion formally to approve his action in arresting Beverley and suppressing the plant cutting (T. 64/88, 75–76) and recommended a recompense to Gen. Smith, although "payment had ceased to the Governor and other General Officers ever since the first of January 1680." For Spencer's advice, see his letter to Jenkins, May 8, 1682, C.O. 5/1356, 73–74. McIlwaine, ed., *Executive Journals of the Council*, I, 19–20, 21; Hening, ed., *Statutes*, III, 543–544. See Beverley's protest, "as I am a free born subject of England," *ibid.*, 545, and also 564–566. For further arbitrary arrests, see McIlwaine, ed., *Executive Journals of the Council*, I, 21–23, 27–28, and *Cal. S.P. Col., 1681–1685*, nos. 731, 747. On the records seizure, see McIlwaine, ed., *Executive Journals of the Council*, I, 20–21, and Hening, ed., *Statutes*, III, 545. See also the suspension of Beverley's supporters and other uncooperative justices by the council, *Cal. S.P. Col., 1681–1685*, no. 520, and McIlwaine, ed., *Executive Journals of the Council*, 41.

the council—afterward backed by Governor Culpeper—refused Beverley bail. They never permitted the prisoner to hear the charges against him, nor was Beverley allowed to confront either the witnesses or the evidence against him. As judges of the general court, the councillors refused to issue a writ of habeas corpus regarding Beverley, nor would they recognize any inferior court's writ. The councillors isolated Beverley from his family, friends, and followers by moving him from ship to ship. Fearful that their prisoner would nonetheless reassert his influence in the fall elections of 1682, the council even ordered Beverley transported across Chesapeake Bay to Accomac.[58]

While the court party thought their incarceration of Beverley was "a great check to the mutineers," they also gave many "thanks to the militia" whom they commanded as county colonels. The councillor-commanders trusted that "the Rod of Correction" would eventually reduce to order the "mass of dirty people with no name" (as well as those of higher status who incited them to riot). They expected to win obedience "by awe rather than willing conformity." Thus, to keep the peace, the courtiers used the prerogative's military and judicial sanctions. Ultimately, they were justified by the crown's direct orders to capture, try, and execute the leading plant cutters. The court party in the reformed and royalized council had applied the techniques of garrison government to rebellious Virginia.[59]

The councillors' imperial attitudes toward political questions contrasted dramatically with the provincial outlook of their predecessors in office and their present rivals, the Berkelean local elite. In 1676, Sir William Berkeley and his associates had waited for months before they hinted to the king's secretaries of state that Virginia had revolted. In 1682, on the outbreak of the plant cutting, the deputy governor, the auditor, and the secretary described the onset of the provincial crisis to King Charles, to both of his secretaries of state, to the privy council's plantations committee, and to the imperial auditor and colonial secretary. The Virginia courtiers did not just report the outbreak, as Governor Berkeley had done; Secretary Spencer and Auditor Bacon asked for royal advice and

58. McIlwaine, ed., *Executive Journals of the Council*, I, 21, 24–27, 28–29; Hening, ed., *Statutes*, III, 545, 551–560. The council responded to Beverley's applications for writs of habeas corpus by noting that they had referred all the proceedings in his case to the crown and could not act further until the king's pleasure was known. Beverley was imprisoned from May 11 to Nov. 3, 1682, and he later testified that some of that term was spent in Accomac (*ibid.*, 563).

59. See. Spencer to See. Jenkins, May 28, 1682, *Cal. S.P. Col., 1681–1685*, no. 524, and Spencer to Blathwayt, May 29, Aug. 12, 1682, Blathwayt Papers, XVI, 1, Williamsburg.

assistance to deal with the riots. And they sought royal orders for the future government of Virginia. The royal officers in the province kept the ministers of the crown fully informed: they wrote by every ship that sailed during the crisis period. Paradoxically, repeated rebellion had strengthened the bonds of empire.[60]

Culpeper's Return

Sir Henry Chicheley's letters of May 8, 1682, marked "A Rebellion in Virginia," reached Whitehall on June 14, 1682. Secretary Spencer's dispatches on the riots arrived simultaneously. The plantations committee met on the same day and recommended to King Charles that Lord Culpeper be hurried back to Virginia "with all possible speed," transported and supported by naval vessels, and ordered to make an example of the leader of the insurrection, whom their lordships strongly suspected to be Robert Beverley. When the governor-general had inflicted due punishment ("to the end the Dignity of the Government may be preserved and all evil minded men deterred from the like attempts for the future"), and when he had enforced with rigor and without exception the royalizing instructions issued to him in the preceding January, he might then call an assembly and make some such concession as a cessation. The king approved these recommendations in council, and Lord Culpeper promised to be ready to sail for his government within the week.[61]

Almost a month later, on July 6, 1682, King Charles read of his Virginia councillors' "hope [that] his Excellency the Lord Culpeper is upon his voyage to Virginia, which may give some stop to these Riotous Actions, and produce a great settlement to this poor distressed country." In reply, King Charles personally convened his privy council's committee for plantations. He told them to expedite Culpeper's departure and to expand the governor-general's naval force, which, "in case of an actual Rebellion," was to remain in Virginia waters under Culpeper's orders. His lordship

60. Chicheley to the king, Middle Plantation, May 8, 1682, C.O. 5/1356, 65–66, Blathwayt Papers, Huntington Lib., and *VMHB*, XXVIII (1920), 117–118; Chicheley to Jenkins, C.O. 5/1356, 66–69; *Cal. S.P. Col., 1681–1685*, nos. 493–494; Sec. Spencer to Sec. Jenkins, May 8, 28, 1682, *ibid.*, no. 495 (and C.O. 5/1356, 69–74), no. 524; Spencer to Blathwayt, May 29, 1682, Blathwayt Papers, XVI, 1, Williamsburg. Chicheley's other letters of May 30, June 12, Aug. 10, and Spencer's letters to Jenkins, June 7, 10, Aug. 12, are in *Cal. S.P. Col., 1681–1685*, nos. 531, 549, 648, 649, 546, 548, 652.

61. Endorsement by Blathwayt on Chicheley's letter to the king, May 8, 1682, Blathwayt Papers, Huntington Lib. See also *VMHB*, XXVIII (1920), 118; C.O. 5/1356, 74–81; and *Cal. S.P. Col., 1681–1685*, no. 561.

was called in to the meeting and ordered to sail on July 15. On August 1, however, he had not yet gone on board. The king agreed with his colonial councillors that some governor-general, but not necessarily the dilatory Lord Culpeper, must be speedily dispatched. Only slightly stirred by this warning, Lord Culpeper began to pay his farewell calls on August 21. He then paused in his preparations for the Virginia voyage in order to shut in a neighbor's right of way across Culpeper property. On August 24 the press announced, somewhat prematurely, that Culpeper "had gone to his government of Virginia." On September 7, however, it was discovered that his commission had not yet passed the seals because Culpeper refused to pay the necessary fees. Finally, on September 19, the king ordered "the Captain of the Frigate appointed to carry my Lord Culpeper to Virginia, that in case his Lordship be not already embarked, he do not receive him on Board."[62]

"In that case," as Blathwayt remarked, Lord Culpeper "will certainly loose his Government at least for some time. These proceedings of his Lordship have occasioned the renewing the enclosed orders." The king commanded that "no Governor or commander in chief of his Majesty's Islands of Jersey and Guernsey or other places and Garrisons beyond the seas to presume henceforward to come into England from the place of their respective Governments." Blathwayt made a special entry in the Virginia records to certify that Governor-General Culpeper had been served with this order personally. Then, to tie this mercenary magistrate more firmly to his duty, his commission was amended to provide that in the governor-general's absence, even with leave, his deputy would receive one-half of the executive's salary and perquisites. The like orders went out to every governor-general in the empire. From such acorns of incident grew constitutional oaks.[63]

62. Bacon to Blathwayt, Aug. 26, 1682, Blathwayt Papers, XIII, 1, Williamsburg; *Cal. S.P. Col., 1681–1685*, no. 597, 612; C.O. 5/1356, 84–86; Conway to admiralty commission, S.P. 44/56, 61. See the report of the privy council committee for plantations, July 21, 1682 (*Cal. S.P. Col., 1681–1685*, no. 623), on the need to send a qualified and instructed person to settle Virginia, and the king's agreement, *ibid.*, no. 637. The final stages of Culpeper's exodus are detailed in W. L. to Lord Hatton, Aug. 21, 26, 1682, Add. MSS 29559, 202, 208b; Luttrell, *Brief Relation*, I, 215; and S.P. 44/56, 64. Culpeper complained to Jenkins of this "severe but unnecessary order." He insisted that "once out of London I needed no quickening" (Oct. 6, 1682, *Cal. S.P. Col., 1681–1685*, no. 742). On the fee episode, see *ibid.*, nos. 641, 678, 742, and the Blathwayt-Culpeper correspondence in Blathwayt Papers, XVII, 2, Williamsburg. Some of this is duplicated in the Huntington Lib., where the fee bill for £61 11s. 10d. also may be found.

63. Blathwayt to Lynch, Sept. 21, 1682, Blathwayt Papers, XXIII, 1, Williamsburg. It is likely that only the surviving influence of Edward Seymour kept Culpeper from losing his government at this time, and that Seymour's disgrace exposed Culpeper to the dismissal for disobedience that ensued coincidentally (Culpeper to Blathwayt, Oct. 6, 1682, and

Lord Culpeper complained bitterly about being ordered to go to his post and to remain there, or lose his command. Writing from Plymouth on October 6, about to sail for Virginia, his lordship sniveled: "I am ashamed to live the time" when to lose a residence in Virginia was considered "a punishment and the stay there an obligation." Culpeper disliked the colony, but he resented even more his personal subordination and political disfavor. "Want of Liberty and Banishment," he called his being ordered to Virginia. Culpeper complained that his sentence of exile was compounded by official "Harshness, and Nonpayment" of his proprietary dues. Culpeper insisted that he would "be better satisfied." He hoped "that my Absence may not be long." And so, greedy and impatient, the governor-general left England for his second voyage to Virginia.[64]

The voyage was "a tedious winter passage," full of unedifying incident. First, the governor-general had the royal frigate *Mermaid* loaded "like a merchantman," which ruined her fighting efficiency and so helped to incite a royal prohibition against freighting warships, one more of Culpeper's perverse contributions to imperial standards. When the *Mermaid* put into Tenerife in the Canaries, his lordship enticed several Portuguese residents on board. He subsequently sold them into servitude in Virginia. A stop in Barbados found him being unhelpful to the guardsman-governor, Sir Richard Dutton, held to his post by the orders Culpeper had provoked. Leisurely, Lord Culpeper thus violated his promise to hasten to his government and block the "wild" proposals he expected from the assembly scheduled for November. It was the evening of Saturday, December 16, before Governor-General Culpeper came ashore in Virginia. He found that the assembly had virtually completed its business.[65]

The Assembly Dissolved

Culpeper responded to this news with an instant exercise of the royal prerogative. He dispatched an express rider to Jamestown to adjourn the assembly until he reviewed what it had done. The

---

Blathwayt to Culpeper, Nov. 2, 1682, Apr. 25, 1683, *ibid.*, XVII, 2). On the residential command, see the order of the king-in-council, July 28, 1682, MS All Souls 211; C.O. 5/1356, 87; and *VMHB*, XXVIII (1920), 228. On the alteration of Culpeper's commission, see C.O. 5/1356, 93; Blathwayt to Culpeper, to Spencer, Dec. 18, 1682, and to Baltimore, Feb. 9, 1683 (Blathwayt Papers, XVI, 2, XVII, 2, Williamsburg).

64. Culpeper to Blathwayt, "Auditor General of His Majesty's Plantations in America," Oct. 6, 1682, Blathwayt Papers, XXXVIII, 21, XVII, 2, Williamsburg.

65. C.O. 5/1356, 92; Capt. Tyrell to admiralty, Mar. 1, 1683, *Cal. S.P. Col., 1681–1685*, no. 983. See also *ibid.*, no. 1035, and n. 66 below. The Barbados visit is questionable, but see *ibid.*, no. 1023.

council joined the governor-general at Green Spring on Sunday morning to discuss the pending legislation. On Monday he came to Jamestown, reconvened the assembly, and announced amendments of one-half of its bills. Culpeper struck politically assertive preambles from judiciary measures. He reduced the scope and penalties of economic proposals. While the burgesses expressed their anger at the amendments and their anxiety to start home for Christmas, the governor-general remembered that he was no longer free to ignore the king's instructions and that they would affect most of the remaining legislation. He sent to the *Mermaid* for the orders he had left behind. Reading them, he concluded that little of the legislation before him would be acceptable to the crown, but he nevertheless passed most of the proposed acts for limited terms. This was an option offered by Culpeper's orders. It conceded something to the assembly while it eventually terminated questionable laws without need for a royal veto. To his own alteration and limited acceptance of the assembly's measures, the governor-general added a warning that the king was particularly concerned with frontier security and might alter the act regarding it at any time.[66]

The king's personal attention to Virginia was political as well as military, Culpeper told the assembly. King Charles and his council had censured him, Culpeper said, for transmitting the assembly resolution of 1680 supporting Robert Beverley, clerk of the assembly, against the royal commissioners in the record-seizing episode. This censure was redoubled when the clerk was implicated in the plant cutting. Culpeper informed the legislators that he was now under royal orders not to permit their former leader to hold any public office whatsoever. Still under arrest, Beverley had not been able to take his place as assembly clerk. Yet the burgesses had voted to pay Beverley fees for current consultation, and they had alleged that large debts were owed their clerk for former services. The council had pared down the proposed payments. Now Culpeper used his fiscal authority to reject all of the burgesses' lavish allowances to Beverley.[67]

66. Culpeper's further representation, Sept. 20, 1683, Effingham Papers, IV, and C.O. 5/1356, 154–155; Spencer to Jenkins, Feb. 15, 1683, *Cal. S.P. Col., 1681–1685*, no. 944; McIlwaine, ed., *Legislative Journals of the Council*, I, 53, 54, 57; "Limitation of this act," Hening, ed., *Statutes*, II, 501.

67. Hening, ed., *Statutes*, II, 155; McIlwaine, ed., *Legislative Journals of the Council*, I, 58–59. The political impact of the ouster of Beverley from his position of legislative leadership was compounded by Culpeper's personal support of that increasingly influential imperial officer, Atty. Gen. Edmund Jennings, *ibid.*, 55–59. See also *Cal. S.P. Col., 1681–1685*, no. 928. Jennings's preparation of the government's case against the plant cutters began his career in the court party. This, together with his relation to Sir Edmund Jennings and the

More important than the political check to the country party by this amendment was its challenge to the assembly's financial authority. By this and other item vetoes, the governor-general not only eliminated the burgesses' especially offensive grant to Beverley, the leader of the opposition party, but also checked the legislators' appropriation of the poll tax proceeds to other burgess favorites. Such appropriation "orders" had been an important element of assembly authority. Acting on a royal command, Culpeper now "denied to pass any one order, (tho from the first Seating of the Country to that day no Assembly had ever sat without passing orders)." Instead Culpeper hustled the assembly into authorizing the public levy, the poll tax, by law. Once the levy became a matter of law, it was not only subject to the governor's item veto but also liable to royal disallowance. As Governor Culpeper discriminated against Beverley in the levy, so King Charles excised particular grants to Culpeper himself. The crown went on to disallow whole categories of assembly appropriations. Thus English executives took a major financial step toward effective imperial sovereignty.

To further constrain the lower house's attempts to regain the authority possessed by the old assembly, and to protect the council courtiers, the governor-general intervened in the debate over the levy law to assert the legislative authority of the council. Prior to Culpeper's return, the burgesses had challenged the council's coequal legislative stature. In retaliation, his lordship insisted on and publicized the new style of legislative enactment "by the Governor Council and Burgesses of this General Assembly."[68]

After he formally consulted his council, Culpeper concluded his attack on the legislative opposition to royal government. He summoned the burgesses to attend him and the council on Friday morning, just five and a half frantic days after his landing in Virginia. He told them that the royal resentment at the late insurrection was so great that he had been ordered "not to call any Assembly att all, till the Dignity of the Government should be first

support this secured him in England, resulted in his presidential administration of Virginia, 1705–1710. See Jenkins to Howard of Effingham, Nov. 13, 1683, S.P. 44/64, 134.

68. McIlwaine, ed., *Legislative Journals of the Council*, I, 56, 57, 59; Culpeper's further representation, Sept. 20, 1683, Effingham Papers, IV, and C.O. 5/1356, 155; Blathwayt to Bacon, Nov. 17, 1683, Blathwayt Papers, XIII, 2, Williamsburg. The imperialists explicitly recognized that revenue control was essential to sovereignty and that increasing the king's authority depended upon wresting fiscal control from the legislature, overseas as at home (Webb, "Blathwayt," *WMQ*, 3d Ser., XXV [1968], 7). On the style of enactment, the relative roles of the house and council in legislation, and the close of the session, see also Culpeper's commission, article 9 and instruction 11, C.O. 5/1356, 19, 33, 126.

asserted by the punishment of the offenders." Now that he had condescended to amend the bills pending at his arrival, and to pass the amended measures into acts, the governor-general was horrified to discover that none of these bills outlawed plant cutting. Therefore, he announced that, with the advice of his council, he had dissolved the assembly. Not until the burgesses had returned to their counties and announced their "Detestation" of the rebellious plant cutting that they had incited, would the governor-general consider calling another assembly. There is no record of any such repentance. There was no meeting of the Virginia assembly for nearly three years. This gap in legislative sessions —unprecedented since the 1620s when the first establishment of royal government in the colony had also suspended assembly meetings—testified to the altered balance of political power. Without assemblies, the authority of the imperial executive in Virginia would grow unchecked and unchallenged.[69]

Even before the assembly's dissolution, some Virginians had been alarmed by the royal suspension or disallowance of provincial legislation by the governor-general or the king. "This Despotic way of Government," as one country partisan called it, had so reduced the prestige of the formerly all-powerful assembly that there was widespread feeling among Virginians that its laws no longer had much force. The younger Beverley put the case plainly: executive repeal of provincial law had led Virginians to look "upon their Acts of Assembly, to be of no more Force, than the Laws of an *Ottoman* Province, which are liable to be suspended or repealed at the Pleasure of the Bashaw."[70]

Such was the anger of the country party at the degradation of the assembly and its laws that, had not the bitter recollection of their own repression by royal troops and commissioners "been so fresh in Memory," a new revolt might have been staged against this "Arbitrary way of doing Business." Indeed, the plant-cutting riots had been an effort by the country partisans to assert assembly authority, as well as being a calculated defiance of the royal government and its courtiers. When this rising failed in the face of court forcefulness, the assembly had tried to reassert its authority by legislating a penalty for denial of the validity of assembly acts.

69. McIlwaine, ed., *Legislative Journals of the Council*, I, 61.
70. Beverley, *History*, ed. Wright, 122–123. Culpeper commented (on his 47th instruction) about the "Jealousies that their laws are insignificant." See Hening, ed., *Statutes*, II, 501–502, and McIlwaine, ed., *Legislative Journals of the Council*, I, 54. Beverley points out that Culpeper's successors down to the time Beverley wrote (1705), continued to use "this *French* method of governing by Edicts."

The governor cut the heart out of this defense of legislative power by an amendment in council that limited the law's vindication to those acts "not repealed, expired, vacated or annulled by the king's most excellent majesty." With such a limitation, Governor-General Culpeper was happy to approve an act that punished all "who shall dare to offend against the Authority and Dignity of the Government in so high a Nature as to speak Contemptuously of the power and Efficacy of our Laws." The viceroy had converted the assembly's self-assertion into one more instrument of executive authority. Now that he had effected the crown's legislative prerogative in a manner at once startlingly comprehensive and, as he said, "beyond my hopes," the governor-general announced to his council what he had intended to place first on his administrative agenda, the crown's proposals to expand its authority and restore social stability in Virginia.[71]

Executions and Persecutions

The first priority of the crown and of its Virginia council was the physical security of the provincial government. The very presence of the governor-general promoted public order, as the king's ministers had presumed it would and as the relieved Virginia council was quick to acknowledge. As soon as Culpeper came ashore, however, the councillors also demanded in "earnest, unanimous and repeated Addresses as most absolutely necessary to the peace and safety of the Country" that the governor-general enlarge the bodyguard that they had raised during the plant cutting. They also insisted on a coast-guard vessel. Without both military and naval force, the councillors said, "the country is not safe, and they cannot be answerable for the Government." Culpeper immediately agreed to these proposals. He put them in operation within two weeks of his arrival, remarking as he did so that the land force was now large enough to adopt regular military drill, as it must be if it were to be an effective police force. More surprising than the speed of the governor-general's response is that he paid both the soldiers and sailors in advance, without conditions or deductions, out of his own pocket. The urgency of the occasion could re-

---

71. Culpeper to Lord Dartmouth, Mar. 18, 1683, HMC, *Dartmouth*, I, 80–81. His orders had commanded the governor to begin his tour of duty by applying the instructions of Jan. 1682 with the help of the council. The existence of the assembly sitting at his arrival had prevented this course. Nonetheless, as Spencer told the privy council plantations committee, the orders and journals of the Virginia council were "an Account of all Political Occurrences in this his Majesty's Government" (May 29, 1683, C.O. 5/1356, 103).

ceive no more profound testimony than this from the avaricious baron.[72]

Under the strictest royal instructions to reassert "the Dignity of the Government" and pressed by the council's courtier majority, Lord Culpeper added law to force to repair the damage done to royal authority by the country revolt. He confirmed the council's opinion that the plant cutting was treason and proclaimed that the cutters and their inspirers and abettors were subject to "all paines, penalties and forfeitures as in open and actual Rebellion." To indict and try four alleged ringleaders for treason, the governor-general impaneled unprecedentedly wealthy and officially connected jurors, as by his instructions he was to do. These legal proceedings utilized English legal forms recently modified by the royal government for political use at home. In reply, just as the whig grand jury of London had rendered an *ignoramus* verdict on the court's charge of treason against Shaftesbury, so country partisans in Virginia tried "to incite Ignoramus Jurus" against the treason prosecution of plant cutters. But these whig tactics failed to prevent the indictment of four plant cutters. Then, despite the "high words and threats" of country spokesmen, a packed jury found three of the accused guilty of treason. Governor-General Culpeper thereupon ordered Somerset Davies hung in Jamestown when the public gathered for the general court session, a human sacrifice to show the judicial power of royal government. Another political use was made of Black Austin. He was strung up in front of the courthouse in Beverley's home county of Gloucester. Such was the governor-general's terrible warning to that county's "country" justices of the physical price of opposition to royal rule. The Gloucester elite "had too much inclined in favor of the insurrection which first broke out there," said the governor-general, and they were still supporting Robert Beverley.[73]

72. Secretary of Virginia to secretary of state, Feb. 15, 1682/3, *Cal. S.P. Col., 1681–1685*, no. 944; McIlwaine, ed., *Executive Journals of the Council*, I, 40–41, 43–44; Spencer to Blathwayt, Apr. 19, 1683, Blathwayt Papers, XVI, 2, Williamsburg. Culpeper's approval of the military proposals is noted in his further representation, Sept. 20, 1683, C.O. 5/1356, 160–163, and in Effingham Papers, IV. The governor-general's advance payment, an expensive concession traditionally made only where the men's loyalty was both crucial and subject to special temptations, is recorded in C.O. 5/1356, 161; see also Treasury warrant, 1684, Blathwayt Papers, Huntington Lib.; and T. 64/88, 100–101, 117.

73. Culpeper to Dartmouth, Mar. 18, 1683, HMC, *Dartmouth*, I, 80; *Cal. S.P. Col., 1681–1685*, nos. 322, 339, 340; McIlwaine, ed., *Executive Journals of the Council*, I, 34–35, 36; C.O. 5/1356, 156, 157. On the jury selection, see C.O. 5/1356, 349; see also *Cal. S.P. Col., 1681–1685*, no. 998; C.O. 5/1356, 158. The Gloucester County justices had also signed Beverley's bail bond (Hening, ed., *Statutes*, III, 553). Note the dismissals of two of these supporters of Beverley from office, Henry Whiting and John Buckner (*Cal. S.P. Col., 1681–1685*, nos. 960–961; McIlwaine, ed., *Executive Journals of the Council*, 41). Having

Beverley badly needed his countrymen's support. Lord Culpeper had exempted from pardon not only fugitives from justice but also those leaders of the country party whom the courtiers identified as "the real contrivers" of the rising: Robert Beverley, John Sackler, and Thomas Amies. Sackler and Amies were kept under the threat of prosecution for treason. Thus the government could compel them to testify against Beverley if he were brought to trial. In the meantime, the viceroy punished Beverley's resistance to royal authority by ousting him from public office: from a lucrative land surveyorship, from the deputy auditor's place, and from large military contracts, as well as from the assembly clerkship. The governor-general also endorsed Secretary Spencer's disbarment of Beverley. After doing all this, and before releasing Beverley from custody, the governor and council, acting as the general court, required from Beverley a bond of £2,000 "for his future good abearance towards his Majesty, and all his liege people." By ouster, disbarment, deprivation, and bond—each indicative of the government's growing range of social sanctions in an increasingly mature, institutionalized, and imperial province—the court party managed to check the political operations of the "Premier" of the country party until the autumn of 1685.[74]

The Rise of the Courtiers:
The Council and the Domestication of Garrison Government

"Having in the first place according to his Majesty's particular Commands" dealt physically and politically with "the Chief Actors and Promoters of the late Insurrection," the governor-general and the council of state took up the crown's more general injunctions. These royal executives were ordered to achieve the "most Security and Safety to his Majesty," by their definition and excision of the causes of civil disorder, if possible, and by their repression of it always. They were ordered to "carry on the Government Securely, improve the Revenues, Cut off unnecessary charges."

---

made two overtly political "examples," Culpeper "thought fit to mingle Mercy with Justice." He asked the king to pardon the third condemned cutter as both young and penitent, and to restore his estate, which was forfeit for treason. By giving up his claim to a share in the felon's estate, the governor hoped that "the whole Country might be convinced that there was no other motive in the thing but purely to maintain Government and their Peace and Quiet" (C.O. 5/1356, 159). Fortunately for the convict in question, his estate was very small.

74. Spencer to Blathwayt, June 19, 1683, Blathwayt Papers, XVI, 2, Williamsburg; Culpeper's further representation, Sept. 20, 1683, Effingham Papers, IV, and C.O. 5/1356, 150; Hening, ed., Statutes, III, 552–553, 557–562, 561–563, 563–564; McIlwaine, ed., Executive Journals of the Council, I, 36, and McIlwaine, ed., Journals of Burgesses, 1659/60–1693, xlix.

Finally, they were asked to suggest what specific imperial measures would "tend most to his Majesty's service, and the Ease and Quiet of the Country." Royal dominion, characterized by public order at a low cost, which would yield a high profit to both the king and his subjects—such was the imperial policy of Charles II.[75]

To implement the crown's policy in the province, the courtiers of the council were second in importance only to the governor-general himself. Lord Culpeper therefore took every occasion to enhance the councillors' increasingly distinctive position in provincial government and so to downgrade the assembly. The governor-general promoted the councillors' power in their local bailiwicks as an extension of his own and of the crown's authority and as a counterweight to the older, Berkelean county court cliques. Thus Culpeper consulted his council on every question of county administration, and, on council advice, he systematically reformed every county office. Encouraged by a chief executive whom they knew would eventually leave Virginia to their administration, and by English bureaucrats who wanted a direct connection with the increasingly important provinces, the courtier-councillors became more self-confident administrators and increasingly devoted imperialists. Both attitudes appeared in the council majority's willingness to erect their own authority on the ruins of the assembly's, to trade the provincial autonomy of the Berkeley era for an Anglo-American political connection, and finally, to shift their allegiance from Culpeper himself to the imperial crown.[76]

Culpeper's administrative negligence, even criminality, finally forced the courtiers to transfer their loyalty from the person of their patron, the governor-general, to the idea of the imperial prerogative, symbolized by the king. Nicholas Spencer, from being Culpeper's attorney and "man of business," became the royal secretary of state for Virginia and president of the king's provincial council. Major General Smith's privileges of military rank and salary were recognized by the imperial privy council in return for police work done in Culpeper's absence. Although Nathaniel Bacon, Sr., was nominated by Blathwayt to the Virginia auditorship as someone subordinate to Culpeper, Bacon ensured Culpeper's disgrace by exposing Culpeper's raid on the provincial treasury.

These members of Culpeper's cabinet were supported in the council by a younger group of Virginia residents, nominated by the governor-general because of their military and administrative

75. McIlwaine, ed., *Executive Journals of the Council*, I, 37, 57.
76. C.O. 5/1356, 18, 124; Add. MSS 30372, 3b.

skills. Colonel William Bridger, the frontier commander, Colonel John Page, manager of the magazine, and William Byrd, Indian trader, when added to the cabinet, made up a court majority in the council of state. It ruled the more effectively because the crown itself degraded the leader of the Green Spring survivors, Philip Ludwell, and Culpeper preoccupied him with proprietorial land management and took Ludwell to England whenever Culpeper himself sailed home. In sum, the governor-general's political finesse was nowhere more apparent than in his development of "a prudent able and Vigorous Council, for the Conduct of almost every individual Member whereof I dare be responsible." They were the indispensable agents of his provincial interest as well as of the crown's authority. The permanence of royal power, however, at last overcame loyalty to the patron. Those councillors who achieved a court identity found themselves tied more firmly to imperial interests than they were to an aristocratic overlord. For Lord Culpeper continued to prefer his personal, proprietary profit to the prerogative of the king and the welfare of the province. [77]

As soon as the spring 1683 receipts came in, Lord Culpeper claimed for himself the entire contents of the Virginia treasury. Every penny in the exchequer, some £9,300, belonged to him, Culpeper said. "He would not be quiet until he had it, and if it had

77. The May 4, 1683, document, endorsed "Account of the Government from the Council Received 29 September 1683," is in C.O. 5/1356, 175–187, and *Cal. S.P. Col., 1681–1685*, no. 1063. Culpeper commented on the elimination or incapacity of old councillors and the promotion of courtiers in his note on his 10th instruction (further representation, Sept. 20, 1683, Effingham Papers, IV). On Bridger, see Effingham Papers, IV, no. 41, and on Page's profits, *ibid.*, no. 45. The list of 13 councillors is in C.O. 5/1356, 32. The seven-member court party in the council included Col. Kemp, whose untimely death was balanced by that of Sir Henry Chicheley, a country partisan. The discredit of Chicheley, even before his death, as the front man of the country party, is eloquently noted by Culpeper to Blathwayt, Mar. 20, 1683, Blathwayt Papers, XVII, 2, Williamsburg. Note also, following Culpeper's own removal and his comment on the crown's lack of care in ranking councillors, the degradation of Ludwell in council seniority, to prevent his succession to the presidency (*Cal. S.P. Col., 1681–1685*, no. 1309). Note Spencer's revelation to Blathwayt that the £200 allocated by the council and issued by Auditor Bacon for an agent at court had been pocketed by the governor, "for which my Lord Culpeper is to make answer" (Spencer to Blathwayt, Mar. 16, 1683, Blathwayt Papers, XVI, 2, Williamsburg). A larger conflict of interest is suggested by the council's recommendation that the proprietorial revenue be placed in a provincial emergency fund, rather than being used to meet the personal claims advanced by Culpeper in his Sept. 20, 1683, comments on his instructions (nos. 47, 48, Effingham Papers, IV). The usefulness to central authority of such patentees as the secretary and the auditor led to clause 21 of Culpeper's instructions (C.O. 5/1355, 324), establishing their relative independence of the governor. This was reemphasized in instruction 65 (C.O. 5/1355, 351). See also the privy council plantations committee's consideration of the relative share of the crown and the viceroys in nominations to these patent places, Oct. 14, 1680, C.O. 5/1355, 391. Note as well the imperial responsibility implied in the veto power given to the secretary and the major general during council administrations (C.O. 5/1355, 365–366).

been 5 times as much more I believe he would have had it," wailed Auditor Bacon. The governor took his loot, packed it away in trunks, and announced to the council that, "since it had pleased God to bless his and the Councils endeavours, with such good Success," he was sailing for England.[78]

The councillors were doubly shocked. "His Excellencies unexpected and sudden return" to England, despite the king's well-known command that governors-general reside in their commands, startled them. They were equally upset by the revelation that Culpeper was still the proprietor of Virginia's revenues. Obviously, he was more a Virginia property holder than a royal dominion's steward. The council could only agree with Culpeper that he should leave. Promising to "use their utmost endeavors to preserve and maintain the Dignity of the Government and secure his Majesty's interest," the councillors politely, if not sincerely, wished "his Lordship a good voyage, good success and a speedy return."[79]

As their price for endorsing his exit, the councillors demanded that the governor-general reaffirm the provincial military establishment. "For the entire satisfaction of the Council," Lord Culpeper ordered the continuance of the garrison, the guardship, and the frontier rangers. He hoped these precautions were unnecessary. He thought that the Seneca, who had informed him of their numbers and the destination of their southward-bound parties, thus had indicated that they meant no harm to Virginia's frontiers.

78. Nathaniel Bacon to Blathwayt, July 23, 1683, Blathwayt Papers, XIII, 1, Williamsburg; announcement of May 22, 1683, McIlwaine, ed., *Executive Journals of the Council*, I, 43; Spencer to the privy council plantations committee, May 29, 1683, C.O. 5/1356, 103–105. The fiscal instructions and some of Culpeper's claims are in C.O. 5/1355, 352. See also T. 64/88, 117b; the draft and agreement of May 24, 1684, Blathwayt Papers, BB no. 47, Huntington Lib.; and C.O. 5/1356, 145–146. Besides demanding all the exchequer of the province from the auditor, Culpeper ordered him to ignore the order of the king-in-council, Dec. 20, 1682, deducting from his Virginia salary the fees that the governor had refused to pay for his new commission (Culpeper to Bacon, May 28, 1683, Blathwayt Papers, XVII, 2, Williamsburg; Blathwayt Papers, BB no. 19, Huntington Lib.). This was one of several outright defiances of orders in council that led to the royal instructions to Culpeper's successor and to all royal governors, making orders of the privy council binding in the provinces of empire as they were in England. Here was one more of Culpeper's unintended contributions to the construction of the imperial prerogative (order of Aug. 31, 1683, *Cal. S.P. Col., 1681–1685*, no. 1226).

79. The command decision is announced and discussed in *Cal. S.P. Col., 1681–1685*, no. 1080; Spencer to Blathwayt, May 9, Aug. 19, 1683, Blathwayt Papers, XVI, 2, Williamsburg; Culpeper's further representation, C.O. 5/1356, 151–152; and Spencer's petition for half-pay as commander-in-chief, T. 64/88, 118b–119. The crucial letter on finance is that which Auditor Bacon finally brought himself to write to Auditor General Blathwayt on July 23, 1683, Blathwayt Papers, XIII, no. 1, Williamsburg. As for the councillors' wishing Culpeper's "speedy return," Spencer at least never expected his lordship to come back to Virginia (Spencer to Blathwayt, Aug. 19, 1683, *ibid.*, XVI, no. 2).

Within the dominion, the governor-general was sure "that the punishment of 2 or 3 of the Plant Cutters . . . for Treason will put us into a Direct Calm till necessity wakes us again." This awakening Culpeper did not expect for at least a year, but he agreed nonetheless to the council's military demands. This confirmation of royal government's armed sanctions in Virginia was Lord Culpeper's last act as the king's lieutenant and governor-general. He turned over the provincial administration to the president and council. At the end of May 1683, the baron of Thoresway sailed from Virginia for the last time.[80]

Governor-General Culpeper Cashiered

The errant officer had picked an especially bad time to be absent without leave from his command. The whigs' Rye House plot to assassinate both the king and his heir, the duke of York, had failed in April 1683. It was exposed on June 13, the day before judgment was entered against the city of London in the *quo warranto* proceeding against its charter. Provoked to profound political reaction, and with the urban center of opposition at its constitutional mercy, the crown began its forceful response to the whigs' "work of Darkness." At the height of this counterrevolutionary fervor, legal aggression, and military repression, early in July 1683, Lord Culpeper arrived in London, from Virginia, without leave.[81]

"My Lord Culpeper is be witched!" Secretary Blathwayt exclaimed. "He is the true instance of what was meant by the adventurous Ulysses's Companions." His lordship was instantly arrested and was charged with being absent from his command, "not only without leave but contrary to His Majestys express commands in Council." On the day of Lord Culpeper's house arrest, William Blathwayt was commissioned secretary at war. "The secretary of war and plantations" (a functional combination, given garrison government as the imperial norm), remarked with amusement that the prisoner now under his supervision "remained

80. C.O. 5/1356, 169; McIlwaine, ed., *Executive Journals of the Council*, I, 43–44; *Cal. S.P. Col., 1681–1685*, no. 1076; Culpeper to Blathwayt, Mar. 20, 1683, Blathwayt Papers, XVII, no. 2, Williamsburg.

81. S.P. 44/68, 293–298. See also *ibid.*, 301, 306, 321, 323; Ogg, *Charles II*, II, 647–648; the officer-governor comments of Sir John Lanier to Lord Hatton, 8br. 1, 1683, Add. MSS 29560, 104; Sec. Jenkins to Sir William Portman, Aug. 18, 1683, S.P. 44/64, no. 69.

confined to his Lodgings, that is to M[istress] Williss, a punishment to both."[82]

An "Inquiry into the Lord Culpeper's Neglect of his Government" began two weeks after his arrest. During this interval, an additional charge was made against the absentee governor-general: that, by failing to name a deputy governor to command in his absence from the post, he had violated his instructions and undermined the unitary, monarchical, and military principle of the imperial executive. Like these charges, the inquisition itself was direct and powerful. The crown issued the commission to enquire on August 2, 1683. The commission members were six senior civil servants. From the privy council, colonial office, and treasury secretariats, they were leading examples of the able administrators who were to make the English monarchy the most efficient in Europe and who were to underpin its approaching imperial triumph. A week after their appointment, these inquisitors ordered the tory sheriff of London to impanel a special, wealthy, court-connected jury, on the same model that Culpeper himself had used against Virginia's plant cutters. On August 16 this jury found correct the inquisitors' presentation that Governor-General Culpeper now had been absent three months from his command, voluntarily, in disobedience to the king's orders and personal wishes, and without appointing a deputy governor. The jury agreed, therefore, that Lord Culpeper's life patent for the government of Virginia should be canceled. Without ever summoning Culpeper to appear before them or the jury, the royal commissioners presented the findings of this "inquisition in chancery" to the king. Charles II thereupon ordered his attorney general to put the sentence into effect. On August 17, 1683, the privy council's plantations committee ordered Secretary Blathwayt to prepare a commission for Francis, Lord Howard of Effingham, as governor-general of Virginia.[83]

82. Blathwayt to Lynch, July 18, 1683, Blathwayt Papers, XXIV, 2, Williamsburg. (Other governors were delighted to be found doing their duty at their posts and out of the way of political trouble [William Longueville to Lord Hatton, July 10, 1683, Add. MSS 29560, 59].) Blathwayt is also quoted from his letter to Bacon, Sept. 8, 1683, Blathwayt Papers, XIII, 2, Williamsburg. On the period of arrest, see Jenkins to Culpeper, July 12, 1683, S.P. 44/68, 328; S.P. 44/164, 97; and Webb, "Blathwayt," WMQ, 3d Ser., XXV (1968), 9–10. The period was a bad one for whig peers: the 13th also witnessed Essex's suicide in the Tower and the beginning of Russell's trial (which ended with his condemnation on the 14th and led to his execution on the 21st of July) (Ogg, Charles II, II, 648–649). The duke of Monmouth, considered by many to be at the heart of the conspiracy, was forced to submit to the duke of York. In this political sense, Culpeper was one more victim of the royalist determination "to disarm all that appeared active or busy in their attendance on the duke of Monmouth" (Jenkins to the duke of Beaufort, Aug. 16, 1683, S.P. 44/64, 67), as Culpeper had so blatantly been (see above, p. 396).

83. Blathwayt to Lynch, July 18, 1683, Blathwayt Papers, XXIV, 2, Williamsburg; Cal.

Lord Culpeper was forced to surrender most of his private property in Virginia, as well as his civil and military authority there, to the imperial crown. In order to obtain his release from arrest, he had to agree to accept a settlement outlined by Blathwayt. Culpeper would receive the usual army pension to ex-governors-general of £600 per year, but only if he resigned to the crown the bulk of his proprietary rights, including quitrents and escheats. Blathwayt summarized this agreement, and concluded Thomas, Lord Culpeper's, fourteen years of involvement in Virginia affairs, when he wrote that "My Lord Culpeper has made a Hodge Podge of his Government, forfeited his Grant, lost his credit, got £600 p.a. for twenty years upon the Establishment for his Quitrents arrears of Salary etc. with which he is not [at] all satisfyed."[84]

Culpeper had political as well as pecuniary reasons to be dissatisfied with his Virginia administration, for it had served the cause of kingship and empire inimical to Culpeper's aristocracy and provincialism. Lord Culpeper's disingenuous moderation,

---

S.P. Col., 1681–1685, nos. 1172, 1182, 1191. The order of this "Inquisition in Chancery" was as follows: commission to enquire, Aug. 2, 1683, summons to the sheriff for a jury, Aug. 10, 1683, the form and findings of the "Inquiry into the Lord Culpeper's Neglect of his Government," and order to the attorney general to proceed on this inquisition, Oct. 6, 1683, all in C.O. 5/1356, 106–111, 112, 113, 114–119 (see esp. 116–117), 244. Meanwhile, Effingham's commission was dated Sept. 28, 1683 (C.O. 5/1356, 188). See also William Longueville to Lord Hatton, Aug. 18, Sept. 13, 1683, Add. MSS 29560, 82–83, 95; Cal. S.P. Col., 1681–1685, no. 1172; Cal. S.P. Dom., 1665–1666, 445; and Stephen P. Baxter, The Development of the Treasury (Cambridge, Mass., 1957), 220–225, 243–246. On the achievement of administrative efficiency, see J. H. Plumb, The Origins of Political Stability in England, 1675–1725 (Boston, 1967), 11–13.

84. As early as Aug. 24, the privy council plantations committee had included in Effingham's instructions a special admonition to investigate Culpeper's management of the public revenue. This order relating to their predecessors became a standing part of instructions to new governors, another example of the inspiration to tightened imperial control provided by Culpeper's maladministration (Cal. S.P. Col., 1681–1685, no. 1208). Effingham's commission was dated Sept. 4, 28 (ibid., no. 1274). As late as Sept. 29, Culpeper wrote to Blathwayt in hopes of retaining his government (ibid., no. 1280), but on that day, the plantations committee recommended that the inquisition against his patent be finally processed (ibid., no. 1279), and Culpeper's release was ordered (Jenkins to Culpeper, Sept. 29, 1683, S.P. 44/64, 109). Blathwayt announced to Spencer and Bacon on Oct. 1 the outlines of the agreement with Culpeper (Blathwayt Papers, XVI, 2, XIII, 2, Williamsburg). Other examples of army pensions to governors-general are Carlisle's, for Jamaica, 1681 (Blathwayt to Lynch, Mar. 3, 1684, ibid., XXIV, 4, which also noted the secretary of war and plantations' care in keeping Lynch, the serving Jamaica governor, on the army payroll), and Lanier's, for Jersey, 1684 (Add. MSS 29578, 37). See also Guy to the attorney general, Mar. 5, 1684, warrant to pay Culpeper £700 arrears and £600 p.a. on the establishment of the armed forces, T. 64/88, 66; and Lord Culpeper's conveyance of his interest in Virginia to the king, May 24 [1684], T. 64/88, 68–69b. The settlement only conclusively covered the "Southern grant." Culpeper renewed the proprietorship of the Northern Neck in 1689 as part of his reward for supporting William of Orange. Culpeper also asked £1,300 in cash for his rights and may have received it, but the amount does not appear in the treasury warrant (T. 64/88, 66; and see Blathwayt to Effingham, Feb. 24, Mar. 8, 1684, Blathwayt

personal royalism, and selfish government had enhanced the prerogative, but his lordship had intended only to enrich himself. The state he had strengthened cast down Culpeper after he had helped to do its work: the provincial legislature had been tamed; the Virginia council had been reformed; a court party and garrison government had been domesticated in the Old Dominion. Centralized, royalized, and militarized, in the seven years since Bacon's rebellion the government of Virginia had been integrated into England's empire.

Papers, XIV, 1, Williamsburg). See also Culpeper to Blathwayt, Nov. 6, 1683 (T. 64/88, 65), and the crown's pledge to devote the revenues taken from Culpeper to support royal government in Virginia, and, in particular, to establish the emergency fund for the suppression of American rebellions so often called for by officers and governors (Blathwayt to Bacon, Nov. 17, 1683, Blathwayt Papers, XIII, 2, Williamsburg; the king to Howard of Effingham, July 25, 1684, and Rochester to Effingham, Dec. 21, 1685, T. 64/88, 69–70, 94). Blathwayt's conclusion was written to Sir Thomas Lynch, Mar. 3, 1684, Blathwayt Papers, XXIV, 4, Williamsburg.

Garrison Government Comes to the Old Dominion, 1676–1683

In Virginia as in England, civil war led to a revival and expansion of garrison government. The precondition of both was the administrative somnambulism of the early Stuarts. It had lingered on in the Old Dominion. There, a leftover governor of Charles I's debased coinage, Sir William Berkeley, became as inadequate to the century of revolution as the sovereign who had appointed him. As in England, so in Virginia, a generation of personal rule and court corruption bred a revolution against the inability of the executive to protect the people, to command their obedience, much less to serve their aspirations. As in the kingdom, so in its colony, the legislature that set out to reform the court was displaced by an army that revolted against both. Finally royal government was restored, more vindictively in Virginia than in England. As in the realm, so in the dominion, the postwar administrations were forced to enlist former rebel commanders, adopt garrison government, and appoint governors-general in order to maintain monarchy, secure public order, and, after years of unrest, achieve political stability. The events of a generation in England—1639 to 1667—were recapitulated in Virginia in the twelve months after April 1676.

When Sir William Berkeley's senility and Nathaniel Bacon's rebellion combined to summon garrison government to Virginia, the imperial crown looked for professional administrators to manage its new investment of men, matériel, and mentation in provincial governance. It found them, as usual, among those of its own military officers who were also veterans of provincial politics: Captain Herbert Jeffreys, guardsman-governor of York; Sir John Berry, the Yorkist captain and colonial investigator; Colonel Francis Moryson, veteran of the civil wars and of Virginia's governorship, and, for a decade past, the agent of the colony at the court of Charles II.

That decade had transformed Moryson from royalist to imperialist. The very objects of his agency became the stuff of empire: naval convoys and court contacts; munitions and questionnaires. Personal loyalty to the prince was replaced by national allegiance to the state. Personal interests in the colony were reshaped by bureaucratic functions for a province. When the members of the Virginia assembly asked Moryson to secure a royal charter that would express a merely titular dependence of the colony on the crown in order to obtain crown confirmation of assembly self-government, the reaction of the English executive forced Moryson to recognize his own conversion from royalism to imperialism. From being the assembly's agent on behalf of the charter in 1675, Francis Moryson became the king's commissioner for garrison government in 1676.

The agent and the charter came before the privy council plantations committee and the cabinet together with news of Indian attacks and Bacon's rebellion. Moryson's imperial auditors held that Berkeley's personal and political debility was to blame for permitting the republican government that the charter described. They felt that assembly self-government had incited Indian uprisings, popular discontents, and civil war. They were sure that the remedy was their own direct government, imposed by royal military force. The king's council and cabinet, dominated by the duke of York, were driven to express this imperialist rationale, to appoint investigatory commissioners, and to organize an expeditionary force, because Virginia's civil war threatened the crown's customs from tobacco. That revenue significantly reduced the royal reliance on politically expensive parliamentary subsidies. To resist the very large encroachments on the royal prerogative intended by the English parliamentarians, therefore, the crown had to squelch the relatively minor annoyance of the Virginia assembly's autonomy. Legislative misgovernment, the imperialists were sure, had caused this costly civil war.

That the habitual royal response to local risings was the imposition of paramilitary government owed much to extant examples in English and Scottish and Irish towns, and in overseas possessions, African, West Indian, and American. From the elements of the king's own Guards that garrisoned London itself, came most of the officers and many of the men for the Virginia expedition. Officers and men from the duke of York's admiralty regiment (commanded by a former governor of Jamaica) also joined the expeditionary battalion, as did regimental subordinates of the earl of Carlisle (then captain general of Jamaica). Further contingents marched or sailed to join the expedition from south-of-England garrisons in royal citadels, county towns, seaport fortresses, coastal forts, and naval dockyards. Eight transports received the infantry, the staff, and the volunteer officers (who, by service in Virginia, would qualify for commands in Tangier and the Leeward Islands). To escort the convoy and to reinforce the commands of the king, his lieutenant, and his commissioners, one of the latter, Sir John Berry, took command of four warships. Berry had previously used the navy as a vehicle of imperial administration in the West Indies and New Hampshire, Newfoundland and Tangier. The expeditionary force that this favorite captain of the duke of York convoyed from England to Virginia demonstrated anew that the transfer of garrison government from metropolis to province was one of professional military men as well as of paramilitary political methods.

A career soldier, Herbert Jeffreys of the Guards, was commissioned colonel, commander-in-chief of the expedition, and governor-designate of Virginia, as well as the senior royal commissioner. He had established Charles II's sovereignty over York with the same agencies of authority that he now deployed in Virginia. Not only did Jeffreys as royal governor again command Guards units as political police, now he also chaired a royal commission of political inquiry like that whose orders he had enforced at York. Once again, a royal commission, backed by the Guards, was to investigate the public excesses of autonomous local oligarchs and to deprive their leaders of office. Their maladministration, it seemed apparent at Whitehall, had provoked the provincial populace to break the king's peace. Therefore, to tame the people at York in 1663, as in Virginia thirteen years later, the crown's expeditionary officers and its political commissioners were named to a commission of oyer and terminer. It conferred on these royal agents power to try rebels. A frieze of severed heads at York, and men hung alive in chains in Virginia, testified terribly to these royal judges' ample authority. The crown also authorized its commissioners to investigate and to limit the much abused institutions of oligarchical power, that is, the agencies of provincial self-government. As a corporate council had been purged and its authority reduced in York, so an assembly seeking a charter was dismembered and degraded in Virginia. In both provinces, moreover, the local law courts were royally regulated, and appeals opened from them to the king. Particular attention was paid to reform of the militia, both by the creation of select units and the removal or reassignment of officers. Restructured, the provincial armed force could serve as a royal constabulary. Finally, all

of these reformed institutions of public authority in the province
—representative, legal, military—were to report their activities
regularly for royal review.

As in the city of York, so in the province of Virginia, pacification was the first task of this puissant administration. In York,
Captain Jeffreys and his companies of the Guards faced republican
rebels, religious dissenters, and the threat of Dutch raiders. In
Virginia, Jeffreys and the Guards battalion countered repeated
Indian raids on the northern and western frontiers of settlement,
repressed Baconian sedition in coastal and Southside counties, and
prepared to resist French landings. The redcoats reinforced frontier garrisons, took quarters in troubled Gloucester County, and
ranged along the porous Carolina border. The regiment's engineers and gunners surveyed coastal defenses, Major Moryson's
"castle in the air" among them, and Colonel Jeffreys ordered the
ships of Sir John Berry's squadron still on the Virginia station to
meet French raiders. The political purpose of this physical activity
was clear. Only a government that provided protection could
command obedience. Such was the negative lesson of Berkeley's
failure and Bacon's rebellion. Such was the positive message of the
Virginia battalion's parade at the Middle Plantation. The regiment physically supported social stabilization and imperial order.
Solemnifying the Indian treaty they enforced on Virginia's frontiers, celebrating the birthday and restoration of the king whose
authority they manifested in his American province, the redcoats
of Colonel Jeffreys's regiment also suggested the post-pacification
stage of provincial discipline: a purge of the Old Dominion's
old elite, Sir William Berkeley and his Green Spring advisers.
"The Souldiers said Hang the Governor and God damn these
Councillours."

Colonel Jeffreys moderated his men's advice. He did not hang
Governor Berkeley. Rather, he deposed him in Virginia, disgraced
him at court, and sent him home to die. Damnation being beyond
him, Jeffreys merely suspended five of Berkeley's councillors,
seized the seal from their surviving chief, cashiered them from
their militia commands, and ousted both the leading Berkeleans
and their relatives and dependents from the county commissions
of the peace and from shrievalties.

Having disciplined the Berkelean plural executive and its
supporters, Colonel Jeffreys separated the legislative roles of the
governor and council from that of the burgesses. He thus destroyed the unitary, republican, assembly system that had survived

the Restoration to dominate the Berkelean regime. The assembly's leader, Clerk Robert Beverley, made himself the particular object of royal wrath. Having successfully urged the assembly to reject the king's call for acts of oblivion and instead substituted laws to kill or fine the late rebels, Beverley capped his contumacy when he refused the royal commissioners access to the assembly's records. Colonel Jeffreys arrested Clerk Beverley and threatened him with a treason trial in England. Jeffreys then attacked the assembly as a whole. He joined his fellow commissioners in successful recommendations that the king take over legislative initiative by composing in council and imposing in Virginia acts that defined treason, taxation, and citizenship. The king also acted on his commissioners' advice to review provincial legislative output (approving, amending, or vetoing assembly acts), and to deny the assembly authority to create courts of law or to hear judicial appeals.

To recast Virginia's traditional institutions and to dismiss the Old Dominion's insubordinate officials was but to open the way to establish imperial government in the province. To man the reformed institutions and to replace the disobedient elite, the crown had to create a party of administration and authority. Such a court party would domesticate the direct government imposed by the royal army. The creation of a group of crown counsellors and court partisans had two phases: the recruitment of imperialists and their professionalization in office.

Jeffreys's ouster of Berkeley's supporters opened provincial politics to men who identified their personal advancement with the king's service. Continued by Culpeper, this process transformed the council of state in Virginia from a bunch of Berkelean barons into a board of imperial administrators. The conversion of local councils from collective executives into advisory and administrative bodies had long been associated with garrison government. It was presently continuing in England in the altered relationship of the king and council. But it prospered particularly on the frontiers of the empire. There, external military dangers were made doubly disruptive by internal social immaturity. To meet either foreign attack or domestic anarchy a chain-of-command administration was required. Whether on Jamaica's Northside and Caribbean frontiers or on Virginia's Southside and western borders, military tasks determined the duties of councillor-colonels as well as those of governors-general. Their soldierly titles conferred social status on these regional administrators, and militia patronage enhanced their political power.

The interrelations of force and politics were apparent, for example, when Matthew Kemp and John Page were rewarded for organizing the court party in the burgesses by elevation to the governor-general's council. They also received fort contracts, militia colonelcies, and Indian agencies. Colonel Page took command of the Middle Plantation arsenal. Colonel Kemp raised a troop of cavalry to replace the regulars who garrisoned Gloucester County. These councillors and their military commands defended the new imperial order against the opposition's "plant cutting" riots in May 1682. Both colonel-councillors were responsive to the linked military and political orders of the crown. One such order required them to list not only every subordinate officer but even the name of every militiaman for royal review. Another order then restricted the franchise to these armed freeholders.

The imperial executive's systematic militarization and provincial penetration roused political opposition in Virginia as they did in England. Threatened with hanging by redcoats, arrested by select militiamen, the old elite were awakened to "the standing army issue." They realized that if "every pitiful little fellow with a periwig" sent by the crown to govern Virginia could suspend councillors, dissolve the assembly, and govern by decree, "the rights of Englishmen" to political participation, representation, and the rule of statute law were endangered. Civil liberties seemed suddenly to require definition and defense by those they privileged, in the province as in the metropolis. As in England, so in Virginia, the creation of a court party produced a country opposition.

Each Virginia faction modeled itself on its English counterpart. From their models they received detailed political instructions. The crown ordered its courtiers overseas to arrest Robert Beverley and to hang the plant cutters. The crown's merchant-bankers and London allies instructed their correspondents on the Virginia council regarding such issues as the Port Act. On the other hand, English merchants of country convictions tutored Virginia planters in whig strategy and tactics. For example, letters from outport merchants in England to Virginia's displaced elite inspired provincial "petitioners" to organize for assembly acts to remedy country grievances. Provincial courtiers, like English ones, were "abhorrers" of this pressure-group politics. They feared that petitioners' success would produce legislative attacks on the militarized executive, and that rebuff of these legislative demands would lead to popular risings. So it happened, in Virginia as in

England. In both colony and kingdom, armed royal government repressed such "civil" disturbances, and political reaction set in against the legislatures that had instigated them. The imperial executive also used law courts against its political opponents, both in England and in Virginia. The executive's political use of its military, legislative, and legal prerogatives proceeded in interlocking patterns in province and metropolis. When the councillor-colonels' cavalry captured or dispersed Virginia's plant cutters, when the crown discontinued assembly sessions for three years, and when the major general of the colony arrested the leader of the opposition and charged him with treason, the parallels with plot, parliament, and Shaftesbury in England were apparent. And we have seen the like in Jamaica.

The closed system of Anglo-American politics also meant that when the crown tried to extend Poynings's Law from Ireland to Virginia and Jamaica, provincial protests were reinforced by English parliamentarians prepared to make the cause of provincial assemblies and colonial elites their own. The moderates pressed the legislative cause on the crown at the one moment in the entire Restoration when the king most needed the swing group's voices and votes. Using the Jamaica case, the moderates convinced King Charles that he had best settle the empire as Lord Culpeper had settled Virginia.

That political settlement—which recognized as it disciplined the legislative role—was consonant with the traditions of garrison government on both sides of the Atlantic. Lord Culpeper knew the truth of Sir Thomas Littleton's remark that, even in a garrison state, the people "are apter to be led than driven." Culpeper recognized that royal rule was most economical and most acceptable if it was exercised in part by representative, respectable, loyal, local leadership. But Governor-General Culpeper's concession to participatory politics in Virginia, like Governor-General Massey's in Gloucester, had a steel backbone. The provincials' "voluntary submission was a witness to his moderation. . . . Only the sword had some influence of fear upon the injurious." Thus the necessity to leaven coercion with consultation in garrison government persuaded Culpeper in Virginia, as it had Carlisle in Jamaica, to help save American assemblies.

In part the product of these governors-general's political moderation, the royal orders of November 1680 permitted the Jamaica assembly to make municipal laws. These orders were followed in July 1681 by the like concession to Virginia's legislature. So, too, when in August and September 1681 the king gave Sir

Thomas Lynch more coercive commands regarding the government of Jamaica, the like orders followed, between October 1681 and January 1682, for Lord Culpeper and Virginia. These imperial dicta reiterated the legal, legislative, and, above all, the military prerogatives of the governors-general. Because the crown's commissions and instructions of 1681 summarized the imperial imposition of garrison government on England's provinces overseas since 1654, and did so in terms of the largest and most powerful of these provinces, they became the fundamental documents of royal government in America. More than that, they largely shaped the political, institutional, and social future of the English empire for a hundred years to come.

Although, by the second quarter of the eighteenth century, the crown's decision to continue provincial assemblies would begin to seem the largest part of the imperial settlement of 1681, for the two generations that immediately followed that settlement it was the royal restrictions on colonial legislatures that were most important. For while King Charles had recognized the creative legislative role of the assemblies, he had also redefined them as tripartite: his viceroy, his council (acting as the upper house), and a lower house (elected by the freeholders). "The Governor Council and Burgesses of this General Assembly," as Culpeper's commission listed them, each possessed equal powers of legislative initiative and amendment, approval and disapproval. The disintegration of the unitary republican assemblies into their constituent parts, together with the adoption of parliamentary procedure, exposed the operations of each legislative component to the view, and the veto, of the crown. Royal review was effected by requiring quarterly or sessional reports from each part of the provincial parliaments. The old assembly clerks, who had refused as Beverley had to reveal "his Masters'" proceedings, were put aside by royal order. Writs of election, summons to meet, times of adjournment, and decisions to dissolve assemblies were prerogative powers insisted on by the crown in the orders of 1681. Henceforward, they were exercised ever more frequently by the crown itself, as well as by the governors-general. "The power and Authority of the Grand Assembly" was so diffused and its subjection to royal influence was so complete that executive orders went far to displace legislation as the voice of government in the empire, whether in Virginia, in Jamaica, or in the other colonies now being royalized. For years after the 1681 orders were enforced in Virginia, the "Grand Assembly" was not even summoned into session

"This Despotic way of Government," as legislative leaders labeled the garrison government codified in 1681, depended on the martial prerogative of the governor-general. This was the largest concern even of so mercenary an executive as Lord Culpeper. It was the most comprehensive authority conveyed to provincial governments by the crown in the imperial commissions of 1681. From the outset of English government in 1655, Jamaica's commander-in-chief had been a general officer. The Virginia viceroy's authority as captain general, however, was practically introduced into the province by overwhelming military force in 1677. The captain general's authority was sustained for more than five years in the Old Dominion by regular troops. These years domesticated garrison government in Virginia. The unrestricted military authority of the crown could no more be resisted in garrisoned Virginia than in occupied Ireland, militarized Scotland, or regimented Jamaica. The regular army elements of the Virginia garrison were gradually withdrawn to help the Stuarts hold England (or disbanded to release funds for the same purpose). By then, however, the king's Virginia council was militarized and royalized. The courtiers in the council commanded select militia units. Culled from the militia masses by Colonel Jeffreys, such companies as the frontier rangers of Colonels Bridger and Byrd, the cavalry patrols of General Smith and Colonel Kemp, and Colonel Page's magazine men, gave these courtiers physical bases for their political authority. Moreover, the councillor-colonels extended their combined military and political influence by nominating their clients as county militia captains and commissioners of the peace. In short, enough of the imperial crown's paramilitary political weapons were in the hands of an expanding court party to preserve the king's peace in the province.

By 1683, the courtier-councillors were, as they would remain for the next decade of Virginia's provincialization, the nerve centers of imperial administration in Virginia. Lord Culpeper himself acknowledged the centrality of the councillors. He identified his authority to suspend councillors (and to nominate their replacements to the crown) as the most important part of his 1681 commission. The greatest achievement of his administration, Culpeper claimed, was his creation of an administratively proficient, royally responsive council.

It was the court party councillors who, as much as the governor-general himself, completed the imposition of garrison government on Virginia. It was they who took over the border commands, the Middle Plantation magazine, and the county patrols from the departing regulars. The councillor-colonels used their military resources to arrest Robert Beverley and to repress the plant cutters. By reporting this unrest to the crown and by requesting executive leadership, the councillors hastened Culpeper's reinstruction and return to Virginia. Finally, it was the councillors' political and fiscal reports that helped end private proprietary power in the province after Culpeper's dismissal from its government. By being cashiered, as much as by his positive admonitions, Governor-General Culpeper reinforced the provincial councillors' understanding of imperial imperatives: particular obedience to royal orders; general use of the royal prerogative in "his Majesty's Interest and Service." The objects of this imperial interest were provincial peace, governmental economy, colonial prosperity. These, court partisans agreed, would "tend most to his Majesty's service, and the Ease and Quiet of the Country." With this assessment of the aims of the royal commission of 1681, there ended the formative period of the first British empire.

Garrison Government: The English Empire to 1681

The First Stage of Empire, 1569–1641

The political and administrative usefulness of military men was impressed on English sovereigns during their long obsession with the conquest of France. Continental experience endowed the monarchy with an imperial title, an imperial ambition, and an imperial instrument. By the reign of Henry VIII, military governors, assisted by councils of military, fiscal, and secretarial officers, controlled the European possessions of "the imperial crown of England." "Governors"—the English title is of Tudor coinage —commanded garrisons in the capitals of the conquered provinces. Their troops marched out from urban citadels to enforce the orders the governor received from the crown and to collect the taxes he levied to support royal government. English soldier-administrators then used the forceful methods they had learned in France to subject England itself to royal authority. As we have seen, this process was concluded at Naworth in 1569/70, when the governor of the Berwick citadel and the soldiers of his garrison shot down the feudal followers of the northern earls. The crisis of the Elizabethan regime was thus decided in favor of royal, central government.

In 1585 Tudor governors and garrisons sailed overseas once more as Spain replaced France in English enmity. Holding fortified commercial towns in the formerly Spanish Netherlands, the English soldier-administrators discovered that wealth followed the flag—that Spain, and through her all of Europe, was enriched by the spoil of conquered kingdoms in America. English officers observed that their nation's entry into the competition for empire could make them the agents and beneficiaries of an English authority extended over England's neighbors and overseas, as well as sustain their position as the instruments of crown control in England itself.

To the army's domestic police function and its American

ambition, the reconquest and colonization of Ireland between 1550 and 1622 added agrarian and societal duties. The settlement of soldier-farmers around the fortified central places of conquered territories was "plantation," a process shaped and labeled by reference to Roman imperial practice. The Irish "first phases of modern English imperialism" led to the implementation of the classic colonial model. By 1609 "the custom of plantation in colonies, whereby the Roman plant was removed into the soil of other nations," was imposed in Munster and in Ulster. Plantation government was defined on the Roman model, modified by the European councilliar tradition: "For Government, let it be in the Hands of one, assisted with some Counsell: and let them have Commission, to exercise Martiall Lawes, with some limitations."[1] Governor, council, and martial law—such was the prescription for English empire in America during the coming century.

English army officers carried these imperial ideas across the Atlantic and applied them in America. Trained in arms and administration in the cities and citadels of France and the Netherlands, experienced, as we have seen, in Irish conquest and plantation, these officers came to command the palisaded centers of settlement on the continent—Jamestown and Henrico; St. Mary's, Sagadahoc, and Saybrook; Plymouth and Piscataqua; Charlestown and Cambridge; and the even more embattled outposts in the West Indies: Providence, St. Christopher, and Barbados. As these settlements grew and required governmental organization, military units helped to define political jurisdictions. In Virginia local squads gave way to plantation companies, which were amalgamated into county commands. In Massachusetts the organization of township militia companies into regiments likewise was fundamental to county definition. And all around the Atlantic circuit of the English empire, town government reflected Netherlands garrison practices, and English settlers obeyed the orders of Netherland veterans.

This militarized social model was established not only at Jamestown, with its triple bastions and uniformed guards, the capital of a dominion in the making, but also at tiny Plymouth, ordered within its palisade, lying down the hill beneath its fort, with "pateroes" pointing from the guard post at the town intersec-

1. Francis Bacon brought the lessons of Irish plantation into the consciousness of the English establishment 16 years after the events cited here, just as the crown was taking over Virginia government, when he amended his essay on the greatness of kingdoms and added one "Of Plantations," both quoted here from *The Essayes or Counsels, Civill and Morall, of Francis Bacon Lo. Verulam, Viscount St. Alban* (London, 1625), 176, 202 (English Books, 1475–1640, microfilm, University of Michigan, Ann Arbor, Mich.).

tion, its men organized by Captain Standish, mustering by squads for guard duty, fire fighting, and religious worship. This simple garrison model was easily duplicated in Captain Graves's Charlestown, Captain Gardiner's Saybrook, Captain Mason's Hartford. Each of these towns was defined by "watch and ward." Each was an outpost, a node of English conquest and colonization in America. The governmental institutions of England's colonies, whether in Ireland, the West Indies, or North America, thus were shaped by military men, intent on establishing security and imposing social order within their jurisdictions and determined to spread crusading Christianity and English authority over conquered territories and "native" peoples.[2] Here were elements of empire.

On the American continent, Virginia was from the first what it would continue to be, the bellwether of English empire. It was the continental colony that contributed most to the development of an imperial constitution, and, prior to the outbreak of the English civil wars, it especially exemplified the effects, and the limits, of military ideas and institutions in the early English colonies. The crises and the captains of early Virginia reflect a general Anglo-American pattern. With a heroism reminiscent of archaic eras, Captain John Smith, soldier, adventurer, imperialist, enacted in Virginia a socially significant scene from a life suffused with military drama. His ideas were institutionalized, and the colony's society stabilized, by a quartet of Netherlands veterans who subjected Virginia to the continent's first English imperial code, the "Lawes Divine, Morall and Martiall."[3] Soldier-advisers and mili-

2. Darrett B. Rutman, "Militant New World, 1607–1640: America's First Generation, Its Martial Spirit, Its Tradition of Arms, Its Militia Organization, Its Wars" (Ph.D. diss., University of Virginia, 1959), is the fullest study of the military bases of the early English settlements on the continent. On the Irish connections and precedents, see Howard Mumford Jones, "Origins of the Colonial Idea in England," American Philosophical Society, *Proceedings*, LXXXV (1942), 451–459; David Beers Quinn, "Sir Thomas Smith (1513–1577) and the Beginnings of English Colonial Theory," *ibid.*, LXXXIX (1945), 543–560; Quinn, "The Munster Plantation: Problems and Opportunities," Cork Historical and Archaeological Society, *Journal*, 2d Ser., LXXI (1966), 19–40, esp. 23, 32. I am indebted to Prof. William Smyth of St. Patrick's College, Maynooth, for a copy of the Munster item. See also Nicholas P. Canny, "The Ideology of English Colonization: From Ireland to America," *WMQ*, 3d Ser., XXX (1973), 575–598. On Dudley and Cambridge, see William Andrew Polf, "Puritan Gentlemen: The Dudleys of Massachusetts, 1576–1686" (Ph.D. diss., Syracuse University, 1973), 6–7, 18, 30–33, 40, 42. Arthur Percival Newton, *The Colonising Activities of the English Puritans: The Last Phase of the Elizabethan Struggle with Spain*, Yale Historical Publications, Miscellany, I (New Haven, Conn., 1914), discusses the Providence and Tortuga settlements. See also Newton, *The European Nations in the West Indies, 1493–1688* (London, 1933); Vincent T. Harlow, *A History of Barbados, 1625–1685* (Oxford, 1926); and Alan Burns, *History of the British West Indies*, 2d ed. rev. (London, 1965).

3. *DNB*, s.v. "Gates, Sir Thomas," and "West, Sir Thomas." On Sir Thomas Dale, see

tary officials defined "plantations," "natives," and "colonists" in terms derived from the conquest and colonization of Ireland. The soldier-statesmen of Virginia also defined the fundamental and perennial divisions of English expansionist thought as they strongly contrasted their imperial and authoritarian programs for Virginia with more legislative, legalistic, civilian, commercial, and oligarchical colonial concepts.

By 1618, after four years of local peace, amidst the first flush of tobacco prosperity and during control of the Virginia Company by partisans of parliamentary authority, the "Lawes Divine, Morall and Martiall" were displaced. There ensued the degraded command, unregulated settlement, and unbridled economic individualism that led to the massacre of 1622. "The cause of the massacre was the want of marshall discipline," John Smith told a royal commission of enquiry. Deficiencies of "marshall discipline," the captain explained, included a variety of social and political elements: dispersed settlement compounded the shortage of soldiers; the excessive number of councillors and counsels, both in England and Virginia, exacerbated the destabilizing, discordant results of overfrequent changes of colonial executives; and all these factors further diluted the Virginia executive's weakened military authority.[4]

Even those English observers of Virginia's plight who did not share Smith's conviction that the crown should institute direct royal rule in Virginia and restore a military governor and government, backed by a regular garrison, nonetheless repeated the martial commonplaces of the age that Smith from the first had applied to the colony. In reaction to the 1622 fighting, George Wyatt wrote to his son, Sir Francis Wyatt, governor of Virginia. The elder Wyatt recalled that Virginia had begun as a combination of Roman "colony" and English "plantation," designed to force "Barbarians to Civilitie and Christianitie." A settlement among savages, Wyatt concluded, should have continued to concentrate

Darrett B. Rutman, "The Historian and the Marshal," *VMHB*, LXVIII (1960), 284–294; Jones, "Origins of the Colonial Idea," Am. Phil. Soc., *Procs.*, LXXXV (1942), 453; Wesley Frank Craven, *The Southern Colonies in the Seventeenth Century, 1607–1689* (Baton Rouge, La., 1949), 91–92, 98, 105–107; David H. Flaherty, ed., *For the Colony in Virginia Brittania Lawes Divine, Morall and Martiall, etc.*, comp. William Strachey (Charlottesville, Va., 1969), 9.

4. Edward Arber and A. G. Bradley, eds., *Travels and Works of Captain John Smith: President of Virginia, and Admiral of New England, 1580–1631*, II (Edinburgh, 1910), 572–578; Craven, *Southern Colonies*, 111–114, 123–127, 133–135.

on "Soldgership, afore better deserving wel, now more to be respected[,] which neclected hathe cost you so deare."[5]

Despite the massacre, "Soldgership" continued to be neglected in Virginia and throughout the infant empire. The death of Prince Henry, the disruption of the Stuart court, and the degradation of the English military combined to thwart such plans as Smith's and Wyatt's for a remilitarized imperialism. "All our plantations have been so foyled and abused," Captain Smith complained in 1630, that "their best good willers have been for the most part discouraged, and their good intents disgraced." He spoke particularly of "Seamen and Soldiers, [who] have beene most worthily honoured and esteemed, but now regarded for most part, but as the scumme of the world." Smith asked English military men to leave the piracy and mercenary employments forced on them by peace. Recover "your wonted reputations," the captain urged his comrades, by an "adventure to those faire plantations of our English Nation."[6]

Those English soldiers, in Virginia and elsewhere, who followed Smith's advice ran up against commercialism and localism. One such soldier was Captain George Donne, the muster-master general and provost marshal of Virginia. He had a wide experience of army, ideology, and empire, for he had fought for the Protestants in France and against the Spaniards in the West Indies. In 1638 Captain Donne presented to Charles I "two Considerations without which this sound limbe of your confirmed Empire cannott bee fast joynted to the full bodie." The first was a "Serious Strict observation" of those laws and rules especially suited to colonies. The second was "ready Instruction in the use of armes." Both should be required in colonial constitutions as "An Injunction by Authority imposed" to which colonial assent need not be secured by the crown. Armed authority would both enforce colonial order and accomplish the conquest of neighbors and natives. The combination of domestic peace and foreign conquest had been "the chiefe Glorye and firmity of the Roman Empire."[7]

Military government, Donne asserted in terms that had be-

5. Arber and Bradley, eds., *Travels and Works of Smith*, II, 588–590; Craven, *Southern Colonies*, 145–147; J. Frederick Fausz and Jon Kukla, eds., "A Letter of Advice to the Governor of Virginia, 1624," *WMQ*, 3d Ser., XXXIV (1977), 112–116.

6. On Henrican militancy and imperialism, see especially, G.P.V. Akrigg, *Jacobean Pageant: Or the Court of King James I* (New York, 1974), 129–131, 135–136, 139–140. Arber and Bradley, eds., *Travels and Works of Smith*, II, 915–916, 925.

7. T. H. Breen, ed., "George Donne's 'Virginia Reviewed': A 1638 Plan to Reform Colonial Society," *WMQ*, 3d Ser., XXX (1973), 449–466, esp. 449–450, 455, 456, 458. See also Craven, *Southern Colonies*, 148–149, 153–155.

come imperialist commonplaces, would check the "search for growing rich to soone." Greed had produced unsuitable political ambition in colonial and commerical elites and had led them into contention with executive authority in general and into "Competition with a Governor for Superiority" in particular. Unwise dependence on "the Wills and counsailes of Men of Trade" had encouraged oligarchic license and councilliar pretensions. Anglo-American opposition to the executive had other springs also. The provost marshal told the king that, as in old England so in New England, religious dissent had inspired political treason. This imperial officer anticipated that, together, social aspiration, political ambition, and religious enthusiasm would excite civil war.[8] He knew that monarchical and military political prescriptions, social regulation, and religious uniformity, all of which the king wished to revive at home and overseas in the later 1630s, "disquieted the Composition of some Mynds in Virginia and of too many (as it appeares) in England."

Within three years Donne's fears became fact: a transatlantic civil war, inimical alike to monarchy, army, and empire, undermined the authority of the executive in America by destroying the monarchy in England. Because it forced the development of autonomous colonial elites and institutions, and provided a republican ideology, the civil war was the essential precondition of American independence. For example, because Sir William Berkeley was commissioned governor of Virginia in 1641 by a monarch whose powers had been limited by the reaction against absolutism, and was recommissioned in 1650 by an exiled prince, he was stripped of the military authority possessed by his veteran predecessors and was reduced to being merely first among equals in the colony's council. Berkeley also lost the institutional model that a strong English executive provided for the dependencies, and he was deprived of direct monarchical support for his provincial government. Concurrent with the abasement of executive authority throughout the empire by civil war, provincial autonomy was enhanced by the political aggression of acquisitive elites. They took control of provincial councils and county courts, and they multiplied ties with English outports, spurning the metropolis as they did the sovereign. Anglo-American republicanism—oligarchic and localist, autarchic alike in religion and commerce—successfully

8. Breen, ed., "George Donne's 'Virginia Reviewed,'" *WMQ*, 3d Ser., XXX (1973), 159, 160, 163 164.

challenged monarchical centralization of politics and imperial uniformity in church and commerce during the civil wars of the
1640s—and of the 1770s and 1780s.

The Interregnum:
Sword Rule and Military Governors

While executive authority shrank overseas, revulsion to the
social disintegration and political factionalization of civil war motivated the champions of authority to strengthen the institutions
of garrison government in England. There, during the 1640s, both
royalist and parliamentary military governors sought to pacify
their commands by firmly establishing the authority of one or the
other of the competing central governments. They thereby introduced a metropolitan focus into local politics. The governors made
"court" and "country" partisanships the political poles of the
English provinces by forcing local leaders either to defend local,
"country" autonomy or to support the "court" and state sovereignty. Thus they forecast the shape of Anglo-American politics as
well. In Nottingham, from 1644 to 1646, as in Virginia from 1676
to 1681, local partisanships were enmeshed in the larger struggle
over the dimensions of metropolitan authority in provincial life.
Established elites saw that the continuation of their sway depended
upon their maintenance of local autonomy. Aspirant outgroups
tied their ascent to an expansion of the role of central government
in local affairs. Appeals to London, to resolve the contest for local
power, produced gubernatorial commissions. These divided authority between the executive and elements of the local elite organized as a council. In these commissions, consultative and judicial
roles were always reserved to the councillors, but the preponder-
ance of power was held by the governor in the form of extensive
military authority.

The governors used their military authority to patronize their
supporters. Thus the executives helped to develop a professional
administrative class—governmental "men of business." The military governors recognized and encouraged these new men because
they paid unprecedented attention to the "middling sort" of people. These were the heart of the governors' militias, the friends of
public order. Their approval of executive authority was in sharp
contrast to both the arrogance of the provincial elites and the
anarchism of the poor.

The governors' social rebalancing, political reorganization, and paramilitary administration were financed in part by local requisitions and taxes, authorized by the state but collected by the governors and spent by them for military purposes. Further financial support for prerogative politics came from the central government's direct grants to localities, disbursed by the governor to pay himself, his staff, his garrison, and their local suppliers. Growing governmental revenues and expenditures, both provincial and national, underwrote politically dictated alternatives to traditional economic arrangements in agriculture, clothing manufacture, food processing, shipping, and finance. The new economic opportunities tended to be monopolized by the growing official "interest" of officers, administrators, court-connected merchants, and farmer-suppliers. Garrison government, whether of nation, province, town, or colony, required the recruitment and organization of masses of men and money, supplies and food. So were laid the economic and bureaucratic bases of prerogative politics.

Yet "men come first, the rest is the result of their labors." As we have seen, twenty-six civil war veterans carried the institutions of garrison government to ten different colonies, seven in America and the West Indies, and one each in Europe, North Africa, and India. These officers had governed a dozen different English cities, towns, and citadels. They subsequently served thirty terms in governorships overseas. Among New World colonies, Jamaica, Barbados, New York, and Virginia were especially influenced by the administration of these civil warriors.[9]

In the British Isles, after 1649, the Celtic kingdoms felt the rough hand of English military rule as Oliver Cromwell extended garrison government from England to the conquest, pacification, and redevelopment of Ireland and Scotland. His officers then transferred their experience of military government, now widened and intensified by its application to Ireland and Scotland, to the overseas units of the empire. Thus the forceful local administrations of the English civil wars were transmuted into an Anglo-American imperial system by royalist and parliamentary officers alike, and by the military executives of the Commonwealth and of the Protectorate.

Basing empire on conquest, Cromwell's legions massacred the defenders of Irish towns and "pacified" the Irish countryside with fire and sword. More constructively, the English troops renewed urban garrison government and agricultural military plan-

9. See the Appendix for details.

tation in Ireland. Together, these operations supported an army of occupation and administration. As frontier police, militia cadres, and seaport patrols, English soldiers redistributed land, regulated political activity, and collected customs. These officer-executives were regularly shifted from Irish posts to provincial service elsewhere in the British Isles, and in Dunkirk, Tangier, Jamaica, Barbados, Massachusetts, New York, and Maryland as well. Repeated Irish revolts ensured that Ireland would continue to employ the English army's largest reserve as a garrison. Ireland was thus the school of governors-general, and of an increasing variety of other officer-administrators, down to the time of the American Revolution.[10] Five officers who afterward commanded Jamaica, New York, and Tangier had served in Ireland before 1660. During the Restoration they were succeeded in Ireland by six officer-executives who later went out to govern New York, New England, and the Leeward Islands. Between 1689 and 1727 fifteen or more veterans of William III's Irish war also served as royal governors-general in Virginia, Gibraltar, Minorca, Jamaica, Barbados, the Leeward Islands, Nova Scotia and Newfoundland, and New York and Pennsylvania.

The first of these classes of military administrators in Ireland, trained as much in social as in military discipline by Cromwell, Monck, and Jones, had gone on to complete their unification of the British Isles by the conquest of Scotland. They were suspicious of merchant motivations. The public order they imposed on the Scots was biased in favor of yeomen and tradesmen. It was distinguished, even among garrison governments, by its high degree of centralization and militarization. After 1654 officer-governors carried the paternalist, regulatory, and coercive methods they had practiced in Scotland to Jamaica. There these methods were successfully applied until they found a wider, but still forceful, expression in the imperial constitution of 1681. After 1688 Williamite repression in Scotland trained seven soldiers who subsequently ruled not only Jamaica but also Virginia, New York, and Barbados. The Union of 1707 refreshed the flow of army administrators from Scotland to the American provinces (and vice versa). A half-dozen veterans of Scottish garrisons, several of whom were themselves Scots, were commissioned as governors-general in America between 1707 and 1727. Whether in expanding the imperial fron-

---

10. The continuing influence on American settlement, society, and politics of the army and the plantations in Ireland is shown in John Christopher Guzzardo, "Sir William Johnson's Official Family: Patron and Client in an Anglo-American Empire" (Ph.D. diss., Syracuse University, 1975), esp. chap. 2.

tier westward, as did Colonel Alexander Spotswood, or in linking provincial and metropolitan political groups, as the earl of Orkney did, Scots officers had an especially marked influence on Virginia in the early eighteenth century.[11]

While this routine transfer of officers from governments in the three British kingdoms to the empire's American provinces continued until the American Revolution, it had begun much earlier, with the Commonwealth's punitive expeditions to Barbados in 1651 and to Virginia in 1652. Next the Protectorate tried to unite the British Isles and every English colony into a single transatlantic state, dedicated by its military executive to the reduction of the Spanish empire. This "Western Design" was planned by a Barbadian, Thomas Modyford. It was directed by a commissioner from the Plymouth Colony, Edward Winslow. Its settlers were recruited by a Massachusetts officer, Daniel Gookin. The governors of Irish plantations and Scottish citadels, Robert Venables and William Brayne, commanded expeditionary regiments drawn from London and the Leeward Islands. The widespread residences of the Design's men attest to the geographic scope of the Protector's imperial vision. And, as this work records, that vision produced the massive expedition of 1654, in which an amphibious force attacked Hispaniola, conquered Jamaica, and so revived and intensified military plantation and garrison government in America after the imperial decadence of the early Stuarts and the imperial disintegration of the civil wars.

The Restoration Empire, 1660–1681

The imperialists of the Restoration, many of them Cromwell's proconsuls, forced a reluctant Charles II to recognize the political and administrative necessity of adopting the Cromwellian system of territorial control and political administration. Thus they kept provincial government, in Britain and overseas, largely a military preserve. As this decision was especially apparent in colonial government, so it was an especially contentious issue in colonial policy. From the outset of English colonization, military-imperial officers had competed with civilian-commercial elements for domination of English expansion overseas, but that struggle was never more severe than it was in the first fifteen years of the Restoration.

11. See the Appendix.

This Anglo-American political conflict was fueled by the incompatibility of imperial social and political values with those of capitalism. Imperial ideals glorified monarchy. Individualist economic pursuits fostered oligarchy. The empire reflected the political authority of the king's governors-general, and it gave priority to the social needs of yeoman farmers and small planters. Commercial exploitation put political power in the hands of rising merchants and engrossing landlords, and it served their social interests.

The country party's Anglo-America was indeed a "commercial connection," but the English empire, as the court party idealized it, was devoted to social order, political obedience, and military security. In pursuit of that imperial ideal, the governors-general menaced merchant-planter property. They embargoed food exports in famine times. They issued ordinances against the engrossment of commodities and land. They imposed restrictions on trade with natives and enemies. They taxed liquor and imported luxuries. Most dangerous of all to private property, the governors-general requisitioned, under martial law, the labor of servants and slaves and the services of ships, carts, and draft animals. In the interest of provincial fortification, defense, and expansion, they even enlisted all free adult males in compulsory service. Agrarian and aggressive, rural yet regulatory, at once patriarchal and public-minded, garrison government restricted the force of statutes, produced by the representatives of the rising, commercial, economic classes, and concluded instead that "it is with an army, not with lawyers, that the sovereign controls multitudes."[12]

Thus the conflict over colonial policy—the overseas direction of men and investment of money—was an issue in the political contest between authoritarian grandees and libertarian elites. The devotees of the Tudor-Cromwellian imperial tradition sought to sustain the militarist and statist outcomes of the Interregnum. They were resisted by the partisans of commercial freedom and local autonomy. From the eve of the Restoration, Anthony Ashley Cooper, afterward the earl of Shaftesbury, sought to ally particularist "country" politicians with the anti-authoritarian elements among the merchants. Cooper tried to bring into this coalition the colonial clients of both the aristocratic and the commercial enemies of imperial policies. By 1674 Shaftesbury had thus defined the proto-whig commercial and colonial program that was restated in

12. The duke of Newcastle's reminder to the king is quoted in Ogg, *Charles II*, I, 145.

1698 by his former secretary, John Locke, and finally realized by the Walpoles after 1722.

The long delay before whig and commercial dominance was attained is the best evidence of the profundity of the monarchical and imperial triumph in 1675. The fall of Shaftesbury and the dissolution of the council of foreign plantations of which he was president gave control of imperial administration to the revitalized, royalist committee of the privy council for the plantations (the so-called lords of trade and plantations). This committee was chaired on occasion by the duke of York, afterward James II, the personification of monarchy, militarism, and empire. It was powerfully influenced by the earl of Danby, whose vision of national unity and achievement was based on absolutism at home and aggression overseas. The privy council committee was informed and guided by its secretariat. First assembled by Sir Robert Southwell, from officers of the council, customs, treasury, and army, it was later developed by William Blathwayt, the imperial fixer. The imperialists' achievement in the six years after 1675 was summarized by the constitution for the empire that they formalized in 1681.

The 1681 Settlement

The materials of the Anglo-American constitution were smelted from the ores of Jamaican and Virginian politics in the fires of the English Exclusion Crisis. They were forged into law in July 1681 as Sir Thomas Lynch's commission to be captain general and governor-in-chief of Jamaica. The structure of the imperial constitution was completed on January 27, 1682, when Lynch's commission became the model also for Virginia's government. It was then imposed on colony after colony, for a century to come, as the organic law of the English empire.[13]

A hundred years of imperial rule so fixed the constitution of 1681 in the minds of Americans that its precepts—about the role of the executive, the shape of the legislature, the dimensions of

13. "MDCCXL Abstract of the Commissions, and Instructions formerly and at the present time given to the Governors of His Majesty's Plantations in America with References to the Books and Papers Showing the Alterations . . . Observations . . . Occurences in each Government especially before the Establishment of this Office in 1696," Add. MSS 30372, British Lib.

prerogative and of privilege, the government's obligations and the governed's rights, the functions of the judiciary, and the relation of the central government of the empire to its constituent provinces —heavily influenced the constitution of the empire's successor states in North America. In 1789, shortly after the close of the third and decisive war in the old empire between alienated elites and assertive metropolitans, American executives assumed their predecessors' duties as commanders-in-chief of an imperial union and as governors-general of its constituent states and territories.

The threat of civil war established the context within which the fundamental decisions of 1681 were made. The country's peace, the crown's authority, the church's unity, the colonies' constitutions, all were imperiled by the conjunction of the Popish Plot and the Exclusion Crisis. The supposed sedition of provincial leaders and the political pretensions of the colonial legislatures were parts of the larger threat to the imperial monarchy from English republicans and the English parliament. The political crisis manifested by the house of commons's passage of the Exclusion Bill on November 11, 1680, forced the king-in-council to reestablish local legislative authority in America. The permanence and privileges of the American assemblies were the result of this decision, not of the 1688 coup against King James, since labeled "the Glorious Revolution." The fundamental concessions to local representative bodies publicly announced in the summer of 1681 were the measure of American self-government, but they were fully balanced by a quid pro quo: the restored assemblies passed laws that levied taxes to support direct royal government and that conceded the full military prerogative of the crown in each royal province. The pelf and power thus produced for the prerogative permanently weighted the executive scale of Anglo-American government. Imperial money and authority counterbalanced provincial legislation and representation.

Immediate limits on legislative capacity and solid additions to prerogative power both followed the defeat of the Exclusion Bill in the house of lords, November 15, 1680. Not only the reenfranchised assemblies, but also the reempowered viceroys, were subjected to a novel degree of royal regulation. The commissions of 1681 redefined the various elements of provincial government in terms of their separate subordinations to the imperial crown. So they exposed the American colonies to the burgeoning bureaucratic and metropolitan agencies of the English state. The commissions and instructions written in 1681 required quarterly journals from the king's provincial secretaries of state, legislative clerks, and financial auditors. They also commanded regular reports from the royal executive and military officers in the provinces. There resulted the bureaucratic linkages and the political, fiscal, and strategic data that made it possible to direct local government from Whitehall.

The royal secretariat, treasury, and courts now joined the military in American government. Within a single generation, the resulting anglicization transformed the isolated, passionate, and principled seventeenth-century autonomous colonies into the relatively cosmopolitan, rationalist, and compromising eighteenth-century imperial provinces. The imperial constitution that helped civilize the American provinces, however, also asserted the imperial right to tax, regulate, judge, and command that ultimately provoked the American Revolution.

The insertion into provincial government of English officials other than the governors-general reduced viceregal authority as much as it did oligarchic autonomy. The appointment of English officers who reported without reference to the governors-general, and often to different imperial agencies, checked the viceroys' political independence. The division of provincial patronage between the crown and the governors-general likewise reduced viceregal absolutism.

Besides proposing a division of provincial patronage with his subordinates, in 1681 the royal commander-in-chief further subjected them to military discipline as his garrison commanders. The king ordered the governors-general to reside at their posts, not to leave them without prior written permission, and to use their tours of duty to strengthen their militias. These military regulations had a variety of social effects. They made the position of governor-general less attractive to the aristocracy, and they enhanced the executives' military, professional, middle-class, administrative character. They reinforced the militia's influence as the skeletal structures of provincial society and increased the militia's protective capacity.

Even before it disciplined the provincial executives, the crown had cast about during the summer of 1681 in search of ways to limit the concessions it had made to the provincial legislatures. The basic settlement of 1681 divided provincial government between the governors-general, their councils, and the assemblies. The last were to be bodies of representatives elected by the colony's enfranchised elements, plus each colony's viceroy and his councillors. The new commissions and instructions emphasized this tri-partite, parliamentary nature of the assemblies in order to reduce their formerly consolidated and overweening power. The legislative authority of the governor-general, and that of the councillors, was detailed: the executive veto power over bills and over the appointment of clerks was insisted on; particular exercises of legislative initiative by the governors-general were ordered in pending military and fiscal matters; the comprehensive legislative power of councils as upper legislative houses was stressed, whereas the representative lower houses' appellate judicial function was denied; all bills were to be thrice read before passage, thus alerting all the agencies of government to legislation pending in the lower house; and, finally, the governor-general's signature was required to make a bill law.

What the separation of powers and the introduction of parliamentary forms did not do to reduce assembly authority was accomplished in 1681 by the assignment to the king of both appellate and veto powers. Henceforward, both law and legislation would be ultimately legitimated only by royal decisions. The 1681 commissions announced that these decisions were to be the basis of a constitutional barter system. The crown traded confirmation of local statutes for grants of money and for extensions of its authority. Provincial pocketbooks and institutions suffered. Chief among these victimized institutions was the assembly, whose stature was to be shrunk still further, under the 1681 orders, by reducing the frequency of its elections, the length of its sessions, and the size of its electorate.

In sum, the commissions written for the governors-general of Jamaica and Virginia during 1681 became the fundamental law of the empire. They expressed a balanced system of Anglo-American government. That system greatly reduced assembly autonomy from its pre-1675 height, but it did not (as the events of the years 1683 to 1689 made clear) authorize an absolute executive. The military, administrative, and political prerogatives of the imperial crown were asserted, but the fiscal and legislative privileges of the provincial assemblies were admitted. If by 1722, when the old empire reached its acme, the imperial crown had more power and the provincial assemblies had less power than their equivalents in England, it was because the 1681 settlement had been reaffirmed in 1688 as the constitution of the empire, whereas in England the elites and their representatives in the parliament had modified the balance of executive and legislature in their favor both in 1689 and in 1701. But these modifications neither crown nor parliament would readily or soon extend to provincial elites and assemblies.

The Governors–General

The imperial code of 1681 framed the work of three generations of the governors-general. Between the restoration of Charles II in 1660 and the death of George I in 1727, the crown commissioned 206 commanders-in-chief of royal provinces overseas. Almost nine in every ten (87.5 percent) of these appointees were English army officers prior to their promotion to the command of colonies. The gubernatorial commissions carried the rank of colonel in the royal army and local rank as general. The prior military service of these governors-general was not nominal, nor was it merely an attribute of social status. These officers had served an average of ten years at the rank of captain or higher before being promoted to provincial commands. Almost two-thirds (65 percent) of the veterans who became governors-general had already seen extensive garrison service in the British Isles, and often in England's possessions as well.[14] In the royal garrisons they had acquired the administrative skills and practiced the paramilitary, prerogative politics that stabilized England itself, long as turbulent a society as any in Europe. Thus these veterans of garrison government were trained to pacify, order, and regulate England's troubled colonies in America.

Through these officers, from these colonies, the English executive shaped an empire between 1654 and 1681. Its principles were territorial conquest and plantation, political coercion and centralization, social regulation and stabilization. More and more territory was seized for the empire from its European rivals or was reclaimed by the imperial state either from private proprietors or from those local oligarchies that claimed royal sanction for their rule but refused to obey the crown's commands. The conquest of Jamaica in 1655 and of New York in 1664, the subsequent reversion of Barbados and the Leeward Islands from proprietary to royal rule, and the royalization of Virginia's government are cases in point during the Restoration. In the persons of the governors-general, with cumulative and lasting effect on provincial polities,

14. See the Appendix.

both in the British Isles and in America and the West Indies, the English executive sought to impose a classic, avowedly Roman, imperial system on its dependencies.

Proconsular government of provinces in the interest of the "imperial princes" of England made use of the existing regional, cultural, and familial ties that bound Englishmen overseas to those at home no less than it drew upon paramilitary techniques. The military cousinage of the Moncks and the Modyfords, and the government service connection of the Nicholas and D'Oyley families, made members of both powerful in Jamaica, as we have seen. In Virginia the influence of the military, banking, and factoring house of Jeffreys had an imperial political effect equaled only by the contributions to empire of the Anglican Morrisons or the Gloucestershire Norwoods and Berkeleys. The political interplay of family, force, fortune, religion, and profession produced a transatlantic imperial interest that looked to the crown for patronage, protection, inspiration, and direction. In return the crown required of its provincial clients (most of whom were both military and economic leaders in their communities) obedience to royal orders. The most functional element in this imperial interest was the union of the military and material friends of the empire. It produced a primitive "military-industrial complex." Arms and munitions for provincial forts and militias became the most common object of solicitation at court by colonial agents in the seventeenth century. The crown's provision of military supplies and its payments to the army officers who commanded colonies and to the soldiers who garrisoned them were the largest fiscal costs of empire.

The crown's colonial commissions analyzed in this work reiterate the military bias of empire. They directed the governors-general to give the largest share of their attention to militia discipline, drill, and command. The social policy enjoined by these commissions opposed land engrossment and poll taxes. Instead, the governors-general were ordered to favor food crops and excise taxes. The dispersion of population caused by unproductive, speculative landholding and by commercial agriculture and the penalty placed on the poor and on families by poll taxes were opposed by the governors-general so as to encourage farm families to settle closely in self-sustaining settlements. Such settlements could support a numerous militia, capable of self-defense and subject to garrison-government discipline.

The provincial militia was consciously designed by the governors-general to discipline both the colonial grandees who served as its officers and the free farmers who were its privates, as well as to repress servants and slaves. The militias were agencies of social order in the significantly named "plantations." Plantation societies, as we have noted, were conceived of as the farming frontiers of empire: their settlers were soldiers; their gentlemen were officers. The militias, commanded by the provincial captain-general, that is, the governor-general, served both to defend the boundaries of empire and to define provincial society. Like the militias, military centers—whether frontier forts, munitions magazines, or urban citadels—provided opportunities for economic and military patronage from the governor-general to his supporters. And in addition to storing public arms, the ultimate instruments of imperial authority, military buildings symbolized state power.

There were other institutions that expressed the imperialists' agrarian, authoritarian, paramilitary social policy. The regimental plantations of Cromwellian soldiers defined the settlement patterns of Jamaica and so shaped the island's social structure. We have also observed that a regiment of Charles II's Guards, elements of which stayed in Virginia for five years, helped a succession of governors-general displace Berkelean oligarchs and repress Baconian rebels. The Guards cleared a social middle ground in Virginia for aspirant, but obedient, planter-militiamen. Regular troops in three New York garrisons, and garrisons in Nova Scotia and Newfoundland, from 1696 until the eve of the Revolution, organized soldier-colonies on the Roman model. Such units manifested the army's social, political, and profoundly imperial influence in colonial America.[15]

"Force gives the rule to law." The laws of religion, of trade,

15. Besides the text's material on the military in Jamaica and Virginia, see Stanley McCrory Pargellis, "The Four Independent Companies of New York," *Essays in Colonial American History Presented to Charles McLean Andrews by his Students* (New Haven, Conn., 1931), 96–123. The survey of garrisons by John Shy, *Toward Lexington: The Role of the British Army in the Coming of the American Revolution* (Princeton, N.J., 1965), 3–44, is unequaled. Note, however, Shy's emphasis indicated in the title of his second chapter, "The Decision of 1763." The other broad treatment of the 18th-century garrisons is the opening chapter of Stanley McCrory Pargellis, *Lord Loudoun in North America* (New Haven, Conn., 1933), in which Andrews's prize student (1929) and junior colleague asserts that "the real problem of colonial defense, before Pitt's time, had nothing to do with empire" (p. 3), and that the words, "Enlarged the Dominion, And upheld the Majesty of these Kingdoms," on a monument commemorating Ticonderoga (1759), "strike a new note in British history; through them breathes for the first time the spirit of Empire" (p. 1). On the 18th-century garrisons, see also D. W. Prowse, *A History of Newfoundland from the English, Colonial, and Foreign Records*, 2d rev. ed. (London, 1896). On the role of the military in Nova Scotia, see R. H. Raymond Smythies, *Historical Records of the 40th (2nd Somersetshire) Regiment* (Devonport, 1894). On the military plantations of New York, see Guzzardo, "Sir William Johnson's Official Family."

of politics, unquestionably important as they were to the shape of the empire, received the color of authority from the palette of physical force. Symbolically as well as actually, executive authority everywhere in the empire was backed by the army. Whether in Carlisle, England, or in Port Royal, Jamaica, the earl of Carlisle took coach to church surrounded by his life guard of cavalry. He sat in a canopied chair of state, the altar at his left hand and the red-coated files of his garrison at his right. He heard the garrison chaplain preach a sermon on the holy duty of obedience to governors. Carlisle's garrison governments thus manifested the authoritarian marriage of the military and the ministry in the service of the state. In Portsmouth or New York, Colonel Richard Nicolls found little fighting for his soldiers, but they enforced the embargoes by which he kept wheat in the port in famine times. They manned patrol boats and (rather roughly) collected customs duties from merchants. The colonel's men not only carried out orders that affected the provincial economy but also competed directly with the local laborers for work. Thus Nicolls's garrisons demonstrated that even the economic impact of English government was a function of its armed force. The corporation of York and the council of Virginia both suffered when Colonel Herbert Jeffreys turned from a civil war career of fighting English and French rebels against royal authority to a peacetime occupation of punishing English and American opponents of crown control. The elements of the king's Guards that composed Jeffreys's garrisons chopped up defiant Yorkshiremen and hanged Baconians. Hearing of the obduracy of some Virginia councillors, rather more provincial-minded than the rest, the Guards asked leave of their colonel to hang them too. The ultimate identity of military force and monarchical—imperial—politics was apparent to all.

There are questions about the efficacy of English soldiers as the physical basis of garrison government in America. The garrisons were diseased, dispersed, and undisciplined, and their numbers were small. In the seventeenth century there were seldom more than one thousand regular soldiers on the North American continent. Often there were no more than three hundred. Both numbers were doubled in the English West Indies. These deficiencies, however, were at least partly offset by the physical debility and the small numbers of the colonists themselves. In proportion to populations, the garrisons often were larger than the armies commanded by the present-day authoritarian regimes.[16] Moreover,

16. The numbers of all branches of the armed services, per thousand of population, in 1974, were: in the United States, 10.2; in the Soviet Union, 15.6; in Spain, 10.5; in North

the garrisons' domestic effect was multiplied many times, both in British and American provinces of the empire, by the militarily weak but politically puissant select militias. The garrisons' greatest reinforcement was psychological. A widespread desire for local peace and social order placed many of the people of almost every province on the side of the armed agents of imperial authority. In addition, when provincials felt exposed to the attacks of hostile natives or alien empires, as was often the case in much of the Atlantic world, the exchange of popular acquiescence in royal rule in return for the protection of garrison government or for the leadership offered by the governors-general was especially easy and natural.

Taxation and Representation: An Imperial View

When the Restoration's military governors and commissioners reported to the imperial crown their efforts to protect and stabilize their provinces, they routinely recommended to the king that he resume the political power previously delegated by charter or custom to local leaders and apply it instead through royally commissioned officers, themselves. The resulting redefinition of provincial authority was expressed in orders, ordinances, and laws that applied local taxation to imperial uses, primarily military. One royal order allocated the customs receipts of Hull to the support of its military governor, his regular garrison, and an urban citadel. Another royal order to the assembly of Virginia elicited a law that assigned local export duties to the royal governor-general. The localities thus paid tribute to the armed authority of the central government. Such taxation was always as much an important symbol of submission to imperial sovereignty as it was a material necessity for imperial administration. It was the last concession provincial parliaments made to royal authority in the era of the empire's formation, and it was the first object of assembly attacks in the period of imperial dissolution a century later.

Korea, 29.4; and in Libya, 11.6 (Bureau of the Census, *The United States Fact Book*, 97th ed. [Washington, D.C., 1977], 894). The numbers of garrison troops only (select militia and royal naval personnel not included) per thousand of population, during the reign of Charles II, approximated: in Jamaica in 1661, 640.0; in Barbados in 1667, 20.2; in Jamaica in 1673, 11.8; in Virginia in 1677, 86.6; in New York in 1681, 20.0; and in Virginia in 1681, 9.0. Three things are impressive about the provincial figures: their range, their magnitude, and their unreliability. But at least the potential for physical coercion in the empire is apparent. The assistance of Mr. and Mrs. Theodore Lustig in compiling these figures is appreciated.

The usefulness of provincial legislatures, properly limited, was recognized by the militarized constitutions associated with the rising national state. The taxes that legislatures raised strengthened national executive agencies: household, navy, and army. The consent to taxation given by the representatives of social estates was fundamental to national or provincial morale, for in order to secure the consent of the political nation to taxation, the executive accepted its petitions and listened to the advice of its representatives. So much was recognized by most monarchs and by almost every governor-general. Overseas, however, the crown denied functional consultation and actual administration to the assemblies and instead conferred them on the governors-general's councils of state and war.

The authority of these provincial councils provides a measure of the influence of "court" or "country" in each royal colony. Acting on their garrison government principles, the governors-general regarded their councils as advisory and executive groups of subordinate officers. In this court view, each of the councillors, if only as an officer of the royal militia, was bound by martial law, first to advise the provincial captain general and governor-in-chief and then "to express his obedience to his General, although it be a service that corresponded not with his own opinion at the first."[17] "Country" politicians took an opposed view of the council model and the councillors' role. As we have seen, in 1674 Shaftesbury and Locke sought to limit the power of provincial executives to suspend councillors or to declare martial law without council consent. They further proposed that councillors be chosen by Shaftesbury and his merchant allies from colonial candidates who combined country principles with wealth. The councillors were to possess freedom to debate and to oppose the executives' proposals. The viceroys' colonial councils were to be restructured on the model of the king's privy council, as it was idealized in country opinion. That is, each colonial council was to represent the various elements of oligarchy in the provincial society. So composed, it would check the authority of the royal executive.

By the 1680s the court-country struggle had divided each royal council into two parties. The majority consisted of men powerful in their communities, possessed of administrative talent, loyal to the prerogative, who held crown office in the colony. The minority was made up of oligarchs whose personal force, economic

17. The quotation is from Elton, *Art Military*, 185.

strength, and country opinions underlay legislative and localist opposition to the executive and to the empire.

The Moderates and the Empire

The opposition councillors had found correspondents in England sympathetic to their criticisms of executive excesses. Since 1675, the party of monarchical and military authority had succeeded in the provinces because the colonists feared foreign attack and because they deeply desired domestic order. When the crown crippled the Jamaica and Virginia assemblies, however, it alerted the enemies of executive power to the menace that garrison government posed to legislative and statutory rule everywhere in the empire. The concern of American elites that "we are to be Govern'd as an army" rather than by legislature and law, was validated in English opinion by regarrisoned Cromwellian citadels and "reformed" corporate charters. As their royal master's power increased physically and politically, his representatives, the local governors, grew more aggressive in England as well as overseas.

As the imperial executive verged on absolutism, political moderates, such as the earl of Halifax, strengthened their position midway between monarchical militarism and legislative republicanism. On the one hand, Halifax rejected the attempt to exclude James, duke of York, from the royal succession because he accepted the argument that James's supporters in Ireland, Scotland, "and the Plantations" would react to exclusion with civil war. Therefore, Halifax joined the garrison government elements that upheld the crown—"Well, if it come to a war," he said to the governor of York, "you and I must go together"—and in parliament he denounced the "popular" program of Shaftesbury and the commons majority.[18] On the other hand, concerned as Halifax was to preserve an effective executive, endangered in England, he was also determined to sustain representative assemblies, attacked in the colonies. Halifax came to dominate the debate in the privy council over the balance to be struck between imperial leadership and provincial representation. The issues in that debate had been raised by the exercise of garrison government during the past gen-

18. The remark to the governor, Sir John Reresby, is noted, Dec. 29, 1680, in James J. Cartwright, ed., *The Memoirs of Sir John Reresby . . . 1634–1689* (London, 1875), 197.

eration and were now considered in the context of the Exclusion Crisis. These issues were summarized in September 1680 when Samuel Long, legislative leader of the Jamaica branch of the Anglo-American country party, appeared before the king-in-council. The governor-general of Jamaica, the earl of Carlisle, had charged Long with treasonable acts. As we have seen, the worst of Long's alleged crimes was his organization of Jamaican resistance to Carlisle's exercise of royal military and fiscal prerogative. Long was also blamed for appealing to country elements in the English parliament against imperial orders designed to eliminate the provincial assembly's authority. The crown denied both that parliament had any jurisdiction over colonial government and that the colonists had any claim to parliamentary privilege. The issues in debate between the king and the colonists, and those being argued by the crown and the parliament were so alike that Long's appeal to parliament seemed to be an additional incitement for exclusion.

The privy council's decision in the Long case shaped the constitution of the English empire for more than a century to come. As we have noted, in two dramatic privy council sessions, the earl of Halifax helped persuade Charles II to re-empower provincial legislatures, at least in part, and to excuse the leaders of their opposition parties, Long chief among them, from prosecution as enemies of the crown. The royal return of legislative initiative and amendment to the assemblies of Jamaica and Virginia was soon followed by the duke of York's grant of a representative body to New York. The sufferance of political opposition and the confirmation of assembly authority (once the assemblies agreed to raise revenues for royal use) were victories for political moderation. These acts defined the governmental structure of the empire and the conduct of Anglo-American politics to and beyond the American Revolution.

Resolution of the imperial crisis of 1681 was thus based on a compromise between the extreme opinions of court and country. Lord Culpeper had worked out just such a compromise while in command of Virginia. Despite royal orders to the contrary, he had preserved the colonial legislature's powers of initiative and amendment. In return for upholding the assembly's privileges, however, Culpeper had exacted a high price in prerogative power. The Virginia assembly accepted a bill, written in the privy council, that provided for a permanent provincial tax to support imperial authority. Equally important to the reduction of local autonomy and to the increase of imperial influence was the acquiescence of the Virginia burgesses in the division of legislative authority among the governor-general, the council, and themselves. Unwillingly, the lower house accepted the governor-general's instruction that they adopt such parliamentary procedures as the multiple reading of bills and the keeping of session records, for these procedures opened the operations of the lower house to prerogative observation and influence. Reluctantly, the burgesses accepted regular royal review of provincial laws. Finally, and most important, the assembly acknowledged in law the absolute military authority of the king's governor-general.

Utilizing both the Virginia model and the Jamaica compromise, Charles II quickly extended the constitutional settlement of 1681 to all the royal colonies. Limited local legislative authority, provincial taxes for imperial use, and an unfettered military prerogative characterized the 1681 settlement. This imposition on American provinces of the civil war formula of governor, council, and martial law testified to the great growth of executive authority in the empire in the generation after 1653. On the other hand, provincial assemblies and courts survived, and they preserved elements of corporate privilege, provincial autonomy, and individual liberty. The imperial balance struck in 1681 between metropolis and provinces, coercion and consultation, military-imperial executive and civilian-localist legislature endured for a century as the constitution of the first English empire. Thus Anglo-American relations were not primarily shaped by a commercial system, in which the strongest political element was "colonial self-government." Rather, they were predominantly directed by a military system, in which the strongest political element was Anglo-American imperial government.

Four Phases of Empire, 1681–1763

Garrison government formed an empire. Such was the political result of the 112 years of English paramilitary provincial administration discussed in this first volume of *The Governors-General*. Yet the forces of empire and their leader, James Stuart, prevailed in 1681 only because of the support of such moderates as Halifax, many of them powerfully placed in the royal army and in James's own household. There, as members of his "shadow cabinet," they greatly influenced imperial administration. These moderates had not dared let James, the personification of monarchical order and social stability, fall before the leveling, republican, and localist forces led by Shaftesbury. So, too, in the garrisoned provinces of Britain and America, the party of authority had succeeded with the aid of imperially ambitious, but not authoritarian, councillor-administrators.[1] The second volume of *The Governors-General* will describe how, during the seven years after 1681, those essential props of empire, the metropolitan and provincial moderates, slowly and reluctantly were driven to join James Stuart's opponents. For he pushed autocratic government (and religious change) to self-destructive extremes: he prosecuted the whig leaders in 1683; massacred the Monmouth rebels in 1685; subverted both the most and the least imperial of the colonial constitutions, those of Jamaica and New England, in 1686; and, in 1687, attacked the sanctuary of social order, the Church of England. The antagonisms James thus accumulated gave social and ideological focus to the army officer corps' dislike of stricter discipline and to their revulsion at the admission of Irish and Catholics to military service. There followed a military coup—the "Glorious Revolution"—against James in 1688 and against his governors-general in America in 1689.[2]

---

1. Webb, "'Brave Men and Servants to His Royal Highness': The Household of James Stuart in the Evolution of English Imperialism," *Perspectives in American History*, VIII (1974), 55–80.

2. Even as the imperial compromise was effected in 1681, moderates in James's own household recognized that, because of his religion, "sooner or later we must all be undone." Col. John Churchill to Col. George Legge, Sept. 12, 1681, in Keith Feiling, *A History of the*

The officers of the English army, compelled to justify their revolt against professional discipline and its concomitant, a cosmopolitan army, voiced three sorts of excuses. These rationalizations proved to be as useful for restoring imperial order as the English officers' coup itself had been in instigating "the Glorious Revolution in America." First, the officers argued, the command of the coup by William, prince of Orange, and his Stuart princess both lent it dynastic legitimacy and gave England executive leadership against the imperial aims of France. Second, those whigs who, under William and Mary, had formed a household government in exile gave the coup republican political principles and so brought to it the support of those aristocrats in England and oligarchs in America who had been alienated by King James's absolutism. Third, the Erastian bishops of the Church of England put the seal of national Protestantism on the coup. On both sides of the Atlantic, this religious coloration was essential to popular acceptance of the coup.

That both Anglicanism and republicanism were but superficial aspects of the military coup d'etat of 1688/1689 was soon apparent in the empire. So was the fundamental monarchism and militarism of its great beneficiary. The new commander-in-chief, even more tolerant in religion than his predecessor, gave small support to the church in the colonies. And there, by 1692, William III, as much a soldier-king and imperialist as James II had been, rebuffed whig-commercialist efforts to return to the status quo ante 1675. Instead, King William restored the 1681 imperial settlement, which balanced military, imperial, and executive dictates with civilian, localist, and legislative demands.[3]

The reestablished imperial constitution proved its worth in inspiring and organizing provincial defenses as far apart as Newfoundland and Jamaica during the first round of England's war

---

Tory Party, 1640–1714 (Oxford, 1924), 181. See also William Coxe, *Memoirs of the Duke of Marlborough, with His Original Correspondence . . .* , I (London, 1872), iii. Besides Feiling's fundamental analysis and the sources named above, particular use has been made here of J. R. Western, *Monarchy and Revolution: The English State in the 1680s* (London, 1972); John Miller, *Popery and Politics in England, 1660–1688* (Cambridge, 1973); J. R. Jones, *The First Whigs: The Politics of the Exclusion Crisis, 1678–1683* (London, 1961); and Jones, *The Revolution of 1688 in England* (New York, 1972). On the motivation of colonial court parties, see Alison Gilbert Olson, *Anglo-American Politics, 1660–1775: The Relationship between Parties in England and Colonial America* (New York, 1973).

3. The reversionary political impact of the coup in the colonies is discussed in Webb, "William Blathwayt," *WMQ*, 3d Ser., XXVI (1969), 373–374, 377–378; Webb, "The Strange Career of Francis Nicholson," *WMQ*, 3d Ser., XXIII (1966), 523–525; and Webb, "The Trials of Sir Edmund Andros," in James Kirby Martin, ed., *The Human Dimensions of Nation Making* (Madison, Wis., 1976), 42–45. See also Olson, *Anglo-American Politics*, 75–78, and J. H. Plumb, *The Origins of Political Stability: England, 1675–1725* (Boston, 1967).

with France for Atlantic empire. The truce in that conflict, from 1697 to 1702, offered whigs and commercialists a chance to reassert the Shaftesbury-Locke program of 1674. In England, they forced William III to establish a board of trade and to appoint John Locke to it. In America, they tried to re-enfranchise the colonial elites in council and assembly, to reinforce the rule of law in the provinces, and to reduce the imperial authority of the governors-general, especially by attacking their military power.[4] After 1702 this whig effort was abandoned, for renewed resistance to French imperialism once again mandated executive authority and military discipline throughout England's empire. William III, just before his death, had chosen a general to provide both.

To mature imperial institutions and to realize imperial ideas in eighteenth-century Anglo-America was the work of that general's subordinates. By their presence and their predilections, the duke of Marlborough's officers insured that the American colonies after 1705 shared more directly than ever before in the conservative political as well as in the victorious military outcomes of England's conflicts with her European rivals for empire. During the five years after the battle of Blenheim, from 1705 to 1710, officers who had served under Marlborough came out to govern Virginia, New York, Massachusetts, Newfoundland and Nova Scotia, Jamaica, and the Leeward Islands.[5] The decade that followed marked the acme of the first British empire. Two thousand regular troops in North America and large garrisons in the West Indies carried out the orders of professional officers deeply imbued with the precepts of garrison government by England's premier general and chief minister. Marlborough's governors-general gave a momentum to imperial administration and a shape to provincial politics and so-

4. On the whig interlude, see Maurice Cranston, *John Locke* . . . (London, 1957); Peter Laslett, "John Locke, the Great Recoinage, and the Origins of the Board of Trade: 1695–1698," *WMQ*, 3d Ser., XIV (1957), 370–402; Gertrude Ann Jacobsen, *William Blathwayt: A Late Seventeenth-Century English Administrator* (New Haven, Conn., 1932); and I. K. Steele, *Politics of Colonial Policy: The Board of Trade in Colonial Administration, 1696–1720* (Oxford, 1968), esp. appendix B. For an application of whig/mercantilism, see the attitudes of the board of trade (without Blathwayt but including Locke) toward Virginia, exemplified in the instructions to Colonel Nicholson as governor of Virginia, Sept. 13, 1698; the representation of the board to the lords justice, Aug. 23, 1698; the additional instructions to Nicholson, May 18, 1699; the circular letter to the governors, June 26, 1699; and the board to Nicholson, June 28, 1699, C.O. 5/1359, 226ff, 252–259, 314–315, 330–332, 333–334.

5. Himself the key to imperial administration from 1704 to 1710, and exercising an indirect but pervasive influence in England's provinces for decades through his former officers, the duke of Marlborough can be pictured in part from published sources, chiefly Sir George Murray, ed., *The Letters and Despatches of John Churchill . . . , 1702–1712* (London, 1845); Coxe, *Memoirs of Marlborough*; and Winston Churchill, *Marlborough: His Life and His Times*, 4 vols (New York, 1933–1938). Further references are assembled by R. E. Scouller, *The Armies of Queen Anne* (Oxford, 1966).

ciety that were not overtly challenged until the mid-1760s, when an overdecisive imperial victory permitted and inspired the Revolutionary generation to enter politics.

Yet in their own eyes, the imperialists suffered decisive defeat as early as 1722. In the previous year the board of trade (headed by a colonel whose qualifications for imperial office seem to have consisted of his translation of Caesar's *Commentaries* into English and its dedication to the duke of Marlborough) had urged on the king-in-council a program of American government prepared by Marlborough's governors-general. This plan proposed the coordination of American commands under a captain general. It would set limits to the colonies and defend them against France by fortifying and garrisoning the inland frontiers. Eight additional regiments would control the Atlantic coast and its population centers.[6] But this summary of imperial aspirations was filed away for a generation when the entire imperialist leadership—Marlborough, Sunderland, and Stanhope—died suddenly in 1721 and 1722.

In their place the whiggish and commercialist Walpole regime came to power. That regime claims a separate study, for it finally, corruptly, destructively, for a generation, put into practice the oligarchical and whig "commercial and colonial" policy. The partisans of aristocrats and merchants took advantage of an abnormally peaceful period in Anglo-American history to debase the administration of the empire into an uncoordinated assortment of patronage posts, reserved for the well-connected and the unqualified. Peace reduced the imperatives of authoritarian politics and allowed the politics of autonomy to vitiate imperial order. Provincial societies became far more concerned with civil profit than with military security. The government of the increasingly autonomous dependencies was gradually assumed by enriched provincial elites, by venal English placemen, and, after 1736, by aggrandizing assemblies. At last, Shaftesbury's alliance of the ambitious classes in the country, the city, and the colonies was fully realized. Commonwealthmen, commercialists, and colonists dominated Anglo-American relations as they had not since the 1640s.[7]

6. Alexander Spotswood to the board of trade, Jan. 16, 1721, Mr. Auditor Walpole's objections, order of the privy council, Aug. 17, 1723; Hugh Drysdale to the board, Nov. 17, 1725, and the earl of Orkney to the board, Dec. 30, 1725, C.O. 5/1319, 3, 35, 52, 91, 92; the case and petition of Colonel Spotswood, C.O. 5/1344, 1, 7, the board to Secretary Carteret, July 17, 1721, C.O. 5/1365, 229–236, the board to the king, "In regard to the Government of the Plantations," Sept. 8, 1721, Add. MSS 35907; *Journals of the Commissioners for Trade and Plantations from November 1718 to December 1722* (London, 1925), 279–280; Steele, *Politics of Colonial Policy*, 167–170; *DNB*, s.v. "Bladen, Martin."

7. J. H. Plumb, *Sir Robert Walpole: The Making of a Statesman* (London, 1956), 262, 263,

With the return of war to English America in the decade 1739 to 1748, the ancient debate between armed authority and moneyed autonomy was resumed, but on much evener terms than had prevailed before 1722. The penultimate phase of Anglo-American empire began when war made its inevitable demands for force-fulness and order on the most pacifistic and oligarchical of English administrations. On the frontiers of empire, in South Carolina, Georgia, Nova Scotia, and in Maroon-menaced Jamaica, the physical imperatives of empire produced a doubling of regular forces and the appointment of militant governors-general by 1748.

Despite the imperialist resurgence, it appeared that the administrative excellence, the political assurance, and the social relevance of the governors-general during the first century of English colonization would not be equaled again. Instead, it was apparent that the anti-imperial forces of acquisitive capitalism, individual liberty, provincial autonomy, and Anglo-American oligarchy had won lasting social and political influence for the local elites who were the eventual authors of the American Revolution.

The final confrontation of empire with autonomy began when four imperial regiments were destroyed or captured on the Ohio and Ontario frontiers in 1754. "The great war for the empire" poured thirty thousand regulars into England's American provinces by 1759.[8] Conquering vast territories, subjugating both natives and planters to English authority (a subjugation symbolized by American service in the English army and by colonial taxes for the army's support), the army achieved at last the imperial ambition coeval with colonization itself.

Undersecretary William Knox's memorandum of February 1763 has been called the fullest expression of the "new" imperialism. Knox anticipated that protection would be offered and obedience enforced by frontier and urban garrisons. Thus the army would "secure the Dependence of the Colonys on Great Britain."[9] This was imperialism, but it was not new. The Knox memorandum of 1763 proclaimed not the arrival but rather the return to Anglo-American political preeminence of coerciveness and power-hunger, of paternalism and militarism. Since 1569,

270, 363–389; Olson, *Anglo-American Politics*, 106–141; Alfred James Henderson, *London and the National Government, 1721–1742* (Durham, Eng., 1945), 92, 109–111, 127–130; James A. Henretta, *"Salutary Neglect": Colonial Administration under the Duke of Newcastle* (Princeton, N.J., 1972), esp. 260–263.

8. Lawrence Henry Gipson, *The British Empire before the American Revolution* (New York, 1936–1969); Shy, *Toward Lexington*; Pargellis, *Lord Loudoun*.

9. Knox, as quoted in Shy, *Toward Lexington*, 64–65.

as this volume has shown, these forces had woven an imperial pattern throughout the fabric we habitually call "the colonial period of American history," but which was really the period of Anglo-American empire. That empire's deepest foundations and strongest buttresses were the garrison-governments of the governors-general.

The Governors-General

Between the restoration of the monarchy in May 1660 and the death of King George I in June 1727 more than two hundred royal commissions were issued to colonial commanders-in-chief and to their lieutenants. Many of these appear in Charles McLean Andrews, "List of Commissions, Instructions, and Additional Instructions Issued to the Royal Governors and Others in America," American Historical Association, *Annual Report for the Year 1911*, I (Washington, D.C., 1913), 393–528. Additional appointments are listed in David P. Henige, *Colonial Governors from the Fifteenth Century to the Present: A Comprehensive List* (Madison, Wis., 1970). While the present appendix contains both names and appointments appearing in neither Andrews nor Henige, presumably it too omits, and certainly it inadequately identifies, some officers commanding colonies. Additions and corrections are invited.

Given the military nature of the imperial executive, the primary source of identification of the governors-general has been *English Army Lists and Commission Registers, 1660–1714*, 6 vols. (1891–1904; repr. London, 1960), tirelessly and meticulously edited by Charles Dalton. Local, regional, and regimental histories, mostly published since he wrote, newspapers, and genealogical sources do offer supplements to Dalton's identifications. Representative citations of these supplementary works appear in the biographical entries. The military entry books of the secretaries of state in State Papers, Class 44, Public Record Office (S.P. 44), occasionally provide commissions not listed by Dalton. But without his scholarly work, sustained for more than thirty years, this study could not have been undertaken.

The information given in the entries follows a basic order. Only the names of those who received royal commissions to command colonies under crown jurisdiction are given as main entries. Each entry is numbered. A star indicates that the subject held regular army rank before the governorship. The class of commission, whether as governor-general (that is, "captain general and governor-in-chief"), governor, lieutenant governor, deputy governor, commander-in-chief, or in reversion, is noted. The year of the commission is followed by that of the end of the commander's service in the colony. Dates in parentheses refer to service prior to King Charles's restoration in May 1660 (usually under the Commonwealth or the Protectorate), under proprietors, or after King George's death in June 1727.

Other governorships held by the subject are listed next, together with the entry numbers of additional colonial appointments. Especially notable garrison commands, apart from governorships, are also indicated. The rise of officers through the commissioned ranks to governorships, and the length of time they had served in the army, are roughly indicated by giving the date and rank of each subject's first known commission. This is followed by a career outline in terms of notable service, successive commissions, and regimental affiliations, in order to suggest the imperial military career pattern of which provincial command was a part. Governors-general serving in the regiment at the same time as the subject are also listed, except in the case of the Guards units, for they always contained viceroys.

The Guards and a few other regiments produced a disproportionate number of officers who came to command as governors-general. At any time, the captains of the royal Guards of horse (cavalry) and foot (infantry) would include both prospective executives and veteran governors-general, for the obvious reasons: the Guards' political connections, court service, and overseas deployment in imperial emergencies (see nos. 5, 6, 8–10, 17, 21, 26, 33, 54, 55, 58, 61, 66, 69, 73, 74, 78, 83, 89, 99, 100, 115, 119, 125, 127, 130, 133, 134, 137, 138, 140, 147, 157, 184, 185, 189–197, 201). The battalion based on Guards cadres that came out to Virginia in the winter of 1676–1677 was one of several such expeditionary forces (see also, 115, 184). (See Jeffreys [189] in particular, and Sir F. W. Hamilton, *The Origin and History of the First or Grenadier Guards . . .* , I [London, 1874], in general.) Other regiments besides Guards battalions saw colonial service, as the names of the Tangier (172–183, 185) and the Barbados (175) regiments suggest. Less obviously imperial units which nonetheless produced numbers of governors-general were the Holland regiment, Holt's (204) Marines, Phillips's (167) and Tufton's (77) regiments of foot, and Bath's (the 10th) regiment (12).

The colonial experience of the officers of these regiments made them obvious candidates for promotion to governorships, as did the practice of naming the officers of a regiment or garrison as successors to their colonel when he served as governor-general (see 59, 60, 75, 76, 77, 79, 82, 88–90, 93, 94, 97, 111, 140, 154, 156, 166–170, 174–179, 181–183, 185, 189–197). Moreover, the exchanged experiences and shared attitudes of regimental messmates were notable sources of imperial ideas, given by Norwood (35, 176, 178) to Jeffreys (189) over the Guards' table at Dunkirk or exchanged by Hunter (68, 158, 205) and Spotswood (206) on Marlborough's staff in the Netherlands. And not only concepts but connections were regimental currency. Influential commanders always sought promotions for their subordinates, and many governorships were awarded for particular military services rendered (see 6, 37, 80, 190, 203, 204, 206, and the above list of imperial regiments). Conversely, gubernatorial service led to regimental promotions (see 138, 140, 175).

Great battles and sieges were concatenations of such services and recognitions. At Namur, for example, the generation of officers whose senior members were commissioned by James II, and all of which was professionalized by William III, came of age. More than a dozen future governors-general were distinguished at Namur, most being wounded and/or promoted (see 17, 39, 40, 57, 58, 59, 67, 74, 76, 132, 138, 158, 203, 205). So, too, the crises of Marlborough's campaigns tested officer candidates for imperial administration. The Blenheim bounty roll lists at least seven of the governors-general (see 206), including the captain general of Virginia (1705–1737) and several of his lieutenants, two of whom ruled the Old Dominion for thirty-two years after 1712. Of equal imperial importance, albeit negative and uncountable, were the deaths of potential provincial commanders at these more-than-military milestones. Given an imperial situation where almost nine in ten of the governors-general were career army officers, every English military event determined the human dimensions of Anglo-American leadership.

The major sociopolitical "interests" of the governors who had no prior army service are given where they are known. Provincial councillors (7, 53, 57, 64, 81), royal navy captains (19, 62, 64), and merchant politicians and/or sea captains (1, 13, 20, 22, 63, 65, 121) were the most common sorts of extra-army governors. The twenty imperial executives whose backgrounds are wholly or partially obscure are included in this nonmilitary cohort, although seven or more of them may have been veteran officers of the royal army, as were 87.5 percent of their colleagues, the governors-general.

A colonial governorship conferred upon an officer, if he had not yet achieved it, the brevet rank of royal army colonel when his command was that of a major royal colony, or of lieutenant colonel in the case of lesser posts. General's rank and jurisdiction, when conferred by a governor's commission, was limited to the assigned province unless otherwise stated. In some cases the constitutional or proprietorial history of a colony affected the appointment patterns of its executives in unusual ways. These particulars are noted under the heading for each colony.

Bahamas

The proprietors' administration of the Bahamas officially gave way to royal government in 1717.

1. WOODES ROGERS. Gov., 1717–1721. Nominated by the proprietors, of whom he was one, the appointment of this famous privateer and circumnavigator, Bristol merchant and son-in-law of Adm. William Whetstone was confirmed by the crown.

2. *GEORGE PHENNEY. Gov., 1721(–1729). Commissioned capt. in 1706, probably of Livesay's (the 12th) regt. of foot, by Handasyde (60) in his capacity as gov.-gen. of Jamaica. This regt. was part of the Jamaica garrison. Its records during its West Indies service are broken, and a number of commissions to officers commanding in the islands are apt to have been lost. But see Douglas (82), capt. with Phenney in the 12th foot, for a parallel case.

Barbados

The constitutional history of Barbados is dealt with in Vincent T. Harlow's very scholarly monograph, *A History of Barbados, 1625–1685* (1926; repr. New York, 1969). The family of Willoughby of Parham entered the government during the civil wars as representatives of both the proprietors and the crown. The government retained this mixed character until the commissioning of Atkins (5).

3. *FRANCIS, LORD WILLOUGHBY OF PARHAM. Lt. gen. (1647–1652); gov.-gen., 1663–1666. Led the English settlement of Surinam, 1650, 1652. Formerly civil war gov. of Gainsborough, Willoughby was commissioned col. of parliamentary foot and of horse in 1642, but he became a royalist vice adm. in 1647. This associate of James, duke of York, in North African operations, drowned while leading an expedition against St. Christopher. On the (imperial) importance of his 1663 commission, see Charles M. Andrews, *The Colonial Period of American History*, 4 vols. (New Haven, Conn., 1934–1937), II, 267–269.

4. WILLIAM, LORD WILLOUGHBY OF PARHAM. Gov.-gen., 1667–1673. Succeeded his brother (3). Courtier. See also 72 for Willoughby's dep. gov.

5. *SIR JONATHAN ATKINS. Gov.-gen., 1673–1680. Atkins served in the Carlisle garrison, acted as gov. ("commissioner") of Guernsey, and commanded the garrison, if not the town, of Rochester prior to this service. Commissioned capt. and col. of the 1st foot Guards in 1664, he was promoted capt. of the king's own company in 1672. Jeffreys (189) succeeded him in this command. In addition to Harlow's *History of Barbados*, see Edward Peacock, ed., *The Army Lists of the Roundheads and Cavaliers, Containing the Names of the Officers in the Royal and Parliamentary Armies of 1642*, 2d ed. (London, 1874), 73, and E. S. de Beer, ed., *The Diary of John Evelyn* (London, 1959), entry of June 2, 1672.

6. *SIR RICHARD DUTTON. Gov.-gen., 1680–1685. Dutton had been gov. of Chester in 1659. A maj. at Sheerness in 1667, he became lt. and lt. col. of the duke of York's troop of the horse Guards in 1672. He commanded cavalry in France, 1672–1673. The imperial scope of the Yorkist officers (for which see Stephen Saunders Webb, "'Brave Men and Servants to His Royal Highness': The Household of James Stuart in the Evolution of English Imperialism," *Perspectives in American History*, VIII [1974], 55–80) is suggested by this report of May 29, 1680: "Here are some alterations in the military employments going on: Mr. [John, afterward duke of Marlborough] Churchill is to command the Duke's regiment of foot and the fort at Sheerness in the room of Sir Charles Littleton [43], who is to be Governor of Jersey; Sir John Lanier [gov. of Jersey] is to be lieutenant of the Duke's troop of Horse Guards in the room of Sir Richard Dutton [6], who is to go Governor of Barbadoes, and Sir Jonathan Atkins [5] is to be recalled home" (Historical Manuscripts

Commission, *Calendar of the Manuscripts of the Marquess of Ormonde, K.P., Preserved at Kilkenny Castle*, N.S., [London, 1902–1920], V, 329–330). Dutton's suggestions about his commission, made to the privy council committee for the plantations, epitomized the command principles of garrison government (W. Noel Sainsbury *et al.*, eds., *Calendar of State Papers, Colonial Series* [London, 1860–], *America and West Indies, 1677–1680*, no. 1505). His behavior in the command summarized Yorkist absolutism (Harlow, *History of Barbados*, 248n).

7. EDYN STEDE. Lt. gov., 1685–1689. Secretary and provost marshal of Barbados from 1673, and ex officio member of the provincial council, Stede was also the factor of the Royal African Company. See Sir Alan Burns, *History of the British West Indies*, 2d ed. rev. (London, 1965), 354–355, and Treasury Group, Class 64, Piece 88, 41, 57b, Public Record Office, London. This commission as lt. gov. may have been a renewal.

8. *JAMES KENDALL. Gov.-gen., 1689–1693. This native of Barbados entered the army in 1675. He became capt. in the Coldstream Guards before 1678, when he commanded Morpeth's regt. as lt. col. He retained his commission in the Guards and was instrumental in the coup of 1688. His reward was the Barbados command. Displaced by a whig (9), Kendall took a tory seat at the admiralty, entered parliament on Bishop Trelawney's nomination, and developed a connection with the earl of Rochester, who, as lord lt. of Ireland, named Kendall to the Irish treasury. He died in July 1708 "and left his estate, value 40,000 £, to his house-keeper" (Narcissus Luttrell, *A Brief Historical Relation of State Affairs from September 1678 to April 1714* [Oxford, 1857], VI, 327).

9. *FRANCIS RUSSELL. Gov.-gen., 1693–1697. Commissioned ens. in the 1st foot Guards in 1678, Russell joined the 2d Tangier regt. as a capt. in 1680 and served in Tangier, before becoming capt. in the 1st foot Guards in 1682. Russell was a capt. of the dragoons raised for the repression of Monmouth's rebellion in 1685 and commanded by Cornbury (155). Like his commander, in 1688 Russell defected to William of Orange, who breveted him col. of horse in 1690. He served through the Irish campaign. Commissioned gov.-gen. in Nov. 1693, Russell was made col. of a foot regt. for Barbados in Feb. 1694.

10. *WILLIAM FORBES, master of Forbes. Lt. gen., 1697. Forbes was commissioned capt. of horse in 1689. He was active against Jacobite forces in Scotland as lt. col. of horse and held this commission until 1697. He was promoted col. of the Scots company in the 1st foot Guards, lt. col. and lt. of the Scots troop of life Guards (col. and capt. the duke of Argyll [133]) and the first col. of the Scots grenadier horse Guards in 1702.

11. RALPH GREY. Gov.-gen., 1697–1702. Brother of Forde Grey, earl of Tankerville, commissioner of trade and plantations.

12. *SIR BEVILL GRENVILLE. Gov.-gen., 1702–1706. Grenville was also gov. of Pendennis Castle, 1696–1703. Commissioned capt. of Bath's regt.

of foot in 1685, he served with Archibald Hamilton (62), Alexander Spotswood (206), and Roger Elliot (37). Grenville became this regt.'s maj. in 1687 and its col. in 1694. He and the regt. served in Flanders. After the peace of Ryswick the regt. was posted to an Irish garrison in 1698, but Grenville resigned the command as soon as his Barbados commission passed the seals. He died on his passage home.

13. MITFORD CROWE. Gov.-gen., 1706–1710. This London merchant and Southampton M.P. was paymaster of the British army in Spain (for which service this commission may have been a quid pro quo). He fancied himself a soldier, having his portrait painted in armor by Thomas Murray, and some sources say Crowe ranked as col. before becoming Queen Anne's agent in Catalonia. Having negotiated the Catalonian declaration of allegiance to Charles III in 1704, Crowe boasted of "the glory of [Queen Anne's] arms when I saw His Royal Person guarded on the throne by two English Grenadiers" (to Sec. Hedges, Nov. 20, 1705, in Lt. Col. John Davis, *The History of the Second Queen's Royal Regiment, Now the Queen's (Royal West Surrey) Regiment*, 4 vols. [London, 1887–1902], II, 337).

14. ★ROBERT LOWTHER. Gov.-gen., 1710–1721. A son of Kendall's (8) predecessor in the admiralty, Lowther was commissioned lt. to Elliot (37) in 1704 and became clerk of the ordnance in the Tower of London in 1708. This nephew of Viscount Lonsdale served as M.P. for Westmoreland in 1705. That his daughter was Wolfe's fiancée suggests both the overlap of generations and the personal associations of the militarized ruling class.

15. ★RICHARD INGRAHM, Viscount Irvine. Gov.-gen., 1721. Did not come out. Commissioned capt. lt. in 1707, col. of foot (commanding Capt. Gooch [208]), and gov. of Hull in 1715, the viscount became col. of horse in 1717. He died of smallpox "on the eve of sailing to Barbados" (Charles Dalton, ed., *George the First's Army, 1714–1727* [London, 1910], I, 156).

16. JOHN, LORD BELHAVEN. Gov.-gen., 1721. Son of the well-known soldier and suspected Jacobite, Belhaven drowned in the wreck of the *Royal Anne* en route to Barbados in Nov. 1721.

17. ★HENRY WORSLEY. Gov.-gen., 1721(–1731). Commissioned ens. in Feb. 1689, Worsley served in Scotland and fought in Flanders at Landen and Namur. He was promoted capt. in 1693, and capt. and lt. col. of the 1st foot Guards in 1700. Fighting in Spain, Worsley succeeded Stanhope (130) as envoy to Charles III in 1708 (see also 13). He was named envoy to Hanover in 1711 and to Portugal in 1714. Besides the diplomatic service so characteristic of his generation of officers, Worsley was M.P. for Newport, Isle of Wight, from 1705 to 1715, succeeding Dudley (124). See Robert Walcott, Jr., *English Politics in the Early Eighteenth Century*, Harvard Historical Monographs, XXVIII (Cambridge, Mass., 1956), 186.

Bermuda

Judgment was entered against the Somers Island (Bermuda) Company in November 1684 (S.P. 44/56), but the serving proprietary governor was continued in what remained a chaotic colony. See Henry C. Wilkinson, *Bermuda in the Old Empire: A History of the Island from the Dissolution of the Somers Island Company until the End of the American Revolutionary War, 1684–1784* (London, 1950).

18. RICHARD CONEY (or CONY). Lt. gov., (1683–)1686. Perhaps this individual was the lt. of this name in Carlisle's (51) regt., 1673. On his gov., esp. his arrest of opponents for mutiny, see the wonderful note in Andrews, *Colonial Period*, I, 246, and see *Cal. S.P. Col., 1681–1685*, nos. 1834, 1899, 2022.

19. SIR ROBERT ROBINSON. Lt. gov., 1686–1689. Robinson had been commodore of Newfoundland in 1680, one of a series of naval governors, beginning with Sir John Berry and including Edward Russell (for whose brother, see 9) and Sir Francis Wheeler ([197] of Virginia, Newfoundland, and West India renown). See "Newfoundland," below.

20. ISAAC RICHIER. Lt. gov., 1689–1693. A London merchant, Richier and Day (22) were the "two broken linen drapers" whose lack of gubernatorial qualifications was much reflected on.

21. *JOHN GODDARD. Lt. gov., 1693–1697. Goddard became brigadier of the 1st troop of the horse Guards before Dec. 1688. Then, as William III afterward put it, he "left his command and came to US upon Our landing in this Kingdom" (War Office Group, Piccc 79, 65; Dalton, ed., *English Army Lists*, III, 174). Goddard was promoted exempt and capt. in 1691. After his term as lt. gov., Goddard was commissioned agent for military transport in Portugal.

22. SAMUEL DAY. Lt. gov., 1697–1700. Samuel was the son of Sir Thomas Day, alderman and M.P. for Bristol. Gov. Day was a merchant (see 20), and he so little provided for his garrison that they were "forced to hoist a palmetto leaf instead of Colours at the Castle" (Burns, *British West Indies*, 401). Day was recalled in disgrace (Luttrell, *Brief Relation*, IV, 285, 648).

23. *BENJAMIN BENNETT. Lt. gov., 1700–1713. Bennett was commissioned capt. of marines (vice Kirke [185]) in 1693 and capt. of an independent company in the Bermudas in 1704. Bennett noted his typical military career pattern and expressed an officer's frustration with political bickering when he wrote, "It would be heart-breaking to me to be recalled in disgrace, after serving the Crown both in the fleet and army these seventeen years, and was never reproached nor disputed till I was prefer'd to this government" (quoted in Wilkinson, *Bermuda in the Old Empire*, 56).

24. *HENRY PULLEYNE. Lt. gov., 1713–1715. Commissioned capt. of foot in 1706 (with Martin Bladen, afterward commissioner of trade and plantations), Pulleyne served in the garrison at Alicante under Richards (138). His regt. was disbanded in 1713.

25. *BENJAMIN BENNETT. Lt. gov., 1715–1721. See also 23. Bennett's petition to the privy council on the needs of his troops noted "that it is about fifteen years since the said Company received any bedding which is long since worn out; having no quarters allow'd them by the Country, but barracks," that the soldiers were ill, and that winter was coming on. By the time the ordnance officers responded, a year or so later, the soldiers were dead. See "The Humble Relation of Benjamin Bennett, Esq., His Majesty's Lieutenant of the Bermuda Islands and Captain of the Independent Company there," W.O. 53/347.

26. *JOHN HOPE. Lt. gov., 1721–1727. Commissioned capt. and lt. col. of the 3d foot Guards in 1708, Hope became lt. col. of the Cameronians (see 161) in 1716. After his governorship he became a col. and inherited a baronetcy. Sir John represented Kinrossshire in parliament from 1727 to 1734 and from 1741 to 1747. Commissioned col. in 1743, Hope was gazetted maj. gen. in 1754 and lt. gen. in 1758. He also served in the Swedish army. Hope died in 1766 (*Dictionary of National Biography*, s.v. "Bruce, Sir John Hope"). He was succeeded in Bermuda by Capt. John Pitt (63, 86).

Bombay

Part of the imperially important dowry of Catherine of Braganza, Bombay was ruled directly by the crown from 1662 to 1667. The royal governors listed here were sorted out from Henige's extensive and undifferentiated list by reference to the work of Sir William Foster, ed., *The English Factories in India, 1618–1669: A Calendar of Documents in the India Office, British Museum and Public Record Office*, 13 vols. (Oxford, 1906–1927).

27. *JAMES LEY, earl of Marlborough. Gov., 1662. Having toured Mass. in 1637, the earl of Marlborough commanded the royal ordnance in 1643, before leading the English colonization of Santa Cruz in 1645 and its reconquest from the Spanish in 1646. He also claimed the proprietorship of Barbados. He was admiral of the expedition that established English authority over the Portuguese outpost of Bombay, and he was subsequently nominated gov.-gen. of Jamaica in 1664 (with Edward Morgan [47] as his lt.). Marlborough was killed at Lowestoft in 1665. See Robert Latham and William Matthews, eds., *The Diary of Samuel Pepys* (Berkeley and Los Angeles, 1970–), VI, 127n; Andrews, *Colonial Period*, II, 150, 150n, 248n, 272n, III, 8n.

28. *SIR GERVASE LUCAS. Gov., 1666–1667. Lucas had governed Belvoir Castle during the civil war.

Dominion of New England

The Dominion was ill-fated in all save its historian, Viola Florence Barnes, whose *The Dominion of New England: A Study in British Colonial Policy* (1923; repr. New York, 1960) remains the standard study. On the first gov.-gen. of New England, 1635 (who did not come out), see "The Stuart Prerogative Assailed: The Case of Sir Ferdinando Gorges," above, pp. 16–21.

29. *PIERCY KIRKE. Gov.-gen., 1685. Did not come out. This thoroughly professional soldier, the penultimate gov.-gen. of Tangier (185), began his career as an ens. in 1666 and was col. of the 2d Tangier foot by 1680. He was deprived of the New England governor-generalship because of his disobedience to James II during the mopping up after Sedgemoor (S.P. 44/56, 260, 266, 268; W.O. 4/1, 12, 13).

30. *SIR EDMUND ANDROS. Gov.-gen., 1686–1689. Andros had previously held provincial commands in Barbados, the Leeward Islands (see under 70), and Ireland and had governed New York (148) for James, duke of York. After his Dominion term Sir Edmund commanded Virginia (201) and Maryland (116) under William III. He closed his career in command of his ancestral domain, Guernsey, in Queen Anne's reign. Apprenticed to arms as a Dutch cuirassier, Andros entered the English army as an ens. in the 1st foot Guards in 1662. He became capt. and maj. in the Barbados regt. (Bridge [175], col., and Stapleton [70], lt. col.) in 1667, and was serving as lt. col. of dragoons when commissioned gov.-gen. Of the many partial studies of Andros, the most illuminating is Edith F. Carey, "Amias Andros and Sir Edmund, His Son," Guernsey Society of Natural Science and Local Research, *Transactions*, VII (1913–1916), 38–66.

31. *FRANCIS NICHOLSON. Lt. gov., 1688–1689. Having previously served in garrisons as far apart as Tangier (where he was aide de camp to Kirke [29, 185] and brevet capt., 1680–1683) and Chepstow Castle, Nicholson spent most of his Dominion term in New York (150). He afterward served as commander-in-chief of Virginia (200, 202), Maryland (117), Nova Scotia (163), and South Carolina (171). Nicholson had been commissioned ens. in 1678 in the Holland regt. (with Collingwood [75] and Hill [73]) for service in Flanders (see 183a), and lt. in 1680 for the Tangier garrison. He was promoted capt. of a garrison company for New England in 1686. See Bruce T. McCully, "From the North Riding to Morocco: The Early Years of Governor Francis Nicholson, 1655–1686," *William and Mary Quarterly*, 3d Ser., XIX (1962), 534–556.

Dunkirk

Captured in 1658 by Cromwellian troops at the Battle of the Dunes, over the desperate opposition of the royalist exiles commanded by the duke of York (see the eloquent description by James himself in *The*

Memoirs of James II: His Campaigns as Duke of York, 1652–1660, trans. A. Lytton Sells [Bloomington, Ind., 1962], 260–276), the important Channel port of Dunkirk passed into Charles II's hands in 1660 and was sold to France. By 1663, elements of its English garrison had sailed for Portugal and Tangier, as well as for England. The model monograph is C. H. Firth, "Royalist and Cromwellian Armies in Flanders, 1657–1662," *Royal Historical Society, Transactions*, N.S., XVII (1903), 67–119.

32. *SIR EDMUND HARLEY. Gov., 1660–1661. Harley had been civil war gov. of Monmouth, Cannon Frome, and Worcester. He also saw notable garrison service in Hertford. Commissioned capt. of parliamentary horse in 1642 and col. of foot, Harley was col. of horse at the time of this governor's commission.

33. *SIR ROBERT HARLEY. Dep. gov., 1660–1661. Sir Robert left Dunkirk and his brother (32) to be chancellor of Barbados under his fellow royalist conspirator, Willoughby (3), but was exiled for insufficient subservience (Historical Manuscripts Commission, *Report on the Manuscripts of His Grace the Duke of Portland, K.G., Preserved at Welbeck Abbey* [London, 1892–1931], III, 273, 281). Formerly col. of horse, at the time of his Dunkirk commission Harley was lt. and maj. under Sir Philip Howard (54) of Monck's life guard. He was also M.P. and a major investor in Surinam. See Sir Charles Firth and Godfrey Davies, *The Regimental History of Cromwell's Army* (Oxford, 1940), index.

34. *ANDREW, LORD RUTHERFORD (afterward earl of Teviot). Gov., 1661–1662. Rutherford was transferred, with his regt. and dep. gov. Norwood (35, 176, 178), to command Tangier (174). This highly regarded Scots soldier of fortune ranked as lt. gen. in the French army before 1660. See Latham and Matthews, eds., *Diary of Pepys*, IV, 408, V, 166, 170.

35. *HENRY NORWOOD. Dep. gov., 1662–1663. Norwood afterward commanded in Tangier (176, 178). Having seen notable garrison duty in Bristol, Worcester, and Virginia (whose auditor he remained for decades) during the civil war and Interregnum, Norwood conspired to restore the monarchy. Succeeding, he became gov. of Sandowne Castle. Commissioned capt. in 1643 and maj. before 1649, Norwood was lt. col. of foot when commissioned dep. gov. of Dunkirk. As dep. gov., Norwood surrendered Dunkirk to its French purchasers before going out to Tangier. He retired from the army to lead the court party in the Gloucester corporation and was M.P. for Gloucester.

Gibraltar

Conquered in 1704, Gibraltar became England's eighteenth-century equivalent of Tangier, where the imperial mix of force, commerce, politics, and diplomacy in garrison government was especially apparent because those elements were peculiarly isolated.

36. *GEORGE, PRINCE OF HESSE. Gov.-gen., 1704–1705. Joining the army of William III in Ireland as brig. gen. and col. of foot, the prince was wounded at the Boyne. He besieged Athlone, was wounded at Aughrim, and led the capture of Gibraltar and commanded its subsequent defense. The prince was "killed at the head of the storming party at the capture of Fort Montjuich" during the siege of Barcelona in 1705. Prior to his English army career, Hesse had fought the Turks (notably at the siege of Negropont in 1685) and the French (being wounded at the sieges of Bonn and Mentz in 1689). (See Dalton, ed., *English Army Lists*, III, 194 n. 3.) This career of sieges, storms, and garrison governorships attests to the centrality of cities and citadels, centralization and militarization, throughout Europe and throughout the century. For further comment on the imperial effect of this general European tendency, see Webb, "Army and Empire: English Garrison Government in Britain and America, 1569 to 1763," *WMQ*, 3d Ser., XXXIV (1977), 7–8.

37. *ROGER ELLIOT. Gov.-gen., 1707–1711. Raised in Tangier with his half brother, Alexander Spotswood (206), Elliot was commissioned ens. under Kirke (29, 185) before 1681, having been wounded in 1680. He was cashiered in 1681 for dueling, but after he served in the ranks and received a recommendation, he was commissioned lt. in 1687 and was promoted capt. of Bath's regt. in 1690 (see Grenville [12]). Wounded at Steinkirk, Elliot was commissioned maj. in 1692. He defended Tongres in 1703 and was promoted col. by Marlborough. Fighting in Spain, Elliot became brig. gen. in Jan. 1707, gov.-gen. in Dec. 1707, and maj. gen. in 1710. He was ousted with Marlborough in 1711 and died in 1714. Note Elliot's multiple family connections with Virginia and North Carolina.

38. *THOMAS STANWIX. Gov.-gen., 1711–1713. Previously lt. gov. of Carlisle, 1705. Stanwix's twenty-year rise to become a gov.-gen. was altogether typical. Commissioned capt. lt. of foot in 1691, capt. in 1692, capt. of horse in 1694, lt. gov. in 1705, and col. of foot in 1706, Stanwix gained distinction in the battle of the Caya in 1709. He was promoted brig. gen. in 1710 and gov.-gen. in 1711.

39. *DAVID COLYEAR, earl of Portmore. Gov.-gen., 1713–1720. In 1674 Colyear enlisted in the Dutch army, where he became capt. before 1685 and lt. col. of the Scots Brigade, the three regts. in Netherlands service since 1572. He led William of Orange's troops ashore at Torbay, Nov. 5, 1688 (see also 61). Under Colyear, the Scots Brigade helped "pacify" Scotland, but it was decimated at Killiecrankie, July 27, 1689. After service in Flanders, Colyear was promoted to brig. gen. in 1693, col. of a Scots regt. in 1694, maj. gen. in 1696, and lt. gen. in 1702. He became col. of the 2d Queen's (ex-Tangier) Regt., gen. in Portugal in 1710, gov.-gen. in 1713, and col. of Scots dragoons in 1714. Colyear had been created Baron Portmore in 1699 and elevated to the earldom in 1703.

40. *RICHARD KANE. Lt. gov., 1720–1727. Kane was also lt. gov. of

Minorca (132). Commissioned lt. of Irish foot in 1689, capt. in 1693, and maj. of the Royal Irish regt. in 1694, Kane was wounded at Namur in 1695. Marlborough breveted him lt. col. in 1706, and Kane commanded a regt. at Malplaquet in 1709. Promoted col. in 1710, Kane was commissioned lt. gov. of Minorca in 1712, lt. gov. of Gibraltar in 1720, col. of the 9th foot in 1725, gov. of Minorca in 1730, and brig. gen. in 1734.

Jamaica

See the text for a study of the governance and the governors-general of Jamaica to 1681. Frank Cundall, *The Governors of Jamaica in the Seventeenth Century* (London, 1936), and its sequel, *The Governors of Jamaica in the First Half of the Eighteenth Century* (London, 1937), are at once indispensable and accessible, but their social context is greatly enriched by such studies as Richard S. Dunn, *Sugar and Slaves: The Rise of the Planter Class in the English West Indies, 1624–1713* (Chapel Hill, N.C., 1972).

41. *EDWARD D'OYLEY. Gov., (1655–)1662. D'Oyley had commanded in Ireland prior to sailing for the West Indies. He was commissioned capt. (of Fairfax's life guard?) in 1647 and was col. of foot at the time he succeeded Lt. Gen. William Brayne in command of Jamaica.

42. *THOMAS (HICKMAN), Lord Windsor (afterward earl of Plymouth). Gov., 1661–1662. Windsor prefaced his Jamaica command with garrison service in Hartlebury Castle during the civil war. Commissioned capt. of royalist horse in 1642, Windsor commanded at Naseby as lt. col. of horse. Active with Littleton (43) in royalist risings during the Protectorate, Windsor was commissioned capt. by Monck in 1660. The restored king restored the Windsor barony and named the baron lord lt. of Worcestershire in 1661. After his return from Jamaica, Windsor was commissioned capt. of an independent troop of horse in 1666 (see 180), to the lord lieutenancy of London in 1667, as lord lt. of the city and county of Worcester in 1670, and as commissioner of the ordnance. Considered as lt. gov. (to the duke of York) of Portsmouth (see 186), in 1682 Windsor was commissioned gov. of Hull and capt. of a garrison company (lt. gov. and capt., Lionel Copley [115]) and was created earl of Plymouth. The earl was commissioned col. of cavalry in 1685 and died in 1687. See S.P. 44/20, 117, 150, 166, 171, n.p.; S.P. 44/29, 1; S.P. 44/164, 154–155; S.P. 44/69, 8–10.

43. *SIR CHARLES LITTLETON. Dep. gov., 1662–1664. Littleton saw civil war service at Colchester, was commissioned capt. of horse in 1648, and served as page to the duke of York in exile. Active in royalist conspiracies during the 1650s, Littleton was commissioned lt. to Lord Windsor (42) in 1661 and chancellor of Jamaica prior to his command as dep. gov. Littleton was afterward successively commissioned capt. and maj. of the duke of York's marine regt. in 1664, lt. col. in 1665, and col. in 1668. He governed Harwich, Sheerness, and Landguard Fort, served with the duke

(and Richard Nicolls [146]) in the desperate battle of Sole Bay in 1672, and commanded the English garrison at Bruges in 1678. Promoted brig. gen. in 1685 and active in the repression of Monmouth's rebellion, Littleton resigned all his commands after the coup of 1688 rather than submit to Marlborough's discipline. Littleton was a lifelong agent for Jamaica.

44. *JAMES LEY, earl of Marlborough. Gov.-gen., 1664. Did not come out. Previously governed Bombay (27). See that entry for Ley's American career.

45. *SIR EDWARD MASSEY. Gov.-gen., 1664. Did not come out, although repeatedly named gov.-gen. from Sept. 1660 on. Parliamentary gov. of Gloucester during the famous siege of 1643, Massey was commissioned maj. gen. in 1645 and lt. gen. in 1647 by the parliament, but he fought as lt. gen. for Charles II at Worcester in 1650. Massey's career is described in the text, beginning with his royalist engineering service (capt., 1639) and his parliamentary infantry command (lt. col., 1642). Massey was gov. of Gloucester in the Restoration and M.P. for that city.

46. *SIR THOMAS MODYFORD, baronet. Gov.-gen., 1664–1671. Gov. of Barbados (1660–1661). Modyford saw civil war and Interregnum garrison service in Exeter and Barbados. He was commissioned maj. before 1647.

47. *EDWARD MORGAN. Dep. gov. and lt. gen., 1664–1665. Commissioned maj. before 1649, Morgan died leading the Jamaican forces at the capture of Eustatia from the Dutch, having been promised the government of the conquest.

48. *SIR THOMAS LYNCH. Lt. gov., 1671–1674. Lynch had been a capt. of Cromwellian foot before 1655 and was aide de camp to D'Oyley (41).

49. *JOHN, LORD VAUGHAN (afterward second earl of Carberry). Gov.-gen., 1674–1678. Lord Vaughan had been commissioned col. of foot in 1673.

50. *SIR HENRY MORGAN. Lt. gov. and lt. gen., 1674–1683. Commissioned maj. of foot in Carlisle's (51) regt. in 1673, Morgan already had acquired vast, if most irregular, military experience as admiral of the buccaneers. His remarkable agreeableness to regular soldiers was surprisingly illustrated by his valued bequest of portraits to Andros (30).

51. *CHARLES HOWARD, earl of Carlisle. Gov.-gen., 1678–1681. Carlisle had previously governed the city of Carlisle, the counties of Cumberland, Westmoreland, and Northumberland, and (in commission) the kingdom of Scotland. Capt. and col. of Cromwell's life guards, 1651–1654, Carlisle was col. of foot and lt. gen. in England when he was commissioned gov.-gen. of Jamaica. For details of his transatlantic career in garrison government, see the text, and see entry 180.

52. *SIR THOMAS LYNCH. Gov.-gen., 1681–1684. See 48.

53. HENDER MOLESWORTH. Lt. gov., 1684–1687. Lynch (52) had secured for Molesworth a commission to command Jamaica in chief, in reversion to himself. Lynch's objective was to keep from command Lt. Gen. Morgan (50), the chief of the privateers, and Maj. Gen. Francis Watson (afterward president of the council and acting gov.-gen.), the leader of the Carlisle coalition. This scheme succeeded in preserving the constitutional settlement of 1681, save for the Albemarle-Watson hiatus (see 56).

54. *SIR PHILIP HOWARD. Gov.-gen., 1685. Did not come out. Howard saw extensive garrison service in London. This brother of the earl of Carlisle (51) was commissioned capt. of foot in 1644. Since 1650 he had been capt. and col. of the troop that was the life guard first of parliament, then of Lord General Monck, and finally of Queen Catherine. See also 180.

55. *CHRISTOPHER MONCK, second duke of Albemarle. Gov.-gen., 1686–1688. Commissioned capt. and col. of foot in 1673 and of horse in 1678, Albemarle was promoted to capt. and col. of the 1st troop of the Life Guards in 1679. As lord lt. of Wiltshire, Albemarle was much criticized for his failure to oppose Monmouth's landing in 1685. The duke thereupon resigned all his commands in England in exchange for a commission as gov.-gen. of Jamaica and commander-in-chief of all military forces in English America.

56. *WILLIAM O'BRIEN, second earl of Inchiquin. Gov.-gen., 1689–1692. The earl had formerly been gov.-gen. of Tangier (181) and had also served in Ireland. Raised by his father as a soldier of fortune in France and Spain (losing an eye to corsairs in 1660), Inchiquin was commissioned col. of foot in 1674 and capt. gen. of the forces in Africa. Out of favor with James II, Inchiquin fought for William III at the Boyne, Dublin, and in county Cork before receiving the Jamaica command with orders to restore the 1681 settlement of Lynch (48, 52) and his clients (53, 57).

57. WILLIAM BEESTON. Lt. gov., 1692–1698; gov.-gen., 1699–1701. Despite a notable series of local commands (including ships of the royal navy) during his twenty years in Jamaica (1660–1680), Beeston held no English military commission prior to that as gov.-gen. (See, however, Dalton, ed., *English Army Lists*, IV, 112–113, for seeming indications that Beeston was at Namur, i.e., nonregimental commissions to the Jamaican commissary-gen. and the dep. judge-advocate, "Dated before Namur, 1 Oct." 1695, and signed by Beeston.) He was one of several absentee planter-merchant-politicians who were recalled to the governorship (see Lawes [65]) after long absence from the island to deal with civil emergencies (here, the Port Royal earthquake). Beeston died on his passage home.

58. *WILLIAM SELWYN. Gov.-gen., 1701–1702. Selwyn had been commissioned gov. of Gravesend and Tilbury Fort. Both commissions were

parts of a standard military career pattern: capt. of 1st foot Guards, 1681; guard duty at Russell's execution for the Rye House Plot, 1683; additional rank of lt. col., 1687. With Robert Hunter (158), Selwyn was one of Princess Anne's escorts in her flight from James II, Nov. 25, 1688. He sailed with the Guards to Flanders, but left them in 1691 to become col. of the 2d Queen's (ex-Tangier) Royal Regt., succeeding Lt. Gen. Kirke (29, 185). Selwyn distinguished himself at Landen and was commissioned brig. gen. at Namur, where numerous officer casualties opened the ranks (see introduction). Selwyn's appointment to Jamaica and Beeston's recall were rumored in Mar. 1701: "the former being a soldier, and more fitt to command in case the French should make any attempt upon them" (Luttrell, comp., *Brief Relation*, V, 28). Taking a more junior regt. out with him, Gov.-Gen. Selwyn became maj. gen. in 1702. He died in office.

59. *RICHARD BREWER. Lt. gov., 1702. Having been commissioned capt. of Henry Sidney's regt. in 1678 for service in Flanders (see 183a, 184), Brewer was well connected for the coup of 1688, upon which he was promoted to lt. col., Dec. 31, 1688. In 1689 Brewer became col., leading his regt. first to the pacification of Scotland, then to the reconquest of Ireland. There Brewer commanded at the Boyne. Newsletters reported his storm of Lanesborough, town and fort, and his installation of a garrison of three hundred men. After garrisoning Guernsey, Brewer's regt. was brigaded with Selwyn's (58) both for amphibious operations out of Portsmouth and for service in Flanders. The brigade fought at Ostend and Namur. Thus it was natural to send the regt. to Jamaica as part of Selwyn's garrison and to make Brewer, as the next senior officer, gov. in reversion. Brewer died only three months after Selwyn, and the command passed by military succession to Handasyde (60).

60. *THOMAS HANDASYDE. Commander-in-chief, 1702; lt. gov., 1703; gov.-gen., 1704–1710. Handasyde had commanded in Newfoundland in 1697 (as maj. to Col. John Gibson of the Portsmouth garrison, the expeditionary organizer for Secretary at War William Blathwayt). On the controversial Newfoundland venture, see Historical Manuscripts Commission, *The Manuscripts of the House of Lords*, N.S. (London, 1900–1962), Vol. III, *1697–1699*, 313–344, and below, s.v. "Newfoundland" and 138. Commissioned capt. of foot by William of Orange in 1688, and capt. of grenadiers in a senior English regt. in 1692, Handasyde had fought in Ireland and Flanders. He was promoted maj. of Gibson's foot in 1694, breveted lt. col. in 1697, and became lt. col. to Sir Henry Belasyse's regt. (afterward Selwyn's [58]). Made lt. gov. and col. of his Jamaica garrison regt. in 1703, Handasyde became brig. gen. in 1705 and maj. gen. in 1710. He resigned his regt. to his son Roger on being succeeded by Hamilton (62). He died in 1712.

61. *CHARLES MORDAUNT, third earl of Peterborough. Gov.-gen., 1702. Peterborough did not come out to Jamaica, but he did see imperial service

in Tangier, the West Indies, Exeter, Barcelona, Valencia, and was gov. of Minorca (134). The son of Henry Mordaunt (172), and perhaps the most controversial soldier of the age, Charles Mordaunt appears in the English army lists, Nov. 10, 1688, amidst the coup, as col. of a regt. of English followers of William of Orange (Mordaunt had signed the invitation to William). He had seen naval service in the Mediterranean in the 1670s and at Tangier in 1680. An ally of Shaftesbury, Mordaunt was implicated in the Rye House Plot. He fled to Holland on the accession of James II and commanded a Dutch squadron in the West Indies in 1687, "to try the temper of the English colonies and their attachment to the reigning sovereign" (John Charnock, *Biographia Navalis; or, Impartial memoirs of the lives and characters of the officers of the navy of Great Britain . . .*, 6 vols. [London, 1794–1798], III, 316–317). He was one of the officers who led William's troops ashore at Torbay (see 39), and he went on to occupy Exeter, Nov. 8, 1688. Created earl of Monmouth, appointed first lord of the treasury, and commissioned col. of horse in 1689, he was disgraced in 1696. Succeeding as third earl of Peterborough in 1697, he was recommissioned lord lt. of Northamptonshire in 1702 and also commissioned as "Captain General and Governor of Jamaica and Admiral and Commander-in-chief" (*DNB*, s.v. "Mordaunt, Charles") of a naval squadron on the Jamaica station. In the latter capacity he was expected to lead the projected invasion of the Spanish West Indies, but that project was aborted by Dutch withdrawal from it. Afterward commissioned gen., admiral, and commander-in-chief of English forces in Spain, 1705–1707, Peterborough became capt. gen. of marines in 1710, envoy to Venice and Hanover, col. of the horse Guards in 1711, and gov. of Minorca in 1713. He is noted here as the most prominent of the series of aristocratic soldier-diplomat-politicians nominated to the Jamaica governor-generalship at this time. These included Granard (137); Lt. Gen. Thomas (Wentworth), Lord Raby, afterward earl of Strafford (1711); and Brig. Gen. Richard Sutton, gov. of Hull and M.P. for Newark. Sutton's clientage to the duke of Newcastle (and his interest in the New York command), like Raby's embassy to the court of the heir-apparent at Hanover, anticipated new ruling elements in Anglo-American politics and imperial administration.

62. LORD ARCHIBALD HAMILTON. Gov.-gen., 1710–1716. Rear admiral at the time of this commission (and since Jan. 1708), Hamilton had a long naval career. His success off La Hogue in 1696 and his mission to Constantinople in 1699 were its most noticed episodes. The military dimensions of the colonial command were physically apparent at Hamilton's departure: "This day about 100 officers, captains, and subalterns attended the lord Archibald Hamilton, governor of Jamaica, for Portsmouth, to embark with him . . . " (Luttrell, *Brief Relation*, VI, 694, entry of Feb. 22, 1711).

63. *THOMAS PITT. Gov.-gen., 1716. Did not come out. Pitt had been president of Fort St. George by appointment from the East India Com-

pany. "Diamond" Pitt was M.P. for Old Sarum until he resigned to accept the governor-generalship of Jamaica, which he never took up. He married a daughter of James Stanhope (130). Their second son was commissioned gov.-gen. of the Leeward Islands (86), and their third son, Capt. John Pitt, commanded Bermuda, 1727–1737.

64. PETER HEYWOOD. Gov., 1716–1718. A protégé of James Stuart and a capt. in the royal navy, Heywood wrecked his ship in the West Indies and settled in Jamaica rather than return home. He was president of the council and acting gov. when commissioned.

65. SIR NICHOLAS LAWES. Gov.-gen., 1717–1722. This native planter-merchant and councillor had retired to England years before his commission as gov.-gen. Handasyde (60) then predicted that Lawes would not return "unless as governor," as Beeston (57) had done (Cundall, *Governors of Jamaica in the Eighteenth Century*, 77).

66. ★WILLIAM HENRY BENTINICK, duke of Portland. Gov.-gen., 1721–1726. Son of William III's most trusted councillor and an experienced soldier, Bentinick was commissioned capt. and col. of the 1st troop of the horse Guards in 1710. He was created duke of Portland in 1716 and died in Jamaica.

67. ★CHARLES DUBOURGAY. Lt. gov., 1721–1726. A quartermaster gen. in Scotland, 1715–1721, Dubourgay had entered the army of William III as ens. of a Huguenot regt. in 1691. He became capt. in 1695 at Namur, and quartermaster gen. in Portugal in 1705. He was breveted as col. after Almanza in 1707 and promoted col. of a French regt. in British service in Spain, 1709. Dubourgay served under Stanhope (130) from 1710 as quartermaster gen. Col. of a new regt., 1715–1718, he was commissioned lt. gov. to provide professional military support to Portland (66). Dubourgay came out to Jamaica, but the refusal of the assembly to authorize a lt. gov.'s salary led to his early return to England, where he was commissioned col. on the Irish establishment in 1723, brig. gen. in 1727, and envoy to Berlin, 1727–1730. Dubourgay died in 1732.

68. ★ROBERT HUNTER. Gov.-gen., 1727(–1734). Formerly (1706–1709) lt. gov. of Virginia ([205] did not come out) and gov.-gen. of New York and New Jersey (158). For reasons of health, Hunter retired from New York and New Jersey in 1719, and exchanged that governor-generalship for a comptrollership of customs with William Burnet (159) in 1720. Hunter recovered health, lost wealth, cultivated Newcastle, and was commissioned gov.-gen. of Jamaica in Feb. 1727. He was ordered to duplicate his New York success in raising a revenue from the assembly, which he did with a twenty-one-year grant in 1728. Promoted maj. gen. in Mar. 1727, Hunter died in Mar. 1734 from fever contracted while fighting the Maroons.

Leeward Islands

When they were separated from Barbados in 1670 because of the economic rivalry, military inefficiency, political resentment, and customs losses inherent in the Caribbee Islands union, the Leeward Islands had already become the cockpit of Anglo-French imperial conflict in the West Indies (the divided island of St. Christopher had been wholly conquered by the French in 1667) and were the scene of enmity between English planters and Irish servants. The ideal professional, racial, and personal qualifications of Sir William Stapleton (70), an Irish-born, French-trained, English-court-connected soldier of extraordinary wit and wisdom, were sufficient to form the Leeward Islands federation. His talents were not equaled by his successors, however, and the jurisdiction became a Hobbesian antisocial nightmare in which successive governors-general were murdered (79, 80).

69. *SIR CHARLES WHEELER. Gov.-gen., 1671–1672. After royalist military service in the civil war, Wheeler had shared the Dunkirk garrison service of the Guards in exile (see 35, 189) with Capt. John Strode, the lt. gov. of Dover, a fellow farmer of the Barbados 4½ percent tax, and organizer of the Leewards separation. Lt. col. of the Guards, Wheeler was commissioned capt. in 1660 and col. in 1678 in Ireland. He was also capt. of an independent troop of horse in 1666 (see 180). His disastrous career in the islands is fully discussed, as is the early constitutional history of the federation, in C.S.S. Higham, *The Development of the Leeward Islands under the Restoration, 1660–1688: A Study of the Foundations of the Old Colonial System* (Cambridge, 1921). See his son Francis (197).

70. *SIR WILLIAM STAPLETON. Gov.-gen., 1671–1686. Also dep. gov. of Montserrat (92). Garrison service in France, Italy, Spain, and Ireland preceded Stapleton's commission as lt. col. of the Barbados regt. in 1668. Its officers included: Sir Tobias Bridge (175), col.; Andros (30), maj.; Capts. Jas. Cotter (dep. gov. of Montserrat) and Cuthbert Morley (who resumed the government of Antigua from the French); Capt. Lt. Jno. Painter (active in Barbados politics with Bridge); and Ens. Abednego Mathew (formerly of the Holland Regt., afterward dep. gov. of St. Christopher, 1678–1681, and founder of a provincial dynasty [78, 83, 114]). Following his distinction in the regt.'s 1667 assault on St. Christopher, Stapleton was commissioned by Willoughby (4) as dep. gov. of Montserrat (the "Irish Island") in 1668. A special royal commission confirmed him in the Montserrat government in 1671. His service as gov.-gen. is eloquently related in the Blathwayt Papers, Colonial Williamsburg Foundation, Williamsburg, Va.

71. *SIR NATHANIEL JOHNSON. Gov.-gen., 1686–1688. Johnson was also proprietary gov. of South Carolina, 1702–1713, where he directed an attack on the Spaniards and the Indians in Dec. 1704 and repulsed the French and Spanish raid of Nov. 1706. The details of his early career remain obscure beyond the generalizations Johnson himself offered when

he rejected the Nevis planters' charge that, because he would not renounce King James, he "who for some time was their Captain-General"
would betray them to Catholics and Frenchmen. Johnson replied that "as
a Englishman, a Protestant, a man of honour and a soldier, I could not
desert this charge in such time of danger till I could find some fit person
to whom to entrust it . . . ," i.e., Codrington (72) (*Cal. S.P. Col., 1689–
1692*, no. 256).

72. ★CHRISTOPHER CODRINGTON (SR.). Gov.-gen., 1689–1698. Codrington had been dep. gov. of Barbados, 1669–1672, but was dismissed
by Willoughby (4) for excessive military spending. A coup organized in
Nevis replaced Johnson (71) with "Major general" Codrington, an act
quickly confirmed by William III and justified by Codrington's recapture
of the English sections of St. Christopher and his defense of the Leeward
Islands against French attack, Irish insurrection, and Carib raids (see
94). For Codrington's civil war service (he was a col. before his 1649
settlement in Barbados), see N. Darnell Davis, *The Cavaliers and Roundheads of Barbados, 1650–1652, With Some Account of the Early History of
Barbados* (Georgetown, British Guiana, 1887), 144. For his West Indian
career (and that of his son [74]), see Vincent T. Harlow, *Christopher
Codrington, 1668–1710* (Oxford, 1928).

73. ★THOMAS HILL. Lt. gen., 1689–1699. Hill was also dep. gov. and
lt. gov. of St. Christopher (110). In 1680 Hill was commissioned lt. and
brig. of the duke of York's troop of horse Guards (col., the duke of
Albemarle [55]). Recommended by the duke of York to Stapleton (70) as
dep. gov. of St. Christopher, Hill had also seen service in France and
Flanders with the Holland Regt., in which he was a lt. in 1678, as was
Henry Holt. On Holt's regt., see 204. See also 31, 75, 76, 93, and 118 for
other governors-general contemporary with Hill in the Holland Regt.,
and note Sir John Berry's command therein. Hill was esteemed as "a
very honest, just trew-hearted man, altogether a souldier" (John Cordy
Jeaffreson, ed., *A Young Squire of the Seventeenth Century. From the Papers
(A.D. 1676–1686) of Christopher Jeaffreson* [London, 1878], I, 322).

74. ★CHRISTOPHER CODRINGTON (JR.). Gov.-gen., 1699–1704. Son of
the gov.-gen. of the Leeward Islands (72), the younger Codrington was
noted for his capture of all of St. Christopher on the renewal of the war
in 1702 and for his invasion of the French islands. Commissioned capt. in
1693 of Goodwyn's regt. in the West Indies and listed as a capt. in Holt's
regt. (see 204) in 1695, Codrington was promoted capt. and lt. col. of the
1st foot Guards at Namur in 1695.

75. ★FRANCIS COLLINGWOOD. Lt. gen. and lt. gov., 1699. Commissioned ens. in the Tynemouth Castle garrison, 1677, Collingwood transferred to the Holland Regt. (see 73) in 1679, was commissioned lt. in the
same year, capt. in 1681, and col. of foot in Flanders in 1692. Collingwood
was sent to the Leeward Islands with his regt. in support of Codrington
(72) in 1698. Within the year he was reported "dead there, as also his lady

and daughter, with many of his officers and soldiers" (Luttrell, comp., *Brief Relation*, IV, 543, 547, entries for Aug. 1, 10, 1699), an epitome of the hazards of fever which led many officers to resign and soldiers to desert rather than risk service in the islands.

76. ★EDWARD FOX. Lt. gen. and lt. gov., 1699–1701. Fox had been commissioned ens. of the Holland Regt. in 1677 (with Collingwood [75]), lt. in 1684, capt. in 1688, and lt. col. to Collingwood in 1692. He was named brigade maj. of foot, 1695, on the same staff list as Hunter (68, 158, 205), Hamilton (203), and Selwyn (58). When half the regt. died in the Leeward Islands, Fox succeeded as regimental col. and as lt. gen. and lt. gov. He commanded the islands in chief in 1700. The regt. was disbanded in 1701, but Fox became col. of marines and brig. gen. in 1702. He died in the defense of Gibraltar in 1704.

77. ★THOMAS WHETHAM. Lt. gen. and lt. gov., 1702. Whetham was commissioned to command Canada in 1709 and Scotland (as the duke of Argyll's [133] dep.) in 1712. Commissioned ens. in 1687 in Tufton's foot, with Maj. Edward Nott (204) and Capts. Thomas Foulke (88) and William Dobbyn (89), Whetham became capt. lt. in 1694 and was promoted col. of the Inskilling foot in the West Indies in 1702, lt. gen., and lt. gov. in reversion. In 1707 he was commissioned brig. gen., and in 1709 he was named commander-in-chief of Canada, as senior officer of the abortive invasion. He became a maj. gen. in 1710, lt. gen. in 1727, and gen. in 1739. He died in 1741.

78. ★WILLIAM MATHEW. Gov.-gen., 1704. This second son of Abednego Mathew (see under 70) was commissioned as ens. in the Coldstream Guards in 1680, lt. in 1687, brevet lt. col. in 1691, and lt. col. in 1702. Edward Southwell wrote to the marquess of Ormond: "The prints say that Mathews of the Guards has got the government of the Leeward Islands. 'I fear he is under contribution'" (HMC, *Ormonde*, N.S., VIII, 52). Mathew's death was announced in Mar. 1705.

79. ★JOHN JOHNSON. Gov.-gen., 1704–1706. Johnson was also lt. gov. of Nevis (106). Commissioned lt. in 1685 to Hamilton (203) in the Royal Scots, Johnson presumably served at Sedgemoor in 1685. He was promoted capt. in the "reformed" regt., Dec. 31, 1688, was made maj. to Whetham's (77) Inskilling foot in 1705, and was murdered in 1706 while commanding the islands, prefacing the violent end of Parke (80).

80. ★DANIEL PARKE. Gov.-gen., 1706–1710. A protégé of Andros (30), this Virginian was aide de camp to Marlborough at Blenheim (see 206). There the duke promised him the governor-generalship of Virginia, but it was given instead to Hamilton (203). Parke was commissioned gov.-gen. of the Leeward Islands in 1706. His career and murder are detailed by Ruth Bourne, "Antigua, 1710: Revolution in Microcosm," in John T. Murray, ed., *Essays in European History* (Bloomington, Ind., 1950), 85–110, and in Ruth Bourne, "John Evelyn, the Diarist, and His Cousin

Daniel Parke II," *Virginia Magazine of History and Biography*, LXXVIII (1970), 2–33.

81. WALTER HAMILTON. Lt. gov., 1710–1711. Previously lt. gov. of St. Christopher (112), and lt. gov. of Nevis (107) simultaneously with this command. Hamilton held the rank of col. from his previous gubernatorial commands. As president of the Leeward Islands council, he succeeded Parke until Douglas (82) was sent out to investigate Parke's murder.

82. ★WALTER DOUGLAS. Gov.-gen., 1710–1715. Douglas was commissioned ens. in 1693 in Lord Cutts's (gov., Isle of Wight) regt. and promoted capt. of Livesay's regt. (part of the Jamaica garrison in which he served with Phenney [2]) by Handasyde (60) in 1702. Becoming a maj. before 1710, Douglas was "kept in England upon promise of preferment" (S.P. Geo. I, 72, printed in Dalton, ed., *English Army Lists*, VI, 384) while his regt. sailed for the Peninsula under the command of Maj. Gen. Whetham (77).

83. ★WILLIAM MATHEW (JR.). Lt. gov., 1714–1715. Mathew also served as lt. gov. of St. Christopher (114) and, some sources say, of Nevis. He had been commissioned lt. and capt. and was also quartermaster of his father's regt., the Coldstream Guards, in 1708.

84. WALTER HAMILTON. Gov., 1714–1721. See 81, 107, 112.

85. JOHN HART. Gov.-gen., 1721–1727. Previously gov. of Maryland (120). Hart was a capt. of foot before 1714 and ranked as brevet col. when commissioned as gov.-gen. of the Leeward Islands. See the account of his forceful administration in Burns, *British West Indies*, 427–428.

86. ★THOMAS PITT, earl of Londonderry. Gov.-gen., 1727(–1729). This second son of Thomas Pitt (63) was commissioned ens. in 1708, capt. of dragoons in 1709, and col. of horse before 1715. Created baron of Londonderry in 1719, he was raised to the earldom in 1726 and commissioned gov.-gen. on June 7, 1727, two days before the death of George I. Pitt died on St. Christopher in 1729. His younger brother, Capt. John Pitt, was gov. of Bermuda, 1727–1737, and may have been aide de camp to Marlborough both at Blenheim and at Ramillies.

Lieutenant and Deputy Governors of Leeward Islands

Four islands of the Leeward Islands federation—Antigua, Montserrat, St. Christopher, and Nevis—each had a lieutenant or a deputy governor. Deputies were appointed by the governor-general, often in response to nominations by crown officials at home. They were "paid at the discretion of the local assemblies and were generally local men" until James Stuart's imperial interest was applied after 1681. In 1683 the deputy governors described themselves as "all soldiers of fortune and through God's mercy and His Majesty's goodness . . . advanced to the station wherein we are." Following Stapleton's (70, 92) retirement from the chief command in 1686, lieutenants were usually appointed directly by the crown. See Higham, *Development of the Leeward Islands*, 219.

Antigua

87. *JAMES EDWARD POWELL. Lt. gov., 1683–1688. Powell had previously commanded Montserrat. Possibly commissioned capt. as early as 1645, Powell was a regimental adjutant in 1678. In 1688 he was pensioned on the army establishment as lt. gov. (T. 64/88, 145, 149b).

88. *THOMAS FOULKE. Lt. gov. and commander-in-chief, 1689. Foulke had commanded in Ireland. Commissioned capt. in 1685 (serving with Nott [204], Whetham [77], and Dobbyn [89]), Foulke was col. of foot by 1689.

89. *WILLIAM DOBBYN. Lt. gov., 1689 (in reversion to Foulke). Dobbyn had been commissioned capt. in 1685 (see 88). He was subsequently commissioned lt. col. of the 1st foot Guards and lt. gov. of Berwick in 1705. He was recommissioned as lt. gov. in 1715.

90. JOHN YEAMANS. Dep. gov., 1698–1715. A John Yeamans is listed as lt. of foot in Holt's regt. in 1702 with: Nott (204), lt. col.; Thomas Delavall (94), maj.; and Nathaniel Blakiston (93, 118) and Codrington (74), capts.

91. *EDWARD BYAM. Lt. gov., 1715(–1741). Brig. Gen. Byam also commanded Montserrat, according to the *Herald and Genealogist*, I (1862), 378. Dalton reports (*George the First's Army*, I, 231) that Byam's brother, Col. Willoughby Byam, had been mortally wounded at St. Christopher (under Codrington's [74] command).

Montserrat

92. *SIR WILLIAM STAPLETON. Dep. gov., 1669–1672. Afterward gov.-gen. of the Leeward Islands (70).

93. *NATHANIEL BLAKISTON. Dep. gov., 1687–1688; lt. gov., 1689–1695. Afterward gov. of Maryland (118). In 1692 Blakiston was commissioned capt. in Holt's regt. with: Nott (204), lt. col.; Delavall (94), maj.; James Norton (111) and Codrington (74), capts.; and Yeamans (90), lt. Breveted lt. col., as lt. gov. of Montserrat, in 1693, Blakiston was mustered "in England" in 1695.

94. *THOMAS DELAVALL. Lt. gov., 1695–1702. Delavall was commissioned capt. of Bolton's 2d (i.e., Holt's) foot in 1689 (see 204). He was a brevet maj. in 1694 when he petitioned the plantations committee of the privy council for the government: "That in April 1690 he went to the West Indies, being a Captain in the Duke of Bolton's Regt., and that he was in all the Expeditions against the French in those parts, in which he lost a brother [at Martinique in 1693, under Codrington (72)], and was

himself wounded. That he is now the eldest Capt. of said Regt., and hath a Breviate to command as Major. That the Government of Montserrat is become vacant by the absence and surrender of Col. Blackeston [93] the Lt.-Govr. thereof. If your Lordships should think fit to recommend him to his Majesty to serve in that government, he will endeavour, with all loyalty, duty, and care, to approve himself therein" (Dalton, ed., *English Army Lists*, IV, 90 n. 2). The petition summarizes the military qualifications for governorships and the seniority principle of military succession to them. On half-pay in 1698, Lt. Gov. Delavall was commissioned capt. in Collingwood's (75), then Fox's (76), regt. in the West Indies, in 1699.

95. ANTHONY HODGES. Dep. gov., 1702–1710.

96. JOHN PEARNE. Dep. gov., 1710–1713. An officer of this (unusual) name was paymaster of the artillery in Spain in 1702 (see 98), while a Henry Pearne was lt. to Codrington (74) in Holt's regt. in 1695.

97. *JOHN MARSHALL. Dep. gov., 1713–1714. Marshall is listed as capt. of Lillingston's regt. in the West Indies in 1710 and 1715.

98. GEORGE HAY. Lt. gov., 1714–1715. Perhaps the lt. col. of artillery under whom Pearne (96) served.

99. *THOMAS TALMARSH. Lt. gov., 1715–1722. Talmarsh was commissioned ens. of the Coldstream Guards in 1697, lt. of the Royal Fusiliers in 1702, lt. of the Coldstream Guards in 1703, capt. of the grenadier company of Mountjoy's regt. in 1704, and was promoted to maj. by Stanhope (130) in 1710. He fought at Cadiz, Vigo, Almenara, and Saragossa. His regt. was decimated at Almanza and disbanded in 1714, after which "Major Thomas Talmarsh [was] to be Lieutenant-Governor of Montserrat" (*London Gazette*, May 20, 1715). An officer of this name was commissioned capt. of the 1st troop of the horse Guards in 1727.

100. *CHARLES DILKE. Lt. gov., 1722–1723. Serving as adj. to the 1st troop of the horse Guards in 1692, brigadier in 1700, and eldest lt. in 1701, Dilke became exempt and the eldest capt. of the 4th troop of the horse Guards in 1712, succeeding Lord George Forbes (gov., Minorca, 1718–1719 [137]; gov.-gen., Leeward Islands, 1729–1731). This Dilke is said to be identical with a maj. of the same name in Munden's dragoons in 1720.

101. *PAUL GEORGE. Lt. gov., 1723(–1728). Commissioned lt. in the Scots Greys in 1720, George had a previous commission in the dragoons that remains untraced. He became capt. of invalids in 1721 and succeeded Dilke ([100] deceased) in Aug. 1723. He is listed as a capt. of Lucas's regt. in the West Indies in 1724.

Nevis

102. SIR AENEAS MACPHERSON. Lt. gov., 1688. A Roman Catholic, MacPherson was commissioned by King James on Dec. 10, 1688, the day

before the king fled from England. Naturally MacPherson did not come out.

103. JOHN NETHERWAY. Lt. gov., 1687–1692. This officer is assumed to be (but not tabulated as)the John Netherway who was a lt. of Hales's regt. in the West Indies in 1692.

104. *SAMUEL GARDINER. Lt. gov., 1692–1699. Gardiner was commissioned ens. at Tangier in 1678 to the earl of Inchiquin (56, 181), afterward gov.-gen. of Jamaica, 1689–1691.

105. ROGER ELRINGTON. Dep. gov., 1699–1702. "Captain."

106. *JOHN JOHNSON. Lt. gov., 1703–1706. Johnson was also gov.-gen. of the Leeward Islands (79) during this period.

107. WALTER HAMILTON. Lt. gov., 1707–1712. Hamilton had previously been lt. gov. of St. Christopher (112). He was also lt. gov. of the Leeward Islands (81) while holding this command, and afterward gov. (84).

108. DANIEL SMITH. Lt. gov., 1712–1722.

109. CHARLES SIBOURG. Lt. gov., 1722(–1732). The high-ranking officer of this name was otherwise unemployed in this period, but, names apart, there is no evidence that he occupied this obscure post.

St. Christopher

110. *THOMAS HILL. Dep. gov., 1682–1688; lt. gov., 1689–1697. Hill was also lt. gen. of the Leeward Islands (73).

111. *JAMES NORTON. Lt. gov., 1697–1701. In 1692 Norton was a capt. in Bolton's 2d (Holt's) regt. with Hill (73, 110) and four other officer-governors (see 74, 93, 94, 204).

112. WALTER HAMILTON. Lt. gov., 1703–1707. Hamilton had commanded Nevis (107) and afterward was lt. gov. and gov. of the Leeward Islands federation (81, 84).

113. MICHAEL LAMBERT. Lt. gov., 1707–1714.

114. *WILLIAM MATHEW (JR.). Lt. gov., 1715(–1733). Mathew had briefly been lt. gov. of the Leeward Islands (83).

Maryland

In Maryland the "Glorious Revolution" strengthened the royal government that it weakened elsewhere, for the Catholic Calverts, lords Baltimore, lost control of the province for twenty-five years. It was thus doubly appropriate that the first royal governor of Maryland was at once a noted Protestant participant in the army coup of 1688 in England and a strong proponent of executive authority in America.

115. *LIONEL COPLEY. Gov., 1691–1693. Copley had served as capt. of the Dublin battalion of the Guards in 1675, and transferred to the 1st foot Guards in 1676. At the height of the Popish Plot the duke of York told the earl of Dartmouth (186): "I am glad Captain Coply is at Hull for I look on him as an honnest man ont [one] that will be my friend" (Historical Manuscripts Commission, *The Manuscripts of the Earl of Dartmouth* [London, 1887–1899], I, 41). When York returned to power in 1681, he commissioned Copley as lt. gov. to Thomas, earl of Plymouth (42). Copley was recommissioned a capt. in the Hull garrison in 1685. During much of the 1680s, Copley was in actual command of Hull, its port and politics, fortifications and garrison. He held a strong "interest" in both the town and troops in 1688. When the then gov., Lord Langdale, was reported to be about to fill all of Hull's offices and commands with Catholics, Copley led the Protestant officers and soldiers in arresting the gov., seizing the town, and declaring for William of Orange. King William commissioned Thomas, earl of Danby, as gov. and made Copley lt. gov. and brevet col. His claim to a gov. was met with Maryland.

116. *SIR EDMUND ANDROS. Gov., 1692–1698 (in reversion to Copley [115] and Nicholson [117]). Andros had previously commanded in the Caribbees (70), New York (148), and New England (30); he held the gov.-gen. of Virginia (201) simultaneously with this command; and he afterward governed Guernsey. Authorized to act in case of the death or incapacity of the gov., Andros physically intervened in Maryland's government only once, following the death of Copley, to the dismay of Nicholson, who arrived in Maryland only to find his treasury substantially diminished by Andros's visit. At the time of this commission, Sir Edmund ranked as lt. col. of horse (1685) and brevet col. (1686).

117. *FRANCIS NICHOLSON. Lt. gov., 1692. Gov., 1694–1698. Nicholson previously served in the Tangier and Chepstow Castle garrisons. He had commanded in New England (31), New York (150), and Virginia (200). After his Maryland service, Nicholson was gov.-gen. of Virginia (202), Nova Scotia (163), and South Carolina (171). Breveted col. in 1689 as gov. of New York, Nicholson had been commissioned ens. in 1678, lt. in 1680, and capt. in 1686.

118. *NATHANIEL BLAKISTON. Gov., 1698–1703. Formerly dep. gov. of Montserrat (93). Blakiston had been breveted lt. col. in 1689 and commissioned capt. in Holt's regt. (204) in 1692.

119. *JOHN SEYMOUR. Gov., 1703–1714. Seymour had been commissioned ens. in the 1st foot Guards in 1674. He became lt. to Copley (115) in 1678, capt. in 1682, and capt. and lt. col. in 1687, and served as such with the Coldstream Guards in Flanders from 1694. "Colonel Seymour of the guards is made governor of Maryland, in the room of Nath. Blackstone, esq." (Luttrell, *Brief Relation*, V, 260, entry of Jan. 21, 1703).

120. *JOHN HART. Gov., 1714(–1720). Hart was afterward gov.-gen.

of the Leeward Islands (85). He had been commissioned capt. of foot before 1714.

Massachusetts

The Bay Colony, whose revolt against James II's regime in New England had been so closely coordinated with that against his rule in England, acquired a modified form of royal government as a result of the negotiations of 1688–1691. Its royalist potential was not effectively developed until after Phips (121) and company led the colony to military disaster, the whigs underwent their sea change in 1694, and the renewal of war in 1702 reemphasized English executive authority and imperial attitudes.

121. SIR WILLIAM PHIPS. Gov., 1691–1694. This sea captain's famous treasure had bought him many friends at court by the time a politically neutral figure was needed to introduce the new charter.

122. WILLIAM STOUGHTON. Lt. gov., 1691. Stoughton, the senior statesman of the Bay Company regime, served as a transitional caretaker at various times in the 1690s.

123. RICHARD COOTE, earl of Bellomont. Gov.-gen., 1697–1701. Bellomont governed New York (153) simultaneously with this command. The son, nephew, and grandson of famous soldiers, Bellomont had fought in Ireland and governed county Leitrim for William III, but no commission was forthcoming. Professor Robert C. Ritchie, citing Additional Manuscripts 41820, 273, British Library, London, reports that Bellomont had commanded a company of English soldiers in the Netherlands for the prince of Orange (afterward William III) in 1687.

124. *JOSEPH DUDLEY. Gov.-gen., 1701–1715. Dudley had been president of the council of New England, 1684–1689, and of New York, 1691–1694, and lt. gov. of the Isle of Wight, 1694–1701. This son of a veteran of Elizabeth's wars (who was also the second gov. of Massachusetts) had made his own military reputation in King Philip's War. Breveted col. as lt. gov. of the Isle of Wight, Dudley was also M.P. for Newton, Isle of Wight, from 1701 to 1702.

125. *THOMAS POVEY. Lt. gov., 1702–1711. Commissioned ens. to the col. of the 1st foot Guards in 1692, adjutant in Mar. 1693, lt. and capt. in Aug. 1693, and renewed in 1702, Povey was the nephew of the secretary of war and plantations and acting secretary of state, William Blathwayt.

126. *WILLIAM TAILER. Lt. gov., 1711–1716. A client of Nicholson ([31] who emulated his own patron, the duke of Bolton, in his solicitation for his subordinates), Tailer was commissioned col. of a regt. raised for service against the French in Canada and Nova Scotia in 1710. Nicholson honored Tailer by sending him to demand the surrender of Port Royal.

Dalton, ed., *English Army Lists*, VI, 337, suggests that this officer may be Capt. William Taylor of Erle's regt. (which saw action in Spain, the West Indies, and with Marlborough in 1708–1709), whose first commission was as ens. in 1702.

127. *ELIZEUS BURGESS. Gov.-gen., 1715. Did not come out. Burgess was commissioned brig. and eldest lt. of the 2d troop of the horse Guards in 1693. In Apr. and May 1696 Burgess killed successive dueling opponents. After the second episode he was rescued from the Gatehouse by a party of the Guards. Pardoned by the king in 1697, Burgess served in Spain under Stanhope (130), who promoted him to lt. col. of dragoons in 1711 and gov.-gen. of Massachusetts in 1715. However, Burgess was bought out by Massachusetts agents. Again commissioned lt. col. of dragoons, in 1716, Burgess was an army pensioner in 1723.

128. *SAMUEL SHUTE. Gov.-gen., 1716–1723. Commissioned capt. of horse in 1694 and wounded at Blenheim (see 206), Shute was breveted maj. in Jan. 1707 and commissioned maj. in Aug. 1707 (commanding capt. lt., John Pitt [63, 86], who was named lt. gov. of Bermuda in Oct. 1727). Shute was breveted col. and commissioned lt. col. in 1712. He left the regt. on becoming gov.-gen. in 1716.

129. WILLIAM DUMMER. Lt. gov., 1716(–1730). Son-in-law of Dudley (124).

Minorca

Minorca was the major British base in the Mediterranean from the time of its capture in 1708 until it was returned to Spain in 1802 (save for the French occupation of 1756–1763 and the Spanish reconquest of 1782–1798). Island governors were usually officers of extensive military experience, wide political influence, and broad imperial interest.

130. *JAMES STANHOPE (afterward Earl Stanhope). Gov., 1708–1711. Commissioned in 1694 as capt. of Gibson's regt. (Handasyde [60], maj.), Stanhope transferred to the 1st foot Guards as a capt. in 1695. In 1702 he was promoted col. of a foot regt. that served in Flanders, Portugal, Spain, and in the Canada expedition of 1711. Made a maj. gen. in 1707, and lt. gen. and commander-in-chief in Spain in 1708, Stanhope was wounded at Almenara and commissioned col. of dragoons (see 145). For his role in capturing Minorca, Stanhope was named gov. in 1708 (he was captured at Brihuega in 1710), created Viscount Stanhope of (Port) Mahon (the island capital) in 1717, and raised to the earldom in 1718. The death of the secretary of state, Earl Stanhope, on Feb. 5, 1721, was a major element in the most profound reshaping of imperial policy and politics in forty years. For Stanhope's influence on imperial personnel, see also 99, 127, 136, 164.

131. *JOHN FERMOR. Lt. gov., 1711–1712. Commissioned ens. in 1702,

capt. (by Marlborough) in 1704, and maj. in 1707, Fermor became a maj. in the duke of Argyll's (133) foot in 1709. Argyll appointed him adj. gen. in Spain, and he was breveted col. in Mar. 1711. Fermor was commissioned lt. gov. in Aug. 1711, became lt. col. of dragoons in 1715, and was elected M.P.

132. *RICHARD KANE. Lt. gov., 1712 (–1729; gov., 1730–1737). Lt. gov. of Gibraltar, 1720–1727 (40). Wounded at Namur in 1695, commissioned maj. in 1702, wounded at Blenheim, and breveted lt. col. in 1706 (with rank from 1704), he commanded a regt. at Malplaquet and was commissioned col. of foot in 1710. Made lt. gov. of Minorca in 1712 and lt. gov. of Gibraltar in 1720, Kane became col. of (9th) foot in 1725, gov. of Minorca in 1730, and brig. gen. in 1734. He died two years later and was buried in Minorca. That he had been, from 1720 to 1727, lt. gov. of both Minorca and Gibraltar, islands 500 miles apart, seems unlikely, but the records are, for the moment, intransigent: "Kane was lieutenant governor of Gibraltar at the same time he was serving in Minorca" (Henige, *Colonial Governors*, 162).

133. *JOHN CAMPBELL, duke of Argyll. Gov., 1711–1713. Argyll served as constable and gov. of Edinburgh Castle and gen. and commander-in-chief in Scotland simultaneously with this command. His staff in Scotland included Maj. Gen. Whetham (77), commander-in-chief in Argyll's absence, and Dubourgay (67), Argyll's quartermaster gen. In 1714 the earl of Orkney (203) replaced Argyll in Scotland. Dubourgay went out to Jamaica in 1721 and was replaced as quartermaster gen. by Spotswood (206), when he came home from Virginia in 1722. Such staff officer transfers between provincial governments manifested the empire's paramilitary character. The "Great Duke of Argyll" was especially influential in the affairs of army and empire, in part because of his rank, his courage, and his military ability, and in part because he was the only possible counterweight to Marlborough. Commissioned col. of the Argyllshire Highlanders in 1696 at the age of fifteen, and col. of the Scots regt. in Holland (fighting at Venlo and Keyservaert) in 1702, Campbell succeeded as the second duke of Argyll and was commissioned col. of the Scots (4th) troop of the horse Guards in 1703 (cf. Dilke [100] and Forbes [10]). Argyll was commissioned brig. gen. and commanded the Scots brigade at Ramillies in 1706; he stormed Menin and became maj. gen. in 1707; he commanded twenty battalions at Oudenarde, was wounded at Lille, and was promoted to lt. gen. in 1709. Wounded at Tournai and distinguished at Malplaquet, Argyll was commissioned commander-in-chief in Spain and gov. of Minorca in 1711, replacing Marlborough's client, Stanhope (130). His next active service was to put down the Scots rising at Sheriffmuir in 1715. For appeals to Argyll against the Marlborough dominance of the empire, see, for example, William Byrd, *The London Diary (1717–1721) and Other Writings*, ed. Louis B. Wright and Marion Tinling (New York, 1958), index. Argyll was recommissioned gov. of Minorca (135) in 1714 and held the post for two years until

Stanhope came to power, but Argyll did not command in the field after 1715. He was commissioned field marshal in 1736 and commander-in-chief of South Britain in 1742. Argyll resigned his commands in 1742 and died in 1743.

134. ★CHARLES MORDAUNT, third earl of Peterborough. Gov., 1713–1714. Peterborough had previously been commissioned gov.-gen. of Jamaica (61) but did not go out. He was capt. gen. of marines and col. of the horse Guards at the time of this appointment.

135. ★JOHN CAMPBELL, duke of Argyll. Gov., 1714–1716. See 133.

136. ★GEORGE CARPENTER. Gov., 1716–1718. Related to Thomas Caulfield (164), Carpenter was commissioned quartermaster of horse in 1685, cornet in 1687, capt. in 1688, maj. in 1691, lt. col. in 1692, and col. in 1703. He distinguished himself in Portugal and Spain as Stanhope's (130) second in command and was created Baron Carpenter in 1719.

137. ★GEORGE, LORD FORBES (afterward earl of Granard). Gov., 1718–1719. Forbes was afterward gov.-gen. of the Leeward Islands (1729–1731). Commissioned lt. of Holt's (204) marines in 1704, Forbes actually served as midshipman under Rooke at the capture of Gibraltar and as aide de camp to the prince of Hesse (36). Forbes became heir to the earldom of Granard by the death of Arthur, Lord Forbes, at Blenheim. He served at the siege of Ostend under Argyll (133, 135), who made Forbes brigadier of the Scots (4th) troop of horse Guards and subsequently exempt and capt. In 1708 Forbes was commissioned lt. of grenadiers in Holt's regt., but he resigned from this regt. in 1711. After serving as a cavalry officer under Argyll in Spain and as lt. gov. of Fort St. Philip, Minorca, Forbes became cornet and maj. of the Scots (4th) troop of horse Guards in 1712, gov. of Minorca in 1718, gov.-gen. of the Leeward Islands in 1729, and envoy to Russia in 1733. At the time of his death in 1765 he was senior admiral of the British navy (Dalton, ed., *English Army Lists*, V, 133).

Newfoundland

Ever since Sir John Berry's investigation and report in 1675, the commodore of the naval convoy for the annual fishing fleet had governed the scattered English settlements on Newfoundland during the summer season. See entries 19, 140, 142, 197. In 1700 a resident lieutenant governor and garrison were established to supplant the local "fishing admirals" in the year-round government and to lead the resistance to the French and Indians. "Government" under the lieutenant governor was highly personal. Other political institutions remained exceedingly weak. Yet the identity of the charges against Thomas Lloyd (139, 141) in 1705 in Newfoundland (see D. W. Prowse, *A History of Newfoundland from the English, Colonial, and Foreign Records* [London, 1895]) and against Francis Nicholson (202) in 1705 in Virginia (see David C. Douglas, ed., *English Historical Documents*, Vol. IX, Merrill Jensen, ed., *American Colonial Docu-*

ments to 1776 [New York, 1955]) suggest that at least some of the dynamics of garrison government applied even to this embryo society.

138. *MICHAEL RICHARDS. Lt. gov., 1700–1702. Richards subsequently governed Alicante. A lt. of Selwyn's (58) regt. and an engineer in the artillery train for Flanders in 1692, Richards was wounded at Namur and also served as adjutant for the bomb and machine vessels of the Channel fleet in 1695. He was commissioned commander-in-chief of the artillery train for Newfoundland in 1697 (see also Handasyde [60]), lt. gov. in 1700, and capt. of a garrison company in 1702. Richards returned to England and was promoted capt. of the 1st foot Guards in 1705, col. of artillery in Spain, and gov. of Alicante (see Pulleyne [24]). He commanded the artillery at Almanza and became col. of foot in 1710, was commissioned brig. gen. and chief engineer of England in 1711, and became surveyor gen. of the ordnance in 1714.

139. *THOMAS LLOYD. Lt. gov., 1703–1704. Commissioned lt. of a garrison company in Newfoundland in 1701, Lloyd was promoted to capt. in 1704. See 141.

140. *JOHN MOODY. Lt. gov., 1704–1706 (acting by commission from Commodore Timothy Bridge). Commissioned ens. of foot in 1697 and lt. of foot (to Richards [138]) in 1703, Moody successfully defended Fort William (St. Johns, Newfoundland) in 1705 and was therefore promoted by Marlborough lt. and capt. of the Coldstream Guards in 1707. He became an adjutant of that regt. in 1712. See 143.

141. *THOMAS LLOYD. Lt. gov., 1705–1708. See 139. Lloyd was breveted lt. col. on his reappointment as lt. gov.

142. *JOHN COLLINS. Lt. gov., 1709–1712 (acting by commission from Commodore Joseph Taylor). Commissioned ens. in Gibson's (60) regt. in 1702, Collins became lt. of Richard Ingoldsby's (156) garrison company in New York in 1715.

143. *JOHN MOODY. Lt. gov., 1713–1719. See 140. On his reappointment as lt. gov., Moody was breveted lt. col. and commissioned capt. of a garrison company that was incorporated in Phillips's (167) regt. in 1717. In 1715 he was assigned a garrison staff for the Newfoundland government that included a chaplain, town maj., and commissary of stores.

144. *MARTIN PURCELL. Lt. gov., 1717. Did not come out. Purcell was commissioned ens. of foot in 1707, capt. of horse in Aug. 1711, maj. in Oct. 1711, and promoted to capt. and lt. col. of Phillips's (167) foot (with Capts. Lawrence Armstrong [169], John Doucett [168], and Alexander Cosby [170]). He was commissioned lt. gov. in 1717. In 1719 Purcell was listed as AWOL in Britain from these commands.

145. *SAMUEL GLEDHILL. Lt. gov., 1719(–1735). Gledhill had been lt. gov. of Carlisle. Commissioned lt. in 1702, Gledhill was lt. col. com-

manding Richard Sutton's (a nominee [61] for the governor-generalship of New York) regt. of foot at Douay. There he was wounded, captured, and stripped. He became capt. of Peterborough's (61, 134) dragoons in Spain in 1712, and capt. of Stanhope's (130) dragoons and lt. gov. of Carlisle in 1713. Gledhill died in office in Newfoundland.

New York and New Jersey

Conquered from the Dutch in 1664 by an expedition commanded by Richard Nicolls (146), and recaptured by the Dutch in 1673, New York was nominally a proprietary province of the duke of York. The duke's status as Charles II's heir, the royal subvention of the garrison government's cost, and the duke's position as the leading imperialist all made the colony more than royal in practice. Officially, it became a royal province when the duke succeeded to the throne as James II. The duke's governors exercised varying degrees of jurisdiction over West Jersey until at least 1676 and over East Jersey until 1681. Both Jersey proprietaries were resumed by the crown in 1701 and were governed by the governors-general of New York until 1736. For a sketch of the duke, parallel in form and intent to these entries, see S. S. Webb, "Household of James Stuart," *Perspectives in American History*, VIII (1974), 55–80. For a discussion of his servants' administrative attitudes, with particular reference to New York, see Webb, "The Trials of Sir Edmund Andros," in James Kirby Martin, ed., *The Human Dimensions of Nation Making: Essays on Colonial and Revolutionary America* (Madison, Wis., 1976), 23–53.

146. *RICHARD NICOLLS. Dep. gov. (to the duke of York), 1664–1668. Nicolls had served in the Portsmouth and Windsor garrisons. Commissioned capt. of royalist horse before 1647, Nicolls served under the duke of York (gov.) in Jersey in 1649 and was on the duke's staff in the French army until 1656. He was commissioned capt. of the duke's company in the garrison of Portsmouth in 1660 and became capt. in the Windsor garrison in 1661. In the spring of 1664, Nicolls was breveted col., named chief investigatory commissioner for New England, and appointed commander-in-chief of the expeditionary force that captured New Amsterdam Sept. 7, 1664. Retiring from New York in 1668, Nicolls was killed at the duke's side at Sole Bay in May 1672. Nicolls has often been confused (as in [William Dicconson], *The Life of James the Second . . . Collected Out of Memoirs Writ of his Own Hand . . .*, ed. Rev. J. S. Clarke, 2 vols. [London, 1816], II, 400, and Andrews, *Colonial Period*, III, 49, 107) with Oliver Nicholas, who was lt. gov. of Portsmouth, groom of the duke's bedchamber, and lt. col. to the duke's (admiral's) regt. (Littleton [43], col.).

147. *FRANCIS LOVELACE. Dep. gov., 1667–1673. Lovelace governed Carmarthen Castle during the civil war. He spent the Interregnum first in exile in Virginia, and then in the French service under the duke of York. A maj. of foot before 1649, Lovelace was commissioned col. and

corp. of Charles II's Life Guards in 1661 and lt. col. of foot in 1667. Disgraced by the Dutch recapture of New York during his absence in Connecticut, July 30, 1673, Lovelace was imprisoned by the duke of York for debts owed the duke from the government of New York. He died in 1675, shortly after his release on bail from the Tower. His grandson (157) ultimately succeeded him in command of New York.

148. *SIR EDMUND ANDROS. Lt. gov., 1674–1681. Andros had served in the West Indies before this appointment and afterward commanded in New England (30), Maryland (116), Virginia (201), and Guernsey. At the time of this commission Andros was maj. of the Barbados regt. of dragoons (the scion of the Barbados foot, commanded by Bridge [175]). Officers serving with Andros in the Barbados regts. included Stapleton (70), Cotter (70), and Mathew (70), and other local commanders in America. Andros's New York garrison subordinates all were former subalterns of the Barbados dragoons: Anthony Brockholes (formerly of the duke of York's troop of horse Guards and afterward twice acting gov. of New York); Rupert Billingsly (lt. col., 1686, commanding Nott [204], Stanhope [130], Foulke [88], Dobbyn [89], and Whetham [77], and lt. gov. of Berwick, 1694); and George Andros (formerly corp. of Prince Rupert's dragoons, subsequently commander at Sagadahoc as one of Sir Edmund's garrison in the Dominion of New England [Blathwayt Papers, XIII, 5, Williamsburg]).

149. *THOMAS DONGAN (afterward earl of Limerick). Gov., 1682–1688. Dongan had previously served as lt. gov. of Tangier (183). An Irish Catholic royalist, Dongan was commissioned maj. before 1647. He joined the duke of York in exile and remained in the French service until 1678. Then in Oct. 1678, Dongan was commissioned successively as col. of a regt. of foot raised in Ireland, brig. of foot and sgt. maj. gen., lt. col. of the Tangier regt. (Inchiquin [56, 181], col.), and lt. gov. of the city, garrison, and territory of Tangier (S.P. 44/44, 85, 99, 107). En route to recruit in Ireland, he and his Irish regimental officers were caught in England at the height of the Popish Plot. So well did their French, Catholic, and military associations fit with the Plot's preconceptions that Charles II bowed to parliamentary and Protestant pressure to disband the regt. and, in Feb. 1680, recalled Dongan from Tangier (182). When the duke of York returned to power, he made Dongan his gov. of New York (Sept. 20, 1682). There Dongan served until replaced by Andros (30) and Nicholson (31) on New York's incorporation into the Dominion. Leaving New York in 1691, Dongan succeeded as Viscount Dongan and earl of Limerick following the deaths of three older soldier brothers. Subsequently, Dongan followed them (and many other English soldiers) into the Portuguese service (see "Dunkirk").

150. *FRANCIS NICHOLSON. Lt. gov., 1689. Having seen garrison service in Tangier and at Chepstow Castle, and having been lt. gov. (resident at New York) of the Dominion of New England, Nicholson was named

lt. gov. of New York, June 30, 1689. He fled the revolution in that colony before his commission reached him, however, and he was sent instead to govern successively Virginia (200, 202), Maryland (117), Nova Scotia (163), and South Carolina (171). Nicholson had previously ranked as capt. of a Dominion garrison company in 1686.

151. HENRY SLAUGHTER (or SLOUGHTER). Gov., 1689–1692. "Colonel" Slaughter's commissions prior to that as capt. of a company to be raised for service in New York (Dec. 6, 1689) have not been found.

152. *BENJAMIN FLETCHER. Gov., 1692–1698. Gov. of Pennsylvania, 1692–1695. Fletcher had risen through the English army in Ireland, from cornet to Lord John Berkeley (president of Connaught, 1662–1663, and brother of Sir William Berkeley [187]) to capt. of an independent company in Connaught quarters, 1672. He was ousted, however, with the rest of the Protestant officers, in Tyrconnel's purge of 1685–1686. Although commissioned capt. (of English foot) in 1688, Fletcher quickly went over to the Protestant prince William III. He won high marks from that soldier-prince as maj. of foot in Ireland. Fletcher was thereupon commissioned gov. of New York, and of Pennsylvania (1692–1695), breveted col. of foot, and commissioned capt. of a New York garrison company in 1692. His effort to bring Pennsylvania into the work of imperial defense is detailed by Andrews, *Colonial Period*, III, 312–317. He was ousted by Secretary of State Shrewsbury to make room for Bellomont (123, 153), but the charges of illegal trading and connivance with pirates that had been carefully prepared against Fletcher by the whigs were blocked by Blathwayt's appeal to the king, who promised Fletcher further employment. It is not known, however, whether the Benjamin Fletcher on the subsequent army lists in Ireland is this same officer.

153. RICHARD COOTE, earl of Bellomont. Gov., 1697–1701. Bellomont also governed Massachusetts (123). His commission here and Nanfan's (154) were issued by the lords justices, not by William III.

154. *JOHN NANFAN. Lt. gov., 1697–1702. Nanfan had been commissioned ens. of foot in 1689 and capt. in 1693. In 1697 he became capt. of a New York garrison company and lt. gov. to Bellomont (153), who had married a cousin of his. Nanfan acted as gov. from Bellomont's death Mar. 5, 1701, to Cornbury's (155) arrival in 1702.

155. *EDWARD HYDE, Viscount Cornbury (afterward third earl of Clarendon). Gov.-gen., 1701–1708. Also gov.-gen. of New Jersey, 1703–1708. Cornbury had been commissioned lt. col. of royal dragoons (col., John Churchill) in 1683. He had commanded four troops of dragoons at Sedgemoor and was promoted col. of dragoons in 1685. As the senior officer with James II's army (Nov. 11, 1685), Cornbury began the desertion to William of Orange by forging orders from the secretary at war, William Blathwayt. Cornbury was nonetheless dismissed from com-

mand by William III because of the Hyde family's toryism. He had to settle for the post of master of the horse to Prince George (husband of Cornbury's cousin, Princess Anne) in 1690. An M.P. from 1685 to 1701, Cornbury was commissioned gov.-gen. of New York in 1701 in anticipation of the accession of his cousin. He was also commissioned gov.-gen. of New Jersey in 1703. He was formally recalled in 1708, after a disastrous maladministration, but he was actually imprisoned for debt in New York until he succeeded as earl of Clarendon in 1709. For Cornbury's military service, see C. T. Atkinson, *History of the Royal Dragoons, 1661–1934* (Glasgow, 1934).

156. *RICHARD INGOLDSBY. Lt. gov., 1702–1709. Ingoldsby was also lt. gov. of New Jersey. Like Fletcher (152), Ingoldsby was promoted because of superior service with the English army in Ireland. Commissioned ens. in 1678, lt. in 1680, and capt. in 1685, Ingoldsby presumably lost his commissions in the purge of Protestant officers. In Dec. 1689 he reappeared in King William's army as capt. lt. On a very favorable report by the king's inspector gen., Ingoldsby was promoted to maj. and then commissioned capt. of a garrison company for New York. His role in the arrest of Jacob Liesler and in the repression of the revolutionary regime in New York is well known. Ingoldsby's ensuing reputation helped him to gain a commission as lt. gov. of New York and New Jersey to Cornbury (155). Breveted lt. col., he was also capt. of a New York garrison company until his death in 1719. For his early service in Ireland and his own report of his American government, see HMC, *Ormonde*, I, II, and N.S., VIII.

157. *JOHN, LORD LOVELACE. Gov.-gen., 1708–1709. Also gov.-gen. of New Jersey, the fourth baron Lovelace was a nephew of the whig leader of the 1688 coup and a grandson of Francis Lovelace (147). He was commissioned guidon and maj. of the 1st troop of the horse Guards in 1699, cornet and maj. in 1700, and col. of a new regt. of foot in 1706. In 1708 Lovelace was commissioned gov.-gen. of New York and New Jersey and capt. of a garrison company in New York in anticipation that he would lead the attack on Montreal, but he died in May 1709.

158. *ROBERT HUNTER. Gov.-gen., 1709–1720. Hunter was also commissioned to command New Jersey. He had been commissioned to govern Virginia (205) in 1706 and afterward (1727–1734) governed Jamaica (68). "The first appearance Mr. Hunter made in the world was at the Revolution as one of the gentlemen [another was Selwyn (58)] who served as a guard under the Bishop of London [lt. horse Guards, 1661; lt. of horse, 1666] to the Princess Anne when she retired from her father's court and he soon afterwards received a commission in King William's army" (Cadwallader Colden to his son, Sept. 25, 1759, in "The Colden Letters on Smith's History, 1759–1760," New-York Historical Society, *Collections*, I [1868], 193). Hunter is said to have had a command at the siege of Derry and he was commissioned aide-maj. of dragoons in 1689.

Promoted capt. of the royal Scots dragoons in 1694, maj. of brigade to the dragoons in Flanders in 1695, and maj. of dragoons in 1698, Hunter was breveted lt. col. of dragoons by Marlborough in 1703. Hunter fought at Blenheim, and as Marlborough's aide de camp at Ramillies (see 206) he is said to have carried Cadogan's battle-winning order. Hunter negotiated the surrender of Antwerp and was rumored as Dudley's (124) replacement in Massachusetts. Instead, he was commissioned lt. gov. of Virginia (205) to Orkney (203; see also 80). Captured by the French en route to Virginia, Hunter was exchanged for the bishop of Quebec and was promised the governor-generalship of Jamaica. However, he was commissioned gov.-gen. of New York and New Jersey in 1709, and brig. gen. in 1711, before he was finally promoted gov.-gen. of Jamaica (68) and maj. gen. in 1727.

159. WILLIAM BURNET. Gov.-gen., 1720–1727. Burnet also governed New Jersey, Massachusetts, and New Hampshire. Even more than Hunter (68, 158, 205), with whom he exchanged offices in 1720, Burnet was a child of the "Glorious Revolution," being born in 1688 at The Hague, where his father, the bishop, had gone to help organize William of Orange's invasion. Prince William was the child's godfather. Commissioned "Our Captain-General and Governour in Chief" of New York and New Jersey in succession to Hunter (Dalton, ed., *George the First's Army*, I, 353), Burnet made way for John Montgomerie, the capt. and col. of the 3d (Scots) foot Guards. Burnet became gov. of Massachusetts at the end of 1727, and of New Hampshire as well in 1729. In that year he died in Boston.

Nova Scotia

Save for the period of English control from 1654 to 1667, and in 1690 (under Phips [121]) Nova Scotia, or "Acadia," was French until the conquest of 1710. The ensuing English government, like that of Newfoundland, was constitutionally embryonic for many years. Yet it displayed the military executives and paramilitary institutions characteristic of imperial garrison government generally.

160. *SIR THOMAS TEMPLE, baronet. Gov., (1654–)1667. A capt. and col. in Bedford's horse (with Oliver Cromwell) in 1642, Temple was commissioned gov. by Cromwell in 1654 and recommissioned by Charles II in 1662, before being forced to return the area to France following the peace of Breda. Temple's deputies included the Cromwellian captains John Leverett (1654–1657), (gov., Massachusetts Bay Colony [1672–1679]) and Thomas Breedon, 1661.

161. *SAMUEL VETCH. Lt. gov. of Annapolis Royal, 1710–1712. Vetch was later commissioned gov. of Nova Scotia (165). Border histories are full of the military pursuit of Vetch's father, the Reverend William Vetch, and the repression of his Covenanter followers by government garrisons

prior to 1689. The children of the family took refuge in Holland until Samuel returned to the British Isles with William of Orange and was commissioned cornet of Scots dragoons. He appears to have joined his brother, William, a lt. of the earl of Angus's foot (the "Cameronians," distinguished by their extraordinary bravery and by their ranking of a Presbyterian elder as an officer of each company) in defense of Dunkeld in 1689. Both Vetches fought at Steinkirk in 1692 and at Landen in 1693, but they left the regt. at the peace to join the Scots colonizing expedition to Darien. Samuel's subsequent career of merchandise, espionage, diplomacy, and politics is summarized by his involvement in 1705 in one of the many "flag of truce" episodes of trading with the enemy. With Nicholson (163), Vetch was the leading organizer of the attack on Canada and was commissioned adjutant gen. of the forces in North America in 1709. He shared command with Nicholson in the capture of Port Royal (Annapolis Royal) in 1710, and he was commissioned lt. gov. and commander-in-chief. He tried to retrieve the disaster at the Isle of Eggs in 1711, and he was succeeded at Annapolis by Nicholson. See the model study by G. M. Waller, *Samuel Vetch: Colonial Enterpriser* (Chapel Hill, N.C., 1960).

162. *SIR CHARLES HOBBY. Lt. gov. of Annapolis Royal, 1711 (in the absence of Vetch [161]). A Boston merchant who was knighted in 1705 (supposedly for services at Port Royal, Jamaica, in 1692), this Nicholson (163) protégé was commissioned col. of a regt. of foot to be raised in New England for the Canada expedition in 1710.

163. *FRANCIS NICHOLSON. Gov. of Nova Scotia and of the town and garrison of Annapolis Royal and gen. of forces in Nova Scotia and Newfoundland, 1712–1715. Nicholson had commanded in New England (31), New York (150), Maryland (117), and Virginia (200, 202). He afterward governed South Carolina (171). Commissioned brig. gen. in 1710, and lt. gen. of North American forces for the 1711 attack on Canada, Nicholson was also a capt. with Vetch (161) and Moody (140, 143) of a garrison company at Placentia in 1713. The gruesome details of this government are in Nicholson's correspondence with his lt. gov., Caulfield (164), in *Nova Scotia Archives*, Vol. II, *A Calendar of Two Letter-Books and One Commission-Book in the Possession of the Government of Nova Scotia, 1713–1714*, ed. Archibald M. MacMechan (Halifax, 1900).

164. *THOMAS CAULFIELD. Lt. gov. of Annapolis Royal, 1712–1716. In 1701 Caulfield was commissioned ens. of his father's (William, Viscount Charlemont) regt. of foot, raised for service in Ireland, but he did not accompany the regt. to the West Indies (1702–1703), where it lost heavily. Instead, he sailed in 1705 for Spain, where he served under Stanhope (130). Named capt. and lt. gov. of Nova Scotia in 1712, Caulfield's service ended with his death in 1717 as a maj. Caulfield said of his government: "There never was a Garrison in the British Establishment so hardly Used as this has been in all Respects" (Caulfield to Clark, Annapolis, June 12, 1716, in MacMechan, ed., *Calendar of Two Letter-Books*, 40).

165. *SAMUEL VETCH. Gov. of Nova Scotia and of the town and garrison of Annapolis Royal, 1715–1717. Did not come out. See 161. Vetch died a prisoner for debt in 1732.

166. *JOHN WILLIAMS. Lt. gov. (acting) of Annapolis Royal, 1716. Commissioned ens. in 1706, and capt. of a garrison company at Annapolis Royal before 1715, Williams became a capt. in Phillips's (167) regt. in 1717.

167. *RICHARD PHILLIPS. Gov.-gen., 1717(–1749). Phillips's first commission was probably as lt. to Morpeth's (heir to Carlisle [51]) regt. in Flanders in 1678 (see 43, 183a). He circulated William of Orange's declaration in England in 1688, was rewarded with a commission as capt. in 1689, and fought at the Boyne. He was commissioned capt. in Flanders in 1692, maj. and brevet lt. col. in 1707, lt. col. in 1710, and col. of the 12th foot (formerly Livesay's) in the West Indies in 1712 (170). Commissioned gov.-gen. of Nova Scotia in 1717, Phillips organized a regt. (the 40th foot) around the four independent companies of the Nova Scotia garrison and the four companies at Placentia and St. Johns, Newfoundland. Phillips's officers included Caulfield (164), Moody (143), Purcell (144), Armstrong (169), Doucett (168), Williams (166), and Cosby (170), as well as John Bradstreet, Paul Mascarene, and John Ligioner among later American commanders. These officers constituted most of the council of state for Nova Scotia. Phillips was commissioned brig. gen. in 1735, maj. gen. in 1739, and lt. gen. in 1743. He left the government in 1749, was commissioned col. of the 35th foot, and married the sister of his lt. col., Cosby (170). Phillips died in 1754. See Capt. R.H.R. Smythies, *Historical Records of the 40th (2nd Somersetshire) Regiment, Now 1st Battalion the Prince of Wales's Volunteers . . .* (Devonport, 1894).

168. *JOHN DOUCETT. Lt. gov. of Annapolis Royal, 1717–1725. Doucett was commissioned lt. of Fox's (76) marines in 1702 and capt. of foot in 1709. He fought at Malplaquet and succeeded Caulfield (164) in 1717 as a capt. in Phillips's (167) regt. and as lt. gov.

169. *LAWRENCE ARMSTRONG. Lt. gov. of Annapolis Royal and commander-in-chief of Nova Scotia, 1725(–1739). Commissioned ens. in 1699 and lt. in 1705, Armstrong served at Oudenarde and Malplaquet. He was commissioned capt. before 1711, when he was wrecked with Meredyth's regt. of foot in the Isle of Eggs disaster. Commissioned capt. of an independent company at Annapolis in 1712, Armstrong sailed home in 1716 but returned as a capt. of Phillips's (167) regt. in 1717. He was promoted lt. col. in 1720, lt. gov. in 1725, and lt. col. commanding Phillips's regt. in 1731. Armstrong committed suicide at Annapolis in 1739 and was succeeded by Mascarene (see 167).

170. *ALEXANDER COSBY. Lt. gov. of Annapolis Royal garrison, 1726(–1728). Commissioned lt. of Livesay's regt. of foot in 1705, capt. in 1708, and recommissioned in the same (12th) regt. (now commanded by Phillips [167]) in 1715, Cosby was promoted maj. in 1717. He transferred to the

Nova Scotia garrison with his col. and became maj. of Phillips's (40th) foot in 1720 and lt. col. in 1740. Cosby died in Nova Scotia in 1743. His eldest brother, William, was col. of the Royal Irish regt. of foot and gov.-gen. of New York, 1732–1736. Alexander's elder brother, Thomas, was capt. of foot and fort maj. of Annapolis Royal in 1722.

South Carolina

171. *FRANCIS NICHOLSON. Gov. 1720(–1729). Nicholson had served in Tangier against the Moors, at Chepstow Castle against the rebels of 1685, at Boston as a garrison capt. of the Dominion of New England, and at New York as the Dominion's lt. gov. (31, 150). He had been lt. gov. of Virginia (200), gov. of Maryland (117), gov.-gen. of Virginia (202), gov. of Nova Scotia and gen. of the forces there and in Newfoundland (163), and inspector gen. ("governor of governors") in North America in 1714 (Webb, "The Strange Career of Francis Nicholson," *WMQ*, 3d Ser., XXIII [1966], 545). Brig. Gen. Nicholson entered the last governorship of his long career when the South Carolinians overthrew the proprietary government and asked for a royal gov. and garrison. These were provided in 1720 to reverse "the great miscarriages and neglect of the government of South Carolina and the incursions of the barbarous Indians etc. etc." (W.O. Commission Book, 1718–1723, Sept. 26, 1720, quoted in Dalton, ed., *George the First's Army*, II, 60). Returning to England in 1725, Maj. Gen. Nicholson died on Mar. 5, 1728.

Tangier

Tangier, like Bombay, had been a part of the dowry of Catherine of Braganza. England's North African and Mediterranean activities focused on it: " 'Tis an out work of the nation, which you know is a principal strength of a fortress, 'tis a safe port, a magazine, a scale of trade, and a community of brave and loyal men" ("A Discourse Touching Tangier . . ." [1680], quoted by Davis, *Second Queen's Royal Regiment*, I, 48). Its political and financial cost, however, and the crown's domestic need for its veteran garrison regiments, led Charles II to order the evacuation and destruction of the town and harbor in 1683. See E.M.G. Routh, *Tangier: England's Lost Atlantic Outpost, 1661–1684* (London, 1912), and Davis, *Second Queen's Royal Regiment*, I.

172. *HENRY MORDAUNT, second earl of Peterborough. Gov.-gen., 1661–1663. Peterborough succeeded his father (gen. of ordnance for parliament) in 1642 and raised a regt. of royalist foot in 1643. Wounded at Newbury, Peterborough was imprisoned and his estate sequestered. He was commissioned capt. of the Tangier troop of horse, col. of the Tangier regt. of foot, and gov.-gen. in Sept. 1661. Following his Tangier tour, Peterborough was pensioned on the Tangier establishment and was commissioned capt. of foot and capt. of horse in 1666 (see 180), col. of foot in

1673, and col. of the duke of York's regt. of horse in 1678 (see 183a). A loyal follower of James II, he lost all his commands and perquisites in 1689 and was impeached for treason. Peterborough died in 1697. His son (61, 134), however, once again reversed the family's politics, reverting to the country attitudes of his grandfather.

173. ⋆SIR JOHN MORDAUNT. Dep. gov., 1661–1663. Commissioned cornet of the Tangier troop of horse in 1661 and capt. of the Tangier foot in 1663, Mordaunt was knighted in 1669 for services at Tangier.

174. ⋆ANDREW RUTHERFORD, earl of Teviot. Gov., 1663–1664. Teviot had previously governed Dunkirk (34). His Dunkirk troops became the Tangier regt. of foot (the 2d Queen's), and he remained their col., with Norwood (35, 176, 178) as lt. col. Capts. Fairborne (182), Robert Needham, and Mordaunt (173) were also among Teviot's imperially significant officers. The earl was additionally a col. of a regt. of horse at Tangier. He was killed in action against the Moors, May 4, 1664.

175. ⋆SIR TOBIAS BRIDGE. Joint commander-in-chief with Norwood (176), 1664. Bridge had seen garrison service in Scotland, England, and Dunkirk prior to serving in Tangier. He afterward commanded English troops in Barbados and the Leeward Islands. Commissioned as capt. in the New Model dragoons before 1647, maj. by 1649, and maj. of English dragoons in Scotland before 1653, Bridge came under Monck's command and patronage in 1654. The maj. was noted for his successes against Scots guerrillas. Bridge also acted as (dep.?) maj. gen. in England. Commissioned maj. of horse in the Dunkirk garrison, 1659–1662, Bridge then went with his men to Tangier, where he commanded three troops of horse from 1663. He assumed the government following the death of Teviot (174), for which service he was knighted and given a medal by Charles II. In 1667 Bridge was commissioned col. of the Barbados Regt. of foot (lt. col., Stapleton [70, 92]; maj., Andros [30, 70, 116, 148, 201]), and by 1674 he was a member of the Barbados council. His provincial role there is memorialized in the name of Bridgetown.

176. ⋆HENRY NORWOOD. Joint commander-in-chief with Bridge (175), 1663–1664. Norwood had previously served as dep. gov. of Dunkirk (35). He came out to Tangier in 1663 as lt. col. of English foot under Teviot (174). Norwood succeeded Teviot as col. and capt. of the 2d battalion of foot at Tangier in 1664. Norwood's commissionership of prizes at Tangier, like his revenue collectorship in Essex (cf. Strode [69], Nicolls [146], Honeywood [of Virginia and Portsmouth], and Massey [45]) and his auditorship of Virginia (1649–1680), is testimony that a gubernatorial salary was the least reward of the governors-general. Note the house property held by Fitzgerald (177), Belasyse (179), Norwood, and Middleton (180) in their Tangier commands, and see Webb review of Beverly McAnear, *The Income of the Colonial Governors of British North America* (New York, 1967), in *WMQ*, 3d Ser., XXVI (1969), 308–309.

177. *JOHN FITZGERALD. Lt. gov., 1664–1666. Fitzgerald had been gov. of Yarmouth. He was commissioned capt. to the earl of Barrymore in 1642. Fitzgerald came out to Tangier as col. of the Irish battalion of the Tangier foot and as a client of the duke of York. Dep. gov. to Peterborough (172) and Teviot (174), Fitzgerald was commissioned lt. gov. in June 1664 and in July took command from Norwood (176) and Bridge (175), with whom he quarreled violently, as much over real estate and fiscal questions as national rivalries between Irish and English. Both officers soon sailed for England, whence Norwood returned with English recruits and a commission as lt. gov. Fitzgerald was retained in England as an advisor on the Mediterranean. To an admiring Samuel Pepys (Treasurer of the Tangier Garrison from 1665, cf. Add. MSS. 28076, 114b), Fitzgerald exemplified the cosmopolitan quality of the empire's military rulers: "I was pleased all the day with his discourse of his observations abroad, as being a great soldier and of long standing abroad and knows all things and persons abroad very well, I mean the great soldiers of France and Spain and Germany, and talks very well" (Latham and Matthews, eds., Diary of Pepys, IX, 274).

178. *HENRY NORWOOD. Lt. gov., 1666–1668. See 35, 176. "This gallant officer, who was an Esquire of the Body to Charles II, succeeded to the command of the garrison as Lt.-Gov., 21 Feb. 1666" (Dalton, ed., English Army Lists, I, 41n; S.P., 44/11, 12–13). See also P. H. Hardacre, "The Further Adventures of Henry Norwood," VMHB, LXVII (1959), 271–282.

179. *JOHN, LORD BELASYSE. Gov.-gen., 1665–1666. The baron had seen extensive and distinguished service in the garrison governments of the civil war, having commanded York and Newark. He became gov. of Hull in 1661. Commissioned col. of foot in 1642 and capt. gen. of horse in 1645, Belasyse became gov.-gen. of Tangier and col. of the Tangier regt. in Jan. 1665. The excellence of his art collection and the fraudulence of his garrison finances were equally remarkable. Belasyse's juggling of the exchange rates of his garrison's pay was a common practice of govs.-gen.

180. *JOHN MIDDLETON, earl of Middleton. Gov., 1668–1675. Middleton had governed Edinburgh and its castle as commander-in-chief of the forces in Scotland, 1661–1663. Commissioned a capt. in 1639, Middleton fought for parliament and was a Covenanter until 1648. Becoming a royalist, he "assisted" Charles II at the battle of Worcester and followed him into exile. Middleton ranked as capt. gen. in 1660. His English commands included the Kent militia and an independent troop of horse (see Carlisle [51], Howard [54], Peterborough [172], Windsor [42], and Wheeler [69] for Middleton's fellow capts. of these military police units). Pepys, announcing Middleton's forthcoming appointment to Tangier on Apr. 15, 1667, termed the earl "a man of moderate understanding, not covetous, but a soldier-of-fortune and poor" (Latham and Matthews, eds.,

Diary of Pepys, VIII, 167). The Tangier treasurer later amended his estimate, concluding that Middleton was "a shrowd man, but a drinking man I think, as the world says—but a man that hath seen much of the world, and is a Scott" (*ibid.*, IX, 326, entry of Oct. 12, 1668). Middleton died in office at Tangier, Jan. 25, 1675.

181. ★WILLIAM O'BRIEN, second earl of Inchiquin. Gov.-gen., 1675–1680. Inchiquin afterward became gov.-gen. of Jamaica (56). His service at Tangier was overshadowed by Fairborne's (182) heroics.

182. ★SIR PALMES FAIRBORNE. Dep. and lt. gov., 1675–1678; lt. gov. and gov., 1680. Having served at the siege of Candia, Fairborne was commissioned capt. of the Tangier foot in 1663, maj. of Norwood's (35, 176, 178) regt. in 1664, dep. gov. in 1675, lt. gov. and lt. col. to Inchiquin (56, 181) in 1677, and commissary gen. in Flanders in 1678. He was recommissioned lt. gov. and lt. col. in Feb. 1680 to replace Dongan (149, 183). As Irish influence at Tangier was reduced, Fairborne became gov. and col. in Nov. 1680 in place of Inchiquin (S.P. 44/164, 54). Fairborne died of wounds at Tangier two weeks before his commission as gov. was issued in England.

183. ★THOMAS DONGAN (afterward earl of Limerick). Lt. gov., 1678–1680. Dongan afterward governed New York (149).

183a. ★THOMAS BUTLER, earl of Ossory. Gov.-gen., 1680. Son of James, duke of Ormond (see text), the earl had commanded the English regiments in the Netherlands (see 31, 43, 59, 73, 76, 167, 172, 184, 185, 186, 204) in 1678 and was distinguished at Mons. Commissioned gov.-gen. in July 1680, he died before the month was out.

184. ★EDWARD SACKVILLE. Lt. gov. and commander-in-chief, 1680–1681. Commissioned capt. of the 1st foot Guards in 1673, lt. col. of foot (while retaining his Guards rank) in 1678 (see 59, 183a), and lt. col. commanding the battalion of the Guards at Tangier in 1680, Sackville succeeded Fairborne (182) as gov. Although the commons had received a bill for "annexing Tangier to the Imperial Crown of England" (*Journals of the House of Commons*, IX, 625, May 20, 1679), Sackville observed that only such expenditures as Charles II could not afford would preserve the colony from the Moors' constant attack. Sackville's health failed in 1681 and in May he left Kirke (185) in command. In 1682 Sackville was commissioned lt. col. in the Coldstream Guards. Having been promoted col. and brig. gen. in 1685, and maj. gen. on Nov. 7, 1688, Sackville resigned all his commissions to the fleeing James II, at Rochester, on Dec. 19, 1688.

185. ★PIERCY KIRKE. Commander-in-chief, 1681; gov.-gen., 1682–1683. Kirke was afterward designated gov.-gen. of New England (29). Commissioned ens. in the duke of York's admiralty regt. (Littleton [43], lt. col.) in 1666, Kirke became cornet of horse in 1670, lt. in 1674, capt. lt. of the 1st foot Guards in 1675 (for service in France, 1673–1674), lt. col.

of dragoons in 1678 (with whom Kirke saw service in Flanders [see 183a]), and capt. of horse and col. of a foot regt. raised for Tangier service in 1680. He succeeded Fairborne (182) as col. of the Tangier regt. (the 2d Queen's, or "Kirke's Lambs"), whose officers included Mathew (78) and Elliot (37). In 1681 Kirke succeeded Sackville (184) as commander-in-chief of Tangier. Nicholson (171) was Kirke's aide de camp. On taking command, Kirke wrote to the earl of Dartmouth (186) asking that the duke of York be told that "I am only heare to searve him, and as he has maid me I will for ever continue his true and faithful servant . . . " (Apr. 29, 1681, quoted in Davis, *Second Queen's Regiment*, I, 193). Kirke remained in Tangier, his command luridly described by Pepys ("Nothing but vice in the whole place, of all sorts . . . ," Edwin Chappell, ed., *The Tangier Papers of Samuel Pepys*, Publications of the Navy Records Society, LXXIII [London, 1935], 89), until Dartmouth (186) destroyed the city, forts, and port in 1683–1684. Kirke mopped up the West Country after Monmouth's rebellion and was promoted brig. gen. in 1685. He was arrested trying to defect to William of Orange, Nov. 28, 1688. Commissioned maj. gen. by William III in 1689, Kirke commanded the expedition that relieved Londonderry. He fought at the Boyne, became lt. gen. in 1690, and died on service in Flanders in Oct. 1691, being succeeded in command of the regt. by Selwyn (58).

186. *GEORGE LEGGE, earl of Dartmouth. Gov.-gen., 1683–1684. Dartmouth had also been lt. of the Tower of London and lt. gov. of Portsmouth (to the duke of York). Only the army service of this noted admiral and favorite of James Stuart can be outlined here. The eldest son of Col. William Legge (who had been educated in arms under Prince Maurice, had served as groom of the bedchamber to Charles I, and had been commissioned gen. of ordnance, 1639, and gov. of Chester and Oxford), George Legge was commissioned capt. of his late father's company in the Tower garrison in 1669. He was promoted lt. gov. of Portsmouth to the duke of York in 1672, col. of foot and gen. of the artillery in Flanders in 1678 (see 183a), master of horse to the duke of York and master gen. of the ordnance in 1681. For Dartmouth's services at Tangier, July 2, 1683–Apr. 3, 1684 (and for those of William "Tangier" Smith, afterward of the New York council) see HMC, *Dartmouth*, I, and Chappell, ed., *Tangier Papers of Samuel Pepys*, where Pepys remarked (p. 93) of Dartmouth that "it is plain even by my lord's discourse [regarding the mayor's jurisdiction at Tangier] . . . that the governors of places do look upon themselves to be meant to govern all the civil officers, and that therefore he did never rest till he had brought it so at Portsmouth."

Virginia

See the text for the careers of Virginia's governors and the development of government in the Old Dominion during Charles II's reign.

187. SIR WILLIAM BERKELEY. Gov. (1641–1652), 1660–1677 (except for absences in 1644 and 1661–1662). No military commissions are forthcoming for Berkeley. Whether his knighthood at Berwick in 1639 was war-related, and how much involvement in imperial administration was implied by his Canada council membership, are unknown. His lack of military title and authority as gov. are discussed in the text.

188. *SIR HENRY CHICHELEY. Lt. gen., 1673; dep. gov., 1674–1682. Chicheley was lt. col. to Sir Richard Willis, the royalist soldier and gov., when he was knighted in 1644. Chicheley's brother was master of the ordnance to Charles II (preceding Dartmouth [186] and presiding over Windsor [42]).

189. *HERBERT JEFFREYS. Lt. gov. and commander-in-chief, 1676–1678. Having seen garrison service in Oxford and Banbury during the civil war, in Dunkirk at the end of the exile period, and in Portsmouth, York, and London after the Restoration, Jeffreys led the expeditionary force to Virginia. Capt. of horse since 1642 and a capt. of the 1st foot Guards from the regt.'s raising in exile, Jeffreys was the Guards' senior capt. (not holding field rank) when the Virginia battalion was organized. He was promoted lt. col. commanding the Guards-based battalion. His capts. were a cross section of English military factions. They have a place here because they were commissioned as Jeffreys's successors both in command of the battalion and in command of Virginia.

190. *JOHN MUTLOWE. Commissioned capt. of the Coldstream (Monck's) Guards in 1661, Mutlowe returned from Virginia to become dep. gov. of Portsmouth (to Dartmouth, then Col. George Legge [186], the lt. gov. to the duke of York).

191. *EDWARD PICTS. In 1664 Picts became lt. in the 1st foot Guards in a company (Strode [see 69], capt.) of exile origin. Commissioned lt. of the king's own company in 1671 and capt. in July 1676, Picts did not go out to Virginia, being replaced by Walters (192).

192. *ROBERT WALTERS. Commissioned maj. before 1647, Walters joined the Guards in exile and served in the Dunkirk garrison in 1661. He retired from the Guards in Oct. 1678.

193. *CHARLES MIDDLETON. A capt. of the duke of York's regt. (Littleton [43], col.) since Oct. 1676, Middleton became capt. in the Holland Regt. in 1682 and capt. of the 1st foot Guards in 1684.

194. *WILLIAM MEOLES (MILES). Meoles was commissioned ens. in the Holland Regt. in 1665, lt. in 1666, and capt. in 1673. His record ended in Virginia. Whether by death or settlement, many battalion officers remained in the Old Dominion after the bulk of the regt. went home in Oct. 1678 (see also 192).

Jeffreys's headquarters staff included:

195. *JOHN TONGUE. Quartermaster and marshal. Commissioned lt. to Atkins (5) in the Carlisle garrison in 1661 and lt. of the Coldstream Guards in 1670, Tongue became a capt. of the 1st foot Guards in 1672. See the text for his service under Carlisle (51).

196. *WILLIAM MORICE. Adjutant. Morice was commissioned an ens. in the 1st foot Guards in 1664, lt. of the duke of York's regt. (Littleton [43], lt. col.) in 1666, and lt. of the 1st foot Guards in 1667. He served as master of the ordnance in Virginia. Culpeper (198) summoned Morice home in 1681 to testify to the privy council committee on the colonies.

197. *FRANCIS WHEELER. Volunteer. Commissioned cornet to his father (69) in 1666 and ens. to Prince Rupert at Windsor in 1674, Wheeler served at Tangier after his return from Virginia and became a capt. of the 1st foot Guards in 1683. This well-known admiral was commodore of the Newfoundland squadron in 1684 (see "Newfoundland" and entry 19). Wheeler was afterward named commander-in-chief in the West Indies, in reversion to Foulke ([88] see Luttrell, *Brief Relation*, II, 551). He was lost at sea in 1693.

Note also Jeffreys's subalterns:

Among the lts.: *John Webb*, the future lt. gen. (distinguished at Wynandel in 1708 and at Malplaquet) and gov. of the Isle of Wight; *Francis Hoblyn*, Nott's (204) subordinate; *Edward Rouse*, commissioned ens. to Sir Philip Howard (54) in the Guards, wounded at Sedgemoor as a capt. of the Guards, and retired in 1697 as lt. col. to become capt. and commissioner of Upnor Castle.

Among the ens.: *William Mathew* (78); *John Jeffreys*, son of the lt. col. and commissioned lt. in the duke of York's regt. (Littleton [43], col.) in 1678.

198. *THOMAS, LORD CULPEPER. Gov., 1675–1678 (in reversion); gov.-gen., 1678–1683. Culpeper had formerly governed the Isle of Wight. He was commissioned capt. of foot in 1661, capt. of a garrison company to be raised for the Isle of Wight in 1666, gov. in reversion to Berkeley (187) in 1675, and lt. and gov.-gen. of Virginia in 1678.

199. *FRANCIS HOWARD, fifth baron Howard of Effingham. Gov.-gen., 1683–1692. Howard was commissioned capt. of Buckingham's foot in 1673. With his succession to the title (one of the twenty Howard family baronies) in 1681 came the patronage of the family head, the duke of Norfolk, and the approval of the duke of York, which together led to the Virginia commission. Howard resigned in 1692 rather than return to the colony he had left on the eve of the coup of 1688. He died in 1694.

200. *FRANCIS NICHOLSON. Lt. gov. to Howard, 1689–1692. See 31, 117, 150, 163, 171, and 202 for his other commands. Nicholson was a brevet col. at this date. His services in Virginia and Maryland are dis-

cussed in Webb, "Francis Nicholson," *WMQ*, 3d Ser., XXIII (1966), 513–548.

201. ★SIR EDMUND ANDROS. Gov.-gen., 1692–1698. See 30, 70, 116, and 148 for his other commands. Andros's Virginia service is discussed in Webb, "Francis Nicholson," *WMQ*, 3d Ser., XXIII (1966), 531–535, and in Webb, "Trials of Sir Edmund Andros," in Martin, ed., *Human Dimensions*, 23–53. Andros retired from this command to the government of Guernsey and there, in 1711, ended an English army career that had begun in the Guards (ens. 1662) 49 years earlier.

202. ★FRANCIS NICHOLSON. Gov.-gen., 1698–1704. See also 200. In "Virginia's Complaint," Nicholson's defenders lamented his recall, for he "with Justice Rules my Bench / My Straggling Cottagers with Strong Defence" protects. His enemies spoke the themes of the coming age: "Thou English Man! be gone, / That we may ride a Native of our own, / Or Scot, who may our Purseproud wishes crown" (Nicholson Papers, Colonial Williamsburg Research Foundation, Williamsburg, Virginia).

203. ★GEORGE HAMILTON, earl of Orkney. Gov.-gen., 1705(–1737). Did not come out. Orkney was also the constable of Edinburgh Castle and commander-in-chief of the forces in Scotland (see 133). This fifth son of the earl of Selkirk (afterward duke of Hamilton) was raised as a soldier by his uncle, the earl of Dumbarton. Commissioned capt. in the royal Scots regt. of foot (col., the earl of Dumbarton) in 1684, Hamilton survived the heavy regimental losses at Sedgemoor to become col. of the Inskilling regt. in 1690. He served at the Boyne, Athlone, and Aughrim. At the last battle, his regt. was decimated and Hamilton was wounded. He replaced Marlborough as col. of the Royal Fusiliers in 1692. After his distinction at Steinkirk, Hamilton was promoted col. of the 1st battalion of the Royal Scots in 1692. The regt. was cut up at Landen in 1693 and again at Namur in 1695. There Hamilton was wounded and commissioned brig. gen. In 1696 he married Elizabeth Villiers, William III's mistress. Her dowry was 95,000 acres in Irish estates confiscated from King James (and from which his mistresses were still maintained) and the earldom of Orkney. On the renewal of hostilities with France, Orkney was commissioned maj. gen. He fought at Stevensvaert and became lt. gen. in 1704. At the battle of Blenheim, his battalion took the village of Blenheim and captured the 13,300 French officers and troops there (see 206). The governor-generalship of Virginia followed. (The administration of the colony was entrusted to Nott, Hunter, Spotswood, Drysdale, and Gooch [204–208], all of whom had served under Orkney and Marlborough.) Orkney relieved Liège in 1705. He led the cavalry pursuit after Ramillies, and commanded at the Dyle and at Menin in 1706. He was elected a representative peer of Scotland to the first parliament of Great Britain in 1707, in which year he led seven battalions in defense of Louvain and at Niville. Distinguished at Oudenarde in 1708, Orkney criticized Marlborough's failure to advance on Paris but remained in

command. He led fifteen battalions in the crucial attack at Malplaquet in 1709. Made privy councillor and gen. of foot in 1710, Orkney directed twenty battalions at Bouchain. He retained his command beyond the Marlborough era and was commissioned col. of the 2d battalion of the Royal Scots in addition to the first battalion. He also became gentleman of the bedchamber to George I. Orkney was named constable of Edinburgh Castle and commissioned commander-in-chief for Scotland in 1714, and recommissioned gov.-gen. of Virginia in 1715 and in 1727. For his staff in Scotland see 133 and Dubourgay (67), Whetham (77), and Spotswood (206). Orkney's last promotion was to be field marshal of England in 1736. He died in 1737.

204. *EDWARD NOTT. (Lt.) gov. and commander-in-chief, 1705–1706. Commissioned in 1677 as ens. to Littleton's (43) company in the duke of York's regt., Nott was promoted to capt. in 1679 and maj. of Herbert's foot in 1686. He appears to have joined William of Orange before King James's flight. He was commissioned maj. of the duke of Bolton's 2d (Holt's) regt., which in 1689 was raised in Yorkshire for West Indies service by the town maj. of Berwick, Henry Holt (formerly lt. and adjutant of the Holland Regt. [see 73], headquartered at Berwick). The new regt. was nominally commanded by the duke of Bolton, who applied his political influence to support his officers' claims to governments (see Nicholson [31] and Collingwood [75]). Nott fought with the regt. in the Martinique expedition of 1693. His fellow officers included Delavall (94), Blakiston (93), Codrington (74), Norton (111), Yeamans (90), and Forbes (137). Nott was commissioned (lt.) gov. of Virginia in 1705 by arrangement with Marlborough and Orkney, but he died of the "seasoning" in 1706.

205. *ROBERT HUNTER. (Lt.) gov., 1706–1709. Captured en route to the province. Afterward gov.-gen. of New York (158) and of Jamaica (68).

206. *ALEXANDER SPOTSWOOD. Lt. gov. and commander-in-chief, 1709–1722. Spotswood followed his Virginia command with one in Scotland (where his grandfather had been secretary of state and had been executed as a royalist in 1646). Spotswood was born in Tangier (see "Tangier," above), where his father was surgeon to the garrison and his half brother, Roger Elliot (37), was an officer. His formal military career began in 1693 as an ens. in Bath's (10th) regt. of foot (afterward Grenville's [12]), in which Elliot was then maj. Spotswood became lt. in 1696, and Marlborough breveted him capt. and appointed him lt. quartermaster gen. of the forces in the Netherlands in 1702. As Spotswood explained, this was "an Employ, that in all other Services of the World, is possest by Men of an higher degree than that of a Captain. Our Government has not made the salary of it very great, but there are accidents in it that may content a man in another manner; and if the War lasts and I live some lucky Hits may happen towards the making of one's Fortune"

(Alexander to John Spotswood, Mar. 15, 1704, in Lester J. Cappon, ed., "Correspondence of Alexander Spotswood with John Spotswood of Edinburgh," *VMHB*, LX [1952], 220). Spotswood was breveted col. by Marlborough in 1706. He appears twice on the Blenheim bounty roll, where Parke (80), Shute (128), John Pitt (see under 86), Hunter (205), Orkney (203), and Gooch (208) are also listed. Captured at Oudenarde in 1708 when his horse was shot from under him and his cavalry escort fled, Spotswood demanded further reward for his staff service after Malplaquet. "[T]his Step of mine was approv'd of by the Chief Officers of our Army" he wrote. Therefore, Virginia's government "was granted to me when the War was judg'd at its last period" (Alexander to John Spotswood, Mar. 20, 1711, *ibid.*, 229). Spotswood commanded Virginia until 1722. He retired in favor and was commissioned quartermaster gen. of the forces in Scotland in 1725. Commissioned col. of an American regt. in 1739 and named quartermaster gen. of the West Indian expedition of 1740 with the rank of maj. gen., Spotswood died at Annapolis on June 14, 1740.

207. *HUGH DRYSDALE. Lt. gov. and commander-in-chief, 1722–1726. Commissioned ens. of foot in 1701, Drysdale rose to become capt. and brevet maj. of Churchill's marines in 1709 and maj. of dragoons in 1715.

208. *SIR WILLIAM GOOCH, baronet. Lt. gov. and commander-in-chief, 1727–1751. Gooch was commissioned capt. of the 15th regt. of foot (col., Lord Irvine [15]) in 1704, fought at Blenheim (see 206), and served throughout Marlborough's campaigns and in the repression of the Scots rebellion of 1715. He resigned his commission in this regt. in 1717. During his governorship of Virginia, Gooch became col. of an American regt. of foot and brig. gen. in 1740. He was wounded at the siege of Cartagena and created a baronet in 1746. When offered command of the 1746 expedition against Canada, he refused it, remarking that he was "fitter for an hospital than a camp" and that "I am next October sixty six years of age and have served the Crown forty five of them" (quoted in Richard L. Morton, *Colonial Virginia* [Chapel Hill, N.C., 1960], II, 535). Gooch retired in 1749 and died in 1751.

Index

This index is organized somewhat differently than the usual scholarly index. Rather than preparing an alphabetized list of indexed items, I have attempted to develop the kind of index that I myself would like to use and that will most assist readers in penetrating this book. Thus, the index is organized in three parts, "Persons," "Places," and "Topics," because students of Anglo-America are apt to approach such a work as this from one of these directions.

As the headings "Persons," "Places," and "Topics" suggest, each of the three parts of this index is organized around a different focus. "Persons" locates individuals and attempts to organize the biographical information about them in the book. Entries in this section are modified as follows: "Ment." indicates a mention of the subject in a significant context. "Ident." assists in identification of the subject. Career references point to the subject's contribution to the leading developments traced by the book.

The entries for especially important persons are further modified. References are made to what I have designated as "Watchwords"—words that are given special emphasis in the book or that were used to classify persons politically in the period treated by the book.

The "Watchwords" are:

Absolute
Arbitrary
Court
Courtier
Country
Elite
Grandee
Household
Moderate
Moderation
Mutiny
Plantation
Popular
Professionals

The elements of the Table of Contents also modify prominent "Persons." The "Watchwords," the Contents, and the names of "Persons" also modify entries in "Places," the locational, geographical index. The

[515]

"Topics" section lists the subjects discussed in the book, especially the institutions, ideas, and "Watchwords" that are most frequently mentioned. The reader should note that the names of "Persons," "Places," "Topics," and "Watchwords" used as modifiers in an index entry are also intended to serve as cross-references. Each section of the index also contains direct cross-references, beginning with *"see also,"* to entries in each of the other sections.

I am grateful for the generous assistance of the members of my family and of Mrs. Helene H. Fineman in the preparation of the index.

Index of Persons

Index of Places

Index of Topics

A

"Absolute": Charles II, 3, 286; James II, 3, 131, 325, 383, 393, 461–462; imperial govt., 3, 98, 214, 261–262, 275, 303; Stuarts, 4, 306; govs.-gen., 29, 36, 165, 193, 196, 201, 216, 219, 232, 285, 295, 317, 352–353; a function of distance, 33, 170, 233–234; garrison govt., 69, 457; "standing army," 296, 323. *See also* Crown, prerogative of

Acts of trade, preface, 148, 156, 186, 340. *See also* Committees and councils for the plantations; Downing, George; Merchants; Trade and commerce

Agents, 299, 307, 337–341, 343, 345–346. *See also* Moryson, Francis; Littleton, Sir Charles

American Revolution, preface, 444, 445, 448, 458; order incites, 4, 143, 449; and contest with "elites," 28, 455; the opposition and, 90; ends political cycles, 316, 348; as "republican revival," 320, 441–442; imperial rivalry and, 400; victory and, 464; authors of, 465

Anglo-American politics: "too much conformity," 269; preface, 3–4, 138–142, 147, 197, Codas I–III, 461–466; rules of, 198, 225, 253–255, 261, 316, 336, 458–459; "country" instructions for, 268–269, 377–378; versus new model, 282–283, 284, 382–383; "court" defense of, 285–286, party, 419; Exclusion Crisis defines, 298–312 *passim*; royal reaction in, 305, 307–308, 310, 324, 461; govs.-gen. in, 318–319, 320; sophistication of, 377; extremes of, 383; "closed system" of, 431–432; councils exhibit, 456–457; oligarchy and, 465. *See also* Army; Assemblies; Committees and councils for the plantations; Councils of state; Garrison government; Governors-General; Imperial settlement; Law; Merchants; Parliament; Poynings's Law; Self-government; Taxation; Western Design; and "Watchwords"

"Arbitrary," 12, 23, 86, 93, 102, 143, 199, 253, 415

Aristocracy: resists executive, 6–7, 23, 284, 396; eroded in civil war, 24, 35, 69–70, by "professionals," 97; military status of, 62, 88, 124–125; feuds of, e.g., 92–93; as traditional ruling class, in colonies, 98, 101, 227, 256, 262, 276; as proprietors, 424. *See also* "Elites"; "Grandees"; Parliament

Army of England, Britain, and the Dominions

OFFICERS: and the empire, preface, conclusion, Appendix *passim*

general officers: qualifications of, 30, 63, 173, 201, 506; govs.-in-chief as, 203, 206, 229, 252, 262, 268, 293, 307–308, 311, 434, 500–501, Appendix *passim*

commanders-in-chief: 4–5; royal, 272, 283–285, 296, 402, 462; in America, 167, 183, 399, 480; of Canada, 486; in Spain, 494; of South Britain, 495; for Scotland, 511 (*see also* Charles II; Cromwell, Oliver; James, duke of York; William, prince of Orange)

captains general: 4; imperial influence of, 60, 225–226, 463–464; and govs.-in-chief, 67, 114–115, 258, 264, 271, 344–348, 362, 381, 501; of marines, 495 (*see also* Churchill, John; Monck, George)

field marshal: 495

sergeant major general: 498

generals (chief executive): e.g., 344; of forces in Nova Scotia and Newfoundland, 504

lieutenants general: duties of, 79, 89–91; colonial, 94, 115, 202, 214, 230, 272, 278, 353, 391, 486; of North American forces, 502, Appendix nos. 45, 51

major generals: military rulers, 76–78, 407–408, 419; colonial, 115, 233, 255, 259, 270, 278, 314, 485, e.g., 37, 505

brigadier generals: govs.-gen. as, e.g., Appendix nos. 58, 149

general staff: as bureaucracy, 124, 197–198